A

CATALOGUE

OF

𝔗𝔥𝔢 𝔏𝔦𝔟𝔯𝔞𝔯𝔶

COLLECTED BY

MISS RICHARDSON CURRER,

AT ESHTON HALL,

CRAVEN, YORKSHIRE.

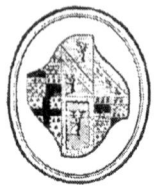

By C. J. STEWART,
BOOKSELLER.

LONDON:
PRINTED FOR PRIVATE CIRCULATION ONLY.

MDCCCXXXIII.

HÆC STUDIA ADOLESCENTIAM ALUNT, SENECTUTEM OBLECTANT, SE-
CUNDAS RES ORNANT, ADVERSIS PERFUGIUM AC SOLATIUM PRÆBENT,
DELECTANT DOMI, NON IMPEDIUNT FORIS, PERNOCTANT NOBISCUM, PERE-
GRINANTUR, RUSTICANTUR

CICERO.

LONDON
J. MOYES, CASTLE STREET, LEICESTER SQUARE.

ADVERTISEMENT.

The Library of which this volume forms the Catalogue, has been collected solely with a view to utility; yet in those works usually considered ornamental and curious it possesses specimens of no common occurrence. In the Natural Sciences, Topography, Antiquities, and History, it is more particularly rich, and the Manuscripts, although not numerous, are both interesting and valuable. The Books individually are in the finest condition, and not a few of them in the richest and most tasteful bindings.

The " *Outlines for the Classification of a Library, submitted to the consideration of the Trustees of the British Museum by the Rev. T. H. Horne,*" was chosen as the latest and best model for the present Catalogue, but has been so modified as to suit a private collection. This plan differs in many respects from those preceding it: its most obvious improvements are the introduction of more comprehensive terms for the Classes, with a more philosophic arrangement of them and their various divisions. Of these may be cited the substitution of *Religion* for *Theology*, *Philosophy* for the *Sciences*, and *Literature* for the *Belles-Lettres*,—the merging of *General Ecclesiastical History* in the title of *History of Religions*, which comprehends every description, and constitutes the last section of the Class Religion,—and the separation of the *Sciences*, or Philosophy as already noticed, and the *Arts*, into distinct classes.

The modifications necessarily introduced into this Catalogue by the compiler relate principally to a reduction of the numerous branches into which the classes of so extensive a Library as that of the British Museum naturally ramify, and, in a few cases, to a deviation from the order laid down in the " Outlines."

The Classic Authors have been kept together, as a separate division, at the close of the volume, but throughout are mentioned under their respective heads, with references to that division; and under Greek and Roman History the period each

ADVERTISEMENT

contains is there adjoined. That principle of analysis has also been adopted, by which the several parts of Polygraphic Authors, Treatises on separate subjects, &c. are placed under their proper heads, with references to their collected sources. Under *Separate Biographical Memoirs*, references are made to such as are, throughout the Catalogue, placed elsewhere, and also to those prefixed to collected works, &c.—a plan still more enlarged in the Index. The order of arranging the works under the minor heads, is such as seemed, on consideration, best suited to the nature or extent of each.

The Index contains the works under their authors' names, except in the cases of translations, biography, and such as are anonymous, which appear under their subjects only; together with the various classes and divisions; and the references are made to where the title is to be found at length.

Four Engravings illustrate the Catalogue,—a View of Eshton Hall, two of the Interiors of the Libraries, and one of the Landscape fronting the House.

CONTENTS.

Class I.—RELIGION.

	PAGE
Sect I.—Holy Scriptures	
Original Texts	1
Ancient Versions	2
Modern Versions	4
Harmonies and Histories of the Bible	8
Apocryphal Books	9
Sect II.—Sacred Philology	
Introductions, Treatises on Interpretation and on Translations of Scripture, and Sacred Literature	9
Commentators and Expositors	11
On the Prophecies	15
Concordances, Dictionaries, and Common-place Books	16
Biblical Antiquities, &c	16
Sect III—Councils	26
Sect. IV—Church Discipline and Government	27
Sect V.—Liturgies and Ecclesiastical Rites	29
Sect VI.—Catechisms and Confessions of Faith	31
Sect VII—Fathers	34
Sect VIII—Miscellaneous Divinity.	
Collected Works	35
Separate Works	37
Sect IX—Sermons	51
Sect X.—History of Religions	
General History of Religions	60
History of the Modern Jews, and Talmudical Writings	60
History of the Christian Religion	61
Ecclesiastical History of particular Countries	62
History of the Popes, and Lives of Saints	64
Religious Orders and Inquisition	65
History of Sects and Missions	65
Mahommedan and Pagan Religions	66

vi   CONTENTS.

Class II.—JURISPRUDENCE.

	PAGE
Sect I.—Introductions, and Treatises on Universal Law	67
Sect II —Ancient, Civil, and Feudal Law	69
Sect III —Canon Law	71
Sect IV.—British Law	
Public and Constitutional Law	71
History and Treatises of the Law of England	72
Statute Law	73
Customary Law and Law of Property	74
Justiciary, Parochial, and Criminal Law	74
Ecclesiastical and Miscellaneous Law	74
Scottish Law	75
Sect V —Foreign Law	75

Class III.—PHILOSOPHY.

Introductory Treatises, &c	76
Sect I —Intellectual Philosophy	
History of Philosophy and Philosophers	76
Metaphysics	76
Occult Philosophy, Physiognomy, &c.	78
Logic	79
Ethics	79
Education	80
Political Philosophy.	
Politics	81
Political Economy	83
Population, Mendicity, &c	84
Finance and Money	85
Commerce and Colonial Policy	85
Sect II.—Natural Philosophy	
Physics, or Natural and Experimental Philosophy	86
Meteorology	86
Chemical Philosophy	87
Natural History	
Dictionaries, Systems, General Treatises, and of various Countries	87
Geology	90
Mineralogy	91
Botany	92

		PAGE
Zoology		96
Ornithology		97
Reptiles, &c.		98
Ichthyology		98
Entomology		98
Conchology		100
Medicine, Anatomy, and Surgery		101

Sect III.—MATHEMATICAL PHILOSOPHY

Histories, Dictionaries, &c of Mathematics	102
Pure Mathematics	102
Mixed Mathematics	103
Astronomy	104
Optics and Perspective	104
Music	105
Navigation and Naval Architecture	105
Military Science	106

Class IV.—ARTS.

General Treatises 106

Sect I.—LIBERAL ARTS
Artificial Memory, Writing, and Printing . . . 107

Sect II.—FINE ARTS
Histories and General Treatises 107
Painting
    History of Painting 109
    Elementary and General Treatises 109
    Particular kinds of Painting 110
    Collections of Engravings after great and eminent Masters 111
    Drawings 116
    Galleries of Paintings 116
    Portraits 117
Engraving 119
Costumes 121
Sculpture 122
Architecture 122

Sect. III.—ECONOMIC ARTS
Agriculture and Gardening 123
Domestic Economy 126
Manufactures 126

Sect IV.—GYMNASTIC AND RECREATIVE ARTS 127

CONTENTS

Class V —HISTORY.

Sect I.—Historical Prolegomena.

	PAGE
On the Study and Use of History, and Historical Atlases	129
Geography	129
Atlases	130
Voyages and Travels, and Foreign Topography	
Introductory Works	130
Navigation of the Ancients	131
Collections of Voyages	131
Voyages round the World	131
Travels in various Quarters of the World	132
Europe	
Travels in various parts	134
Northern Countries of Europe	135
Germany	137
Switzerland	137
Italy	137
France	140
The Netherlands	141
Spain and Portugal	141
Turkey	142
Greece	142
Africa	144
Central, North, West, and South Africa	144
Egypt, Nubia, and Abyssinia	146
Asia	147
Asiatic Turkey	147
Arabia	148
Persia, &c.	148
East Indies	149
China, &c.	151
Asiatic Russia	152
America	152
North-west Passage	152
North America	153
West Indies	154
South America	154
South Sea, Polynesia, and Australia	157
Chronology	158
Antiquities — Numismatics	
Dictionaries, Treatises, and Collections of Antiquities	159
Antique Monuments	170
Numismatics	173
Inscriptions	176

CONTENTS

	PAGE
Sect. II.—UNIVERSAL HISTORY	176
Sect. III.—ANCIENT HISTORY.	
Origin of Nations	177
General Ancient History, and particular History of several Ancient Nations	177
Grecian History	179
Roman History	180
Byzantine History	181
Sect. IV.—HISTORY OF THE MIDDLE AGES	183
Sect. V.—MODERN HISTORY	
Europe.—General History	183
English History.	
Topography and Antiquities	185
Roman Topography	186
Ecclesiastical and Monastical Topography	186
Surveys, Descriptions, Itineraries, and Tours	187
Architectural and Sepulchral Antiquities, and Graphic Illustrations	190
Miscellaneous Antiquities	193
Topography of the several Counties, in alphabetical order	195
Narrative	
Introduction	219
Collections of Ancient English Historians	220
Particular Histories before the Conquest, Chronicles, and General Histories	221
Particular Histories since the Conquest, in chronological order	226
Naval and Military History	243
Political and Parliamentary History	244
Documentary History	246
Ecclesiastical History	251
History of Wales	
Topography	256
Narrative	257
Scottish History	
Topography and Antiquities	258
Narrative	261
History of particular periods	262
Documentary History	267
Ecclesiastical History	268
Irish History	
Topography and Antiquities	269
Narrative	270
Ecclesiastical History	273

CONTENTS.

	PAGE
General History of Northern Nations	273
History of Denmark and Norway, including Greenland and Iceland	274
History of Sweden, including Lapland	275
History of Russia	276
History of Poland	277
History of Germany	277
History of the Low Countries	278
History of France	279
French Ceremonials, Monuments, &c.	289
Provincial History	289
History of Switzerland	290
History of Spain	290
History of Portugal	292
History of Italy	292
History of the Ottoman Empire	299
History of the Gipsies	300
Asia —General History	300
History of the Arabs and Saracens	301
History of Persia and Armenia	302
History of India	302
History of China, Tartary, and Siam	305
History of the Asiatic Isles	306
Africa —General History	306
History of Egypt and Abyssinia	307
History of Barbary and other parts of Africa	307
America —General History	308
History of South America	309
History of North America	309
History of the West India Islands	310

Sect VI —Biographical and Monumental History

Biographical History.	
General Biography.	311
Ecclesiastical Biography	312
Ancient Biography	312
Modern Biography	
British Biography	312
Foreign Biography	314
Biography of Artists	314
Biographical Anecdotes	314
Portraits, with Biographical Notices	315
Separate Biographical Memoirs	316
Heraldic and Genealogical History	
Heraldry, History of Knighthood, Nobility, &c.	330
Genealogical History	333

Class VI.—LITERATURE.

Sect I.—History of Literature and Bibliography.

	PAGE
History of Literature	336
History of Writing and Diplomatics	339
History of Literary and Philosophical Societies, Literary Journals, &c	339
Bibliography	340
History of Printing	340
General Bibliographers	342
National and Professional Bibliographers	343
Anonymous and Pseudonymous Works	345
On Libraries	345
Catalogues of Public and Private Libraries	345

Sect. II.—Polite Literature

Introductions to the Study and Courses of Polite Literature	347
Grammar	
On the Origin, &c of Language, and Universal Grammar	348
Grammars and Dictionaries	
Various Languages	348
Oriental Languages	349
Greek Language	350
Latin Language	351
Anglo-Saxon Language	352
English Language, including Provincial Dialects and Lowland Scotch	352
Celtic, including Cornish, Welsh, Gaelic, and Irish Languages	354
French Language	354
Italian Language	355
Spanish and Portuguese Languages	356
Dutch Language	356
German Language	356
Northern Languages	356
African and American Languages	357
Criticism	358
Rhetoric and Oratory	359
Poetry.	
On the Art of Poetry	359
Greek Poets	360
Latin Poets	360
English Poetry	
History of, and Dissertations on, English Poetry	362

CONTENTS

	PAGE
Collections and Extracts of English Poetry..	362
English Songs	364
Separate English Poets	365
Scottish Poetry	372
Welsh and Irish Poetry	374
French Poetry	374
Italian Poetry	375
Spanish and Portuguese Poetry . .	377
German, Dutch, and Northern Poetry . .	377
Oriental Poetry	378
Romances and Novels.	
History of Romance	379
Greek, Latin, and Chivalric Romances	379
English Novels	381
French Novels	385
Italian Novels	387
Spanish Novels	388
German and Northern Novels	388
Oriental Romances.	388
Dramatic Poetry	
Treatises on Dramatic Poetry	389
Greek and Latin Drama.	389
English Drama	
History of the English Theatre and Drama .	389
English Dramatic Works	390
French Drama	394
Italian Drama.	395
Spanish Drama	396
German Drama	396
Oriental Drama	396
Polygraphy, in all languages	396
Fables	400
Satirical Works	400
Proverbs, Apothegms, Ana, &c.	401
Emblems	402
Epistolary Writings	402
Essayists	405
Miscellanies	406
AUCTORES CLASSICI	408
MANUSCRIPTS	431
APPENDIX	438
INDEX	441

CATALOGUE

OF

ESHTON HALL LIBRARY.

CLASS I.—RELIGION.

SECT I.—HOLY SCRIPTURES.

Original Texts.

BIBLIA HEBRAICA. Pentateuchus, Prophetæ Priores, Chetavim, et Prophetæ Minores, cum Punctis et Commentariis D Kimchi, ex recog F Vatabli, 4 vols 4to *Parisiis, R. Stephani,* 1541–45

Biblia Hebraica, secundùm ultimam editionem J Athiæ, à J Leusden recognitam, recensita, atque ad Masoram et Correctiones Bambergi, Stephani, Plantini, aliorumque editiones exquisitè adornata, variisque Notis illustrata ab E Vander Hooght, 8vo *Amstel* 1705

Biblia Hebraica, digessit, et graviores Lectionum Varietates adjecit Jahn, 4 vols. 8vo. *Viennæ,* 1806

Biblia Hebraica; Vetus Testamentum Hebraicum sine Punctis, cum variis Lectionibus; edidit Benj Kennicott, 2 vols. folio *Oxonii,* 1776–80

Biblia Hebraica Varias Lectiones Kennicotti continuavit Jo Bern De Rossi, et adjecit alias ex immensâ MSS editorumq Codicum congerie haustas, et ad Samar. Textum, ad vetustiss Versiones, ad accuratiores S Criticæ Fontes ac Leges examinatæ, 4 vols 4to *Parmæ,* 1784–88

Biblia Hebraica, De Rossi Scholia Critica in V T, seu Supplementum ad varias Sacri Textûs Lectiones, 4to *Ibid.* 1799

Novi Testamenti omnia, Græcè, cum Versione et Adnotationibus D Erasmi, folio *Basileæ, ap J Bebelium,* 1535.

Novi Testamenti omnia, ex Bibliothecâ Regiâ, 16mo Editio "O mnificam!" *Lutetiæ, ex officinâ R Stephani,* 1546

Novi Testamenti omnia, ex Regiis aliisque optimis Editionibus, cum curâ expressum, 16mo "Textus receptus." *Lugduni Bat ex offic. Elzeviriana,* 1624

Novum Testamentum, unà cum Scholiis Græcis, è Græcis Scriptoribus desumptis, operâ ac studio Jo. Gregorii, folio, large paper. *Oxonii,* 1703

RELIGION

Novum Testamentum Græcum, editionis receptæ, cum Lectionibus var. Codicum MSS., Editionum aliarum, Versionum, et Patrum, necnon Commentario pleniore ex Scriptoribus vet Hebr Gr et Lat, operâ et studio J J Wetstenii, 2 vols, folio *Amstelod* 1751-2

Novum Testamentum Græcum, ad fidem Cod MSS expressum, adstipulante Jo Ja. Wetstenio, juxta Sectiones J A Benzelii divisum, et novâ Interpretatione sæpiùs illustratum, curâ J Bowyer, 4to. *Londini,* 1783

Novum Testamentum Græcè, ex recensione J J Griesbachii, cum selectâ Lectionum Varietate, 4 vols in 2, folio *Lipsiæ, typis Goschenis,* 1803-7

Novum Testamentum Græcum, è Cod MS Alexandrino descriptum à C G Woide, cum Appendice [curâ et operâ H Ford], 2 vols. large folio *Londini,* 1786, et *Oxonii,* 1799

Novum Testamentum Græcum (Evangelia et Acta Apostolorum), ad exemplar Codicis Th Bezæ, Cantabrigiensis expressa. Quadratis litteris Græco-Latinus Edidit, Codicis Historiam præfixit, Notasque adjecit, Tho Kipling, 2 vols large folio. *Cantabr impensis Academiæ,* 1793

Novum Testamentum Græcum (Acta Apostolorum), Græco-Latinè, litteris majusculis è Codice Laudiano characteribus uncialibus exarato, et in Bib Bodleiano adservato, descripsit, edidituque T Hearnius, qui et Symbolum Apostolorum ex eodem Codice subjunxit, royal 8vo *Oxonii, sumptibus editoris,* 1715.

BIBLIA SACRA POLYGLOTTA, complectentia Textus Originales, Hebraicum cum Pentateucho-Samaritano, Chaldaicum, Græcum; Versionumque Antiquarum, Samaritanæ, Græcæ LXXII. Interp Chaldaicæ, Syriacæ, Arabicæ, Æthiopicæ, Persicæ, Vulg Latinæ, quicquid comparari poterat, cum Textuum et Versionum Orientalium Translationibus, et Apparatu, Annotationibus, Tabulis, variis Lectionibus, &c Edidit Brianus Waltonus. 6 vols folio *Londini,* 1657.

Biblia Sacra Polyglotta. Paraphrasis Chaldaica in Librum priorem et posteriorem Chronicorum, cum Versione Latinè à D. Wilkins, 4to. *Cantab* 1715.

Ancient Versions.

Βιβλια Sacræ Scripturæ Veteris Novæque omnia [Græcè ex multis vetustissimis exemplaribus excusa, curâ Andreæ Ausulani], folio, editio princeps *Venetiis in ædib Aldi et And. Soceri, M D.XVIII*

A remarkably fine and large copy, the margins almost rough

Vetus Testamentum, ex Versione LXX secundùm exemplar Vaticanum, unà cum Scholiis ejusdem editionis, variis Lectionibus, nec non Fragmentis Versionum Aquilæ, Symmachi, et Theodotionis, summâ curâ edidit L Bos, 2 vols in one, 4to *Franequeræ,* 1709.

Vetus Testamentum, ex Versione LXX Interpretum, secundùm exemplar Vaticanum Romæ editum. Accedunt variæ Lectiones è Cod. Alexandrino, necnon Introductio J. B Carpzovii, 6 vols. 8vo. *Oxonii,* 1817

Vetus Testamentum Græcum, cum variis Lectionibus, editionem à R. Holmes inchoatam continuavit Jac Parsons, 5 vols folio. *Oxonii,* 1818-27.

Vetus Testamentum Græcum, è Codice MSS Alexandrinûm qui Londini in Bib Musæi Britannici asservatur; Typis ad similitudinem ipsius Codicis Scripturæ fideliter descriptum [cum Notis et Prolegomenis], curâ et labore H. H Baber, 4 vols imperial 4to *Londini,* 1816–28

Hexapla Originis quæ supersunt, edidit Notisque illustravit C. F Bahrdt, 2 vols 8vo *Leips* 1769–70

S Evangeliorum Versio Syriaca Philoxeniana, ex Cod MSS nunc primùm edita; cum Interp et Annotat Jos White, 2 vols 4to *Oxonii, è Typ Clar* 1778.

V. Libri Moysis Prophetæ, et Nov Testamentum in Linguâ Ægyptiâ, vulgò Copticum, ex MSS Vaticano, Parisiensi, Bodleiano descripsit, ac Latinè vertit D Wilkins, 2 vols 4to *Londini,* 1731, *et Oxonii,* 1716

Fragmenta Novi Testamenti, juxta interp Dialecti Superioris Egypti, quæ Thebaica vel Sahidica appellatur, è Cod MSS Oxoniensis, cum Diss. de Versione Ægyptiacâ. (Appendix ad N T. Gr. Alexandr. Woide.)

Biblia Armenicè, cum variis Lectionibus, &c curâ Zohrab. 4to. *Venetiis,* 1805.

S. Evang Versio Gothica, ex Cod Argenteo, emendata atque suppleta cum Interp Latinè et Annotat E Benzelii. Edidit, Observationes adjecit, et Grammatica Gothica præmisit, E Lye, 4to. *Oxonii,* 1750

Bibliorum Sacrorum Latinæ Versiones Antiquæ, seu Vetus Italica, etc Accedunt Præfationes, Observationes, ac Notæ; operâ et studio D P Sabatier, 3 vols. folio. *Romæ,* 1743–49.

Biblia Sacra, V et N. Testamentum complectentia, Latinè, secundùm editionem Vulgatam, ad fidem vetustiss Cod MSS et editionum antiquarum emendata; studio et operâ R Stephani, folio *Parisiis, ex off R Stephani,* 1540.

Biblia Sacra Vulgatæ editionis, ad Concil Tridentini præscriptum, emendata et à Sixto V P. M recognita et approbata, folio. *Romæ, ex typ Apost Vaticanâ,* [*Aldi Fil*] *M D.XC.*

Biblia Sacra Vulgatæ editionis, Sixti V Pont jussu recognita, et edita [Clementis VIII Pont Max], folio. *Romæ, ex typ Apost. Vatic* [*Aldi Fil*] *M D XCII.*

Biblia Sacra Vulgatæ editionis, Sixti V jussu recognita, et Clement VIII auctoritate edita, 8vo *Coloniæ Agrippinæ* [*Amsterd ap Elzevium*], 1682

Heptateuchus, Liber Jobi, et Evang Nicodemi, Anglo-Saxonicè, Historia Judith, Fragmentum Dano-Saxonicè edidit nunc primùm ex MSS. Cod E Thwaites, 8vo *Oxonii,* 1699

Psalterium Davidis Latino-Saxonicum Vetus, à Jo. Spelmanno editum è vet exempl MS 4to *Londini,* 1640

The Gospels of the Fower Evangelists, translated in the olde Saxons tyme out of Latin into the Vulgare Toung of the Saxons, newly collected out of auncient Monumentes of the seyd Saxons, and now published for testimonie of the same [with Preface by John Fox, the Martyrologist], 4to *London, by John Daye,* 1571.

RELIGION

Psalterium Davidicum è Lat. in Theotiscam Vet. Ling versum, et Paraphrasi illustratum Notkero, curavit J Schilterus. (Schilteri Thes Vol I)

Cantica Canticorum, Paraphrasis Lat et Vet Francica Willerami. Accedunt var. Lect et Notæ vai. necnon J G Schezii (Schilteri Thes. Vol I)

Evangeliorum Volumen, Vet Franc et Lat Otfridi Weissenburgensis; Observationibus exornatum à J. G Schezio (Schilteri Thes. Vol I)

Modern Versions.

Biblia Sacra ex S Castalionis postremâ recognitione, cum Annotationibus ejusdem et Historico Supplemento ab Esdrâ ad Machabæos, inde usque ad Christum, ex Josepho, folio *Basileæ, per P. Pernam,* 1573.

Biblia Sacra · Test Vet Latinè recens ex Hebræo facti, brevibusque Scholiis illustrati ab Im Tremellio et F Junio; accesserunt Libri Apocryphi Latinè redditi et Notis quibusdam aucti à F. Junio Quibus etiam adjunximus Nov Test ex Sermone Syro ab eodem Tremellio, et ex Græco à T. Bezâ in Latinum versos, Notisque itidem illustratos, secundâ curâ F. Junii, 4to. *Genevæ, ap. J. Tornæsium,* 1590.

New Testament, translated from the Latin in the year 1380 by J. Wicliff, edited by H. H. Baber, 4to *London,* 1810

BIBLIA the Bible, that is, the Holy Scriptures of the Olde and New Testament, faithfully and truly translated of Douche [German] and Latyn into Englysche [by Miles Coverdale], black letter, folio [*Zurich, prynted by Frischover,*] *and fynished the fourthe day of October, in the yeare* M D XXXV

> The first complete English version an exceedingly fine copy, and deficient only in the title, address to Henry VIII, the prologue, table of the bookes, and title to Apocrypha.

The Bible, which is all the Holy Scripture; in which are contayned the Olde and Newe Testament, truly and purely translated into Englysh by Thomas Matthew [John Rogers], black letter, folio [*Abroad, at the expense of R Grafton and E Whitchurch*], M D XXXVII

> The second, being partly Tindal's and partly Coverdale's, with alterations.

The Byble in English, that is to saye, the content of all the Holye Scripture, both of the Olde and Newe Testament, truly translated after the veryte of the Hebreu and Greke Textes, by the dylygente studye of dyverse excellent learned men, experte in the foresayde tonges, black letter, folio. [*London, by R. Grafton and E Whitchurch*], M D XXXIX.

> The third, called Cranmer's Bible, on account of the preface and prologue written by him, and the Great Bible, on account of its increased size.

The moste Sacred Bible, which is the Holy Scripture; conteyning the Old and New Testament, translated into English, and newly recognised with great diligence after most faythful exemplars, by Rychard Taverner, black letter, folio. *London, by John Byddell, for Tho. Barthlet,* M D XXXIX.

> The fourth, by some said to be an entire new version, and by others a mere revisal or correction of Matthew's

RELIGION.

The Byble; that is to say, all the Holy Scripture contained in the Olde and Newe Testament, faythfully set forth according to y⁰ copy of Tho Matthewe's Translacion; whereunto are added certain learned Prologes and Annotacions, for the better understanding of many hard places throughout the whole Byble, [by Edmund Becke,] black letter *London, by Jhon Day, M.D LI*

> The fifth, a correction of all the editions before it, agreeing principally with Taverner's, and the first that contains the third book of Maccabees

The Holie Bible, conteyning the Olde Testament and the Newe, folio, black letter *London, by R Jugge, M D LXVIII*

> The sixth English version, made under the direction of Archbishop Parker, and commonly called the Bishops' Bible.

The Bible and Holy Scriptures, conteyned in the Olde and New Testament, translated according to the Ebrue and Greeke, and conferred with the best translations in divers languages; with most profitable Annotations upon all the hard Places, and other things of great importance, 4to *Geneva, by Rouland Hall, M D LX*

Holy Bible, conteyning the Olde Testament and the Newe; newly translated out of the originall tongues, and with former translations diligently compared and revised, by his Majestie's especiall commandement, black letter, folio. *London, by R Barker, M DC.XI.*

> The first edition of the present authorised version

Holy Bible, 2 vols 4to, large paper. *London, Baskett*, 1767.

Holy Bible [carefully collated and corrected, with the addition of Marginal References, by R. Blayney] "The Standard Edition," 4to *Oxford*, 1769

The Holy Bible and Apocrypha [the latter containing the Third Book of Maccabees, from Becke's]; with Notes by Bishop Wilson; and various Renderings collected from other Translations, by Clement Cruttwell 3 vols. 4to *Bath*, 1785

The Holy Bible [with Tables of the Marginal Readings and Parallel Passages from the edition of 1611, prefixed], 2 vols 4to *Oxford, Clarendon Press*, 1807

The Holy Bible [the latest standard Edition, 4to] *London, Eyre and Strahan [Woodfall]*, 1813

Holy Bible of the Old and New Testament, with Apocrypha; embellished with Engravings from Pictures and Designs of the most eminent English Artists Published by Thomas Macklin, 8 vols large folio, a subscription copy bound in morocco, with joints, by Staggemeir *London, Bensley*, 1800–16

Newe Testament, both Latine and Englyshe, ech correspondent to the other, after the Vulgar Texte, communely called St Jerom's. Faythfully translated by Johan Hollybushe [Miles Coverdale], 4to, black letter. *Southwarke, by J Nicolson, M D XXXVIII.*

The Old Covenant, commonly called the Old Testament, translated from the Septuagint, the New Covenant, translated from the Greek. By Charles Thomson, 4 vols 8vo *Philadelphia*, 1808.

> The only English translation of the LXX

RELIGION.

The Old and New Testaments, faithfully translated out of the authenticall Latin, diligently conferred with the Hebrew, Greeke, and other editions in divers languages, with Arguments, Annotations, Tables, &c By the English College of Douay, 3 vols 4to *Douay, by L. Kellam*, 1609–10; *Rheims, by John Fogny*, 1582

Book of Job, literally translated from the original Hebrew, and restored to its natural arrangement, with Notes critical and illustrative, and an Introductory Dissertation on its Scene, Scope, Language, Author, and Object, by John Mason Good, 8vo. *London*, 1812

The Book of Job, translated from the Hebrew by Elizabeth Smith; with a Preface and Annotations, by F Randolph, 8vo *London*, 1810.

The Book of Psalms, translated from the Hebrew; with Notes explanatory and critical, by Sam. Horsley, 2 vols. 8vo. *London*, 1816.

The Psalms of David, translated into divers and sundry kindes of Verse; begun by Sir Philip Sidney, and finished by the Countess of Pembroke, his sister Printed from the original MS. small 8vo. *Lond* 1823.

The Book of Proverbs; an attempt towards an improved Translation from the original Hebrew, with Notes critical and explanatory, and a preliminary Dissertation, by Geo Holden, 8vo. *London*, 1819

The Book of Ecclesiastes; an attempt to illustrate by a Paraphrase, in which the expressions of the Hebrew Author are interwoven; with a Commentary by John Holden, 8vo. *London*, 1822.

The Song of Songs, or, Sacred Idyls, translated from the original Hebrew, with Notes critical and explanatory, by J. M Good, 8vo. *London*, 1803.

Isaiah: a new Translation; with a preliminary Dissertation, and Notes critical, philological, and explanatory, by Robt Lowth, 2 vols 8vo *Glasgow*, 1822.

Jeremiah and Lamentations · a new Translation; with Notes critical, philological, and explanatory, by B Blayney, 8vo *Edinb* 1810

Ezekiel. an Attempt towards an improved Version, a Metrical Arrangement, and an Explanation, by Archb Newcome, 4to *Dublin*, 1788.

Daniel an improved Version attempted; with Notes, critical, historical, and explanatory, by Thomas Wintle, 4to *London*, 1807.

XII Minor Prophets: an Attempt towards an improved Version, a Metrical Arrangement, and an Explanation, by Archb. Newcome, 8vo. *Pontefract*, 1809

Hosea translated from the Hebrew, with Notes explanatory and critical (Horsley's "Bibl Criticism," Vols III and IV)

Zechariah: a new Translation; with Notes critical, philological, and explanatory, by B. Blayney, 4to *London*, 1797.

Four Gospels, translated from the Greek, with preliminary Dissertations, and Notes critical and explanatory, by Geo. Campbell, 4 vols. 8vo *Aberdeen*, 1814

The Apostolical Epistles, a New Literal Translation from the original Greek, with a Commentary and Notes, to which is added, a History of the Life of the Apostle Paul, by John Macknight, 4 vols 8vo *London*, 1816

The Apocalypse; or, Revelation of Saint John, translated, with Notes critical and explanatory; to which is prefixed, a Dissertation on the Divine Origin of the book; by J. C. Woodhouse, 8vo. *Lond.* 1806

Bible in Welsh [translated by Bishops Morgan, Davis, &c], black letter, folio. *London, by C. and R Barker*, 1588

Bible in Irish, [translated by King and Daniel, edited by Bishop W. Bedell, and printed at the expense of the Hon Robt Boyle,] 4to *London*, 1681-85

Bible in Irish, 12mo. *London*, 1690

Bible in the Manks Language [translated by Bishops Wilson and Hildesley], 4to *Whitehaven*, 1775.

Bible in Gaelic [translated by Drs James and John Stewart and Dr. Smith, and revised by a Committee of the General Assembly], 4to *Duneidin*, 1826.

Biblia Bohemica [from the Originals, by A Nicolai, J. Capito, and other Reformers, at the expense of the Baron Zerotinus], 4to. [*In Castello Krahtz*], 1579-93.

Biblia Belgica [from the Hebrew and Greek, by J Bogermann, W. Baudart, G. Bucer, A Walæus, &c., by order of the Synod of Dort], 8vo. *Leyden* [1638]

La Sainte Bible, revue, et conférée sur les Textes Hébreux et Grecs par les Pasteurs et Docteurs de l'Eglise de Genève, 4to *Genève*, 1588.

La même, avec un Index par Lieux-communs, 8vo, ruled red lines, a very fine copy in old morocco *Amstelod* 1635

La Sainte Bible, nouvelle traduction, conforme à la Vulgaire du Sexte V, [par Jacques Corbin], et approuvée par l'Université de Poictiers, 8 vols 16mo, old morocco. *Paris*, 1643

"Coll. per H. Drury è libris Comitis Mac Carthy, venditis apud Parisios, 1817"

Pseaumes nouvellement mis en Vers Français, enrichis de Figures, gravées par L Chevron, 8vo ——

Le Nouveau Testament, traduit en Français sur le Vulgate, avec les Différences du Grec [par De Sacy, Arnauld, Nicole, &c], 2 vols. 12mo, in morocco by Pardeloup. *Mons* [*Leyde par Elzev.*], 1667

Biblia Germanica, das ist die gantze heilige Schrift, aufs neu zugericht D Mart Luther, black letter, 2 vols. folio *Wittemberg, gedruckt durch A Lufft, M D XLI*

The latest revised edition by the Reformer himself, and that on which his greatest care was bestowed

Bible, Swiss-German [translated by Leo Juda, and revised, by order of the Helvetian magistrates, by J Hottinger, J Muller, J C Suicer, J. H. Ottius, J H Heidegger, &c], 2 vols 4to *Zurich*, 1665-7.

Biblia Hungarica, [translated from the originals by C Caroli] 4to *Wysolyin*, 1589

Biblia tradotta in Lingua Italiana, e commentata da Giov Diodati, con l'Aggiunta de' S Salmi messi en rime per lo medesimo, folio. *Geneva*, 1641

Biblia Polonica, [translated by the Calvinists] 8vo. *Berlin*, 1813.

RELIGION.

Biblia Hispanica, que es, los sacros Libros del Viejo y Nuevo Testamento [transladada por Cassiodoro de Reyna], revista y conferida con los Textos Hebreos y Griegos, y con diversas Translaciones, por Cyprian de Valera, folio *En Amsterdum* 1602

New Testament in Sungskrit, translated from the original Greek by the Missionaries, 4to. *Serampore*, 1808

Four Gospels, and the Acts of the Apostles, translated into the Malayan Language [by J Marshall, and edited by T Hyde], 4to. *Oxonii*, 1677.

New Testament, translated into the Indian Language [by J. Elliot], 4to. *Cambridge [New England]*, 1661

Harmonies and Histories of the Bible.

Harmonia Evangelica in Ling Theotiscam antiquiss Tatiano Syro [cum Vers Lat] ad duo MSS et curas J. Schilteri posthumas studiosè recensita, subjectis Notulis. Accedit Fragmentum aliud Theotiscum quo Christi cum Samaritanâ Muliere Colloquium rhythmo vet exhibetur. (Schilteri Thesaurus, Vol II)

Harmony and Chronicle of the Old Testament, by J Lightfoot. (Works, Vol II)

Harmony, Chronicle, and Order of the New Testament, by J Lightfoot (Works, Vol. III.)

Harmony of the IV Evangelists among themselves, and with the Old Testament (Works, Vols IV and V)

The Old and New Testament, arranged in Historical and Chronological order; with copious Notes, by George Townsend, 4 vols 8vo *London*, 1821–5

Harmony of the Four Gospels; with a Paraphrase and Notes by J Macknight, 2 vols 8vo *London*, 1809

Harmony of the IV Gospels, by Philip Doddridge. (Family Expositor, Vol. I)

Harmony of the Four Gospels in Chinese, by the Jesuit Missionaries, with forty-eight large Cuts illustrative of our Saviour's Life, small folio *See* First Report of Bible Society, Butler's Confessions of Faith, p 151 [*China, printed* ——]

Reconciler (The) of the Bible enlarged, wherein above 3000 seeming Contradictions throughout the Old and New Testament are fully and plainly reconciled, by J T and T [homas] M [an], folio *Lond*. 1662

Fuller's (Thos) Pisgah Sight of Palestine and the Confines thereof, with the Historic of the Old and New Testament acted thereon, front plate of arms, &c *London*, 1650

Wesley's (Sam) History of the Bible, in Verse; and adorned with 330 Sculptures by J Sturt, 3 vols small 8vo. a fine copy, old morocco. *London*, 1701–16

Stackhouse's (Thos) History of the Holy Bible; with Answers to Infidel Objections; Dissertations on the most remarkable Passages, and a Connexion of the Profane with the Sacred Writings, with Additions and Corrections by Bishop Geo. Gleig, 3 vols 4to *London*, 1817.

RELIGION

Watts's (Isaac) View of Scripture History, with a Continuation of the Jewish Affairs from the Old Testament till the time of Christ, 12mo *London*, 1717

Apocryphal Books

Apocrypha (The Books of the), with critical and historical Observations, and Introductory Discourses, explaining the Distinctions between Canonical and Apocryphal Writings, and illustrating the intimate Connexion between the Old and New Testament, by C Wilson, 8vo *Edinburgh*, 1801

Collection of Authentic Records belonging to the Old and New Testament, translated into English by W Whiston, 2 vols royal 8vo, large paper *London*, 1727–8

Sect II —SACRED PHILOLOGY

Introductions, Treatises on the Interpretation, on Translations of the Scripture, and on Sacred Literature.

Horne's (T H) Introduction to the Critical Study and Knowledge of the Holy Scriptures, 4 vols 8vo *London*, 1828

Walton (Brian) in Biblia Polyglotta Prolegomena specialia, recognovit Dathianisque et variorum Notis suas immiscuit Fr Wrangham, 2 vols royal 8vo *Cantabr.* 1827
_{Presentation copy from the Editor.}

Gray's (Robt) Key to the Holy Bible, giving an Account of the several Books, their Contents and Authors, including Bishop Percy's Key to the New Testament, 8vo *London*, 1818

Lightfoot's (John) Rules for a Student of the Holy Scriptures (Works, Vol II)

Tyndall's (Wm) Pathway into the Holy Scripture (Works.)

Tyndall's (Wm) Prologues to his Translation of the Bible (Works)

Ostervald's (J F) Arguments of the Books and Chapters of the New Testament, with Practical Observations, translated from the original MS by J Chamberlayne, 8vo, thick paper *London*, 1718

Pritii (J G) Introductio in Lectionem Novi Testamenti, curâ C G. Hoffmann, 8vo *Lipsiæ*, 1764

Michaelis's (John David) Introduction to the New Testament, translated, and augmented with Notes and a Dissertation on the Origin and Composition of the Three first Gospels, by Herbert Marsh, 6 vols 8vo *London*, 1819

Jones's (Jeremiah) New and Full Method of settling the Canonical Authority of the New Testament, with a Vindication of St Matthew's Gospel from Mr Whiston's charge of Dislocations, 3 vols. 8vo *Oxford, Clarendon Press*, 1798

Butler's (Charles) Horæ Biblicæ a Series of Notes on the Text and Literary History of the Bible, 2 vols 8vo *London*, 1807

Townley's (James) Illustrations of Biblical Literature, exhibiting the History and Fate of the Sacred Writings, from the earliest Period to the present Century, including biographical Notices of Translators and other eminent Biblical Scholars, 3 vols 8vo *London*, 1821

Clarke's (J B B) Concise View of the Succession of Sacred Literature, in a Chronological Arrangement of Authors and their Works, from the Invention of Alphabetic Characters to A D. M.CCC., 2 vols 8vo *London*, 1832.

Orme's (William) Bibliotheca Biblica a Select List of Books on Sacred Literature ; with Notices biographical, critical, and bibliographical, 8vo *Edinburgh*, 1824

Warburton's (Bishop) Directions for the Study of Theology (Works, Vol X)

Waterland's Advice to a Young Student in Theology (Works, Vol VI)

Bickersteth's (E) Christian Student , designed to assist Christians in general in acquiring Religious Knowledge , with Lists of Books adapted to various Classes of Society, 12mo *London*, 1829

Bibliotheca Sacra, post J. Lelong et C. F Boerneri iteratas curas, ordine disposita, emendata, suppleta continuata ab A G Masch 2 vols 4to *Halæ*, 1778–83
   A bibliographical account of the various editions of the original texts, Vulgate and Oriental versions

Baber's (H. H) Historical Account of the Saxon and English Versions of the Scriptures, previous to the opening of the XVth Century (Wiclif's New Testament)

Lewis's (John) History of the English Translations of the Bible, 8vo. *London*, 1739

Cruttwell's (Cl) Account of English Translations of the Bible, and List of their various Editions (Preface to Wilson's Bible)

Boyle (Hon Robt) on the Style of the Holy Scriptures (Works, Vol II)

Simpson's (David) Sacred Literature ; shewing the Holy Scriptures to be superior to the most celebrated Writings of Antiquity, by the Testimony of above 500 Witnesses , and also by a Comparison of their several Kinds of Composition, 4 vols 8vo *Birmingham*, 1788

Jones (W) on the Figurative Language of Scripture (Works, Vol II)

Keach's (Benj) Key to open the Scripture Metaphors and Types , to which are prefixed, Arguments to prove the Divine Authorship of the Holy Scriptures, folio *London*, 1779.
   See also Bampton Lectures Conybeare and Chevallier.

Cappelli (Ludov) Critica Sacra, sive de variis quæ in Sacris Vet Test Libris occurrunt Lectionibus. Recensuit, etc G J L Vogel , cum Appendice var Scriptorum ad eam se referentium, recens J G Schafenberg, 3 vols 8vo *Halæ Magd* 1775–86

Lowth (Robt) de Sacra Poesi Hebræorum, cum Notis et Epimetris J D Michaelis, edidit E F C Rosenmuller, 8vo *Oxonii*, 1821

Lowth's (Robt) Sacred Poetry of the Hebrews, translated, with the Notes of Michaelis and others, by G Gregory, 2 vols 8vo *London*, 1816.

Jebb's (Bp John) Sacred Literature , comprising a Review of the Principles of Composition laid down by Bp Lowth, and an Application of those Principles to the Illustration of the New Testament, 8vo *Lond* 1820.

Wilson's (W) Illustration of the Method of Explaining the New Testament by the Early Opinions of Jews and Christians concerning Christ [in refutation of Priestley's Early Opinions], 8vo *Cambridge*, 1797

Middleton's (Bp T F) Doctrine of the Greek Article applied to the Criticism and Illustration of the New Testament, 8vo. *London*, 1808

Commentators and Expositors.

Lutheri (Mart.) Comment in S Scripturam, vid. in Lib Deut (Opera, Vol III), XXII Psalmos priores, Psalmos Grad, et in Psalmos XLV et LI (Vols II, III, et IV), Ecclesiasten, (Vol IV), Canticum Canticorum, (Vol IV), Esaiam, (Vol III), Hoseam et Joelem, (Vol IV), Amos et Abiam, (Vol III), Micham, (Vol IV), Mattheam, (Vol IV), Epist ad Galatas, (Vols I, II, et III)

Melancthonis (Ph) Commentarii in S. Scripturam (Opera, Vols II, III, et IV)

Zuinglii (Huld) Annotationes in Genesim et Exodum, Enchiridion Psalmorum, Complanationes Isaiae et Jeremiae Prophetae, Annotationes in Evangelia et Epistolas Pauli, &c (Opera, Vol III)

Calvini (Joh) Commentaria, Homiliae, et Conciones in S Script (Opera, Vols I to VII)

Critici Sacri, sive, Annotata doctiss Virorum in Vetus ac Novum Testamentum Quibus accedunt Tractatus varii Theologico-Philologici, 8 vols. in 9, folio *Amstelod* 1698 — Thesaurus Theologico-Philologicus, sive, Sylloge Dissertationum ad illustr Vet et Nov Testamenti loca, 2 vols folio *Amstelod* 1701 — Thesaurus Novus Theologico-Philologicus, sive, Sylloge Dissertat exegeticarum ad V et N Instrumenti loca Ex museo T Hasæi et C Ikenii, 2 vols folio *Lugduni Bat* 1732

Poli (Matthæi) Synopsis Criticorum aliorumque S Scripturæ Interpretum, 4 vols in 5, folio, large paper *Londini*, 1669-76

Bloomfield's (S T) Recensio Synoptica Annotationis Sacræ, being a Critical Digest and Synoptical Arrangement of the most important Annotations on the New Testament, 8 vols 8vo *London*, 1826-8

Gill's (John) Exposition of the Old and New Testaments, in which the Sense of the Sacred Text is given, difficult Passages explained, seeming Contradictions reconciled, and whatever is material in the various Readings and the several Oriental Versions is observed, 9 vols 4to *London*, 1809.

Patrick, Lowth, Arnald, Whitby, and Lowman's Critical Commentary and Paraphrase on the Old and New Testament and the Apocrypha, edited by J R Pitman, 6 vols large 4to *Lond* 1822

Henry's (Matt) Exposition of the Old and New Testament, with Practical Remarks and Observations, 6 vols 4to *Lond* 1792

Scott's (Tho) Holy Bible, with Explanatory Notes, Practical Observations, and copious Marginal References, 6 vols 4to *Lond* 1823

Hall's (Bp Joseph) Contemplations upon the principal Passages in the Holy Story (Works, Vols I and II)

Hall's (Bp Joseph) Plain and Familiar Explication, by way of Paraphrase, of all the Hard Texts of the Old and New Testament (Works, Vols III and IV)

Saurin (Jacques), Discours historiques, critiques théologiques, et moraux, sur les Evenemens les plus memorables du Vieux et Nouveau Testament, 11 vols 8vo *La Haye*, 1720

RELIGION.

La Sainte Bible [connu sous le nom de BIBLE DE VENCE], en Latin et François, avec des Notes littérales, critiques, et historiques, des Préfaces et des Dissertations, tirées du Commentaire de Calmet, de l'Abbé de Vence, et des Auteurs le plus célèbres, revue, corrigée, et augmentée de Notes, 25 vols 8vo *Paris*, 1820–24.

Lightfoot (Joh.) ΛΕΙΨΑΝΑ de Rebus ad LXX Vers spectantibus, Versiones Proph Minorum Græca et Vulgaris, nec non Targum, cum Hebræo fonte collatæ (Works, Vol X.)

Baxter's (Rich) Paraphrase on the New Testament, 8vo. *Lond* 1695

Burkitt's (W) New Testament, with Observations and Practical Instructions, abridged by S Glasse, 2 vols. 4to. *Lond* 1806

Doddridge's (Philip) Family Expositor, or, a Paraphrase and Version of the New Testament, with Critical Notes and a Practical Improvement, with Life of the Author by Job Orton, 4 vols. 4to *Lond* 1808

Gilpin's (Wm) Exposition of the New Testament, pointing out the leading Sense and Connexion of the Sacred Writers, 2 vols 8vo *Lond* 1793

Le Nouveau Testament, avec des Réflexions Morales sur chaque Verset [par Pasq. Quesnel], 8 vols 12mo *Amst* 1736

Blunt's (J J) Veracity of the V Books of Moses, argued from the undesigned Coincidences to be found in them, when compared in their several parts, 12mo *Lond* 1831

Townsend's (Joseph) Character of Moses established for Veracity, as an Historian recording Events from the Creation to the Deluge and subsequently, 2 vols 4to *Bath*, 1813

Kennedy's (James) Ten Lectures on the Philosophy of the Mosaic Record of the Creation, delivered in Trinity College, Dublin, 2 vols 8vo *Lond* 1827

Shuckford (Sam) on the Creation and Fall of Man. (Connexion, Vol IV)

Lightfoot's (John) Observations on Genesis ; Gleanings out of Exodus; and de Creatione Itineribus, et Mansione Israelit , Expositio Hoseæ (Works, Vol II.)

Graves' (Richard) Lectures on the Four last Books of the Pentateuch, designed to shew the Divine Origin of the Jewish Religion from Internal Evidence, 2 vols 8vo *Dublin*, 1807

Boys' (Tho) Key to the Book of Psalms, 8vo *London*, 1825

Horne's (Bp Geo) Commentary on the Psalms, 2 vols 8vo *Oxford*, 1798

Leighton s (Abp) Meditations, practical and critical, on Psalms IV , XXXII , and CXXX , translated from the Latin by P Doddridge (Works, Vol II)

Hall (Bp. Jos) Some few of David's Psalms metaphrased (Works)

Reynold's (Bp Edward) Exposition of the CXth Psalm. (Works, Vol II)

Reynold's (Bp Edward) Annotations on the Book of Ecclesiastes (Works, Vol IV)

Mede's (Jos) Treatises on Obscure Passages in Daniel (Works)

RELIGION. 13

Blunt's (J. J.) Veracity of the Gospels and Acts of the Apostles argued from their undesigned Coincidences, 12mo Lond. 1828

Lardner's (N) Credibility of the Gospel History, or, the Facts occasionally mentioned in the New Testament confirmed by Passages of contemporary ancient Authors   (Works, Vol I)

Stabback's (Tho) Four Gospels and Acts of the Apostles, illustrated with Annotations, critical, explanatory, and practical, selected from the most able Commentators, and accompanied with Reflections. 2 vols 8vo   Falmouth, 1809

Trapp s (Joseph) Explanatory Notes upon the Four Gospels, with Three Discourses explaining the illustrious Prophecies of the Old and New Testament, 8vo   Oxford, 1805

Lightfoot s (John) Hebrew and Talmudical Exercitations on the Evangelists and part of Romans and I Corinthians   (Works, Vols. XI and XII)

Townson (Tho) on the Four Gospels, (Works, Vol 1), on Evangelical History   (Vol II)

Elsley's (J) Annotations on the Four Gospels and the Acts of the Apostles, 2 vols 8vo   Lond. 1824

Adams's (Tho) Exposition of St. Matthew.   (Works, Vols. III and IV)

Tyndall's (Wm) Exposition uppon the V, VI, VII Chapters of Matheu, whiche three Chapters are the Keye and Dore of the Scripture, and the restoring agayne of Moses' lawe, corrupte by the Scribes and Pharises   And the Exposition is the restoring agayne of Christe's Lawe, corrupte by the Papistes   (Works)

Gray's (And.) Delineation of the Parables of our Blessed Saviour; to which is prefixed, a Dissertation on Parables and Allegorical Writings in general, 8vo   Lond 1814

Gardiner's (James) Exposition of our Saviour's Sermon on the Mount, 8vo, large paper   Lond 1720

Biscoe's (Rich) History of the Acts of the Holy Apostles confirmed from other Authors, and considered as full Evidence of the Truth of Christianity   (Boyle Lectures)

Lightfoot's (John) Commentary and Hebrew and Talmudical Exercitations on the Acts of the Apostles.   (Works, Vol VIII)

Slade's (J) Annotations on the Epistles, 2 vols. 8vo.   Lond 1824

Pearson (Jo) Annales Paulini   (Randolph's Enchiid Vol I)

Locke's (John) Essay on the Understanding of St Paul's Epistles, with Paraphrase and Notes to the Epistles of St Paul to the Romans, Corinthians, Galatians, and Ephesians   (Works, Vol VIII)

Adams's (Tho) Paraphrase on the first XI Chapters of the Epistle to the Romans, 8vo   Lond 1771   (Works Vol I)

Davenant's (Bp John) Exposition of the Epistle to the Colossians, translated from the original Latin, with a Life of the Author, and Notes illustrative of the Writers and Authorities referred to in the Work, by Josiah Allport to which is added, a Translation of de Morte Christi, by the same Prelate, 2 vols 8vo   Lond 1831

Jewell s (Bp) Exposition upon the Two Epistles to the Thessalonians   (Works Vol II)

14   RELIGION.

Owen's (J) Exposition of the Epistle of St Paul to the Hebrews, with
    Preliminary Exercitations, 4 vols royal 8vo, large paper   *Edin*
    1812-13

Stuart's (Moses) Commentary on the Epistle to the Hebrews, [edited by
    Eben Henderson], 2 vols 8vo   *Lond* 1828

Leighton's (Abp R) Practical Commentary on the 1st Epistle of Peter
    (Works, Vol I)

Jones (W) on the Epistle to the Hebrews shewing the Harmony between
    the Mysteries, Doctrines, and Morality of the Old and New Testa-
    ment   (Works, Vol III)

Mede's (Joseph) Paraphrase and Exposition of St Peter, 2d Epist
    chap iii , on the Day of Christ's Second Coming   (Works)

Tyndall's (Wm) Exposition of the First Epistle of St John, set forth
    1531   (Works)

Mede (Joseph) Clavis et Commentationes Apocalypticæ , Opuscula ad
    Rem Apocalypticam spectantia   (Works)

Daubuz' (Charles) Commentary on the Revelation of St John, with a
    Preliminary Discourse, new modelled and abridged by P Lancaster,
    4to   *Lond* 1730

Gauntlett's (Henry) Exposition of the Book of Revelation, 8vo   *Lond*
    1821

Cunningham's (W) Dissertation on the Seals and Trumpets of the Apo-
    calypse, and the Prophetical Period of 1260 years, 8vo   *Lond* 1817

Horsley's (Bp S) Biblical Criticism on the first XIV Historical Books
    of the Old Testament, also on the first IX Prophetical, 4 vols 8vo
    Lond 1820

Lightfoot's (John) Explanation of difficult Places of Scripture.   (Works,
    Vol V)

Allix's (Peter) Reflections upon the Books of the Holy Scripture, to
    establish the Truth of the Christian Religion, 8vo   *Oxford*, 1822
    (Works, Vol. I)

King's (Edw) Morsels of Criticism, tending to illustrate some few Pas-
    sages in the Holy Scriptures upon Philosophical Principles, 3 vols 8vo.
    Lond 1800

Roberts's (W H) Corrections on various Passages in the English Version
    of the Old Testament, upon the Authority of Ancient MSS and An-
    cient Versions, 8vo   *Lond* 1794

Newton's (Bp T) Dissertations on some Parts of the Old and New
    Testament   (Works, Vols I to IV)

Jones (W) on the Use and Intent of some remarkable Passages of Scrip-
    ture not commonly understood   (Works, Vol III)

Callaway's (John) Oriental Observations and Occasional Criticisms, more
    or less illustrative of several hundred Passages of Scripture, 12mo
    Lond 1827

Barrington's (Hon Daines) Miscellanea Sacra.   (Works)

Bowyer's (W) Critical Conjectures and Observations on the New Testa-
    ment, collected from various Authors, 4to   *Lond* 1782.

Newton's (Sir I) Historical Account of Two Notable Corruptions of
    Scripture, viz 1 John, v 7. and Tim. iii 16   (Works, Vol V)

On the Prophecies.

Keith's (A) Evidences of the Truth of the Christian Religion, derived from the literal Fulfilment of Prophecy, as illustrated by the History of the Jews, and by the Discoveries of recent Travellers, 8vo   *Edin* 1832

Kett's (Henry) History the Interpreter of Prophecy, or, a Scriptural View of the Prophecies and their Fulfilment, 2 vols 8vo   *Lond* 1805

Newton (Bp Tho) on the Prophecies which have remarkably been fulfilled, and at this time are fulfilling, 2 vols 8vo   *Lond* 1817

Newton's (Sir I) Observations on the Prophecies of Holy Writ, particularly those of Daniel and the Apocalypse of St. John (Works, Vol V.)

Robinson (Tho), Prophecies of the Messiah, from the beginning of Genesis to the end of the Psalms of David, considered and improved, 8vo   *Lond* 1812

Zouch's (Tho) Attempt to illustrate the Prophecies of the Old and New Testament (Works, Vol I)

Faber's (G. S.) Calendar of Prophecy; or, a Dissertation on the Prophecies which treat of the Grand Period of Seven Times 3 vols. 8vo   *Lond* 1828

Faber's (G S) General and Connected View of the Prophecies relative to the Conversion, Restoration, Union, and future Glory of Israel and Judah, 2 vols   *Lond* 1808

Faber (G S) on the Prophecies that have been fulfilled and are now fulfilling, or will hereafter be fulfilled, relative to the Great Period of 1260 Years, the Papal and Mohammedan Apostacies, Reign of Antichrist, and Restoration of the Jews, 3 vols 8vo   *Lond* 1807–18

Faber (G S) on Daniel's Prophecy of the Seventy Weeks, 8vo   *Lond* 1811

Warburtonian Lectures on Prophecy —

    Hurd's (Bp Richard) Introduction to the Study of the Prophecies concerning the Christian Church, and particularly concerning the Church of Papal Rome, 8vo   *London*, 1772

    Hallifax (Bp Sam) on the Prophecies of the Christian Church, and in particular concerning the Church of Papal Rome, 8vo   *Lond* 1776

    Bagot (Bp Lewis) on the Prophecies concerning the first Establishment and subsequent History of Christianity, 8vo   *London*, 1780

    Apthorp's (East) Discourses on Prophecy, 2 vols. 8vo   *London*, 1786

    Nares' (Robt) Connected and Chronological View of the Prophecies relating to the Christian Church, 8vo   *London*, 1805

    Pearson's (Ed) Lectures on the Subject of the Prophecies relating to the Christian Church, 8vo   *London*, 1811

    Allwood (Ph) on the Prophecies relating to the Christian Church, and especially to the Apostacy of Papal Rome, 2 vols 8vo   *Lond* 1815

    Davison (John) on Prophecy, in which are considered its Structure, Use, and Inspiration, 8vo   *London*, 1825.

Concordances, Dictionaries, and Commonplace Books

Buxtorfii (Jo) Concordantiæ Bibliorum Hebraicæ et Chaldaicæ, folio. *Basileæ*, 1632

Williams' (J) Concordance to the Greek Testament. with the English Version to each Word, 4to. *London*, 1767

Cruden's (Alex) Complete Concordance to the Holy Scriptures; or, a Dictionary and Alphabetical Index to the Bible, 4to *London*, 1763.

Cruttwell's (C) Concordance of Parallels, collected from Bibles and Commentaries, which have been published in the Hebrew, Latin, French, Spanish, and other Languages, with the Authorities of each, 4to *London*, 1790

Calmet's Dictionary of the Holy Bible, historical, critical, and geographical; with Fragments, or continued Appendix, illustrating the Manners, Incidents, and Phraseology of the Scriptures, selected from the most esteemed and authentic Voyages and Travels into the East; with Remarks, Observations, and Plates. Revised, corrected, and enlarged, by C Taylor, 5 vols 4to *London*, 1823

Brown's (Jo) Dictionary of the Bible, edited by his Sons, 2 vols 8vo *Edinburgh*, 1807

Robinson's (John) Theological, Biblical, and Ecclesiastical Dictionary, 8vo *London*, 1816.

Locke's (John) Commonplace Book to the Holy Bible, or, the Scriptures' Sufficiency practically demonstrated, wherein the Substance of Scripture respecting Doctrine, Worship, and Manners, is reduced to its proper heads Revised and improved by W Dodd, 8vo *London*, 1824

Biblical Antiquities, Connexions of Sacred and Profane History, &c.

Josephi (Flavii) Opera Omnia, Gr et Lat cum Notis et Novâ Versione J Hudsoni, acced Notæ varior &c ; omnia collegit, disposuit, et ad Codices ferè omnes recensuit, Notasque suas adjecit S. Havercampus, 2 vols folio *Amst.* 1726

Josephus's Works, or, History and Antiquities of the Jews, translated by W Whiston, 4 vols. 8vo *London*, 1806

Ugolini (Blasii) Thesaurus Antiquitatum Sacrarum, complectens selectissima clarissimorum Virorum Opuscula, in quibus veterum Hebræorum Mores, Leges Instituta, Ritus Sacri et Civiles illustrantur, 34 vols folio *Venetiis*, 1744–69

 Vol 1 R Chija Additamenta ad Codicem de Die Expiationum
  R Martini in Pugionem Fidei Proœmium
  Observationes Jos De Voisin ad Proœmium
  J Meyeri Tractatus de Temporibus Sacris et Festis Diebus Hebræorum, cum Animadversionibus in Joh Spenceri libros de Legibus Ritualibus Hebræorum
  J. Triglandius de Origine et Caussis Rituum Mosaicorum
  H Witsii Ægyptiaca, sive de Ægyptiacorum Sacrorum cum Hebraicis Collectione libri tres

 Vol. 2 Chr Wormii de corruptis Antiquitatum Hebræarum apud Tacitum, &c Vestigiis libri 2.
  G Caspiris Kirchmeyeri Exercitatio ad C. Taciti Histor lib 5, de Rebus Moribusque Judæorum

RELIGION

        H Relandi Antiquitates Sacræ, amplissimus commentariis philologicis illustratæ.

Vol. 3 T Goodwini Moses et Aaron, cum Hottingeri notis
        P Cunæi Libri 3 de Republ Hebræorum, cum Nicolai notis
        J H Hottingeri Jus Hebræorum

Vol. 4 B Corn Bertramus de Rep Hebræorum, cum commentario Constantini l'Empereur
        C. Sigonii Libri 7 de Rep Hebræorum, cum Nicolai notis.
        J Buxtorfii Synagoga Judaica
        A Pfeiffer Antiquitates selectæ, ab Ugolino notis illustratæ

Vol. 5 Eusebii Onomasticon, cum Latina interpretatione S. Hieronymi, cum notis Bonfrerii, et Joh Clerici Animadversionibus
        J Bonfrerii Annotationes in promissæ Terræ Chorographicam Tabulam.
        J. Rhenferdii Periculum criticum in loca depravata Eusebii Cæsariensis et Hieronymi, de situ et nominibus locorum Hebraicorum
        Ejusdem Exercitatio philologica 2da, ad loca deperdita Eusebii et Hieronymi de situ, &c
        Ejusdem Exercitatio philologica 3tia ad loca vexata Eusebii, &c
        Ejusdem Exercitatio philologica 4ta ad loca depravata et vexata Eusebii et Hieronymi de locis Hebraicis S Sc
        Ejusdem Notæ Criticæ et Observationes in Eusebii et Hieronymi Onomasticon
        Ejusdem Exercitatio Eusebio Hieronymiana de Angulo Arabiæ et Batanæ
        N Sansonis Animadversiones in duis Tabulas geographicas, ex Veteri et Novo Testamento desumptas.
        Ejusdem Index Geographicus
        Joh Clerici Notæ in Indicem Geographicum N Sansonsis
        N Sansonis Descriptio Judææ.
        Ejusdem Jesu Christi Vita
        Ejusdem Petri Apostoli Vita
        Ejusdem Pauli Apostoli Vita
        J Lightfooti Centuria Chorographica in S Matthæum
        Ejusdem Decas Chorographica in S Marcum.
        Ejusdem Chorographica pauca in S Lucam
        Ejusdem Disquisitio Chorographica in S Johannem

Vol. 6 H. Relandi Palestina
        Bochardi Monachi Descriptio Terræ Sanctæ
        T. Quistorpii Nebo
        J. H. Hottingeri Dissertatio de Geographia Terræ Chanaan.
        J Millii Dissertatio de Nilo et Euphrate
        R Petachiæ Itinerarium, cum Versione Wagenseilii

Vol 7 Ab Peritsol Itinera Mundi, Hebraicè et Latinè, cum Interpretatione et Notis Th Hydæ
        R S Sancti Itinerarium, Hebraicè et Latinè
        P Dan Huetii Commentarium de Navigationibus Salomonis
        M. Lipenii Dissert de Navigio Salomonis
        Ejusdem Dissert de Ophir
        J Chr Wichmanshausen Dissert de Navigatione Ophiritica
        J. C Jehringii Dissert de Regione Tharsis.
        I Hassæi Dissert de תובח
        H Relandi Dissert de Ophir
        Ejusdem Dissert de Mari Rubro
        P Dan Huetii Tractatus de Situ Paradisi Terrestris
        H Relandi Dissert de Situ Paradisi Terrestris
        T Hopkinsonii Descriptio Paradisi
        Sam Bocharti Epistola de Paradisi Situ
        Steph Morini Dissert de Paradiso Terrestri
        Joh Vorstii Dissert de Paradiso
        H Relandi Dissert de Monte Garizim
        Harkenrothii Dissert de Monte Sublimi
        T Hassæi Observatio de Monte Sublimi
        Haremborgii Oculus Moysis et Christi, a monte editissimo Palæstinum spectans
        Harkenrothii Periculum Criticum, quo Λιβάδων Heyschii, aliaque ejus depravata loca explicantur
        H Van Alphen Dissert de Terra Chadrach et Damasco ejus quiete ad Zach ix

RELIGION.

Chr Cellarii Dissert de Excidio Sodomæ
T Hasæi de Zabulonis præ Sidone præstantia ad Gen. xlix
Ejusdem Dissert de Nephthalitide, Apostolorum patria, ad illustrationem
    Oriculi Jacobæi, Gen xlix
J C Wickmanshausen Dissert de Thermis Tiberiensibus.
J Philidelphii Dissert de Valle Josaphat et Excidu
C B Ottonis Dissert de Flumine Sabbathico.
M Liebentantii Dissert de Terra Morijah, et Monte Visionis Dei
Gh Outoven Observationes de Montibus Sionis et Morijah.
J F Harkenrothi Dissert de Rachele.
Ejusdem Disseit. de Ænon prope Salim.
P Zornii Dissert de Ænone prope Salim
Ejusdem Liber singularis de Historia et Antiquitatibus No-Amon
F Hasæi Dissert de Gente פפ *Kau Kau* ad Isaiæ xviii
C Cellarii Dissert de Amœnitatibus geographicis et historicis, ex Itine-
    ribus S Pauli collectis.
Lucherii, Episcopi, Epistola ad Faustum presbyterum.
Antonii Placentini Itinerarium

Vol 8 S Van Til Commentarius de Tabernaculo Moysis
    J Buxtorfii Historia Arcæ Fœderis
    T Hasæi Dissert. de Lignis Sittim
    Ejusdem Dissert de Rubo Moysis
    Ejusdem Dissert de Lapide Fundamenti
    J H A Dorien, Dissert. de Cherubinis Sancti Sanctorum.
    J Buxtorfii Dissert de Manna
    Maimonidis Vita, ab J. Buxtorfio descripta, in Præfatione in More Ne-
      vochim
    R Claveringii Dissert de Maimonide.
    H Prideaux Præfatio ad Tractatus Maimonidis de Jure Pauperis et
      Peregrini.
    Lud Compiegne de Veil Præfatio in Opera Maimonidis.
    Maimonidis Constitutiones de Templo, Vasis Sanctuarii, et de Ingressu
      Sanctuarii, Heb et Lat a Ugolino notis illustratæ
    I C Sturmii Scenographia Templi Hierosolymitani

Vol 9 R Abrahami Ben David Commentarius de Templo, ab Ugolino Latina
      Interpr illustratus, Heb et Lat
    J Lightfooti Descriptio Templi Hierosolym.
    Ejusdem Ministerium Templi
    F Opitii Commentar. de Templi Custodia nocturna
    H Relandi Lib. de Spoliis Templi Hierosolym. in Arcu Titiano conspicuis
    T Dassovii Imagines Hebræarum rerum

Vol 10 M Plesken Dissert de Columnis æneis
    J J Crameri Dissert de Ara exteriori Templi Secundi.
    D Mihi Dissert de Cornibus Altaris exterioris
    J Buxtorfii Historia Ignis Sacri
    J. G Bornhii Dissert de Igne Gentilium sacro
    D Mihi Dissert de Altari Mediatore.
    B Ugolini Altare exterius
    C L Schlichter Dissert. de Mensa Facierum, ejusque Mysterio
    Ejusdem Dissert de Pane Facierum
    B. Ugolini Dissert de Mensa et Panibus Propositionis

Vol 11 B Ugolini Altare interius
    R Abrahami Ben David Commentarius de Suffitu, ab Ugolino ex Heb
      Latine redditus et notis illustratus
    J Meyeri Dissert de Suffitu
    D Weymari Dissert de Suffitu
    P Alpini Dialogus de Balsamo
    J G Michaelis Dissert de Thuribulo Adyti
    G F Rogal Thuribulum
    J Braunii Dissert de Adolitione Suffitûs
    G M Doederlini Exerc de Candelabris Judæorum
    B Ugolini Dissert de Candelabro.
    D F Jani Exercit de Vite aurea Templi Hierosolym.

Vol 12 J Sauberti Lib de Sacerdotibus Hebræorum
    J Krumbholtz Sacerdotium Hebraicum
    E C Boldich Pontifex M Hebræorum.
    J Braunii Dissert de Sanctitate Pontif. Max.

RELIGION

J Seldeni Lib 2 de Successione Pontificum Hebræorum
B D Carpzovii Dissert de Pontificum Hebræorum Vestitu sacro
J. Buxtorfii Historia Urim et Thummim.
N Polemanni Dissert de Urim et Thummim
J Spenceri Dissert de Urim et Thummim
P Ribouldealdi Dissert de Urim et Thummim contra Joh Spencerum
C. L Schichter Dissert de Lamina aurea Pont Max.
H A Toepffer Dissert de Tiara Summi Sacerdotis
Ejusdem Dissert de Tiaris minorum Sacerdotum
B Scheidii Oleum Unctionis
D Weymar Dissert de Unctione Sacra Hebræorum, et inaugurali.
J J Quandt Dissert de Pontificis Max Suffraganeo
T R Latii Dissert de Sacerdote Castrensi
B. Ugolini Dissert de Sacerdote Castrensi

Vol 13 R Abrahami Ben David Dissert. de Vestitu Sacerdotum Hebræorum, Heb et Lat
שי״י, שש, משור, רכלת, ארגמן, תורער I C Harembergii Dissert de Vocibus
I C Biel Dissert de Purpura Lydia ad illustrationem loci Act xvi 11.
B Ugolino Sacerdotium Hebraicum
D Pfeffingeri Dissert de Nathinæis

Vol 14 Mechiltha, Commentarius vetustiss et eruditiss in Exodum, ab Ugolino ex Heb Latinè redditus
Siphre, Commentar vetustiss et eruditiss. in Leviticum, ab Ugolino ex Heb Latinè redditus

Vol. 15 Siphre, Commentar antiquiss et eruditiss in Numeros, ab Ugolino ex Heb Lat redd
Siphre, Commentar. &c. in Deuteronomium, ab Ugolino ex Heb Lat redd
Pesiktha Minus, Commentarius vetustus et philologicus in Leviticum, Numeros, et Deuteronomium, ex Heb &c

Vol. 16. Residuum Pesikthæ complectitur.

Vol 17 N Muleri Judæorum Annus Lunæ Solaris, et Turc-Arabum Annus mere Lunaris
J Seldeni Dissert de Anno Civili Judæorum
Maimonidis Constitutiones de Consecratione Novilunii, Heb et Lat
Chr Languasen Dissert de Mense Iunii veterum Hebræorum
Additamenta ad Codicem de Sabbatho, ab Ugolino ex Heb Lat reddita
Additamenta ad Codicem de Commixtionibus Sabbaticis, ab Ugolino, ex Heb Lat redd
J G Outhovii Dissert de Sabbatho sec indo-primo
J J. Syrbii Dissert de Sabbatho Gentili
Additamenta ad Codicem de Pascha, ab Ugolino ex Heb Latine reddita
Codex de Pascha, Ghemara Hierosolymitana illustratus, ab Ugolino ex Heb Lat redd
I R Gruner Diatribe de Oblatione Primitiarum.
Ugolini Dissert de Ritibus in Cœna Domini, ex Antiquitatibus Paschalibus illustratis

Vol 18 Additamenta ad Codicem Sekalim de Siclis, ab Ugolino ex Heb Lat redd
Tractatus Sekalim, Ghemara Hierosolym
Additamenta ad Tractatum Joma
Tractatus Ioma, Ghemara Hierosolym illustratus
Additamenta ad Tractatum Succah
Tractatus Succah, Ghem Hierosol
G Groddekii Dissert de Ceremoniis Palmarum
Additamenta ad Tractatum Rosh-Haschana, ab Ugolino ex Heb Lat redd
Tractatus Ros-Haschana, Ghem Hierosol
Additamenta ad Tractatum Tahanijoth
Tractatus Tahanijoth, Ghem Hierosol
Additamenta ad Tractatum Meghilah
Tractatus Meghilah, Ghem Hierosol
Additamenta ad Tractatum Chaghigah
Tractatus Chaghigah, Ghem Hierosol
Additamenta ad Tractatum Betzah
Tractatus Betzah, Ghem Hierosolym
Additamenta ad Tractatum Mohed Katon
Tractatus Mohed Katon, Ghem Hierosol.

RELIGION

Vol. 19 Additamenta ad Tractatum de Sacrificiis, ab Ugolino ex Heb. Lat. redd.
Tractatus de Sacrificiis, Ghemara Babylonica illustratus
Additamenta ad Tractatum de Muneribus
Tractatus de Muneribus, Ghem Babylon
Additamenta ad Tractatus de { Profanis, Primogenitis, Sacrificiorum Commutatione, Prevaricatione, Exciduis, Rerum Votarum Æstimatione
Tractatus Misnicus de Sacrificio Jugi, ab Ugolino notis philologicis illustratus
H G Clemens de Labro æneo
L C Sturmii Mare æneum

Vol 20 Additamenta ad Tractatus de { Benedictionibus, Angulo, Re dubia, Separationibus, Anno Septimo, Heterogeneis
J. C. Hottingeri Commentar de Decimis Hebræorum
Additamenta ad Tractatum de Decimis
Tractatus de Decimis, Ghem Hier illustratus
Additamenta ad Tractatum de Decima Secunda
Tractatus de Decima Secunda, Ghem Hier &c.
J Spencer Dissert de Solutione Primitiarum et Decimarum
Ejusdem Dissert de Professione Decimarum.
Additamenta ad Tractatum de Placenta
Tractatus de Placenta, Ghem Hier &c
Additamenta ad Tractatum de Præputio Arborum
Tractatus de Arbore Præputiata, Ghem Hier &c
Additamenta ad Tractatum de Primitivis
Tractatus de Primitivis, Ghem Hier &c

Vol 21 J. Rhenferdii Dissert 2 de decem Otiosis Synagogæ
Ejusdem Investigatio Præfectorum, et Ministrorum Synagogæ
C Vitringa Liber de Decemviris Otiosis
C. Bornitii Exercitationes Philologicæ tres de Synagogis veterum Hebræorum
I Sauberti Dissert. de Precibus Hebræorum
N Polemanni Dissert. de Ritu precandi veterum Hebræorum.
F W Jahn Dissert. de Precibus Gentilium expiatoriis
M Hilleri Dissert de Vestibus Fimbriatis Hebræorum.
C Lubeci Exercitatio de Decisionibus Peniculamenti Hebræorum
B Ugolini de Phylacteriis Hebræorum
T Dassovii Dissert Ritibus Mezuzæ
G Ursini Antiquitates Hebraicæ, Scholastico-Academicæ
J. L Heubneri Dissert de Academiis Hebræorum
I J Scrupii Dissert de Titulo Rabbi
I. H. Otthonis Historia doctorum Misnicorum, cum notis Relandi
G E Geiger Commentatio de Hillele et Sammai

Vol. 22 B Ugolini Trihæresium, sive Dissert de tribus Sectis Judæorum, scil de Pharisæis, Sadducæis, et Essenis
J Schmid Dissert de Secta Pharisæorum
H Opitii Exercitatio philologica de Pharisæis
L A Rechenberg Dissert. de Pharisæis
S Barthel Scbed historicum de Sadducæis.
J Drusii Libellus de Hasidæis.
P Slevogti Disputatio de Metempsychosi Hebræorum
I Triglandii Diatribe de Secta Karæorum.
L Waineri Dissert de Karæis.
R A Karæi Excerpta in Librum Josuæ
Institutio Karæorum, ab Ugolino ex Heb Lat redd
H Relandi Dissert. de Samaritanis
C Cellarii Collectanea Historiæ Samaritanæ
Epistolæ duæ Sichemitarum ad Jobum Ludolfum
J Rhenferdii Dissert. de fictis Judæor Hæresibus
Ejusdem Dissert de Sethianis
Ejusdem Dissert de Redemptione Marcosiorum et Heracleonitarum.

RELIGION. 21

P Slevogti Dissert de Proselytis Judæorum
J G Muller Dissert de Proselytis
J. Reiskii Dissert de Baptismo Judæorum
J A Danzii Baptismus Proselytorum Judaicus.
J Spenceri Dissert de Lustrationibus et Purificationibus Hebræorum.
J H Mau Dissert. de Lustrationibus et Purificationibus Hebræorum contra J Spencerum
Ejusdem de Purificatione mirabili singulari, et singulariter mirabili
J Spenceri Dissert de Circumcisione.
S Deylingii Observatio de Origine Circumcisionis Judaicæ
J J Quandt Dissert de Cultris Circumcisoriis et Secespitis Hebræorum.
H. B Gedæi Dissert de Instrumento Circumcisionis à Zippora et Josua adhibito
G Groddecki Dissert de Judæis Præputium attrahentibus
H Lossii Dissert de Epispasmo Judaico

Vol 23 J Seldeni Syntagmata duo de Diis Syris
A. Beyeri Additamenta ad Seldeni Syntagmata
J C Wichmanshausen Dissert. 4. de Divinationibus Babyloniorum
J Clodii Dissert. de Magia Sagittarum.
D Milii Dissert de אוב et אובות
Ejusdem Dissert de חרטמ
J C Wichmanshausen Dissert de Theraphim
A Pfeifferi Exercitatio de Theraphim.
P. E Jablonski Remphan, Egyptiorum Deus, ab Israelitis in deserto cultus, nunc ex lingua et antiquitate Ægyptiaca erutus et illustratus
J H Mau Dissert de Kijun et Remphan.
J C Schwabii Dissert de Moloch et Remphan.
D Milii Dissert de Idolo אחד
Ejusdem Dissert de Bahalzebub et Miphlezeth.
Ejusdem Dissert de Gad et Meni
J P. Lakmacheri Dissert de Gad et Meni
H Relandi Dissert de Diis Cabiris
Z. B Pochari Dissert. de Simulacris Solaribus Israelitarum
J Spenceri Dissert de Tyriorum Gammadim et Hammanim.
F Mayeri Dissert de Idolo אשרה.
G. F. Meinhardi Dissert. philolog de Selenolatria
J Crausii Dissert de Succoth Benoth
D Dietzschii Dissert de Cultu Molochi
C S Ziegra Dissert. 3 de crudelissima Liberorum Immolatione Molocho facta
C G. Meyeri Dissert. de Hominibus Piacularibus
I. Roser Dissert de Dagone, Philistæorum Idolo.
S Deylingii Dissert de Fletu super Thamuz.
T Hasæi Diatribe de vera Origine et Significatione Vocis Astartes
Joh a Lent Schediasma histor philol. de Judæorum pseudo-Messiis
D Milii Dissert de Mohamedismo ante Mohamedem.

Vol 24. J Spenceri Dissert de Theocratia Judaica.
C Blechschmidi Dissert de Theocratia in populo sancto instituta
Deylingii Exercitatio de Israele, Jehova Domino
T Goodwini Dissert. de Theocratia Israelitarum
J. L Michaelis Dissert. philol num Deus dicatur אלהים, &c
H Hulsii Dissert de Jehova, Deo, Rege, ac Duce Militari in prisco Israele
Ejusdem Dissert de Sechinah, seu propinqua Dei in Israele Præsentia et Habitatione
J C Danhaueri Politica Biblica
H Conringii Exerc de Politia, sive de Rep Heb
C B Michaelis Dissert. philol. de Antiquitatibus Œconomiæ Patriarchalis
W Schickardi Jus Regium Hebræorum, cum notis J B Carpzovii.
R J Abarbanelis Dissert de Statu et Jure regio
Ejusdem Dissert de Judicum et Regum Differentia
N Serarii S J Herodes.
J Hardinii Prolusio de Nummis Herodiadum
A. Calovii Dissert historico-theologica de Statu Judæorum Ecclesiastico et Politico, ab anno primo nativitatis Christi, usque ad excidium Hierosolymæ.
J Rhenferdii Dissert de Arabarcha, vel Ethnarcha Judæorum.

RELIGION

P. Wesselingii Diatribe de Judæorum Archontibus, ad Inscriptionem Berenicensem

Vol. 25. Tractatus de Synedriis, Ghemara Hierosol. illustratus ab Ugolino ex Heb. Lat. redd.
Tractatus de Pœnis, Ghem. Hier. &c.
Tractatus de Synedriis Ghem. Babylon. &c.
J. Vorstii Dissert. de Synedriis Hebræorum.
S. F. Bucheri Synedrium Magnum
H. Witsii Dissert. de Synedriis Hebræorum
J. D. Jacobi Dissert. de Foro in Portis

Vol. 26. D. Henrici Dissert. de Judiciis Hebræorum.
J. Nicolai Tract. de Synedrio Ægyptiorum
J. B. Michaelis Tract. de Judiciis Pœnisque capitalibus in S. Scriptura commemoratis
F. W. Bierling Dissert. philolog. de veterum Hebræorum, circa Vitulam decollandam, Ritibus
Æ. Strauchii Dissert. de flagellandi Ritu apud Hebræos
J. J. Seyppelli Dissert. de flagellandi Ritu apud Romanos
J. G. Bindrin, Dissert. de Gradibus Excommunicationis apud Hebræos.
J. A. Osiandri Dissert. de Asylis Hebræorum.
J. Lydii Dissert. de Juramento
J. Nicolai Diatribe de Juramentis Hebræorum, Græcorum, Romanorum, aliorumque Populorum
J. Seldeni Dissert. de Juramentis
B. L. Molembecii Dissert. de Juramento per Genium principis
J. Spenceri Dissert. de Juramento per Anchialum
J. C. Miegii Constitutiones Servi Hebraei
J. C. Wagenseilii Dissert. de Sceptro Juda, ad Genes. xlix
P. Zornii Historia Fisci Judaici, sub Imperio veterum Romanorum
Ejusdem de Patriarcharum Judæorum Auro Coronario, sive Canone Anniversario
D. S. Deylingii Observatio de Sceptro Judæ, ad Genes. xlix.
Ejusdem de Judæorum Jure Gladii, tempore Christi ad loc. Joh. xviii.
C. Cellarii Dissert. de Cn. Pompeii M. Expeditione Judaica
Ejusdem Dissert. qua Flavii Josephi de Herodibus Historia à νόθως contra Joh. Harduinum justis vindiciis asseritur et nummis antiquis conciliatur
D. S. Deylingii Observatio de Familia et Genealogia Herodiadum.

Vol. 27. H. Relandi Oratio de Galli Cantu Hierosolymis audito.
J. G. Altmanni Observatio philol. de Gallicinio Hierosolymis in Ædibus Pontificis audito
J. C. Biel Animadversiones ad præcedentem Observationem.
Αλικτροφωνιας Evangelica Significatio genuina defensa
C. J. Ansaldi Liber de Forensi Judæorum Buccina
J. Lydii Syntagma sacrum de Re Militari, cum notis S. Van-Til
J. A. Danzii Dissert. de Re Militari Hebræorum
J. C. Ortlob Conjectura de Scutis et Clypeis Hebræorum.
J. B. Carpzovii Dissert. de Crethi et Plethi.
H. Opitii Dissert. de Crethi et Plethi, Davidis et Salomonis Satellitio
J. Seldeni de Jure Naturali et Gentium juxta Disciplinam Hebræorum, libri septem.

Vol. 28. J. G. Walchii Præfatio ad B. Bevernii, &c
B. Bevernii Syntagma de Ponderibus et Mensuris.
J. C. Eisenschidii Disquisitio de Ponderibus et Mensuris veterum Romanorum, Græcorum, Hebræorum, nec non de Valore Pecuniæ veteris
S. Epiphanii Liber de Ponderibus et Mensuris, Gr. et Lat.
D. Petavii Animadversiones ad eundem librum de Ponderibus et Mensuris
O. Sperlingii Dissert. de Nummis non cusis, tam veterum, quam recentiorum.
H. Coringii Paradoxa de Nummis Hebræorum
S. Græpii Dissert. de Multiplici Siclo et Talento Hebræorum item de Mensuris Hebraicis, tam aridorum, quam liquidorum
D. Deylingii Observatio de Re Nummaria veterum Hebræorum, &c.
A. Beyeri Siclus sacer, et regius appensus
J. C. Kessler Oratio de Dimidio Siclo argenteo, sancto, lytro animarum Israelis
D. Wulferi Dissert. de Siclo
J. H. Gradonici Dissert. de Siclo argenteo, &c.

J Buxtorfi Dissert de Literarum Hebraicarum genuina Antiquitate
J Harduini Expositio de 2 nummis Samaritanis.
Ejusdem Epistola de Nummis Samaritanis
H Relandi Dissert de Nummis Samaritanis, item Epistola de Nummis Samaritanis
J B Otti Epist de quibusdam Nummis Samaritanis
J. Gagnieri Epist de Nummis Samaritanis
C D Koch Dissert de Nummorum Hebraicorum Inscriptionibus Samaritanis
H Hottingen Dissert de variis Orientalium Inscriptionibus
Ejusdem Dissert. de Nummis Orientalium
J. Rhenferdi Periculum Phœnicium, sive Literaturæ Phœniciæ eruendæ Specimen.
J C Harembergii Observatio Critica de רכמך, דרבון, ארדבון
L B Carpzovii Disput de Nummis, Effigiem Moysis cornutam exhibentibus
S Schmidt Disput de Drachmis à Christo solutis

Vol. 29 Ugolini Comment de Re Rustica veterum Hebræorum
C Schoetgenii Antiquitates Triturae in S L occurrentes
C L Hoheisel Disput philol de Molis manualibus veterum
F L Goetzii Dissert de Molis et Pistrinis veterum
P Zornii Dissert de Hortis Opobalsami
J. G Schelhornii Dissert de דנים רלב ad Job. xl.
J Hasæi Dissert de רגאל דנים et בלל כנכים
T Hisæi Supplement ad præcedentem Dissertat
P Zornii Dissert de veterum Hebræorum hibernis et æstivis Domibus.
J C Harembergii Observatio de Domo inducta Minio.
C Schoetgenii Antiquitatis Fulloniæ
M H Schaibau Dissert de Luxu Hebiæorum.
P Lyseri Dissert philol de עכסים, &c
J C Biel Dissert de Purpura Lydia, ad Actorum xvi
G Altmanni ad dictum locum Act de Lydia Thyatirensi Observationes
J C Biel Animadversiones ad Altman de Lydia Thyatirensi.
J Hasæi Dissert de Inquinatis Sardiensium Vestimentis ad illustrationem loci Apoc iii
C F Pezoldi Dissert de promiscua Vestium utriusque Sexûs Usurpatione.
J. Schmidii Dissert historica de Usu Vestium albarum
L R Rot Exercitatio historica de Velamine Capitis virilis
F Bucheri Dissert de Velito Hebræorum Gynæceo
I D'Outreini Dissert philologico-theologica de velando Capite Muliebri propter Angelos, &c
G. Croesii Cogitationes de eadem re
J D Outreini in easdem Cogitationes Epicrisis
A Bynæi de Calceis Hebræorum Libri duo
A Platineri Dissert de Sandaligerulis Hebræorum
J G Carpzovii Discalceatio religiosa in loco sacro
J C Wichmanshausen Dissert. de Calceo Hebræorum in Sacris deponendo.
C Sagittarii Dissert de Nudipedalibus veterum
J Q Hedeni Scissio Vestium Hebræis ac Gentilibus usitata
J Rhorenseensii de Ritu scindendi Vestes

Vol 30 J Buxtorfii Dissert de Sponsalibus et Divortus
B Ugolini Uxor Hebræa
Tractatus Kiddusein, seu de Sponsalibus, Ghemara Hier illustratus, ab Ugolino ex Heb Lat redd
Tractatus Sotah, seu de Muliere Adulterii suspecta, Ghem Hier &c
Tractatus Chethuboth seu de Dotibus, Ghem, &c
F Dassovii Vidua Hebræa
G Groddekii Exercitatio de antiquorum Hebræorum Purgationibus Castitatis
G F Gudii Exercitatio philol de Hebraica Obstetricum Origine
F B Carpzovii Exercitatio de Chuppa Hebræorum
J Buxtorfii Dissert de Conviviis veterum Hebræorum.
J H Mau Dissert de Philothesiis veterum Hebræorum, Græcorum, atque Romanorum
D G Werner Dissert de Poculo Benedictionis
G Goezii Philologema de Osculo
I Iomijeni Dissert de Osculis
I Nicolai Tractatus de Phyllobolia

RELIGION.

J. C. Dieterici φυλλοβολια, seu Sparsio Florum
J. N. Graberg Dissert. de Unctura Christi in Bethania facta
S. F. Bucheri Dissert. de Unctione in Bethania
R. Verwey Dissert. de Unctionibus.
J. Spenceri Dissert. de Lege Tonsuram orbicularem prohibente.
T. Bartholini Paralytici N. T. medico et philologico Commentario illustrati.
Ejusdem de Morbis Biblicis, Miscellanea Medica

Vol. 31. T. Eberti Poetica Hebraica, Harmonica, Metrica, &c.
J. Eberti Tetrasticha Hebræa in Textus Evangelicos, &c.
R. Lowth de Sacra Poesi Hebræorum, Prælectiones Academicæ
R. Lowth Oratio Creweiana, in memoriam publicorum Benefactorum, Acad. Oxon.
F. Gomari Davidis Lyra, seu nova Hebræa S. Scr. Ars Poetica, &c.
Abbatis Fleury Exercitatio in Poesin universam, et Hebræorum potissimum
J. C. Schrammii Dissert. de Poesi Hebræorum in Cod. Sacro
I. C. Danhaueri Oratio Pentecostalis de Sacrosancta Spiritûs Sancti Poesi.
A. Pfeifferi Diatribe de Poesi Heb. recognita
Ejusdem Manuductio nova et facilis ad Accentuationem, &c
P. Leyseri Dissert. de frustra quæsita Poesi in Codice Sacro Hebræo
I. Clerici Dissert. de Poesi Hebraorum
E. Hare, S. T. P. Psalmorum Liber, in versiculos metrice divisus.

Vol. 32. Tractatus de Musica veterum Hebræorum
H. Horchii Dissert. de Igne sacro, et de Musica.
J. A. Glaseri Exercitatio philologica de Instrumentis Hebræorum Musicis נחילות et נגינות
J. G. Dreschleri Dissert. de Cithara Davidica
J. Hasæi Disputatio de Inscriptione Psal. xxii. אילת השחר.
S. Van-Til Cantus Poeseos, &c.
A. Kircheri Liber philologicus de Sono artificioso, sive Musica, &c
Ejusdem Liber diacriticus de Musurgia antiquo-moderna
J. Bartolocci Tract. de Musicis Instrumentis Hebræorum.
M. Mersennus de Musica, &c.
J. Spenceri Usus Musicæ in Sacris celebrandis
B. Lamy Dissert. de Levitis Cantoribus
J. I. Schudt Dissert. de Cantricibus Templi
A. Pfeifferi Specimen de Monialibus Vet. Test.
J. H. Bocrisii Dissert. de Musica Hebræorum.
A. Calmet Dissert. de Psalmis Graduum
A. Pfeifferi Specimen de Psalmis Graduum
J. Bartolocci Excerpta de Voce סלה
M. J. Paschii de סלה philologica Enucleatio
A. Calmet de סלה
M. H. G. Reine de סלה
M. H. J. Bytmeysteri Dissert. de סלה contra Gottheb. Reine
C. A. Heumanni Programma de סלה Hebræorum Interjectione musica
A. Pfeifferi Specimen de Voce vexata סיר
P. J. Buretti Dissert. de veterum Symphonia
A. Calmet Dissert. de Musica, &c
Ejusdem Dissert. in Musica Instrumenta Hebræorum
F. Scachii Dissert. de Inauguratione Regum Israel.
J. G. Abichi Dissert. de Lapsu Murorum Hierichuntinorum.
I. Meursii F. de Tibiis Collectanea
Aldi M. Pauli, F. Aldi, N. Dissert. de Tibiis veterum, &c
F. A. Lampe Dissert. de Cymbalis veterum.
I. Vossius de Instrumento Hydrauli, &c
J. Laurentii Collectio de Cithara dis, Fistulis, et Tintinnabulis.
I. D'Outrein de Instrumento מנרפה, &c
A. Calmet Dissert. de למצח
I. Spenceri Dissert. de Ritu saltandi et Ramorum Circumgestatione
M. J. E. Mulleri Dissert. de Davide ante Arcam Fœderis saltante
J. A. M. Nagelii Dissert. de Ludis secularibus veterum Romanorum, in Ghemara Babylonica commemoratis
L. Cappelli Animadversiones in novam Davidis Lyram Francisci Gomari.

Vol. 33. R. M. Maimonidis Constitutiones de Luctu, ab Ugolino ex Heb. Lat. redd.
M. Geyeri Liber de Hebræorum Luctu
I. Spenceri Ritus funebres et sepulchrales veterum Hebræorum.
J. Nicolai Libri quatuor de Sepulchris Hebræorum.

RELIGION.

    J A Quenstedii Tractatus de Sepultura veterum
    J B Carpzovii Disput. philol de Sepultura Josephi Patriarchæ.
    H Hulsii Disput de Corpore, Velo, et Sepulchro Moysis.
    P Dorffer Exercitatio philol de Sepulchro Christi
    J. J Chitlenus de Linteis Sepulcralibus Christi, &c
    J C Rostousch Dissert de Sepulcris Calce notatis.
    Z Grapii Dissert de Percussione Sepulerali
    M F Beckii Monumenta antiqua Judaica.
    I H Hottingeri Cippi Hebraici
    M H Reinhardi Dissert de Sacco et Cinere
    J T. Garmanni Dissert. de Pane Lugentium
    J C Wichmaushausen Dissert de Laceratione Vestium
    C Ikenii Dissert de Funere, Sepultura, et Luctu
    H Ugolini Dissert de veterum Funere et Præficis
    Wolfii Epitaphia Judaica, Heb et Lat. passim collecta et editi.
Vol 34 Index I Auctorum
    Index II Locorum S Scripturæ
    Index III Dictionum Hebraicarum.
    Index IV Rerum et Verborum

Godwyn's (Thos) Moses and Aaron : Civil and Ecclesiastical Rites of the ancient Hebrews, observed and opined for the clearing of many obscure Texts, 4to   *London*, 1685

Jennings' (David) Jewish Antiquities, or, a Course of Lectures on Godwin's Moses and Aaron, to which is annexed, a Dissertation on the Hebrew Language [edited by P Furneaux], 2 vols 8vo   *Lond.* 1808

Lightfoot's (John) Prospect of the Temple, especially as it stood in the Days of our Saviour. (Works, Vol IX)

Fleury's (Claude) Manners of the Ancient Israelites; containing an Account of their peculiar Customs, Ceremonies, Laws, Polity, Religion, Sects, Arts, and Trades, translated   [Enlarged by Dr Adam Clarke]. 8vo   *London*, 1809

Lowman's (Moses) Rational of the Ritual of the Hebrew Worship, in which the wise Designs and Usefulness of that Ritual are explained, 8vo   *London*, 1748

Lightfoot (John) on the Temple Service, as it stood in the Days of our Saviour (Works, Vol IX)

Lowman (Moses) on the Civil Government of the Hebrews, in which the true Design and Nature of their Government are explained, 8vo. *London*, 1816

Michaelis's (Sir John D) Commentaries on the Laws of Moses, translated by Alex Smith, 4 vols 8vo   *London* 1814

Selden (Jo) de Synedris et Præfecturis Juridicis veterum Ebræorum (Opera, Vol I)

Selden (Jo) de Successionibus in Bona Defunctorum, et de Successionibus in Pontificatum Ebræorum   (Opera, Vol II)

Wells's (Edward) Historical Geography of the Old and New Testaments, 2 vols 8vo   *Oxford*, 1819

Bocharti (Sam) Geographia Sacra   (Opera, Vol I)

Lightfoot (John) Chorographic Pieces, viz of the memorable Places in the Land of Israel, whereof mention is made in the Evangelists Fragmenta Terræ Sanctæ, Animadversiones in Tabulas Chorog. Terræ Sanctæ   (Works, Vol X)

Bochart (Sam) de Animalibus, Avibus, Serpentibus, Insectis, &c Sacræ Scripturæ   (Opera, Vols II and III)

RELIGION

Brown's (Sir T.) Observations on several Plants mentioned in Scripture, and on the Fishes eaten by our Saviour after his Resurrection (Works.)

Scheuchzer (J. J.), Physique Sacrée; ou, Histoire Naturelle de la Bible, traduit du Latin, 8 vols folio   *Amst* 1732-37

Gray's (Bishop Robt.) Connexion between the Sacred Writings and the Literature of Jewish and Heathen Authors, particularly that of the classical ages, illustrated, 2 vols 8vo   *London*, 1819

Shuckford's (Sam.) Sacred and Profane History of the World connected, from the creation of the world to the death of Joshua, 4 vols 8vo   *London*, 1808

Russell's (Mich.) Connexion of Sacred and Profane History, from the death of Joshua to the decline of the kingdoms of Israel and Judah, 3 vols 8vo   *London*, 1827-32

Prideaux's (Humph.) Old and New Testament connected in the History of the Jews and neighbouring nations to the time of Christ; with Life of the Author, 4 vols 8vo.   *London*, 1821

Lightfoot's (John) Erubhin; or, Miscellanies, Christian and Judaical. (Works, Vol IV.)

Calmet's Miscellaneous Illustrations of the Manners, &c. of the Jews (Fragments, see Dictionary.)

Harmer's (Thomas) Observations on various Passages of Scripture, from relations incidentally mentioned in Voyages and Travels, with Notes by Adam Clarke, 4 vols 8vo.   *London*, 1808

Burder's (Samuel) Oriental Customs; or, an Illustration of the Sacred Scriptures, by an explanatory application of the Customs and Manners of the Eastern Nations, and especially the Jews, therein alluded to Collected from the most eminent Travellers and Critics, 4 vols 8vo   *London*, 1827

Sect III.—COUNCILS

[Salmon] Traité de l'Etude des Conciles et de leurs Collections, avec un Catalogue des principaux Auteurs, 4to   *Paris*, 1724

Fabricii Bibliotheca Græca, Lib VI. quibus enarrantur Collectiones Canonum veteris Ecclesiæ et Conciliorum, tam universalium quam particularium, nec non de Epistolis ac Decretis Pontificum Rom Notitia traditur Accedit Synodicum vetus à Jo Pappio, curante G. C. Harles (Vol XII.)

Beveregii Pandectæ Canonum SS. Apostolorum et Conciliorum, ab Ecclesia Græca receptorum, nec non Canonicarum SS. Patrum Epistolarum; cum Scholiis antiquorum, Gr et Lat et Notis, 2 vols folio   *Oxonii*, 1672

Grier's (Ri.) Epitome of the General Councils of the Church, to the conclusion of the Council of Trent in 1563, 8vo   *Dublin* 1828

Lenfant (J.), Histoire du Concile de Pise, et de ce qui s'est passé de plus mémorable depuis ce Concile jusqu'au Concile de Constance, 2 vols. in one, 4to   *Utrecht*, 1731

Lenfant (J.), Histoire du Concile de Constance, 2 vols in one, 4to   *Amsterdam*, 1727

RELIGION.

Lenfant (J), Histoire de la Guerre des Hussites et du Concile de Basle, 2 vols. in one, 4to *Amsterdam*, 1731

Sarpi (Fra Paoli), Histoire du Concile de Trent, traduit en Français, avec des Remarques par P F. Le Courayer, 3 vols 4to. *Amsterdam*, 1751

Justelli (Ch) Codex Canonum Ecclesiæ Africanæ ex MSS Gr et Lat. Notis illustravit, 8vo. *Lutet Par* 1614.

Pithœi Canones Ecclesiæ Romanæ (Corpus Juris Canonici)

Burriel (Andrea) Præfatio Historico-critica in veram et genuinam Collectionem Vet Canonum Ecclesiæ Hispanicæ à Divo Isidoro, cum var. lect ornatam, possidet C de la Serna Santander, 8vo. *Br ux* 1800 (Catalogue Santander)

Wilkins (D) Concilia Magnæ Britanniæ et Hiberniæ ad A D 1717; accesserunt Constitutiones et alia ad Historiam Eccles Ang spectantia, 4 vols. folio *Londini*, 1737

Professionum Antiquorum Angliæ Episcoporum Formulæ de Canonum Obedientia Archiep Cant præstanda, è Coll MSS T Smithi (Textus Roffensis.)

Heineccius (J G) de Colloquiis Religiosis, 4to, 1719

Acta Wormaciensia, Ratisbonensia, et Smalcaldensia (Melancthonis Opera, Vol IV)

Reformatio Legum Ecclesiasticarum, ex Auth primum Henrici VIII inchoata, deinde per Edouardum VI provecta, atque nunc ad pleniorem ipsarum Reformationem in lucem edita, 4to *Londini*, 1640

Constitutiones Ecclesiæ Anglicanæ. (Wilkins' Concilia, Vol IV)

Constitutions and Canons Ecclesiastical, and the XXXIX Articles of the Church of England (Homilies)

Clergyman's Assistant , or, a Collection of Acts of Parliament, Forms and Ordinances, relative to the Duties and Rights of Parochial Clergy · to which are prefixed, the Articles of Religion, the Constitutions and Canons of the Church of England, 8vo *Oxford*, 1807.

Canons of the Church of Scotland, drawn up by the Provincial Councils held at Perth, A D 1242 and 1269 (Hailes's Scottish Tracts)

Dalrymple's (Sir D.) Historical Memorials concerning the Provincial Councils of the Scottish Clergy to the Era of the Reformation (Hailes's Scottish Tracts)

Sect IV —CHURCH DISCIPLINE AND GOVERNMENT, AND ON TOLERATION.

Dominis (Antonio de) de Republica Ecclesiastica, 3 vols folio *Lond* 1617-20, *and Francof* 1628

Barrow (Isaac) on the Pope's Supremacy, and on the Unity of the Church (Works, Vol 1)

Clarendon's (Edward Hyde Earl of) Religion and Policy, and the Countenance and Assistance each should give to the other , with a Survey of the Papal Power and Jurisdiction in the Dominions of other Princes, 2 vols 8vo *Oxford* 1811

RELIGION

Bramball's (Abp.) Vindications of the Church of England against Catholics and Presbyterians (Works.)

Daubeny's (Charles) Vindiciæ Ecclesiæ Anglicanæ, in which the false Reasonings, Misrepresentations, &c. of the True Churchman, ascertained by J. Overton, are pointed out, 8vo *Bath*, 1803

Hall's (Bishop Joseph) Apology against the Brownists,—Episcopacy by Divine Right asserted,—Remonstrance for Liturgy and Episcopacy, with Defence against Smectymnus and Answer,—Apostolic Institution of Imposition of Hands (Works, Vol. IX.)

Hooker's (Richard) Works, containing Ecclesiastical Polity, and other Treatises, with Life by Isaac Walton, 3 vols. 8vo *Oxford*, 1807

Jones's (W., of Nayland) Essay on the Church, and State of the Argument between Churchmen and Dissenters (Works, Vol. V.)

Locke's (John) Four Letters on Toleration (Works, Vol. VI.)

Melancthon's Defensio Conjugii Sacerdotum, missa ad Regem Angliæ (Opera, Vol. II.)

Milton's (John) Treatise of Civil Power in Ecclesiastical Causes, shewing that it is not lawful for any Power on earth to compel in matters of Religion (Prose Works, 4to, Vol. I., 8vo, Vol. III.)

Milton's (John) Considerations touching the likeliest means to remove Hirelings out of the Church (Prose Works, 4to, Vol. I., 8vo, Vol. III.)

Milton (John), of Reformation touching Church Discipline in England. (Prose Works, Vol. I. 4to and 8vo.)

Milton (John), of Prelatical Episcopacy, and whether it may be deduced from Apostolical Times,—Reason of Church Government, urged against Prelacy (Prose Works, Vol. I. 4to and 8vo.)

Milton's (John) Animadversions upon the Remonstrant's Defence against Smectymnus,—an Apology for Smectymnus (Prose Works, Vol. I. 4to and 8vo.)

Potter (John) on Church Government, wherein the Rights of the Church and the Supremacy of Christian Princes are vindicated and adjusted *London*, 1724

[Rawlinson (Th.)?] Vindication of the King's Sovereign Rights, together with a Justification of his royal exercises thereof in all causes and over all persons ecclesiastical (Antiquities of Salisbury Cathedral.)

Stillingfleet's (Bishop E.) Ecclesiastical Cases relating to the Duties and Rights of the Clergy and Ecclesiastical Jurisdiction (Works, Vol. III.)

Stillingfleet's (Bishop E.) Irenicum a Weapon Salve for the Churche's Wounds, or the divine right of particular Forms of Church Government examined (Works, Vol. II.)

Stillingfleet's (Bishop E.) Power of Excommunication (Works, Vol. II.)

Stillingfleet's (Bishop E.) Unreasonableness of Separation from the Communion of the Church of England (Works, Vol. II. and end of Vol. III.)

Swift's (Jonathan) Tracts in support of the Church Establishment, and on the Test Act (Works, Vol. VIII.)

RELIGION.

Taylor (Bishop Jer) on the Liberty of Prophesying ; with its just Limits and Temper   (Works, Vol VII and VIII)

Taylor (Bishop Jer), of the Sacred Order and Offices of Episcopacy   (Works, Vol. VII)

Thuanus's [De Thou] Preface or Dedication of his History to Henry IV , translated by Collinson   (Life)

[Travers (Walter)] a Full and Plaine Declaration of Ecclesiasticall Discipline, owt off the Word of God, and off the Declininge off the Churche off England, from the same [translated, reviewed and perfected, with a Preface, by Cartwright,] 4to, **black letter.** *Imprinted* M D LXXIII

> This is printed in type similar to Coverdale's Bible, and therefore likely to have been executed at Zurich or Marlborough. It was carefully suppressed by Archbishop Parker

Warburton's (Bishop) Alliance between Church and State   (Works, Vol VII)

Witherspoon's (John) Ecclesiastical Characteristics , or, the Arcana of Church Policy   (Works, Vol VI)

Steuart s (Walter, of Pardovan) Collections and Observations concerning the Worship, Discipline, and Government of the Church of Scotland, 8vo   *Edin* 1770.

Sect. V.—LITURGIES AND ECCLESIASTICAL RITES.

Taylor's (Bishop Jer) Apology for authorised and set Forms of Liturgy, against the Pretence of the Spirit   (Works, Vol VII)

Brett's (Thos) Collection of the principal Liturgies of the Christian Church on the Celebration of the holy Eucharist , with a Dissertation shewing their usefulness, authority, &c 8vo   *London*, 1720

Renaudoti (Eus) Collectio Liturgiarum Orientalium, 2 vols   4to   *Parisiis*, 1715–16

Goar's (Jac) Euchologion, sive Rituale Græc Gr et Lat   *Par* 1647

Liturgia Armena, Arm et Ital , per cura del P Gabriele Avedichian, 8vo   *Venezia*, 1826.

Liturgia Armena, 32mo. [*Venet*], 1793

Missale SS Patrum Latinorum, J Pamelio digesta, 2 vols 4to   *Coloniæ*, 1610

Missale Romanum   an illuminated MS on vellum, of the fifteenth century, executed in France, the borders of each page are grotesquely and humorously ornamented, the Gospels and various Offices having illustrative miniatures very beautifully executed   the initial letters, &c are also illuminated   4to. in excellent condition, and bound in velvet

Missale Romanum, ex decreto S Conc Tridentini restitutum, Pii V Pont Max jussu editum et Clementis VIII primum, nunc denuo Urbani VIII auctoritate recognitum   in quo Missæ propriæ de Sanctis ad longum positæ sunt ad majorem celebrantium commoditatem, folio   *Coloniæ* 1700

Missæ Defunctorum, juxta usum Ecclesiæ Romanæ, cum Ordine et Canone extensæ, folio   *Antverpiæ*, 1684

RELIGION.

Pontificale Romanum, Clementis VIII primum, nunc denuo Urbani VIII auctoritate recognitum, ac demum, ad plurium usum, in commodiorem formam redactum, 8vo *Coloniæ*, 1682.

Rituale Romanum, Pauli V Pont. Max jussu editum, 4to *Antverp. Plantin*, 1625.

Breviarium Romanum, ex decreto S Concilii Tridentini restitutum, Pii V. Pont Max jussu editum, et Clementis VIII auctoritate recognitum; additis aliquot Officiis Sanctorum ex Præcepto Pauli V, Gregorii XV, et Urbani VIII., 8vo. *Colon* 1628

Missale mixtum, secundum Regulam B Isidori, dictum Mozarabes, Præfatione, Notis et Appendice, ab Alex Lesleo, 4to *Romæ*, 1755

Palmer's (W) Origines Liturgicæ; or, Antiquities of the English Ritual; and a Dissertation on Primitive Liturgies, 2 vols 8vo *Oxford*, 1832

The Primer, set furth by the King's Majestie and his Clergy, to be taught, lerned, and red, black letter, small 8vo (Reprint) *London, by R Grafton*, 1546

The Booke of Common Praier and Administracion of the Sacramentes and other Rites and Ceremonies of the Churche, after the Use of the Churche of Englande, folio, black letter *London, in officina R. Graftoni, mense Martii*, M D XLIX
    The " First Book of Edward VI "

The Booke of Common Praier, &c, [or second of Edward VI] black letter, folio *London, R Grafton*, M D LII.
    This differs from the preceding in the omission of the oil in baptism, unction for the sick, prayers for the dead, &c &c.

The Primer, in Englishe and Latine, set out all along after the use of Sarum, with many godlie and devoute Praiers, black letter, 4to *London, by J. Kingston and H Sutton*, 1557

The Booke of Common Prayer, and Administracion of the Sacramentes, &c, [revised, with alterations and additions, under the direction of Archbishop Parker], folio, black letter *Londini, in officina R Jugge et J. Cawood*, 1559

Book of Common Prayer, &c [revised in consequence of the Hampton Court Conference], folio, black letter *London*, 1605.

Book of Common Prayer, &c [revised by Archbishop Laud], for the Use of the Church of Scotland, with the Psalms translated by K James, folio *Edin. R. Young*, 1637.

Book of Common Prayer, &c. [revised by royal commission, the standard of the present editions, and usually termed the "Sealed Book,"] black letter *Lond* 1662.

Book of Common Prayer, 24mo. *Edin J. Watson*, 1717

Book of Common Prayer, engraved and illustrated on silver plates by Sturt, a large copy, bound in velvet, with silver corners and clasps, 8vo *Lond* 1717

Book of Common Prayer, with Notes explanatory, practical, and historical, selected by Richard Mant, 4to *Oxford*, 1820

L'Estrange's (Ham) Alliance of Divine Offices, exhibiting all the Liturgies of the Church of England, as also of the Scotch Service-Book [Laud's], with their respective variations, folio *Lond* 1690

Liturgia Eccles Anglicana in Ling Græcam translat. 12mo. *Londini*, 1818

The Forme of Prayers and Administration of the Sacramentes, according to the Church of Scotland [a reprint of that adopted by Knox], small 8vo. *Aberdene, by E Raban*, 1633

Reformed Liturgy, by Richard Baxter (Works, Vol XV)

The Directory for the Publique Worship of God throughout the Three Kingdoms, together with the Ordinance of Parliament for taking away the Book of Common Prayer, 4to. *Lond*. 1644

Downes' (Sam) Lives of the Compilers of the Liturgy, with an Historical Account of its several Revisors, 8vo *Lond* 1722.

Index Evangeliorum Dominicalium et Festorum apud Veteres Anglo-Saxones, Calendarium Alemannicum ex Cod MS. Sæc XIII (Schilteri Thes Vol I)

Melancthonis (P) Annotationes in Evangelia, quæ usitato more Diebus Dominicis et Festis proponuntur (Opera, Vol III)

Biddulph's (T) Practical Essays on the Morning and Evening Services, and on the Collects of the Church of England, 3 vols. 8vo *Lond.* 1822

Hole's (Matthew) Practical Discourses on all the Parts and Offices of the Liturgy, 5 vols 8vo. *Lond* 1716, &c

Reading's (W) CXVI Sermons on the Lessons, 4 vols 8vo *Lond* 1728

Rogers (Tho.) on the Morning Prayer and Litany (Sermons)

Shepherd's (John) Critical and Practical Elucidation of the Book of Common Prayer, according to the use of the United Church of England and Ireland, [edited, with Memoir of the Author, by Eliza Shepherd], 2 vols 8vo; one of twelve copies printed on coloured paper *Lond* 1817

Wheatley's (Charles) Illustration of the Book of Common Prayer of the Church of England, 8vo *Lond* 1741.

Nelson's (Robt) Companion for the Fasts and Festivals of the Church, 8vo *Lond* 1805

Beveridge (Bishop W) on the Necessity and Advantage of Public Prayer and frequent Communion (Works, Vol I)

Beveridge's (Bishop W) Defence of the Old Singing Psalms (Works, Vol I)

Heber's (Regd) Hymns, written and adapted for the Weekly Church Service throughout the Year, 8vo *Lond* 1827

Mason's (W) Essays, historical and critical, on English Church Music. (Works, Vol III

Latrobe's (J A) Music of the Church considered in its various branches, congregational and choral, an historical and practical Treatise for the general reader, 8vo *Lond* 1831

SECT VI.—CATECHISMS AND CONFESSIONS OF FAITH.

Catechismus Romanus, ex decreto Concilii Tridentini et Pii V Pont Max editus, studio et industriâ A. F Leodii, 8vo *Antverpiæ*, 1606

RELIGION.

Bellarmini (Roberti, Cardinalis) Doctrina Christiana, ex Italico idiomate in Arabicum translata per V. Scialac et G. Sionitam, ad Fidei propagationem et orientalium Christianorum commodum. Arab et Lat. 8vo. *Rom.* 1613

Ορθοδοξος, &c. hoc est Orthodoxa Confessio Catholicæ atque Apostolicæ Ecclesiæ Orientalis, cum interp. Latinâ et versione Germanicâ præmissa est Historia hujus Catechismi à D. C. G. Hofmann, 8vo. *Wratslaviæ*, 1751

Cyrilli Patriarchæ Constant. Confessio Christianæ Fidei. Gr. et Lat. 4to. *Genevæ*, 1633

Corpus et Syntagma Confessionum Fidei, quæ in diversis Regnis et Nationibus Ecclesiarum nomine fuerunt authentice editæ, edidit G. Laurentio. 4to. *Genevæ*, 1654

Confessions of Faith of the Waldenses, Albigenses, &c. (Leger Hist des Vaudois.)

Confessions of Faith of the Bohemians. (Hist. du Concile de Bâle.)

Lutheri Confessio Fidei. (Opera.)

Propositiones Theologicæ M. Lutheri et P. Melancthonis, continentes summam Doctrinæ Christianæ, scriptæ et disputatæ Wittebergæ, inde usque ab anno 1516, cum Præfat. Melancthonis (Melancthonis Opera, Vol. IV.)

Melancthonis (P.) Catechesis; Confessio Doctrinæ Saxonicarum Ecclesiarum exhiberetur Synodo Tridentinæ 1551, Ennaratio Symboli Niceni (Opera, Vol. I.)

Confessio Augustana (Melancthonis Opera.)

Articuli Smalcaldensis (Lutheri Opera.)

Repetitio Augustanæ Confessionis, sive Confessio Doctrinæ Sax. Ecc. Melancthonis Opera.)

Formularies of Faith, set forth by the King's Authority during the reign of Henry VIII, 8vo. *Oxford*, 1824

Catechisma Brevis, Christianæ Disciplinæ summam continens, authoritate regiâ [Edwardi VI.] commendatus, adjuncti sunt Articuli Synodi Londinensis, anno 1552. small 8vo. *Londini, ap. R. Wolfium*, 1553

A Shorte Catechisme, conteyninge the Summe of Christian Learninge set forth by King Edward VI. (Randolph's Enchird. Vol. I.)

Noelli (Alex.) Catechismus, sive Prima Institutio Disciplinaque Pietatis Christianæ (Randolph's Enchird. Vol. I.)

Articles of the Church of England (Gibson's Codex and Clergyman's Assistant.)

Waterland's Critical History of the Athanasian Creed (Works, Vol. IV.)

Barrow's (Isaac) Exposition of the Creed, the Lord's Prayer, and the Decalogue, to which is added the Doctrine of the Sacraments (Works, Vol. I.)

Beveridge's (Bishop) Exposition of the XXXIX Articles of the Church of England (Works, Vol. IX.)

Beveridge's (Bishop W.) Church Catechism explained (Works, Vol. I.)

[Collins's (A.)] Historical and Critical Essay on the XXXIX Articles of the Church of England, 8vo. *London*, 1724

RELIGION.

Nares' (Edward) Discourses on the Three Creeds, and on the Homage offered to our Saviour as expressed in the Evangelical Writings 8vo *London*, 1819

Jackson's (Thos) Commentaries on the Creed. (Works, Vol I.)

Leighton's (Abp R.) Exposition of the Creed, Lord's Prayer, and the X Commandments (Works, Vol III)

Lightfoot's (John) Exposition of Three Articles in the Apostles' Creed (Works, Vol VI)

Pearson's (Bp John) Exposition of the Creed with Index Folio, with a few MS Notes, port *London*, 1741

Secker's (Abp) Lectures on the Church Catechism (Works, Vol VI)

Articles of Religion agreed upon by the Archbishops and Bishops and the rest of the Clergy in Ireland, in the Convocation held in Dublin in 1615, for the avoiding of diversities of opinions and the establishing of consent touching true religion. [by Archbishop James Usher, and in force till 1634] 4to *London*, 1628.

Dunlop's (W) Collection of Confessions of Faith, Catechisms, Books of Discipline, &c of public authority in the Church of Scotland, together with the Acts of Assembly 2 vols 8vo *Edin* 1719–22

Confession of Faith, together with the Larger and Lesser Catechisms, composed by the Assembly of Divines 4to *London*, 1658

Declaration of the Faith and Order owned and practised in the Congregational Churches in England, agreed upon and assented to by their Elders and Managers, in their Meeting at the Savoy, Oct 12, 1658 8vo. *Reprinted, London* 1729

Belgicarum Ecclesiarum Doctrina et Ordo; hoc est Confessio, Catechesis, Liturgia, Canones Ecclesiastici, Gr et Lat interpretibus F Sylburgio et J Revio 8vo *Haerderuici*, 1637

Confessio sive Declaratio Sententiæ Pastorum. qui in Fœderato Belgio Remonstratenses vocantur, super præcipuos Articulos Religionis Christianæ 4to *Haerderuici*, 1622

La Discipline Ecclésiastique des Eglises Réformées de France, avec les Observations des Synodes Nationaux sur tous les Articles, à quoi l'on a joint la conformité de la dite Discipline avec celle des anciens Chrétiens, et à la Discipline du Synode de Dordrect 4to *Amst* 1610.

Catechesis Racoviensis, seu Liber Socinianorum primarius, ad fidem editionis anno MDCIX recensuit Socinianam vero impietatem in hoc libro traditam à recentioribus assutam accuratè profligavit G L Oederus 8vo *Francof* 1739

Confession of the Unitarians (Lardner on the Logos Works, Vol V)

Barclay's (Robert) Apology for the True Christian Divinity, being an Explanation and Vindication of the Principles and Doctrines of the Persons called Quakers 4to *Birmingham, Baskerville* 1765

Oratio Dominica in diversas omnium fere Gentium Linguas versa, et propriis cujusque Linguæ characteribus expressa, editore Jo Chamberlayne 4to *Amstelodami*, 1715

Catecheticæ Versiones Variæ, sive Catechismus communis Quadrilinguis, tam Prosâ, quam Carmine, Hebraicè, Græcè, Latinè, et Anglicè, cum Præfatione G S[andys] 12mo *Lond* 1638

Boone's (Charles) Book of Churches and Sects, or, the Opinions of all Denominations of Christians differing from the Church of England traced to their Source by an Exposition of the various Translations and Interpretations of the Sacred Writings. 8vo *London,* 1826

Sect VII —FATHERS.

SS Patrum Apostolicorum, Barnabæ, Hermæ, Clementis, Ignatii, Polycarpi Opera genuina, unâ cum Ignatii et Polycarpi Martyriis, Versionibus antiquis et recentioribus, variantibus lectionibus, selectisque variorum Notis illustrata Accesserunt S Ignatii Epistolæ, tum interpolatæ, tum suppositæ, curâ Ri Russell The 4 parts in 2 vols royal 8vo, large and thick paper *Lond* 1746

Reliquiæ Sacræ, sive Auctorum fere jam perditorum II et III. Sæculi Fragmenta quæ supersunt. Accedunt Epistolæ Synodicæ et Canonicæ Nicæno Concilio antiquiores Ad Cod MSS recensuit, Notisque illustravit M. J. Routh 4 vols 8vo *Oxonii,* 1814–18

Lactantii (C) Firmiani Opera omnia, Notis var, variis lect recensuit J L Bunemann 2 vols 8vo. *Lips* 1739

Lactantii (C) Opera omnia quæ exstant, studiis Soc Bipontinæ 8vo *Bipont* 1786

Minutius Felix Octavius, ex iteratâ recensione Jo Davisii, cum ejusd Animadversionibus ac Notis integris D Heraldi et N Rigaltii, nec non selectis aliorum Accedit Commodianus ævi Cyprianici Scriptor, cum Observat antehac editis 8vo, large paper *Cantabr.* 1712

Bryant (Jacob), the Sentiments of Philo-Judæus concerning the ΛΟΓΟΣ or Word of God, together with large Extracts from his Writings compared with the Scriptures, on many other Doctrines of the Christian Religion. 8vo *Cantabr* 1797

Apologies of Justin Martyr, Tertullian, Minutius Felix, and Vincentius Lirensis, in defence of the Christian Religion, translated, with Notes, by W Reeves 2 vols 8vo *London,* 1709

Suiceri (J C) Thesaurus Ecclesiasticus è Patribus Græcis, ordine alphabetico, exhibens quæcunque Phrases, Ritus, Dogmata Hæreses, et hujusmodi alia huc spectant 2 vols folio *Amst* 1728

Sculteti (Abr) Medulla Theologiæ Patrum, qui à temporibus Apostolorum ad Concilium usque Nicenum floruerunt; methodo analyticâ et syntheticâ expressa, cum Præfatione D Paræi 2 vols 4to *Amberg* 1603-9

RELIGION 35

Sect VIII.—MISCELLANEOUS DIVINITY

Collected Works

Adam's (Thos. of Wintringham) Collected Works 5 vols. 8vo *London and York*, 1771–86.

Arminius's (James) Works, translated from the Latin; to which are prefixed, the Life of the Author by C. Brandt, Extracts from his Letters, and an Account of the Synod of Dort, by James Nichols 3 vols. 8vo *London*, 1822–25.

Barrington's (Shute, 1st Viscount) Theological Works, including the Miscellanea Sacra, the Essay on the Dispensations, and his Correspondence with Dr Lardner, with a Life of the Author, and a brief Memoir of his Son, the late Lord Bishop of Durham, by Geo Townsend 3 vols 8vo *London*, 1828.

Barrow's (Isaac) English Works, edited, with some Account of the Author, by Archbishop Tillotson 3 vols in 2, folio *London*, 1722.

Baxter's (Richard) Practical Works, with Life and Times of the Author by W. Orme 23 vols 8vo *London*, 1827–31.

Berkely's (Bp Geo.) Works, to which are added, an Account of his Life and several of his Letters 3 vols 8vo *London*, 1820.

Beveridge's (Bp William) Works, with a Memoir of the Author, and a Critical Examination of his Writings, by T H Horne. 9 vols 8vo *Lond* 1824.

Bramhall's (Archbishop John) Works, edited, with Life, [by Bishop John Vesey] Folio *Dublin*, 1677.

Bull (Geo.) Opera omnia Latinè, curâ et Annotat J E Grabe Folio. *Lond* 1703.

Calvini (Joannis) Opera omnia Editio ad fidem emend Codicum recognita et Indicibus adornata 9 vols folio *Amstelodami*, 1671.

Cecil's (Richard) Works, edited, with Life by Josiah Pratt 3 vols 8vo. *London*, 1816.

Charnock's (Stephen) Works, edited by Edward Parsons 9 vols 8vo *London*, 1815.

Chillingworth's (William) Works, [with Life by Birch, and Letters] 3 vols 8vo *London*, 1820.

Flavel's (John) Whole Works 6 vols 8vo *London*, 1820.

Hall's (Bp Joseph) Works, with Life and Sufferings by himself, arranged and revised by Joseph Pratt 10 vols 8vo *London*, 1808.

Hall's (Robert) Entire Works, with Memoir of his Life by Sir James Mackintosh, and a critical Estimate of his Writings by O Gregory 6 vols 8vo *Lond* 1831.

Horberry's (Matthew) Works 2 vols 8vo *Oxford*, 1828.

Hopkins' (Ezek.) Works, collected, with a Life of the Author, by Joseph Pratt 4 vols. 8vo *London*, 1809.

Jackson's (Thomas) Works, with his Life by Edward Vaughan 3 vols folio. *London*, 1673.

See Jones's Life of Bishop Horne.

RELIGION.

Jewell's (Bp John) Workes; [with Life of the Author, and Prefatory Dedication to K James, by Bishop Overall,]. 𝔅lack letter, 2 vols. folio *Lond* 1611
> "This book was bought at the parish of St Giles's in the Field's charges, anno 1613, it cost 20s, Mr Thomas Fuke being curate, and John Lorchin and John Bruer churchwardens."—*MS Note*

Jones's (William, of Nayland) Theological Works; with an Account of his Life and Writings, by W Stevens 6 vols 8vo. *Lond* 1810

Lake's (Bp Arthur) Works, with Life of the Author Folio, port by Payne *Lond* 1629

Lardner's (Nathaniel) Works, with Life by A Kippis 5 vols 4to *Lond* 1815

Leighton's (Abp Robt) Whole Works, with Memoir of the Author by Robt Jerment 4 vols 8vo. *Lond* 1820

Lightfoot's (John) Whole Works; edited by J R Pitman 13 vols 8vo. *Lond.* 1825

Luther (Mart) Opera, cum Præfatione Nic Amsdorfii. 4 vols folio. *Jenæ, excud Christ Rhodius*, 1556–70.

Mede's (Joseph) Works, with Life by J Worthington Folio *Lond* 1677

Melancthonis (Phil) Opera omnia [collegit, &c Caspar Peucerum] 4 vols folio. *Wittebergæ, excud. J Crato*, 1562–3.

Newton's (Bp Thos) Works, with some Account of his Life, and Anecdotes of several of his Friends, written by himself 6 vols 8vo *London*, 1777

Reynolds's (Bp Edward) Whole Works, with his Funeral Sermon by Rively, and a Memoir of his Life by Alexander Chalmers, edited by J R Pitman 6 vols. 8vo *London*, 1826.

Scott's (John) Works 6 vols 8vo *Oxford, Clarendon Press*, 1826.

Scott's (Thomas) Theological Works. 5 vols 8vo *Buckingham*, 1805

Secker's (Abp Thos) Works, with a Review of his Life and Character by Bishop Porteus 6 vols 8vo *London*, 1811

Sherlock's (Bp Thos) Works 5 vols 8vo *Oxford*, 1812, &c

Stillingfleet's (Bp) Works, with his Life and Character 6 vols folio. *London*, 1710.

Taylor's (Bp Jeremy) Whole Works, with Life of the Author, and critical Examination of his Writings, by Bishop Reginald Heber 15 vols 8vo *London*, 1822

Tillotson's (Abp) Works, edited with Life by J Birch 3 vols. folio. *London*, 1752.

Townson's (Thos) Works, with an Account of the Author, &c. by Ralph Churton *London*, 1810.

Tyndall (W.), John Frith, and Robt Barnes's (three worthy Martyrs and principal Teachers of the Churche of Englande) Whole Workes, collected and compiled in one tome [with their several Lives by John Foxe] 𝔅lack letter, folio *At London by John Daye. M D LXXIII*

Warburton's (Bp W) Works, with Life by Bishop Hurd 12 vols. 8vo *London*, 1811

Wilson's (Bp Thomas) Works; with Life, and History of the Isle of Man, by C Cruttwell 8 vols 8vo *Bath*, 1817–22

RELIGION

Waterland's (Daniel) Works, now first collected and arranged, to which is prefixed, a Review of the Author's Life and Writings by Bishop W Van Mildert. 10 vols 8vo *Oxford*, 1824

Zuinglii (Huldrici) Opera omnia, cum Præfatione apologeticâ R Gualtheri. 4 vols folio *Tiguri*, 1581

Separate Works.

Fathers (The) of the English Church, or, a Selection from the Writings of the Reformers and early Protestant Divines, with Memorials of their Lives and Writings [By Legh Richmond] 8 vols 8vo *London*, 1807–12

Addison (Jos) on the Christian Religion (Works, 8vo Vol VI 4to. Vol IV)

Adams's (Thos) Private Thoughts on Religion (Works Vol II)

Allix's (Peter) Judgement of the Ancient Jewish Church against the Unitarians in the Controversy upon the Holy Trinity and the Divinity of our Saviour 8vo *Oxford*, 1821 (Works, Vol II.)

Bacon's (Lord) Meditationes Sacræ (Works, Vols I. and XI)

Bacon's (Lord) Theological Tracts (Works, Vol VII)

Balguy's (Thos) Divine Benevolence asserted, and vindicated from the Objections of Sceptics. 12mo *London*, 1803

Barnes's (Robert) Supplication unto the most gracious Prince King Henry VIII,—His Articles condemned by Popishe Byshops,—Whole Disputation betweene the Byshops and Hym on the Doctrines and Discipline of the Church. (Works)

Bartas's (Du) Divine Weekes and Workes (Poetry)

Bates's (Ely) Christian Politics 8vo *London*, 1806

Baxter's (Richard) Christian Directory; or a Sum of Christian Theology. (Works, Vols. II–VI)

Baxter's (R) Treatise on Conversion, and Call to the Unconverted (Works, Vol VII)

Baxter's (R) Sound Conversion,—Directions for weak or disturbed Christians,—and Character of a sound Christian (Works, Vol VIII)

Baxter's (R) Method for a settled Peace of Conscience (Works, Vol IX)

Baxter's (R) Saint or a Brute;—the One Thing necessary,—and Cain and Abel Malignity (Works, Vol X)

Baxter (R) on Self-Denial, and Obedient Patience (Works, Vol XI)

Baxter's (R) Life of Faith (Works, Vol XII)

Baxter's (R) Divine Life, or, the Knowledge of God,—and Divine Appointment of the Lord's Day (Works, Vol XIII)

Baxter's (R) Gildas Salvianus; or, Reformed Pastor, shewing the Nature of the Pastoral Office. (Works, Vol XIV)

Baxter's (R.) Confirmation and Restauration the necessary Means of Reformation and Reconciliation (Works, Vol XIV.)

Baxter's (R) Knowledge and Love compared, Counsel to all Young Men, a Moral Prognostication of what is expected in the Church of Christendome (Works, Vol XV)

Baxter's (R.) Mischiefs of Self-Ignorance, True Catholic and Catholic Church described; Catholic Unity, or the only way to bring us all of one Religion. (Works, Vol. XVI.)

Baxter's (R.) Dying Thoughts, and Mother's Catechism. (Works, Vol. XVIII.)

Baxter's (R.) Catechising of Families, and Poor Man's Family-Book. (Works, Vol. XIX.)

Baxter's (R.) Unreasonableness of Infidelity, and Reasons of the Christian Religion. (Works, Vols. XX. and XXI.)

Baxter's (R.) Saint's Everlasting Rest. (Works, Vols. XXII. & XXIII.)

Bennet's (Benj.) Christian Oratory, or, the Devotions of the Closet displayed. 2 vols. 8vo. *London*, 1811.

Bentley on Free-Thinking. (Randolph's Enchirid. Vol. II.)

Berkeley's (Bp.) Alciphron, or, the Minute Philosopher, containing an Apology for the Christian Religion against Free-Thinkers. (Works.)

Beveridge's (Bp. W.) Private Thoughts upon Religion. (Works, Vol. I.)

Biddulph (Thos.) on the Divine Influence or Operation of the Holy Spirit. 8vo. *Bristol*, 1824.

A Profitable and Necessarye Doctryne, with certayne Homelies adioyned therunto, set forthe by the Reuerende Father in God, Edmonde [Bonner] Byshop of London, for the Instruction and Information of the People beynge within his diocese, and of his cure and charge. 𝔅lack letter, 4to. A remarkably fine copy. *Imprinted at London by Ihon Cauodde* [1555].

"Prepared," says Strype, "by the study of his chaplains, John Harpesfield and Henry Pendleton."

Boyle (Hon. Robert) on Some Motives to the Love of God. (Works, Vol. I.)

Boyle (Hon. R.) on the Excellency of Theology compared with Natural Philosophy. (Works, Vol. IV.)

Boyle (Hon. R.) on the Reconcilableness of Reason and Religion, and on the Possibility of the Resurrection. (Works, Vol. IV.)

Boyle's (Hon. R.) Dissuasive from Swearing. (Works, Vol. V.)

Boyle's (Hon. R.) Christian Virtuosa. (Works, Vols. V. and VI.)

Boyle (Hon. R.) on the Final Causes of Natural Things. (Works, Vol. V.)

Bramhall's (Archbishop) Controversies about the Sabbath clearly stated. (Works.)

Bridges' (Charles) Christian Ministry, with an Inquiry into the Causes of its Inefficiency, with an especial reference to the Ministry of the Establishment. 12mo. *London*, 1830.

[Brightwell's (Richarde)] Pistle to the Christen Reader,—the Revelation of Antichrist,—Antithesis, wherein are compared togeder Christes Actes and oure Holye Father the Popes. 𝔅lack letter, small 8vo. *At Malborow, in the lande of Hesse, by me Hans Lust, the XII day of Julye,* 1529.

With Tyndall's Parable of the Wicked Mammon.

RELIGION

Brewster's (John) Meditations of a Recluse, chiefly on Religious Subjects 12mo *London*, 1802.

Brown's (Sir Thos) Religio Medici, with Annotations, also, Observations by Sir K Digby. (Works)

Bulli (G) Defensio Fidei Nicœnœ, ex Scriptis Cath Doct qui intra tria prima Ecc Christ Sæc. floruerunt (Opera)

Bulli (G) Judicium Eccl Cath trium primorum Sæculorum de Necessitate credendi quod J Christus sit verus Deus (Opera)

Bulli (G) Primitiva et Apostolica Traditio de Jesu Christi Divinitate (Opera)

Bulli (G) Harmonia Apostolica, seu binæ Dissert de Doct Jacobi de Justificatione ex Operibus, et Consensu Pauli cum Jacobo Responsio ad Animad et Apologia (Opera)

Bunyan's (John) Pilgrim's Progress, with Life by R Southey, and illustrated with Engravings by Martin Royal 8vo *London*, 1830.

Burnet's (Gilb) Discourse of the Pastoral Care 8vo First edition *Lond* 1692

Burton's (Edward) Testimonies of the Ante-Nicene Fathers to the Divinity of Christ 8vo *Oxford*, 1826

Butler's (Bp) Analogy of Religion, Natural and Revealed, to the Constitution and Course of Nature, with a Life of the Author by Bishop Samuel Halifax 8vo *London*, 1809

Calvini (Jo) Tractatus Theologici omnes (Opera, Vol VIII)

Calvini (J) Institutiones Christianæ Religionis (Opera, Vol IX)

Calvin's (J) Institutes of the Christian Religion, translated by John Allen 3 vols 8vo *London*, 1813

Calvini (J) Epistolæ et Responsa Ecclesiæ Dei Virorum (Opera, Vol IX)

The Mynde of the Godly and Excellent Lerned Man, M Ihon Caluyne; what a faithful Man whiche is instructe in the Worde of God ought to do, dwellinge amongest the Papistes Black letter, small 8vo *Ipswiche, imprinted by Ihon Oswen (cum privilegio*, 1548)

Campbell (Geo) on Miracles, in answer to Hume, with a Correspondence on the subject by Mr Hume, Dr Campbell, and Dr Hugh Blair 8vo *Edin* 1812

Campbell (G) on Christian Temperance and Self-denial (Eccles Hist Vol II)

Cecil's (Richard) Practical Tracts and Miscellanies (Works)

Cecil's (R) Remains. (Life)

Chalmers's (Thos) Evidence and Authority of the Christian Revelation 8vo *Edinburgh*, 1824

Charnock (Samuel) on the Existence and Attributes of God (Works, Vols I to III)

Charnock (S) on Divine Providence, and on Regeneration (Works, Vols III to V)

Charnock (S) on the Knowledge of God and Christ,—the Lord's Supper,—and Minor Pieces (Works, Vols VI to IX)

Cheke's (Sir John) Treatise of Superstition (Life by Strype)

RELIGION.

Chillingworth's (William) Charity maintained by Catholics (Works, Vols. 1 and II.)

Chillingworth's (W.) Tracts in Controversy with the Catholics (Works, Vol III.)

Clark's (N.) Compleat Body of Divinity, consonant to the Doctrine of the Church of England   8vo.   *London*, 1718

Copleston's (Bp. Ed.) Inquiry into the Doctrines of Necessity and Predestination; with Notes and an Appendix on the XVIIth Article of the Church of England   8vo   *London*, 1821.

Cranmer's (Abp. Thomas) Confutation of unwritten Verities, both by the Holye Scriptures and moste auncient Autors, and also probable Arguments and pithy Reasons, with plaine Aunswers to all, translated and set forth by E. P.   Black letter, small 8vo   Bishop Burnet's copy [*London, by R. Wolfe* ——]
  "A short but excellent treatise, almost wholly lost and extinct."—*Strype* It contains stories of the visions of the holy maids of Lemster, Kent, &c.

Cranmer's (Abp. T.) Defence of the True and Catholic Doctrine of the Sacraments of the Body and Blood of Christ, by H. J. Todd.   8vo   *London*, 1825

Cudworth (R.) de Verâ Notione Cœnæ Domini, ex Anglico vertit, Observat. &c. addidit J. L. Mosheimus   (Syst. Intel.)

Cudworth (R.) Conjunctio Christi et Ecclesiæ in Typo, ex Anglico vertit, Annot. subjecit J. L. Mosheimus   (Syst. Intel.)

Davy's (Sir Humphry) Consolations in Travel, or, the Last Days of a Philosopher   Small 8vo   *London*, 1830.

De Courcy's (Rich.) Essay on the Nature, &c. of Pure and Undefiled Religion   (Sermons.)

Dewar's (Daniel) Nature, Reality, and Efficacy of the Atonement.   12mo. *Edinburgh*, 1831

Dewar (D.) on the Nature and Obligations of Family Religion, with Prayers for Individuals and Families   8vo   *Glasgow*, 1821

Ditton (Humphry) on the Resurrection of Jesus Christ, wherein the Consequences of the Doctrine are stated, the Nature and Obligation of moral Evidence explained, and the Proofs of the Fact are demonstrated to be conclusive   8vo large paper   *London*, 1712

Douglas's (Bp. John) Criterion; or, Rules by which the True Miracles recorded in the New Testament are distinguished from spurious Miracles of Pagans and Papists   Abridged by W. Marsh   12mo   *Colchester*, 1824

Drummond's (W. of Hawthornden) Cypresse Grove.   (Hist. of Scotland.)

Dwight's (Timothy) Theology explained and defended, in a series of Sermons, with a Memoir of the Author's Life   5 vols 8vo.   *Lond.* 1822.

Edwards's (Jonathan) History of the Work of Redemption; with Notes 8vo   *Lond.* 1788

Edwards's (J.) Treatise concerning Religious Affections   8vo   *Edinburgh*, 1772

Edwards's (J.) Careful and Strict Inquiry into the modern prevailing Notions of that Freedom of the Will, which is supposed to be essential to Moral Agency, Virtue, &c   8vo   *Lond.* 1773.

RELIGION.

Edwards's (J) Great Christian Doctrine of Original Sin defended, Evidences of its Truth produced, and Arguments to the contrary answered. 8vo. *London*, 1767

Erasmus's (Desid) Preparation to Deathe, a Boke as devout as eloquent. 𝕭lack letter, small 8vo. *London, T Berthelet*, 1543.

Erasmus's Antipolemus; or the Plea of Religion, Reason, and Humanity against War Translated, with a Preface, by V. Knox (V. Knox's Works, Vol. V.)

Faber (George Stanley) on Infidelity. 8vo. *London*, 1824.

Faber's (G S) Difficulties of Romanism. 8vo. *London*, 1826

Faber (G. S.) on the Ordinary Operations of the Spirit. 12mo. *London*, 1829.

Faber (G. S.) on the Apostolicity of Trinitarianism ; or, the Testimony of History to the positive Antiquity and to the Apostolical Inculcation of the Holy Trinity 2 vols 8vo. *London*, 1832.

Faber (G. S) on the Genius and Object of the Patriarchal, Levitical, and the Christian Dispensations 2 vols 8vo *London*, 1823.

Faber (G. S) on the Origin of Expiatory Sacrifice 8vo *London*, 1826.

Flavel s (John) Treatise on the Soul of Man, (Works, Vols II. and III); On Fear; Righteous Man's Refuge, and Causes and Cure of Mental Errors, (Vol III); Mystery of Providence, (Vol. IV)

Flavel's (J.) Husbandry and Navigation Spiritualised ; Saint Indeed ; Touchstone of Sincerity ; and Token for Mourners, (Vol. V)

Flavel's (J) Preparation for Sufferings, and Balm of the Covenant; Exposition of the Assembly's Catechism ; Sacramental Meditations; and Personal Reformation, (Vol. VI)

[Foster's (John)?] Natural History of Enthusiasm. 8vo *London*, 1832.

[Foster's (J)?] Saturday Evening 8vo *London*, 1832

Frith's (John) Booke concernyng the Saciament of the Body and Bloud of Christ, in aunswere to M. More; with the Articles of hys Examination before the Bishops of London, Winchester, and Lyncoln en Paule's Churche (Works)

Frith's (J) Aunsweres unto Rastall's Dialogue, to Sir Thos. More, and unto Fysher, Bishop of Rochester, on Purgatory ; and Bulwark against Rastall (Works)

Frith's (J.) Letter written from the Tower to Christe's Congregation, anno 1532. (Works)

Frith's (J) Myriour or Glasse to knowe thyself, anno 1532 (Works.)

Frith's (J) Antithesis, wherein are compared together Christe's Actes and the Pope's (Works)

Frith's (J) Sacrament of Baptism described. (Works.)

Fuller's (Thos) Holy and Profane States. 2 vols. in one, folio *Cambridge*, 1642

Gale's (Theoph) Court of the Gentiles ; or, a Discourse touching the Original of Human Literature both Philologie and Philosophie, from the Scriptures and Jewish Church 5 parts in 2 vols 4to. *London*, 1672–8

Gastrell (Bp.) on the Trinity (Randolph's Enchiridion, Vol I)

G

RELIGION

Gibson's (Bp) Pastoral Letters   (Randolph's Enchiridion, Vol II)

Gisborne's (Thos) Survey of the Christian Religion, and of History as connected with Christianity and with its Progress to the present time   8vo   *London*, 1799.

Gribalde (A notable and marvetlous Epistle of Dr. Matthewe) concerning the terrible Judgemente of God upon [Francis Spira] hym, that for feare of men denieth Christ and the known Veritie; with a Preface by Doctor Calvine. Now newlie imprinted, with a godly and wholesome Preservative against Desperation, at all tymes necessarie for the Soule   [Translated by Edward Aglionbye]. **Black letter**, small 8vo *London, by H. Denham* [1548].

<small>This copy has the autographs of Wm. Herbert and David Laing.</small>

Griffith (Brief Notes upon a late Sermon entitled the Fear of God and the King, by Matthew), by John Milton.   (Prose Works, 4to. Vol. I. 8vo. Vol. III.)

Grotius (Hugo) de Veritate Religionis Christianæ   24mo.   *Amstel Elzev.* 1675.

Grotius (H) de Veritate Religionis Christianæ [in Ling Arab. trans. Ed Pocockio]   12mo.   [*Oxonii*, 1660.]

Grotii (Hug.) Baptizatorum Puerorum Institutio, et Eucharistia; unà cum ejusdem Annotat. ad Decalogum et ad Sermonem Christi in Monte habitum   8vo.   *Oxonii*, 1706.

Gurnall's (W) Christian in Complete Armour; or, a Treatise on the Saint's War with the Devil. 2 vols. 8vo.   *London*, 1826

Hale's (Sir Matthew) Letters to his Children;—Three Discourses on Religion—on Immortality, the Day of Pentecost, and the Works of God; —On doing as we would be done by   (Works, Vol. I.)

Hale's (Sir M.) Contemplations moral and divine.   (Works, Vol. II)

Hall's (Bp. Joseph) Meditations and Vows; Holy and occasional Meditations, Holy Rapture; Select Thoughts; Supernumeraries; Breathings of a Devout Soul; Soliloquies; Soul's Farewell to Earth, Mystery of Godliness; and Invisible World.   (Works, Vol. VI)

Hall's (Bp J.) Heaven upon Earth; Art of Divine Meditations; Characters of Virtue and Vice, Epistles; Henochismus, or the Manner of Walking with God; Remedy for Prophaneness; Christian Moderation, and Devout Soul   (Works, Vol VII)

Hall's (Bp. J) Remedy of Discontentment, the Peace-Maker, Balm of Gilead, Christ Mystical; the Christian; Satan's Fiery Darts quenched, and Pax Terris   (Works, Vol VIII)

Hall's (Bp. J) Resolutions and Decisions of divers Cases of Conscience; the Holy Order; and Songs in the Night. (Works, Vol. VIII.)

Hall's (Bp J) Serious Dissuasion from Popery; No Peace with Rome, Honour of the Married Clergy maintained; Old Religion, or the true Difference between the Reformed and Roman Church; The Reconciler, Catholic Propositions; Censurer to Pope Urban's Inurbanity; and Christ's Presence in the Sacrament. (Works, Vol. IX.)

Hall's (Bp. J) Via Media, in the V. Articles commonly known by the name of Arminius. (Works, Vol. IX.)

RELIGION.

Hall's (Bp. J) Solomon's Divine Acts, Ethics, Politics, and Economics;—and Revelation revealed, concerning the 1000 Years' Reign of Christ upon Earth. (Works, Vol. X)

Hall's (Robert) Tracts on Terms of Communion, and John's Baptism. (Works, Vol. II.)

Hamilton's (Bp. Hugh) Existence and Absolute Perfection of the Supreme unoriginated Being proved. (Works, Vol. II.)

Hamilton (Bp. H) on the Permission of Evil, and the necessary Connexion between Intelligence and Free-Agency. (Works, Vol II)

Horberry (Matthew) on the Scripture Doctrine of the Duration of Future Punishments (Works.)

Hervey's (James) Meditations and Contemplations 2 vols. 12mo. *Lond.* 1764.

Hervey's (J.) Letters. 8vo *London*, 1811.

Holmes's (Robt.) Treatises on Religious and Scriptural Subjects Royal 8vo. *Oxford*, 1806

Hooker (Rich) on Justification. (Works, Vol. III)

Hopkins's (Bp E) Vanity of the World (Works, Vol I.)

Hopkins's (Bp. E) Exposition of the Lord's Prayer, and of the X. Commandments. (Works, Vol. I.)

Hopkins's (Bp. E) Doctrine of the Two Covenants and of the Two Sacraments, and on Regeneration (Works, Vol. II.)

Hopkins's (Bp E) All-Sufficiency of Christ; Heavenly Treasures; Practical Christianity, Assurance; the Attributes, Almost Christian, Conscience, Mortification. (Works, Vol. III)

Hopkins's (Sam) System of Doctrines contained in Divine Revelation explained and defended. 2 vols 8vo *Boston* [*New England*], 1811.

Horne's (T H) Scripture Doctrine of the Trinity briefly stated and defended. 12mo. *Lond.* 1826

Horsley's (Bp S) Tracts in Controversy with Priestley on the Belief of the First Ages in our Lord's Divinity 8vo *Dundee*, 1812.

Hunter's (Henry) Sacred Biography; or, the History of the Patriarchs, and part of the History of Jesus Christ. 5 vols. 8vo *Lond* 1814.

Jackson (Thos) on the Attributes of the Deity (Works, Vol II)

Jackson (T) on the Holy Catholic Faith and Church, &c (Works, Vol. III.)

Juelli (Jo.) Apologia Ecclesiæ Anglicanæ. (Randolph's Enchiridion, Vol I.)

Jewell's (Bp. John) Defence of the Apologie of the Church of England, containing an Answer to Mr. Harding's Booke. (Works, Vol. I)

Jewell's (Bp J.) Replie unto Mr. Harding's Answer. (Works, Vol II)

Jewell's (Bp. J) Treatise of the Sacraments (Works, Vol II)

Jewell's (Bp J) Sermon preached at Paule's Cross; with true Copies of the Letters between the Bishop and Dr. Cole upon the occasion of it (Works, Vol I)

Johnson's (Sam.) Prayers. (Works, Vol XII.)

RELIGION.

Jones (William) on the Catholic Doctrine of the Trinity. (Works, Vol I.)
Jones's (W.) Preservative against Socinianism, Trinitarian Analogy; Answer to an Essay on the Spirit (Works, Vol I)
Jones's (W) Remarks on a Work entitled the Confessional. (Works, Vol II)
Jones's (W) Zoologica Ethica; a Disquisition on the Mosaic Distinction of Clean and Unclean Animals. (Works, Vol II)
Jones (W) on Christ's Temptation, and on Life and Death (Works, Vol II)
Jones (W.) on the Metaphorical Use of Sleep in the Scriptures; and on the Signification of Spring as described in Solomon's Song. (Works, Vol II)
Jones's (W) Essay on Man, according to the Holy Scripture (Works, Vol V.)
Jones's (W) Book of Nature, or, the True Sense of Things explained (Works, Vol V.)
Jones's (W) Letters, &c (Works, Vol. VI.)
[Jortin's (John)] Discourses concerning the Truth of the Christian Religion. 8vo. Lond. 1746.
Ireland's (John) Paganism and Christianity compared. 8vo Lond. 1809.
Kempis (Thomas à), the Imitation of Jesus Christ, translated, with an Introduction and Notes by T. F. Dibdin. Royal 8vo Lond 1828
Kidder's (Bp Richard) Demonstration of the Messias, in which the Truth of the Christian Religion is proved against all the Enemies thereof, especially against the Jews. (Boyle Lectures.)
Klopstock's (F. T) Messiah; a new Translation; edited by T Raffles 3 vols. 12mo Lond 1814
Knox's (Vic) Christian Philosophy (Works, Vol. VII.)
Knox's (V) Considerations on the Lord's Supper (Works, Vol VII)
Lake's (Bp. A) Religious and Divine Meditations. (Works)
Lardner (N.) on the Logos, on the Epistles of Clement of Rome; Remarks on Ward s Dissertations (Works, Vol V)
Law (William) on Christian Perfection; with the Absolute Unlawfulness of Stage Entertainment. 8vo. Lond 1807
Law's (W) Serious Call to a Devout and Holy Life 8vo London, 1807.
Leland's (John) View of the principal Deistical Writers that have appeared in England in the last and present century, and of the Answers that have been published against them; with a View of the present times with regard to Religion and Morals, by Professor W L Brown 2 vols 8vo London, 1798.
Leland (J) on the Advantage and Necessity of the Christian Revelation shewn from the State of Religion in the ancient Heathen World. 2 vols 8vo Glasgow, 1819
Leslie's (Charles) Short and Easy Method with the Deists. (Randolph's Enchirid Vol. II)
Leighton's (Abp) Theological Lectures. (Works, Vol IV)
Lightfoot (Letters to and from Dr. John). (Works, Vol. XIII.)

Limborchii (Phil. à) Theologia Christiana.   Folio   *Amstel* 1730
Locke's (John) Reasonableness of Christianity, as delivered in the Scriptures, and Two Vindications of it   (Works, Vol V.)
Locke's (J) Discourse on Miracles   (Works, Vol IX.)
Locke's (J) Replies to Bishop Stillingfleet's Observations on certain Passages in the Essay of Human Understanding on the Trinity   (Works, Vol IV)
Locke's (J) Examination of Malebranche's Opinion of seeing all Things in God   (Works, Vol. IX.)
Lupsete (Thos), a Compendious and a very Fruiteful Treatyse, teachynge the Waye of Dyenge Well   Sm 8vo, black letter   *Londini, ex ædibus T. Berthelet, MDXLI.*
A Briefe Collection of all such Textes of the Scripture as do declare ye most blessed and happie estate of them that be vyseted wyth syccknes and other visitations of God, and of them that be departinge out of this lyfe · wyth most godly prayers and general confessions, verie mete to be read to all sicke persones, to make them wylling to dye. Whereunto are added, two fruitfull and comfortable Sermons, made by the famous Clarke, Doctor Martin Luther, very mete also to be reade at the burialles. Small 8vo, black letter. [*London*], *by Gaulter Lynne, MDLXIX*
With the preceding work and both Herbert's copies
Lyttleton (George Lord) on the Conversion and Apostleship of St. Paul. (Misc Works)
Magee (Abp William) on the Scriptural Doctrines of Atonement and Sacrifice, and on the principal Arguments advanced by the Opponents of those Doctrines, as held by the Established Church. 3 vols. 8vo   *London*, 1816.
Mason (W.) Conjectural Essay, in which the meaning of the word Angel, as used by St Paul, is attempted to be ascertained   (Works, Vol IV.)
Mede (Joseph) on the Apostasie of the Latter Times   (Works)
Mede's (J) Several Discourses and Treatises of Churches and the Worship of God therein   (Works)
Mede's (J) Epistles, being Answers to divers Letters of learned Men. (Works)
Mede's (J) Fragmenta Sacra, or Miscellanies of Divinity (Works.)
Melancthon de Usu integri Sacramenti   (Opera, Vol II.)
Melancthonis Loci Theologici et Examen eorum   (Opera, Vol I)
Milner's (Joseph) Reply to Bishop Marsh's Objections against the British and Foreign Bible Society   8vo   *London*, 1813
Milton (John), of True Religion, Heresy, Schism, Toleration, and the best means to be used against the growth of Popery. (Prose Works, 4to. Vol II, 8vo Vol IV)
Miltoni (Joannis) de Doctrinâ Christianâ, libri posthumi, quos ex schedis MS. deprompsit, et typis mandari primus curavit C R Sumner, 4to.   *Cantab* 1825
Milton's (J) Treatise on Christian Doctrine, compiled from the Holy Scriptures alone; translated from the original by C. R Sumner, 4to   *Cambridge*, 1825.

RELIGION.

More's (Hannah) Practical Piety, or, the Influence of the Religion of the Heart on the Conduct of Life. 2 vols. 8vo. *London*, 1811.

More's (H.) Christian Morals. 2 vols 8vo *London*, 1813.

More's (H.) Essay on the Character and Practical Writings of St. Paul 2 vols. 8vo. *London*, 1816

Newcome's (Abp W) Observations on our Lord's Conduct as a Divine Instructor, and on the Excellence of his Moral Character. 8vo *London*, 1795.

New Whole Duty of Man 8vo. *London*, 1798.

Niersis (S) Clajensis, Armeniorum Patriarchæ, Preces, XXIV. Linguis editæ [Paschal Aucher] Sm. 8vo. *Venetus*, 1823.

Nye (Stephen) on Natural and Revealed Religion 12mo. *Glasgow, Foulis*, 1752

Overton's (John) True Churchman ascertained; or, Apology for the Established Clergy, sometimes called Evangelical Ministers 8vo. *York*, 1802

Oxlee's (John) Christian Doctrines of the Trinity and Incarnation considered and maintained on the Principles of Judaism 2 vols 8vo. *London*, 1815; *and York*, 1820.

Paley's (William) View of the Evidences of Christianity. 2 vols. 8vo. *London*, 1807

Paley's (W) Horæ Paulinæ; or, the Truth of the Scripture History of St Paul evinced 8vo *London*, 1807.

Paley's (W) Natural Theology; or, Evidences of the Existence and Attributes of God, collected from Appearances in Nature. 8vo. *London*, 1809.

Paley's (W) Clergyman's Companion for Visiting the Sick. (Sermons and Tracts)

Pascal (Blaise), Pensées sur la Religion, avec sa Vie par Mad Perrier. 12mo. *Paris*, 1714

. Pascal's (B) Thoughts on Religion, translated, with Memoirs of his Life 8vo, large paper. *Lond*. 1803

Pascal's (B) Letters relating to the Jesuits; with Life by Madame Perrier, translated by W. A 2 vols sm 8vo, thick paper *London*, 1744.

[Plymley (Archd John)] Catholic Doctrines of the Church of England asserted and explained. 18mo ——— 1788

Predestination and Providence (a Collection of Tracts on), by Playfere, Potter, Womack, &c 8vo *Cambridge*, 1719.

Progress of the Pilgrim Good-Intent in Jacobinical Times 12mo *London*, 1803

Prynne's (W) Histrio-Mastrix, the Players' Scourge; wherein the Sinfulness of Stage-Playes is largely evinced (Introd to Drama)

Quarles' (Francis) Manual of Devotion; or, Judgment and Mercy for afflicted Souls, consisting of Meditations, Soliloquies, and Prayers; with a Biographical and Critical Introduction by the Rev. T. F Dibdin. 8vo. *Lond*. 1809

RELIGION 47

Rambach's (J) Meditations and Contemplations on the Sufferings of our Saviour with Preface by J Richardson 8vo York, ——.

Randolph's (John) Enchiridion Theologicum; or, Manual of Divinity. 2 vols 8vo *Oxford*, 1825

Reynold's (Bp Edward) Three Treatises, on the Vanity of the Creature; Sinfulness of Sin, and Life of Christ. (Works, Vol 1)

Reynold (Bp E) on the Sacrament of the Lord's Supper. (Works, Vol III)

Reynold (Bp. E) on the Fall and Rising of Peter. (Works, Vol IV)

Ridley's (Bp.) Treatise against Transubstantiation and Protestatio. (Randolph, Vol. I.)

Robinson's (Thomas) Scripture Characters; or, a Practical Improvement of the principal Histories of the Old and New Testament 4 vols. 8vo *London*, 1793

Robinson's (T) Christian System, unfolded in a series of Essays on the Doctrines and Duties of Christianity 3 vols 8vo *London*, 1812

Robinson's (T) Vindication of the Philosophical and Theological Exposition of the Mosaick System of the Creation; with moral Inferences and Conclusions. 8vo *London*, 1709; (Natural History of Westmoreland)

Sancroft's (Abp W.) Fur Prædestinatus (Life by D'Oyly)

Scott's (John) Christian Life, from its Beginning to its Consummation in Glory; together with the several Means and Instruments of Christianity conducting thereunto (Works, Vols. I. to III)

Scott's (Thomas) Force of Truth. (Works, Vol I)

Scott's (T) Rights of God, in Answer to the Rights of Man and to the Age of Reason (Works, Vol III)

Scott's (T.) Essays on the most important Subjects of Religion. (Works, Vol V.)

Scott (T) on Repentance, Faith in Christ, Growth in Grace, and Family Prayers (Works, Vol IV)

Scott's (T) Remarks on Bishop Tomline's Refutation of Calvinism. 2 vols. 8vo. *London*, 1811

Scougal's (Henry) Works · viz Life of God in the Soul of Man, Sermons, Reflections, and Essays. 12mo. *London*, 1822.

[Serle's (Amb)] Horæ Solitariæ; or, Essays upon the Nature, Names, Titles, and Attributes of the Holy Spirit; and on the Trinity. 2 vols. 8vo *London*, 1804.

Shepherd's (John) Divine Origin of Christianity deduced from some of those Evidences which are not founded on the Authenticity of Scripture. 2 vols 12mo *London*, 1829.

Sherlock's (Bp Thos) Trial of the Witnesses of the Resurrection of Jesus (Works, Vol. IV)

Sherlock's (Bp. T) Dissertations on the Authority of the 2d Epistle of Peter; the Sense of the Ancients on the Circumstances and Consequences of the Fall, the Blessing of Judah; and Christ's Entry into Jerusalem. (Works, Vol. IV.)

RELIGION.

Simpson's (David) Plea for Religion and the Sacred Writings [in answer to Paine] 8vo. *London*, 1818.

Smith's (John Pye) Scripture Testimony to the Messiah, an Inquiry, with a View to a satisfactory Determination of the Doctrine taught in the Holy Scriptures concerning Christ 3 vols 8vo *London*, 1818–21.

Stebbing's (Henry) Christianity justified upon the Scripture Foundation; being a summary View of the Controversy between Christians and Deists. 8vo large paper. *London*, 1750.

Stewart's (James Haldane) View of the Redeemer's Advent, in a Series of Discourses. 8vo. *London*, 1826.

Stillingfleet's (Bp E) Mysteries of the Christian Faith asserted (Randolph's Enchiridion, Vol I.)

Stillingfleet's (Bp E) Origines Sacræ; or, a rational Account of the Grounds of natural and revealed Religion. (Works, Vol II)

Stillingfleet (Bp. E) on the Doctrine of Christ's Satisfaction; and Vindication of the Doctrine of the Trinity. (Works, Vol. III.)

Stillingfleet's (Bp. E.) Rational Grounds of the Protestant Religion. (Works, Vol IV)

Stillingfleet's (Bp E) Works in Controversy with Roman Catholics. (Works, Vols V and VI)

Sturm's (C C) Reflections on the Works of God, and of his Providence throughout all Nature. 2 vols. 8vo *Lond* 1804.

Suckling's (Sir John) Account of Religion by Reason. (Works.)

Sumner (Bp John Bird) on the Records of the Creation, and Moral Attributes of the Creator 2 vols 8vo. *Lond* 1825

Sumner's (Bp J B.) Apostolical Preaching considered, in an Examination of St. Paul's Epistles 8vo *Lond* 1826

Sumner (Bp J. B) on the Evidences of Christianity, derived from its Nature and Reception 8vo. *Lond*. 1826.

Sumner's (Bp J B) Ministerial Character of Christ practically considered. 8vo. *Lond*. 1824.

Swift's (Jonath) Tracts in Defence of Christianity. (Works, Vol. VIII)

Taylor's (Bp Jeremy) History of the Life and Death of the holy Jesus. (Works, Vols II. and III)

Taylor's (Bp J.) Contemplations of the State of Man in this Life and in that which is to come (Works, Vol III)

Taylor's (Bp J.) Rule and Exercises of Holy Living and Dying (Works, Vol IV)

Taylor (Bp J) on the Doctrine and Practice of Repentance (Works, Vols VIII. and IX.)

Taylor (Bp J) on Original Sin (Works, Vol. IX.)

Taylor (Bp J), the Real and Spiritual Presence of Christ in the Sacrament proved against Transubstantiation. (Works, Vol IX.)

Taylor's (Bp. J.) Dissuasive from Popery. (Works, Vol. X)

Taylor's (Bp J.) Discourse of Confirmation. (Works, Vol. XI)

Taylor (Bp J.) Ductor Dubitantium; or, the Rule of Conscience (Works, Vols XI to XIII)

RELIGION

Taylor (Bp J.) on the Office Ministerial   (Works, Vol XIV)

Taylor's (Bp J) Golden Grove; or, a Manual of Daily Prayers and Litanies   (Works, Vol XV.)

Taylor's (Bp J) Psalter of David; with Titles and Collects, according to the matter of each Psalm; and Devotions in all occasions and necessities   (Works, Vol XV)

Taylor's (Bp J.) Worthy Communicant, or, a Discourse of the Nature, Effects, and Blessings of the Lord's Supper.   (Works, Vol XV)

[Tempest's (Stephen)] Religio Laici; or, a Layman's Thoughts upon his Duty to God, his neighbour, and himself   8vo   *London*, 1764

Tillotson's (Abp) Rule of Faith, or, an Answer to J. S[argent's] Treatise entitled Sure-footing.   (Works, Vol I)

Tomline's (Bp. George) Elements of Christian Theology, containing Proofs of the Authenticity of the Scriptures, Summary of the History of the Jews, Contents of the Books of the Old and New Testaments, &c.   2 vols 8vo.   *Lond* 1820

Tomline's (Bp G) Refutation of Calvinism   8vo   *London*, 1811.

Tucker's (Abraham) Light of Nature pursued, with his Life by Sir H P. St John Mildmay.   7 vols 8vo   *Lond* 1805

Twyne (Thos), the Garlande of Godly Flowers, bewtifully adorned, as most freshly they flourish in the Gardeins of right faithfull Christian Writers.   Black letter, small 8vo.   *London, W. How*, 1574

Tyndall's (William) Frutefull and Godly Treatise, expressing the right institution and usage of the Sacramentes   (Works.)

Tyndall (W), the Supper of the Lord, after the true meaning of John, vi and 1 Corinth xi   (Works.)

Tyndall (W), the Parable of the Wicked Mammon,—that Fayth, the mother of all good workes, justifieth us before we can bringe forth anye good works   Small 8vo black letter   *Marlborowe, by Hans Lust, M D XXVIII.*   (Works)

Tyndall (W), the Obedience of a Christen Man, and how Christen Rulers ought to governe, set forth 1528.   (Works)

Tyndall (W), an Aunswere unto Syr Thomas More's Dialogue, made 1530, wherein he declareth what the Church is, and giveth a reason of certaine words which Master More rebuketh in the Translation of the New Testament; after that he aunswereth particularly every Chapter.   (Works)

Tyndall's (W) Practise of Papistical Prelates, made in 1530   (Works)

Venn's (Henry) Complete Duty of Man, or, a System of Doctrinal and Practical Christianity   12mo   *London*, 1817

Venn's (H) Mistakes in Religion exposed   an Essay on the Prophecy of Zacharias   12mo   *Lond* 1807.

Wall's (W) History of Infant Baptism, being an impartial Collection of all such Passages in the Writers of the Four first Centuries as make for or against it   with a Defence of the History against Mr. Gale and others   3 vols 8vo   *Lond* 1819

Warburton's (Bp) Divine Legation of Moses demonstrated on the principles of a Religious Deist   (Works, Vols I to VI)

Warburton's (Bp) Rational Account of the Nature and End of the Lord's Supper (Works)

Warburton's (Bp) Doctrine of Grace (Works, Vol VIII)

Warburton's (Bp) Controversial Tracts. (Works, Vols XI and XII.)

Wardlaw (Ralph) on the principal Points of the Socinian Controversy. 8vo *Lond.* 1819

Wardlaw's (R) Unitarianism incapable of Vindication, in Reply to Yates 8vo *Lond* 1816.

Waterland's (Daniel) Vindications of Christ's Divinity. (Works, Vols I and III)

Waterland's Answer to Dr. Whitby's Reply respecting his Disquisitiones Modestæ (Works, Vol II.)

Waterland's Case of the Arian Subscription considered, with Supplement. (Works, Vol II)

Waterland's Answer to some Queries relating to the Arian Controversy,—the Scriptures and Arians compared;—V. Letters to Mr Staunton,—on the Argument, *à priori*, for proving the Existence of a First Cause. (Works, Vol IV)

Waterland's Importance of the Doctrine of the Trinity. (Works, Vol. V)

Waterland's Remarks on Dr. Clarke's Exposition of the Church Catechism (Works, Vol V)

Waterland's Nature, Obligation, and Efficacy, of the Christian Sacraments considered; with Supplement (Works Vol V)

Waterland's Scripture Vindicated, in Answer to Christianity as Old as the Creation (Works, Vol VI)

Waterland's Defence of the Bishop of St David's,—and Regeneration stated and explained. (Works, Vol VI)

Waterland's Review of the Doctrine of the Eucharist, as laid down in Scripture and Antiquity (Works, Vol VII)

Waterland's Summary of the Doctrine of Justification,—Inquiry concerning the Antiquity of Infant Communion. (Works, Vol IX)

Waterland's Letters on Lay-Baptism, to the Rev. Mr Lewis and others, and Notes by Dr W on his own Writings. (Works, Vol X)

Watson's (Bp Richard) Apologies for Christianity and for the Bible, in Answer to Gibbon and Paine 8vo *Lond.* 1806

Watson's (Bp R) Collection of Theological Tracts [on the most interesting subjects of Sacred Literature] 6 vols. *Lond* 1791

West's (Gilbert) Observations on the History and Evidences of the Resurrection of Jesus Christ 8vo *Lond* 1785

Wilberforce's (William) View of the prevailing System of professed Christians in this Country, contrasted with real Christianity 8vo. *Lond* 1818

Wilson (Bp Thomas) on the Lord's Supper,—Sacra Privata (Works, Vol II)

Wilson's (Bp T) Instructions for the Indians (Works, Vol III.)

Wilson's (Bp T) Parochialia;—Maxims of Piety (Works, Vol IV)
Witherspoon (John) on Regeneration. (Works, Vol I)
Witherspoon's (J) Address to Students;—and on the Nature and Effects of the Stage. (Works, Vol VI)
Witherspoon's (J) Lectures on Divinity   (Works, Vol. VIII.)
York (Duchess of)—Controversy between Dryden and Stillingfleet concerning the Duchess of York's Paper [on the Grounds of her Conversion to the Catholic Faith]   (Dryden's Works, Vol XVII.)
Zeal without Innovation; or, the Present State of Morals and Religion considered. *Lond* 1808.
Zuinglii (Huld) Opus Articulorum ;—de licitis Sacerdotum Connubiis ;—de Canone Missæ   (Op Vol I)
Zuinglius (H) de Certitudine Verbi Dei,—de Divinâ et Humanâ Justitiâ, de Providentiâ Dei   (Op Vol I)
Zuinglii (H) in Evang. Doctrinæ brevis Pastorum Isagoge; et Pastor   (Op Vol I)
Zuinglius (H) contra Catabaptistos; Ecclesiastes, sive de Ratione et Officio concionandi liber. (Op Vol II)
Zuinglius (H) de Baptismo; de Peccato Originali (Op Vol. II)
Zuinglius (H) de Verâ et Falsâ Religione (Op Vol II)
Zuinglius (H.) de Eucharistiâ; ad Lutheri Librum de Sacramento Responsio; ad Lutheri Confessionem Responsiones. (Op. Vol II)
Zuingli (H) ad Carolum Imp Fidei Ratio; Fidei Christianæ Expositio, Acta Disputat quæ Tigurini consensum est (Op Vol II)

Sect. IX —SERMONS.

Cooke's (John) Preacher's Assistant; containing a Series of the Texts of Sermons and Discourses, published by Divines of the Church of England, and by the Dissenting Clergy, since the Restoration. 2 vols 8vo *Oxford*, 1783.

Boyle Lectures in Defence of Natural and Revealed Religion —

   1692 Confutation of Atheism, by R Bentley. 8vo

   1693 and 4. Demonstration of the Messias, by Bp. R Kidder 3 vols 8vo

   1695 and 6. On Divine Revelation, by Bp J. Williams 4to

   1697 The Certainty and Necessity of Revelation, by Bp. F Gastrell 8vo

   1698 On the Attributes, by J Harris 4to.

   1699 On the Credibility of Revelation, by Bp S. Bradford 4to

   1700 The Sufficiency of Revelation, by Bp. O Blackhall 8vo

   1701 The Truth and Excellency of the Christian Religion, by Bp G. Stanhope 4to

   1704 On the Attributes, by S Clarke 8vo

   1705. On Natural and Revealed Religion, by S Clarke. 8vo

   1706. Proving the Being of a God, by J. Hancock 8vo

RELIGION.

Boyle Lectures :—

1707. The Accomplishment of Scripture Prophecies, by W Whiston 8vo

1708 On Redemption, by J. Turner. 8vo.

1709 Religion no Matter of Shame, by L Butler 8vo.

1710 Divine Original, &c. of the Christian Religion, by J. Woodward 8vo.

1711 and 12. Physico-Theology, by W. Derham 8vo

1713 and 14. On Freethinking, by B Ibbot 2 vols 8vo.

1717 and 18 Natural Obligations to believe Revelation, by Bp. J. Leng 8vo.

1719 and 20 On the Origin of Evil, by J. Clarke. 2 vols 8vo.

1721 and 22. Difficulties no excuse for Infidelity, by R. Gurdon. 8vo.

1724 and 25. Demonstration of True Religion, by T. Burnett. 2 vols 8vo

1730 to 32 Gradual Revelation of the Gospel, by W. Berriman 2 vols 8vo.

1736 to 38 On the Acts of the Apostles by R Biscoe. 8vo

1739 to 41 [On various subjects] by L. Twells. 8vo.

1747 to 49. Christianity justified on Scripture Foundation, by H Stebbing 8vo.

1766 to 68 Evidence of Christianity deduced from Facts, by W. Worthington 2 vols 8vo

1769 to 71 Intent of Scripture Miracles, by H. Owen 2 vols 8vo.

1778 to 80. Comparison of Revelation with the Mind, by J. Williamson. 8vo

1802 to 4. Rise and Progress of Infidelity, by Bp. W. Van Mildert. 2 vols 8vo.

Moyer Lectures in Defence of the Divinity of Christ —

1719 and 20. On the Divinity of Christ, by D Waterland. (Works)

1720 and 21 The Divinity of Christ proved from the Old Testament, by J Knight. 8vo.

1723 and 24 Historical Account of the Trinitarian Controversy, by W Berriman. 8vo

1724 and 25 On the Errors and Absurdities of the Arian Scheme, by T Bishop 8vo

1728 and 29. Christian Faith asserted, by H Felton 8vo

1729 and 30. Summary View of the Trinitarian Controversy, by J. Trapp 8vo

1731 and 32 [On various subjects] by J. Browne. 8vo

1732 and 33 [On various subjects] by J. Seed. 2 vols 8vo

1734 and 35. The Nicene and Athanasian Creeds explained and confirmed, by C Wheatley 8vo.

1737 and 38 Critical Dissertation on 1 Timothy, iii. 16, by J Berriman 8vo

1738 and 39. On several Subjects, by E Twells 8vo

RELIGION.

Moyer Lectures :—
    1739 and 40. Incarnation of Christ proved from the Testimony of the most ancient Jews, by A Bedford. 8vo.
    1740 and 41 On the Holy Ghost, by G. Ridley 8vo.
    1757 On several Subjects, by W Clements. 8vo.
    1764 and 65. On the Logos, by B Dawson. 8vo.

Bampton Lectures :—
    1780 On the Christian Faith and Character, by J Bandinel. 8vo
    1781. Proving Jesus Christ to be the Saviour, by T Neve. 8vo.
    1782. On the Prophecies of John the Baptist, by R Holmes. 8vo.
    1783 Christian Happiness, by J. Cobb. 8vo.
    1784 Comparison of Mahommedism and Christianity, by J. White. 8vo
        Gabriel's (R. B) Facts relating to Dr White's Bampton Lectures,—Dr White's Statement of his Literary Obligations to Mr. Badcock and Dr Parr   1 vol 8vo. *Oxford*, 1790.
    1785 Destruction of Jerusalem, by R Churton 8vo
    1786 Defence of Church of Englandism, by G Croft. 8vo.
    1787 Scripture Mysteries, by W. Hawkins 8vo
    1788 Ground and Credibility of the Christian Religion, by R. Shepherd 8vo
    1789. On the Conduct and Opinions of the Primitive Christians, by H. Kett 8vo
    1790 Chart and Scale of Truth, by which to find the Cause of Error, by E. Tatham 2 vols. 8vo.
    1791 On Faith, by R. Morres 8vo.
    1792 On Christian Theology, by J. Eveleigh 8vo.
    1793 On the Truth, &c of the Scriptures, by J Williamson 8vo.
    1794 Christian Redemption illustrated, by T Wintle 8vo
    1795 On the Doctrine of the Atonement, by D Veysie. 8vo.
    1796. Principles of the Reformation in England, by R Gray 8vo.
    1797. Objections against Christianity answered, by W. Finch 8vo
    1798 On the Fulness of Time, by C H Hall 8vo
    1799 Variety of Opinions, &c on Christianity, by W. Barrow. 8vo.
    1800 Divine Origin of Prophecy, by G Richards 8vo.
    1801 Horæ Mosaicæ, or, Dissertation on the Credibility and Theology of the Pentateuch, by G S Faber 2 vols 8vo.
    1802 Religious Enthusiasm considered, by G. F Nott 8vo.
    1803 The Mission and Character of Christ, and the Beatitudes, by J. Farrer. 8vo.
    1804 The Articles termed Calvinistical of the Church of England, by R Lawrence. 8vo
    1805 The Evidences of Christianity at the close of the Age of Reason, by E Nares. 8vo.
    1806. Divine Revelation, by J. Browne. 8vo

RELIGION.

Bampton Lectures :—

- 1807. Nature and Guilt of Schism considered, by T Le Mesurier 8vo.
- 1808. The Truth of Christianity proved from the Wisdom of its original Establishment, by J. Penrose. 8vo
- 1809. View of the Brahminical Religion, by J B S Carwithen 8vo.
- 1810. Evanson's Dissonance of the Evangelists examined, by T. Falconer. 8vo.
- 1811. The Truth and Consistency of Divine Revelation, by J Bidlake 8vo.
- 1812. That the Gospel is preached by the National Clergy, by R Mant 8vo.
- 1813. Key to the Writings of the Fathers of the first Three Centuries, by J Collinson 8vo
- 1814. Principles of Scripture Interpretation, by W. Van Mildert. 8vo.
- 1815. Personality and Office of the Christian Comforter, by Bp. R Heber. 8vo
- 1816. Christian Unity considered, by J H. Spry. 8vo.
- 1817. Divine Authority of the Holy Scripture asserted from its adaptation to Human Nature, by J Miller 8vo
- 1818. Doctrines of Unitarians examined, by C A Moysey 8vo.
- 1819. Religious Principles and Practices of the Age, by H D. Morgan 8vo
- 1820. Claims of the Established Church to exclusive support, by G Fausset 8vo
- 1821. Moral Tendency of Divine Revelation, by J Jones. 8vo
- 1822. Party Feeling in Matters of Religion, by R Whately 8vo.
- 1823. The Mental Condition necessary to a due Inquiry into Religious Evidence, by C. Goddard 8vo
- 1824. Secondary and Spiritual Interpretation of Scripture, by J J. Conybeare. 8vo
- 1825. Divine Revelation in connexion with the Progress of Society, by G. Chandler. 8vo
- 1826. The Benefits arising from a participation in Baptism and the Lord's Supper, by Wm. Vaux. 8vo
- 1827. The Character and Conduct of the Apostles considered as an Evidence of Christianity, by H H Milman. 8vo.
- 1828. The Religious Necessity of the Reformation asserted, and the extent to which it was carried in England vindicated, by T. Horne 8vo
- 1829. An Inquiry into the Heresies of the Apostolic Age, by E. Burton. 8vo
- 1830. An Inquiry into the Doctrines of the Anglo-Saxon Church, by H Soames 8vo
- 1831. The Popular Evidence of Christianity stated and examined, by T. W Lancaster 8vo
- 1832

RELIGION. 55

Hulsean Lectures —
    1821. On the Evidences of Christianity in the Discourses of our Lord, by J C Franks 8vo
    1822 On Scripture Difficulties, by C. Benson 8vo
    1823. On the Apostolical Preaching, by J C Franks. 8vo.
    1824

Andrews's (Bp) XVII Sermons, modernised by Charles Daubeny. 8vo London, 1821

Adams's (Thomas) Sermons   (Works, Vols II and IV)

Adams's (T) Evangelical Sermons. (Vol. V.)

Barrow's (Isaac) XXXII Sermons. (Works, Vol. I)

Barrow's (I) Sermons and Expositions of the Creed, and on Contentment, &c. (Works, Vols II and III)

Beveridge's (Bp W.) Sermons. (Works, Vols II. to VI.)

Beveridge's (Bp W) Thesaurus Theologicus , or, Complete System of Divinity, in skeletons of Sermons (Works, Vols. VII. and VIII)

Binning's (Hugh) Works [or Sermons]; with Life of the Author. 4to. Edinburgh, 1735.

Blair's (Hugh) Sermons 5 vols 8vo London, 1785—1801

Blair's (James) Sermons on our Saviour's Divine Sermon on the Mount. To which is prefixed, a Paraphrase on the whole Sermon; with a recommendatory Preface by Dr. Waterland. 4 vols 8vo. London, 1740

Blackall's (Bp Ofspring) Practical Discourses upon our Saviour's Sermon on the Mount With a Preface by Sir William Dawes, Abp of York 8 vols 8vo, large paper London, 1718

Bossuet (J J.), Sermons, Panégyriques, et Oraisons Funèbres 7 vols 8vo. Versailles, 1816.

Bouillier (J R), Sermons sur divers Textes. 8vo Amsterdam, 1803-4.

Bourdaloue (L). Sermons. 6 vols 8vo. Versailles, 1812-13.

Bradley's (Charles) Sermons at High Wycombe, Glasbury, and Clapham. 4 vols 8vo London, 1819, 1831.

Brewster's (John) Lectures on the Acts of the Apostles 2 vols 8vo London, 1807

Brown's (David) Sermons, preached at Calcutta (Life)

Buchanan's (Claudius) Sermons. 8vo London, 1812.

Campbell's (George) Sermons. (On Miracles.)

Cecil's (Richard) Sermons (Works)

Chalmers's (Dr Thos) Discourses on the Christian Revelation, viewed in connexion with Modern Astronomy. 8vo. Glasgow, 1817.

Chalmers's (Dr T) Sermons, preached at St John's Church, Glasgow 8vo. Glasgow, 1823.

Chalmers's (Dr T) Sermons, preached at the Tron Church, Glasgow. 8vo. Glasgow, 1821

Chalmers's (Dr. T) Sermons on the Application of Christianity to the Commercial and Ordinary Affairs of Life 8vo Glasgow, 1820.

RELIGION.

Charnock's (Stephen) Sermons   (Works)
Chillingworth's (W) Sermons   (Works, Vol III.)
Conybeare's (Bp John) Sermons ; with IX. separate and on particular occasions, collected. 3 vols. 8vo   *London* 1757, 1749, &c
Cooper's (Edward) Sermons, designed to elucidate some of the leading Doctrines of the Gospel   2 vols 12mo   *London*, 1805–6
Cooper's (E) Sermons, particular and familiar. 7 vols. 12mo.   *London*, 1813–15
Cunningham's (J W) Sermons   2 vols 8vo.   *London*, 1823–4
Davies (Samuel), of New Jersey, Sermons on useful and important Subjects   5 vols 8vo.   *London*, 1767–71
Daubeny's (Charles) Discourses on the connexion between the Old and New Testaments   8vo   *London*, 1802
Dawes's (Sir W) Sermons on several Occasions. 8vo   *Cambridge*, 1707.
De Courcy's (Richard) Sermons.   8vo.   *London*, 1810.
Debon's (Bp. Theodore) Sermons on the Public Means of Grace, the Fasts and Festivals of the Church, &c. 2 vols. 8vo.   *London*, 1825.
Doddridge's (Philip) Sermons on various Subjects   4 vols 8vo   *London*, 1826.
Drant's (Thomas) Two Sermons preached, the one at S. Maries Spittle, on Tuesday in Easter Weeke, 1570 ; and the other at the Court at Windsor the Sonday after Twelft-day, being the VIII of January, before, in the year 1569. Small 8vo. 𝔅lack letter   *London, by John Daye,* [1570]
Dwight's (Tim) Sermons, [from the original MSS] 2 vols 8vo.   *Edinburgh*, 1828.
Evans's (John) Practical Discourses concerning the Christian Temper. With Life of John Erskine   2 vols 12mo   *London*, 1812
Family Lecturer on Faith and Practice ; selected from the most celebrated Divines, by Vicesimus Knox. 2 vols royal 8vo.   *London*, 1798
Flavel's (John) Sermons.   (Works, Vols I II IV)
Gallatin's (Ezech) Sermons sur divers Textes   8vo   *à Genève*, 1720
Gilpin's (W) Sermons to a Country Congregation.   8vo   *Lymington*, 1799.
Gisborne's (Thomas) Sermons, including those on Christian Morality   3 vols 8vo   *London*, 1802–9.
Hall's (Bp Joseph) Sermons   (Works, Vol V.)
Hall's (Robert) Sermons, from his own MSS   (Works, Vol V)
Hall's (R) Sermons, from Notes taken while they were preached   (Works, Vol VI)
Hall's (R) Sermons, Charges, and Circular Letters. (Works, Vol II)
Heber's (Bp Reg) Sermons preached in England   8vo   *London*, 1829.
Heber's (Bp R) Sermons preached in India   8vo   *London*, 1829.
Henry's (Matt) Select Sermons, edited by John Palmer 8vo   *London*, 1802.

RELIGION

Hill's (John) Sermons 8vo *London*, 1823
Homilies (Sermons, of), appointed to be read in Churches in the time of Queen Elizabeth 8vo *Oxford*, 1810
Hooker's (Richard) Sermons (Works, Vol III)
Hopkins's (Bp E) Sermons (Works, Vols II. and IV)
Horberry's (Matthew) Sermons on important subjects. (Works)
Horne's (Bp Geo) Discourses 4 vols 8vo *London*, 1799.
Horne's (Bp G) XVI. Sermons 8vo *London*, 1800
Horsley's (Bp Samuel) Sermons 3 vols 8vo *London*, 1816
Horsley's (Bp S) IX Sermons on the Resurrection 8vo *London*, 1817
Horsley's (Bp S.) Charges. 8vo *Dundee*, 1813
Hurd's (Bp R) Sermons (Works, Vol. V to VIII)
Jebb's (Bp John) Sermons, chiefly practical, with illustrative Notes, and an Appendix on the Character of the Church of England. 8vo *London*, 1815
Jewell's (Bp) Sermons, preached before the Queen's Majestic at St Paul's Cross. (Works, Vol II)
Jones's (Thomas Snell) Sermons on various subjects 8vo *Edin* 1816
Jones's (W), of Nayland, Sermons. (Works, Vols III and IV)
Knox's (V) Sermons (Works, Vol VI)
Lake's (Bp A) Sermons (Works)
Lardner's (N.) Sermons and Discourses on the Trinity (Works, Vol V)
Latimer's (Bp Hugh) Sermons, collated by the early impressions, and illustrated with Notes and a Life of the Author, by W Watkins 2 vols 8vo *London*, 1824.
Lavington's (Samuel) Sermons and Discourses, with Memoir of the Author 3 vols 8vo *London*, 1815-24.
Leighton's (Abp. R) Lectures and Sermons (Works, Vols II and III)
Lightfoot's (John) Sermons (Works, Vols. V. and VI)
Le Maitre (J H), Sermons, prononcéz dans des occasions extraordinaires, &c *Lemgo*, 1737
Maclaine's (Archibald) Discourses preached at the Hague 8vo. *London*, 1801.
Mant's (R) Sermons for Parochial and Domestic Use 2 vols 8vo *Oxford*, 1813
Marriott's (Harvey) Four Courses of Practical Sermons, expressly adapted to be read in Families 4 vols 8vo *London*, 1825-29
Martyn's (Henry) XX Sermons 8vo *London*, 1822
Mason (John), The Lord's Day Evening Entertainment, containing Fifty-two Discourses 4 vols 8vo *London*, 1752
Mason's (J) Christian Morals, or, a Sequel to the Lord's Day Entertainments 2 vols 8vo *London*, 1761
Mason's (W) XVI Sermons (Works, Vol. IV)
Massillon (J B), Sermons 13 vols 8vo *Paris*, 1811
Massillon, Petit Carême 8vo, pap vélin *Paris*, 1812
Mede's (Joseph) Discourses for every Sunday in the Year (Works)

RELIGION.

Middleton's (Bp. T F) Sermons and Charges, with Memoirs of his Life by Henry Kaye Bonney 8vo *London*, 1824
Miller's (John) Sermons, intended to shew a sober application of Scripture Principles to real life 8vo. *Oxford*, 1830
Milner's (John) Practical Sermons, with an Account of the Life and Character of the Author. 8vo *York*, 1800
Milner's (Dean Isaac) Sermons 2 vols 8vo. *London*, 1800.
Nardin (J F) le Prédicateur Evangélique, ou Sermons pour les Dimanches et les principaux Fêtes de l'Année 4 vols 8vo *Par* 1821
Newton's (Bp Thos) Sermons. (Works, Vol III)
Ogden's (Samuel) Sermons, with Life by Bp S Halifax 2 vols 8vo. *London*, 1788
Paley s (Wm) Sermons and Tracts 2 vols 8vo. *London*, 1808
Paley's (W) Sermons on several occasions 8vo *London*, 1809
Paley's (W) Posthumous Sermons, edited by his Son 2 vols 8vo *London*, 1825
Patrick's (Bp Simon) Sermons on Contentment 8vo *London*, 1719
Porteus's (Bp Beilby) Sermons on several occasions. 8vo *Lond* 1789
Porteus's (B) Lectures on St Matthew 2 vols 8vo. *Lond* 1803
Reynolds' (Bp E.) Sermons (Works, Vols IV and V.)
Richardson's (Wm) Sermons and Expository Discourses; with a brief Memoir of the Author. 3 vols 8vo *London*, 1824, 5
Riddoch's (James) Sermons on several Subjects 2 vols 8vo *London*, 1831.
Rogers' (Thos) Lectures on the Morning Prayer and Litany of the Church of England 4 vols 8vo *London*, 1804.
Sancroft's (Abp W) Three Sermons (Life, by D'Oyly)
Sanderson's (Bp Robt) XXXIV Sermons Folio, port *Lond.* 1689
Sandys' (Abp Edwin) Sermons; with a Life of the Author, edited by J D Whitaker 8vo *London*, 1812
Saurin (J), Sermons 12 vols 8vo *La Haye*, 1776
Scattergood's (Sam) Sermons on several occasions. 2 vols. 8vo. *Oxford*, 1810
Scotch Preacher; a Collection of Sermons by the most eminent Ministers of the Church of Scotland 4 vols 12mo *Lond* 1776
Scott's (Thos) Sermons. (Works, Vols I to III)
Scott's (John) Sermons. (Works, Vols IV to VI)
Secker's (Abp) Sermons (Works, Vols I to V)
Sherlock's (Bp Thos) Discourses, preached at the Temple and on different occasions. (Works, Vols I to III)
Sherlock's (Bp T) VI on the Use and Intent of Prophecy (Works, Vol. IV)
Sherlock's (Bp T) Charges (Works, Vol IV)
Simeon's (Charles) Horæ Homiliticæ; or, Discourses in the Form of Skeletons upon the whole Scriptures 11 vols 8vo *Lond* 1819-20.

RELIGION

Skeeler's (Thos) XIV Sermons preached at St Mary's, Oxford 8vo large paper *Oxford*, 1740

South's (Robert) Sermons   7 vols 8vo   *Oxford*, 1823.

Sterne's (Laur) Sermons   (Works, Vols. VI to VIII)

Stillingfleet's (Bp) Sermons   (Works, Vol I)

Sumner's (J B) Sermons on Christian Faith and Character   8vo *Lond* 1826

Sumner (J B) on the principal Festivals of the Christian Church   8vo *Lond* 1827.

Superville (Daniel), Sermons sur divers Textes. 4 vols. 8vo. *Rotterd* 1714–43

Superville (D., le Fils), Sermons sur divers Textes. 4 vols 8vo *Amst* 1763

Swift's (Jonathan) Sermons. (Works, Vols VII and VIII.)

Taylor's (Bp Jeremy) Sermons   (Works, Vols. V and VI.)

Tillotson's (Abp) Sermons, published by himself   (Works, Vol I)

Tillotson's (Abp) Sermons, published by R. Barker. (Works, Vols. II and III)

Townsend's (Geo) Sermons on the most interesting Subjects in Theology.   8vo   *Lond* 1830

Townson's (Thos) Practical Discourses, a selection from his unpublished MSS with a biographical Memoir by Archdeacon Churton Edited by Bp J. Jebb.   8vo   *Lond* 1830

Twell's (Rich) XXIV Sermons at Boyle Lectures   2 vols royal 8vo, large paper   *Lond* 1743

Venn's (John) Sermons   2 vols 8vo   *Lond.* 1827.

Walker's (Sam) Fifty-two Sermons, for each Sunday in the Year, edited by Sam Burder.   2 vols 8vo   *Lond* 1810

Walker's (Robt) Sermons on Practical Subjects; with Character of the Author by Hugh Blair   4 vols. 8vo.   *Lond* 1806.

Warburton's (Bp) Sermons and Discourses on various Subjects (Works, Vols IX and X.)

Wardlaw's (Ralph) Lectures on the Book of Ecclesiastes   2 vols. 8vo. *Glasgow*, 1821.

Wardlaw's (R) Miscellaneous Sermons   8vo.   *Edinburgh*, 1829

Waterland's (D) VIII Sermons in Vindication of the Divinity of Christ (Works, Vol II)

Waterland's Charges and occasional Sermons.   (Works, Vol VIII)

Waterland's Sermons on several Subjects   (Works, Vol. IX)

Watson's (Bp R) Two Sermons and Charge in Defence of Revealed Religion   (Two Apologies)

Whichcote's (Benj) Sermons   4 vols 8vo   *Aberdeen*, 1751.

Wilkinson (Robt) the Merchant Royall, a Sermon preached at Whitehall, before the King's Majestie, at the Nuptials of Lord Hay and his Lady   4to   *Lond* 1607

Wilson's (Dan) Sermons   8vo   *Lond* 1818

Wilson's (D) Sermons and Tracts   2 vols 8vo   *Lond* 1825
Wilson's (Bp Thos) Sermons.   (Works, Vols V to VIII)
Wisheart's (Wil) Theologia , or, Discourses of God, in CXX Sermons   2 vols 8vo   *Edinburgh*, 1716
Witherspoon's (John) Sermons   (Works, Vols II to V)
Wrangham's (Francis) Sermons, practical and occasional   (Works, Vols. I. and II)

SECT. IX — HISTORY OF RELIGIONS.

General History.

Cérémonies et Coutumes Religieuses de tous les Peuples du Monde, representées par des Figures dessinées de la main de B Picard, avec une Explication historique et quelques Dissertations curieuses, [rédigées sur divers Auteurs par J F et Ja. Bernard, Bruzen de la Martinière, &c]   9 vols folio.   *Amsterdam*, 1723–43

Superstitions Anciennes et Modernes [de M Thiers], Préjugés Vulgaires, qui ont induit le Peuple à des Usages et des Pratiques contraires à la Religion [du Père Le Brun , rédigées avec des Remarques par J F Bernard]   2 vols folio   *Amsterdam*, 1733–36.

Stukeley's (W) Particular Account of the First and Patriarchal Religion , and of the Peopling of the British Islands   (Antiquities of Abury)

Broughton's (Thomas) Historical Dictionary of all Religions to this present time   2 vols. in one, folio   *London*, 1756

History of the Modern Jews and Talmudical Writings.

*** Ancient Jewish History — see Biblical Antiquities

Basnage (Jacques) Histoire des Juifs depuis Jésus-Christ jusqu'à présent.   15 vols 12mo   *La Haye*, 1716–17

Jahn's (John) History of the Hebrew Commonwealth from the earliest times to the destruction of Jerusalem, translated and continued to the time of Adrian by M Stuart   2 vols 8vo   *Lond* 1829.

Lightfoot's (John) Parergon on the Fall of Jerusalem, and the Condition of the Jews in that land after   (Works, Vol III)

Wilkins' (Geo) History of the Destruction of Jerusalem as connected with the Scripture Prophecies   8vo   *Nottingham*, 1816

Warburton's (Bp) Julian ; or, a Discourse concerning the Earthquake and Fiery Eruption which defeated that Emperor s attempt to rebuild Jerusalem   (Works, Vol VIII)

[Stehlin's (Peter)] Traditions of the Jews , or, the Doctrines and Expositions contained in the Talmud and other Rabbinical Writings . with an Inquiry into the Origin, Progress, Authority, and Usefulness of those Traditions , wherein the mystical sense of the Allegories in the Talmud, &c is explained   2 vols 8vo   *London*, 1742

Allen's (John) Modern Judaism ; or, a brief Account of the Opinions, Traditions, Rites, and Ceremonies of the Jews in Modern Times   8vo   *London*, 1816

Wotton's (W) Miscellaneous Discourses relating to the Traditions and Usages of the Scribes and Pharisees in our Saviour's time 2 vols 8vo. *London*, 1718

Shaw's (Duncan) History and Philosophy of Judaism, or, a Critical and Philological Analysis of the Jewish Religion 8vo *London*, 1788

Lightfoot (John) Index Talmudis Hierosolymitani, &c. (Vol X)

History of the Christian Religion.

[Trittenhem (Johannes de)] Liber de Scriptoribus Ecclesiasticis [cura F Johannis de Lapide] Folio Editio Princeps *Basileæ*, [per J Amerbachium] M.CCCC XCIII

Dupin's (L E) History of Ecclesiastical Writers, containing an Account of the Authors of the several Books of the Old and New Testament, of the Lives of the Primitive Fathers, and of the Authors, to the end of the XVIth Century of the Church with a Compendious History of the Councils and Chronological Tables [translated and revised by W Wotton] 3 vols folio Mr Williams's copy, in morocco. *Dublin*, 1723, 4

Campbell's (Geo) Lectures on Ecclesiastical History, with some Account of the Life and Writings of the Author by Geo Skene Keith 2 vols 8vo *Aberdeen*, 1815.

Spanheim's Ecclesiastical Annals, from the Commencement of the Scripture History to the XVIth Century, a compressed translation, with Notes, by Geo Wright 8vo *London*, 1828

Eusebii Pamphili Chronicon Bipartitum [Græco-Armenio-Latinum], nunc primùm ex Armeniaco Textu in Latinam conversum, Adnotationibus auctum, Græcis Fragmentis exornatum Opera J B Aucher 2 vols folio, large paper *Venetiis*, 1818

Severi (Sulpitii) Opera [vid Historia Sacra, de Vitâ B Martini, Epistolæ, Dialogi] 24mo *Lugd. Bat. ap. Elzev* 1643.

Eusebii Pamphili, Socratis, Sozomeni, Theodoreti, Evagrii, et Philostorgii Historiæ Ecclesiasticæ, Gr et Lat. Notis Valesii et Reading. 3 vols folio *Cantabr* 1720

Cave's (William) Apostolici et Ecclesiastici, or, Lives of those who were contemporary with the Apostles; of the Primitive Fathers of the First Three Centuries, and of the Fathers of the Church that flourish't in the Fourth Century with Appendix 2 vols. folio, large paper. *London*, 1677–83

Lardner's (N) History of the Apostles and Evangelists, Writers of the New Testament   (Works)

Lardner's (N.) History of the Heretics of the Two First Centuries after Christ   (Works)

Kay's (Bp) Ecclesiastical History of the IId and IIId Centuries illustrated from the Writings of Tertullian 8vo *Cambridge*, 1829

Lightfoot (John) Fragmenta Historiæ Romanæ et Christianæ de Rebus et Persons IV. primorum Sæculorum   (Works, Vol VIII)

Mosheim's (J L) Commentaries on the Affairs of the Christians before the time of Constantine the Great, translated by S Vidal 2 vols 8vo *London*, 1813

Usserius (Jac.) de Christianarum Eccles. in occidentis præsertim partibus, ab Apost. temp. ad nostram usque ætatem, continuâ Successione et Statu. (De Ant. Ecc. Britan.)

Centuriatorum Magdeburgensium Historia Ecclesiastica, secundùm singulas centurias, ex vetustissimis et optimis Historicis, Patribus, et aliis Scriptoribus congesta [ad annum MCCC], per studiosos ac pios aliquot Viros [M. F. Illyricus, J. Vuigandus, M. Judex, B. Faber, &c.], recens Lucu. 3 vols folio *Basileæ*, 1624.

Mosheim's (J. L.) Ecclesiastical History, translated, and illustrated with Notes and Chronological Tables, by Arch. Maclaine, and continued to the end of the XVIIIth Century by Charles Coote. 6 vols 8vo *London*, 1811.

Milner's (Joseph) History of the Church of Christ; with Additions and Corrections by Isaac Milner. 4 vols. in five, 8vo. *Cambridge*, 1800–9

Milner's (J.) Church History, continued by John Scott from A.D. MDXXX. 3 vols 8vo *Lond.* 1828–31

Bingham's (Joseph) Antiquities of the Christian Church, and other Works, with a Set of Maps of Ecclesiastical Geography. Edited by Richard Bingham. 9 vols. 8vo. *London*, 1829.

Ecclesiastical History of particular Countries.

. Ecc. Hist. of Great Britain—see English and Scottish History
History of Councils—see page 26

Perrin (J. P.), Luther's Fore-runners; or, a Cloud of Witnesses deposing for the Protestant Faith, gathered together in the History of the Waldenses; translated out of the French by Samuel Lennard. 4to. port *Lond.* 1624

Moreland's (Sir Sam.) History of the Evangelical Churches of the Valleys of Piedmont containing a faithful account of their Doctrines, Persecutions, &c. to the year 1658. Folio, port. map, and plates. *London*, 1658

Leger (Jean), Histoire Générale des Eglises Evangéliques des Vallées de Piemont, ou Vaudoises. Folio *Leyde*, 1669.

Allix's (Peter) Remarks upon the Ecclesiastical History of the Ancient Churches of Piedmont. 8vo *Oxford*, 1821. (Works, Vol. III.)

Allix's (P.) Remarks upon the Ecclesiastical History of the Ancient Churches of the Albigenses. 8vo. *Oxford*, 1821. (Works, Vol. IV.)

Peyran's (J. R.) Historical Defence of the Albigenses or Vaudois, Inhabitants of the Valleys of Piedmont, with an Introduction and Appendices by Thos Sims. 8vo *London*, 1826

Gilly's (William Stephen) Narrative of an Excursion to the Mountains of Piedmont, in the Year 1823; and Researches among the Vaudois or Waldenses, Protestant Inhabitants of the Cottian Alps. 8vo *London*, 1825.

Gilly's (W. S.) Waldensian Researches during a second Visit to the Vaudois of Piedmont, with an introductory Inquiry into the Antiquity and Purity of the Waldensian Church. 8vo *London*, 1831

Lenfant, Histoire de la Guerre des Hussites. (Concile de Basle.)

RELIGION

Hayne's (Thos) Life and Death of Martin Luther taken out of his owne and other godly and most learned Men's Writings who lived at his time 4to, portrait by Holtner *London*, 1641

Bower's (Alex.) Life of Martin Luther, with an Account of the early Progress of the Reformation. 8vo *London*, 1813

Luther's Pieces regarding the Reformation. (Opera.)

Cox's (F A) Life of Philip Melancthon, comprising an Account of the most important Transactions of the Reformation. 8vo *Lond* 1813

A Famose Cronicle of our Time, called Sleidane's Commentaries, concerning the State of Religion and Commonwealth during the raigne of the Emperour Charles V ; translated oute of Latin into Englishe by Jhon Daus here unto is added, also, an Apology of the Authoure 𝔅lack letter, folio *London, by John Daye*, 1560

Frarin (Peter), an Oration against the Unlawfull Insurrections of the Protestantes in our Times, under pretense to refourme Religion, made and pronounced in Latin at Louvaine, anno 1565, and now translated with the advise of the Author [by Jhon Fouler] 𝔅lack letter, small 8vo *Antverpiæ, ex off J Fouleri*, M.D.LXVI.

> At the end is " The table of this booke set out, not by order of alphabet or numbre, but by expresso figures, to the eye and sight of the reader, and of him also y^t cannot reade," or cuts representing the cruelties practised by the Protestants, with descriptions in rhyme

Seckendorfii (V. L. à) Commentarius Historicus et Apologeticus de Lutheranismo, sive, de Reformatione Religionis ductu D. Mart. Lutheri 2 vols folio *Francof* 1692

Gerdesii (Dan) Historia Reformationis, sive, Annales Evangelii Sæc. XVI passim per Europam renovati doctrinæque reformatæ Accedunt varia Monumenta Pietatis et Rei Litterariæ ut plurimum ex MSS. eruta. 4 vols 4to portraits *Groning* 1744-52

Gerdesii (Dan) Scrinium Antiquarium, sive, ad Historiam Reformationis Ecclesiast. præcipue spectantia inseruntur Tractatus varii generis, Epistolæ, Orationes, Biographiæ, &c 4 vols 4to. *Groning*. 1748-51

Brandt's (Gerard) History of the Reformation in the Low Countries, from the beginning of the VIIIth Century to the famous Synod of Dort Translated from the Dutch [by John Chamberlayne] 4 vols folio. *London*, 1720-23.

Brandt's (G.) Life of Arminius, with considerable Augmentations, and a copious Account of the Synod of Dort and its Proceedings (Arminius's Works, Vol I)

Limborchii (P. à) Relatio historica de Origine et Progressu Controversiarum in Fœderato Belgio de Prædestinatione. (Theologia.)

Laval's (S A) History of the Reformation in France 7 vols 8vo *Lond*. 1737-41

Zwingle (The Life of Ulrich) the Swiss Reformer, by J G Hess, translated by Lucy Aikin 8vo. *London*, 1812

Ruchat, Histoire de la Réformation de la Suisse 6 vols 12mo *Genève*, 1727.

Gerdesii (Dan) Specimen Italiæ Reformatæ, sive, reformata quædam renati Italia tempore Reformationis Evangelii 4to *Lugd Bat*. 1765

RELIGION.

Macrie's (Thomas) History of the Progress and Suppression of the Reformation in Italy, including a Sketch of its History in the Grisons 8vo *Edinburgh*, 1827

Macrie's (T) History of the Progress and Suppression of the Reformation in Spain during the XVIth Century 8vo *Edinburgh*, 1829

Milner's (T) History of the VII Churches of Asia, their Rise, Progress, and Decline, with Notices of the Churches of Tralles, Magnesia, Colosse, Hierapolis, Lyons, and Vienne designed to shew the Fulfilment of Scripture Prophecy 8vo *London*, 1832

Eutychii Ecclesiæ suæ Origines, Arabicè, ac Versione et Commentario auxit J Selden (Opera. Vol II)

Croze (De la), Histoire du Christianisme des Indes 12mo *Haye*, 1724

Buchanan s (Claud) Apology for promoting Christianity in India 8vo *London*, 1813

Geddes's (Mich) History of the Church of Malabar, giving an Account of its Persecutions by the Roman Prelates, together with the Synod of Diamper, celebrated 1599. 8vo *London*, 1694.

Lettres Edifiantes et Curieuses, écrites des Missions étrangères [publiée par l'Abbé de Querbeuf], Nouvelles des Missions Orientales, reçues en 1785 et 6, Nouvelles Lettres Edifiantes des Missions de la Chine et des Indes Orientales 36 vols 12mo *Paris*, 1780–1819

Geddes' (M) History of the Church of Ethiopia, wherein, among other things, the two great Roman Missions into that Empire are placed in their true light 8vo *London*, 1696.

Lobo, Histoire de l'Eglise Chrétienne de l'Abyssinie (Relation Historique de l'Abyssinie)

Mather (Cotton) Magnalia Christi Americana; or, the Ecclesiastical History of New England, from the first planting in 1620 to 1698. Folio *London*, 1702.

History of Popes, and Lives of the Saints.

Platina's (Bapt) Lives of the Popes, from the time of Christ to the reign of Sextus IV.; translated into English, and continued to the present time by Paul Rycault Folio *London*, 1658.

Bower's (Archibald) History of the Popes, from the Foundation of the See of Rome to the present time. 7 vols 4to *London*, 1749–66

Bower's History (Pamphlets relative to), with the Author's Answers *London*, 1756–7.

[Jacobi de Voragine] Legenda Sanctorum quæ Lombardica nominatum Hystoria Black letter. Folio *Impressa Coloniæ, M CCCC LXXXV*

Panzer quotes this ed.tion from Maittaire, but styles it "editio dubia." A very fine copy, the capitals inserted in red

Butler's (Alban) Lives of the Fathers, Martyrs, and other principal Saints; illustrated with the Remarks of judicious modern Critics and Historians. 12 vols 8vo *Dublin*, 1779–80.

Wicelii (M Geo) B Martyris S Bonifacii, in Germania quondam Apostoli, vera Historia, carmine heroico 4to *Coloniæ, ex offic hæred J Quintel*, 1553

Boyle (Robert) on the Martyrdom of Theodora and Dydimus   (Works, Vol V)

Religious Orders and the Inquisition.

[Helyot], Histoire des Ordres Monastiques, Réligieux, et Militaires, et des Congrégations Séculaires, qui ont été établies jusqu'à présent 8 vols 4to plates   *Paris*, 1721

Keronis Interp Regulæ S Benedicti Theotisca, ex MS antiq nunc primùm eruta per R P Franckium, recensuit Notisque illust J. G Scherzius   (Schilteri Thes , Vol I.)

History of the Jesuits, with a Reply to Mr. Dallas's Defence of that Order   2 vols 8vo   *London*, 1816

Racine (Jean), Abrégé de l'Histoire de Port-Royal, Réponse à l'Auteur [Desmarets] des " Hérésies Imaginaires "   (Œuvres, Vol IV)

Clemencet (Charles), Histoire de Port-Royal 10 vols 12mo *Amst* 1755

Lancelot s (Dom Claude) Journey, in 1667 to La Grande Chartreuse and Alet; including some Account of De Rancé, Du Verger de Hauranne Abbé de St Cyran, C Jansensius and a brief Sketch of the Institution of Port-Royal, with Notes, &c by Mrs. Schemmelpennick   8vo   *London*, 1813

Llorente (J. A), Histoire Critique de l'Inquisition d'Espagne depuis l'époque de son établissement par Ferdinand V jusqu'au règne de Ferdinand VII 4 vols 8vo *Paris*, 1818

Dellon's (Le Sieur) Account of the Inquisition at Goa, translated from the French, with an Account of the Escape of Archibald Bower from the Inquisition at Maceratæ, in Italy   8vo   *Hull*, 1812

History of Sects and Missions

Servetus (an Impartial History of Michael) burnt alive at Geneva for Heresie   8vo   *London*, 1724

Mosheimi (Jo L) de Turbatâ per recentiores Platonicos Ecclesiâ Commentatio   (Cudworth Systema Intellectuale)

Crantz's (David) Ancient and Modern History of the Unitas Fratrum, translated, with Notes, by Benjamin La Trobe 8vo *London*, 1780

Holmes's (John) History of the Protestant Church of the United Brethren. 2 vols 8vo   *London*, 1825–30

Sewell's (William) History of the Rise and Progress of the Quakers Folio   *London*, 1725.

Browns (W) History of the Propagation of Christianity among the Heathen since the Reformation 2 vols 8vo *Edinburgh*, 1823

Buchanan's (Claudius) Christian Researches in Asia, with Notices of the Translation of the Scriptures into Oriental Languages   8vo   *Lond* 1819.

Jowett's (William) Christian Researches in the Mediterranean, from 1815 to 20, and in 1823 and 4. 2 vols 8vo. *London*, 1824–6

Crantz's (David) Relation of the Mission carried on in Greenland by the Unitas Fratrum   (History of Greenland)

Loskiel's (G H) History of the Mission of the United Brethren among the Indians of North America translated by C J Latrobe 3 parts in one vol 8vo *London*, 1794

Mahommedan and Pagan Religions.

Butler's (Charles) Connected Series of Notes on the Koran, Zend-avesta, Vedas, Kings, and Edda, the sacred books of the Mahometans, Hindus Parsees, Chinese, and Scandinavians (Horæ Biblicæ, Vol II)

The Koran, or, Alcoran of Mohammed, translated with Notes and a Preliminary Discourse on Mohammedism, &c by Geo Sale 2 vols 8vo *London*, 1795

Mishcat-ul-Masabih, or, a Collection of the most authentic Traditions regarding the Actions and Sayings of Muhammed; exhibiting the Origin of the Manners and Customs, the civil, religious, and military Policy of the Musslemans, [and forming a Supplement to the Koran], translated from the Arabic by Captain Matthews 2 vols 4to *Calcutta*, 1809

Galland, Récueil des Rits et Cérémonies du Pélerinage de la Mecque, auquel on a joint divers Ecrits rélatifs à la Réligion, aux Sciences, et aux Mœurs des Turcs 12mo *Amst* 1754.

White's Comparison of Mahometism and Christianity (Bampton Lectures)

Faber's (Geo Stanley) Origin of Pagan Idolatry, ascertained from historical Testimony and circumstantial Evidence 3 vols 4to *London*, 1816

Christie's (James) Essay on the earliest Species of Idolatry, the Worship of the Elements 4to *Norwich*, 1814

Banier (l'Abbé), la Mythologie et les Fables expliquees par l'Histoire. 3 vols 4to. *Paris*, 1738–40

Bryant's (Jacob) New System or Analysis of Ancient Mythology 3 vols. 1774–6

D Hancarville, Système de la Mythologie (Antiquities)

Millin, Galerie Mythologique. (Antiquities)

Faber (Geo. S) on the Mysteries of the Cabiri, or, the Great Gods of Phœnicia, Samothrace, Egypt, and Greece 2 vols 8vo. *Oxford*, 1803

Bell's (John) New Pantheon, or, Historical Dictionary of Gods, Heroes, &c of Antiquity 2 vols in one, 4to *London*, 1790

Dictionary of Polite Literature, or, Fabulous History of Heathen Gods and Heroes 2 vols 12mo. *London*, 1804.

Lenoir (Alex), la Mythologie des Egyptiens et des Grecs (Explication des Hieroglyphes)

Ahmad ben Abubeki's Account of the Egyptian Priests, their Classes, Initiation, and Sacrifices (Ancient Alphabets.)

Champollion (J F), Panthéon Egyptien, Collection des Personnages Mythologiques de l'Ancienne Egypte, d'après les Monumens, avec un Texte explicatif 4to Parts I.–XV *Paris*, 1825.

Aristoteles de Divinûm Sapientiâ secundùm Ægyptos (Opera, Vol II)
Hyde (Thomæ) Veterum Persarum et Parthorum, et Medorum Religionis Historia, Zoroastris Vitam et Præcepta seu Canones complectens, ejusdem et aliorum Vaticinia de Messiah, primitivas Opiniones de Deo, orig Orient Sibyllæ, &c 4to *Oxonii* 1760
Zoroastre le Zend-Avesta ; ouvrage contenant les Idées Théologiques, Physiques, et Morales, de ce Législateur, les Cérémonies du Culte Réligieux qu'il a établi et plusieurs Traits importans rélatifs à l'Ancienne Histoire des Perses, traduit sur l'original Zend avec des Remarques, et accompagnés de plusieurs Traités propres à éclaircir les matières qui en sont l objet, par Anquetil du Perron 3 vols 4to *Paris*, 1771
Selden (Jo) de Diis Syris (Opera, Vol II)
Oupnek'-hat (id est, secretum tegendum), opus continens antiquam et arcanam, seu theologicam et philosophicam Doctrinam è IV Sacris Indorum Libris exceptam, studio et operâ Anquetil du Perron. 2 vols 4to *Argent*, 1801–2
Moor's (Edw) Hindu Pantheon 4to *London*, 1810
Carwithen on the Brahminical Religion (Bampton Lectures)
Confucius Sinarum Philosophus ; sive, Scientia Sinensis Latinè exposita, studio et operâ P P. Soc Jesu Folio *Parisiis*, 1687
Catechism of the Shamans , or, the Laws and Regulations of the Priesthood of Buddha in China. Translated from the Chinese original with Notes and Illustrations by C F Neumann. 8vo *London*, 1831
Edda Sæmundar Hinns Froda, Edda Rhythmica seu Antiquior, vulgò Sæmundina dicta, Odas Mythologicas, à Resenio non editas, ex Cod Perg Bib Reg Hafniensis et aliorum, cum Interpret Latinâ, Lectionibus variis, Notis, Glossario Vocum, et Indice Rerum Sumpt Legati Magnæani et Gydendalii 4to *Hafniæ*, 1787
The Edda , or, System of Runic Mythology, and other Pieces, from the ancient Islandic Tongue, from the French of Mallet ; with additional Notes by the English Translator [Bp Percy], and Goranson's Latin version of the Edda (Mallet's Northern Antiquities, Vol II)
Rowland's (Thos) Account of the Ancient Druids of the Isle of Mona or Anglesey, to the Dissolution of their Hierarchy (Mona Antiqua)
Davies' (Edward) Mythology and Rites of the British Druids, ascertained by National Documents, and compared with the general Traditions and Customs of Heathenism, with an Appendix of ancient British Poems and Extracts, and some Remarks on ancient British Coins Royal 8vo *London*, 1809

CLASS II.—JURISPRUDENCE

Sect I —INTRODUCTIONS AND TREATISES ON UNIVERSAL LAW

Butler's (Charles) Horæ Juridicæ Subsecivæ, a Connected Series of Notes respecting the Geography, Chronology, and Literary History of the Grecian, Roman, Feudal, and Canon Law Large paper, royal 8vo *London*, 1807

JURISPRUDENCE

Camus, Lettres sur la Profession d'Avocat, et Bibliothèque choisie des Livres de Droit Augmentée par Dupin 2 vols 8vo *Paris,* 1818

Platonis Minos, sive, de Legibus (Opera)

Cicero de Legibus. (Opera)

Montesquieu (C. de), de l'Esprit des Loix, et l'en Défense, avec l'Eloge de l'Auteur et Analyse de l'Ouvrage, par D'Alembert. 4 vols. 12mo. *Paris,* 1805

Harrington's (James) Art of Lawgiving (Works)

Filangieri (Gaet.), la Sienza della Legislatione 6 vols 8vo *Milano,* 1822

Bentham's (Jeremy) Introduction to the Principles of Morals and Legislation 2 vols 8vo *London,* 1823

Grotii (Hug) de Jure Belli ac Pacis Lib. III., cum Annotat Variorum et J F Gronovii, accesserunt Diss de Mare Libero, et Libellus sing de Æquitate, Indulgentiâ, et Facilitate 8vo, large paper *Amstelod ex Off Wetsteniana,* 1712

Grotius (H) de Jure Belli ac Pacis, cum Notis, ex alterâ recensione Jo Barbeyracii 8vo *Amst.* 1735

Puffendorf (S) de Officio Hominis et Civis secundùm Legem Naturalem, cum Obs et Annot C Barbeyracii et variorum 2 vols roy. 8vo large paper *Lugd Bat* 1769

Wolfii (Christ) Institutiones Juris Naturæ et Gentium 8vo *Halæ,* 1754

Burlamaqui (J J) Principes du Droit de la Nature et des Gens, avec la Suite du Droit de la Nature, le tout augmenté par De Felice. 8 vols. 8vo *Yverdon,* 1766-68

Vattel (E. de), le Droit des Gens, ou Principes de la Loi Naturelle appliquée à la conduite et aux Affaires des Nations et des Souverains, augmentée, revue, et corrigée 2 vols 8vo *Paris.* 1820

Selden (Jo) de Jure Naturali et Gentium, juxta Disciplinam Hebræorum (Opera, Vol. I.)

[Mably], le Droit Public de l'Europe, fondé sur les Traités 3 vols 12mo *Genève,* 1776

Koch, Histoire Abrégé des Traités de Paix entre les Puissances de l'Europe depuis la Paix de Westphalie, revue et augmentée par Schœll jusqu'à 1815 15 vols 8vo *Paris,* 1817-18

Rymer (Thomæ) Fœdera, Conventiones, Litteræ, et cujuscunque generis Acta Publica inter Reges Angliæ et alios ab anno 1101 (Eng Documentary History)

Montagu's (Edward Wortley) Reflections on the Rise and Fall of the Ancient Republicks, adapted to the present state of Great Britain 8vo. *Lond* 1769

Young on the Principles, Policy, and Practice of Republican Governments (Hist of Athens)

Adams's (John) History of the principal Republics in the World 3 vols 8vo *Lond* 1794

Humbert, Manuel du Publiciste et de l'Homme d'Etat, contenant les Chartes et les Lois Fondamentelles, &c., et tout ce qui est rélatif aux Constitutions de l'Ancien et du Nouveau Monde. 4 vols 8vo. *Rouen*, 1826

Temple's (Sir W.) Survey of the Constitutions and Interests of the Empire, Sweden, Denmark, Spain, Holland, France, and Flanders, with their Relation to England in 1671. (Works, Vol II.)

Grotius (H.) de Mare Libero, et P. Merula de Maribus. 24mo. *Lugd Bat* 1633

Selden (Jo.) Mare Clausum, seu, de Dominio Maris, ex Jure Naturæ seu Gentium, &c. (Opera, Vol II.)

Azuni, Origine et Progrès du Droit et de la Législation Maritime, avec des Observations sur le Consulat de la Mer. 8vo. *Paris* 1810

Sect II.—ANCIENT, CIVIL, AND FEUDAL LAW

*** For Mosaic and Jewish Law—see "Biblical Antiquities"

Leges Atticæ, Gr. et Lat.; collegit et Comment. illustravit S. Petit, cum Observationibus Wesselingii et variorum. Folio. *Lugd Bat* 1742

The Speeches of Isæus, in causes concerning the Law of Succession to Property at Athens. (Sir W. Jones's Works, Vol IV.)

Chapman (T.) on the Roman Senate. 8vo, large paper. *Lond* 1750

Gravinæ (Jo. V.) Origines Juris Civilis, seu, de Ortu et Progressu Juris Civilis, cum Notis Mascovii. 4to. *Lipsiæ*, 1737

Savigny's History of the Roman Law during the Middle Ages, translated from the German by E. Cathcart. 2 vols 8vo. *London*, 1830

Waltheri (J. L.) Lexicon Juridicum, Indices utriusque Juris exhibens locupletissimos. 8vo. *Francof.* 1754

Taylor's (John) Elements of Civil Law. 4to. *London*, 1756

Fontes IV Juris Civilis in unum collectæ, putà, Leges XII Tab. et Leges Juliæ et Papiæ Fragmenta, cum Notis; Edicti perpetui ut et Sabinianorum librorum ordo seriesque. Edente Jac. Gothofredo. 4to. *Genevæ*, 1653

Jurisprudentia Vetus antè Justinianea, ex recensione et cum Notis Schultingii Nova collata cum Codd MSS de illustratione Juris Civilis Antiqui, ex lectione classicorum; præfatus est D. G. H. Ayler. 4to. *Lipsiæ*, 1737

Continens—Quæ supersunt ex Cau Inst Lib. IV
 Pauli Sententiarum receptarum lib V
 Fragmentum ex Institut Lib II.
 Tituli ex corpore Ulpiani XXIX.
 Codd Gregoriani et Hermogeniani Fragmenta.
 Mosaicarum et Romanarum Legum Collatio, cum quibusdam aliis Fragmentis.
 Consultatio Veteris cujusdam Jurisconsulti
 Papiani Responsorum liber
 Dosithei Magistri Liber III Gr et Lat

Codex Theodosianus, cum perpet Commentariis J. Gothofredi. Editio emendata et Observationibus aucta à J. D. Ritter. 6 vols folio, *Lipsiæ*, 1736–45

Theodosiani Codicis Fragmenta inedita, ex Codice palimpsesto Bib
R. Taurinensis Athenæi in lucem protulit atque illustravit A Peyron
4to *Augustæ Taur* 1824

Theodosiani Codicis genuina Fragmenta, ex Membranis Bib Ambrosianæ Mediolanensis, nunc primum edidit W F. Classius. 8vo. *Tubingæ*, 1824.

Theodosiani Codicis libri V. priores; recognovit, additamentis insignibus à W F Classio, et A Peyron repertis aliisque auxit, Notis Subitaneis tum criticis tum exegeticis, nec non quadruplici Appendice, instruxit C F. C Wenck. 8vo *Lipsiæ*, 1825

Leges Novellæ V., Anecdotæ Imper. Theodosii Junioris, et Valentiniani III; cum cæterarum etiam Novellarum editarum Titulis, &c, studio J C Amaduti Folio *Romæ*, 1767

Justinianæ Institutiones Additi sunt Tituli Digestor de Verborum Significatione et Regulis Juris 32mo, large paper. *Lugd Bat ap Dan à Gaesbeeck*, 1678.

Justiniani Imp Corpus Juris Civilis, cum Notis D Gothofredi et variorum, ex editione S Van Leeuwen 2 vols folio *Lugd Bat Elzev* 1663

Voet (J. E) Commentarius ad Pandectas 2 vols folio *Hagæ-Comit* 1734.

Wieling (Abr.) Jurisprudentia Restituta, sive, Index Chronologicus in totum Juris Justinianæi Corpus, ad modum J Labitti, &c nova tamen et faciliore methodo collectus 8vo *Amstelod*. 1727
    Accesserunt—J Labitti Usus Pandectarum, cum Notis W. Schmaucen
               H Hahn de Usu Chronologiæ in Jure.
               H Brencmann de Legum Inscriptionibus
               B. H Reinoldi Oratio de Inscriptionibus Legum Dig et Cod

ΒΑΣΙΛΙΚΩΝ Libri IX, Car A. Fabrotus Latinè vertit et Græcè edidit 7 vols folio *Paris*, 1647.

ΒΑΣΙΛΙΚΩΝ Supplementum, continens Libros IV Basilicorum, 49–52, Gr et Lat vertit et castigavit Ruhnkenius Folio *Lugd Bat* 1765

Constitutiones Vetustæ Imperatorum, ex MS. à J. B. Schiltero. (Schilteri Thes Vol. II)

Lindenbrogii (F) Codex Legum Antiquarum, in quo continentur Leges Wisigothorum, Edictum Theoderici Regis, Lex Burgundiorum, Salica, Almannorum, Bajuvariorum, Decretum Tassilonis Ducis, Leges Ripuariorum, Saxonum, Anglorum, et Wermorum, Frisorum, Longobardorum; Capitularia Caroli Magni, &c Folio *Francof* 1613.

Legis Salicæ Antiquissimæ textus vet, ex Bib Parisiensi Regiâ descriptus Recensuit et Editioni paravit Jo Schilterus Adjuncta est accurata subnotatio variationum insignium ex edit Heraldi et ex aliis vetustis Cod Accedit pactus Legis Salicæ textus recentior, Notis Baluzii, Pithoei, Bignonii (Schilteri Thes Vol II)

Jus Provinciale Alemannicum, ex Cod MS Membr Dni R Krafft. Lectiones variantes excerpsit et Latinam versionem juxta textum donavit, Notis illustrat B Schilterus (Schilteri Thes Vol. II)

Jenichen (G A) Thesaurus Juris Feudalis, continens optima atque selectissima Opuscula quibus Jus Feudale explicatur 3 vols 4to *Francof* 1750

JURISPRUDENCE. 71

Beccaria's (Marquis) Essays on Crimes and Punishments, translated, with the Commentary by Voltaire, 8vo *Lond* 1804.

Montagu (Basil), the Opinions of different Authors upon the Punishment of Death   3 vols 8vo   *Lond* 1809–13

Sect. III.—CANON LAW

Corpus Juris Canonici ex Edit et cum Notis P et F Pithæorum, curâ Fr Desmares   2 vols folio   *Parisiis*, 1687

Selden (Jo) Uxor Ebraica, seu, de Nuptiis et Divortiis ex Jure Civili, id est, Divino et Talmudico, Vet Ebræorum   (Opera, Vol II)

Milton's (John) Doctrine and Discipline of Divorce restored from the Bondage of the Canon Law, and other mistakes, to the Meaning of True Scripture,—the Judgment of Martin Bucer concerning Divorce,—Tetrachordon; Expositions upon the four chief places of Scripture that treat of Marriage,—Colasterion, a Reply to a Nameless Answer against the Doctrine and Discipline of Divorce   (Prose Works, 4to. Vol I ; 8vo Vols I and II)

Sect. IV —BRITISH LAW.
Public and Constitutional Law.

Smith (Sir Thomas) De Republicâ Anglorum the Manner of Government or Policie of the Realme of England   𝔅𝔩𝔞𝔠𝔨 𝔩𝔢𝔱𝔱𝔢𝔯.   4to *London, by Henrie Middleton*, 1583.
   <small>The first published Work on the English Government.</small>

Acherley (Roger), The Britannic Constitution; or, Fundamental Form of Government in Britain   Folio. *London*, 1727.

De Lolme (J L), the Constitution of England, or, an Account of the English Government.   8vo   *London*, 1807

Wentworth (Peter), a Pithie Exhortation to her Majestie for establishing her successor to the crowne, whereunto is added, a Discourse containing the Author's opinion of the true and lawful successor to her Majestie, [wherein the title is briefly and plainely set down, Dolman's objections refuted, and inconveniences removed]   Small 8vo *Imprinted (abroad)* 1598
   <small>The "Exhortation" was presented in 1593 as a supplication to the Queen, and cost its author an imprisonment in the Tower. Both were now first printed with a view to favour James's succession.</small>

[Hearne's (Thomas)] Vindication of those who take the Oath of Allegiance to his present Majestie, from Perjurie, Injustice, and Disloyaltie, charged upon them by such as are against it   Royal 8vo, large paper, port by Vertue.   [*Oxford*], *printed* 1731

Harrington's (James) Grounds and Reasons of Monarchy considered, Answer to Wren's Monarchy asserted, and Letters and Answer to Stubbs and Rogers   (Works)

Milton (John), the Tenure of Kings and Magistrates, proving that it is lawful to call to account a Tyrant or Wicked King   (Prose Works, 4to, Vol. I, 8vo, Vol III)

Milton (J) Defensio pro Populo Anglicano, contra Salmasium; Defensio secunda contra A Morum, pro se Defensio contra idem liber, et ad A Mori Supplementum Responsio   (Prose Works, 4to Vol II, 8vo Vol V)

JURISPRUDENCE.

Philippi (Jo) Responsio ad Apologiam anonymi cujusdam Tenebrionis pro Rege et Populo Anglicano infantissimam (Milton's Prose Works, 4to Vol II , 8vo Vol V)

Cruise (W) on the Origin and Nature of Dignities and Titles of Honour Royal 8vo *London*, 1823.

Betham's (Sir W) Dignities, Feudal and Parliamentary; the Constitutional Legislature of the United Kingdom , the Nature and Functions of the Aula Regis, the Magna Concilia and the Communia Concilia of England, &c 2 vols. 8vo *London*, 1831

Selden (Jo) on the Office of Lord Chancellor of England (Works, Vol III)

Selden's (J) Privileges of the Baronage of England (Works, Vol III)

The Antiquity, Power, Order, State, Manner, Persons, and Proceedings of the High Court of Parliament, by Agarde, Tate, Camden, &c (Curious Discourses, Vol. I.)

Ralegh's (Sir W) Prerogative of Parliaments in England ; proved in a Dialogue between a Counsellor of State and a Justice of Peace (Works, Vol VIII.)

Prynne's (W) Soveraigne Power of Parliaments and Kingdomes , with an Appendix, wherein the superiority of our owne, and most other foraine Parliaments, States, &c (collectively considered) over and above their lawful Kings, is abundantly evidenced. 4to. *Lond* 1643.

Selden (John) of the Judicature in Parliament (Works, Vol. III)

Dugdale's (Sir W) Perfect Copy of all Summons of the Nobility to the Great Councils and Parliaments of England, from 49th of Henry III. until these times Folio *London*, 1685.

Palgrave's (Francis) Parliamentary Writs, and Writs of Military Summons , together with the Records and Muniments relating to the Suit and Service due and performed to the King's High Court of Parliament and the Councils of the Realm, or affording Evidence of attendance given at Parliaments and Councils 2 vols fol *Lond* 1827

Harrington (James), a Word concerning a House of Peers (Works)

Stillingfleet (Bp) on the Bishops' Right to vote in Parliament in Cases capital (Works, Vol III)

Hatsell's (John) Precedents of Proceedings in the House of Commons, with Observations 4 vols. 4to *London*, 1796

History and General Treatises of the Law of England.

Herbert's (W.) Concise History of English Law (Antiquities of Inns of Court)

Selden (Jo) ANALECTON ANGLO-BRITANNICON , quibus ea maximé quæ ad Civilem illius, quæ jam Anglia dicitur, Mag. Brit antiquitàs, Administrationem, Statûsque Catastrophas usque ad Normanni adventum attinet. (Opera, Vol II)

Dugdale's (Sir Wm) Origines Juridiciales , or, Historical Memorials of the English Laws, Courts of Justice, Forms of Tryall, Punishments in Cases criminal, Law Writers, Law Books, Innes of Court and Chancery , also, a Chronology of the Lord Chancellors, Judges. &c Folio First edition *London*, 1666

JURISPRUDENCE.

Selden's (Jo) England's Epinomis ;—Notes on Sir John Fortescue de Laudibus Legum Angliæ, and on Sir Ralph de Hengham's Summæ. (Works, Vol III)

Wynne's (Edward) Eunomus , or, Dialogues concerning the Law and Constitution of England 2 vols 8vo. *Lond* 1809.

Lambardi (Gul) ΑΡΧΑΙΟΝΟΜΙΑ, sive, de Priscis Anglorum Legibus Libri, Saxonicè et Latinè 4to Herbert's copy *Lond. J Dau*, 1568.

Selden (Jo) Janus Anglorum, à primo Henrici II ad usque abitionem quod occurrit prophanum Anglo-Britanniæ Jus resipiens (Opera, Vol II)

Selden (J) Dissertatio ad Jus Angl. Vet Fletam dictum. (Opera, Vol. II.)

Leges Anglo-Saxonicæ Eccl et Civiles. Accedunt Leges Edwardi, Guilielmi Conquest , et Henrici I. Subjungitur H Spelmanni Codex Legum Vet Stat Regni Angliæ ad Hen III Præmit Dissert Guil Nicolsoni de Jure Feudali Vet Saxonum Notas, Vers , et Gloss adjecit David Wilkins Folio *Lond* 1721

Leges Walhcæ Eccles et Civilis Hoel Boni, Wal et Lat , cum Notis Guil. Wottoni Folio *London*, 1730

Coke's (Sir Edward) Four Institutes of the Laws of England , or, a Commentary upon Littleton's Tenures, &c ; with Notes by Charles Butler and Francis Hargrave. 6 vols roy 8vo *London*, 1817

Blackstone's (Sir W) Commentaries on the Laws of England , with Notes by J. T Coleridge 4 vols 8vo *London*, 1825.

Jacob's (Giles) Law Dictionary, improved by T E Tomkins. 2 vols 4to *London*, 1820

Comyn's (Sir John) Digest of the Laws of England , with Additions by Ant Hammond. 8 vols royal 8vo. *London*, 1822

Statute Law.

Magna Charta Regis Johannis, A D M CCXV Et Conventio inter Regem Johannem et Barones Folio *Londini, apud J Whittaker*, 1816–19

> On vellum printed in gold, and one of the copies sumptuously ornamented with emblematical and grotesquely painted margins, containing the arms and banners of the barons emblazoned in their proper colours , with portraits of King John, George IV (to whom, as Prince Regent, the work was dedicated), &c , and a representation of John affixing his signature to the charter , all richly executed in body colours on the vellum, in the highest style of miniature paintings. Miss Currer's genealogical escutcheon on the first leaf Splendidly and appropriately bound in blue morocco by Whittaker, and enclosed in a case

The Boke of Magna Charta, with divers Statutes, translated out of Latyn and French into Englyshe by George Ferrers Black letter, small 8vo *Lond by Rob Redman*, 1534

Johnson's (Samuel) History and Defence of Magna Charta ; with an Introductory Account of the Rise and Progress of National Freedom Also the Liberties which are confirmed by the Bill of Rights, and an Essay on Parliaments 8vo *London*, 1772

The Statutes of the Realm printed, by authority, from original Records and authentic MSS , with Indexes alphabetical and chronological 11 vols folio [*London*], 1810, &c

JURISPRUDENCE.

Customary Law and Laws of Property.

Somner's (W) Treatise of Gavel Kind, with sundry emergent Observations, both pleasant and profitable to be known, of Kentish Men, and of the Ancient Custume or the Common Law of this Kingdom; with Life of the Author by Bp White Kennet 4to Lond 1726

Ritson's (J) Jurisdiction of the Court Leet exemplified. 8vo. Lond 1809.

Nicolson's (Bp Wm) Leges Marchiarum, or, Border Laws, containing several original Articles and Treatises for the better preservation of Peace upon the Marches, from the reign of Henry III to the Union of the Crowns in King James I. 8vo London, 1705

Johnson's (J) View of the Jurisprudence of the Isle of Man, with the History of its Ancient Constitution, Legislative Government, Extraordinary Privileges, &c 8vo *Edinburgh*, 1811

Ralegh (Sir W), of Tenures which were before the Conquest (Works, Vol VIII)

Blount's (Thomas) Fragmenta Antiquitatis, or, Ancient Tenures of Land and Jocular Customs of Manors; with Additions by J Beckwith 4to Lond 1815.

Dalrymple's (Sir John) History of Feudal Property in Great Britain. 12mo Lond 1759

Cruise's (W) Digest of the Laws of England respecting Real Property. 6 vols royal 8vo *London*, 1824.

Sugden (Sir E) on the Law of Vendors and Purchasers of Estates Royal 8vo *London*, 1826

Coote (R. H.) on the Law of Mortgage; with an App of Precedents Royal 8vo. *London*, 1827.

Scriven (J) on Copyholds, Customary Freeholds, Ancient Demesne, &c. 2 vols 8vo Lond 1823

Justiciary, Parochial, and Criminal Law.

Burn's (Richard) Justice of the Peace and Parish-Officer, by Sir G. Chetwynd 5 vols 8vo *London*, 1825

Nolan's (Mich) Treatise of the Laws for the Relief and Settlement of the Poor 3 vols 8vo *London*, 1825.

Jones' (Sir W) Essay on the Law of Bailments (Works, Vol VI)

Tomlins' (H N) Digest of the Criminal Statute Laws of England. 2 vols royal 8vo *London*, 1819

Cary's (H) Law of Jury and Jurors, as amended by 6 Geo IV 12mo *London*, 1826

Smith's (J G) Principles of Forensic Medicine applied to British Practice 8vo Lond. 1824

Ecclesiastical and Miscellaneous Law.

Gibson's (Edmund) Codex Juris Ecclesiastici Anglicani, or, the Statutes, Constitutions, Canons, Rubricks, and Articles of the Church of England with a Commentary historical and juridical, and an Introduction on the present state of the Power, Discipline, and Laws of the Church of England 2 vols folio. *Oxford, Clarendon Press*, 1761

JURISPRUDENCE

Burn's (Richard) Ecclesiastical Law, with Additions by R Philip Tyrwhitt 4 vols 8vo *Lond* 1824

Bearblock (James) on Tythes, with an Estimate of Titheable Articles, and the Modes of compounding for them. 8vo *Lond* 1818

Selden's (John) History of Tythes, and Tracts relative to it. (Works, Vol III)

Selden (J), of the Original of Ecclesiastical Jurisdiction of Testaments (Works, Vol III)

Liber Niger Scacarii, è codice Ri Gravesii nunc primum edidit Tho Hearnius. 2 vols 8vo *Oxonii*, 1728.

Madox's (Tho) History and Antiquities of the Exchequer of the Kings of England, from the Norman Conquest to the end of the reign of Edward II , taken from the Records 2 vols 4to *London*, 1769

Bacon's (Lord) Judicial Tracts and Charges. (Works, Vols VI and VII), Law Tracts (Works, Vol XIII.)

Scottish Law.

Bell's (G J.) Principles of the Law of Scotland. 8vo. *Edinburgh*, 1830.

Bell's (G. J.) Dictionary of the Law of Scotland, to which is annexed, Skene de Verborum Significatione 2 vols 8vo *Edinburgh*, 1826

Dalrymple's (Sir D) Examination of some of the Arguments for the high Antiquity of Regiam Majestatem, and an Inquiry into the Authenticity of Leges Malcolmi (Hailes's Scottish Tracts)

Regiam Majestatem, the Auld Lawes and Constitutions of Scotland, fra the Dayes of Malcolm II untill the Time of James I., translated out Latine into Scotish Language by Sir John Skene. Folio *Edinburgh*, 1609

Foreign Law

Coras (Jean de), Arrest Memorable du Parlement de Toulouse, prononcé Sep 12, 1560; contenant une Histoire prodigieuse d'un supposé Mary [Martin Guerre] advenue de nostre temps enrichie de CXI. belles et doctes Annotations Small 8vo *Paris, Du Pre*, 1572.

Jones (Sir W), the Mahommedan Law of Succession to Property of Intestates,—Al Sira'jiyyah; or, the Mahommedan Law of Inheritance. (Works, Vol III)

Jones' (Sir W) Institutes of Hindu Law, or, the Ordinances of Menu, according to the Gloss of Calluca (Works, Vol III)

Jones' (Sir W) Extracts from the Vedas (Works, Vol VI)

Ta Tsing Leu Lee; being the Fundamental Laws, and a Selection from the Statutes, of the Penal Code of China; translated from the Chinese, with illustrative Appendix, Notes, &c by Sir Geo Staunton 4to *London*, 1810

CLASS III.—PHILOSOPHY.

Introductory Treatises, &c.

Bacon's (Lord) Advancement of Learning (Works, Vol II)
Bacon (Ld) de Augmentis Scientiarum (Works, Vols VIII and IX.)
Bacon (Ld) Novum Organum. (Works, Vols. IX. and XIV)
Borde (Andrew), the Boke of the Introduction of Knowledge. [Reprint edited by W. Upcott, Esq] Black letter, 4to *Lond.* 1814
Bartholomei (Fratris) [de Glanvilla] Anglici Tractatus de Proprietatibus Rerum Folio, black letter *Impressus sub die vero Decembri X anno M CCCC LXXXII*
Encyclopædia Britannica; or, a Dictionary of Arts, Sciences, and Miscellaneous Literature, enlarged and improved Sixth Edition, with Supplement, containing Preliminary Dissertations on the History of the Sciences, and Additions to former Editions Edited by Macvey Napier 28 vols 4to. *Edinburgh*, 1823, 4

Sect. I.—INTELLECTUAL PHILOSOPHY

History of Philosophy and Philosophers.

Enfield's (William) History of Philosophy, from the earliest times to the beginning of the present Century, drawn up from the Historia Critica Philosophiæ of Brucker 2 vols 8vo. *London,* 1819.
Buhle (J C.), Histoire de la Philosophie Moderne depuis la Renaissance des Lettres jusqu'à Kant, précédée d'une Abrégé de la Philosophie depuis Thales jusqu'au XIV Siècle. Trad. de l'Allemand par Jourdan. 7 vols 8vo *Paris,* 1816–17
Diogenis Laertii de Vitis, Dogmatibus, et Apothegmatibus clarorum Philosophorum (Classics)
Gillies' (John) Critical History of the Life of Aristotle, New Analysis of his Speculative Works, and an Account of the Interpreters and Corrupters of his Philosophy, in connexion with the History of the Times in which they respectively flourished (Aristotle's Ethics, and Politics)
Gray (Thos.), some Account of the Dialogues and Epistles of Plato (Works, by Mathias, Vol II)
Spens (H) on the Philosophy of the Ancients (Plato)
Ameer Khoawend Shah's Account of Philosophers, Persian and English. (Gladwin's Persian Moonshee.)

Metaphysics.

Abercrombie's (John) Inquiries concerning the Intellectual Powers and the Investigation of Truth. 8vo *Edinburgh,* 1831

PHILOSOPHY.

Aristotelis Organon et Metaphysica (Opera.)

Baxter's (Andrew) Inquiry into the Nature of the Human Soul, wherein its Immateriality is evinced from the Principles of Reason and Philosophy, with Appendix. 3 vols 8vo *London*, 1745-50

Beattie (James), an Essay on the Nature and Immutability of Truth, in opposition to Sophistry and Scepticism 8vo *London*, 1774

Berkeley's (Bp.) Principles of Human Knowledge. (Works.)

Boyle (Hon. Robt.) on Things above Reason, and whether a Philosopher ought to admit there are any such (Works, Vol IV.)

Boyle's (Hon. R.) Free Inquiry into the received Notion of Nature, and Disquisition about the Final Causes of Natural Things. (Works, Vol V.)

Brown's (Sir Thos.) Pseudodoxia Epidemica, or, Inquiries into very many received Tenets and commonly presumed Truths. (Works.)

Brown's (Prof. Thos.) Lectures on the Philosophy of the Human Mind. 4 vols. 8vo *Edinburgh*, 1824.

[Buck's (Ch.)] Philosophy of Human Nature, or, the Influence of Scenery on the Mind and Heart 2 vols 8vo *Lond* 1813

Buffon, Histoire Naturelle de l'Homme (Hist. Nat.)

Burke's (Edmund) Vindication of Natural Society (Works, Vol. I.)

[Burton (Robert)], the Anatomy of Melancholy Folio, front *Lond* 1652.

Ciceronis Academicarum Quæstiones,—de Finibus Bonorum et Malorum,—Tusculanorum Quæstiones,—Natura Deorum,—de Fato (Opera.)

Confucius Sinarum Philosophus, sive, Scientia Sinensis Latinè exposita (Paganism.)

Cudworth (Rudolphi) Systema Intellectuale. J. L. Mosheimius omnia ex Anglico vertit, recensuit, variisque Observat. et Dissertat. illustravit et auxit Folio *Jenæ*, 1733

Cudworthi (R.) de Æternâ et Immutabili Rei Moralis, Latinè vertit et Notularum aliquid subjecit J. L. Mosheimius. (Syst. Int.)

Darwin's (Erasmus) Temple of Nature; or, the Origin of Society, a Poem, with Philosophical Notes 4to *London*, 1803

Harris's (James) Philosophical Arrangements (Works, Vol. II.)

Hume's (David) Treatise of Human Nature, being an Attempt to introduce the experimental Methods of Reasoning into Moral Subjects 2 vols 8vo *London*, 1817

Hume (D.) on the Human Understanding, the Passions, and Natural History of Religion (Essays, Vol. II.)

Hamilton's (Eliz) Series of Popular Essays, illustrative of Principles connected with the Improvement of the Understanding, the Imagination, and the Heart 2 vols 8vo *Edinb*. 1813

Kaimes's (Henry Home, Lord) Sketches of the History of Man 4 vols 8vo *Edinb* 1788

Locke's (J.) Essay concerning the Human Understanding, with Defences, and on the Conduct of the Understanding. (Works, Vols. I to III.)

Lucretius de Rerum Naturâ (Classics.)

78   PHILOSOPHY.

Maximi Tyrii Dissertationes   (Classics.)
Monboddo's (James Burnett, Lord) Antient Metaphysics, or, the Science of Universals [containing the History and Philosophy of Men], and an Examination of the Principles of Sir Isaac Newton's Philosophy. 6 vols in 3   4to   Edinb 1779–99
Plato de Rebus Divinis, et Phœdo   (Opera)
Ralegh's (Sir W.) Treatise on the Soul, and the Sceptic. (Works, Vol VIII)
Reynolds' (Bp. E) Treatise on the Passions and Faculties of the Soul (Works, Vol VI)
Reid's (Thomas) Essays on the Powers of the Human Mind   3 vols 8vo   Edinburgh, 1808
Seneca de Consolatione, de Providentiâ, de Tranquillitate Animi, de Sapientis Constantiâ, de Otio Sapientis, de Brevitate Vitæ, de Beneficiis, de Vitâ beatâ. (Opera)
Stewart's (Dugald) Elements of the Philosophy of the Human Mind. 3 vols 4to   London, 1792
Stewart's (D) Philosophical Essays.   4to   Edinburgh, 1810
Stillingfleet (Bp. E.) on the Human Understanding. (Works, Vol III)
Tucker's (Abraham) Light of Nature pursued. (Theology)
Xenophontis de Socrate Commentarii, et Socratis Apologia   (Opera)
Young's (Edward) True Estimate of Human Life, in which the Passions are considered in a new Light. (Works, Vol. V)
Zimmermann (M) on Solitude, considered with respect to its Influence on the Mind and Heart, from the French of J. B Mercier   Royal 8vo large paper   London. 1792

Occult Philosophy, Physiognomy, &c.

Agrippa's (Hen Corn) Three Books of Occult Philosophy, translated out of Latin by J F   4to   London, 1651
Antonini (Marci) Imperatoris ad Seipsum Lib XII. (Classics)
Artemidori Oneirocritica   (Classics)
Cardanus Comforte, translated into Englishe [by — Bedingfielde], and published by commaundement of the Earl of Oxenford. Black letter, 4to. London, by Tho. Marshe, 1573.
Censorinus de Die Natali   (Classics)
Cicero de Divinatione , Scipionis Somnium   (Opera)
Glanvil's (Joseph) Sadducismus Triumphans; or, a full and plain Evidence concerning Witches and Apparitions; with Dr H More's Letter to the Author on this subject   8vo   London, 1726
Julius Obsequens de Prodigiis   (Valerius Max , Classics)
Lilly's (Mr William) History of his Life and Times, written by himself to his friend Elias Ashmole , containing an Account of Dr Forman, Dr Napier, Dr. Booker, Dr. Dee, Kelly, and all other Astrologers and Conjurers his contemporaries, &c   Small 8vo   London, 1715
Lilly's (W) Ænigmatical Types of the Future State of England , Grebner his Prophecy, and other English, Latin, Saxon, Welch, and Scotish Prophecies (Monarchy and No Monarchy)

PHILOSOPHY

[Loire's (Peter de)] Treatise of Specters or Straunge Sights, Visions, and Apparitions, appearing sensibly unto Men, wherein is delivered the Nature of Spirits, Angels, and Divels, their Power and Properties, as also of Witches, Sorcerers, Enchanters and such like Newly done out of French [by Zacharie Jones]   4to   *London*, 1605

Richard (l'Abbé) Théorie des Songes   12mo   *Paris*, 1766

Scot's (Reg) Discovery of Witchcraft, proving the Compacts of Witches with Devils, &c. are but erroneous Novelties and imaginary Conceptions; to which is added, a Discourse of the Nature and Substance of Devils and Spirits.   Folio   *London*, 1665.

"The damnable opinions of Scot '—*James the First's Dæmonologie.*

Evelyn (John) on Physiognomy   (On Medals)

Lavater's (John Caspar) Essays on Physiognomy, translated by Thomas Hunter, and illustrated by more than 800 Engravings, executed by or under the direction of Thomas Holloway, [with prefatory Advertisement by H. Fuseli.] 3 vols in 5, imperial 4to   *London*, 1789–98.

Schimmelpenninck's (Mary-Anne) Theory on the Classification of Beauty and Deformity, and their Correspondence with Physiognomic Expression exemplified.   4to.   *London*, 1815

Spurzheim's (J. G) Physiognomical System of Drs. Gall and Spurzheim, founded on the Anatomical and Physiological Examination of the Nervous System, and of the Brain in particular   Royal 8vo   *Lond* 1815

Logic.

Miltoni (Jo) Artis Logicæ plenior Institutio, ad P Rami Methodum concinnata, adjecta est Praxis analytica et P Rami Vita. (Prose Works, Vol. II 4to, and VI 8vo)

Watts's (Isaac) Logick, or, the right Use of Reason in the Inquiry after Truth.   8vo   *London*, 1790

Wilson's (Sir Thos.) Rule of Reason, conteining the Arte of Logique, set forth in English.   Small 8vo   **black letter.**   *London, by Richard Grafton*, 1552

Ethics.

Aristotelis Ethica   (Opera)

Bacon's (Lord) Essays or Counsels, Civil and Moral   (Works, Vol I)

Bacon's (Lord) Wisdom of the Ancients   (Works, Vols III and XI)

Bates's (Ely) Rural Philosophy, or, Reflections on Knowledge, Virtue, and Happiness, in a Life of Retirement   8vo   *London*, 1805

Butler's (Samuel) Characters [of modern Men]   (Remains, Vol II)

Cicero de Officiis, de Amicitiâ, &c   (Opera)

Cornewallys's, the younger, (Sir Wm) Essayes   Both parts in one vol small 8vo   *London*, 1606

Epicteti Enchiridion.   (Classics)

Evelyn's (John) Public Employment, and an Active Life with all its Appendages, such as Fame, Command, Riches, &c. preferred to Solitude   (Misc Works)

PHILOSOPHY.

Flecknoe's (Richard) Characters, made at several times and on several occasions Small 8vo *London, printed* 1673

Gisborne's (Thomas) Enquiry into the Duties of Men in the higher and middle Classes of Society of Great Britain. 2 vols 8vo *London,* 1795

Gisborne's (T) Enquiry into the Duties of the Female Sex. 8vo. *Lond* 1798

Hall's (John) Horæ Vacivæ, or Essays, and some Occasionall Considerations 12mo portrait by Marshall. *London,* 1646

Hume's (David) Essays and Treatises on Moral Subjects 2 vols. 8vo. *Edinburgh,* 1809.

Hurd's (Bp.) Moral and Political Dialogues (Works, Vols. III. & IV)

Mothe le Vayer (F de la) on Liberty and Servitude, translated by John Evelyn (Evelyn's Misc Works)

Paley's (Wm.) Principles of Moral and Political Philosophy 2 vols 8vo *London,* 1809

Platonis Republica (Opera)

Ralegh (Sir W) on the Original and Fundamental Cause of natural, arbitrary, necessary, and unnatural War (Works, Vol VIII)

Sady (the Pundnameh of), a Compendium of Ethics, Persian and English (Gladwin's Persian Moonshee]

Seneca de Irâ, de Clementiâ. (Opera.)

Shaftesbury's (Earl of) Characteristicks of Men, Manners, Opinions, and Times. 3 vols. royal 8vo. large paper. *Birming.* [*Baskerville*], 1773.

Smith's (Adam) Theory of Moral Sentiments. 2 vols. 8vo *Lond* 1790

Stephens' (John) New Essays and Characters, with a New Satyre in defence of the Common Law and Lawyers, mixt with Reproofe against their Enemye Ignoramus Small 8vo. *London,* 1631.

Theophrasti Characteres Ethici (Classics)

Taylor (Bp Jer) on Friendship (Works, Vol XI)

Temple's (Sir W) Essays on Heroic Virtue, Excesses of Grief, and on the different Conditions of Life. (Works, Vol III)

Valerii Maximi Dictorum Memorabilium Libri IX (Classics.)

Witherspoon's (John) Lectures on Moral Philosophy (Works, Vol VII)

Witherspoon's (J) Letters on Marriage. (Works, Vol VIII)

Education

Argyle's (Archibald, Marquess of) Instructions to a Son ; with Maxims of State Small 8vo, port *London,* 1661

Ascham's (Roger) Schoolmaster (Works)

Chapone's (Mrs) Letters on the Improvement of the Mind ; with Life of the Author. 12mo *London,* 1815

Chrysostom's (St. John) Golden Book, concerning the Education of Children, translated out of the Greek by John Evelyn (Evelyn's Miscellaneous Works)

Edgeworth's (R. L) Essays on Professional Education 4to. *London,* 1809

Edgeworth's (Maria and R. L.) Practical Education 2 vols 4to
  London, 1798
James I.—A Prince's Looking-glass, or, a Prince's Directions, containing sundrie Precepts and Instructions, out of that most Christian and vertuous ΒΑΣΙΛΙΚΟΝ ΔΩΡΟΝ, or his Majestie's Instructions to his dearest Sonne Henrie, translated into Latin and English Verse, (his Majestie's consent and approbation being first had and obtained thereunto) for the more delight and pleasure of the said Prince, now in his younger yeares, by William Willymat 4to, port of James by J Meyssens, and of P Henry inserted *Cambridge, printed by John Legat*, 1603
Jones' (W), of Nayland, Letters from a Tutor to his Pupils (Works, Vol. V)
[Kames' (Henry Home, Lord)] Loose Hints upon Education, chiefly concerning the Culture of the Heart 8vo *Edin* 1782
Knox's (Vicesimus) Liberal Education, or, a Practical Treatise on the Methods of acquiring Useful and Polite Learning (Works, Vols III and IV)
Knox's (V) Remarks on Grammar Schools (Works, Vol IV)
Knox's (V) Letters to a Young Nobleman (Works, Vol V)
Locke's (John) Thoughts concerning Reading and Study for a Gentleman (Works, Vol III)
Locke's (J) Thoughts concerning Education (Works, Vol IX)
Milton (John) on Education (Prose Works, 4to and 8vo. Vol 1)
More's (Hannah) Essays on various subjects, designed for Young Ladies 12mo *Lond* 1785
More's (H) Strictures on the Modern System of Female Education 2 vols 8vo. *Lond* 1799
More's (H) Hints towards forming the Character of a Young Princess. 2 vols 8vo *Lond* 1805
Quarterly Journal of Education 8vo *Lond* 1831, &c
Ralegh's (Sir W) Instructions to his Son and to Posterity (Works, Vol VIII)
Witherspoon's (John) Letters on Education (Works Vol VIII)

Political Philosophy.

Politics   See also Jurisprudence, Sect 1

Aristotelis Politica et de Republicâ (Opera)
Bentham's (Jeremy) Fragment on Government 8vo *Lond* 1823
Burke's (Edmund) Political Letters (Works, Vols II, III, VI, and VIII)
Cunninghame's (W) Principles of the Constitution of Governments, with Illustrations from the Classics 8vo *Lond* 1813
De Brosses, Discours Politiques sur le Gouvernement des Romains (Salluste)
Douglas (James) on the Advancement of Society in Knowledge and Religion 8vo *Edinburgh*, 1825

PHILOSOPHY.

Falconer (W) on the Influence of Climate, Situation, Nature of Food, and Way of Life, on the Dispositions and Temper, Manners and Behaviour, Intellect, Laws and Customs, Forms of Government, and Religion, of Mankind 4to *Lond* 1781

Franklin's (B.) Political and Commercial Pieces. (Works, Vol VI)

Hall's (Robt) Political Tracts (Works, Vol III)

Harrington's (James) System of Politics delineated (Works)

Harrington's (J) Prerogative of Popular Governments (Works)

Harrington's (J) True Forme, and Seven Models, of a Popular Commonwealth,—the Rota, or, a Model of a Free State or Equal Commonwealth (Works)

Harrington's (J) Commonwealth of Oceana, and Letters on it with Dr. Ferne (Works)

Hume (David) on National Characters. (Essays, Vol I)

Jones' (Sir W.) Principles of Government. (Works, Vol IV)

Knox's (V) Spirit of Despotism (Works, Vol V)

Leckie's (Gould Fr) Historical Research into the Nature of the Balance of Power in Europe; with an attempt to establish clear and distinct Ideas on the subject. 8vo *London*, 1817.

Locke (John) on Civil Government (Works)

Millar's (John) Origin of the Distinction of Ranks; or, an Inquiry into the Circumstances which gave rise to Influence and Authority in the different Members of Society, with Life of the Author by John Craig 8vo *Edin*. 1806

More (Thom) de Optimo Reipublicæ Statu, deque Novâ Insulâ Utopiâ; ex prioribus edit collatis accuratè expressus Small 8vo *Glasguæ, excud R and A Foulis*, 1750

More (Sir T), a most pleasant, fruitful, and witty Work, of the best State of a Public Weal, and of the new Isle of Utopia, written in Latin by Sir T More, and translated into English by Raphe Robinson, a new edition, with Notes and Introduction by T. F Dibdin Large paper, 4to *London*, 1808

More's (Sir T) Utopia, translated by Cayley (Life of More)

Milton's (John) present Means and brief Delineation of a Free Commonwealth, the ready and easy Way to establish a Free Commonwealth (Prose Works, 4to Vol I , 8vo Vol III)

Ralegh's (Sir W) Maxims of State (Works)

Ralegh's (Sir W.) Cabinet Council, containing the chief Arts of Empire and Mysteries of State, discabineted in political and polemical Aphorisms, grounded on authority and experience, and illustrated with the choicest examples and historical observations Published by John Milton (Works)

Southey's (Robert) Sir Thomas More, or, Colloquies on the Progress and Prospects of Society 2 vols 8vo. *London*, 1831

Reynard the Fox, a political Satire to represent a wise Government (Romances)

Temple (Sir W) on the Original and Nature of Governments (Works, Vol I)

Temple (Sir W.) on Popular Discontents (Works, Vol III)

Witherspoon's (John) History of a Corporation of Servants discovered in the Interior of South America. [A political Romance] (Works, Vol. VI.)

Finetti Philoxenis, some choice Observations of Sir John Finett, Knt, and Master of the Ceremonies to James I and Charles I, touching the Reception and Precedence, the Treatment and Audience, the Puntillios and Contests of forren Ambassadors in England; [with Preface by James Howell] Small 8vo *London*, 1656

<small>This also forms a narrative of the Embassies to England, from the marriage of the Queen of Bohemia to 1627.</small>

Sydney's (Algernon) Discourses concerning Government, with his Letters, Trial, Apology, and some Memoirs of his Life [by T Hollis] 4to. *London*, 1763

Political Economy

Campbell's (John) Political Survey of Britain, intended to shew that we have not as yet approached near the summit of improvement, but that it will afford employment to many generations before they push to the uttermost extent the Natural Advantages of Great Britain 2 vols 4to *London*, 1774

Chalmer's (Thomas) Political Economy, in connexion with the Moral State and Prospects of Society 8vo *Glasgow*, 1832.

Colquhoun's (P.) Treatise on the Wealth, Power, and Resources of the British Empire in every Quarter of the World; with the Rise and Progress of the Funding System explained 4to *London*, 1814

Ganilh, des Systèmes d'Economie Politique, de la Valeur comparative de leurs Doctrines, et de celle qui parait la plus favorable au Progrès de la Richesse, avec des Additions relatives aux Controverses récentes de Malthus, Buchanan, et Ricardo. 2 vols 8vo *Paris*, 1823

Ganilh, Théorie de l'Economie Politique 2 vols. 8vo *Paris*, 1822

Hamilton's (Robert) Progress of Society, as regards Human Welfare, Industry, Capital, Money, Rent, Tithes, Distribution, and Equalisation of Wealth, Property, Education, Commerce, Population, &c 8vo *London*, 1828

Hume (David) on Commerce, Money, Interest, Trade, Taxes, and Public Credit (Essays, Vol 1)

[Marcet's (Mrs)] Conversations on Political Economy, in which the Elements of that Science are familiarly explained. 12mo *London*, 1827

Ricardo (David) on the Principles of Political Economy and Taxation 8vo *London*, 1821.

Say (J Baptiste), Cours complet d'Economie Politique pratique 6 vols 8vo. *Paris*, 1828–30

Say's (J B) Political Economy, or, the Production, Distribution, and Consumption of Wealth, translated from the 4th edition, with Notes, by C. R Prinsep. 2 vols 8vo *London*, 1821

PHILOSOPHY

Smith's (Adam) Inquiry into the Nature and Causes of the Wealth of Nations, with an introductory Discourse, Notes, supplemental Dissertations, and Life of the Author, by J R M'Culloch 4 vols 8vo *Edinburgh*, 1828

Skarbek, Théorie des Richesses Sociales, suivie d'une Bibliographie d'Economie Politique 2 vols 8vo *Paris*, 1829

Population Mendicity, &c.

Chalmer's (Thos) Christian and Civic Economy of large Towns 3 vols 8vo *Glasgow*, 1821-26

Colquhoun's (P) Treatise of Indigence, exhibiting a general view of the National Resources for Productive Labour, with Propositions for ameliorating the Condition of the Poor 8vo *London*, 1806

Colquhoun (P) on the Police of the Metropolis, containing a Detail of the various Crimes, &c by which Public and Private Property is injured and endangered 8vo *London*, 1806

Eden's (Sir F M) State of the Poor, or, an History of the Labouring Classes in England, together with Parochial Reports relative to the administration of Work-houses, &c 3 vols 4to. *London*, 1797

Godwin (W) on Population, an Enquiry concerning the Power of Increase in the numbers of Mankind, in answer to Malthus 8vo *London*, 1820

Graunt's (John) Natural and Political Observations made upon the Bills of Mortality, with reference to the Government, Growth, Air, Diseases, &c. of the City of London (Eng. Topography—London)

Howard's (John) State of Prisons in England and Wales, with an Account of some foreign Prisons and Hospitals 4to *London*, 1792

Howard's (J) Account of the Principal Lazarettos in Europe, with various Papers relative to the Plague 4to *London*, 1791

Hume (David) on the Populousness of Ancient Nations (Essays, Vol I)

Malthus (T R) on the Principles of Population, or, a View of its past and present effects on Human Happiness 2 vols 8vo *London*, 1826

Marshall (J), a variety of Statistical Accounts illustrative of the Progress and Extent of the Amount expended for the Maintenance of the Poor in each county of England and Wales, and in each parish of the Metropolis, from 1775 to 1830 (Marshall's Mortality of the Metropolis *See* Eng Topography—London)

Rickmann (John), the Population Returns of 1831, as printed for the House of Commons Royal 8vo *London*, 1832

Sadler (M T), the Law of Population, a Treatise in disproof of the Superfecundity of Human Beings, and developing the real Principle of their Increase 2 vols 8vo *London*, 1830

Wallace's (Robt) Dissertation on the Numbers of Mankind in ancient and modern times 8vo *Edinburgh*, 1809

Weyland's (John) Inquiry into the Policy, Humanity, and past Effects of the Poor Laws 8vo. *London*, 1807

Weyland's (J) Principles of Population and Production 8vo *Lond.* 1816

Finance and Money

[Arbuthnot's (John)] Tables of Ancient Coins, Weights, and Measures, explained and exemplified in several Dissertations 4to *London*, 1727

Fleetwood's (Bishop) Chronicon Preciosum, or, an Account of English Money, Price of Corn and other Commodities, and of Salaries, Stipends, Wages, &c for the last six hundred years 8vo *Lond* 1745.

Gaudin (M C), Notices Historiques sur les Finances, la Banque, &c de la France, de l'an 1800 au 1814 (Mémoires du Duc de Gaete)

Jacob's (Wm) Historical Inquiry into the Production and Consumption of the Precious Metals, from the earliest Ages, and into the Influence of their Increase or Diminution on the Prices of Commodities 2 vols 8vo *London*, 1831

Locke (John) on the Consequence of lowering the Interest and raising the Value of Money, and on the Silver Coin (Works, Vol V)

Sinclair's (Sir John) History of the Public Revenue of the British Empire. 3 vols. 8vo *London*, 1802–3

Witherspoon's (John) Essay on Money as the Medium of Commerce. (Works, Vol IX)

Commerce and Colonial Policy.

[Anderson's (Adam)] Historical and Chronological Deduction of the Origin of Commerce, from the earliest accounts, [edited by Macpherson] 4 vols 4to. *London*, 1787–9

[Dee's (John)] General and Rare Memorials pertayning to the perfect Arte of Navigation. Folio *London, by John Day*, 1577
_{This work relates to naval policy, and furnishes many suggestions which may even now be valuable This copy contains a leaf completely occupied with the arms of Sir C Hatton, not mentioned by Herbert}

East India Company (History of India)

Evelyn's (John) Navigation and Commerce, their Original and Progress, containing a Succinct of Traffick in general, its Benefits and Improvements (Miscellaneous Works)

Jacob's (W) Tracts relating to the Corn Trade and the Corn Laws, including the Second Report ordered to be printed by Parliament 8vo *London*, 1828

Macpherson's (David) History of the European Commerce with India, to which is subjoined a Review of the Arguments for and against the Trade with India, and the management of it by a Chartered Company 4to *London*, 1812

M'Culloch's (J R) Dictionary, practical, theoretical, and historical, of Commerce and Commercial Navigation 8vo *Lond* 1832

Malynes (Gerard de), Treatise on the Canker [the abuse of the exchange of money] of England's Commonwealth Small 8vo *Lond* 1601

Milburn's (William) Oriental Commerce, containing a Geographical, Nautical, and Commercial Account of the maritime parts of India, China, Japan, and neighbouring Countries, by T Thornton Royal 8vo *London*, 1825

86 PHILOSOPHY.

Ralegh's (Sir W.) Observations touching the Trade and Commerce with the Hollander and other Nations, wherein is proved, that our Sea and Land Commodities serve to enrich and strengthen other Countries against our own (Works, Vol VIII)

Brougham's (Henry Lord) Inquiry into the Colonial Policy of the European Powers. 2 vols 8vo *London*, 1803

Sect II.—NATURAL PHILOSOPHY.

Physics, or Natural and Experimental Philosophy.

Boyle (Hon Robert) on the Usefulness of Natural and Experimental Philosophy (Works, Vols II and III)

Boyle's (Hon. R) Christian Virtuoso, shewing that by being addicted to Experimental Philosophy, a man is rather assisted than indisposed to be a Christian (Works, Vols V and VI)

Cowley's (Abr) Proposition for the Advancement of Experimental Philosophy (Works, Vol III.)

Journal of Science of Art, edited at the Royal Institution of Great Britain [by W. T. Brande] 8vo *London*, 1816, &c

Newtoni(Is) Philosophiæ Naturalis Principia. (Opera, Vols. II and III)

Locke's (John) Elements of Natural Philosophy (Works, Vol III)

Leslie's (Sir John) Elements of Natural Philosophy Vol I. 8vo. *Edinb* 1823

Bacon (Roger) Opus Majus, ex MS. Codice Dublinensi cum aliis quibusdam collato, nunc primùm edidit S Jebb Folio, large paper *Lond* 1733.

Meteorology, &c

Aristotelis Meteorologica (Opera, Vol I)

Bacon's (Lord) Historia Ventorum, et Historia Densi et Rari. (Works, Vol X)

Boyle's (Hon. Rob) Experimental History of Cold; and on the Temperature of the Subterraneal and Submarine Regions (Works, Vols II and III)

Boyle's (Hon R) General History of Air (Works, Vol V)

Boyle (Hon R) on the Spring and Weight of Air (Works, Vols II, III., and IV)

Forster's (Thomas) Researches about Atmospheric Phenomena. 8vo. *London*, 1823

Hamilton's (Bp. Hugh) Philosophical Essays on Vapours, Clouds, Rain, Dew, &c , on the Nature of the Aurora Borealis, and the Tails of Comets; on the Improvement of Barometers (Works, Vol II)

Priestley's (Josh) Experiments and Observations on different kinds of Air, and other branches of Natural Philosophy connected with the subject 3 vols 8vo *Birmingham*, 1790.

Thomson's (Thomas) Outlines of the Sciences of Heat and Electricity 8vo *London*, 1830

Cavallo's (Tiberius) Complete Treatise on Electricity, in theory and practice with Original Experiments 3 vols 8vo *London*, 1795

Franklin's (Ben) Experiments on Electricity, and Papers on Philosophical Subjects (Works)

Cavallo's (T) Treatise on Magnetism 8vo *London*, 1800

Wilkinson's (C H) Elements of Galvanism, with a view to its history. 2 vols 8vo *London*, 1804

Chemical Philosophy.

Aikin's (A and R C) Dictionary of Chemistry and Mineralogy, with an Account of the Processes used in Chemical Manufactures 2 vols. 4to. *London*, 1807.

Bancroft's (Edw) Experimental Researches concerning the Philosophy of Permanent Colours, and the best means of procuring them, by dyeing, calico printing, &c 2 vols 8vo *London*, 1813

Boyle's (Hon R) Various Chemical Treatises (Works)

Brande's (W T) Manual of Chemistry ; containing the principal Facts of the Science, in the order in which they are discussed and illustrated at the Royal Institution 3 vols. 8vo *London*, 1821

Davy's (Sir H) Elements of Chemical Philosophy 8vo. *Lond* 1812.

Davy's (Sir H) Elements of Agricultural Chemistry 8vo *London*, 1827

Parkes' (Sam) Chemical Catechism. with Notes, Illustrations, and Experiments 8vo *London*, 1808.

[Marcet's (Mrs)] Conversations on Chemistry, in which the Elements of that Science are familiarly explained. 2 vols 12mo *Lond* 1828

Thomson's (Thomas) System of Chemistry Part I , Inorganic 2 vols 8vo *London*, 1831

Natural History

Dictionaries, Systems, General Treatises, and of various Countries.

Gronovii (L. A) Bibliotheca Regni Animalis atque Lapidei , seu, Recensio Auctorum et Librorum qui de Regno Animali et Lapideo methodicè tractant, in usum Nat Hist Studiorum 4to *Lvgd Bat sumptibus Auctoris*, 1740

" Ex dono F Gronovii, Laurentii patris "

Dictionnaire des Sciences Naturelles, dans lequel on traite méthodiquement des différens Etres de la Nature, considerés soit en eux-mêmes, soit relativement à l'utilité qu'en peuvent retirer la Médecine, l'Agriculture, le Commerce, et les Arts suivi d'une Biographie des plus célèbres Naturalistes Par plusieurs Professeurs du Jardin du Roi, &c. 60 vols 8vo *Paris*. 1830

Linné's (Sir Charles) General System of Nature ; or, the three grand kingdoms of Animals, Vegetables, and Minerals, systematically divided into their several Classes. Orders, Genera, &c , translated from Gmelin, Fabricius Wildenow, &c by W Turton, and including various modern arrangements and improvements. 7 vols 8vo *London*, 1806

Bingley's (Wm) Useful Knowledge, or, an Account of the various Productions of Nature, Mineral, Vegetable, and Animal   3 vols 12mo   *London*, 1816

Good's (J M.) Book of Nature, being a Popular Illustration of the General Laws and Phenomena of Creation   3 vols. 8vo.   *London*, 1826

Aldrovandi (U) Opera, scil —
  Ornithologia   3 vols   *Bononiæ*, 1599–1603
  De Insectis   *Bononiæ*, 1634
  De Reliquiis Animalibus ex Anguibus   *Bononiæ*, 1606
  De Piscibus et de Cetis, curâ J C Uterhi et M A Bernire   *Bononiæ*, 1638
  De Quadrupedibus solidipedibus   *Bononiæ*, 1616
  Quadrupedum bisulcorum Historia   *Bononiæ*, 1621.
  De Quadrupedibus digitatis, viviparis, et oviparis   *Bononiæ*, 1637
  Serpentum et Draconum Historia.   *Bononiæ*, 1640
  Monstrorum Historia, cum Paralipomenis Hist omnium Animalium   *Bononiæ*, 1642
  Museum Metallicum   *Bononiæ*, 1648
  Dendrologiæ Naturalis Lib II   *Bononiæ*, 1668
  Together, 13 vols folio

  Aldrovand, besides the natural history of his various subjects, has collected all that the ancients ascribed to them — their parts in religious services, then hieroglyphic, symbolic, or figurative meanings, their use in armorial bearings, &c. &c.

Bacon's (Lord) Sylva Sylvarum, or, a Natural History, in X Centuries. (Works, Vol IV)

Buffon (G. L Leclerc, Comte de), Histoire Naturelle, générale et particulière, nouvelle édition, accompagnée de Notes, &c , ouvrage formant un Cours complet d'Histoire Naturelle, rédigé par C S Sonini   27 vols 8vo   *à Paris*, 1798–1807
  Buffon (G L), Théorie de la Terre, et Epoques de la Nature (Vols I. to IV)
  Buffon (G L), Minéraux   (Vols V to XVI)
  Buffon (G. L.), Histoire des Animaux. (Vols. XVII. and XVIII)
  Buffon (G L), Histoire de l'Homme   (Vols XIX to XXI)
  Buffon (G L), Hist des Quadrupèdes   (Vols XXII to XXXIV)
  Buffon (G L), Hist des Singes   (Vols XXXV and XXXVI)
  Buffon (G L), Hist des Oiseaux   (Vols XXXVII to LXIV)
  Daudin, Hist des Reptiles   8 vols
  Denys-Montfort, Hist des Mollusques   6 vols
  Latreille, Hist des Crustacées et Insectes   14 vols
  Sonini, Hist des Poissons   13 vols.
  Sonini, Hist des Cétacées   1 vol
  Brisseau-Mirbel, &c , Hist des Plantes   18 vols
  Tables Générales   3 vols

Buffon —Cuvier (M F), Supplément à l'Histoire Naturelle de Buffon, offrant la Description des Mammifères et des Oiseaux les plus remarquables découvertes jusqu'à nos jours   3 vols 8vo   *Paris*, 1831.

Deleuze Histoire et Description du Muséum Royale d'Histoire Naturelle. 2 vols 8vo.   *Paris*, 1823.

Fond (Sigaud de la), Dictionnaire des Merveilles de la Nature   3 vols 8vo   *Paris*, 1802

PHILOSOPHY.

Lucretius de Rerum Naturâ   (Classics)

Plinii Historia Naturalis   (Classics.)

Sebæ (Alberti) Rerum Naturalium Thesauri accurata Descriptio, et Iconibus artificiosissimis expressis, Lat et Gal   Vols I and II. Large folio   *Amstelodami, apud Wetstenium*, 1734–5

Smith's (Sir Jas Ed) Selection of the Correspondence of Linnæus, and other Naturalists, from the original Manuscripts   2 vols 8vo. *London*, 1821

Spectacle de la Nature; ou, Entretiens sur les Particularites de l'Histoire Naturelle   3 vols in 6, 12mo   *Utrecht*, 1733.

Wood's (W) Zoography, or, the Beauties of Nature Displayed, in select Descriptions from the Animal, Vegetable, and Mineral Kingdoms, illustrated with Plates from designs by Daniel. 3 vols imperial 8vo large paper   *London*, 1807

Barrington's (Hon Daines) Essays on Natural History   (Miscellanies)

Edwards's (G) Representations of many curious and undescribed Animals, such as Quadrupeds, Serpents, Fishes, and Insects, with Descriptions and Gleanings of Natural History   (Birds)

The Journal of a Naturalist   8vo   *London*, 1830

Loudon's (J C) Magazine of Natural History.   8vo.   *London*, 1828, &c.

Plott's (Robert) Natural History of Oxfordshire, being an Essay towards the Natural History of England   (Oxfordshire)

Pulteney's (Richard) Catalogue of the Birds, Shells, and some of the more rare Plants of Dorsetshire, with a Biographical Memoir of the Author. Folio.   *London*, 1813. (Hutchins's Dorset, Vol. III)

White's (Gilb) Works in Natural History, comprising Natural History of Selborne, Naturalist's Calendar, and Miscellaneous Observations; with Observations, &c by W Markwich   2 vols 8vo   *London*, 1802

Sibbaldi (R) Prodromus Historiæ Naturalis Scotiæ   (Hist Scotland.)

Forbes (James) on the Natural History of India   (Oriental Memoirs)

Kalm's (Peter) Natural History, Plantations, and Agriculture of North America   (Travels)

Hernandez (Fr) Nova Plantarum, Animalium, et Mineralium Mexicanorum Historia, à J Terentio, J Fabro, et F. Columna Lyceis, Notis et Additionibus illustrata   Cui access. Theatris Naturalis Phytosophicæ Tabulæ, et Historiæ Animalium et Mineralium Novæ Hispanicæ Lib I   Folio   *Romæ*, 1651

Bancroft (Ed) on the Natural History of Guiana in South America. 8vo   *London*, 1769

Stedman's Natural History of Surinam   (Voyages and Travels)

Catesby's (Mark) Natural History of Carolina, Florida, and the Bahama Islands   2 vols folio, first edition   *London*, 1731

Hughes' (Griffith) Natural History of Barbadoes   Folio   *Lond*. 1750.

Sloane's (Sir Hans) Natural History of Jamaica   (Voyages and Travels.)

Smith's (Wm) Natural History of Nevis, and the rest of the English Leeward Charibee Islands   8vo   *Cambridge*, 1745.

PHILOSOPHY.

Geology

Beche's (Henry T de la) Geological Manual   8vo   *London*, 1832

Lyell's (Charles) Principles of Geology; being an Attempt to explain the former changes on the Earth's Surface, by reference to Causes now in operation.   2 vols 8vo   *London*, 1830–32

Conybeare's (W D) and Wm Phillips's Outlines of the Geology of England and Wales, with an Introductory Compendium of the General Principles of that Science, and Comparative Views of the Structure of Foreign Countries   8vo   *London*, 1822

Burnet's (Thomas) Sacred Theory of the Earth   2 vols 8vo   *London*, 1759

Keill's (J) Examination of Dr Burnet's, with some Remarks on Mr Whiston's, Theory of the Earth   8vo   *London*, 1734

Hutton's (James) Theory of the Earth, with Proofs and Illustrations.   2 vols 8vo   *Edinburgh*, 1795

Playfair's (Professor John) Illustrations of the Huttonian Theory of the Earth.   8vo   *London*, 1802

Cuvier's (G S) Essay on the Theory of the Earth, translated by R Kerr; with Mineralogical Notes, and an Account of Cuvier's Geological Discoveries by Professor Jameson   8vo   *London*, 1822

Turner's (Sharon) Sacred Theory of the World, as displayed in the Creation and subsequent Events to the Deluge, attempted to be philosophically considered   8vo   *London*, 1832

Barrington (Hon Daines) on the Deluge.   (Miscellanies)

Buckland's (Wm) Reliquiæ Diluvianæ, or, Observations on the Organic Remains contained in Caves, Fissures, and Diluvial Gravel, and on other Geological Phenomena attesting the Action of an universal Deluge   4to   *London*, 1823

Townsend's (Joseph) Character of Moses as an Historian established from Geology   (Sacred Philology)

Kircher (Anth) Mundus Subterraneus, quo Divinum Subterrestris Mundi Opificium, immersæ denique Naturæ Majestas et Divitiæ, summâ Rerum Varietate exponuntur. 2 vols in one, folio   *Amstel.* 1665

De Luc's (J) Geological Travels in the North of Europe and in England, translated from the French MS   3 vols 8vo   *London*, 1811.

Pennant's Physical Geography of the Arctic Circle   (Arctic Zoology. Vol I)

Wilson's (Joseph) History of Mountains, Geographical and Mineralogical accompanied by a picturesque View of the principal in their respective proportions, by Robert Andrew Riddle   3 vols 4to   *London*, 1807

Smith's Chart of the Comparative Heights of Mountains   (Coll of Prints, Vol XVIII)

Humboldt (Alex de), Physique Générale, et Géologie Equinoxiale.   (Voyage de l'Amérique.)

Ordinaire's (Abbé) Natural History of Volcanoes, including submarine Volcanoes, and other analogous Phenomena, translated by R. C. Dallas   8vo   *London*, 1801

Hamilton's (Sir W.) Campi Phlegræi · Observations on the Volcanoes of the Two Sicilies, with a Supplement, being an Account of the great Eruption of Mount Vesuvius in August 1779   English and French, edited by P Febris   3 vols in one, folio, largest paper, the Plates coloured after nature.   *Naples*, 1776–9

Boyle's (Robt) Memoirs of the Natural and Experimental History of Mineral Waters   (Works, Vol IV)

Mineralogy.

Accum's (Fr) Manual of Analytical Mineralogy   2 vols 12mo   *Lond* 1808

Bacon's (Lord) Articles of Questions touching Minerals   (Works, Vol VI)

Boyle (R) on the Growth of Minerals   (Works, Vol IV.)

Brogniart (Alex), Traité Elémentaire de Minéralogie, avec des Applications aux Arts   2 vols 8vo   *Paris*, 1807

Hauy (Réné-Just), Traité de Mineralogie, publié par le Conseil des Mines.   4 vols 8vo, and Atlas in 4to.   *Paris*, 1801

Jameson's (Robert) System of Mineralogy   3 vols 8vo   *Edin.* 1820

Werner's (Abr Gott) Theory of the Formation of Veins, with its application to the art of working Mines, translated, with illustrative Notes, by Ch Anderson   8vo.   *Edinburgh*, 1809.

Williams's (John) Natural History of the Mineral Kingdom, relative to the Strata of Coal, Mineral Veins, and the prevailing Strata of the Globe, enlarged by James Millar.   2 vols. 8vo   *Edinb* 1810

Ray's (J) Account of preparing some of our English Metal Minerals. (Proverbs)

Cuvier (M le Baron), Recherches sur les Ossemens Fossiles de Quadrupèdes   4 vols 4to   *Paris*, 1812

Parkinson's (James) Organic Remains of a former World · an Examination of the Mineralized Remains of the Vegetables and Animals of the Antediluvian World   3 vols 4to   *London*, 1804–1811

Brander (G) Fossilia Hantonensia collecta, et in Museo Britannico deposita   [cum Descriptionibus Specierum Solanderi]   4to, plates by Green   *London*, 1766

<small>This work was privately printed, at the expense of Mr Brander the fossils which it describes were found between Christchurch and Lymington, and are of species unknown in England.</small>

Mawe's (John) Mineralogy of Derbyshire, with a Description of the most interesting Mines in the North of England, in Scotland, and in Wales, and an Analysis of Williams's Mineral Kingdom   Subjoined is a Glossary of the Terms and Phrases used by the Miners in Derbyshire.   8vo   *London*, 1802

Martin's (Will) Petrificata Derbiensia, or, Figures and Descriptions of Petrifactions collected in Derbyshire   4to   *Wigan*, 1803.

Robinson's (Thos) Essay towards a Natural [Mineral] History of Westmoreland and Cumberland   8vo   *London*, 1709

Thomson's (Thomas) Mineralogy of Sweden   (Travels in Sweden)

Pinkerton's (J) Petralogy   a Treatise on Rocks   2 vols 8vo.   *Lond.* 1811.

Theophrastus' History of Stones   (Classics)

Boyle (R) on the Origin and Virtues of Gems   (Works, Vol IV)

Boot (A B de), le Perfaict Joaillier, ou, Histoire des Pierreries, enrichi des belles Annotations par André Toll   Small 8vo   *Lyon*, 1644

Mawe's (John) Treatise on Diamonds and Precious Stones   8vo   *London*, 1826.

Botany

Rousseau's (J. J.) Letters on the Elements of Botany, translated, with Notes and full Explanation of the System of Linnæus, and illustrative Plates, by Thomas Martyn. 2 vols. 8vo   *London*, 1791–9

Withering's (W) Elements of Botany.   (Arrangement of B Plants)

Milne's (Colin) Botanical Dictionary; or, Elements of Systematic and Philosophic Botany   8vo coloured Plates   *London*, 1805.

Miller's (Philip) Gardener s and Botanist's Dictionary; with a complete Enumeration and Description of all Plants hitherto known, &c, by Thomas Martyn   2 vols in four, folio   *London*, 1807

Loudon's (J. C) Encyclopædia of Plants, comprising the Description, Specific Character, Culture, History, application to the Arts, and every other desirable particular respecting all the Plants, indigenous, cultivated in, or introduced to, Britain   8vo   *London*, 1829

Rau (Joan) Historia Plantarum   3 vols in two, folio   *London*, 1686–1704.

Gerarde (John), the Herball; or, Generall Historie of Plants, enlarged by Th. Johnson. Folio, front by Payne.   *London*, 1636

Brisseau-Mirbel, Elémens de Physiologie Végétale et Botanique. 2 vols. 8vo   *Paris*, 1815

Stillingfleet (Benj) on the Irritability of Flowers; and Swedish Calendar of Flora   (Works, Vols II and III)

Curtis' (W) Botanical Magazine; or, Flower-Garden displayed. 55 vols royal 8vo.   *London*, 1786–1828

LXXIII exquisitely finished Drawings of Flowers and Insects, executed, in colours on a black ground, by Ditche, for the late Marquess of Bute, and from that nobleman's library   Large folio

LXIII exquisitely finished Drawings, principally Wild Flowers, executed, in colours on a white ground, by A Schouman; also for the Marquess of Bute, and from his library   Large folio

Smith's (James Ed) Exotic Botany, consisting of Coloured Figures and Descriptions of such Plants as are worthy of Cultivation in Great Britain   the Figures by James Sowerby. Large paper, 2 vols in one, 4to   *Lond* 1804–5

Hooker's (W. J.) Exotic Flora, containing Figures and Descriptions of New, Rare, or otherwise Interesting Exotic Plants, especially of such as are deserving of being cultivated in our Gardens, with Remarks on their Characters, History, Culture, &c   3 vols 8vo.   *Edin* 1823.

Greenhouse Companion; comprising Greenhouse and Conservatory Practice and Arrangement, and a Descriptive Catalogue of the most desirable Plants to form a collection.   8vo.   *London*, 1824.

PHILOSOPHY.

Turner's (Dawson) Fuci; or, Coloured Figures and Descriptions of the Plants referred by Botanists to the Genus Fucus 2 vols large 4to. *London*, 1808–1809

Chandler's (A) Illustrations of the Plants which compose the Natural Order Camelliæ, and of the variety of the Camellia Japonica, cultivated in the gardens of Britain; with Descriptions by W B Booth Imperial 4to coloured Plates *London*, 1831

Redouté (P J.), les Roses, avec le Texte par C A Thory Folio, coloured Plates *Paris*, 1817.

Sweet's (Robert) Cistineæ, an Account of the Family of Cistus or Rock-Rose, with coloured Figures, and Directions for their Cultivation and Propagation. Royal 8vo *London*, 1825–30

Ehret's (G D) History and Analysis of the parts of Jessamine which flowered in the curious garden of R Warner, at Woodfort Folio, coloured Plates. [*London*, 1759]

Buchoz (P J), Collection des plus belles Variétés de Tulipes qu'on cultive dans les Jardins des Fleuristes Folio, coloured Plates *Paris*, 1781–97.

Buchoz (P J), Collection de Jacinthes Folio, coloured Plates *Paris*, 1781.

Redouté (P J), les Liliacees 8 vols folio, coloured Plates *Paris*, 1803–16

Sweet's (Robert) Geraniaceæ; the Natural Order of Geraniæ, containing coloured Figures, Descriptions, and Directions for their treatment 5 vols royal 8vo. *London*, 1820–32

Hooker (W J) and R K Greville's Icones Filicum, or, Figures and Descriptions of Ferns, principally of such as have been altogether unnoticed by Botanists, or as have not yet been correctly figured Folio. *London*, 1827–32

Hooker (W) and T Taylor's Muscologia Britannica, containing the Mosses of Great Britain and Ireland, systematically arranged and described 8vo coloured Plates *Lond* 1818

Hooker's (W.) Musci Exotici, containing Figures and Descriptions of new and little-known foreign Mosses and other Cryptogamic Plants 4to coloured Plates *London*, 1818–20

Sowerby's (James) Coloured Figures of English Fungi or Mushrooms, with Descriptions 3 vols folio *London*, 1797–1803.

Greville's (R K) Scottish Cryptogamic Flora, or, coloured Figures of Plants belonging chiefly to the Order Fungi, with Descriptions. 6 vols 8vo. *Edin* 1823–31

Greville's (R K) Algæ Britannicæ, or, Descriptions of the Marine and other Inarticulated Plants of the British Islands belonging to the Order Algæ 8vo *Edinburgh*, 1830

Woodville's (W) Medical Botany, enlarged and improved by John Frost. 5 vols 4to, plates, coloured *London*, 1829.

Withering's (W.) Arrangement of British Plants, according to the latest improvements of the Linnæan System 4 vols 8vo *London*, 1830

Turner's (Dawson) and L W Dillwyn's Botanist's Guide through England and Wales 2 vols 8vo *London*, 1805

Darwin's (Erasmus) Botanic Garden, a Poem, with Philosophical Notes
4to *London*, 1791

Mason's (W) English Garden, a Poem, with Commentary and Notes by W. Burgh (Works, Vol I)

Sowerby's (James) English Botany; or, Coloured Figures of British Plants, with their Essential Characters, Synonymes, and Places of Growth to which are added, occasional Remarks by Sir J. E Smith 36 vols 8vo *London*, 1790–1831

Smith's (Sir James E) English Flora 2 vols 8vo *London*, 1824

Curtis's (Wm) Flora Londinensis, or, a History of Plants indigenous to Great Britain [First series], enlarged by George Graves Plates coloured 3 vols folio *London*, 1817–26.

Curtis's (W) Flora Londinensis; a Continuation by George Graves and W J Hooker Folio *London*

Aiton's (W) Hortus Kewensis, or, Catalogue of Plants cultivated in the Royal Botanic Garden at Kew 5 vols 8vo *London*, 1810

Relham (Rich) Flora Cantabrigiensis secundum Systema Sexuale digesta 8vo *Cantab* 1802

[Richardsoni] (Hen) Index Horti Bierleiensis, Plantas tàm Britannicas notabiliores quàm Exoticas complectens. juxta Raii Methodum dispositas A C. M DCC XXXVII 4to MS.

Richardsoni Deliciæ Hortenses, sive, Horti Richardsoniani Index Alphabeticus, quá Plantæ omnes quotquot hactenùs horti sui fuere alumnæ, tàm insulæ hujus spontaniæ quàm aliundè delatæ, fideliter in ordinem reducuntur. Curá et studio R R[ichardson]. 1676. 2 vols 4to MS

Lightfoot's (John) Flora Scotica, or, a Systematic Arrangement of the Native Plants of Scotland and the Hebrides 2 vols 8vo *Edinburgh*, 1792

Besleri (Bas) Hortus Eystettensis, sive, Plantarum, Florum, Stirpium, ex variis orbis terræ partibus singulari studio collectarum, quæ in celeberrimis Viridariis Arcis Episcopalis, Delineatio et ad vivum Representatio; [with the Explanations and the Winter Part] Large folio. [*Norimbergæ*] 1613

Wallich (N) Plantæ Asiaticæ rariores, or, Description and Figures of a select number of unpublished East India Plants 3 vols folio *Lond* 1829–32

Van Rhede (H) et T Janson Hortus Malabaricus [continens Regni Malabarici Plantas rariores ad vivum exhibitas, additâ insuper accuratâ earundem Descriptione] Notis adauxit et Commentariis illustravit Jo Commelinus 12 vols folio *Amstelodami*, 1686–1703.

Van Rhede — Casparis Commelini Flora Malabarica, sive, Horti Malabarici Catalogus, in ordinem alphabeticum digessit Folio *Lugd Bat* 1696

Van Rhede — Joannis Burmanni Flora Malabarica, sive, Index in omnes tomos Horti Malabarici Folio. *Amstelodami*, 1769

Rumphii (Geo Er) Herbarium Amboinense, plurimas complectens Arbores Frutices, Herbas, Plantas, terrestres et aquaticas, quæ in Amboiná et adjacentibus insulis, quod et insuper exhibet varia Insectorum Animaliumque Genera Belgicè conscripsit, nunc primùm in lucem edidit et Latinam Versionem adjecit Jo Burmannus 7 vols. in six Folio Large paper *Amstelodami*, 1741–55

Hooker's (W J) Flora Boreali-Americana, or, the Botany of the Northern Parts of British America; compiled principally from the Plants collected on the Northern Land Expeditions under Sir John Franklin, and those of Mr Douglas. 4to *London*, 1829.

Hooker's and G A W Arnot's Botany of Captain Beechey's Voyage, comprising an Account of the Plants collected by Messrs Lay and Collie, and other Officers of the Expedition, during the voyage to the Pacific and Behring's Straits performed in 1825 4to *Lond* 1830

Barton's (W P C) Compendium Floræ Philadelphicæ, containing a Description of the Indigenous and Naturalised Plants found within ten miles around Philadelphia 2 vols. small 8vo *Philadel* 1818

Humboldt (Alex de) Plantes Equinoxiales (Voyage de l'Amérique)

Evelyn's (John) Silva, or, a Discourse of Forest Trees and the Propagation of Timber, together with an Historical Account of the Sacredness and Use of Standing Groves, with Notes by A Hunter 2 vols. 4to. *York*, 1801

Strutt's (J G.) Sylva Britannica; or, Portraits of Forest Trees distinguished for their Antiquity, Magnitude, or Beauty Folio *London*, 1822

Brown (Sir Thos.), the Garden of Cyrus, or, the Quincuncial, Lozenge, or Net-work Plantations of the Ancients considered. (Works)

Phillips's (Henry) Silva Florifera, the Shrubbery historically and botanically treated, with Observations on the Formation of Ornamental Plantations and Picturesque Scenery 2 vols in one, 8vo *Lond* 1823

Duhamel du Monceau, Traité des Arbres Fruitiers, augmenté par A. Poiteau et P Turpin Les Figures imprimées en couleur, et retouchées au pinceau par les Auteurs mêmes. 6 vols folio *Paris*, 1807. &c.

Phillip's (Henry) Pomarium Britannicum, an Historical and Botanical Account of Fruits known in Great Britain 8vo *London*, 1823.

Ferrarii (Jo Bapt) Hesperides, sive, de Malorum Aureorum Cultura et Usu Folio *Romæ*, 1646

Ronald s (Hugh) Pyrus Malus Brentfordiensis, or, a Concise Description of selected Apples, with a Figure of each sort drawn from nature on stone and carefully coloured, by his Daughter 4to. *London*. 1831

Kerner (J S) le Raisin, ses Espèces et Variétés, dessinés et colories d'après Nature Folio *Stouttgard*, 1803–10

Kerner (J S) les Melons, contenant XXXVI Espèces, dessinés et colories d'après Nature Folio *Stouttgard*, 1811

Risso et Poiteau (A), Histoire Naturelle des Orangers 4to coloured Plates *Paris*, 1818

Kæmpfer's Natural History of the Japanese Tea, and its Preparation (History of Japan, Vol II)

Ellis's (John) Natural History of many curious and uncommon Zoophytes, systematically arranged and described by the late Dr. Solander and published by his Daughter. 4to. *London*, 1786

Zoology

Aristoteles de Animalibus (Opera, Vol I)

Shaw's (Geo) Zoological Lectures, delivered at the Royal Institution, with Plates from the best Authorities 2 vols 8vo *London*, 1809

Shaw's (Geo) General Zoology ; or, Systematic Natural History, continued by James Francis Stephens , with Plates from the first Authorities, and most select Specimens, engraved by Mrs. Griffith and Mr Heath 28 vols 8vo *London*, 1800–26

Cuvier's (the Baron) Animal Kingdom, described and arranged in conformity with its Organisation , with additional Descriptions, and other original matter, by Edward Griffiths and others 9 vols. royal 8vo, large paper, coloured Plates *Lond* 1827–31.

Cuvier's (the Baron) Fossil Mammalia, by Pidgeon. Royal 8vo large paper, coloured *London*, 1830

Bingley's (W) Animal Biography , or, Authentic Anecdotes of the Lives, Manners, and Economy of the Animal Creation. 3 vols. 8vo *Lond* 1805.

Waltoni (E) de Differentiis Animalium Libri X , ad Seren Aug Regem Edwardum VI Folio *Lutetiæ, apud Vascosanum*, 1552.

Landseer's (Thos) Characteristic Sketches of Animals, drawn from the Life and engraved , with Descriptive Notices by John Barrow. Imp. 4to. proofs on India paper. *London*, 1829–32

Pennant's (Thomas) British Zoology 4 vols. 4to. *Warring*. 1776–7.

Sowerby's (James) British Miscellany ; or, Coloured Figures of new, rare, or little-known Animal Subjects, inhabitants of the British Isles. 8vo. *London*, 1806.

Pennant's (Thomas) Arctic Zoology. 2 vols. 4to. *London*, 1784

Richardson's (John) Zoology of the Northern Parts of British America ; containing Descriptions of the Objects of Natural History collected on the Expeditions under Sir John Franklin. 4to *London*, 1829.

D'Obsonville's (M F) Philosophic Essays on the Manners of various foreign [Asiatic] Animals, translated by Thomas Holcroft. 8vo. *London*, 1784

Pennant s (T) Indian Zoology 4to *London*, 1790.

Gray's (J E) Illustrations of Indian Zoology, consisting of coloured Plates of new or hitherto unfigured Indian Animals, from the collection of Major-General Hardwicke 2 vols folio *London*, 1829.

Prichard's (J C) Researches into the Physical History of Mankind. 2 vols 8vo. *London*, 1826

Bewick's (T) General History of Quadrupeds, the Figures engraved on Wood 8vo *Newcastle*, 1792

Geoffroi Saint Hilaire et F Cuvier, Histoire Naturelle des Mammifères, avec des Figures originales coloriées, dessinées d'après des Animaux vivans Folio *Paris*, 1819

Pennant's (Th) History of Quadrupeds 2 vols 4to *London*, 1793

Topsell's (E) Historie of Four-footed Beastes, collected out of Conrad, Gesner, and all other Writers. Folio, Cuts *London, by W. Jaggard*, 1607

Ornithology.

Pennant's (Thos) Genera of Birds   4to.   *London*, 1781.

Pennant's (T) Index to the Ornithology of Buffon, and Systematic Catalogue.   4to.   *London*, 1786

Willughby's (Francis) Ornithology, translated, with Three Discourses on the Art of Fowling, the ordering of Singing Birds, and of Falconry, by John Ray   Folio   *London*, 1678

[Latham's (John)] General Synopsis of Birds, the Plates elaborately coloured   3 vols in 6.   Both Supplements   2 vols.   Index Ornithologicus, sive Systema Ornithologiæ, cum Supplemento 2 vols.; 10 vols in 8, 4to.   *London*, 1781–1802

Edwards's (Geo) Natural History of Birds, with Figures exactly coloured after the original drawings   7 vols in 4, folio.   Only 25 copies of this size executed   *London*, 1802–6.

Bewick's (T) History of Birds   Figures engraved in wood.   2 vols. 8vo first edition   *Newcastle*, 1797–1804

Themminck (C J.), Histoire Naturelle des Pigeons; les Figures coloriées par Mdme. Knip, née Pauline de Courcelles   Folio.   *Paris*, 1811

Audebert (J. B) et L P Vieillot, Histoire Naturelle et Générale des [Oiseaux Dorés, viz.] Colibris, Oiseaux-Mouches, Jacamars et Promerops, Grimpereaux, et des Oiseaux de Paradis   2 vols folio, large paper, Plates highly finished in colours.   *Paris*, 1802

Vaillant (Fr le), Histoire Naturelle des Oiseaux de Paradis, des Toucans, et des Barbus; suivie de celle de Promerops, Guépiers, et des Couroucous   3 vols. folio, coloured Plates   *Paris*, 1803–16

Lesson (R P), Histoire Naturelle des Oiseaux-Mouches   Royal 8vo coloured Plates   *Paris*, 1829

Desmarest (A G), Histoire Naturelle des Tangaras, des Manakins, et des Todiers; avec Figures coloriées d'après les desseins de Mlle Pauline de Courcelles   Folio   *Paris*, 1805

Vaillant (Fr le), Histoire Naturelle des Perroquets   2 vols folio, coloured Plates   *Paris*, 1801–5.

Gould's (J) Coloured Figures of the Birds of Europe, with Descriptions   Large folio   *London*, 1832

Montagu's (Col G) Ornithological Dictionary of British Birds   Second edition, with a Plan of Study, and many new Articles, by James Rennie   8vo.   *Lond* 1831

Lewin (W) on the Birds of Great Britain, systematically arranged, with their Eggs accurately engraved and painted from nature.   8 vols royal 4to   *London*, 1795–1801

Donovan's (E) Natural History of British Birds, or, a Selection of the most rare, beautiful, and interesting, which inhabit this country, with Figures coloured from the original specimens.   10 vols royal 8vo   *London*, 1794–1818

Frisch (J L), Représentation des Oiseaux d'Allemagne, et occasionellement de quelques Oiseaux etrangers, peints avec leurs couleurs naturelles   2 vols folio   *Berlin*, 1763.

Vieillot (L P). Histoire Naturelle des plus beaux Oiseaux Chanteurs de la Zone Torride   Folio, Plates coloured   *Paris*, 1806.

Gould's (J) Century of Birds from the Himalaya Mountains, coloured from nature, with Descriptions by N. Vigors. Large folio *London*, 1831

Vaillant (Fr le), Histoire Naturelle d'une partie des Oiseaux nouveaux et rares de l'Amérique et des Indes. Folio, Plates coloured *Paris*, 1804

Wilson's (Alex) American Ornithology, or, the Natural History of the Birds of the United States, illustrated with Plates, coloured from original drawings taken from nature. [With Life of the Author by Geo Ord] 9 vols 4to *Philadelphia*, 1808–14

Audubon's (John James) Birds of America, from Drawings made during a residence of Twenty-five Years in the United States and its Territories 3 vols. folio. *Edinburgh*, 1831

Audubon's (J. J.) American Ornithological Biography. Royal 8vo. *London*, 1831.

Waterton's (C) Original Instructions for the Perfect Preservation of Birds &c for Cabinets of Natural History. (Travels in South America)

Reptiles, &c

Cordiner's (Charles) Natural History of Scottish Marine Animals, &c. (Antiquities of Scotland)

Topsell's (Ed) Historie of Serpents, collected out of Divine Scriptures, Fathers, Philosophers, Physicians, and Poetes. Folio *London*, by *W Jaggard*, 1608.

Ichthyology

Willughben (Fr) Historia Piscium, recognovit, coaptavit, supplevit Joan. Raius *Oxonii*, 1686

Cuvier (le Baron) et M Valenciennes, Histoire Naturelle des Poissons, décrits d'après nature, et distribués conformément à leurs rapports d Organisation , avec des Observations sur leur Anatomie, et des Recherches critiques sur leur Nomenclature ancienne et moderne 15 vols 8vo coloured Plates *Paris*, 1828

Albin's (E) History of Esculent Fish , with North's Essay on Fish and Fish-Ponds. 4to coloured Plates. *London*, 1794

Donovan s (E) Natural History of British Fishes ; with accurately finished coloured Plates 5 vols. royal 8vo. *London*, 1808

Jovius (Paulus) de Romanis Piscibus (Descriptiones)

Entomology.

Kirby (W.) and W. Spence's Introduction to Entomology , or, Elements of the Natural History of Insects with Plates 4 vols 8vo. *London*, 1818–26

Swammerdam (J) Biblia Naturæ , sive, Historia Insectorum, in linguâ Bataviâ et Latinâ Accedit Præfatio, in quâ Vitam Auctoris descripsit H Boerhaave 2 vols folio, large paper *Leydæ*, 1737

Olivier (G. A), Entomologie , ou, Histoire Naturelle des Insectes. 6 vols 4to, coloured Plates *Paris*, 1789–1808

Stoll (Caspar), Représentation, exactement coloriée d'après nature, des Punaises, des Cigales, des Spectres ou Phasmes, des Mantes, des Sauterelles, des Grillons, des Criquets, et des Blottes, qui se trouvent dans les quatre parties du monde, rassemblés et décrits, Hollandois et François 3 vols 4to, fine paper   *Amsterdam*, 1788–1813
 "Exemplaire retouché au pinceau sur les originaux dans le cabinet de M Raye de Breukelerwoert."—*MS Note*

Voet (J E.), Catalogue Systématique des Coléoptères 2 vols 4to. Plates beautifully coloured *à la Haye* [1805].
 "Exemplaire retouché," &c as Stoll, above

Curtis's (John) British Entomology; containing coloured figures, from nature, of the most rare and beautiful species of British Insects, and of the Plants on which they are found. Royal 8vo. *Lond* 1824

Donovan's (E) Natural History of British Insects, including such as require investigation by the microscope. Illustrated with figures coloured from the living specimens 16 vols royal 8vo *London*, 1792–1813.

Harris's (Moses) Exposition of English Insects, arranged according to the Linnæan system Plates coloured after nature, 4to. *London*, 1781.

Harris's (M) Aurelian, a Natural History of English Moths and Butterflies together with the Plants on which they feed. Plates coloured from nature, folio, large paper. *London*, 1776

Harris's (M) Aurelian (Index of Modern Generic Names to) (Retrospective Review, New Series, Vol I)

Lee (Coloured Specimens from the Collection of Mr), of Hammersmith, to illustrate the Natural History of Butterflies. With Descriptions Folio *London*, 1806
 These are carefully coloured by the author on etched outlines, and the number of copies executed was very limited.

Haworth (A H) Lepidoptera Britannica, adjunguntur Dissertationes ad Hist. Nat spectantes 4 parts, 8vo *London*, 1803–28

Ernst (M), Papillons d'Europe, peints d'après nature, gravés et coloriées sous sa direction [et sous celle de Gigot d'Arcy], décrits par R. P. Engramelle. 8 vols 4to, fine paper *à Paris*, 1779–92
 "Exemplaire retouché," &c as Stoll, above.

Cramer (Pierre), Papillons Exotiques des trois parties du monde, l'Asie, l'Afrique, et l'Amérique, rassemblés, décrits, et dessinés sur les originaux, par l'Auteur, et gravés et enluminés sous sa direction Avec le Supplement par C. Stoll, contenant ceux de Surinam Hollandois et François 5 vols 4to fine paper *Amsterdam*, 1779–91
 "Exemplaire choisi, dont les objets ont été repeint," &c as Stoll, above.

Palissot de Beauvois (A M F J), Insectes recueillis en Afrique et en Amérique, dans les Royaumes de Benin, à S Domingue, &c pendant les années 1786–97. 2 vols folio, coloured Plates *Paris*, 1804–7

Donovan's (E.) Natural History of the Insects of India and the Islands of the Indian Seas Figures coloured from the specimens 4to *London*, 1800

Donovan's (E.) Natural History of the Insects of China. Figures coloured from the specimens 4to. *Lond* 1798

Donovan's (E) Natural History of the Insects of New Holland, New Zealand, and other islands of the Indian, Southern, and Pacific Oceans Figures coloured from the specimens. 4to   *Lond* 1805

Merian (M S) de Generatione et Metamorphosibus Insectorum Surinamensium. His adjunguntur Bufones, Lacerti, Serpentes, alæque Animalculæ. Accedit Appendix Transformationum Piscium in Ranas et Ranarum in Pisces. Folio   *Amstelodami*, 1719

Smith's (Sir J E) History of the Lepidopterous Insects of Georgia, with the Plants on which they feed, collected from the Observations of Mr Abbot   2 vols folio, coloured Plates   *Lond* 1797.

Lewin's (J W) Natural History of Lepidopterous Insects of New South Wales , collected, engraved, and faithfully painted after nature. 4to   *London*, 1805

Wildman's (Th) Treatise on the Management of Bees; containing a Natural History of these Insects, and of Wasps and Hornets   8vo   *Lond* 1770

Huber's (Fr) New Observations on the Natural History of Bees, translated. 12mo   *Edin* 1808

Huber's (F) Natural History of Ants, translated, with Notes, by J R. Johnson   12mo   *Lond* 1820

Dandalo's (Count) Art of Rearing Silk-worms, translated   8vo. *London*, 1825.

Adams' (Geo) Essays on the Microscope , containing a General History of Insects, their Transformation, General Habits, and Economy [and Instructions for Collecting and Preserving them]   with Additions and Improvements by F Kanmacher   4to   *Lond* 1798

Hooke's (R) Micrographia · or, some Physiological Descriptions of Minute Bodies made by Magnifying Glasses , with Observations and Inquiries thereupon   Folio. *Lond*. 1665

Conchology

Mawe's (John) Linnæan System of Conchology; describing the Orders Genera, and Species of Shells, arranged into Families   8vo, coloured Plates   *London*, 1823.

Lister (Martin) Historia, sive Synopsis methodica Conchyliorum, quorum omnium Picturæ ad vivum delineatæ exhibentur , cum Appendice figurarum anatomicarum. Folio, large paper   *Lond* 1685.

Perry's (Geo) Conchology, or, Natural History of Shells · containing a new Arrangement of the Genera and Species, illustrated by coloured Engravings from the natural specimens [by Jo. Clarke]. Folio. *London*, 1811

Audebert de Ferussac (J B L d'), Histoire naturelle, générale, et particulière des Mollusques Terrestres et Flûviatiles. Folio, coloured Plates   *Paris*, 1819

Dillwyn's (L W) Descriptive Catalogue of recent Shells, arranged according to the Linnæan System, with particular attention to the Synonymes   2 vols 8vo   *London*, 1817

Montague's (Geo) Testacea Britannica, or, Natural History of British Shells, systematically arranged , with the Supplement   3 vols 4to   *London*, 1803, *and Exeter*, 1808.

Donovan's (E) Natural History of British Shells, with coloured Figures 5 vols royal 8vo *London*, 1804

Sowerby's (James) Mineral Conchology of Great Britain; or, coloured Figures and Descriptions of those Remains of Testaceous Animals or Shells which have been preserved at various times and depths in the earth 6 vols 8vo *London*, 1812–24

Ellis's (John) Essay towards a Natural History of the Corallines, and other Marine Productions of the like kind, found on the coasts of Great Britain 8vo *London*, 1755.

Medicine, Anatomy, and Surgery.

Hamilton's (W) History of Medicine, Surgery, and Anatomy, to the commencement of the XIXth Century 2 vols. 12mo. *Lond.* 1831.

Aristoteles de Generatione et Corruptione (Opera, Vol I)

Bacon's (Lord) Historia Vitæ et Mortis (Works)

Bell s (John) Principles of Surgery, containing the ordinary Duties of a Surgeon, and a System of Surgical Operations 3 vols in 4, 4to *Edinb. and Lond.* 1801–8.

Berkeley's (Bp) Siris; a Chain of Philosophical Reflections and Inquiries on the Virtues of Tar-Water in the Plague (Works)

Boyle's (Robt) Natural History of the Human Blood. (Works, Vol IV)

Boyle's (R) Receipts for the Cure of Diseases. (Works, Vol V)

Boyle's (R) Effects of Motion on the Salubrity and Insalubrity of the Air (Works, Vol V.)

Brande's (W Thos) Manual of Pharmacy. 8vo *London*, 1825.

Buchan's (Wm) Domestic Medicine, edited by A. P. Buchan. 8vo. *London*, 1826

Cavallo's (Tit) Practice of Medical Electricity. (Electricity)

Celsus (A Corn) de Medicinâ, ex recensione et cum Notis variorum, edidit Leon Targa 2 vols 8vo *Argent* 1806

Cheyne's (Geo) Essay of Health and Long Life 8vo. *Lond* 1725

Cooper's (Sam) Dictionary of Practical Surgery 8vo. *London*, 1830.

Darwin's (Eras) Zoonomia; or, the Laws of Organic Life 2 vols *London*, 1796

Dioscoridis (P A Matthioli Commentarii in Libros) à Medicâ Materiâ ab ipso Auctore recogniti, et locis plus mille aucti; adjectis magnis ac novis Plantarum ac Animalium Iconibus ad vivum delineatis Folio *Venetiis, ap F. Valgrisium*, 1583

Gold-Headed Cane; [or, Sketches of Radcliffe, Mead, Askew, Pitcairn, and Baillie] Small 8vo. *London*, 1827

Good's (J M) Study of Medicine, by Sam Cooper 5 vols 8vo. *London*, 1829

Graham's (T J) Modern Domestic Medicine, or, a Popular Treatise on Diseases 8vo *London*, 1828

Gratarolus' (Guil) Direction for the Health of Magistrates and Students, namely, suche as bee in their consistent age, or neere thereunto, Englished by T[h] N[ewton] 𝔅𝔩𝔞𝔠𝔨 𝔩𝔢𝔱𝔱𝔢𝔯, small 8vo. *London, by W How*, 1574

PHILOSOPHY.

Hippocratis Opera (Classics.)

Home's (Sir Everard) Lectures on Comparative Anatomy, in which are explained the Preparations in the Hunterian Museum, with Supplement, and including a Synopsis of the Classes and Orders of the Animal Kingdom 6 vols. 4to. *London*, 1814–28

Hooper's (Rob) Medical Dictionary. 8vo *London*, 1831

Kæmpfer on the Cure of Colic by Acupuncturation, of Moxa, Ambergrease, &c (History of Japan, Vol II.)

Lizars's (John) System of Anatomical Plates, accompanied with Descriptions and Observations Folio, Plates coloured. *Edinb* 1822–6

Paris (J A) on Diet, with a view to establish, on Practical Grounds, a System of Rules for the Prevention and Cure of Diseases incident to a Disordered State of the Digestive Functions 8vo. *London*, 1824

Russell's (T) Description and Treatment of the Plague. (Natural History of Aleppo)

Tissot (M), de la Santé des Gens de Lettres 8vo. *Lausanne*, 1768.

Sect. III —MATHEMATICAL PHILOSOPHY

Histories, Dictionaries, &c.

Montucla (J. F.), Histoire des Mathématiques, achevée par J. De la Lande. 4 vols 4to *Paris*, 1799–1802

Hutton's (Charles) Mathematical and Philosophical Dictionary; with numerous Additions and Improvements 2 vols 4to *Lond* 1815

Hutton's (C) Tracts on Mathematical and Philosophical Subjects. 3 vols 8vo *London* 1812

Hutton's (C) Recreations in Mathematics and Natural Philosophy; containing amusing Dissertations and Inquiries on a variety of subjects. 4 vols 8vo. *London*, 1814.

Pure Mathematics.

Ben Musa's Algebra; edited and translated by Frederick Rosen 8vo. *London*, 1831

Bridges (B) Lectures on the Elements of Algebra 8vo *Lond* 1819.

Cowley's (J Lodge) Illustration and Mensuration of Solid Geometry, containing movable schemes for forming the various Solids revised by W. Jones 4to. *London*, 1787.

Euclidis Elementa Geometriæ (Classics)

Hutton's (Charles) Mathematical Tables, containing the Common, Hyperbolic, and Logistic Logarithms, &c. 8vo. *London*, 1811

Hutton's (C) Elements of Conic Sections, with select Exercises in various branches of Mathematics and Philosophy 8vo *Lond* 1787.

Hutton's (C) Treatise of Mensuration, both in Theory and Practice 8vo. *London*, 1788.

Hamilton (Bp H) de Sectionibus Conicis. (Works, Vol I)

Lacroix (S. F), Traité du Calcul Différentiel et du Calcul Intégral, revue, corrigée, et augmentée 3 vols 4to *Paris*, 1810-19

PHILOSOPHY.

Leslie's (Sir John) Philosophy of Arithmetic; exhibiting a progressive view of the Theory and Practice of Calculation 8vo *Edin* 1817

Maseres' (Baron Francis) Scriptores Logarithmici, or, a Collection of Tracts on the Nature and Construction of Logarithms. 6 vols 4to, fine paper *London*, 1791–1807.

Newtoni (Sir I) Tractatus ad Fundamenta Geometriæ sublimioris pertinentes (Opera, Vol 1)

Newtoni (Sir I) Arithmetica Universalis (Opera, Vol I)

Playfair's (John) Elements of Geometry, containing the first Six Books of Euclid with Elements of Trigonometry, 8vo *Edinb* 1804

Simson's (Rob) Elements of Euclid, with a Treatise on Trigonometry and Logarithms 8vo *London*, 1806

Wilson's (Ri) System of Plane and Spherical Trigonometry to which is added, a Treatise on Logarithms 8vo *Cambridge*, 1831

Baily's (F) Doctrine of Interest and Annuities, and of Life Annuities and Assurances, with Appendix 2 vols 8vo *Lond* 1809–10

Baily's (F) Tables for the Purchase and Renewing of Leases 8vo. *London*, 1807

Morgan's (W) Principles and Doctrine of Assurances, Annuities, and Contingent Reversions 8vo *London*, 1823

Place (P S. De la), Théorie Analytique des Probabilités 4to *Paris*, 1820

Rouse's (W) Doctrine of Chances, or, the Theory and Probability of Gaming 8vo *London*, 1814.

Adams' (Geo) Geometrical and Graphical Essays, containing a general Description of the Mathematical Instruments used in Geometry, Civil and Military Surveying, Levelling, and Perspective, enlarged by W Jones: with an Appendix by John Gale, containing Tables of Southing 2 vols 8vo *London*, 1791–1803

Brewster's (David) Treatise on New Philosophical Instruments, for various purposes in the Arts and Sciences, with Experiments on Light and Colours 8vo *Edinb* 1813

Mixed Mathematics.

Archimedis Opera. (Classics)

Aristotelis Quæstiones Mechanicæ (Opera, Vol I)

Emerson's (Wm) Principles of Mechanics, explaining and demonstrating the general Laws of Motion 4to *London*, 1800

Hamilton (Bp Hugh) on the Principles of Mechanics, and Introductory Lectures on Natural Philosophy (Works, Vol II)

Robison's (John) Mechanical Philosophy, by Sir D Brewster. 4 vols 8vo *Edinb* 1822

Wood's (James) Principles of Mechanics 8vo *Camb*. 1811

[Worcester's (Marq of)] Century of the Names and Scantlings of such Inventions as he tried and perfected 12mo *London*, 1746

Worcester's (Marq of) Century of Inventions; with Historical and Explanatory Notes, and a Biographical Memoir by C F Partington Small 8vo. *London*, 1825.

Astronomy.

Adams's (Geo) Astronomical and Geographical Essays, containing the general Principles of Astronomy, the Use of the Globes, Planetarium, Tellurium, and Lunarium, enlarged by Wm Jones 8vo *London*, 1803.

Bode (J E), Représentation des Astres, sur XXXIV Planches, avec une Instruction sur la manière de s'en servir. 4to. *Berlin*, 1805

Delambre (J B J), Tables Astronomiques 4to. *Paris*, 1806.

Ferguson's (James) Astronomy explained upon Sir I Newton's Principles, with Notes and Supplementary Chapters by David Brewster. 2 vols 8vo with 4to volume of illustrative Plates *Edinb* 1811.

Long's (Roger) System of Astronomy 2 vols 4to *Camb* 1742.

Maskelyne's (Nevil) Astronomical Observations made at the Royal Observatory, Greenwich, from 1765 to 1797 3 vols folio *London*, 1776–1800.

Maupertius (M de) on the different Figures of Celestial Bodies, with a summary Exposition of the Cartesian and Newtonian Theories. (Keill's Examination of Burnet)

Place (le Comte la), Exposition du Système du Monde. 2 vols. 8vo. *Paris*, 1813.

Place (le Comte la), Traité de Mécanique Céleste 4 vols 4to *Paris*, 1799–1805

[Recorde's (Rob)] Castle of Knowledge, containing the Explication of the Sphere, bothe Celestiall and Materiall, and divers other things incident thereto. 4to *London, by Rey Wolfe*, 1556.

Somerville's (Mary) Mechanism of the Heavens 8vo *London*, 1831.

Theodosii Tripolensis Sphæræ   (Classics)

Vince's (James) Elements of Astronomy 8vo. *Cambridge*, 1810

Wharton's (Geo) Calendarium Carolinum; or, a New Almanack after the old fashion, for the Year of Man's Creation 5612—Redemption 1663, to which is added, Gesta Britannorum, or a Chronology for 62 Years, from 1600 to 1663. Small 8vo port *London*, 1663

Optics and Perspective.

Brewster's (David) Experiments on Light and Colours. (Treatise on Phil. Inst.)

Newton's (Sir I) Optics. (Opera, Vol. I)

Wood's (James) Elements of Optics 8vo *Cambridge*, 1811

Wood's (J G) Lectures on Perspective, illustrated with Plates and a Mechanical Apparatus 4to. *London*, 1804

Le Clerc's Practical Geometry, or, an Introduction to Perspective, from the French; with Additions by C. Nattes. Plates by Pyne 8vo. *London*, 1805

Music.

Burney's (Charles) General History of Music, from the earliest ages to the present period, with a Dissertation on the Music of the Ancients 4 vols 4to. *London*, 1776-89

Hawkins' (Sir John) General History of the Science and Practice of Music 5 vols 4to *London*, 1776

Montucla, Histoire de la Musique. (Hist des Mathematiques, Vol IV)

Burney's (C.) Present State of Music in Germany, the Netherlands, and United Provinces. 3 vols. 8vo. *London*, 1773.

Busby's (Thomas) Complete Dictionary of Music 12mo. *Lond.* 1806.

Calcott's (Dr) Musical Grammar. 12mo. *London*, 1809.

Euclidis Introductio Harmonica (Opera)

Harris (James) on Music (Works, Vol. I)

King's (M P) General Treatise on Music, particularly on Harmony and Thorough-Bass, and its application in composition Folio *Lond.* 1808.

Zarlino (Gioseffo), Le Institutioni Harmoniche, nelle quale le materie appartenenti alla musica Folio *Venet* 1558.

Bonanni (Père), Description des Instrumens Harmoniques en tout genre, augmentée par l'Abbé Ceruti. Ital et Franc 4to *Roma*, 1776

[Ritson (Jos.)] on the Songs, Music, and Instrumental Performance of the ancient English. (Ancient Songs.)

Tytler (W) on Scottish Music (James the First's Remains)

Dissertation on Scottish Music (Arnot's Edinburgh, App. No. VIII)

Gunn's (John) Historical Inquiry respecting the Performance on the Harp in the Highlands of Scotland, until discontinued about 1734 4to *Edinburgh*, 1807

Walter (Joseph C.) on the Music and Musical Instruments of Ireland (Irish Bards)

[Coxe's (W.)] Anecdotes of Geo. F Handel and John Christ Smith, with select Pieces of Music composed by J C. Smith, never before published. 4to. *London*, 1799.

Barrington's (Daines) Account of a very remarkable young Musician [Mozart], and of Charles and Samuel Wesley, little Crotch, and the Earl of Mornington. (Miscellanies)

Purcell's (Henry) Orpheus Britannicus; a Collection of the choicest Songs for one, two, and three Voices; with Symphonies and a Thorough-Bass to each Both parts in one vol folio *London*, 1706-11.

Navigation and Naval Architecture.

Charnock's (John) History of Marine Architecture, including a view of the Nautical Regulations and Naval History of all Nations, especially that of Great Britain, deduced to the present time. 3 vols 4to large paper *London*, 1800-2

Clerk (John) on Naval Tactics, systematical and historical. 4to. *Edin.* 1804

Falconer's (Wm) Universal Dictionary of the Marine; being a copious Explanation of the Technical Terms and Phrases, modernised and much enlarged by W Burney   4to   *London*, 1815

Ralegh (Sir W) on the Invention of Ships, the several Uses, Defects, and Supply of Shipping; the Strength and Defects of the Sea Forces of England, France, Spain, and Venice; with Observations on the Royal Navy and Sea Service   (Works, Vol VIII)

Military Science

Æliani Tactica,—Arriani Ars Tactica,—Frontini Stratagematicon,—Vegetius de Re Militari,—Scriptores Veteres de Re Militari   (Classics.)

Duncan's (W) Discourse concerning the Roman Art of War.   (Cæsar)

Folard (Le Chev de), Commentaire sur Polybe, ou un Cours de Science Militaire, avec un Supplément, contenant les Nouvelles découvertes de la Guerre   (Polybius)

Grose's (Francis) Military Antiquities   (English Military History.)

Meyrick's (Sam Rush) Critical Inquiry into Ancient Armour, as it existed in Europe, but particularly in England, from the Norman Conquest to the reign of Charles II; with a Glossary of Military Terms of the Middle Ages   3 vols imperial 4to   *Lond* 1824.

An original copy, coloured under the immediate inspection of the author

Muller's (John) Treatise, containing the elementary part of Fortification, regular and irregular   8vo   *Lond* 1807

CLASS IV.—ARTS.

General Treatises.

Roujoux (P. G. de), Essai d'une Histoire des Revolutions arrivées dans les Sciences et les Arts depuis les temps héroïques jusqu'à nos jours   3 vols 8vo   *Paris*, 1811

Beckmann's (John) History of Inventions and Discoveries, translated by W Johnston   4 vols 8vo.   *London*, 1814

Dutens (M L), Origine des Découvertes attribuees aux Modernes   3 vols 8vo   *Paris*, 1812

Smith's (G) Laboratory, or School of Arts; containing a large collection of valuable Secrets, Experiments, and manual Operations in Arts and Manufactures   2 vols 8vo   *Lond*. 1799

Transactions of the Society instituted at London for the Encouragement of Arts, Manufactures, and Commerce, from 1783 to the present time, with Index to first 25 vols   29 vols 8vo   *Lond* 1783–1808

Sect. I.—LIBERAL ARTS.

Artificial Memory, Writing, and Printing.

∗ See also Literary History and Bibliography

Grey's (Rich) Memoria Technica, or, a new method of Artificial Memory 12mo. *London*, 1737

Ahmad bin Abubekr bin Washih's Ancient Alphabets and Hieroglyphic Characters explained Translated from the Arabic by Jos Hammer 4to. *London*, 1806.

Champollion (le Jeune), Précis du Système Hiéroglyphique des anciens Egyptiens, ou, Recherches sur les Elemens premiers de cette Ecriture Sacrée Augmentée de la Lettre à M. Dacier relative à Alphabet des Hieroglyphes Phonétiques employés par les Egyptiens sur leurs Monumens de l'Epoque Grecque et de l'Epoque Romaine 2 vols roy 8vo *Paris*, 1829

Kircheri (Athanasii) Sphinx Mystagoga; sive, Diatribe Hieroglyphica Folio. *Amstelodami*, 1676

Lenoir (Alex), Nouvelle Explication des Hieroglyphes, ou des anciennes Allégories sacrées des Egyptiens. 3 vols 8vo *Paris*, 1809-10

Beck's (Cave) Universal Character, by which all the Nations of the World may understand one another's conceptions, reading out of one common writing their own mother tongue Small 8vo, front *London*, 1657

Bridges' (Noah) Stenographie and Cryptographie; or, the Arts of Short and Secret Writing. Small 8vo. *London*, 1659.

Morland's (Sir Samuel) New Method of Cryptography, or Secret Writing Folio, port by Lombard. —— 1666

Smith's (W) Introduction to Common Decyphering (History of Nevis)

Johnson's (J.) Typographia; or, the Printer's Instructor 2 vols 8vo, large paper *London*, 1824

Savage's (Wm) Practical Hints on Decorative Printing, with Illustrations engraved on wood, and printed in colours at the Type Press 4to *London*, 1822

Sect II —FINE ARTS

Histories and General Treatises.

Winkelmann (Jean-Joach), Histoire de l'Art chez les Anciens, traduite de l'Allemande, avec des Notes historiques et critiques de différens Auteurs [et Mémoires sur la Vie et Ouvrages de l'Auteur, par Huber, et revue par Jansen] 3 vols in two, 4to *Paris*, 1801-3
See also " Monumens de l'Antiquité "

Seroux d'Agincourt (J B L C), Histoire de l'Art par les Monumens, depuis sa décadence au IV Siècle, jusqu'à son renouvellement au XVI (pour servir de suite à l'Histoire de l'Art chez les Anciens) 4 vols folio *Paris*, 1823

ARTS.

Hume (D) on the Rise and Progress of the Arts   (Essays, Vol 1)

Hoare's (Prince) Epochs of the Arts, including Hints on the Use and Progress of Painting and Sculpture in Great Britain   8vo   London, 1813.

Alberti (L B) de Picturâ. (Vitruvius à de Laet)

Junius (Fr.) de Picturâ Veterum. Accedit Catalogus adhuc ineditus Architectorum, Mechanichorum, sed præcipuè Pictorum, Statuariorum, Cælatorum, Tornatorum, aliorumque Artificum et Operum quæ fecerunt [curâ et studio J. G Grævii]. Folio. *Rotterdami*, 1694

Turnbull (Geo) on Ancient Painting; containing Observations on the Rise, Progress, and Decline of that Art amongst the Greeks and Romans; its Connexion with Poetry and Philosophy; and the Use that may be made of it in Education   Illustrated with 50 pieces of ancient Painting, engraved from Drawings by Camillo Paderni   Folio, large paper. *London*, 1740.

D'Hancarville, Recherches sur l'Origine et Progrès des Arts dans la Grèce   (Antiquities)

Winkelmann's Reflections on the Painting and Sculpture of the Greeks, with Instructions for the Connoisseur, and an Essay on Grace in Works of Art, translated by Henry Fuseli   8vo.   *London*, 1765

Spence's (Joseph) Polymetis, or, an Inquiry concerning the Agreement between the Works of the Roman Poets and the Remains of ancient Artists, being an attempt to illustrate them mutually from one another. Folio   *London*, 1747.

Vasari (Georgio), Vite de' piu Eccelenti Pittori, Scultori, ed Architetti; illustrate con Note. 17 vols 8vo.   *Milano*, 1807–11

Memoirs of Benvenuto Cellini, containing a variety of information regarding the Arts of the 16th Century   (Biography)

Barry's (James) Works; viz Correspondence, Lectures at the Royal Academy; Observations of different Works of Art in Italy and France; Inquiry into the Causes which have obstructed the Progress of the Fine Arts in London; with some Account of the Life and Writings of the Author   2 vols 4to   *London*, 1809

Notizia d' Opere di Disegno, nella prima metà del secolo XVI esistenti in Padova, Cremona, Milano, Pavia, Bergamo, Crema, e Venezia; scritta da un Anomino di quel tempo, pubblicata ed illustrata da D. J. Morelli   8vo   *Bassano*, 1800

Richardson's (John), Account of some of the Statues, Bas-reliefs, Drawings, and Pictures in Italy, &c ; with Critical Remarks on their Productions   8vo   *London*, 1722

Lenoir (Alex), Recueil de Gravures, pour servir à l'Histoire des Arts en France, prouvée par les Monumens   Folio.   *Paris*, 1811.

[Chaussard], le Pausanias Français; Etat des Arts du Dessin en France à l'ouverture du XIX siècle   Royal 8vo.   *Paris*, 1806

Reynolds' (Sir Joshua) Journey to Flanders and Holland in 1781 [containing accounts of the Specimens of Painting, &c.]   (Works, Vol II)

Vertue's (Geo) Anecdotes of Painting in England; with some Account of the principal Artists, and Incidental Notes on other Arts, digested and published from the Author's original MSS, by Horace Walpole, with considerable Additions by the Rev James Dallaway   5 vols. royal 8vo, large paper, proofs   *London*, 1826.

ARTS.

Walpole's (Horatio, Earl of Orford) Anecdotes of Painters, Statuaries, and Medallists, in England   (Works, Vol III)

Edwards's (Geo) Anecdotes of Painters who have resided or been born in England, with Critical Remarks on their Productions, intended as a continuation of those of the late Lord Orford.   *Lond* 1808

Dallaway's (James) Anecdotes of the Arts in England; or, comparative Remarks on Architecture, Sculpture, and Painting. 8vo *London,* 1800

Christ (M), Dictionnaire des Monogrammes, Chiffres, Lettres Initiales, Logogryphes, Rebus, &c , sous lesquels les plus célèbres Peintres, Graveurs, et Dessinateurs, ont dessiné leurs noms; trad et augmenté par M. [Sellius]. 8vo   *Paris,* 1762.

Painting.

History of Painting.

Pilkington's (Matth) Dictionary of Painters, edited by H Fuseli   New edition, with numerous additions. 2 vols 8vo   *London,* 1829

Heinecker (le Baron), Dictionnaire des Artistes   (Engraving)

Buchanan's (W) Memoirs of Painting, containing a Chronological History of the Importation of Pictures by the great Masters since the period of the French Revolution with Critical Remarks thereon, and Sketches of the Characters of leading Masters of various Schools of Painting. 2 vols 8vo   *London,* 1824.

Serie di Ritratti degli eccelenti Pittori, dipinti di propria mano, che esistono nell' Imperiale Galleria di Firenze, colle Vite in compendio de' medesimi, descritte da Fran Moucke. 4 vols folio. *Firenze,* 1752-62.

Lanzi (Luigi), Storia Pittorica della Italia; dal risorgimento delle Belle Arti fin presso al fine del XVIII secolo. 6 vols 8vo   *Bassano,* 1818.

Lanzi's (Luigi) History of Painting in Italy, translated from the original Italian by Thomas Roscoe. 6 vols 8vo   *London,* 1828

Life of Michel Angelo Buonarotti   (Biography.)

Pinkerton (John) on the Rise and Progress of Painting in Scotland   (Scottish Gallery)

Cumberland's (Rich) Anecdotes of eminent Painters in Spain during the 16th and 17th centuries, with Remarks on the present state of the Arts in that kingdom. 2 vols. 12mo   *London,* 1787.

Bermudez (Don Juan A. C.) upon the Style and Taste of the School of Seville   (Life of Murillo.)

[Beckford's (W)] [Satirical] Biographical Memoirs of Extraordinary Painters   8vo   *London,* 1780.

Elementary and General Treatises.

Bell's (Char) Essays on the Anatomy of Expression in Painting. 4to. *London,* 1806.

Burnet's (John) Practical Hints on Composition and on Colour in Painting, illustrated by Examples from the great Masters of the Italian, Flemish, and Dutch Schools. 4to. *London,* 1822-27

ARTS

Du Fresnoy (C A) de Arte Graphicâ, the Art of Painting with Remarks translated, with a Parallel between Painting and Poetry, by John Dryden Also a short Account of the most eminent Painters, ancient and modern, by [Richard Graham] Large paper, 4to. *London*, 1695.

Du Fresnoy's (C A) Art of Painting, with Remarks, translated, with an original Preface, containing a Parallel between Painting and Poetry, by John Dryden (Dryden's Works, Vol XVII)

Du Fresnoy's (C A) Art of Painting, translated into English verse by W Mason, with Notes by Sir Joshua Reynolds, and Chronological List of modern Painters by Gray (Gray's Works, Vol. III., and Sir J Reynolds' Works, Vol III)

Du Piles' (M) Art of Painting, with the Lives of the most eminent Painters, Reflections on their Works, and Essay towards an English School 8vo *London*, 1743

Du Piles' (M) Principles of Painting, with an Account of Athenian, Roman, Venetian, and Flemish Schools 8vo. *London*, 1743

Evelyn (John), an Idea of the Perfection of Painting, demonstrated from the principles of the art. (Misc. Works)

Fuseli's (Henry) Lectures on Painting, delivered at the Royal Academy 4to *London*, 1801

Gilpin's (W) Essays on Picturesque Beauty, Picturesque Travel, and on sketching Landscape, with an Account of the Principles and Mode in which the Author executed his own drawings. 8vo *Lond.* 1808

Gilpin's (W) Collected Works, relating chiefly to Picturesque Beauty 10 vols large 8vo *London*, 1792–1809

Harris (James) on Painting (Works, Vol I)

Hogarth's (Wm) Analysis of Beauty, with a view to fix the fluctuating Ideas of Taste 4to *London*, 1753

Northcote's (J) Varieties of Art. (Memoirs of Sir J Reynolds)

Price's (Uvedale) Essays on the Picturesque, as compared with the Sublime and Beautiful, and on the use of studying Pictures for the purpose of improving real Landscape 3 vols 8vo *London*, 1810

Reynolds' (Sir Joshua) Discourses, delivered at the Royal Academy. (Works, Vols I and II)

Richardson's (John) Essay on the Theory of Painting 8vo. *London*, 1715

Richardson's (J) Two Discourses on the Art of Criticism as it relates to Painting, and on the Science of a Connoisseur 8vo *London*, 1719

Shee's (Sir M A) Elements of Art, a poem, with Notes and a Preface, including Strictures on the state of the Arts, Criticism, Patronage, and Public Taste 8vo *London*, 1809

Shee's (Sir M.) Rhymes on Art; or, the Remonstrance of a Painter, with Notes 8vo *London*, 1805

On particular kinds of Painting

Muntz's (J H) Encaustic, or, Count Caylus's Method of Painting in the manner of the Ancients, to which is added, a sure and easy way of fixing of Crayons. 8vo *London*, 1760

Lenoir (Alex), Histoire de la Peinture sur Verre, et Description des Vitraux anciens et modernes, pour servir à l'Histoire de l'Art relativement à la France. 8vo *Paris*, 1803

Hawkins's (J S) Inquiry into the mode of Painting upon and staining Glass, as practised in the Ecclesiastical Structures of the Middle Ages (Gothic Architecture)

Collections of Engravings after great and eminent Masters.

Landon (C P), Vies et Œuvres des Peintres les plus célèbres de toutes les écoles, viz Peintres Antiques, M. Ange, Raphael, Corrège, Dominiquin, L da Vinci, Titien, Guide, P Veronèse, C Albane, Baccio Bandinelli, Daniel de Volterre, Poussin, Le Sueur, et Jouvenet 25 vols in eleven, 4to. *Paris*, 1803, &c.

Engravings (XLVIII) after Poussin, Salvator Rosa, Claudio Gellée, Lorense, Panini, &c. by Chatelain and his Pupils, Vivares, Wood, Mason, &c Folio 1744

From the Italian School, after C Allori; F Albani, by Sir F Dorigny, and including the Rape of Proserpine by Rosabina, M Angelo, including the Crucifixion by Folo, Baccio, including Presentation in the Temple by Perfetti, Barocci, including the Annunciation and St Francis, by himself, Bassano; Berettini; Della Bella ; Vinc Camuccini, including the Death of Cæsar, and other classical subjects, A Carracci, including the Dead Christ by Roullett, the Frescos of the Magnani Palace at Bologna by Tortebat ; Lud Carracci, Cignani; Cipriani, Conca, Corregio, including Holy Family by Bonato, La Madonna col Divoto by Bettelini, Madelena by Rahl, and others by Sornique, Duchange, &c (Coll of Prints, Vol. I.)

From the Italian School after Pietro de Cortona, Carlo Dolci, Dominichini, including the Martyrdom of St Agnes by Audran, the Communion of St. Jerome by Frey and by Fardieu, the Four Cardinal Virtues, or Angels, by Frey, and the Four Evangelists by Dorigny, Feti; Franco, Francisco Bolognese, Gauli, including the St John by l'Epicier, Guercino da Cento, Guido, including St John by Raphael Mengs, Ecce Homo by Bartolozzi, plain and coloured, the Crucifixion by Chereau, St Andrew by G Audran, Bacchus and Ariadne by Frey, Aurora by Frey and Raphael Morghen, and Liberality and Modesty by Strange, Giulio Romano, Filipo Lauri, including St John, &c by Sympson, jun , and Jacob's Departure by Major (Coll of Prints, Vol II)

From the Italian School after Ber Luino, including the Nativity by Piotti, Madonna by Bisi, Baptist's Head by Garavaglia, C Maratti, including Sleeping Jesus by Strange, the Repose and the Martyrdom of St Andrew by Frey, the Martyrdom of St Blas by Audenaerd, Murillo, G delle Notti, Ochiale, Paulo Veronese, including the Marriage at Cana by Vanni, Il Parmigiano, Pellegrini by Bartolozzi, Perugino ; Piazzeti, F Railbolini, including a Madonna by Lecomte, Raphael including the Marriage of the Virgin by Dissard and Longhi, the Madonna di Fuligno by Fosetti, di Sisto by Muller, dell' Impanata by Sotomajor, and others by Bloemaert, Brebriette, Frey Laurnessin, Desnoyers, Bettelini, N. Vinch, Gio Della Bella, Raphael Morghen, and Jesi, St John by

Chereau, the Cartoons by Holloway (proofs), the Transfiguration by Raphael Morghen (proof, No. 454), the Frescos in the Vatican by Carlo Maratti, Dorigny, and P Thomassin. (Coll of Prints, Vol. III.)

From the Italian School, after Raphael, continued · the Battle of Constantine by Aquila, the Frescos in the Vatican by Valpato, Fabri, and Salandri; the Archangel by Rousselet and Chatillon, the Dream by G. Ghisi, and Mount Parnassus by Matham; M Ricci; Salvator Rosa, including the Prodigal Son by Ravenet, Jason by Boydell, Belisarius by Strange, Sasso Faratto, by Folo, &c.; J Rossi; A Sacchi, byFrey and Strange; A del Sarto, Tintoretto, including St Anthony by Berteli; Titian, including the Virgin adoring the Infant Jesus by Morin, Madonna by Bettelini, the Woman taken in Adultery by Anderloni, St Peter the Martyr by Zuliani (proof, No 56, before the letters), the Assumption by Schiavoni, &c., Tobar; L. da Vinci, including Madonna del Lago by Longhi, and with St. Catharine and Barbara by Steinmuller, and the Last Supper by Raphael Morghen (Coll. of Prints, Vol. IV.)

Ottley's (W Young) Italian School of Design; being a Series of Fac-Similes of original Drawings, by the most eminent Painters and Sculptors of Italy, with Biographical Notices of the Artists, and Observations on their Works Folio *London*, 1823.

Caracci (Annibale) [The Cries of Bologna] Diverse Figure, disegnate di penna nell' hore di ricreazione, intagliate e lavate degli originali da Simone Guilino [Guillain] Folio *Roma*, [1646.]

Caracci (A) Galeria nel Palazzo Farnese in Roma, intagliata da Carlo Cesio [con Argomento nel quali spiegarsi e reducersi allegoricamente alla moralità le Tavole Poetiche in essa rappresentate]. Folio *Roma*, 1657.

Giulio Romano Sigismundi Augusti Mantuam Adventus. Profectus, ac Triumphus, opus ex archetypo Julii Romani à Fr. Primatico, Mantuæ in Ducali Palatio, quod del T nuncupatur, sculpturâ mirè elaboratum, cum Notis J P. Bellori; à P Sancto Bartolo ex vet exemplari traductum, ærique incisum. Oblong folio. *Romæ*, 1680

Raphaele Sancto Urbinato (Imagines V et N Testamenti à), in Vaticani palatio xystis mirâ picturæ elegantiâ expressæ, J. J. Rubeis curâ ac sumptibus delineatæ, incisæ, ac typis editæ. Oblong folio *Romæ*,

Raphael — Nicol Dorigny's Pinacotheca Hamptoniana; Engravings from the Cartoons of Raphael de Urbino at Hampton Court, on VII Plates; with the Descent from the Cross, and the Transfiguration Brilliant impressions · the Harley copy Large folio

M. Angelo and Raphael — R Duppa's Dissertation on the Picture of the Last Judgment, in the Sistine Chapel, by M Angelo, accompanied with XII Heads, and XII. from the Fresco Pictures of Raffaelo in the stanze of the Vatican, traced from the originals, and engraved of the same size, with Life of Raffaelo Folio. *London*, 1801-2

Salvator Rosa (Etchings by), viz a Set of LXII. of Soldiers, Banditti, &c, and VI. of Tritons, &c, in 8vo; Fall of the Giants, Finding of Œdipus, and Deaths of Regulus and Polycrates, large oblong plates; with X Engravings after S Rosa, by Goupy. Folio.

ARTS 113

Titianus Vecellus Cadubriensis et Paulus Calliari Veronensis (Opera selectiora quæ) inventârunt ac pinxerunt, quæque V Le Febre delineavit et sculpsit Folio [*Venetiis*], 1682

From the French School, after Baudoin, by Launoy; Boucher, by Cochin and Aveline; Bourdon, including Laban and the Baptism of the Eunuch by Boissevin, Holy Family by Van Schuppen, Dead Christ by Boulanger, &c , Corbelet, including Holy Family by Boulanger, Claude Lorraine, including Landscapes by Major, the Roman Edifices by Woolet, Landing of Eneas by Mason, and others by Goupy and Haldenwang; J Callot, including Les Misères, &c de la Guerre by Israel, 18 plates, and the famous Temptation of St Anthony by Cheron, De la Hire; Israel, including 12 Landscapes and 12 Views in Rome, Jouvenet, including Mary Magdalen washing the Feet of our Saviour by Duchange, the Resurrection of Lazarus by Audran, and the Magnificat by Thomasin, one of the works of Jouvenet's left hand; Largilhère, Christ bearing the Cross, and the Crucifixion, by Roettiers, P Marriette, Meillan, by himself; N Mignard, including Holy Family by Masson, P Mignard, including Holy Family by Pailly, Christ led to Crucifixion, and the Pest, by G Audran, Monamy, by Canat, T M Moreau; Moucheron, Patel; Retout, including the Agony by Drevet, Le Sueur, including Paul at Athens by B Audran, Martyrdom of St. Lawrence by G. Audran, &c , Rousseau; Vernet, Watteau, including l'Accorrlée de Village by Larmesin (Collection of Prints, Vol V.)

From the French School, after Poussin, viz Sacrifice of Noah, by Frey; Finding of Moses, by Marriette and C Stella; Moses trampling on Pharaoh's Crown, by Baudet, Moses's Defence of the Priests of Midian, by Anderloni; Moses striking the Rock, by C Stella, the Worship of the Golden Calf, by Baudet, Ahasuerus and Esther, Marriage of the Virgin, and Adoration of the Shepherds, by J Pesne, a Repose, by Raphael Morghen; Holy Family, by C Stella, by Anderloni (proof), and by Baudet, Baptism of Jesus, Christ giving the Keys to Peter, Mary washing our Saviour's Feet, and Last Supper, by J. Pesne, Crucifixion, and Peter restoring Sight to the Blind, by C Stella, Death of Sapphira, Confirmation, Extreme Unction, and Testament of Eldamidas, by J Pesne, Continentio Scipionis, by Du Bosc, Tancredus Emonia, by Vandergucht, Bacchus and Ariadne, by Beauvois, Death of Germanicus, by Marriette; the Seasons, by Raphael Morghen, the Saving of Pyrrhus by G Audran, Habitation of Polyphemus, and VI other Landscapes, by Baudet, Sea Storm, including Jonah by Vivares, and Land Storm by Goupy (Collection of Prints, Vol VI)

Poussin —A Collection of XXXII Engravings of Landscapes after Poussin. Fine impressions, mounted, in one vol folio

Le Brun's (C) Battles of Alexander, 4 large Engravings, on 13 Plates, by G Audran, the Tent of Darius by Edelinck, and F Verdier's Passage of the Red Sea, engraved by G Audran Large folio

The splendid prints illustrative of Alexander are usually considered the chefs d'œuvre of this "greatest engraver." The impressions forming this copy are proofs, having the printer's name, "Goyton," etched on the margins

Q

114   ARTS.

Le Brun (C), Le Grand Escalier de Versailles, gravé par E Baudet, et le Plafond par C Simmoneau; La Franche-Conté conquise pour la seconde fois, gravée par C. Simmoneau; La Voûte de la Chapelle de Séaux, dont le sujet est l'Ancienne Loi accomplie par la Nouvelle, gravée par C Audran   In one vol large folio. [*Paris*, 1674–81]
   Beautiful impressions, from the royal collection, the French arms stamped on the sides and back.

From the Dutch and Flemish Schools, after L Bakhuisen , Berghem, by himself and J Vischer, including Berghem's Ball, others by Avelne, Vivares, and Boydell, Jo Both, by Maetham; Breenberg; Brouwer, by Vischer and M'Ardell; G. Douw; Elchout, including the Fifty-guilder Print by Baillie , Genoels , Ferg, by Wagner , Gheiner, including the Sorcery and Tobit by Goudt , C du Jardin; J Jordaens, including Bacchus and Philemon by N Lawers; A Kuyp, P. de Laer, F Mielly, F. de Neue; A Van Ostade, including the Painter, Cottage Dinner, Fair, &c &c by himself, and the Peasant's Quarrel by Sayderhoef, Poelenburg and Bout; Rembrandt, including Haman and Mordecai, (in a very early state,) Little la Tombe, Tribute to Cæsar (early impressions), Christ driving the Money-changers out of the Temple, Christ and the Samaritan Woman, the Hundred-guilder Piece, or Christ Healing the Sick, Ecce Homo (a finished impression), and the Descent from the Cross (companions), Death of the Virgin—Landscapes, including the Cottage and Barn, that with the Mill-sail, and the pair, the second of which contains a square tower—Portraits, including John Lutma and three of Rembrandt by himself—Copies, Rembrandt's Mother by M'Ardell, and others by Earlom, Simon Ravenet, Pether, and Wood; Rubens, including Elizabeth and Mary by De Jode, Christ bearing his Cross, Murder of the Innocents, "Christus Funus," and the Assumption, by P Pontius, the Education of the Virgin by S. A Bolswaert, and the Crucifixion and a Hunting Piece by A Bolswaert; Mutius Scævola, and Diana Hunting, by Goupy, the Ceiling of Whitehall by Gribelin, and the Chapeau de Paille by Reynolds (proof) (Collection of Prints. Vol. VII)

From the Dutch and Flemish Schools, after S Ruysdael; F Snyders, by Zaal , P Stevens, including the Seasons, &c by Giles Sadeler, and others by Marco Sadeler , Teniers, including the Sebat by Ahamet, Chemist and Surgeon by Major, Prodigal Son and two Flemish Feasts by Le Bas, and others by Laurent , Ant Vandyke, including Holy Family and Crucifixion by S E Bolswaert, Belisarius by Goupy, Rinaldo and Armida by P de Jode, and its companion by P Baillu; J Van Eyck including the Adoration of the Infant Jesus by the Three Holy Kings by C Van Hess, Vandermeer, Vandervelde; C Visscher, including the Rat-catcher and Pancake Woman (first impressions) , N Vleughels , Van Vliet; Waterloo, Vries, P Wouvermans, by J Vischer, Strange, Lament, and including the Meage, and Death of the Stag, by Major   (Collection of Prints, Vol VIII)

Brun (le), Galerie des Peintres Flamands, Hollandais, et Allemands, CCI Planches gravées d'après les meilleurs tableaux de ces maitres. 3 vols folio   *Paris*, 1792

Abr Bloemart —Hagar and two Landscapes by Sanredam and Maetham. Folio   (Rubens' Landscapes)

Rubens (XXV Landscapes, &c after) by S Bolswaert, and a Flemish Landscape by Major Folio
  Copies from Rubens are considered Bolswaert's best performances
Rubens (La Galerie du Palais du Luxembourg, peinte par), dessinée par Nattier, et gravée par les plus illustres graveurs La fol *Par* 1710

From the German School, after Albert Durer, including the Prodigal Son, and Melancholy, W Hollar including Theatrum Mulierum (14 Plates), Tower of London, Peace proclaimed at Antwerp, Holbein, including Henry VIII. presenting the Barber-surgeons their Charter by B Baron, and St Barbara, Raphael Mengs, and nine anonymous Prints   (Collection of Prints, Vol VIII)

Lithographic Engravings (LXXI) of Scriptural and Religious Subjects, after Hammeling, J Van Eyck, M. Coxis, J. von Meckenem, C Hemskirk, J Patenier, Mabuse, H Vandergoes, J von Melem, M Wilhelm von Koln, J Schwartz, B de Bruyn Hemling, Alb Durer, L Kranach, B Von Orley, T T Walch, M Grunewalde, J Schoorel, M Schon, Holbein, J. Kalcar, P de Mares, L Van Leyden, Hans Burgmaier. Large folio *Gedruckt unter der Direction von Strixner, in Stuttgart und Munchen,* 1820–30.

From the English School, after Sir W Beechey, including the Fortune-Teller by Young , E Bird, including Chevy Chase and Surrender of Calais by Young , T Frye; Hogarth, the original published Plates, including Calais Gate, Gin Lane, Beer Street, Cockpit, Superstition and Enthusiasm, Paul before Felix, the Good Samaritan, and Pool of Bethesda, by Ravenet , Ang Kauffman, including Blind Man's Buff and Cornelia by Bartolozzi , J Mortimer, including King John by Ryland , Geo Lambert ; Sir J Reynolds, including Garrick between Tragedy and Comedy by Fisher , H Richter, including Christ giving Sight to the Blind by Young , G. Morland, by Williamson , John Smith, by Woollett , Stothard, including Pilgrimage to Canterbury by Schiavonetti and Heath (India proof) , Stubbs; B. West, including Penn's Treaty by Hall, the Death of Wolfe by Woollett, Alfred dividing his Loaf with the Pilgrim by W Sharp, and Christ Healing the Sick by Heath (India proof) , R Westall, including Telemachus and Calypso by Scriven and Williamson , Wheatley, including the Cries of London by Vendramini and Schiavonetti , D Wilkie, including the Jew's Harp and Blind Fiddler by Burnet , B Wilson , R Wilson, by Woollett and Wooton   (Coll of Prints, Vol IX)

Britton (John), the Fine Arts of the English School, illustrated by a series of Engravings from Paintings, Sculpture, and Architecture of eminent English Artists , with Biographical, Critical, and Descriptive Essays by various Authors   Folio   *London,* 1812

Hogarth —Original Impressions of the Rake's and Harlot's Progresses, the Poet, Bartholomew Fair, Morning, Noon, Evening, and Night, Strolling Players, the Enraged Musician, and Illustrations of Hudibras   Large folio

Hogarth (the genuine Works of), illustrated with Biographical Anecdotes, a Chronological Catalogue, and Commentary, by J Nichols and Geo Steevens   3 vols 4to large paper   *London,* 1808–17

Hogarth (Graphic Illustrations of), from Pictures, Drawings, and scarce Prints; edited by Samuel Ireland. 2 vols 8vo *Lond* 1794

Martin's (John) Illustrations of the Bible Proofs before the letters Folio. *London*, 1831

Martin's (John) Illustrations of Paradise Lost (Poetry.)

Gallery of the Society of Painters in Water Colours India Proofs. Imp 4to *London*, 1832

Drawings

Original Drawings and Sketches, viz Four illustrative of Ovid's Metamorphoses, apparently by one of the old Italian Masters, by F. Parmigiano, Batt Franco, Polidoro, Carlo Maratti, Guido, Primaticcio, A Carracci, B Bandinelli, Guercino, Gaysar, Claude Lorraine, Moucheron, Chatelain, three Studies by Vandyke, Genoels, C Berghem, Bird's-eye Views of Prague and Passau, "W Hollar delin Aug. 1636," beautifully executed, and various Chalk Studies, anonymous but evidently by some of the old Masters. (Coll of Prints, Vol. XIII)

Galleries of Paintings.

The British Gallery of Pictures, selected from the most admired productions of the old Masters in Great Britain, accompanied with Descriptions, historical and critical, by Henry Tresham, William Young Ottley, and Peltro William Tomkins Folio, India proofs *Lond* 1818

British Gallery of Engravings, from Pictures in the most celebrated Collections in Great Britain, edited by Edward Forster Folio, India proofs. *London*, 1815

Angerstein Gallery.—Young's (J) Catalogue of the Collection of Pictures of the late J J Angerstein, with a finished Etching and Description of every picture Imp 4to proofs *London*, 1823.

Blenheim Collection — Smyth's (John) Mezzotinto Engravings from Pictures of Titian at Blenheim, with Frontispiece by Vertue, the Holy Family from Carlo Maratti, and Portraits of Wing, Anthony Leigh. Rembrandt, first Earl of Athlone, and the equestrian one of the Duke of Schomberg Folio *London*, 1709

Derby Gallery.—Winstanley's (Hamlet) Twenty Etchings from the Earl of Derby's Collection of Pictures at Knowsley, with Portrait of his Lordship Folio 1728–29.

Grosvenor Gallery — Young's (John) Catalogue of the Pictures at Grosvenor House London, with Etchings from the whole Collection, executed, and accompanied by historical Notices Imp. 4to proofs *London* 1820.

Leicester Gallery —Young's (J) Catalogue and Etchings of the Pictures of British Artists in the possession of Sir P. Leicester, Bart.; with Descriptions Imp 4to proofs *London*, 1821

Leigh Court —Young's (J.) Catalogue and Etchings of the Pictures at Leigh Court, near Bristol, the seat of J P Miles, Esq Imp 4to proofs *London*, 1822

Stafford Gallery.— Engravings of the Pictures in the Marquess of Stafford's Collection in London, arranged according to schools, and in chronological order; with Remarks on each picture by William Young Ottley and P W Tomkins Proofs on India paper, 4 vols in 2, folio. *London*, 1818

Strawberry Hill — Walpole's (Horatio) Description of the Furniture, Pictures, Curiosities, &c at Strawberry Hill (Orford's Works, Vol II)

Dresde (Galerie Royale de), ou, Recueil d'Estampes d'apres les plus célèbres de ses Tableaux, avec une Description en Ital. et Fran 2 parts in one vol folio *Dresde*, 1753-7

Dusseldorf (la Galerie Electorale de); ou, Catalogue raisonné et figuré de ses Tableaux, par N de Pigage 2 vols folio *Basle*, 1778.

Florence Gallery. — Reale Galleria di Firenze illustrata. 10 vols 8vo *Firenze*, 1817-25

Galerie de Florence (Tableaux, Statues, Bas-reliefs, et Camees de la) et du Palais Pitti, dessinés par M Wicar, avec l'Explications par M. Mongez l'aîné Original edition. 4 vols in 2, folio *Paris*, 1789-1807

French Royal Collection —Tableaux du Cabinet du Roi. Folio *Paris*, 1679.

<small>This has the descriptions by Felibien, often wanting, and contains the 38 plates. The Holy Family by Fdchuck, and Christ at Emmaus, commonly known as "la Nappe de Masson," are, especially the latter, fine impressions</small>

Couche (J), Galerie du Palais Royal, gravée d'après les Tableaux de différentes écoles qui la composent, avec une Description de chaque Tableau par De Fontenai, Morel, &c 3 vols folio *Paris*, 1786-1808

Landon (C. P), Annales du Musée et d Ecole moderne des Beaux Arts. Recueil des Gravures au trait d'après les principaux ouvrages de Peinture, Sculpture, &c du Musée , Paysages et Tableaux de Genre, gravées en taille douce; Annales du Musée, seconde collection, comprenant Partie Ancienne, les Galeries Giustiniana et Massias, et Salons de 1808-31, avec des Notices historiques et critiques 42 vols 8vo *Paris*, 1801-31.

Galerie de Lucien Bonaparte (Choix de Gravures à l'eau forte, d'après les Peintures originales et les Marbres de la) The Plates executed in Italy Folio *Londres*, 1812

Lucien Bonaparte —The Catalogue of the Originals sold at Buchanan's, Pall Mall 8vo *London*, 1815

Russian Imperial Collection —A Set of Prints, engraved after the most capital Paintings in the Collection of her Imperial Highness the Empress of Russia (Catherine II), lately in the possession of the Earl of Orford, Houghton Hall; with Plans, Elevations, &c by J and J. Boydell 2 vols. large folio. *London*, 1788

<small>A fine set of the original impressions, 1775, &c</small>

Vienna —Galerie Impériale au Belvidère à Vienne, d'après les dessins de S de Perger, avec un Texte explicatif, critique, et historique, sur chaque objet 4to *Vienne*, [1830]

Portraits.—See also "Biography"

Portraits Jane Seymour, after Holbein, by Hollar , Mary Queen of Scots, by Vertue, Charles I by Gaywood , Princess Charlotte, after C Jones, by Agar , Princess Royal (Queen Dowager of Wirtemberg), after Fischer, by Skelton Duke and Duchess of Cambridge and the young Prince George and Princess Augusta, Clement IX , after Carlo Maratti, by J Hall , Clement XIII , after J B Pirenesi by Cunego,

Margaret of Scotland, Queen of Louis XI. (Dr Dibdin's private plate), Young Napoleon, after Ender, by Stemmuller, Louis XVIII by Colnaghi, Charles X, Louis Antoine and Marie Thérèse, Duc et Duchesse d'Angoulême, in mezzotinto by Turner, Anna, Empress of Russia, after Wandelaer by Houbraken, Nicolas I and Alexandrina, Emperor and Empress of Russia, after Krugner, William I, King of the Netherlands, after Cels, Wilhelmine, his Queen, after Vanderkhoven; Prince of Orange, after Copley, by C Turner, the same, and the Princess Anna, by Sinati, on stone, Prince Frederick, and the Princesses Louise and Marianne, Frederick William III King of Prussia after Arnold, Frederick Augustus, King of Saxony, after Vogel, by Steinla; Augusta, Princess of Liegnitz, after Kruger, Charles Frederick, Duke of Brunswick and Lunenberg, George, Duke of Buckingham, and his brother Francis, 1636, after Vandyke, by M'Ardell, the Pembroke Family, after Vandyke by B. Baron, Earl of Arundel, after Vandyke; Frederick, Lord North, after Dance, by Burke, Lord Lovat by Hogarth, Countess of Clarendon, after S G Kneller, by Faber; Countess of Coventry, by M'Ardell; Duke of Rutland, after Hoppner, by C. Turner, Earl and Countess Spencer, after Hoppner, by Reynolds, Marquess of Stafford, after Owen by Meyer, Duchess of Northumberland, after Robertson, by Dean, Markham, Abp of York, after Sir Joshua Reynolds, by J. R Smith, Bp. of Carlisle, after Hoppner, by C. Turner, Bp Heber, after Phillips, by Reynolds; Sir Hans Sloane, after Kneller, by Faber, Sir Joseph Banks, after Reynolds, by Dickinson, Sir W. Scott, after Raeburn, by C Turner, Dr. Aldrich, after Kneller, by J Smith, Lawrence Sterne, after Reynolds, by Fisher, Dean Cyril Jackson, after Owen, by C Turner; Claudius Buchanan, after Slater, by Lewis; John Graham, after Marshall, by Wood, Ed Irving, after Robertson, by Meyer, John Wesley and George Whitfield, after Hone, by Grenwode · John Watson, by Williams; Arthur O'Leary, after Murphy, by Keating, Spencer Perceval, Two Ladies, after Ramsay, by M'Ardell; Miss F Murray, after H Morland, by M'Ardell, Mrs Bouverie and Mrs Cruse, after Sir J Reynolds, by Marche, T T Mayern, after Rubens, by Simm, Dr Radcliffe, after Kneller, by Vertue; Capt Thos Coram, after Hogarth, by M'Ardell, M Prior, M Isaac, after Goupy, by White, A Sharp (the Mathematician) by Vertue, Geo Holmes, after Van Bleeck, by Vertue, Sir Joseph Radcliffe, after Owen, by Heath, G Gibbons (the Sculptor), after Kneller by Smith, Henry Jenkins, John Bellingham, Mrs Hunt, Mrs. Pope; Thos Stothard, after Harlow, by Worthington, Barth Johnson, Cardinal Julius di Medicis, after Raphael, by Edelinck, Cardinal Bentivoglio, after Vandyke, by Morin, Cardinal Fleury, after Rigaud, by Drevet, Abp Fenelon, after Rigaud, by Smith, Le Masle, Prior des Roches, Castiglione, after Raphael, by Edelinck, Comte d'Harcour, after Mignard, by Masson, Ninon de l Enclos by Scriven (Dr Dibdin s private plate), Agnes, Albert Durer s Frau, by Focbers, a Lady, after Carlo Dolci, by Raphael Morghen, Ignatius Loyola and Giov Francesco, Jesuits, after Carlo Maratti, by Wagner, I nd Hesselin, by Nanteuil; Seg. Havercamp, after Mieris, by Houbraken, Const Hugens, after Vandyke, by P Ponsius, Goethe and Klopstock, on stone, by Bendixen, Ez Spanheim, after Arlaud, by Simon, Ant. Vitré, by Morin. (Coll of Prints, Vol. X.)

Portraits: Raphael and La Fornarina, after Raphael, by Raphael Morghen, Titian and his Mistress, after Titian, by Vandyke, Rembrandt, after himself, by Earlom, Bindo Altoviti, after Titian, on stone, by Hackenecker, Monna Lisa, moglie di Fr del Giocondo, after Da Vinci, on stone, by Lecomte, Vandyke, after himself, on stone, by Winterhalter, N Couston, by Dupuis, Guil Coustou, by l'Armessin, Robert de Cotte, by Drevet, Ant Coyzevox, by Audran; P Dupuis, by Ant Masson, Herb Vander Eynden, after Vandyke, by Vosterman, C de la Fosse, by Duchange, Fr. Guardon, by Duchange, Cl Halle, by l'Armessin, P de Jode, jun, after Vandyke, by De Jode, J Jouvenet, by Trouvain, N de Largillière, by Dupuis, Raph Morghen, by L Bardi, and Bardi himself, J Nogari, by Marcus; Hyac Rigaud, by Daulle, P. P Rubens, after Vandyke, by Visscher; F Verdier, by Desrochers, L da Vinci, a Head, after Vandyke, by M'Ardell, after Piazzetta, by J C Leopold, Cunne Shote, an Indian Chief, by M'Ardell, Statue of Cicero, by Worlidge; Rossini, on stone, by Constans, Paganini, on stone, by Kriechuber; Talma, after Picat, by Lignon; Madlle Mars, on stone, by Constans and by Weber; Mde Pasta, on stone, by Bellard; Antonia Bianchi, on stone, by Kriechuber; Madlle Cinti, on stone; Five Greek Chiefs, by Fridel, and Gen L Pfyffer de Wyher. (Coll of Prints, Vol XI)

Portraits after Sir Thos Lawrence of K. William IV (Q. Adelaide, after Sir W. Beechey), Duke of York, Duke of Wellington, Marquess of Clydesdale and Lady Susan Hamilton, Earl Grey, Countess Grey and her Daughters (now Ladies Durham and E Bulteel), Countess Gower and Lady E Levison Gower, Lady Dover and her son Hon Agar Ellis, Ladies Burghersh, Lady Georgiana Fane, Hon Master Lambton, Sir Robert and Lady Peel, Sir H Davy, Sir Thomas Lawrence and Miss Bloxam and Susan (his Nieces), Mrs Wolff, a study (Mrs Newdigate), the Daughters of C B Calmady, Esq Miss Macdonald, Miss Croker, a study (a Lady),—Duke of Reichstadt, Cardinal Gonsalvi, La Comtesse de Lieven;—Hamlet, Little Red Riding-Hood, and Rural Amusement

(Coll of Prints, Vol XII)

Engraving.

Evelyn's (John) Sculptura, or, the History and Art of Chalcography and Engraving on Copper; with an ample enumeration of the most renowned Masters To which is annexed, a new manner of Engraving in mezzotinto, communicated by Prince Rupert Small 8vo, with the Plate etched by Prince Rupert *London*, 1662 (and in Misc Works)

Ottley's (W Y) Inquiry into the Origin and early History of Engraving upon Copper and in Wood, with an Account of Engravers and their Works, from the invention of Chalcography to the time of Marc Antonio Raimondi 2 vols 4to *London*, 1816

Dibdin (T F) on the Origin of Engraving, &c (Ames's Typ. Antiquities, Vol. 1)

Landseer's (John) Lectures on the Art of Engraving 8vo London, 1807

Gilpin's (Wm) Essay on Prints 8vo London, 1802

Heinecken (le Baron), Idée générale d'une Collection Complète d'Estampes, avec une Dissertation sur l'Origine de la Gravure, et sur les premiers Livres d'Images. 8vo. *Leipsic*, 1771.

Heinecken (le Baron), Dictionnaire des Artistes dont nous avons des Estampes, avec une Notice détaillée de leurs ouvrages gravés 4 vols 8vo *Leipsic*, 1778-90

Strutt's (Joseph) Biographical Dictionary of Engravers, from the earliest period of the Art; a short List of their Works, with the Cyphers, Monograms, and particular Marks, used by each Master. To which is prefixed, an Essay on the Rise and Progress of Engraving, both on Copper and Wood 2 vols 4to London, 1785.

> W. Ford, of Manchester's, copy, enriched with numerous marginal MS. remarks and additions

Bartch (Adam), le Peintre Graveur. 21 vols 8vo *Vienne*, 1803-23.

Walpole's (Horatio) Catalogue of Engravers, with Life of Geo. Vertue, and List of his Works. (Orford's Works, Vol IV)

Bromley's (Hen) Catalogue of Engraved British Portraits, from Egbert to the present time; with Appendix of Foreign Portraits 4to. London, 1793.

[Vertue's (Geo.)] Description of the Works of Winceslaus Hollar; with some Account of his Life 4to. London, 1745

Daulby's (D.) Descriptive Catalogue of the Works of Rembrandt, and of his scholars, Bol, Livens, and Van Vliet, compiled from the original Etchings Large paper in 4to *Liverpool*, 1796

> W Ford, of Manchester's, copy, with his MS notes and prices

---

Sadeler (Raphael) Bavaria Sancta LX Tabulis æreis expressa Small folio, very fine impressions *Monaci*, 1615

Vænii (Ott) Historia VII Infantum Laræ [tabulis æreis expressit excud Gilbert Vænio]. Oblong 4to *Antverpæ*, 1612.

> This collection consists of forty plates, engraved by Gilbert Van Vien or Venius, after designs by his brother Otho, exhibiting the history of the seven brothers of the house of Lara, celebrated by Dr Southey in the History of the Cid, with explanations at the bottom of each plate in Latin and Spanish It is neither mentioned by Brunet nor by Strutt

Baillie's (Capt) Collection of Prints, engraved by, after Pictures and Drawings in various Collections 2 vols in one, folio. London. 1792

Flaxman's (John) Compositions from Æschylus, the Iliad and Odyssey of Homer and the Hell, Paradise, and Purgatory of Dante, engraved [at Rome] by Tho. Pirolı 4 vols oblong 4to London, 1795, 1805, and 7

Canova (the Works of Antonio), engraved in Outline by Henry Moses; with Descriptions from the Italian of the Countess Albrizzi, and a Biographical Memoir by Count Cicognara 3 vols 4to London, 1823-29

Costumes.

Malliot (J), Recherches sur les Costumes, les Mœurs, les Usages Religieux, Civils et Militaires, des anciens Peuples, ouvrage mêlé de critiques et préceptes utiles aux Peintres, Sculpteurs, Architectes, et autres Artistes ou Amateurs, revue et corrigé par P Martin 3 vols 4to *Paris*, 1809

Hope's (Thomas) Costume of the Ancients 2 vols in one, 4to. *London*, 1809

Baxter's (Thomas) Illustration of the Egyptian, Grecian, and Roman Costume, with Descriptions 4to *London*, 1810

Costumi Varie A Collection of Italian coloured Drawings illustrative of Italian Costume, and coloured Prints of Swiss Costume Folio

Austria —The Costume of the Hereditary States of the House of Austria displayed in 50 coloured Engravings, with Descriptions and an Introduction by Bertrand de Molville 4to *London*, 1804

Britain (the Costume of Great), designed, engraved, and written by W H Pyne Folio *London*, 1808

China —Original Chinese Drawings, most exquisitely finished, 100 illustrating the Costume, Trades, and Occupations of the Country, and 35 of the Flowers and Butterflies Large folio

China —Costume of China, in XLVIII coloured Engravings, by W Alexander Folio *London*, 1805

China —Costume of China, illustrated in LX coloured Engravings, by G H Mason, with Explanations 4to *London*, 1800

China —Punishments of China, in XXII coloured Engravings, with Descriptions Folio *London*, 1801

France —Costumes des Départmens de la Seine Inférieure, du Calvados, de la Manche, et de l'Oine Dessinées par Lanté, et gravées par Gatine, les Planches coloriées 4to

Germany and France —Lewis (Geo), a Series of Groups illustrating the Physiognomy, Manners, and Character of the People of Germany and France 4to *London*, 1823

Hindostan —Solvyns' (B) the Hindoos: a Picturesque Delineation of the Persons, Manners, Customs, and Religious Ceremonies of that People, accurately distinguished into their several castes, together with the Arts, Manufactures, and Curiosities natural and artificial, of Hindostan, and several islands of the Indian Seas 4 vols large folio, Plates highly finished and coloured *Paris*, 1808–12

Hindostan (the Costume of), with Descriptions by B Solvyns. Folio *London*, 1804

Russian Empire (the Costume of) illustrated by a Series of 73 Engravings, with Descriptions. 4to *London*, 1803

Russian Empire —Atkinson (J A) and James Walker's Picturesque Representation of the Manners, Customs, and Amusements of the Russians, in 100 coloured Plates, with Explanations 3 vols in one, folio *London*, 1812

Turkey (the Costume of), illustrated by a Series of Engravings, with Descriptions 4to *London*, 1802

Sculpture

Carradori (Fi) Instruzione Elementale pei gli Studiosi della Scultura Folio. *Firenze*, 1802

Architecture.

Seroux d'Agincourt, Histoire de l'Architecture (Hist de l'Art, Vol I)

Felibien (A), Principes de l'Architecture, de la Sculpture de la Peinture, et les autres Arts qui en dépendent , avec un Dictionnaire des Termes 4to *Paris*, 1697.

Palladio's (Andrea) Four Books of Architecture , wherein, after the Five Orders, those Observations that are most necessary in building Private Houses, Streets, Bridges, Piazzas, Xisti, and Temples, are treated of Published by Isaac Ware Folio. *London*, 1738

Vitruvius (M P) de Architectura ; cum Notis, Castigat , Observat , et Lexico Vitruviano B Baldi Urb à J De Laet Folio. *Amst. apud Elzev* 1649

Vitruvius (M P) de Architectura Libri X studio Societatis Bipontina Accedit anonymi Scriptoris Veteris Architecturæ Compendium ; cum Indicibus 8vo *Argent* 1808

Wottoni (Hen) Elementa Architecturæ, ex Ang. in Lat versa à S de Laet (Vitruvius)

Nicholson's (Peter) Architectural Dictionary 2 vols 4to *Lond* 1821.

Repton's (H) Remarks on Grecian and Gothic Architecture (Landscape Gardening)

Castell (Rob), the Villas of the Ancients illustrated Folio, large paper. *London*, 1728

Hawkins' (J S) History of the Origin and Establishment of Gothic Architecture ; and an Inquiry into the mode of painting upon and staining Glass, as practised in the Ecclesiastical Structures of the Middle Ages 8vo *Lond* 1813

Hall's (Sir J) Essay on the Origin, History, and Principles of Gothic Architecture Imperial 4to *London*, 1813

Murphy on Gothic Architecture. (Church of Batalha)

Essays on Gothic Architecture, from the works of Warton, Taylor, Bentham, Grose, and Milner. Royal 8vo *London*, 1808

Whittington's (G D.) Rise and Progress of Gothic Architecture in Europe illustrated (Whittington's France)

[Taylor's (J)] Specimens of Gothic Ornaments, selected from the Parish Church of Lavenham, Suffolk 4to *London*, 1796

Britton's (John) Chronological and Historical Illustrations of the Ancient Architecture of Great Britain (Arch Ant Vol V)

Hunt's (T F) Exemplars of Tudor Architecture, adapted to modern habitations , with illustrative details, selected from ancient edifices , and Observations on the Furniture of the Tudor period Royal 4to *London*, 1830

Whitaker's (T D) Origin and Progress of Domestic Architecture (Hist of Whalley)

Clarke (Charles) on early English Architecture   (Archit Ecc Londini.)

Norris's (C) Illustrations of early Flemish Architecture, from ancient edifices in Tenby   (Wales)

Campbell's (Colin) Vitruvius Britannicus, or, the British Architect; containing the Plans, Elevations, and Sections of the regular buildings, public and private, in Great Britain   With Supplement by John Woolfe and James Gandon. 4 vols folio.   *Lond.* 1715–67

Hunt's (T F) Architettura Campestre, displayed in Lodges, Gardeners' Houses, and other Buildings   Royal 4to   *London*, 1828.

Hunt's (T F) Designs for Parsonage-houses, Alms-houses, &c &c Royal 4to   *London*, 1827

Hope's (Thos) Designs for Household Furniture and Interior Decorations   Folio, large paper   *Lond* 1807

Smeaton's (John) Reports made on various occasions in the course of his employment as a Civil Engineer. [Edited by the Committee of Civil Engineers] 3 vols. 4to.   *Lond* 1812

Smeaton's (J) Miscellaneous Papers, comprising his Communications to the Royal Society, printed in the Philosophical Transactions   4to *London*, 1814.

Nicholson's (P.) Mechanical Exercises; or, the Elements and Practice of Carpentry, Joining, &c   8vo   *Lond* 1815

Nicholson's (William) Treatise on Masonry and Stone-cutting. Royal 8vo   *London*, 1827

Stevenson's (Robt) Account of the Bell Rock Lighthouse; including the details of the erection and peculiar structure of the edifice   To which is prefixed, a Historical View of the Institution and Progress of the Northern Lighthouses   4to   *Edin.* 1824

Dugdale's (Sir William) History of Imbanking and Draining of divers Fens and Marshes, both in foreign parts and in this kingdom, and of the Improvements thereby, by Charles Nalson Cole   Folio, large paper   *Lond* 1772.

Sect. III.—ECONOMIC ARTS

Agriculture and Gardening.

See also " Botany "

Stillingfleet's (B) Memoranda for a History of Husbandry   (Works, Vol II)

Evelyn's (John) Terra, a Philosophical Discourse of the Earth, its Culture and Improvement for Vegetation   (Silva, Vol. 1.)

Geoponica, sive de Re Rustica   (Classics)

Scriptores Rei Rusticæ   (Classics)

Cato (M P) de Agricultura   (Classics)

Virgilii Bucolica et Georgica   (Classics)

Dickson's (R W) Practical Agriculture, or, a Complete System of Modern Husbandry   2 vols 4to   *London*, 1807

ARTS

Loudon's (J C) Encyclopædia of Agriculture, comprising the Theory and Practice of the Management of Landed Property, and the Cultivation and Economy of Animal and Vegetable Productions 8vo London, 1825

Potts' (Th) British Farmer's Cyclopædia, or, Dictionary of Modern Husbandry 4to London, 1808

Amos's (W) Minutes of Agriculture and Planting, illustrated with Specimens of natural Grasses, &c 4to Boston, 1810

Anderson's (James) Recreations in Agriculture, Natural History, &c 6 vols 8vo London, 1799–1802.

Bligh's (Walter) English Improver improved; or, the Survey of Husbandry surveyed 4to frontispiece. London, 1653

Darwin's (Eras) Phytologia, or, the Philosophy of Agriculture and Gardening, with the Theory of Draining Mosses 4to London, 1800

Dugdale's Imbanking and Draining. (Civil Architecture)

Loudon (John) on the forming, improving, and managing of Country Residences, so as to combine architectural fitness with picturesque effect 2 vols 4to London, 1806.

Martyn's (Th.) Flora Rustica; exhibiting Figures of such Plants as are either useful or injurious in Husbandry. drawn and engraved by T Nodder 4 vols in 2, 8vo coloured Plates London, 1792–94

Price (Uvedale) on the Picturesque for improving real Landscape. (Painting)

Stillingfleet's (Benj) Observations on Grasses (Works, Vol II)

Tusser's (Thos) Five Hundred Points of Good Husbandry together with a Book of Huswifery; being a Calendar of rural and domestic Economy for every month in the year, and exhibiting a Picture of the Agriculture, Customs, and Manners of England in the XVIth Century, with Notes georgical, illustrative, and explanatory, a Glossary, and other improvements, by William Mavor Large paper, 4to. Lond 1812

Agricultural Surveys, drawn up by order of the Board of Agriculture, videl

    Bedfordshire, by Thos Batchelor 8vo London, 1808
    Berkshire, by W Mavor 8vo London, 1809
    Buckinghamshire, by St John Priest 8vo London, 1810
    Cambridgeshire, by W Gooch 8vo London, 1811
    Cheshire, by Henry Holland 8vo London, 1808
    Devonshire, by Charles Vancouver 8vo London, 1808.
    Durham, by John Bailey 8vo London, 1810
    Essex, by the Secretary to the Board 2 vols 8vo Lond 1807
    Gloucester, by Thos Rudge 8vo London, 1807
    Hampshire, including the Isle of Wight, by Charles Vancouver. 8vo London, 1810
    Hereford, by John Duncumb 8vo London, 1805
    Hertfordshire, by the Secretary 8vo London, 1804
    Huntingdonshire, by R Parkinson 8vo London 1811
    Kent, by John Boys 8vo London, 1805
    Leicester, by Wm Pitt } 8vo London, 1809
    Rutland, by R Parkinson.

Lincolnshire, by the Secretary 8vo. *London*, 1808
Middlesex, by John Middleton 8vo *London*, 1807
Norfolk, by the Secretary 8vo *London*, 1804
Norfolk, by N. Kent 8vo *London*, 1796.
Northampton, by W Pitt 8vo *London*, 1809.
Northumberland, by J Bailey and G Culley 8vo *Lond* 1805
Nottingham, by R Lowe 8vo. *London*, 1798
Oxfordshire, by the Secretary 8vo *London*, 1809.
Shropshire, by Jos Plymley. 8vo *London*, 1803
Somerset, by John Billingsley. 8vo *London*, 1798
Staffordshire, by W Pitt 8vo *London*, 1808
Suffolk, by the Secretary 8vo. *London*, 1804
Surrey, by W Stevenson 8vo *London*, 1809
Sussex, by Arth Young 8vo *London*, 1808
Wiltshire, by Thos Davies 8vo *London*, 1811
Worcester, by W Pitt 8vo *London*, 1819
Yorkshire (West Riding), by Robt Brown 8vo *London*, 1799
Yorkshire (North Riding), by John Tuke 8vo *London*, 1800
North Wales, by Walter Davies 8vo *London*, 1810
Argyle, by John Smith 8vo *London*, 1805
Berwickshire, by Robt. Keir 8vo *London*, 1809
Clydesdale, by John Naismith 8vo *London*, 1806
Galloway, by S Smith 8vo *London*, 1810.
Inverness-shire, by James Robertson. 8vo *London*, 1808.
Kincardineshire, or the Mearns, by Geo Robertson 8vo *Lond* 1810
East Lothian, by Robt Somerville 8vo *London*, 1805
Nairn and Moray, by Wm. Leslie 8vo *London*, 1811.
Ross and Cromarty, by Sir Geo Steuart Mackenzie. 8vo. *Lond* 1810
Roxburgh and Selkirk, by Robt Douglas 8vo *Lond* 1798

[Aikin's (John)] Woodland Companion, or, a Brief Description of British Trees, with some account of their uses 8vo *Lond* 1802

Boutcher's (Wm) Treatise on Forest-trees, their Culture, Transplanting, &c 4to *Edinburgh*, 1775.

Evelyn's Silva (Botany)

Pontey's (Wm) Profitable Planter. a Treatise on the Theory and Practice of Planting Forest-trees 8vo *London*, 1809.

Pontey's (W) Forest Pruner, or, Timber-Owner's Assistant a Treatise on the Training and Management of Timber-trees 8vo *London*, 1810

Steuart's (Sir Henry) Planter's Guide, or, a Practical Essay on the best Method of giving immediate effect to Wood, by the removal of large trees and underwood, interspersed with Observations on general Planting, and the improvement of real Landscape 8vo *Edin* 1820

London's (J C) Encyclopædia of Gardening, comprising the Theory and Practice of Horticulture, Floriculture, Arboriculture, and Landscape Gardening, including all the latest Improvements, a general History of Gardening in all Countries, and a statistical view of its present state, with Suggestions for its future Progress in the British Isles 8vo *London*, 1822

Browne's (Sir T.) Garden of Cyrus, or, the Quincuncial Plantations of the Ancients considered   (Works.)

Evelyn's (John) Kalendarium Hortense; or, the Gard'ner's Almanack, directing what he is to do monthly throughout the year, and what Fruits and Flowers are in prime   (Misc Works.)

Evelyn's (J.) Acetaria, a Discourse of Sallets   (Misc Works.)

Forsyth's (William) Treatise on the Culture and Management of Fruit-trees   8vo.   *London*, 1824

Horticultural Society of London's Transactions   First series.   7 vols 4to.   *London*, 1815–30

Locke (John) on the Culture of Vines and Olives, the Preservation of Fruit, &c   (Works.)

Loudon's (J. C.) Gardener's Magazine   *London*, 1826, &c.

Mawe and Abercrombie's Gardener's Calendar.   12mo   *Lond* 1829

Phillips's (Henry) History of Cultivated Vegetables, comprising their botanical, medicinal, edible, and chemical Qualities, Natural History and relation to Art, Science, and Commerce   2 vols 8vo   *London*, 1822

Repton (H.) on the Theory and Practice of Landscape Gardening.   4to.   *London*, 1805

Temple's (Sir W.) Essay on Gardening.   (Works, Vol III.)

Walpole (Horatio) on Modern Gardening   (Orford's Works, Vol. II.)

Topography of all known Vineyards; containing a Description of the Kind and Quality of their Products, and a Classification   12mo   *London*, 1824

Domestic Economy.

Dods's (M.) Cook and Housewife's Manual   12mo   *Edinb.* 1829

Pegges' Forme of Cury   (English Misc Antiq.)

Warner's Antiquitates Culinariæ   (English Misc Antiq.)

Ude's (L. E.) French Cook   8vo   *London*, 1827

Jarrin's (G. A.) Italian Confectioner, or complete Economy of Desserts, containing the Elements of the Art   8vo   *London*, 1827.

[Henderson's (Alex.)] History of Ancient and Modern Wines, &c.   Large paper   *London*, 1824.

Manufactures.

Locke (John) on the Production of Silk   (Works, Vol X.)

Kæmpfer's Account of Japanese Paper Manufactories   (History of Japan, Vol II.)

Schaffer's (Ja. Ch.) Sämtliche Papierversuche; nebst 81 Mustern, und 13 illumeverten Theils schwazen Kupfertafeln   6 vols in 2, square 12mo fine paper   *Regensberg*, 1772

<small>The 81 Mustern are so many various specimens of differently manufactured papers.</small>

Sect. IV —GYMNASTIC AND RECREATIVE ARTS

West's (Gilbert) Dissertation on the Olympick Games   (Pindar)

Strutt s (Joseph) Sports and Pastimes of the People of England   (Eng Miscellaneous Antiquities)

Ascham's (Ro) Toxophilus, the School, or Partitions of Shooting [with the Bow]   (Works)

Wood (W), The Bowman's Glory, or, Archery revived   8vo   *Lond* 1682.
    King Charles II 's copy, with his initials, &c. on the side

[Markham's (Gervase)] Cavalrice ; or, the English Horseman, containing all the Art of Horsemanship, as much as is necessary for any man to understand, whether he be Breeder, Rider, Hunter, Farrier, &c   4to   *London*, 1607

Clater's (F) Every Man his own Farrier.   8vo   *London*, 1811.

Middleton's (Chr) Short Introduction for to learne to Swimme gathered out of Master Digbie's Booke of the Art of Swimming, and translated into English   4to   Cuts   *London, by James Roberts*, 1595

Parkyns (Sir Th), The Inn-play, or Cornish-hugg Wrestler, digested in a Method which teacheth to break all Holds, and throw most Falls mathematically   4to.   *Nottingham*, 1714

[Weaver's (John)] Essay towards a History of Dancing   Small 8vo   *London*, 1712

Rei Accipitariæ Scriptores, accessit Liber de Curâ Canum   (Classics)

Barnes' (Juliana) Book ; containing the Treatises of Hawking, Hunting, Coat-armour, Fishing, and Blasing of Arms, as printed at Westminster by W de Worde, M CCCC LXXXXVI [Edited verbatim et literatim, with biographical and bibliographical Notices, by Joseph Haslewood]   Black letter.   Small folio   *London*, 1810

Beckford's (Peter) Thoughts on Hunting.   8vo.   *London*, 1796

Daniel's (W B) Rural Sports.   2 vols   4to.   large paper, coloured Plates   *London*, 1801–2

Lloyd's (L) Field Sports of the North of Europe, comprised in a personal Narrative of a Residence in Sweden and Norway.   2 vols   8vo   *London*, 1830

Osbaldiston's (W A.) British Sportsman   4to   *London*, [1792]

Oppian de Piscatu et de Venatione   (Classics)

Vliti (Jan) Venatio Novantiqua   24mo   [Lugd Bat]   *Ex off Elzev*   1645

Williamson's (Capt Th.) Oriental Field Sports, or, Wild Sports of the East   Oblong folio   Designs by S Howett, coloured Plates   *London*, 1807

Williamson's (Capt T) Oriental Field Sports   3 vols 4to   Designs by S Howett   *London*, 1808

Campbell's (James) Treatise on Modern Faulconry, with an Introduction, shewing the Practice of Faulconry in remote Times   8vo   *Dublin*, 1780

Latham's (Symon) Falconry, or, the Falcon's Lure and Cure. Both parts in one volume 4to *London*, 1633

Willughby's (Francis) Art of Fowling, ordering of Singing Birds, and of Falconry (Ornithology.)

[Davy's (Sir Humphry)] Salmonia, or, Days of Fly-fishing. In a series of conversations. With some account of the habits of Fishes belonging to the Genus Salmo 12mo *London*, 1829

Walton's (Isaac) Complete Angler, or, Contemplative Man's Recreation, being a Discourse on Fishing, &c edited by Sir J Hawkins 4to *London*, 1808.

[Christie (James)], An Inquiry into the ancient Greek Game [Πεττεια] supposed to have been invented by Palamedes, antecedent to the Siege of Troy, with reasons for believing the same to have been known from remote antiquity in China, and progressively improved into the Chinese, Indian, Persian, and European Chess also two Dissertations on the Athenian Skirophoria, and on the Mystical Meaning of the Bough and Umbrella in the Skiran Rites 4to. *London*, 1801

Mandragorias seu Historia Shahiludii, viz ejusdem Origo, Antiquitas, Ususque per totum Orientem celeberrimus Accedunt de eodem Rabbi Abi Aben-Ezræ Poema; R Bonsenior Abben-Jachiæ Oratio; Liber Deliciæ Regum per innominatum, Heb et Lat Historia Nerdiludii, hoc est dicere Trunculorum, cum quibusdam aliis Arabum, Persarum, Indorum, Chinensium, et aliarum Gentium Ludis Congessit Thomas Hyde 3 vols in 1, small 8vo. *Oxonii*, 1694

Barbier (Jo.) The famous Game of Chesse Play 18mo *Lond* 1673.

Kenny's (W S.) Practical Chess Grammar 4to *London*, 1817

Studies of Chess, containing Caissa, a Poem by Sir W Jones; a Systematic Introduction to the Game, and the whole Analysis of Chess, composed by A D. Philidor, with original critical Remarks 2 vols 8vo. *London*, 1803

[Twiss (Richard)], Chess, [a Compilation of all the Anecdotes and Quotations that could be found relative to the Game, with an Account of the Books published on it] 2 vols 8vo *London*, 1787.

Vida (M H) Scacchia Ludus; the Game of Chess, with poetical Translation by A Murphy (Murphy's Works, Vol VII)

Singer's (S W.) Researches into the History of Playing Cards, with Illustrations of the Origin and Progress of Engraving on Wood. 4to *London*, 1816

CLASS V.—HISTORY.

Sect I —HISTORICAL PROLEGOMENA.

On the Study and Use of History and Historical Atlases.

Lucianus quo modo Historia conscribenda sit (Opera)
Cassagne (l'Abbé), Discours sur l'Art Historique (Salluste.)
Bigland (John) on the Study and Use of Ancient and Modern History 8vo *London*, 1808.
Du Fresnoy's (Langlet) Short Way of Studying History. (Chronology)
Introduction to the Study of History. (Hearne's Ductor Historicus)

Le Sage [Las Cases], Atlas historique, généalogique, et chronologique, nouvelle édition, très augmentée, et continuée jusqu'à la mort de Napoléon   Large folio *Bruxelles* 1829

Geography.

*** Sacred Geography—see Biblical Antiquities

Dionysii Alexandrini Orbis Descriptio,—Pomponius Mela de Situ Orbis,—Strabonis Geographia (Classics)
D'Anville's (J. B B) Compendium of Ancient Geography, translated from the French, illustrated with Maps, and one of ancient Britain from Horsley Prolegomena and Notes by the Translator. 2 vols. 8vo. *London*, 1810
Rennel's (James) Geographical System of Herodotus examined and explained, by a Comparison with those of other ancient Authors, and with modern Geography 4to *London*, 1800
Rennel's (J) Illustrations, chiefly geographical, of the History of the Expedition of Cyrus, and the Retreat of the Ten Thousand Greeks 4to with folio volume of Maps *London*, 1816.
Kinneir's (J M.) Remarks on the Marches of Alexander, and the Retreat of the Ten Thousand Greeks. (Travels in Asia Minor)
Gell's (W) Itinerary of Greece, with a Commentary on Pausanias and Strabo. (Travels in Greece)

Jovii (P) Descriptiones quotquot extant Regionum atque Locorum Small 8vo *Basileæ*, 1571.
Maltebrun's Universal Geography, or, a Description of all parts of the World, according to the great natural divisions of the Globe accompanied with analytical, synoptical, and elementary Tables 10 vols 8vo. *Edinburgh*, 1822–32
Myers' (Thomas) New and Comprehensive System of modern Geography, mathematical, physical, political, and commercial 2 vols. 4to *London*, 1822

Martinière (B de la), Le Grand Dictionnaire géographique, historique, et critique   6 vols folio   *Paris*, 1768

The Edinburgh Gazetteer, or Geographical Dictionary, containing a Description of the various Countries, Kingdoms, &c of the World   6 vols 8vo   *London*, 1827

Tuckey's (J H) Maritime Geography and Statistics, or, a Description of the Ocean and its Coasts, maritime Commerce, Navigation, &c.   4 vols 8vo.   *London*, 1815

Atlases.

Scripture Atlas; a series of Maps to illustrate the Old and New Testament   4to   *London*, 1812.

D'Anville's Atlas and Geography of the Ancients   Folio   *Lond* 1815

Faden's (Wm) General Atlas   Folio   *London*, 1802.

Pinkerton's (John) General Atlas   Folio   *London*, 1815

The British Atlas, comprising a complete set of County Maps of England and Wales, a general Map of navigable Rivers and Canals, and Plans of Cities and Principal towns.   Folio.   *London*, 1810.

Carey's (John) English Atlas, being a set of County Maps from actual Surveys   4to   *London*, 1787

Crosthwaite's (P) Maps of the Lakes of Cumberland and Westmorland. Royal 8vo   *Keswick*, 1809

County Atlas of Scotland   Large folio   *Edin Thomson*, 1821, &c

Dalbe (Bacler), Carte Générale des Royaumes de Naples, Sicile, et Sardaigne, ainsi que des Isles de Malte et de Goze   Large folio   *Paris*, 1802

Chauchard's (Capt) General Map of the Empire of Germany, Holland, the Netherlands, Switzerland, the Grisons, Italy, Sicily, Corsica, and Sardinia   Folio   *London*, 1800

Arrowsmith's (A) Atlas to Alcedo's Dictionary of America and the West Indies, collated from all the most recent Authorities, and composed chiefly from scarce and original Documents for that Work   Folio.   *London*, 1816

Voyages and Travels, including Foreign Topography.

Introductory Works

Hall's (Bp Jos) Quo vadis? a just Censure of Travel   (Works)

Howell's (James) Instructions for Forreine Travel, shewing by what cours, and in what compasse of time, one may take an exact survey of the Kingdomes and States of Christendome, and arrive to the practicall knowledge of the languages to good purpose   Small 12mo, front by Hollar and port of Charles II by Gaywood   *Lond* 1642

Evelyn's (John) Navigation and Commerce, their Origin and Progress   (Miscel Works.)

Locke's (John) History of Navigation, from its original to this time (1702), with a Catalogue and Character of most Books of Voyages and Travels   (Works, Vol X)

Stevenson's (W) Historical Sketch of the Progress of Discovery and Navigation and Commerce, from the earliest Records to the beginning of the XIXth Century, including a Catalogue of Voyages and Travels. (Kerr's Coll of Voyages, Vol XVIII)

Richardere (B. de la), Bibliothèque Universale des Voyages 6 vols 8vo, papier vélin *Paris*, 1808

Navigation of the Ancients

Vincent's (W) Voyage of Nearchus from the Indus to the Euphrates, collected from Arrian and illustrated, containing an Account of the first Navigation attempted by Europeans in the Indian Ocean;— Periplus of the Erythrean Sea, containing an Account of the Navigations of the Ancients from the Sea of Suez to the Coast of Zanguebar, and from the Gulf of Elana, in the Red Sea, to the Island of Ceylon;— Voyage of Nearchus, the Periplus, Part III, and part of Arrian's History, Gr. and Eng 3 vols 4to. *Lond.* 1807, *and Oxford*, 1809.

Ancient Voyages. (Purchas, Vol I)

Oetheres' Voyage to the Northern Seas, translated, and the Geography of the IXth Century illustrated (Barrington's Miscellanies)

Collections of Voyages.

Ramusio (Geo Bat) Raccolta delle Navigationi e Viagi. 3 vols folio *In Venetia, appresso i Giunti*, 1559, 1583, and 1556.

Hakluyt (R), The principal Navigations, Voyages, Discoveries, and Traffiques of the English Nation, made by sea, or over land, to the remote and farthest distant quarters of the Earth, with Supplement [containing a Selection of early Voyages and Travels, published separately by Hakluyt Edited by R H Evans]. 5 vols imperial 4to, large paper. *London*, 1809–12.

Hakluytus Posthumus, or, Purchas his Pilgrimes containing a History of the World, in Sea Voyages and Land Travells, by Englishmen and others. Some left written by Mr Hakluyt at his death, more since added His also perused and perfected, all examined, abbreviated, illustrated with Notes, enlarged with Discourses, adorned with Pictures, and expressed in Mapps By Samuel Purchas With Relations of the World. 5 vols folio, sc front *London*, 1625–6

Kerr's (Robert) General History and Collection of Voyages and Travels, arranged in systematic order 18 vols 8vo *Edin* 1811–24

Thevenot (Melch), Relations de divers Voyages curieux, qui n'ont point été publiés, et qu'on a traduites ou tirées des originaux des Voyageurs de toutes les Nations. 4 vols. folio *Paris*, 1672

Shipwrecks and Disasters at Sea, or, Historical Narratives of the most noted Calamities and Providential Deliverances that have resulted from Maritime Enterprise, with a Sketch of the various Expedients for preserving the Lives of Mariners 3 vols 8vo *Edinb* 1812

Voyages round the World

Burney's (Capt James) Chronological History of the Discoveries in the South Sea from 1579–1723; including a History of the Buccaneers of America 4 vols 4to *London*, 1803

Circumnavigations of the Globe (Purchas's Pilgrimes, Vol. I.)

Dampier's (W) Collection of Voyages [round the World, viz those of Dampier, Lionel Wafer, W Funnel, Cowley, Sharp, Wood, and Roberts] 4 vols 8vo. *London*, 1729

Hawkesworth's (John) Account of the Voyages undertaken for making Discoveries in the Southern Hemisphere, and successively performed by Commodore Byron, Capt Wallis, Capt Carteret, and Capt Cook [first Voyage] accompanied by Sir Joseph Banks 3 vols *London*, 1773 —Cook's (Capt) Voyage towards the South Pole, 1772–5 in which is included Capt Furneaux's Narrative of his Proceedings during the separation of the ships 2 vols *London*, 1777 —Captains Cook, Clarke, and Gore's Voyage to the Pacific in 1776–80, to determine the position and extent of the West Side of North America, and the practicability of a Northern Passage to Europe By Captains James Cook and J. King. With an Introduction by Bp Douglas, and a Narrative of the Death of Capt Cook, by David Samuel. 3 vols *Lond* 1784–86 —8 vols 4to, and Atlas of Plates, large folio V Y

<small>All bound from uncut copies, with very early impressions of the plates.</small>

Vancouver's (Geo) Voyage of Discovery to the North Pacific Ocean, and round the World, principally to ascertain the existence of any navigable communication between the North Pacific and the Atlantic 3 vols. 4to. Atlas in folio. *London*, 1798

Sparrman's (Andrew) Voyage round the World, (Southern Africa)

Kotzebue's (Otto Von) Voyage of Discovery into the South Sea and Beering's Straits, for the purpose of exploring a North-east Passage, undertaken in the years 1815–1818. [Translated by H. E. Lloyd] 3 vols. 8vo *London*, 1821.

Beechey's (Capt F W) Narrative of a Voyage to the Pacific and Behring's Straits, to co-operate with the Polar Expeditions, in 1825–8 2 parts in one vol 4to *London*, 1831

Dillon's (P) Narrative and Successful Result of a Voyage in the South Seas, to ascertain the actual fate of La Perouse's Expedition 2 vols 8vo. *London*, 1829.

Travels in various Quarters of the World.

Mandeville's (Sir John) Travels (Manuscripts.)

Ibn Batūta's Travels [in Barbary, Egypt, Syria, Arabia, Persia, Tartary, Hindustan, and Spain, A D 1324–53], translated from the Arabic, with Notes by Samuel Lee. 4to *Lond* 1829

[Lavender (Thos)] the Travels of Foure Englishmen and a Preacher into Africa and Asia Begunne in the Yeere of Jubile 1600, and by some of them finished the yeere 1611, the others not yet returned. Black letter, 4to *Lond* 1612

<small>The names of the travellers are "Master W Biddulph (preacher to the companie of English merchants at Aleppo), Jeffrie Kirbie, Edward Abbot, John Elkin, and Jasper Tyon."</small>

Coryat's (Thomas) Crudities: Travels in France, Savoy, Italy, Rhaetia, Switzerland, &c, to which are now added, his Letters from India, and Extracts relating to him, from various Authors. 3 vols. 8vo *London*, 1776.

Herbert's (Thos) Travels into Afrique and the Greater Asia, particularly the Persian Monarchie, begunne 1626 Folio *Lond* 1634

Sandys' (George) Travels, containing an History of the Turkish Empire, of Greece, of Egypt, of the Holy Land, and of Italy Folio *London*, 1673

Valle (Pietro della), Viagi descritti da lui medesimo in 54 Lettere, da diversi luoghi all' erudito, &c M Schipiano, cioè, la Turchia, la Persia, et l'India, col Ritorno in patria 4 vols 18mo *In Venetia*, 1667.

Thevenot's (M de) Travels in the Levant, viz into Turkey, Persia, and the East Indies Folio *London*, 1687.

Thevenot (Jean), Voyage en Europe, Asie, et Afrique. 5 vols. 12mo. *Amsterdam*, 1729

Pococke's (Richard) Description of the East and some other countries [Egypt, Palestine, Syria, Mesopotamia, Greece, the Archipelago, &c] 3 vols folio. *Lond* 1763–5

Sandwich's (Earl of) Voyage performed round the Mediterranean, in 1738–39. Written by himself. To which are prefixed, Memoirs of the Author's Life by John Cooke 4to *London*, 1807

Forbes's (J.) Oriental Memoirs, including Observations on parts of Africa and South America, and a Narrative of Occurrences in four Indian Voyages (India)

Olivier's (G A) Travels in the Ottoman Empire, Egypt, and Persia, undertaken by order of the French Republic, translated 2 vols. 8vo and Atlas in 4to *London*, 1801

Wittman's (Wm) Travels in Turkey, Asia Minor, Syria, and across the Desert into Egypt, in 1799, 1800, and 1801 4to *London*, 1803.

Valentia's (Lord Viscount) Voyages and Travels in India, Ceylon, the Red Sea, Abyssinia, and Egypt, in 1802–6 3 vols 4to large paper *London*, 1809

Valentia —XXIV. Views taken in St Helena, the Cape of Good Hope, India, Ceylon, Abyssinia, and Egypt, by Henry Salt [with Descriptions in 4to] The plates highly coloured in imitation of the original drawings Large folio *London*, 1809.

Ali Bey's [Domingo Badiah y Leblich] Travels in Morocco, Tripoli, Cyprus, Egypt, Arabia, Syria, and Turkey, between the years 1803 and 1807 2 vols 4to *London*, 1816.

Abu Taleb Khan's (Mirza) Travels in Asia, Africa, and Europe, translated by Charles Stewart 2 vols 8vo *London*, 1810.

Clarke's (E D.) Travels in various countries of Europe, Asia and Africa. 6 vols. 4to. *London*, 1810–19

Galt's (John) Voyages and Travels, containing Observations on Gibraltar, Sardinia, Sicily, Malta, Serigo, and Turkey 4to *London*, 1812

Blaquiere's (E) Letters from the Mediterranean, containing a Civil and Political Account of Sicily, Tripoly, Tunis, and Malta; with Biographical Sketches, Anecdotes, and Observations illustrative of the present state of those countries 2 vols 8vo *London*, 1813

Keatinge's (Colonel) Travels in Europe and Africa, comprising a Journey through France, Spain, and Portugal, to Morocco, with a particular account of that empire. 4to *London*, 1816

Richardson's (Robert) Travels along the Mediterranean and parts adjacent, in company with the Earl of Belmore, during 1816, 17, and 18, extending to the Second Cataract of the Nile, Jerusalem, Damascus, Balbec, &c. 2 vols. 8vo. *London*, 1822

Carne's (John) Letters from the East; written during a recent tour through Turkey, Egypt, Arabia, the Holy Land, Syria, and Greece. 2 vols 8vo *London*, 1830

Carne's (J) Recollections of Travels in the East. 8vo. *London*, 1830

Hall's (Captain Basil) Fragments of Voyages and Travels, including Anecdotes of a Naval Life. 3 vols. 18mo *Edin*. 1831

Hall's (Captain B) Fragments of Voyages and Travels, Second Series. 3 vols. 18mo *Edin*. 1832

Europe.

TRAVELS IN VARIOUS PARTS

Bullet (J B), Description Etymologique des Villes, Rivières, Montagnes, Forêts, Curiosités Naturelles des Gaules, de la meilleure partie de l'Espagne et de l'Italie, de la Grande Bretagne, dont les Gaulois ont éte les premiers habitans. (Bullet, Mem sur la Langue Celtique, Vol I.)

Starke's (Mariana) Travels on the Continent, written for the use and particular information of travellers 8vo *London*, 1820

Chauchard's Geographical, Historical, and Political Description of the Empire of Germany, Holland, the Netherlands, Switzerland, Prussia, Italy, Sicily, Corsica, and Sardinia, with a Gazetteer of reference, compiled and translated from the German To which are added, Statistical Tables of all the states of Europe, translated from the German of J. C. Boetticher, with Continuation by Playfair. 4to. *London*, 1800

Hentzner (Paul) Itinerarium Germaniæ, Galliæ, Angliæ, et Italiæ. 4to *Norinbergæ, sumptibus auctoris*, 1612

Morysine's (Fynes) Itinerary, containing his Ten Yeares' Travel through the XII Dominions of Germany, Bohmerland, Sweitzerland, Netherland, Denmark, Poland, Italy, Turky, France, England, Scotland, and Ireland Folio *London*, 1617

> The author was secretary to Sir C Blunt, afterwards Lord Mountjoy, and his account of Ireland, which is in this copy complete, contains the result of his official knowledge

Reresby's (Sir John) Travels, exhibiting a View of the Governments and Society in the principal states of Europe during the time of Oliver Cromwell (Reresby's Memoirs)

Brown's (Ed) Travels in divers parts of Europe, viz Hungary, Macedonia, Thessaly, a great part of Germany, &c Folio *Lond* 1687

Brydges' (Sir E) Letters from the Continent 2 vols 8vo. *Lee Priory*, 1821

Batty's (Robert) Select Views of the principal Cities of Europe, viz. Oporto, Gibraltar, Lisbon, Edinburgh, Amsterdam, Rotterdam, Brussels, and Antwerp India proofs 4to *London*, 1830-31.

Granville's (A B) St Petersburgh, a Journal of Travels to and from that capital, through Flanders, the Rhenish Provinces, Prussia, Russia, Poland, Silesia, Saxony, the Federated States of Germany, and France 2 vols 8vo *London*, 1829

Tennant's (Charles) Tour through parts of the Netherlands, Holland, Germany, Switzerland, Savoy, and France, in 1821-2, with an Appendix of fac-simile copies of eight Letters in the handwriting of Napoleon Bonaparte to Josephine 2 vols 8vo *London*, 1824

Cogan (Thos), the Rhine, or, a Journey from Utrecht to Frankfort on the borders of the Rhine, and passage down the river from Mentz to Bonn 2 vols. 8vo. *London*, 1794.

Batty's (Robt) Scenery of the Rhine, Belgium, and Holland, from drawings made in 1824 4to. *London*, 1826

Schrieber (A), Description générale et particulière des Pays du Rhin, depuis Schafhause jusqu'en Hollande, et des Contrées adjacentes ; traduite par M l'Abbé Henry. 40 Plates, oblong 4to *Heidelberg*,

Brockedon's (W) New Illustrated Road-Book of the Route from London to Naples, from Drawings by Prout, Stanfield, and Brockedon, engraved by W and E Finden. Roy 8vo India proofs *Lond* 1831

Moore's (John) View of the Society and Manners in France, Switzerland, and Germany, with Anecdotes of some eminent Persons 2 vols 8vo *London*, 1783

NORTHERN COUNTRIES OF EUROPE

Barrington (Daines) on the Possibility of reaching the North Pole (Miscellanies)

Pennant's (Thomas) Description of the Arctic World (Arctic Zoology, Vol 1)

Scoresby's (Wm) Account of the Arctic Regions, with a History and Description of the Northern Whale Fishery 2 vols 8vo *Edinb* 1820

Troil's (Uno von) Letters on the Civil, Literary, Ecclesiastical, and Natural History of Iceland, from Observations made during the Voyage undertaken by Sir Joseph Banks in 1772, assisted by Drs. Solander, Lind, and Von Troil To which are added, the Letters of Dr Ihre and Dr Bach on the Edda and the Elephantiasis of Iceland 8vo *Lond* 1780

Prefixed is a catalogue of writers on Iceland

Hooker's (W J) Journal of a Tour in Iceland, in 1809 8vo *London*, 1811

Mackenzie's (Sir G S) Travels in Iceland in 1810 4to *London*, 1811

Henderson's (Eb) Iceland, or, a Journal of a Residence in that island during 1814 and 15, containing Observations on its Natural Phenomena, History, Literature, and Antiquities, and on the Religion of the Inhabitants 2 vols 8vo *Edinb* 1818

Skioldebrand's (A F) Picturesque Journey to the North Cape, translated from the French. 8vo *London*, 1813

[Klingsted (Timothee-Merzahn)], Mémoire sur les Samojedis et les Lappons 8vo *Copenhague*, 1766

Linnœus —Lachesis Lapponica, or, a Tour in Lapland, now first published from the original MS Journal [in Swedish] of the celebrated Linnœus, by J E Smith. 2 vols 8vo *London*, 1811

Scheffer's (John) History of Lapland; containing a Geographical Description and a Natural History of that country, with an Account of the Inhabitants, &c translated from the Latin. To which are added,
The Travels of the King of Sweden's Mathematicians into Lapland;
The History of Livonia, and the Wars there, also,
A Journey into Lapland, Finland, &c by Olof Rudbeck. 8vo *London*, 1784

Acerbi's (Jos) Travels through Sweden, Finland, and Lapland, to the North Cape, in 1798-9 2 vols 4to *London*, 1802

Brooke's (Arthur de Capell) Winter in Lapland and Sweden; with Observations relative to Finmark and its Inhabitants Plates from drawings made by Sir Thos Dyke Acland 4to *Lond* 1827.

Buch's (L. von) Travels through Norway and Lapland, translated from the original German by John Black, with Notes and Illustrations, and some Account of the Author, by Professor R. Jameson. 4to *London*, 1813.

Heber's (Bp Reg) Journal of a Tour in Norway, Sweden, Hungary, and Germany. (Life, Vol. I)

Lamotte (A), Voyage dans le Nord de l'Europe, principalement en Norvège et en Suède, dans 1807 4to *London*, 1813

Lloyd's (L.) Narrative of a Residence in Sweden and Norway in 1827 and 8. (Northern Field Sports)

Batty's (Robt) Danish Scenery, from drawings made in 1828. 4to. *London*, 1829

Boisgelin's (Louis de) Travels through Denmark and Sweden. 2 vols in one, 4to *London*, 1810

Macdonald's (James) Travels through Denmark and part of Sweden, in 1809 2 vols 12mo. *London*, 1809

Thomson's (T) Travels in Sweden, during the autumn of 1812 4to *London*, 1813.

Clarke's (E. D.) Travels in Russia and in Scandinavia. (Travels, Vols I. and VI)

Coxes (W) Travels in Poland, Russia, Sweden, and Denmark, interspersed with Historical Relations and Political Inquiries 3 vols. 4to. *London*, 1784-90.

Porter's (Sir R K.) Travelling Sketches in Russia and Sweden, in 1805-8. 2 vols 4to *London*, 1808

Jovii (Pauli) Moschovia, in quâ Situs Regionis Antiquis incognitus, Religio Gentis, Mores, &c referuntur. (Descriptiones.)

Macartney's (Sir Geo) Account of Russia in 1767 (Life)

Muller (D Chret), Tableau de Pétersbourg; ou, Lettres sur la Russie, écrites en 1810, 11, et 12, et traduites de l'Allemand par C Leger 8vo. *Paris, (Mayence)*, 1814

Pallas (P S), Voyages en differentes provinces de l'empire de Russie, et dans l'Asie Septentrionale, traduits par Gausbier de la Peyronie 6 vols and Plates in 4to. *Paris*, 1788-93.

Burnet's (Geo) View of the present State of Poland 12mo *London*, 1807.

TRAVELS.

GERMANY

Hodgskin's (Thos) Travels in the North of Germany, describing the present state of the Social and Political Institutions, the Agriculture Manufactures, Commerce, Education, Arts, and Manners, particularly in the kingdom of Hanover   2 vols 8vo. *Edinburgh*, 1820

Russell's (John) Tour in Germany, and some of the Southern Provinces of the Austrian Empire in 1820-22 2 vols small 8vo. *Edinburgh*, 1825.

Notes and Reflections during a Ramble in Germany   8vo   *Lond* 1827

Bright's (Rich) Travels from Vienna through Lower Hungary, with Observations on the state of Vienna during the Congress in 1814   4to   *Edinb* 1818

Batty's (Robert) German Scenery, from Drawings made in 1820   4to Proofs   *London*, 1821

Batty's (R) Hanoverian and Saxon Scenery   4to Proofs   *Lond* 1829

Views in Germany, coloured   (Coll of Prints, Vol XVIII)

Views in Prague, Berlin, and Toplitz   Oblong 4to   ———

Views in Dresden, Heidelberg, and Potsdam   Oblong 4to

SWITZERLAND

Coxe's (W) Travels in Switzerland and the Country of the Grisons, in a series of letters to W. Melmoth, Esq 2 vols 4to. *London*, 1794

Latrobe's (Charles Joseph) Alpenstock ; or, Sketches of Swiss Scenery and Manners, 1825-6   8vo. *London*, 1829

Simond's (L.) Switzerland ; or, a Journal of a Tour and Residence in that country in 1817-19 ; followed by an Historical Sketch of the Manners and Customs of ancient and modern Helvetia. 2 vols 8vo   *London*, 1823

[Stapfer], Voyage Pittoresque de l'Oberland, ou, Description des Vues prises dans l Oberland.   4to.   Plates coloured   *Paris*, 1812

Zurlauben et La Borde, Tableaux Topographiques, Pittoresques, Physiques, Historiques, Moraux, Politiques, et Littéraires, de la Suisse, avec la Table analytique et raisonnée des Tableaux, par M Quetant   5 vols folio   *Paris*, 1780-88

Cockburn s (Major) Swiss Scenery   4to Proofs. *London*, 1820

Roscoe's (Thos.) Tourist in Switzerland and Italy   (Landscape Annual, 1830.)

ITALY

Addison's (Joseph) Remarks on several parts of Italy in 1701-3   (Works, 4to and 8vo Vol II)

Batty's (Miss E F) Italian Scenery, from drawings made in 1817.   4to Proofs   *London*, 1817

Barthelemy's (Abbe) Travels in Italy, in a series of letters to the Comte Caylus, with several unpublished pieces by the Abbé Winkelman, Father Jacquier, the Abbe Zarillo, &c. Translated from the French   8vo   *London*, 1802

Bourrit's (M) Journey to the Glaciers in the Duchy of Savoy translated by C and F Davy   *Norwich*, 1775

HISTORY.

Beaumont's (Albanis) Travels through the Rhœtian Alps, in 1782, from Italy to Germany through the Tyrol   Large folio.   *London*, 1792.

Beaumont's (A) Travels through the Maritime Alps, from Italy to Lyons across the Col de Tende, by the way of Nice, Provence, Languedoc &c   Folio   *London*, 1795

Beaumont s (A) Travels from France to Italy through the Leopontine Alps, or, an Itinerary of the road from Lyons to Turin, by the way of the Pays de Vaud, the Vallois, and across the Mont Great St Bernard, Simplon, and St Gothard, with topographical and historical descriptions, including observations on the natural history and elevation of that part of the Alps   To which are added, remarks on the course of the Rhone, from its source to the Mediterranean Sea   Folio   *London*, 1800

> The above are unique copies, as they contain the plates, coloured on the outline, from the actual scenes they represent, as patterns for those afterwards done on the aquatint.

Blunt's (John James) Vestiges of ancient Manners and Customs discoverable in modern Italy and Sicily.   8vo   *Lond* 1823

Eustace's (J. C.) Tour through Italy, exhibiting a view of its Scenery, its Antiquities, and its Monuments, particularly as they are objects of classical interest and elucidation, with an account of the present state of its Cities and Towns, and occasional observations on the recent spoliations of the French   2 vols 4to   *London*, 1813

Forsyth's (Jas) Remarks on Antiquities, Arts, and Letters, during a Tour in Italy, in 1802 and 3.   2 vols in one, 8vo.   *London*, 1824.

Hakewell's (James) Picturesque Tour through Italy, from drawings made in 1816-17   4to   Proofs   *London*, 1820

Hoare's (Sir R C) Classical Tour in Italy and Sicily   4to   *London*, 1819

Hoare's (Sir R C) Hints to Travellers in Italy   12mo.   *London*, 1815.

Kotzebue's (A von) Travels through Italy, in 1804-5   4 vols 12mo.   *London*, 1806.

Labat, Voyage en Italie   (Spain)

Montaigne (Mich de), Journal du Voyageur en Italie par la Suisse et l'Allemagne, en 1580 et 81 ; avec des Notes par M de Querlon 4to. large paper.   *Rome [Paris]*, 1774.

Moore's (John) View of the Society and Manners in Italy, with Anecdotes of some eminent Characters.   2 vols 8vo.   *London*, 1783

Petit-Radel (P), Voyage Historique, Chorographique, et Philosophique dans l'Italie, en 1811 et 12   3 vols 8vo   *Paris*, 1815.

Ritchie's (Leitch) Travelling Sketches in the North of Italy, the Tyrol, and on the Rhine   (Picturesque Annual for 1832)

Roscoe's (Thos) Tourist in Italy   (Landscape Annual for 1831 and 2)

[Rose's (W S)] Letters from the North of Italy   2 vols in one, 8vo   *London*, 1819

Sketches descriptive of Italy in 1816 and 17, with a brief Account of Travels in various parts of Switzerland   4 vols. small 8vo   *London*, 1820.

Smollett's (Tobias) Travels through France and Italy, with a particular Description of the Town, Territory, and Climate of Nice   (Works, Vol V)

Williams' (H W) Travels in Italy, Greece, and the Ionian Islands, in a series of letters, descriptive of Manners, Scenery, and Fine Arts. 2 vols 8vo *Edin.* 1820

Bosio (Ant), Roma Sotteranea, opera postuma, compita, disposta, ed accresciuta del Giov. Severani nella quale si tratta de' sacri Cimeterii di Roma, dei Cubiculi, Oratorii, Imagini, Ieroglifici, Iscrittioni, ed Epitaffi, che vi sono, nuovamente reconosciuta dal Ottavio Pico Large folio *Roma,* 1632

Burton's (Ed) Description of the Antiquities and other Curiosities of Rome. 8vo. *Oxford,* 1821.

Ferrerio (Pietro), Palazzi di Roma di più celebri Architetti 2 vols in one, oblong folio ———

Fea (M Charles), Description de Rome, traduite de l'Italien, ornée des Vues, et publiee par Ange Bonelli 2 vols 12mo. *Rome,* 1825

[Merigot's (J)] Select Collection of Views in Rome and its vicinity, from drawings made in 1791, with Descriptions Folio Plates, highly coloured as drawings *London,* 1797

Nardini (Famiano), Roma Antica, riscontrata, ed accresciuta delle ultime scoperte, con Note et Osservazioni critico-antiquarie di Antonio Nibby ; e con Disegni di Antonio di Romanis 4 vols 8vo *Roma,* 1818–20

Nibby (Antonio), Viaggio Antiquario ne' contorni di Roma. 2 vols 8vo *Roma,* 1819

Rome in the XIXth Century ; containing a complete Account of the Ruins of the ancient City, the Remains of the Middle Ages, and the Monuments of modern times 3 vols 12mo *London,* 1823

Rossini (Luigi), Vedute di Roma Oblong folio *Roma,* 1823
This consists of 101 plates, but without title or descriptions

[Knight's (E C)] Description of Latium ; or, the Campagna di Roma *London,* 1805

Kelsall's (Charles) Classical Excursion from Rome to Arpino 8vo *Geneva,* 1820

[Maffei (Scipione)], Verona illustrata 4 vols in one, folio *Verona,* 1732

Views in Rome, Florence, and Bologna. Oblong 4to.

Views in Venice, Milan, and Pisa. Oblong 4to

Vedute di Firenze, de' Laghi di Como e Maggiore, e dell' Isole Borromeo (Coll of Prints, Vol. XVIII)

Le Fabriche più cospicue di Venezia, mesurate, illustrate, ed intagliate dai Membri della Veneta Reale Academia di Belle Arti 2 vols folio *Venezia,* 1815

Artaria (Fr), Il Duomo di Milano, ossia Descrizione storico-critica di questa insigne Tempio, e degli Oggetti d'Arte che le adornano LXV plates 4to. large paper *Milano,* 1823

Saint Non (Abbé), Voyage Pittoresque, ou Description des Royaumes de Naples et de Sicile 5 vols folio *Paris,* 1781–6

Balsamo's (the Abbate) View of the present State of Sicily, its rural Economy, Population, and Produce (from a Tour in 1808), with Notes by Thomas Vaughan 4to *London,* 1811

Smith's (W H) Memoir, descriptive of the Resources, Inhabitants, and Hydrography of Sicily and its Islands, interspersed with antiquarian and other notices   4to   *London*, 1824

Swinburne's (Hen) Travels in the Two Sicilies, in 1777–80. 4 vols 8vo   *London*, 1790

Light's (Capt.) Sicilian Scenery   4to proofs   *London*, 1821.

Veduta di Napoli da Vito; a Collection of Italian coloured Drawings   folio

De Non's (M) Travels in Sicily and Malta   8vo   *London*, 1789

Brydone's (M) Tour through Sicily and Malta   8vo.   *Lond* 1806

Goupy's Views of Malta   (Coll. of Prints, Vol XVII)

FRANCE

[Borde (A de la)], Guettarde, &c , Description générale et particulière de la France   12 vols in six, folio   Sir M M Sykes's copy.   *Paris*, 1781–96

Batty's (Robt) French Scenery, from drawings made in 1819   4to.   Proofs   *London*, 1822.

Whittington's (G D) Historical Survey of the Ecclesiastical Antiquities of France [with Preface by the Earl of Aberdeen]. 4to.   *London*, 1809

Young's (Arthur) Travels in France in 1787–9, with a view of ascertaining the Cultivation, Wealth, Resources, and National Prosperity of that kingdom   2 vols 4to   *London*, 1794.

Kotzebue's (A von) Travels to Paris, 1804   3 vols. 12mo   *Lond* 1806

Scott's (John) Visit to Paris, being a review of the moral, political, intellectual, and social condition of the French Capital   8vo.   *London*, 1815.

Promenades aux Cimetières de Paris, aux Sépultures royales de S. Denis, et aux Catacombes   8vo   *Paris*, 1818.

Stothard's (Charles) Letters written during a Tour through Normandy, Britanny, and other parts of France, in 1818 ; including local and historical Descriptions   4to   *London*, 1820

Cotman's (J S) Architectural Antiquities of Normandy, accompanied with descriptive Notices by Dawson Turner. 2 vols. in one, folio.   *London*, 1822

Ducarel's (A. C) Anglo-Norman Antiquities considered, in a Tour through Normandy   Folio   *London*, 1767.

Turner's (Dawson) Account of a Tour in Normandy, undertaken chiefly to investigate the architectural antiquities of the duchy   2 vols in one, royal 8vo   *London*, 1820

Beaumont's (Albanis) Select Views in the South of France, with topographical and historical Descriptions   Folio   *London*, 1794.
   A similarly unique copy to those of Beaumont's other works   See page 138

Hughes' (John) Views in the South of France, chiefly on the Rhone, with Descriptions   Large paper, royal 8vo   *London*, 1825

Hughes' (J) Itinerary of the South of France   4to   *London*, 1825

TRAVELS.

Wery's Views of Lyons and its Environs, and of Rouen Cathedral, by Knaus   (Coll of Prints, Vol XVIII)

Views in the Pyrenees, with Descriptions [by Miss Young]. 4to proofs   London, 1832

THE NETHERLANDS

Carr's (Sir John) Tour through Holland in 1806   4to   Lond 1807

Views in the Netherlands. (Views in Dresden, &c)

SPAIN AND PORTUGAL

Bradford's (William) Sketches of the Country, Character, and Costume of Portugal and Spain, made during the campaign, and on the route of the British Army, in 1808–9, with appropriate Descriptions, and Supplement containing Sketches of the Military Costume   Folio, large paper   London, 1809–10.

[Porter's (Sir R K.)] Letters from Spain and Portugal, written during the march of the British troops under Sir John Moore   8vo.   London, 1809.

Recollections of the Peninsula, by the Author of the Sketches of India   8vo   London, 1825

Southey's (Robert) Letters, written during a Journey and Residence in Spain and Portugal. 2 vols 12mo   London, 1808

Twiss's (Richard) Travels through Portugal and Spain in 1772–3, with Summaries of the History, and some Account of the Literature of these countries   4to   London, 1775

Borde (Alex de la), Voyage pittoresque et historique de l'Espagne   4 vols in two   Folio   Paris, 1807–20

Borde's (A de la) View of Spain, comprising a descriptive Itinerary of each province, and a general Statistical Account of the country, translated from the French, with Atlas. 6 vols. 8vo   London, 1809.

Bourgoing (J Fr.), Tableau de l'Espagne Moderne   3 vols 8vo and Atlas in 4to   London, 1808

Jacob's (Will) Travels in the South of Spain in 1809–10   4to Plates coloured   London, 1811

Inglis's (Henry D) Spain in 1830   2 vols 8vo   London, 1831

Labat (le Père), Voyages en Espagne et en Italie   8 vols. 12mo   Paris, 1730

Rehfues (J F), l'Espagne en 1808, ou, Recherches sur l'état de l'Administration, des Sciences, des Lettres, &c , faites dans un Voyage à Madrid en 1808   Suivis d'un Fragment Historique, intitulé les Espagnols du XIV siècle   2 vols 8vo   Paris, 1811

Swinburne's (Henry) Travels through Spain in 1775–6, in which several Monuments of Roman and Moorish Architecture are illustrated   2 vols 8vo   London, 1787

A Year in Spain, by a young American   2 vols 8vo   London, 1831

Chatelet's (Duc de) Travels in Portugal, with Notes by J F Bourgoing, translated by J J Stockdale   2 vols 8vo   London, 1809

Kinsey's (William) Portugal, illustrated in a series of letters   Royal 8vo London, 1829

Murphy's (James) General View of the state of Portugal, including a topographical description thereof 4to *London*, 1798

Murphy's (J) Travels in Portugal in 1789–90 4to *London*, 1795

Baillie's (Marianne) Lisbon in the years 1821, 22, and 23 2 vols small 8vo *London*, 1824

Murphy's (James) Plans, Views, and Elevations of the Church of Batalha in the province of Estremadura, in Portugal, and the History and Description by Fr Luis de Sousa, with Remarks Large folio. *London*, 1795

TURKEY.

Busbequius's (A G) Travels in Turkey, translated Small 8vo *Lond* 1744

Clarke's (E D) Travels in Turkey (Travels, Vol I)

Eton's (W) Survey of the Turkish Empire, in which are considered its Government, State of the Provinces, Causes of its Decline, and of the British Commerce with that country 8vo. *London*, 1809

Mayer's (Luighi) Views in the Ottoman Empire, chiefly in Caramania; with some curious selections from the islands of Rhodes and Cyprus, and the cities of Corinth, Carthage, and Tripoli, with incidental Illustrations of the Manners and Customs of the nations Folio, large paper. *London*, 1803.

Nicholay's (Nicholas) Navigations, Peregrinations, and Voyages, made into Turkie; with LX Figures, set furth, as wel men as women, according to the diversitie of nations, &c [by Cæsar Titian]; translated out of the French by T Washington, the younger 4to Black letter. *London, by Thomas Dawson*, 1585

Walpole's (Robert) Memoirs relating to European and Asiatic Turkey, edited from the MS Journals of Morritt, Sibthorp, Hunt, Raike, Squire, Davison, Hume, Light, Hawkins, Wilkins, Whittington, Browne, Leake, E D Clarke, &c 2 vols 4to *London*, 1817–20

Melling (M), Voyage pittoresque de Constantinople et des Rives de Bosphore 2 vols large folio *Paris*, 1819

Macfarlane's (Charles) Constantinople in 1828, a residence of sixteen months in the Turkish Capital and Provinces, with an Appendix of Observations to 1829 2 vols 8vo. *London*, 1830

Frankland's (C C) Travels to and from Constantinople in 1827–8 2 vols 8vo *London*, 1829

Macmichael's (W) Journey from Moscow to Constantinople in 1817–18 4to *London*, 1819

Walsh's (R) Narrative of a Journey from Constantinople to England. 8vo *London*, 1829

GREECE

Douglas's (T S N) Essay on certain points of Resemblance between the ancient and modern Greeks 8vo. *London*, 1813

Choisseul-Gouffier (M de), Voyage pittoresque de la Grèce 2 vols in three, folio *Paris*, 1782–1809

Clarke's (E D) Travels in Greece (Travels, Vol II to IV)

Dodwell's (Edward) Views in Greece Large folio, the Plates highly coloured after the original drawings *London*, 1821

Dodwell's (E) Classical and Topographical Tour through Greece 2 vols. 4to and Plates in folio *London* 1819

Gell's (W) Itinerary of Greece; with a Commentary on Pausanias and Strabo, and an Account of the Monuments of Antiquity at present existing in that country. Compiled in 1801-6 4to *Lond.* 1810

Guys' (M de) Journal through Greece, in a series of letters, translated. 3 vols 12mo *London*, 1772.

Pouqueville (F C H L), Voyage dans la Grèce, comprenant la Description ancienne et moderne de l'Epire, de l'Illyrie, &c , avec des Considérations sur l'Archéologie, la Numismatique, les Mœurs, les Arts, l'Industrie, et le Commerce des Inhabitans de ces Provinces 5 vols 8vo *Paris*, 1820-21

Pouqueville's (F C. H L) Travels in Greece, translated by Anne Plumtre. 4to *London*, 1813.

Spon (Jacob) et Geo Wheeler, Voyage de Dalmatie, de Grèce, et du Levant, fait aux années 1675-6 [avec une Liste des Cabinets et Palais à Rome; un petit Dictionnaire du Grec vulgaire, et des Inscriptions antiques qui sont citées] 2 vols 8vo *Amst* 1679

Wheeler's (G) Journey into Greece, in company with Dr Spon. Folio *London*, 1682.

Bryant's (Jacob) Observations upon the Vindication of Homer, and of the ancient Poets and Historians who have recorded the Siege and Fall of Troy, written by J. B S Morritt 4to *Eton*, 1799

Chandler's (Rich) History of Ilium, or Troy. 4to *London*, 1802

Chevalier's (M) Description of the Plain of Troy, translated from the original, accompanied with Notes, by Andrew Dalzel 4to *Lond* 1791

Gell's (W.) Topography of Troy and its vicinity, illustrated and explained by XLV coloured Drawings. and Descriptions Folio *London*, 1804.

Rennel's (James) Observations on the Topography of the Plain of Troy, and on the principal objects within and around it, described or alluded to in the Iliad 4to. *London*, 1814

Gell's (Wm) Geography and Antiquities of Ithaca. 4to. *Lond* 1807.

Hobhouse's (J C) Journey through Albania, and other provinces of Turkey in Europe and Asia, to Constantinople 4to. *Lond.* 1813.

Holland's (Henry) Travels in the Ionian Isles, Albania, Thessaly, Macedonia, &c. in 1812 and 13 4to *London*, 1815.

Lavallée (J), Voyage pittoresque et historique de l'Istrie et de la Dalmatie, redigé d'après l'Itinéraire de L F Casas Folio *Par* 1802

Leake's (W M) Travels in the Morea 3 vols 8vo. *London*, 1830

Macarius (Travels of), Patriarch of Antioch, written in Arabic by his attendant, Archdeacon Paul of Aleppo Part I, Anatolia, Romelia, and Moldavia Translated by F C Belfour 4to *London*, 1829

Stanhope's (Jo Spencer) Topography illustrative of the Battle of Platæa 8vo *London*, 1817

Stanhope's (J S) Olympia, or, the Topography illustrative of the actual state of the Plain of Olympia, and of the Ruins of the City of Elis. Folio, Plates *London*, 1824.

144   HISTORY.

Vaudoncourt's (Guil. de) Memoirs of the Ionian Islands, considered in a commercial, political, and military view, including a Character of Ali Pacha. Translated from the inedited MS by William Walton. 8vo   London, 1816

Forbin (M. le Comte de), Voyage dans le Levant. Plates in aquatinta and lithography. Large folio   Paris, 1819

Tournefort's (M.) Voyage into the Levant; containing the ancient and modern state of the Islands of the Archipelago, as also of Constantinople the Coasts of the Black Sea, &c. with the Author's Life by M. Began, and his Eulogium by Fontenelle. Translated by J. Ozell   2 vols. 4to   London, 1718

Turner's (W.) Travels in the Levant. 3 vols. 8vo   London, 1820

Africa

Murray's (Hugh) Historical Account of Discoveries and Travels in Africa, from the earliest ages to the present time, including the substance of the late Dr. Leyden's work on that subject. 2 vols. 8vo   Edinburgh, 1818.

Leonis Africani (Jo.) de totius Africæ Descriptione Libri IX; quibus non solùm regionum, &c. complexus est, sed regum familias, bellorum causas et eventus, resque in eâ memorabiles, descripsit: recens in Latinam linguam conversi J. Floriano interprete. Small 8vo   Antverpiæ, ap. Jo. Latium, 1556
    Stephen Baluzius's copy, with his autograph

CENTRAL, NORTH, WEST, AND SOUTH AFRICA

Caillié's (Réné) Travels through Central Africa to Timbuctoo, and across the Great Desert to Morocco, performed in 1824-8. 2 vols. 8vo. London, 1830.

Denham's (Major Dixon) and Capt. Hugh Clapperton's Narrative of Travels and Discoveries in Northern and Central Africa in the years 1822-4. 4to   London, 1826

Lyon's (Capt. G. F.) Narrative of Travels in Northern Africa in the years 1818-20; accompanied by Geographical Notices of Soudan, and of the Course of the Niger. 4to   London, 1821

Beechey's (F. W. and H. W.) Proceedings of the Expedition to explore the Northern Coast of Africa, from Tripoly eastward, in 1821-2, comprehending an Account of the Greater Syrtis and Cyrenaica, and the ancient cities composing the Pentapolis. 4to   London, 1828

Pananti's (Sig.) Narrative of a Residence in Algiers, comprising an historical account of the Regency, biographical sketches of the Dey and his Ministers, and Observations on the Relations of the Barbary States with the Christian Powers; with Notes and Illustrations by E. Blaquiere. 4to   London, 1830

Jackson's (James Grey) Account of the Empire of Morocco and the districts of Susa and of Timbuctoo, the great emporium of Central Africa. 4to   London, 1809

Shaw's (Thomas) Travels, or Observations relative to several parts of Barbary and the Levant; with Supplement. Folio   Oxford, 1738

Narrative of a Ten Years' Residence at Tripoli, from the original Correspondence of Richard Tully, British Consul there. 4to. *London*, 1816

Adams's (Robert) Narrative of his Shipwreck on the Western Coast of Africa in 1810, and residence for several months at Timbuctoo 4to *London*, 1816.

Bowditch's (T E) Mission from Cape Coast Castle to Ashantee ; with a Statistical Account of that kingdom, and Geographical Notices of other parts 4to coloured Plates *London*, 1819

Clapperton's (Hugh) Journal of a Second Expedition into the Interior of Africa, from the Bight of Benin to Soccatoo. To which is added, the Journal of Richard Lander from Kano to the Sea-coast. 4to *London*, 1829.

Dupuis' (Jos.) Journal of a Residence in Ashantee, comprising Notes and Researches relative to the Gold Coast and the Interior of Western Africa, chiefly collected from Arabic MSS. and information communicated by the Moslems of Guinea To which is prefixed an Account of the origin and causes of the present War. 4to. *London*, 1824.

Lander's (Richard) Records of Captain Clapperton's last Expedition to Africa; with the subsequent Adventures of the Author 2 vols 8vo *London*, 1830

Landers' (R and J.) Journal of an Expedition to explore the Course of the Niger, with a Narrative of a Voyage down that river to its termination 3 vols 18mo *London*, 1832.

Norris's (Robt.) Journey to Abomey, in the kingdom of Dahomy 8vo. *London*, 1789

Park's (Mungo) Travels in the Interior Districts of Africa, performed in 1795, 6, and 7 ; with an Account of a subsequent Mission to that country in 1805 To which is added, an Account of the Life of Mr Park, and Geographical Illustrations of Africa, by Major Rennel 2 vols 4to *London*, 1816.

Riley's (James) Loss of the American brig Commerce, wrecked on the Western Coast of Africa in 1815, with an Account of Tombuctoo, and the hitherto undiscovered city of Wassanah 4to. *London*, 1817

Smith's (W) Voyage to Guinea in 1726, describing the manners and customs of the inhabitants, the soil, climate, &c 8vo *London*, 1744.

Tuckey's (J H.) Narrative of an Expedition to explore the river Zaire, usually called the Congo, in 1816. To which is added, the Journal of Professor Smith, containing the Natural History of the kingdom of Congo 4to *London* 1818

Barrow's (John) Travels in Africa, in which are described the character and the condition of the Dutch colonists of the Cape of Good Hope, and of the several tribes of natives beyond its limits 2 vols 4to. Plates by Daniel *London*, 1806.

Barrow's (J.) Account of a Journey made, in the years 1801-2, to the residence of the Chief of the Booshuana Nation, by Truter, Somerville, &c. (Cochin China)

Burchell's (W J) Travels in the Interior of Southern Africa   2 vols
4to   *London*, 1822

Campbell's (John) Travels in South Africa, undertaken at the request of
the London Missionary Society   8vo   *London*, 1815

Campbell's (J) Second Journey in South Africa.   2 vols in one, 8vo.
London, 1822

Daniel's (Sam.) African Scenery and Animals   Oblong folio, the Plates
coloured after the original drawings   *London*, 1805.

Lichentstein's (Hen) Travels in Southern Africa in 1803, translated from
the German by Anne Plumptre   2 vols. 4to   *London*, 1812.

Sparrman's (Andrew) Voyage to the Cape of Good Hope, and in the
Country of the Hottentots and Caffres   2 vols 4to   *Lond* 1785.

Vaillant (Fr Le), Voyage dans l'Intérieur de l'Afrique, par le Cap de
Bonne Espérance, dans 1780 et 82   2 vols in one, 4to   *Paris*, 1790.

Vaillant (Fr Le), Second Voyage dans l'Intérieur de l'Afrique, 1783,
84, et 85   2 vols 4to   *Paris*, 1798

EGYPT, NUBIA, AND ABYSSINIA

Belzoni's (G) Narrative of the Operations and recent Discoveries within
the Pyramids, Temples, Tombs, and Excavations, in Egypt and
Nubia, and of a Journey in search of the ancient Berenice, and
another to the Oasis of Jupiter Ammon , with Mrs Belzoni's Account
of the Women of Egypt, Nubia, and Syria   4to   *London*, 1820

Belzoni's (G) Fifty Plates illustrative of his Researches and Operations
in Egypt and Nubia   Folio   *London*, 1820–22.

Burckhardt's (John Lewis) Travels in Nubia and in the Interior of N -E
Africa   4to   *London*, 1819

Burckhardt's (J L) Manners of the Modern Egyptians illustrated.
(Arabic Proverbs)

Clarke's (E D) Travels in Egypt   (Travels, Vols II —IV)

Denon's (Vivant) Travels in Upper and Lower Egypt, translated by
Arthur Aikin   3 vols 8vo the Plates inserted   *London*, 1803

Edmonstone's (Sir Arch.) Journey to Two of the Oases of Upper Egypt
8vo   *London*, 1822

Finati's (Gio) Life and Adventures in the campaigns against the Waha-
bees to recover Mecca and Medina   2 vols. 12mo   *London*, 1830

Hamilton's (William) Ægyptiaca , or some Account of the ancient and
modern State of Egypt, as obtained in the years 1801–2.   4to.   Accompanied by Etchings from drawings of the late Charles Hayes.
Folio   *London*, 1809

Legh's (Thom) Narrative of a Journey in Egypt and the country beyond
the Cataracts.   8vo   *London*, 1817

Mayer's (Luigi) Views in Egypt, from original drawings taken during
Sir Robert Ainslie's embassy to Constantinople , with illustrations of
the manners and customs of the natives of that country   Folio,
large paper   *London*, 1801

Norden's (F L) Travels in Egypt and Nubia, enlarged with observations
from ancient and modern authors, by Peter Templeman.   2 vols
in one, folio, largest paper   *London*, 1757.

Salamé's (Ab) Itinerary, with some particulars of the present government of Egypt (Expedition to Algiers)

Sonini (C. S), Voyage dans la Haute et Basse Egypte 3 vols 8vo and Plates in 4to *London*, 1799

Bruce's (James) Travels to discover the Source of the Nile; containing the Annals and Natural History of Abyssinia, 1768–73 5 vols. 4to. *Edinburgh*, 1790.

Pearce's (Nath) Life and Adventures during a residence in Abyssinia from 1810 to 1819; together with M. Caffin's Account of his Visit to Gondar · edited by J J. Halls 2 vols 8vo. *London*, 1831.

Salt's (Hen) Voyage to Abyssinia, and Travels into the Interior of that country, executed under the orders of the British Government in 1809–10, including an account of the Portuguese settlements on the east coast of Africa, &c 4to the Plates inserted. *London*, 1814.

Waddington (G.) and B Hanbury's Journal of a Visit to some parts of Ethiopia 4to *London*, 1822.

Drury (Robt.), Adventures of, during Fifteen Years' Captivity on the island of Madagascar, containing a description of that island, its produce, &c 8vo. *London*, 1807

Barrow's (John) Description of the islands of Madeira, Teneriffe, St. Jago, &c. (Cochin China)

Asia.

Murray's (H) Historical Account of Discoveries and Travels in Asia, from the earliest ages to the present time. 3 vols 8vo *Edin* 1820.

Jones's (Sir W) Description of Asia. (Works, Vol. V.)

Marco Polo's Travels in the Thirteenth Century, being a description by that early traveller of remarkable places and things in the eastern parts of the world; translated from the Italian, with Notes, by Wm Marsden. 4to *London*, 1818

Pinto (Historia Oriental de las Peregrinaciones de F Mendez), trad. en Castellano, con Apologia en favor de Pinto y desta Historia, por F. de Harrera Maldonado Folio *Valencia*, 1645.

Rennel's (James) Comparative Geography of Western Asia. 2 vols 8vo. *London*, 1831

ASIATIC TURKEY.

Brocquiere's (B. de la) Travels in Palestine, 1432–33, translated by Th Johnes 8vo large paper *Hafod*, 1807

Buckingham's (J S) Travels in Palestine, through the countries of Bashan and Gilead, east of the Jordan; including a visit to the cities of Geraza and Gamala in the Decapolis 4to A presentation copy, with the author's autograph *London*, 1821.

Buckingham's (J S) Travels in Mesopotamia, including a journey from Aleppo to Diarbekr, and thence to Mardin, and by the Tigris to Mousul and Bagdad, with Researches on the Ruins of Babylon, &c. 4to. *London*, 1827.

Burckhardt's (J L) Travels in Syria and the Holy Land. 4to. *Lond.* 1822

HISTORY.

Casas (L. F.), Voyage pittoresque de la Syrie, de la Phénicie, de la Palestine, et de la Basse Egypte   2 vols folio   *Paris*, 1799, &c.

Chandler's (Rich.) Travels in Asia Minor   4to   *Oxford*, 1775

Chateaubriand (F. A), Itinéraire de Paris à Jerusalem. 3 vols. 8vo. *Paris*, 1811

Clarke's (E D) Travels in the Holy Land   (Travels, Vols II to IV.)

Hasselquist's (Fred.) Voyages and Travels in the Levant in 1749–52; containing observations on natural history, physic, agriculture, and commerce, particularly on the Holy Land and the natural history of the Scriptures [translated from the German version of C Linnæus]   8vo   *London*, 1766

Kinneir's (J. M) Journey through Asia Minor, Armenia, and Koordistan, in 1813 and 1814   8vo. with Map   *London*, 1818

Legh's (Thomas) Journey through Syria   (Macmichael's Journey to Constantinople)

Maundrell's (Henry) Journey from Aleppo to Jerusalem, 1697, and to the banks of the Euphrates and Mesopotamia. 8vo. large paper, *Oxford*, 1740

Mayer's (Luigi) Views in Palestine, from original drawings; with historical and descriptive account of the country   Folio, large paper. *London*, 1804.

Russell's (Alex.) Natural History of Aleppo, containing a description of the city, the principal natural productions, &c. edited by Pat. Russell   2 vols 4to   *London*, 1794

Walpole's Memoirs of Asiatic Turkey   (Turkey in Europe)

ARABIA.

Buckingham's (J S) Travels among the Arab Tribes inhabiting the countries east of Syria and Palestine; including a journey from Nazareth to the mountains beyond the Dead Sea, and from thence through the plains of Houran to Bozra, Damascus, Tripoly, Baalbeck, and by the valley of the Orontes to Seleucia, Antioch, and Aleppo   4to   *London*, 1825

Burckhardt's (J I) Notes on the Bedouins and Wahabys, collected during his travels in the East; [edited by Sir W Ouseley]   4to. *Lond* 1830.

Burckhardt's (J L) Travels in the Hedjaz   4to   *London*, 1824.

Michaelis (J D), Recueil des Questions proposées à une Société de Savans qui font le Voyage de l'Arabie.   4to   *Amst* 1774.

Niebuhr (C.), Voyage en Arabie et en d'autres pays circonvoisins 2 vols. 4to   *Amst* 1776.

Niebuhr (C), Description de l'Arabie   4to.   *Amst* 1774

PERSIA &c

Buckingham's (J S) Travels in Assyria, Media, and Persia; including a journey from Bagdad by Mount Zagros to Hamadan the ancient Ecbatana, researches on Ispahan and the ruins of Persepolis, &c. 4to   *London*, 1829.

Chardin (Jean), Voyages en Perse et autres lieux de l'Orient, par L Langles. 10 vols 8vo. and Atlas in folio   *Paris*, 1811.

Franklin's (W) Observations on a Tour from Bengal to Persia, in 1786 and 7; with an account of the remains of the celebrated Palace of Persepolis. 8vo London, 1790.

Fraser's (J B) Narrative of a Journey into Khorasan, in 1821–2, including some account of the countries to the north-east of Persia, with remarks upon the national character, government, and resources of that kingdom. 4to. London, 1825

Kinneir's (J M) Geographical Memoir of the Persian Empire, accompanied by a Map. 4to. London, 1813

[Malcolm's (Sir John)] Sketches of Persia, from the Journals of a traveller in the East 2 vols 8vo London, 1827.

Mandelslo (Jean Albert), Voyages faits de Perse aux Indes Orientales, mis en ordre et publiéz par Adam Olearius, et traduits de l'original par le Sr Wicquefort 2 vols in one, folio, large paper Leide, 1719

Morier's (James) Two Journeys through Persia, Armenia, and Asia Minor, to Constantinople, in 1808–9, and between 1810 and 16; including an account of his majesty's missions to the court of Persia under Sir Harford Jones and Sir Gore Ouseley, Baronets 2 vols 4to London, 1812–18

Olearius (Adam), Voyages faits en Muscovie, Tartarie, et Perse, traduits de l'original et augmentéz par le Sr Wicquefort 2 vols in one, folio, large paper. Leide, 1719.

Olearius' (Adam) Voyages and Travels of the Ambassadors sent by Frederick Duke of Holstein to the Great Duke of Moscovy and the King of Persia, from 1633 to 1639, containing a complete History of Moscovy, Tartary, and Persia. To which are added, the Travels of John Albert de Mandelslo from Persia into the East Indies, faithfully rendered into English by John Davies of Kidwelly Folio, with two titles of the same date, the second with the addition of Mandelslo, and the scarce frontispiece by Chantry London, 1662

Ouseley's (Sir W) Travels in the East, more particularly Persia, illustrating many subjects of antiquarian research, history, geography, philology, and miscellaneous literature, with extracts of rare and valuable Oriental MSS. 3 vols 4to. Brecknock, 1819-23

Porter's (Sir Robert Ker) Travels in Georgia, Persia, Armenia, ancient Babylonica, &c during 1817–20 2 vols 4to London, 1821

Waring's (E. S) Tour to Sheeraz, by the route of Cazroon and Ferouzabad, with various remarks on the manners, customs, laws, language, and literature of the Persians; and a History of Persia from the death of Kureem Khan to the subversion of the Zund dynasty. 4to. London, 1807.

EAST INDIES

Rennel's (James) Memoir of a Map of Hindostan, with an introduction illustrative of the geography and present divisions of that country The Maps forming a separate volume 2 vols 4to London, 1792

Forster's (J R) Essay on India, its Boundaries, Climate, Soil, and Sea, translated by John Aikin (Pennant's Indian Zoology)

Gray's (Th) Geographical Disquisitions relating to some parts of India and Persia (Works, by Matthias, Vol. II)

HISTORY.

Hamilton's (Walter) East India Gazetteer; containing particular descriptions of the empires, kingdoms, principalities, &c &c of Hindostan and the adjacent countries, India beyond the Ganges, and the Eastern Archipelago 8vo. *London*, 1815.

Hamilton's (W) Geographical, Statistical, and Historical Description of Hindostan and the adjacent countries. 2 vols. 4to. *Lond* 1820.

Pennant's (Thomas) View of Hindoostan, India extra Gangem, China, Japan, the Malayan Isles, New Holland, &c. 4 vols 4to. *London*, 1798–1800

Bernier (F), Voyages; contenant la description des états du Grand Mogol, de l'Indoustan, de Kachemire, &c. 2 vols 12mo. *Amsterdam*, 1710

Broughton's (J D) Letters written in a Mahratta Camp, descriptive of the character, manners, habits, &c of the Mahrattas, in 1809. 4to. *London*, 1813

[Choissy (l'Abbé de)], Journal du Voyage de Siam, fait en 1685 et 6. 12mo. *Amsterdam*, 1687

Covert's (Robt) True and almost incredible Report of an Englishman, who travelled by land to Cambaya, thorow many unknowne kingdomes and great cities ; with the discovery of a great Emperour, called the Great Mogul, a prince till now unknown to our English nation. Black letter, 4to *London*, 1631

Daniel's (T. and W.) Picturesque Voyage to India by the way of China. Folio *London*, 1810.

Daniel's (T.) Oriental Scenery , or Views in Hindostan The six series in 2 vols oblong folio *London*, 1795–1808.

Daniel's (Samuel) Picturesque Illustration of the Scenery, Animals, and Natives of the island of Ceylon. Oblong folio *Lond* 1808

These works of the Daniels are all early impressions of the plates, carefully coloured after the original drawings, under the inspection of the authors

Fraser's (J B) Journal of a Tour through part of the snowy range of the Himala Mountains, and to the Sources of the rivers Jumna and Ganges. [Including historical sketches of Nepal and of the Ghoorka conquest] 4to. *London*, 1820.

Fraser's (J B) Views in the Himala Mountains Large folio. Early impressions, carefully coloured after the drawings *London*, 1820

Graham's (Maria) Journal of a Residence in India. 4to *Edinburgh*, 1812.

[Hamilton] Buchanan's (Francis) Journey from Madras through the countries of Mysore, Canara, and Malabar 3 vols. 4to *London*, 1807

Heber's (Bp Reginald) Narrative of a Journey through the Upper Provinces of India from Calcutta to Bombay, 1824–5 , with Notes upon Ceylon, an Account of a Journey to Madras and the southern provinces in 1826, and Letters from India. 3 vols 8vo *Lond* 1828

Hodges' (W.) Travels in India during 1780–83. 4to Plates. *London*, 1793

Hodges' (W) Select Views in India, drawn on the spot in 1780–3, and executed in aquatinta. 2 vols. folio. *London*, 1786

TRAVELS.

Kirkpatrick's (Colonel) Account of the Kingdom of Nepaul; being the substance of observations made during a mission to that country in 1793   4to.   *London*, 1811.

Meer Hassan Ali's (Mrs) Observations on the Mussulmauns of India; descriptive of their manners, customs, habits, and religious opinions, made during a 12 years' residence in their immediate society.   2 vols 8vo   *London*, 1832

Pottinger's (Henry) Travels in Beloochistan and Sinde, accompanied with a geographical and historical account of those countries.   4to *London*, 1816

Seely's (J B) Wonders of Elora, or, the Narrative of a Journey to the excavated Temples and Dwellings in the Elora Mountain, East Indies. with observations on the people and country.   8vo   *London*, 1824

[Tachard (Guy)], Voyage de Siam des Pères Jésuites.   12mo.   *Amsterdam*, 1688

Terry's (Edward) Voyage to the East Indies; wherein some things are taken notice of in our passage thither, but many more in our abode there, within that rich and most spacious empire of the Great Mogul. Small 8vo Port   *London*, 1655

Tombe (C F), Voyages aux Indes Orientales, revus, et augmentés de Notes par M Sonini   2 vols. 8vo. Atlas in 4to   *Paris*, 1810.

Wathen's (James) Journal of a Voyage, in 1811 and 12, to Madras and China, returning by the Cape of Good Hope.   4to. Plates.   *London*, 1814

CHINA, &c

Abel's (Clarke) Narrative of a Journey in the Interior of China, containing an account of Lord Amherst's embassy to the court of Pekin. 4to   *London*, 1818

Barrow's (John) Travels in China. Plates by Alexander.   4to   *Lond* 1806

Barrow's (J) Voyage to Cochin China, in the years 1792 and 93, and account of such European settlements as were visited on the voyage. 4to   *Lond*. 1806

Ellis' (Henry) Journal of the Proceedings of the late Embassy to China; comprising a narrative of the public transactions of the Embassy, and of the voyage to and from China.   4to.   *Lond*. 1817.

Finlayson (Geo) on the Mission to Siam and Hué, the capital of Cochin China, in the years 1821–2, with a Memoir of the Author by Sir Stamford Raffles   8vo.   *London*, 1820.

Hall's (Basil) Voyage of Discovery to the West Coast of Corea, and the great Loo-Choo Islands   4to.   *London*, 1818.

Keate's (Geo.) Account of the Pelew Islands, compiled from the Journals of Capt H. Wilson   4to   *London*, 1788.

Keate's (Geo) Account of the Pelew Islands (J P Hockin's Supplement to), compiled from the oral communications of Capt H Wilson   4to.   *Lond* 1803

Macartney's (George Earl) Journal of an Embassy to the Emperor of China, in 1792, 3, and 4   (Life)

HISTORY

M'Leod's (John) Narrative of a Voyage in his Majesty's late Ship the Alceste to the Yellow Sea, along the Coast of Corea to the Island of Loo-Choo   8vo   *London*, 1817

Pennant's (J.) View of China and Japan   (Hindoostan.)

Staunton's (Sir Geo.) Account of Lord Macartney's Embassy to the Emperor of China   3 vols 8vo. with Plates in folio   *London*, 1798.

Turner's (Samuel) Account of an Embassy to the Court of the Teshoo Lama in Tibet.   4to.   *London*, 1806.

ASIATIC RUSSIA

Bell's (John) Travels from Russia to divers parts of Asia, to Ispahan in Persia, and to Pekin in China, through Siberia.   2 vols. 4to   *Glasgow, Foulis*, 1763

Coxe's (Wm.) Account of the Russian Discoveries between Asia and America, to which are added, the Conquest of Siberia, and the History of the Transactions and Commerce between Russia and China.   4to   *London*, 1780.

Chappe d'Auteroche (l'Abbé), Voyage en Sibérie, fait en 1761   3 vols. 4to and Atlas   *Paris*, 1768

Cochrane's (Captain John Dundas) Narrative of a Pedestrian Journey through Russia and Siberian Tartary, from the Frontiers of China to the Frozen Sea and Kamschatka   2 vols 8vo   *London*, 1824.

Olearius (Adam), Voyage en Tartarie   (Persia.)

America.

Murray's (Hugh) Historical Account of Discoveries and Travels in North America, including the United States, the shores of the Polar Sea, and the voyages in search of a North-west Passage   2 vols. 8vo. *Lond* 1829

Memoir of Sebastian Cabot, with a Review of the History of Maritime Discovery, illustrated by documents from the Rolls, now first published   8vo.   *London*, 1831

Irving's (Washington) History of the Life and Voyages of Christopher Columbus.   4 vols small 8vo   *Paris*, 1828.

NORTH-WEST PASSAGE

Ellis's (Henry) Voyage to Hudson's Bay by the Dobbs Galley and California [Captains W. Moor and F. Smith] in 1746 and 47, for discovering a North-west Passage; with a fair view of the facts, and arguments from which the future finding of such a passage is rendered probable, and an historical account of the attempts hitherto made. 8vo large paper   *London*, 1748.

Chappel's (Edward) Narrative of a Voyage to Hudson's Bay; containing some account of the north-east coast of America, and the tribes inhabiting that region · with Preface by E. D. Clarke.   8vo   *London*, 1817

Ross's (John) Voyage of Discovery for the purpose of exploring Baffin's Bay, and Inquiry into the probability of a North-west Passage 4to.   *London*, 1819.

TRAVELS

Parry's (Sir W. E.) Journal of a Voyage for Discovery of a North-west Passage from the Atlantic to the Pacific, performed in the years 1819-20 with North Georgia Gazette, or Winter Chronicle, written by the Officers. 4to *London*, 1821

Fisher's (Alex) Journal of a Voyage of Discovery to the Arctic Regions, in 1819 and 20 8vo *London*, 1820

Parry's (Sir W. E.) Journal of a Second Voyage for the Discovery of a North-west Passage, performed in 1821-3 4to *London*, 1824.

Parry's (Sir W. E.) Journal of a Third Voyage for the Discovery of a North-west Passage, performed in 1824-5 4to *London*, 1826.

Parry's (Sir W. E.) Narrative of an Attempt to reach the North Pole, in 1827, by boats fitted for the purpose 4to *London*, 1828

Lyon's (G. F.) Private Journal of H M S Hecla, during the recent [Second] Voyage of Discovery under Capt Parry. 8vo. *Lond.* 1824.

Franklin's (Sir John) Narrative of a Journey to the Shores of the Polar Sea, in the years 1819-22, with an Appendix on various subjects relative to Science and Natural History. 4to *London*, 1823

Franklin's (Sir J) Narrative of a Second Expedition to the Shores of the Polar Sea, in 1825-7, including an Account of the progress of a Detachment to the Eastward, by Dr John Richardson 4to. *Lond.* 1828.

Mackenzie's (Alex) Voyages from Montreal, through the Continent of North America, to the Frozen and Pacific Oceans; with an Account of the rise, progress, and present state of the Fur-trade. 4to. *Lond.* 1801.

NORTH AMERICA

Carver's (J) Travels through the interior parts of North America, 1766, 7, and 8 8vo large paper *Lond* 1778

Kalm's (P) Travels into North America, translated by J R Foster 3 vols 8vo *Warrington*, 1770

Weld's (Isaac) Travels through the States of North America and the Canadas, in 1795, 6, and 7 2 vols 8vo *Lond* 1800.

Rochefoucalt's (Liancourt, Duke de) Travels through the United States of North America, the country of the Iroquois, and Upper Canada, in 1795-7, with an authentic Account of Lower Canada 2 vols 4to *Lond.* 1799

Lambert's (John) Travels through Canada and the United States, in 1804-8, with biographical Notices and Anecdotes of leading Characters in the United States 2 vols 8vo *Lond* 1816.

Duncan's (John M) Travels through part of the United States and Canada, in 1818 and 1819 2 vols. 8vo *Glasgow*, 1823

Hall's (Capt Basil) Travels in North America, in 1827-8 3 vols 8vo. *Edinburgh*, 1829

Hall's (Capt B) Forty Etchings from Sketches made with the Camera Lucida in North America, in 1827-8 Imp 4to *London*, 1829

Heriot's (Geo) Travels through the Canadas, with a comparative view of the Manners and Customs of the Indian Nations. 4to. *London.* 1807

Howison's (John) Sketches of Upper Canada, and some Recollections of the United States of America 8vo *Edin.* 1822.

HISTORY.

Head's (Geo) Forest Scenes and Incidents in the Wilds of North America. Crown 8vo *Lond* 1829

Faux's (W) Memorable Days in America, being a Journal of a Tour to the United States, principally to ascertain the condition and probable prospects of British Emigrants 8vo. *Lond* 1823

Dwight's (Timothy) Travels in New England and New York 4 vols. 8vo *London*, 1823

[Cooper's (J. F)] Notions of the Americans, by a Travelling Bachelor. 2 vols. 8vo *Lond* 1828

Trollope's (Mrs) Domestic Manners of the Americans. 2 vols cr. 8vo. *London*, 1832

Pike's (Z M) Exploratory Travels through the Western Territories of North America, in 1805, by order of the Government of the United States 4to. *Lond* 1811

Lewis and Clarke's Travels to the Source of the Missouri River, and across the American Continent to the Pacific Ocean, in 1804, 5, and 6 3 vols 8vo *Lond* 1815

Hunter's (John D) Memoirs of a Captivity among the Indians of North America, from childhood to the age of nineteen, with Anecdotes descriptive of their Manners and Customs 8vo *Lond* 1824

Maurelli's (Don F A) Journal of a Voyage, in 1775, to explore the Coast of America northward of California (Barrington's Miscellanies)

Bullock's (W) Six Months' Residence and Travels in Mexico; containing remarks on the present state of New Spain, &c 8vo *Lond* 1824

Ward's (H. G) Mexico, with an Account of the Mining Companies, and of the Political Events in that Republic, to the present day. 2 vols 8vo *London*. 1829

Mexico (View of the great Square in the City of). (Coll of Prints, Vol XVIII)

WEST INDIES

Bayley's (F W N) Four Years Residence in the West Indies, during the years 1826–9. To which is added, a Narrative of the Hurricanes in Barbadoes and St. Lucia, in 1831 8vo *Lond* 1832.

Mackenzie's (Charles) Notes on Haiti, made during a residence in that Republic 2 vols 8vo *London*, 1830

Sloane's (Sir Hans) Voyage to the Islands Madeira, Barbadoes, Nieves, St Christopher's, and Jamaica; with the Natural History of the last of those Islands, and an Introduction, wherein is an Account of the Inhabitants, Air, Water, Diseases, Trade, &c. of that place. 2 vols folio *London, printed for the Author*, 1707–25

" Donum illustrissimi authoris Riccardo Richardson, M D '—R R.

SOUTH AMERICA

Schmidel (Huld) Vera Historia admirandæ Navigationis, ab Anno M D XXXIV usque ad Annum M D LIV., in Americam vel Novum Mundum, juxta Brasiliam et Rio della Plata Ab ipso Schmidelio Germanicè descripta; nunc verò, emendatis et correctis urbium, &c nominibus, adjecta etiam tabula geographica, figuræ, &c [à Levinio Hulsio] 4to *Norimbergæ*, 1599

Condamine (M. de la), Voyage dans l'Intérieur de l'Amérique Meridionale, depuis la Côte de la Mer du Sud, jusqu'aux Côtes du Brésil et de la Guiane, en descendant la Rivière des Amazones 8vo *Paris,* 1745

Ulloa (G Juan) and Ant Ulloa's Voyage to South America, describing at large the Spanish Cities, Towns, Provinces, &c on that extensive Continent, undertaken by command of the King of Spain. Translated from the original Spanish, with occasional Notes and Observations, and an Account of some parts of the Brazils hitherto unknown to the English nation, by John Adams. 2 vols 8vo *Lond* 1772.

Humboldt (Alex de), A Bonpland, [J. Oltmanns, et C. S. Kunth], Voyage dans l'Intérieur de l'Amérique, dans l'années 1799–1804. 4 vols 8vo ; 11 vols 4to ; and 17 vols folio *Paris,* 1807–29

 Viz I. Partie —[Relation Historique d'un] Voyage aux Régions Equinoxiales du Nouveau Continent, fait en 1799–1804. 4 vols. 4to *Paris,* 1814
  Atlas Géographique et Physique Large folio *Paris,* 1814
  Vues des Cordillières, et Monumens des Peuples indigènes de l'Amérique. Large folio *Paris,* 1810.
 II Partie — Recueil d'Observations de Zoologie et d'Anatomie comparee, faites dans un Voyage aux Tropiques 2 vols. 4to *Paris,* 1811.
 III Partie — Essai Politique sur le Royaume de la Nouvelle Espagne 2 vols 4to *Paris,* 1811
  Atlas Physique et Géographique. Large folio *Paris,* 1810.
 IV. Partie — Recueil d'Observations Astronomiques, d'Opérations Trigonométriques, et des Mesures Barométriques, faites pendant le cours d'un Voyage aux Régions Equinoxiales de Nouveau Continent, rédigées et calculées d'après les Tables les plus exactes, par J Oltmanns. 2 vols 4to. *Par* 1808.
 V Partie — Physique Générale et Géologie Essai sur la Géographie des Plantes, accompagné d'un Tableau Physique des Régions Equinoxiales, fondé sur des mesures exécutées depuis le 10me degré de latitude boréale jusqu'au 10me de latitude australe 4to *Paris,* 1806.
 VI Partie — (1) Plantes Equinoxiales recueillies au Mexique, dans l'Ile de Cuba, dans les Provinces de Caraccas, de Cumana, et de Barcelona, aux Andes de la Nouvelle Grenade, de Quito, et de Pérou, et sur les bords du Rio-Nigro, de l'Orénoque, et la Rivière d'Amazones, rédigé par M A Bonpland. 2 vols large folio *Paris,* 1805
  (2) Monographie des Melastoma et autres genres du même ordre, recueillis et dirigés par M A. Bonpland. 2 vols large folio. *Paris,* 1806
  (3) Nova Genera et Species Plantarum quas in peregrinatione ad Plagam Æquinoctialem Orbis Novi collegerunt, descripserunt, partim adumbraverunt A Bonpland et A de Humboldt è schedis autographis A Bonplandi ; in ordinem digessit, et cum synopsi ejusdem adjecit C S Kunth. 7 vols folio, and 4 vols. 8vo. *Parisiis,* 1815, 22, &c.
  Révision des Graminées publiées dans les "Nova Genera, &c Plantarum," précedée d un Travail sur cette Famille, par C S Kunth Folio. *Paris,* 1829
  (4) Mimoses et autres Plantes Légumineuses du Nouveau Continent, rédigées par C. S Kunth Large folio *Paris,* 1819

156 HISTORY

De Pons' (Fr.) Travels in South America in 1801, 2, 3, and 4; containing a description of the Captain-generalship of Caraccas, with a View of the Manners and Customs of the Spaniards and the Native Indians 2 vols 8vo *London*, 1807

Walton's (W.) Present State of the Spanish Colonies in South America; with a general Survey of the Settlements on the South Continent of America, as relates to history, trade, population, &c 2 vols. 8vo. *London*, 1818

Stevenson's (W B) Historical and Descriptive Narrative of Twenty Years' Residence in South America, containing Travels in Arauco, Chile, Peru, and Colombia, with an Account of the Revolution, its rise, progress, and results 3 vols 8vo *London*, 1825

Caldcleugh's (Alex) Travels in South America, during the years 1819–21, containing an Account of the present state of Brazil, Buenos Ayres, and Chile 2 vols 8vo *London*, 1825.

Waterton's (Charles) Wanderings in South America, north-west of the United States and the Antilles, in 1812–24. 4to. *Lond* 1825.

Ralegh's (Sir W.) Voyage for the Discovery of Guiana, and his Apology for his Voyage. (Works, Vol VIII)

Ralegh (Gualth) Brevis et admiranda Descriptio Regni Guianæ, auri abundantissimi, in Americâ, seu Novo Orbe, sub lineâ æquinoctiali siti; nunc verò in Latinum sermonem translata [à Lavinio Hulsio]. 4to *Norimbergæ*, 1599

Fermin (Phil), Description générale, historique, géographique, et physique de la Colonie de Surinam. 2 vols 8vo. *Amst* 1769.

Stedman's (J G) Narrative of a Five Years' Expedition against the revolted Negroes of Surinam, from the year 1772 to 1777, elucidating the history of that country, and describing its natural productions; with an Account of the Indians of Guiana and Negroes of Guinea. 2 vols 4to large paper, Plates of natural history, &c. coloured *London*, 1806.

Koster's (Hen.) Travels in Brazil, from Pernambuco to Searo, also a Voyage to Maranam, exhibiting the state of society in that country during a residence of six years, illustrated by plates of costume 4to *Lond* 1816

Maximilian's Prince of Wied-neuwied's Travels in the Brazil, in 1815–17 4to *Lond* 1820.

Von Spix (J B) and C. F P. Von Martius's Travels in Brazil, in the years 1817–20, undertaken by command of the King of Bavaria; translated by H E Lloyd 2 vols. in one, 8vo *Lond* 1824

Lindley's (Thos) Narrative of a Voyage to Brazil, the Imprisonment of the Author by the Portuguese, and description of St Salvadore and Port Seguro 8vo *Lond.* 1805

Mawe's (John) Travels in the Interior of Brazil, particularly in the Gold and Diamond Districts of that country. 4to *Lond* 1812

Walsh's (R) Notices of Brazil in 1828 and 1829 2 vols 8vo *Lond* 1830

Head's (Capt F B.) Rough Notes taken during some rapid Journeys across the Pampas and among the Andes. 8vo *Lond* 1828

Schmidtmeyer's (Peter) Travels into Chile, over the Andes, in the years 1820 and 21 4to *Lond* 1824

Hall's (Basil) Extracts from a Journal written on the coasts of Chili, Peru, and Mexico, in the years 1820, 1821, and 1822 2 vols 8vo. *Edinburgh*, 1824

Mollien's (G) Travels in the Republic of Colombia, in 1822 and 1823 8vo *Lond* 1824.

Andrews's (Joseph) Journey from Buenos Ayres, through the provinces of Cordova, Tucuman, and Salta, to Potosi, thence by the deserts of Caranja to Arica, Santiago de Chili, and Coquimbo, undertaken on behalf of the Chilian Mining Company 2 vols 8vo *Lond* 1827

Miers's (John) Travels in Chile and La Plata; including Accounts respecting the geography geology, statistics, government, and the mining operations in Chile 2 vols 8vo. *Lond* 1826

South Sea, Polynesia, and Australia.

*** See also Voyages round the World

Weddel's (James) Voyages towards the South Pole, performed in 1822; containing an Examination of the Antarctic Sea to the 74° south latitude, and a visit to Tierra del Fuego To which are added, Observations on the probability of reaching the South Pole, and an Account of a Second Voyage to the same seas. 8vo. *Lond* 1827

Missionary Voyage to the Southern Pacific Ocean, in 1796-8, in the ship Duff, Capt. J. Wilson, compiled from the Journals of the Officers and the Missionaries; with a preliminary Discourse on the geography and history of the South Sea Islands, and an Appendix on the natural and civil state of Otaheite 4to *London*, 1799

Ellis's (Will.) Narrative of a Tour through Hawaii or Owyhee; with Observations on the natural history of the Sandwich Islands, and on the manners, customs, traditions, history, and language of their Inhabitants 8vo *London*, 1827

Ellis's (W.) Polynesian Researches, during a Residence of nearly Six Years in the South Sea Islands 2 vols 8vo *London*, 1829

Tongataboo (Narrative of Four Years' Residence in) 8vo *London*, 1810

Manner's (W) Account of the Natives of the Tonga Islands, in the South Pacific Ocean; with an original Grammar and Vocabulary of their language compiled and arranged by John Martin 2 vols. 8vo *London*, 1817.

Phillips' (Governor Arthur) Voyage to Botany Bay, with an Account of the establishment of the Colonies of Port Jackson and Norfolk Island To which are added, the Journals of Lieutenants Shortland, Watts, Ball, and Capt Marshall 4to *London*, 1789

Hunter's (John) Historical Journal of the Transactions at Port Jackson and Norfolk Island, with the Discoveries which have been made in New South Wales since the publication of Phillips's Voyage, including the Journals of Governors Phillips and King, and Lieutenant Ball 4to *London*, 1793

Collins's (David) Account of the English Colony in New South Wales; with some particulars of New Zealand, from a MS. of Governor King, and an Account of the Voyage for ascertaining the Strait separating Van Diemen's Land from the Continent, by Flinders and Bass 4to *London*, 1804

Flinders' (Matthew) Voyage to [and circumnavigating] Terra Australis, in 1801–3; with an Introduction containing the prior discoveries in that country 2 vols large 4to with Atlas, large folio *Lond* 1814

Field's (Barron) Geographical Memoirs on New South Wales, by various hands, together with other papers on the Aborigines, the Geology, the Botany, the Timber, the Astronomy, and the Meteorology of New South Wales and Van Diemen's Land 8vo *Lond* 1825

Oxley's (John) Journals of Two Expeditions behind the Blue Mountains and into the interior of New South Wales, undertaken by order of the British Government, in the years 1817–18. 4to. *Lond.* 1820.

King's (Philip P.) Narrative of a Survey of the Intertropical and Western Coasts of Australia, performed between the years 1818 and 22, with an Appendix containing various subjects relating to hydrography and natural history 2 vols 8vo *London*, 1827

Cunningham's (P) Two Years in New South Wales; comprising Sketches of the actual state of society in that colony, its topography, natural history, &c. 2 vols 8vo *Lond* 1824.

Savage's (John) Account of New Zealand, particularly the Bay of Islands 8vo *Lond.* 1807.

Nicholas's (J. L) Narrative of a Voyage to New Zealand, performed in 1814, in company with the Rev S Marsden, principal Chaplain of New South Wales 2 vols 8vo. *Lond* 1817

Cruise's (Richard A.) Journal of Ten Months' Residence in New Zealand. 8vo. *Lond.* 1824

Chronology.

Hales' (William) New Analysis of Chronology and Geography, History and Prophecy, harmonised upon scriptural and scientific principles 4 vols 8vo *Lond* 1830.

Newton's (Sir I) Chronology of ancient Kingdoms amended, and short Chronicle from the first memory of things in Europe to the conquest of Persia by Alexander (Works, Vol. V)

Williams's (William) Primitive History, from the Creation to Cadmus. 4to *Chichester*, 1789.
    This is an attempt to a new reconciliation of discordant chronologies.

Selden (John) on the Birth-day of our Saviour (Works, Vol III)

Marmora Arundelliana, sive, Saxa Græce incisa. Accedunt Inscriptiones aliquot Veteres Latin, Gr et Lat, publicavit, Apparatus ad Gr. Chron. Comment &c adjecit J. Selden. (Seldeni Opera, Vol. II)

Clinton's (H. F) Fasti Hellenici, the civil and literary Chronology of Greece, from the LVth Olympiad to the death of Augustus 2 vols 4to. *Oxford*, 1824–32

Mure (W) on the Calendar and Zodiac of ancient Egypt, with Remarks on the first introduction and use of the Zodiac among the Greeks 8vo *Edinb* 1832

Selden (J) de Anno Civili veteris Ecclesiæ, seu Reipublicæ Judaicæ (Opera, Vol 1)

Brady's (John) Clavis Calendaria; or, a compendious Analysis of the Calendar, illustrated with ecclesiastical, historical, and classical Anecdotes   2 vols 8vo.   *London*, 1812.

Nicolas's (Nich. H) Notitia Historica; containing tables, calendars, and miscellaneous information for the use of historians and the legal profession   8vo.   *London*, 1824

Eusebii Chronicon.   (Hist. of the Christian Religion)

Petav (P), Abrégé Chronologique de l'Histoire Universelle [traduit par Moreau de Mantour et Dupin], continué jusqu'à présent   5 vols. in four, 12mo.   *Paris*, 1715

Du Fresnoy's (Lenglet) Chronological Tables of Universal History, sacred and profane, ecclesiastical and civil, from the creation of the world to 1743, translated and continued down to the death of Geo II. [by Thos Floyd].   2 vols. 8vo.   *London*, 1762

L'Art de vérifier les Dates des Faits historiques, des Inscriptions, des Chroniques, et autres anciens monumens, avant et depuis la Naissance de Jésus-Christ jusqu'à nos jours, [par Clement, D'Antine, Clemencet, et Durand].   7 vols. folio.   *Paris*, 1783-1830.

Antiquities—Numismatics.

Dictionaries, General Treatises, and Collections

Fosbrooke's (T D) Encyclopædia of Antiquities, and Elements of Archæology, classical and mediœval   2 vols 4to   *London*, 1825

Fosbrooke's (T D) Foreign Topography, or, an encyclopedic account of the ancient remains in Asia, Africa, and Europe, (the United Kingdom excepted)   4to   *London*, 1827

Wilson's (Thos) Archæological Dictionary, or, classical Antiquities of the Jews, Greeks, and Romans   8vo   *Lond* 1793.

Lempriere's (J.) Classical Dictionary, containing a copious account of all the proper names mentioned in ancient authors, with the value of coins, weights, and measures   4to large paper   *London*, 1804

Pownal (Thomas) on the Study of Antiquities as the commentary to historical learning, sketching out a general line of research   8vo   *London*, 1782.

Montfaucon's (Bern de) Antiquity explained and represented in Sculptures, with Supplement   Translated from the French by David Humphreys   7 vols folio   *London*, 1721-5

[D'Hancarville], Recherches sur l'Origine, l'Esprit, et le Progrès des Arts dans la Grèce, sur leur Connexion avec les Arts et la Religion des plus anciens peuples connus, sur les Monumens antiques de l'Inde, de la Perse, du reste de l'Asie, de l'Europe, et de l'Égypte   Avec le Supplément, contenant des observations nouvelles sur l'origine des idées employées dans les anciens emblèmes religieux, &c   3 vols 4to   *Londres*, 1785

> This contains the principles of M. D'Hancarville's System of Ancient Mythology   The work was printed at the expense of Mr Charles Townley, the eminent collector of the Townley marbles

Malliot (J). Recherches sur les Costumes, les Mœurs, et les Usages des anciens peuples (Costumes)

Hope (Thos) on the Costume of the Ancients   (Costumes)

Grævii (J G), Jac Gronovii, &c. Thesaurus Antiquitatum Græcarum et Romanarum 35 vols fol Videl

 Thesaurus Græcarum Antiquitatum, congestus à J Gronovio 13 vols. folio *Lugd Bat* 1697-1702

 Vol 1. 2 et 3, continent effigies virorum et mulierum illustrium, ex Fulvio Ursino, Caucæo, Leon Augustino, et aliis

 Vol 4 Nicolai Gerbelii in Michaelis Sophiani descriptionem Græciæ explicatio
  Joannis Taurembergii ennarratio Græciæ antiquæ, cum tabulis geographicis
  Ubbonis Emmii vetus Græcia, in tres tomos distincta, quorum I habet descriptionem regionum à Græcis habitatarum II complectitur res gestas Græcorum III repræsentat statum ac formam præcipuarum ejus gentis rerum publicarum, cum additamentis auctoris ante hâc ineditis
  Item de inclinatione et interitu reipubl Atticæ, Spartanæ, et Carthaginensis
  Item de situ, amplitudine, et magnificentiâ portûs Carthaginis
  Joannes Meursius de populis et pagis Atticâ, cum supplementis autoris et Jacobi Sponii
  Joannis Meursii Athenæ Atticæ, sive de præcipuis Athenarum antiquitatibus libri 3
  Ejusdem Cecropia, sive de Athenarum arce.
  Ejusdem Ceramicus geminus, sive de Ceramici Atheniensium utriusque antiquitatibus
  Ejusdem regnum Atticum, sive de regibus Atheniensium, eorumque rebus gestis, libri 3
  Ejusdem archontes Athenienses, sive de iis qui Athenis summum istom magistratum obierunt libri 4

 Vol 5. Guillelmi Postelli tractatus de republicâ seu magistratibus Atheniensium
  Antonii Thysii de republ. Atheniensium discursus politicus.
  Joannis Meursii Pisistratus, sive de ejus vitâ et tyrannide.
  Caroli Sigonii de republ. Atheniensium libri 4.
  Idem de Atheniensium temporibus
  Ejusdem Lacedæmoniorum tempora
  Joannis Meursii fortuna Attica, sive de Athenarum origine, incremento, magnitudine, potentiâ, gloriâ, vario statu, decremento, et occasu
  Ejusdem Atticarum lectionum libri 4, in quibus antiquitates plurimæ proferuntur
  Ejusdem Piræeus, sive de Piræeo Atheniensium portu
  Ejusdem themis Attica, sive de legibus Atticis libri 2
  Ejusdem Solon, sive de ejus vitâ, legibus, dictis, atque scriptis
  Ejusdem Areopagus, sive de senatu Areopagitico
  Marquardi Freheri decisionum Areopagiticarum sylvula
  Martini Schoockii Achaia vetus, ejus situs, antiquitas, respublica, reges, tyranni, leges, bellum, &c
  Joannes Meursius de regno Laconico
  Ejusdem miscellanea Laconica.
  Nicolaus Cragius de republicâ Lacedæmoniorum.

 Vol 6 Joachimus Stephanus de jurisdictione veterum Græcorum.
  Joachimus Perionius de magistratibus Græcorum et Romanorum
  Heraclides Ponticus de politiis Græcorum.
  Joan Adamus Osiander de asylis gentilium.
  Joan Bat Crophii antiquitates Macedonicæ
  Petri Hendreich Massilia, ejus situs, administratio, respublica, &c
  Burcherdi Niderstedt Melita vetus et nova
  Petrus Gyllius de Bosphoro Thracio libri 3
  Idem de Topographia Constantinopoleos libri 4
  Georgius Douza de itinere suo Constantinopolitano
  Leonardi Aretini commentaria rerum Græcarum
  Wolfgangi Lazii Græciæ antiquæ variis numismatibus illustratæ, libri 2

ANTIQUITIES

Josephus Laurentius de rebuspublicis, suffragiis, consiliis, accusationibus, et tormentis veterum
Everhardi Feithi antiquitates Homericæ
Nicolaus Damascenus de moribus græcorum aliarumque gentium

Vol 7 Danielis Claseni theologia gentilis, quâ probatur gentilium theologiam ex fonte Scripturæ originem traxisse
Josephi Laurentii varia sacra Gentilium
Abrahami Ortelii deorum dearumque capita, ex antiquis numismatibus collecta, cum figuris
Julii Cæsaris Bulengeri de oraculis et vatibus liber.
Idem de templis ethnicorum
Johan Henrici Eggelingii mysteria Cereris et Bacchi
Johan Meursii panathenæa, sive de Minervæ illo gemino festo.
Ejusdem Eleusinia, sive de Cereris Eleusiniæ sacro ac festo
Johan Nicolai de ritu antiquo et hodierno Bacchanaliorum commentatio.
Johan Jacobus Helleus de deo ignoto Atheniensium
Jacobi Sponii ignotorum atque obscurorum quorundam deorum aræ, notis illustratæ
Stephani Byzantini grammatici de Dodone fragmentum, quo tota veterum doctrina de perantiquo oraculo isto continetur
Jacobi Triglandii conjectanea ad quædam obscura fragmenti de Dodone loca
Johan. Antonius Venerius de oraculis et divinationibus antiquorum
Claudii Menetrii symbolica Dianæ Ephesiæ statua exposita, cum figuris
Lucas Holsteinius de fulcris seu verubus Dianæ Ephesiæ simulacro appositis, cum figuris
Joan Petri Bellorii nota in numismata apibus insignita, cum figuris
Ejusdem expositio symbolici deæ Syriæ simulacri
Laurent. Theod Gronovii marmorea basis Colossi Tiberio Cæsari erecti ob civitates Asiæ restitutas, post horrendos terræ tremores, defensi
Laurent Pignorii magnæ deûm matris Idææ et Attidis initia, cum fig.
Joan Favoldi Græcorum veterum hierologia
Petri Castellani heortologium, sive de festis Græcorum
Joan Meursii Græcia feriata, seu de festis Græcorum, cum figuris
Joan Jonstonus de festis Græcorum
Julius Cæsar Bulengerus de ludis veterum
Joan Meursius de ludis Græcorum
Danielis Souterii Palimedes, sive de tabula lusoria, alea, et variis ludis
Andreas Senftlebius de alea veterum.
Cœlius Calcagninus de talorum, tesserarum, et calculorum ludis

Vol. 8. Johan Meursii orchestra, sive de saltationibus veterum.
Johan Bapt Casalius de ritu nuptiarum veterum
Joseph Laurentius de sponsalibus et nuptiis antiquorum
Barnabas Brissonius de adulteriis
Joseph Laurentius de adulteris et meretricibus
Johan Meursius de puerperio
Joseph Laurentius de natalitiis.
Idem de præconibus, citharœdis, fistulis, ac tintinnabulis
Lilius Gregorius Gyraldus de comœdia
Julius Scaliger de comœdia et tragœdia
Idem de versibus comicis
Joach Camerarius de comicis versibus
Johan Baptista Casalius de tragœdia et comœdia
Albericus Gentilis de actoribus et spectatoribus fabularum non notandis disputatio
Evanthius et Donatus de tragœdia et comœdia.
De fabularum, ludorum, theatrorum, scenarum, ac scenicorum antiquâ consuetudine libellus
Johan Ludov Fabricius de ludis scenicis
Petrus Faber de re athletica ludisque veterum gymnicis
Octavii Falconerii inscriptiones athleticæ notis illustratæ.
Barnabas Brissonius de spectaculis
Joseph Laurentius de agytis, histrionibus, acclamationibus, et osculis.
Johan Meursius fil de tibiis
Musonius philosophus de luxu Græcorum.
Petrus Bellonius de admirabili operum antiquorum præstantiâ
Philo Byzantius de septem orbis spectaculis, Gr Lat Leo Allatii
Phlegon Trallianus de rebus mirabilibus.

Phlegon Trallianus de longævis
Johan. Frideric Gronovius de museo Alexandrino.
Luodolph Neocorus de museo Alexandrino.

Vol 9 Janus Cornarius de conviviis veterum Græcorum
Andreas Baccius de conviviis antiquorum, deque solemni in eis vinorum usu.
Johan Bapt Casalius de trichiniis, conviviis, hospitalitate, et tesseris veterum, cum figuris
Joseph Laurentius de conviviis, hospitalitate, tesseris, et strenis.
Jacob Sponius de origine strenarum
Jac Philippus Tomasinus de tesseris hospitalitatis, cum figuris.
Joseph. Laurentius de prandio et cœnâ veterum
Petri Castellani kreophagia, sive de esu carnium.
Hieronym Mercurialis de potionibus ac edulis veterum.
Ioan Frelinshemius de calido potu
Adrian. Turnebus de vino, ac ejus usu et abusu
Johan Henr. Meibomius de cervisiis veterum
Johan Bapt Casalius de thermis et balneis veterum.
Petrus Servius de odoribus
Lazarus Bayfius de vasculis
Pomponius Gauricus de sculpturâ sive statuariâ
Ludovicus Demontiosius de sculpturâ, cælaturâ gemmarum, &c
Aldus Manutius P F de cælaturâ et picturâ veterum
Philostratus de picturâ
Julius Cæsar Bulengerus de picturâ, plastice, statuariâ
Joan Bapt Casalius de insignibus, annulis, fibulis, &c
Joseph Laurentius de re vestiariâ
Otto Sperlingius de crepidis veterum
Theodorus Gaza de mensibus Atticis
Joan Perrellus de ratione lunæ epictarum, &c.
Petri Haguelomi calendarium trilingue, seu de mensibus Hebræorum, Græcorum, et Romanorum
Joan. Lalamantius de tempore, de anno Macedonum seu Græcorum, et de anno Attico.
Petrus Castellanus de mensibus Atticis
Samuel. Petitus de anno Attico
Steph Pighii Themis dea, seu de lege divinâ
Ejusdem mythologia in horis
Jacob. Usserius de Macedonum et Asianorum anno solari.
Joseph Laurentius de annis, mensibus, diebus, horis, &c
Phlegon Trallianus de Olympiis
Joan. Meursii denarius Pythagoricus, sive de nummorum usque ad denarium qualitate
Erycii Puteani Olympiades
Ioachimi Camerarii historia rei nummariæ
Leonardus Porcius de re pecuniariâ veterum
Joseph Scaliger de re nummariâ antiquorum.
Willebrod Snellius de re nummariâ
Carolus Patinus de numismate antiquo Augusti et Platonis
Sebastianus Fœschius de nummo Pylamensis Evergetæ

Vol 10. Ludovici Cresollii theatrum veterum rhetorum, oratorum, declamatorum
Origenis philosophumenon fragmentum
Guilel Morellius de veterum philosophorum origine, successione, ætate, et doctrinâ
Davidis Chytræi tabula philosophica, sive series philosophorum.
Desiderius Jacotius de philosophorum doctrinâ.
Johan Meursii Æschylus, Sophocles, Euripides, sive de tragœdiis eorum.
Plutarchi Alexandrinâ proverbia Græca
Johan Meursii Theseus, sive de ejus vitâ
Raphael Trichetus Dufresne de Charondæ effigie in Catanensi, nummo argenteo
Johan Meursii Dionysius, sive de auctoribus istius nominis.
Ejusdem de Heraclide aliisque ejus nominis
Ejusd Theophrastus, sive de illius libris
Ejusd lectiones Theophrasteæ
Adolfi Vorstii epistola de obitu Johan Meursii
Jacob Philip Tomasini manûs Lnea Cecropii votum referentis dilucidatio.

Octavius Falconerius de nummo Apamensi, Deucalionei diluvii typum exhibente
Georgii Schubarti enarratio Metamorphoseos Ovidianæ de diluvio Deucalionis
Tanaquilli Fabri vitæ poetarum Græcorum
Joseph Barberius de miseriâ poetarum Græcorum
Petri Castellani vitæ veterum et illustrium medicorum
Joh Hem Bacleri de scriptoribus Græcis et Latinis, ab Homero ad initium sæculi 16
Helladii Besantinoi chrestomathiæ, Gr Lat J Meursii
Johan à Wower de polymathia.
Jos Laurentius de professoribus, oratoribus, nomenclatoribus, et litteris
Johan Meursii bibliotheca Græca
Ejusdem bibliotheca Attica
Leo Allatius de patriâ Homeri
Ejusdem natales Homeri

Vol. 11 Dicæarchi geographia quædam sive de viâ Græciæ
Henrici Stephani dialogus, Dicæarchi sympractor, vel de Græcorum moribus.
Erasmi Vindingii Hellen, in quo antiquæ Græciæ populorum incunabula, migrationes, coloniarum deductiones, et res præcipuæ gestæ exponuntur
Lazarus Baifius de re navali, cum figuris
Stephan Doletus de re navali
Cænius Calcagninus de re nauticâ
Johan Schefferus de varietate navium
Joseph. Laurentius de varietate navium
Joachim Camerarii hippocomicus, seu de curandis equis, item de nominibus equestribus Græcis et Latinis collectio
Julius Cæsar Bulengerus de triumphis, spoliis bellicis, trophæis, arcubus triumphalibus, et pompâ triumphi
Franciscus Modius de triumphis, ludis, et spectaculis veterum
Johan Meursius de funere
Joseph Laurentius de funeribus antiquorum
Johan Andr Quenstedius de sepulturâ veterum
Petri la Seine Homeri nepenthes, seu de abolendo luctu liber.

Vol 12 Petri Sancti Bartoli et Johan Petri Belloni veterum sepulchra, seu mausolea Romanorum et Etruscorum, cum figuris
Ejusdem veterum lucernæ sepulchrales, cum figuris
Johan Potteri archæologia Græca, sive antiquitatum Græciæ corpus absolutissimum, ex Anglo in Latinum versum, cum figuris

Vol 13 Index locupletissimus in universos 12 tomos

Thesaurus Antiquitatum Romanarum, congestus à J G Grævio 12 vols folio *Traject ad Rhen* 1694

Vol. 1 Ferrarius de origine Romanorum
Paullus Manutius de civitate Romanâ
Carolus Sigonius de antiquo jure civium Romanorum
Onuphrius Panvinius de civitate Romana
Idem de imperio Romano
Paullus Manutius de comitiis Romanorum
Nicolaus Gruchius de comitiis Romanorum
Caroli Sigonii posterior cum Nicolao Gruchio disputatio de binis comitiis et lege curiatâ
Nicolai Gruchii ad posteriorem Sigonii disputationem refutatio.
Carolus Sigonius de lege curiatâ magistratuum et imperatorum, et eorum jure
Paullus Manutius de senatu Romano
Johan Sirius Zamoscius de senatu Romano

Vol. 2. Paullus Manutius de legibus Romanis.
Antonius Augustinus de legibus Romanis, cum notis Fulvii Ursini.
Carolus Sigonius de antiquo jure Italiæ
Idem de antiquo jure provinciarum
Idem de judiciis
Sibrandus Tetardus Siccama de judicio centum virali
Franciscus Hottomannus de magistratibus Romanorum
Idem de senatu et senatus consulto
Idem de formulis antiquis.

Nicolai Rigaltii, Ismaelis Bulliuldi, et Henrici Valesii, observationes de populis fundis
Carolus Sigonius de nominibus Romanorum
Onuphrius Panvinius de antiquis Romanorum nominibus
Josephi Castalionis adversùs feminarum nominum assertores disputatio
Ejusdem de antiquis puerorum prænominibus

Vol 3 Fr. Robortellus de provinciis Romanorum et earum distributione atque administratione
Fr Robortellus de judiciis apud Romanos
Junius Rabirius de hastarum et auctionum origine
Franciscus Robortellus de magistratibus imperatorum
Idem de gradibus honorum et magistratuum Romanorum
Guido Pancirollus de magistratibus municipalibus
Idem de corporibus artificum
Sextus Rufus de regionibus urbis
P Victor de regionibus Romæ
Burtholom Marliani urbis Romæ topographia, cum notis Fulvii Ursini.
Onuphrii Panvinii antiquæ urbis imago
Guidonis Pancirolli urbis Romæ descriptio
Ejusdem de quatuor urbis regionibus comment
Georgii Fabricii descriptio urbis Romæ
Alexandri Donati Roma vetus ac recens, utriusque ædificiis ad eruditam cognitionem expositis, cum figuris à J Goeree

Vol 4. Famiani Nardini Roma vetus libri 8, ex Italicâ in Latinam linguam translati à Jacobo Tollio
Octavii Falconerii de pyramide C Cestii epulonis dissertatio
Ejusdem epistola de latere ex ædificii veteris ruderibus eruto
Isaacus Vossius de antiquâ urbis Romæ magnitudine
Olai Bornichii de antiquâ urbis Romæ facie
Sexti Julii Frontini de aquæductibus urbis Romæ commertarius
Raphael Fabrettus de aquis et aquæductibus veteris Romæ
Johan Chiffletti Aqua Virgo, fons Romæ celeberrimus, et priscâ religione sacer
Lucæ Holstenii commentariolus in veterem picturam nymphæum referentem, ubi typus nymphæi appositus est
Petri Ciacconii in columnæ rostratæ inscriptionem explicatio
Antiquæ inscriptionis quâ L Scipionis Barbati F expressum est elogium explanatio.
Josephus Castalio de Templo Pacis, atque ex occasione de Jani gemini templo, bellique portis
Ejusdem explicatio ad inscriptionem Augusti, quæ in basi est obelisci statuti per Sixtum V. pont
Petri Angeli Bargæi de privatorum publicorumque ædificiorum urbis Romæ eversoribus epistola
Ejusdem commentarius de obelisco
Joseph Castalio de columnâ triumphali imperatoris Antonini
Jo Petri Bellorii fragmenta vestigii veteris Romæ, ex lapidibus Farnesianis
Livini Cruylii descriptio faciei variorum locorum, quam prospectum vocant, urbis Romæ, tàm antiquæ quàm novæ, in 15 tabulis æri incisa

Vol 5 Jacobus Gutherus de veteri jure pontificio urbis Romæ.
Johan Andr Bosius de pontifice maximo Romæ veteris
Idem de pontificatu maximo imperatorum Romanorum
Michael Angelus Causeus (de la Chausse) de insignibus pontificis maximi, flaminis dialis, auguris, et instrumento sacrificantium.
Augustinus Niphus de auguriis
Julius Cæsar Buleugerus de sortibus
Idem de auguriis et auspiciis
Idem de ominibus.
Idem de prodigiis.
Idem de terræ motu et fulminibus
Johan Baptista belli de partibus templi auguralis
Johan Pierius Valerianus de fulminum significationibus.
Justus Lipsius de Vestâ et vestalibus
Ezechiel Spanhemius de nummo Smyrnæorum, seu de Vestâ et prytanibus Græcorum
Hieronymi Aleandri jun antiquæ tabulæ marmoreæ solis effigie symbolisque exsculptæ explicatio.

ANTIQUITIES

        Michaelis Angeli Causei deorum simulacra
        Johan Bapt Hansenius de jure jurando veterum
        Stephanus Trehenus de jure jurando
        Erycius Puteanus de jure jurando antiquorum
        Marci Zuerii Boxhornii quæstiones Romanæ, quibus sacri et profani ritus, eorumque caussæ et origines explicantur
        Plutarchi quæstiones Romanæ, Gr et Lat

Vol 6 Franc Bernard Ferrarius de veterum acclamationibus et plausu
        Pet Berthaldus de aris
        Bened Bacchinus de sistris
        Caspar Sagittarius de januis veterum
        Lazarus Bayfius de re vestiariâ
        Octavius Ferrarius de re vestiariâ
        Albertus Rubenius de re vestiariâ
        Octavii Ferrarii analecta de re vestiariâ
        Johan Bapt Donius de utraque pœnula
        Aldus Manutius de togâ Romanorum
        Idem de tunicâ Romanorum
        Idem de tibiis veterum
        Theophilus Raynaudus de pileo

Vol 7 Richard Streinnius de gentibus et familiis Romanorum
        Antonius Augustinus de familiis Romanorum
        Familiæ Romanæ nobiliores, è Fulvii Ursini commentariis
        Guidonis Panciroli notitia dignitatum utriusque imperii orientis scilicet et occidentis ultra Arcadii Honoriique tempora
        Val Chimentelli marmor Pisanum de honore Bisellii

Vol 8 Vetus kalendarium Romanum è marmore descriptum in ædibus Mafiæorum.
        Petri Ciacconii Toletani notæ in vetus Romanorum kalendarium
        Fulvii Ursini notæ ad kalendarium rusticum Farnesianum
        Kalendarii fragmentum, quod visitur in ædibus Capranicorum
        Sibrandi Siccamæ commentarius in fastos kalendares Romanorum
        Vetus kalendarium quod in libris antiquis præfigitur Fastis Ovidii
        Kalendarium Romanum sub Constantini circa annum Christi 354 compositum
        Lambecii notæ in kalendarium vetus
        Thomæ Dempsteri kalendarium Romanum
        Dionysii Petavii kalendarium vetus Romanum.
        Petri Gassendi kalendarium Romanum expositum
        Petrus Viola de veteri nováque Romanorum temporum ratione
        Hadrianus Junius de annis et mensibus.
        Ejusdem fastorum liber
        Johannes Lalamantius de anno Romano.
        M Jacobus Christmannus de calendario Romano
        Franc Robortellus de mensium appellatione ex nominibus imperatorum.
        Josephus Scaliger de veteri anno Romanorum
        Sam. Petiti eclogæ chronologicæ de anno et periodo veterum Romanorum
        Wilhelmus Langius de vetere anno Romanorum.
        Erycii Puteani de bisexto liber
        Petrus Laffinus de veterum Romanorum anno seculari
        Erycii Puteani de nundinis Romanis liber
        Greg Tholosanus de nundinis et mercatibus
        Johan Bapt. Bellus de Pharsalici conflictus mense et die
        Petri Morestelli Philomusus, sive de triplici anno Romanorum
        Ejusdem Alypius, sive de priscorum Romanorum feriis.
        Julius Cæsar Bulengerus de tributis et vectigalibus populi Romani
        Vincentius Contarenus de frumentariâ Romanorum largitione.
        Johan Schefferi Agrippa Liberator, seu dissertatio de novis tabulis
        Barnabas Brissonius de ritu nuptiarum et jure connubiorum
        Antonius Hotmanus de veteri ritu nuptiarum
        Idem de sponsalibus, de veteri ritu nuptiarum, et jure matrimoniorum
        Idem de spuriis et legitimatione
        Johan Meursius de luxu Romanorum
        Stanislaus Kobierzykius de luxu Romanorum
        Joach Johan Maderus de coronis, nuptiarum præsertim, sacris et profanis

Vol 9 Onuphrius Panvinius de ludis circensibus, cum notis Joh Argoli, et additamento Nicolai Pinelli.
        Jul Cæsar Bulengerus de circo Romano, ludisque circensibus, ac de theatro

Onuphrius Panvinius de ludis secularibus
Agesilaus Mariacottus de personis et larvis earumque usu et origine.
Marquardi Freheri Cecropistromachia antiqua duelli gladiatorii, sculptura in Sardoniche exposita, cum notis Hen. Guntheri Thulemarii
Justi Lipsii saturnalioram libri duo de gladiatoribus.
Idem de amphitheatro
Onuphrius Panvinius de triumpho, cum notis et figuris Ioach Johan Maderi

Vol 10 Nicolai Bergieri de publicis et militaribus imperii Romani viis libri 3
Henr Chr Hennini notæ ad Bergierum
Francisci Patricii res militaris Romana, à Ludolpho Neocoro
Hygini et Polybius de castris Romanis, notis R H Schelii
Ratbodus Herminnus Schelius de sacramentis
Idem de custodiâ castrorum
Idem de stipendio militari
Idem de stipendio equestri
Idem de stipendio ductorum
Idem de die stipendii
Idem de frumento et veste.
Idem de tributo et ærario
Idem de prædâ
Idem de victu militum
Idem de itinere.
Idem de agmine Polybiano
Idem de agmine Vespasiano
Idem de cohortibus legionis antiquæ.
Cl Salmasii de re militari Romanorum liber
Johan Henr Bœclerus de legione Romana
Franc Robortellus de legionibus Romanorum
Erycius Puteanus de stipendio militari apud Romanos
Vinc Contarenus de militari Romanorum stipendio.
Michael Angelus Causeus de signis militaribus
Pet Rami liber de militiâ C Julii Cæsaris

Vol 11 Ezechielis Spanhemii orbis Romanus
Stephani Vinandi Pighii fasti magistratuum Romanorum ab urbe conditâ ad tempora Vespasiana.
Integri fasti consulares, idaciani dicti, studio Philippi Labbe
Tironis Prosperi chronicon integrum, ab Adamo ab Romam captam, à Generico Wand rege
Fasti consulares anonymi, cum dissertatione Hen Noris
Anonymus de præfectis urbis ex temporibus Gallieni, ex editione Ægidii Bucheri.
Epistola consularis, supplem et illust. Henrici Noris.
Sortorius Ursatus de notis Romanorum
Ludovicus Savot de nummis antiquis Lud. Neocoru
Albertus Rubenius de gemmâ Tiberianâ et Augusteâ
Idem de urbibus Neocoris diatribe
Marquardus Freherus de re monetariâ veterum Romanorum
Robertus Cenalis de verâ mensurarum ponderumque ratione.
Lucas Pætus de mensuris et ponderibus Romanis et Græcis
Prisciam Cæsariensis, Rhemnii Fannii, Bedæ Angli, Volusii Metiani, Balbi ad Celsum, libri de nummis, ponderibus, mensuris, numeris, eorumque notis, ab Elia Vineto emendati, ut et à Joh Frid Gronovio.
Alexandri Sardi Ferrariensis de nummis liber

Vol. 12 Vincentius Butius de calido, frigido, et temperato antiquorum potu.
Julius Cæsar Bulengerus de conviviis
Erycii Puteani reliquiæ conviviii prisci
Andreas Baccius de thermis veterum
Francisci Robortelli laconici, seu sudationis, quæ adhuc visitur in ruinâ balnearum Pisanæ urbis, explicatio.
Francisci Mariæ Turrigii notæ ad vetustissimam ursi togati, ludi pilæ vitreæ inventoris inscriptionem
Martini Lipenii strenarum historia, à primâ origine ad nostra usque tempora
Marcus Meibomius de fabricâ triremium
Constantinus Opelius de fabricâ triremium Meibomianâ
Isaac Vossius de triremium et liburnicarum constructione
Jacob Philip Thomasinus de donariis et tabellis votivis

Vincentius Alsarius de invidia et fascino veterum
John Schefferus de antiquorum torquibus
Michael Angelus Causeus de vasis, bullis, armillis, fibulis, annulis, clavibus, tesseris, stylis, strigilibus, guttis, phialis lacrymatoriis, de mutuis simulacris et de æneis antiquorum lucernis
Octavius Ferrarius de veterum lucernis sepulcralibus
Picturæ antiquæ sepulchri Nasonorum in Viâ Flaminiâ, delineatæ, æri incisæ Pet Sancto Bartolo, explicatæ vero et illust a Ioh Pet Bellorio
Jacobus Guthcrius de jure manium, seu de ritu, more, et legibus prisci funeris
Ejusdem Choartius major, vel de orbitate toleranda
Petri Morestelli pompa feralis, sive justa funebri veterum.

Novus Thesaurus Antiquitatum Romanarum, congestus ab Alb H de Sallengre 3 vols. folio *Hayæ Comit* 1716.

Vol 1 J Minutoli dissert de urbis Romæ origine et fundatione.
　Idem de urbis Romæ incrementis et casu
　Idem de urbis Romæ topographiâ.
　Idem de Romanorum domibus
　Idem de Romanorum templis
　Idem de Romanorum sepulchris
　Idem de Romanorum ædificiis judicialibus
　L Faunus de antiquitatibus urbis Romæ.
　J M Suaresius de foraminibus lapidum in priscis ædificiis.
　A. Alciatus de magistratibus civilibusque et militaribus officiis
　L. Joubertus de gymnasiis et generibus exercitationum apud antiquos celebrium
　Idem de balneis antiquorum.
　H Noris de duobus nummis Diocletiani et Licinii, diss duplex.
　Idem de votis decennalibus imperatorum ac Cæsarum.
　Poggii Florentini de fortunæ varietate urbis Romæ, et de ruinâ ejusdem descriptio
　F Contelorius de præfecto urbis.
　Marmoris Patavini inscripti obscuri interpretatio, triplici comment
　Delineatio Dianæ Arelatensis à Francesco de Rebatu
　Geminæ matris sacrorum titulus sepulcralis explicatus. Vetus exequiarum ritus unâ detectus à J J Chifletio
　H Th Chifletii diss de Othonibus æreis
　C Chifletius de antiquo numismate
　G. Grenius de rusticatione Romanorum
　Idem de villarum antiquarum apud Rom structura
　A Manutius de Reatina urbe agroque, Sabinaque gente
　Idem de aquis in urbem Romam olim influentibus
　Idem de ratione intercalandi.
　Idem de accumbendi et comedendi ratione
　Idem de convivio tempestivo seu intempestivo.
　Idem de auspiciis
　Idem de trabeâ
　Idem de subselliis
　Idem de signo et statuâ
　Idem de parmâ, clypeo, scuto, peltâ, ancile.
　Idem de primipilo
　Idem de drachmis
　Idem de sestertiis
　P Jovius de Romanis piscibus
　J B Donius de restituendi salubritate agri Romani
　G Guiruni explicatio duorum vetustorum numismatum Nemausensium ex ære
　J Grasseri antiquitates Nemausenses
　Fybenius de ordine equestri veterum Rom morum
　J Servilius de mirandis antiquorum operibus, opibus, &c.
　P L Hannekenii de curâ domesticâ Romanorum diss 4.

Vol 2 A Cirino de urbe Roma ejusque rege Romulo.
　C Salmasius de secretariis
　O Ferrarius de pantomimis et mimis
　N Calliachius de ludis scenicis mimorum et pantomimorum.
　I A Astori epistola de Deo Brotonte

J. A. Astorii comment. in antiquum Alcmanis poetæ Laconis monumentum allatum è Græcia
J. A. Crusius de nocte et nocturnis officiis apud veteres
P. Bertius de aggeribus et pontibus hactenùs ad mare extructis
I. Ferdinandi Comitis Marsilii epistola de ponte sub imperio Trajani supra Danubium exstructo
P. Petavii antiquariæ suppellectilis portiuncula
Ejusdem veterum nummorum ΓΝΩΡΙΣΜΑ
C. Bretus de ordine antiquo judiciorum civilium apud Romanos.
Il Magius de tintinnabulis, notis F. Sweertii
Idem de Equuleo, notis Jungermanni
F. Angelus Roccha de campanis
H. Bossius de togâ Romanâ.
Idem de senatorum lato clavo
Ejusdem Isiacus, sive de sistro opusculum
Ejusdem Janotatius, sive de strenâ.

Vol 3 G. Cuperi de elephantis in nummis obviis exercitationes 2
J. Gutherius de officiis domûs Augustæ publicæ et privatæ
H. F. Salomon de judiciis et pœnis Romanorum
Idem de officiis vitæ civilis Romanorum
P. Lanzoni de coronis et unguentis in antiquorum conviviis
H. Baruffaldus de armis convivalibus
Idem de præficis, &c
P. Lanzoni de luctu mortuali veterum.
L. J. Mohn de clavibus veterum.
Incerti auctoris interpretatio inscriptionum et epitaphiorum, quæ antiquariæ quâ urbis est Boetica in Hispaniâ reperiuntur
Phil. à Turre explicatio inscriptionis taurobolii Lugdunensis
Purpurini à Faventia ad kalendarium Romanum Amiterni effossum minuscula commentaria.
D. Aulisii de gymnasii constructione et mausolei architectura opuscula duo
Idem de colo Mayerano
C. F. Menestrier de colo Mayerano
R. Volaterranus de magistratibus et sacerdotiis Romanorum
J. Guhelmus de magistratibus reip. Rom. dum in libertate urbs fuit
G. Vauchopius (Scotus) de magistratibus veteris populi Romani
Æ. Prævotius de magistratibus populi Romani
H. Bebelius de sacerdotiis et magistratibus Romanorum.
P. Fabri de magistratibus Romanorum commentarius.
E. Putemi pecuniæ Romanæ ratio facillimo ad nostram calculo revocata.
H. Conringius de studiis liberalibus urbis Romæ et Constantinop
C. Cellarius de studiis Romanorum literariis in urbe et provinciis

Utriusque Thesauri Antiquitatum Romanarum Græcarumque Nova Supplementa, congesta à J. Poleno 5 vols folio Venet 1737

Vol 1 Paul Merula de legibus Romanorum
Idem de comitiis Romanorum
P. Ott. Aicher de comitiis veterum Rom
Franc. Poleti historia fori Romani restituta
M. Antonii Majoragii de senatu Romano
Mathæi Ægyptii senatûs consulti de Bacchanalibus explicatio.
Pet. Burmann de vectigalibus populi Romani.
Balth. Bonifaci de archivis liber singularis.
Albert. Barisoni de archivis commentarius.
Scipionis Gentilis disputationum illustrium, sive de jure publico populi Romani, liber
A. G. de armis Romanis libri 2

Vol 2 Gisberti Cuperi apotheosis, vel consecratio Homeri.
Ejusdem explicatio gemmæ Augusteæ.
Ejusdem numismata antiqua explicata
Ejusdem inscriptiones et marmora antiqua exposita et illust.
Ejusdem de utilitate, quam ex numismatis principes capere possunt dissertatio
Schott Homericæ apotheosis in antiquo lapide designatæ nova explanatio
Jacobi Le Roy Achates Tiberianus.
Gisberti Cuperi Harpocrates

ANTIQUITIES

  Ejusdem monumenta antiqua inedita
  Steph Le Moine de Melanophoris epistola
  Claudii Salmasii duarum inscriptionum veterum explicatio
  Ejusdem ad Dosiadæ aras, Simmiæ Rhodii ovum, alas, securim, Theocriti fistulam, notæ
  Georgii d'Arnaud de diis praediis commentarius
  Job Gutberleth de mysteriis deorum Cabirorum
  Joh Astorii de diis Cabiris dissertatio
  Math Brouer de Niedese
  Caroli Patini in tres inscriptiones Græcas commentarius
  Ejusdem in antiquum monumentum Marcellinæ commentarius
  Ejusdem in antiquum cenotaphium Marci Antoni commentarius

Vol. 3 Ant Fran Gorii descriptio monumenti, sive columbarii libertorum et servorum Liviæ, Augustæ, et Cæsaris, notis Ant Salvini
  Octavii Ferrarii dissertatio de balneis
  Ejusdem dissertatio de gladiatoribus
  Nicol Calliachii dissertatio de gladiatoribus
  Dissertatio de suppliciis servorum
  Wilh à Loon eleutheria, sive de manumissione servorum apud Romanos
  Joh Jac Claudii diatribe de nutricibus et paedagogis
  Hieron Mercurialis de arte gymnastica
  Anton Bombardin de carcere
  Christ Schattgenii historia librariorum et bibliopolarum veteris et medii ævi.
  Joh Andr Eschenbachius de scribis veterum Romanorum
  Joh Clerici de stylis veterum, et variis cartarum generibus dissertatio
  Laurentius Pignorius de servis
  Ant Velseri ad Hieron Fabrum medicum de Zeta et Zetario, sive diæta et diætario epistola
  Titi Popmæ Phrysii de operis servorum liber

Vol 4 Gisberti Cuperi et Ottonis Sperlingii dissertationes, sive epistola mutuæ de variis rebus et quæstionibus quæ pertinent ad antiquitates Græcas et Romanas
  Nic Calliachii dissertatio de Osiride
  Ejusdem dissertatio de sacris Eleusiniis et eorundem mysteriis
  Adr Relandi dissertatio de diis Cabiris
  Tobiæ Gutberlethi conjectanea in monumentum Heriæ, Thisbes monodiariæ, et Titi Claudii glaphyri choraulæ
  Ejusdem animadversiones philologicæ in antiquam inscriptionem Græcam Smyrnæ repertam.
  Jac Sponii rei antiquariæ selectæ quæstiones in varias dissertationes distributæ
  Ejusdem miscellanea eruditæ antiquitatis, in quibus marmora, statuæ, musiva, toreumata, gemmæ, numismata referuntur ac illustrantur

Vol 5 March Scip Maffei de amphitheatro Veronensi
  Ejusdem de amphitheatris Galliæ, epistola ad Marchionem Johannem Polenum.
  Ejusdem de antiquis Galliæ theatris, epistola ad Bernardinum Zendrinum.
  Eman Martini de theatro Saguntino
  Jos Emman Minianæ Valentini de theatro Saguntino
  Ejusdem de circi antiquitate et ejus structura dialogus
  Nicol Calliachii dissertatio de ludis scenicis
  Ejusdem dissertatio de circensibus ludis.
  Alexii Symmachi Mazzochii in mutilum Campani amphitheatri titulum aliasque nonnullas Campanas inscriptiones commentarius
  Tobias Gutberleth de Saliis Martis sacerdotibus apud Romanos
  Joh Scheffer de militia navali veterum libri 4, ad historiam Græcam Latinamque utiles
  Ejusdem de re vehiculari veterum
  Pyrrhi Ligorii de vehiculis antiquorum diatriba
  Johannis Schefferi in diatribam Pyrrhi Ligorii de vehiculis antiquorum nota.

Lexicon Antiquitatum Romanarum, auctore S. Pitisco. 2 vols folio *Leorardiæ*, 1713

HISTORY.

Potter's (Jo) Antiquities of Greece, edited, with a concise history of the Grecian States, and a short account of the Lives and Writings of the most celebrated Greek Authors, by G Dunbar 2 vols. 8vo *London* 1813

Boeckh's (Aug) Public Economy of Athens To which is added, a Dissertation on the Silver Mines of Laurion Translated from the German 2 vols 8vo *London*, 1828

Godwyn's (T) English Exposition of the Roman Antiquities, wherein many Roman and English offices are paralleled, and divers obscure phrases explained. 4to *London*, 1689

Adam's (Alex) Roman Antiquities, or, an account of the Manners and Customs of the Romans 8vo *London*, 1807

[Rollin's (Chas)] Treatise on the Revenue and False Money of the Romans 8vo *Lond* 1741.

Sacy (S. de), Mémoires sur divers Antiquités de la Perse. 4to *Par* 1793.

Antique Monuments

Caylus (le Comte A C P), Recueil d'Antiquités Egyptiennes, Etrusques, Grecques, Romaines, et Gauloises, et De la Sauvagère, Recueil d'Antiquités dans les Gaules. 8 vols 4to *Paris*, 1752-70

Millin (A L), Galerie Mythologique, ou Recueil de Monumens pour servir à l'étude de la Mythologie, de l'Histoire de l'Art, des Antiquités, &c des Anciens 2 vols 8vo *Paris*, 1811

Winckelmann (J G), Monumens inédits de l'Antiquité, Statues, Peintures antiques, Pierres gravées, Bas-reliefs de marbre et de terre-cuite expliqués, gravés par David et Mlle Sibire, trad de l'Ital par A F Désodoards, pour compléter l'Histoire de l'Art chez les Anciens, et faire une suite aux Antiquités d'Herculaneum, aux Vases Etrusques d'Hamilton, et au Musée de Florence. 3 vols in two, 4to *Paris*, 1808

Museum Florentinum, exhibens insigniora vetust monumenta quæ extant in Thesauro Mediceo, cum observationibus Ant Franc Gorii 10 vols. folio. *Florentinæ*, 1731-42

Wilton House — A Description of the Antiquities and Curiosities in Wilton House illustrated with Engravings of the capital Statues, Bustos, and Relievos, with the Anecdotes and Remarks of Thomas Earl of Pembroke 4to *Sarum*, 1786

Museum Worsleyanum; or, a Collection of antique Basso-relievos, Bustos, Statues, and Gems, with views of places in the Levant, taken on the spot, in 1785, 6, and 7, in the possession of Sir R Worsley 2 vols in one, folio *London, privately printed*, 1792-4

This is the presentation copy to Lord Nelson, which was afterwards sold by Lady Hamilton It contains proof impressions, and, inserted loosely, is the Analysis, from Savage's Librarian

Blundell's (Henry) CLV Engravings of the principal Statues, Bas-reliefs, Sepulchral Monuments, Urns, and Paintings, in the Collection at Ince-Blundell, [with views of the Pantheon and a portrait of the proprietor] Folio *London, privately printed*, 1809

A presentation copy from Mr Blundell

ANTIQUITIES

Blundell's (H) Account of the Statues, Busts, Bas-reliefs, Cinerary Urns, and other ancient Marbles and Paintings at Ince. 4to *Liverpool, privately printed*, 1803

Museum Thoresbyana, or, a Catalogue of the Antiquities, and of the Natural and Artificial Rarities, preserved in the Repository of Ralph Thoresby, at Leeds, A D 1712, with Notes and Additions by T D Whitaker (Whitaker's Leeds)

Piroli (T H), Antiquités d'Herculaneum, avec une Explication ; publiées par F et P Piranesi 6 vols 4to *Paris*, 1804, &c

Drummond (Sir W) and Robt Walpole's Herculaneum, or, Dissertations [on the City of Herculaneum], containing a MS found among the ruins 4to *London*, 1810

Gell (Sir W) and John P Gandy's Pompeiana, the Topography, Edifices, and Ornaments of Pompeii Imp 8vo Proofs *Lond* 1821.

Gell (Sir W) and John P Gandy's Pompeiana New Series 2 vols imp 8vo Proofs *London*, 1830

Antiquities of Palmyra, alias Tadmor, containing a history of that city and its emperors 8vo *London*, 1715

Wood's (Robt) Ruins of Palmyra, otherwise Tadmor, in the Desart Folio *London*, 1753

Wood s (Rob) Ruins of Balbec, otherwise Heliopolis, in Cœlo-Syria Folio. *London*, 1757

Stuart (James) and Nicholas Revett's Antiquities of Athens, with Supplement of Antiquities of Athens and other places in Greece, Sicily, &c delineated and illustrated by R Cockerell, W Kinnaird, T L Donaldson, W Jenkins, and W Railton 5 vols folio *London*, 1762–1830

The unedited Antiquities of Attica, comprising the architectural remains of Eleusis, Rhamnus, Sunium, and Thoracius By the Dilettanti Society Folio *London*, 1817

Chandler's (R) Ionian Antiquities; published by the Society of Dilettanti 2 vols folio *London*, 1769–97

Clarke (E D) on the Sarcophagus of Alexander the Great, &c. (Plates illustrating) Folio *London*, 1805 (Belzoni's Egypt)

Hobhouse's (John) Dissertations on the Ruins of Rome (Illustrations of Byron)

Taylor (G L) and Edward Cresy's Architectural Antiquities of Rome measured and delineated 2 vols in one, folio *London*, 1821

Rome — LXXIV Engravings of Antiquities in and about Rome, by Piranesi, Busiri, Jolli, G B Natali (Coll. of Prints, Vol XV.)

Bellori (J P) Veteres Arcus Augustorum Triumphis Insignes, ex reliquiis quæ Romæ adhuc supersunt, cum imag restituti antiqui nummis Notasque illustrati Folio *Romæ* 1690

Ciaccone (Alf), Colonna Trajana scolpita, con l'Istoria della Guerra Dacica, &c. movamente designata ed intagliata da Pietro Santo Bartoli Oblong folio *Roma*, ——

Bartoli (P. S) Columna Antoniniana del ci mcisa, cum Notis excerptis ex Declarationibus Oblong folio ——

Rossini (Luigi), le Antichità dei Contorni di Roma, ossia le più rinomata Città del Lazio. Oblong folio *Roma*, 1826.

Adams' (R.) Ruins of the Palace of the Emperor Dioclesian at Spalatro in Dalmatia Folio *Lond* 1764

Morghen (Fil.), le Antichità da Pozzuoli, Baja, e Cuma, incise in rame. Folio. *Napoli*, 1769

Wilkins' (Wm.) Antiquities of Magna Græcia Folio *Cambridge*, 1807.

Capmartin de Chaupy, Découverte de la Maison de Campagne d'Horace; ouvrage utile pour l'intelligence de cet auteur, et qui donne occasion de traiter d'une suite considérable de lieux antiques 3 vols 8vo. *à Rome*, 1767.

Dodwelli (Hen.) de Parmâ Equestri Woodwardiana Dissertatio Recensuit ediditque Tho. Hearne 8vo large paper. *Oxonii*, 1713.

This was suppressed by order of the University of Oxford.

Chifflet (Jo. Jac.) Portus Iccius Julii Cæsaris demonstratus 4to. *Antverp Plantin* 1627.

Ancient Remains in England (English Topography.)

Laborde (Alex.), Description d'un Pavé découvert dans l'ancienne ville d'Italica [près de Seville] Folio, coloured Plates. *Paris*, 1802

Murphy's (James Cav.) Arabian Antiquities of Spain, representing, in 100 Engravings, the principal remains of the Architecture, Sculpture, Painting, and Mosaics of the Spanish Arabs Large folio *Lond* 1815

Antiquities of Mexico; comprising Fac-similes of ancient Mexican Paintings and Hieroglyphics Translated, and illustrated with Notes, by Lord Kingsborough The Drawings, on Stone, by Aglio 9 vols. folio *London*, 1830

Statuæ antiquæ Deorum et Virorum illustrium quæ extant in Thes. Florentino, cum obs A. F. Gori Folio *Florent* 1734

Rossi (Domenico de), Raccolta di Statue, antiche e moderne, data in luce sotto i auspicii della Papa Clemente XI Illustrata colle Spazioni à ciascheduna imagine di P. A. Maffei Large folio, Proof impressions *Roma*, 1704

Des Bustes et des Statues antiques au Palais des Thuilleries, gravés par Baudet et Melan Folio, 1671-80

Thomassin (Simon), Recueil de LXXI des plus belles figures, antiques et modernes, de celles qui sont placées dans les appartements et parc de Versailles; et XII représentant les Saisons Folio, ——

Seroux d'Agincourt, Recueil de Fragmens de Sculpture antique et terre-cuite 4to. *Paris*, 1814

Specimens of ancient Egyptian, Etruscan, Greek, and Roman Sculpture, selected from collections in Great Britain by the Dilettante Society 2 vols folio *London*, 1809

Combe's (Taylor) Description of the Collection of ancient Terra-cottas and Marbles in the British Museum, with Engravings 3 vols imp 4to. large paper *London*, 1810-12

Bellori (J. P.) et P. Sancti Bartoli admiranda Romanorum Antiquitatum ac veteris Sculpturæ Vestigia Oblong folio *Romæ*, 1693

ANTIQUITIES

Clarke's (Edw. D) Greek Marbles brought from the Shores of the Euxine, Archipelago, and Mediterranean, and deposited in the vestibule of the Public Library, Cambridge Small folio. *Camb.* 1809

Stosch (Ph de), Pierres Antiques gravées, sur lesquelles les gravures ont mis leurs noms, dessinées et grav. par B Picart, Iat et Franc. par M de Limiers Folio, large paper. *Amsterdam*, 1724

Worlidge's (Thos) Drawings from Antique Gems, etched after the manner of Rembrandt 2 vols 4to *Lond* 1768 [1780]

Gemmæ Antiquæ, ex Thes Mediceo et privatorum Dactyliothecis Florent , cum Obs A. F Gorn. 2 vols. folio *Florent*. 1731-2

Dactyliotheca Smithiana, complectens Enarrationes et Historiam Glyptographici Ant Fr Gorn 2 vols folio. *Venetiis*, 1767

A Collection of 401 Italian Casts, in sulphur, of ancient Gems, with a Catalogue In a case

---

[Christie's (James)] Disquisition upon Etruscan Vases, displaying their probable connexion with the Shews at Eleusis and the Chinese Feast of Lanterns, with explanations of a few of the allegories depicted upon them Imp 4to *London* [*privately printed*], 1806

Christie's (J) Disquisitions upon the Painted Greek Vases, and their probable connexion with the Shews of the Eleusinian and other mysteries 4to *London*, 1825

Hamilton —Collection of Etruscan, Greek, and Roman Antiquities, from the Cabinet of Sir William Hamilton, with Introduction and Descriptions, in English and French, by D'Hancarville 4 vols in two, folio *Naples*, 1766-7

Hamilton —Tischbien's (W) Engravings from ancient Vases, mostly of pure Greek workmanship, discovered in sepulchres in the kingdom of the Sicilies, but chiefly in the neighbourhood of Naples, during 1789 and 1790, now in the possession of Sir W Hamilton With remarks on each vase by the collector, in English and French 4 vols large folio *Naples*, 1791-5

Hamilton's (Sir W) Outlines from the Figures and Compositions upon the Vases, with engraved borders, by the late W Kirk 4to *Lond* 1804

Vases from the Collection of Sir H Englefield, Bart, drawn and engraved by Henry Moses 4to large paper, Proofs *London*, 1819

Piranesi (C B), Vasi, Candelabri, Cippi, Sarcofagi, Tripodi, Lucerne, ed Ornamenti. Large folio *Roma*, 1778

Numismatics

Evelyn's (John) Numismata a Discourse of Medals, ancient and modern, together with some account of heads and effigies of illustrious persons of whom we have no medals extant Folio *London*, 1697

Pinkerton's (John) Essay on Medals, or, an Introduction to the Knowledge of ancient Coins and Medals 2 vols 8vo *London*, 1808

Addison's (S) Dialogues upon the Usefulness of Ancient Medals (Works, Vol I 4to and 8vo)

HISTORY

Arbuthnot (John) on Ancient Coins   (Commerce.)

Gibbon (Ed.), Principes des Monnoies des Anciens   (Misc Works, Vol III)

[Rollin's (Charles)] Manner of distinguishing Antique Medals from such as are counterfeit   (Revenue of the Romans)

Cardwell's (T) Course of Lectures on the Coinage of the Greeks and Romans, delivered in the University of Oxford   8vo   *Oxford*, 1832.

Rasche (J. C.) Lexicon universæ Rei Nummariæ Veterum, et præcipuè Græcorum ac Romanorum, cum observationibus antiquariis, geographicis, chronologicis, historicis, et criticis Præfatus est C S. Heyne   7 vols in 14, 8vo   *Lipsiæ*, 1785–1805

Sestini (Abati Don) Classes Generales Geographiæ Numismaticæ, seu, Monetæ Urbium, Populorum, et Regum, ordine geographico et chronologico dispositæ, secundùm systema Eckhelianum   2 vols in one, 4to   *Lipsiæ*, 1797

Pedrusi (Paulo), I Cesari in oro raccolti nel Farnese Museo, e publicati colle loro congrue interpretazioni   10 vols. folio   *Parma* 1694–1717

Gori (A F) Antiqua Numismata, aurea et argentea præstantiora, et ærea maximi moduli, quæ in Regio Thesauro M Ducis Ltruriæ adservantur, cum Observationibus   3 vols folio   *Florent* 1740–42

Combe (Car.) Nummorum veterum Populorum et Urbium qui in museo G Hunter asservantur, Descriptio, figuris illustrata   4to   *Londini*, 1782

[Combe (T)] Veterum Populorum et Regum Nummi qui in Museo Britannico adservantur   4to   *Londini*, 1814

Wise (Fr) Nummorum Antiquorum scriniis Bodleianis reconditorum Catalogus, cum Commentario, Tabulis æneis, et Appendice   Folio. *Oxonii*, 1750

Pembrochiæ (Thomæ, Comitis) Numismata antiqua et recentiora omnis generis metalli et moduli, ære incisa, &c. in IV. partes divisa [cum Indice Jo. Ames]   4to   *Londini*, 1746

Northwick (Lord).—Selection of Ancient Greek Coins, chiefly from Magna Grecia and Sicily, from the cabinet of the Right Hon the Lord Northwick, drawn by Del Frate, and engraved by H Moses the Descriptions by Dr Noehden. Imperial 4to   *London*, —

Marsden's (W.) Numismata Orientalia illustrata; the Oriental Coins, ancient and modern, in his collection described   4to   *London*, 1823

Vaillant (J. F.) Seleucidarum Imperium; sive, Historia Regum Syriæ, ad fidem numismatum accommodata   Folio.   *Hagæ Comit* 1732.

Combe (C) Index Nummorum omnium imperatorum Augustorum et Cæsarum à Julio Cæsare usque ad postumum, qui ex ære magni moduli signabantur   4to   *Londini*, 1783

Tabulæ Nummorum Antiquorum qui sunt in Notis J Harduini ad Plinium illustrati   (Plinii Hist Nat. Vol III)

Quinones (Juan de), Explication de Unas Monedas de oro de Emperadores Romanos, que se han hallado en el Puerto de Guadarrama 4to   *Madrid*, 1620

ANTIQUITIES

Clarke's (Wm) Connexion of the Roman, Saxon, and English Coins, deduced from Observations on the Saxon Weights and Money   4to   *London*, 1767

Davies (E) on Ancient British Coins   (Druidical Mythology)

Stukeley's (W) Medallic History of M A Carausius, Emperor of Britain   2 vols 4to   *London*, 1757–9

Sharpe (Abp John) on English Coins   (Manuscripts)

Pembrochiæ (T) Nummi Anglici et Scotici.   (Numism Ant et Recent)

Fleetwood's (Bp) Historical Account of Coins, from William the Conqueror to the Restoration   8vo   *London*, 1745   (Chronicon Preciosum)

Leake's (S Martin) Historical Account of English Money, from the Conquest to the present time; including those of Scotland from the union of the two crowns   8vo   *London*, 1745

Folkes's (M) Tables of English Silver and Gold Coins   [With explanation of the Plates by Drs Ward and Gifford, and Supplement by F Perry]   4to   The Roxburgh copy   *London, by the Society of Antiquaries*, 1763

[Snelling's (Thomas)] View of the Silver Coin and Coinage of England, from the Norman Conquest to the present time   Folio.   *Lond* 1762.

[Snelling's (T)] View of the Gold Coin and Coinage of England, from Henry III to the present time.   Folio   *London*, 1763

Snelling's (T) View of the Copper Coin and Coinage of England , including the Leaden, Tin, and Latten Tokens of Tradesmen and Corporations   Folio   *London*, 1766

Ruding's (Rogers) Annals of the Coinage of Britain and its dependencies, from the earliest period to the close of 1818   5 vols 8vo and Plates in 4to   *London*, 1819

Pegge's (Samuel) Assemblage of Coins fabricated by order of the Archbishops of Canterbury , with Observations on a Coin of Alfred the Great and on the famous Unwic of the late Mr Thoresby   4to   *London*, 1772

[Combe's (T)] Description of the Anglo-Gallic Coins   4to   *Lond*   1827

Snelling s (Thomas) Miscellaneous Views of the Coins struck by English Princes in France, counterfeit Sterlings, Coins struck by the East India Company, in the West India colonies, and in the Isle of Man, also of Pattern Pieces for Gold and Silver Coins and Gold Nobles struck abroad in imitation of English   Folio   *London*, 1769

Snelling s (T) View of the Silver Coin and Coinage of Scotland, from Alexander I to the union of the kingdoms   *London*, 1774

Simon's (James) Essay towards an Historical Account of Irish Coins, and of the currency of Foreign Monies in Ireland   4to   *Dublin*, 1749

Vertue's (George) Medals, Coins, and Great Seals, from the elaborate works of Thomas Simon, chief engraver to the Mint, from Charles I to Charles II   4to   *London*, 1753

Tindal's Medallic History of England, from the Revolution to the death of George I   (Rapin's History of England, Vol V.)

Series of Medals illustrative of English Victories in the reign of George III. In a 4to case, bound in morocco

Snelling's (T) View of the Coins at this time current throughout Europe
8vo   *London*, 1766

Médailles sur les principaux Evenemens du règne de Louis le Grand, avec des Explications historiques [par Fr Charpentier, P Tallemand, J Racine, Boileau, &c]   Folio   *Paris*, 1723
    The preface, which was suppressed before the publication of the first edition, is contained in this   It is an historical account of the progress of the study of medals, and states that the famous Colbert was the first who introduced the descriptive terms, *Légende, Type* and *Exergue*

Lastanosa (Vinc Juan de), Museo de las Medallas des conocidas Españolas. Illustrado con tres discursos del P Paulo de Rajas, del Dr Franc Ximenez de Urrea, i del Dr J F A de Uztarroz   4to Port Plates and Front   *Huesca*, 1645

Sacy (Silv de), les Medailles des Rois de la dynastie des Sassanides (Antiq de la Perse.)

Inscriptions

Gruteri (J) Inscriptiones antiquæ totius orbis Romani   4 vols folio *Amst* 1707

Muratori (L. A) Novus Thesaurus veterum Inscriptionum   4 vols folio *Mediolani*, 1739–42

Donati (Seb) ad Novum Thesaurum vet Inscriptionum Muratori Supplementum   2 vols folio   *Lucæ*, 1765

Chandler (Ric) Inscriptiones antiquæ pleræque nondùm editæ, in Asiâ Minori et Græciâ collectæ   Folio   *Oxonii*, 1774

Chishull (Edm) Inscriptio Sigea antiquissima Βουστροφηδὸν exarata. Folio. *London*, 1721

Chishull (E) Antiquitates Asiaticæ Christianam æram antecedentes, cum Notis et Comment. illustratæ.   Folio   *London* 1728

Sect. II —UNIVERSAL HISTORY.

Struvii (B G) Bibliotheca Historica, aucta à C G Budero , nunc verò à J G Meuselio ita digesta, amplificata, et emendata   11 vols 8vo.   *Lipsiæ*, 1782–1804

Hearne's (Thomas) Ductor Historicus; or, a short System of Universal History, and an Introduction to the study of it.   8vo.   *London*, 1714–23

Anquetil (L. P), Précis de l'Histoire Universelle, ou, Tableau Historique, présentant les vicissitudes des nations, depuis le tems où elles ont commencé à être connues jusqu'au moment actuel   9 vols. 12mo *Paris*, 1799

Bossuet (J B), Discours sur l'Histoire Universelle jusqu'à l'empire de Charlemagne   4 vols. 18mo   *Paris, Didot*, 1784

Gibbon's (Edward) Outlines of the History of the World. (Misc Works, Vol II)

Millot's (Abbé) Elements of General History, translated   5 vols 8vo *London*, 1778–9

Purchas' (Sam) Relations of the World, and the Religions observed in all ages and places discovered from the creation unto this present. Folio *Lond* 1626

Tytler's (A F) Elements of General History, ancient and modern, with Continuation to the demise of George III by Edward Nares 3 vols 8vo *Lond* 1824–5

Universal History, from the earliest accounts to the present time, compiled from original authors 60 vols 8vo *London*, 1779–85.

Sect III — ANCIENT HISTORY.
Origin of Nations.

Cumberland's (Bp R) Origines Gentium antiquissimæ, or, Attempts for discovering the times of the first planting of Nations. 8vo *London*, 1724

Drummond's (Sir W) Origines, or, Remarks on the Origin of several ancient Oriental Empires, States, and Cities 2 vols 8vo *London*, 1824.

Fourmont (M), Réflexions sur l'Origine, l'Histoire, et la Succession des anciens peuples, Chaldeens, Hebreux, Pheniciens, Egyptiens, Grecs, &c jusqu'au tems de Cyrus. 2 vols 4to *Paris*, 1747.

Prichard (J C.) on the Eastern Origin of the Celtic Nations 8vo *London*, 1831

General Ancient History, and particular History of several Ancient Nations.

History of the World, from the creation to the birth of Abraham (An. Univ. Hist Vol I)

Ralegh's (Sir W) History of the World, from the creation until the conquest of Asia and Macedon by the Romans, with a Chronological Table, shewing the years of the Julian period, World, Patriarchs, &c , printed after the edition of 1614 (Works, Vol II to VII)

Rutherford's (Wm) View of Ancient History, including the progress of Literature and the Fine Arts 2 vols 12mo *London* 1809

Heeren's (A H L) Manual of Ancient History, particularly with regard to the Constitutions Commerce, and Colonies of the States of Antiquity, translated 8vo *Oxford*, 1831

Diodori Siculi Historia Egypti, Persiæ, Syriæ, Mediæ, Romæ, et Carthaginis (Classics)

Bryant's (Jacob) History of the Babylonians, Chaldeans, Egyptians, Canaanites, &c &c (System of Mythology)

Gibbon (Edward), sur la Monarchie des Mèdes, les principaux Epoques de la Grèce et de l'Egypte, et sur la Succession de l'Empire Romain (Misc Works, Vol III)

Rollin's (Charles) Ancient History of the Egyptians, Carthaginians, Assyrians, Babylonians, Medes and Persians, Grecians and Macedonians, revised and corrected, to which is prefixed, a Life of the Author by R Lynam. 6 vols 8vo *London*, 1823

HISTORY

Heeren's (A H L) Historical Researches into the Politics, Intercourse, and Commerce of the Carthaginians, Æthiopians, and Egyptians; with a general Introduction, translated   2 vols. 8vo.   *Oxford*, 1831

History of Egypt to the time of Alexander the Great, and from the foundation of that monarchy by Ptolemy Soter to its becoming a Roman province. (Ancient Un Hist Vols I and VIII)

Champollion (le Jeune), l'Egypte sous les Pharaons, ou, Recherches sur la Géographie, la Religion, la Langue, l'Ecriture, et l'Histoire de l'Egypte, avant l'invasion de Cambyse   2 vols 8vo   *Paris*, 1814.

Champollion-Figeac, Annales des Lagides, ou, Chronologie des Rois Grecs de l'Egypte, successeurs d'Alexandre le Grand 2 vols 8vo. *Paris*, 1819.

History of the Moabites, Ammonites, Midianites, Edomites, Amalekites, Canaanites, and Philistines, and of the ancient Syrians   (Ancient Univ Hist Vol 1)

History of the Jews, to the destruction of Jerusalem by Titus Vespasian. (Ancient Univ Hist Vols. II and III , also Hist of Religion)

Sanchoniathon's Phœnician History, translated from the first book of Eusebii Præparatio Evangelica with a continuation by Eratosthenes Cyrenæus's Canon   Illustrated by historical and chronological remarks by Bp R Cumberland   8vo.   *London*, 1720

History of the Phœnicians   (Ancient Univ Hist Vol II.)

History of the Assyrians, Babylonians, Phrygians, and Trojans. (Anc Un Hist Vol III)

History of the Lycians, Lydians, and ancient Cilicia   (An Un. Hist Vols III and IV)

History of the Medes, Persians, and Parthians (An Un Hist. Vols IV and IX)

History of the Scythians, Gomerians, and Mysians   (An Un Hist Vol IV)

History of the Seleucidæ in Syria, the Armenians, and the kingdom of Pontus   (An Un Hist Vol VIII)

History of the Cappadocians, Bithynians, and the kingdoms of Colchis, Iberia, Albania, Bosphorus, Medea, Bactria, Edessa, Emesa, Adiobene, Characene, Elymais, Comagene, and Chalcidene   (An Un Hist Vol. IX)

History of the King of Pergamus, Thrace, and Epirus. (An Un. Hist. Vol. IX)

History of the Carthaginians, Numidians, Mauritanians, Gætulians, and Æthiopians   (An Un Hist Vols XV. and XVI)

History of the Etruscans   (An Un Hist Vol XVIII)

Pinkerton (John) on the Origin and Progress of the Scythians and Goths, being an Introduction to the ancient and modern History of Europe. 8vo. *London*, 1787   (Hist of Scotland, Vol II)

Grecian History.

Pausaniæ Græciæ Descriptio.
Herodotus, - containing Olympiads 14– 75
Thucydides, - - - 75– 92
Xenophon, - - - 55–104
Ctesia, Theopompus, Agatharchides, Memnon, &c 55–94
Diodorus Siculus, - - - 75–120
Plutarchus, Arrianus, et Curtius de Rebus Alex. M. 111–113
See Classics

Cramer's (J A) Geographical and Historical Description of ancient Greece; with a Map, and a Plan of Athens. 3 vols 8vo   *Oxford*, 1828

History of the Fabulous and Heroic Times; containing the history of the ancient kingdoms of Sicyon, Argos, Attica, Bœotia, Arcadia, Thessaly, Corinth, of Sparta to Lycurgus, &c.   (An Un Hist Vol. V)

Mitford's (Wm) History of Greece. 5 vols. 4to. *London*, 1789–1818.

Gillies' (John) History of ancient Greece, its Colonies and Conquests, from the earliest accounts till the division of the Macedonian empire in the East, including the history of Literature, Philosophy, and the Fine Arts. 4 vols 8vo *London*, 1809

Gillies' (J) History of the World, from the reign of Alexander to that of Augustus, comprehending the later ages of European Greece, and the history of the Greek kingdoms in Asia and Africa, from their foundation to their destruction   2 vols 4to *London*, 1807

Heeren's (A H L) Sketch of the Political State of ancient Greece, translated. 8vo *Oxford*, 1831

Barthélemy (Jean Jacq), Voyage du Jeune Anacharsis en Grèce, avec Mémoires sur la Vie de l'Auteur par lui-même 7 vols 8vo *Paris*, 1799.

Anacharsis —Recueil de Cartes Géographiques, Plans, Vues, et Médailles de l'ancienne Grèce, relatifs au Voyage du Jeune Anacharsis, précédé d'une analyse critique des cartes [par J D. Barbie du Bocage]. 4to *Paris*, 1799

Muller's (C. O) History and Antiquities of the Doric Race, translated by H Tufnell and G C Lewis 2 vols 8vo *Oxford*, 1830

History of the Athenians and Spartans   (An Un Hist. Vol. V.)

Young's (Sir W) History of Athens, including a commentary on the principles, policy, and practice of Republican Governments Royal 8vo *London*, 1804

Athenian Letters, or, the Epistolary Correspondence of an agent of the King of Persia, residing in Athens during the Peloponnesian War, [by the Earl of Hardwicke, Hon E Yorke, Dis. Rooke, Green, Heberden, Birch, Salter, &c &c] 2 vols 4to *London*, 1798

Theban History, in which the Phocian, or Sacred War, and the Histories of the Arcadians, Corinthians, Argives, Thessalians, Eleans, and other inferior states, are continued (An Un Hist Vol VI)

History of the Macedonians (An Un Hist Vols VII and VIII)

Leland's (Tho) Life and Reign of Philip King of Macedon, the father of Alexander 2 vols 8vo *London*, 1806

History of the Islands of Sicily, Crete, Samos, Rhodes, &c. to their becoming subject to the Romans   (An. Un Hist Vols VI and VII)

Raoul Rochette (M), Histoire Critique de l'établissement des Colonies Grecques   4 vols 8vo   *Paris*, 1815.

Roman History.

Dionysius Halicarnassus, containing An Urbis cond			1– 312
Livius,	-	-	-	1– 587
Polybius,	-	-	-	365– 609
Sallustius,	-	-	-	640– 706
Cæsar,	-	-	-	695– 709
Ciceronis Epistolæ,	-	-	684– 710
Dion Cassius,	-	-	-	1– 684
Tacitus,	-	-	-	766– 845
Suetonius,	-	-	-	669– 848
Herodianus,	-	-	-	932– 991
Historia Augusta,	-	-	868–1036
Ammianus Marcellinus,	-	-	1105–1130
Zosimus,	-	-	-	9–1162

Appian, Eutropius, Florus, Justin, C Nepos, S. Rufus, Valerius Maximus, Victor, Historiæ Romanæ Scriptores max. et minores

See Classics.

Fragmenta Historiarum, collecta ab Antonio Augustino, emendata à Ful Ursino, et ejusdem Notæ ad Sallustium, Cæsarem, Livium, Tacitum, Suetonium, et alios   8vo   *Antv. ex off. Plantin* 1595.

Gibbon (Ed) Nomina Gentis Antiquæ Italiæ   (Mis. Works, Vol III)

History of the ancient State of Italy, to the building of Rome.   (An. Un Hist. Vol. IX)

Roman History, from Romulus to the removal of the imperial seat to Constantinople   (An Un Hist Vols. IX to XIV)

Niebuhr's (B. G) History of Rome. Translated from the third edition of the original, by J C Hare and C Thirlwall   2 vols 8vo   *Cambridge*, 1831

Hooke's (N) Roman History, from the building of Rome to the ruin of the Commonwealth.   4 vols. 4to   *London*, 1770–71

Ferguson's (Ad.) History of the Progress and Termination of the Commonwealth   5 vols 8vo   *Edin* 1813

Crevier's (J B L) History of the Roman Emperors, from Augustus to Constantine , translated by John Mill   10 vols 8vo   *London*, 1814

Lyttleton's (Geo Lord) Observations on the Life of Cicero, and on the Roman History   (Misc Works)

[Montesquieu], Considerations sur les Causes de la Grandeur des Romains et de leur Décadence   A laquelle on a joint un Dialogue de Scylla et d'Eucrate, et la Défense de l'Esprit des Lois, avec quelques éclaircissemens   Large paper, royal 8vo.   *Edinb* 1751

Leigh's (Edw) Select and Choyce Observations on all the Romane Emperours.   Small 8vo   *London* 1657

ANCIENT 181

Byzantine History.

Byzantinæ Historiæ Scriptores varii scilicet
   Labbe (P) de Hist. Byz Scriptoribus publicandis Protrepticon. Folio *Parisiis, è typ. Reg* 1648
   Procopii Historia sui temporis, Gr et Lat ; cum Notis C Maltreti 2 vols folio. *Parisiis, typ Reg* 1662
   Agathias de Rebus Gestis Imperat Justiniani, Gr. et Lat ex interp et cum Notis Bon Vulcanii. Folio *Parisiis, typ Reg* 1660.
   Theophylacti Simocattæ Historia, Gr. et Lat ex interp J Pontani, et Glossario Græco-barbaro auctior, studio et operâ C A. Fabroti Folio *Parisiis*, 1647.
   Nicephori Patr Const Breviarium Historicum de Rebus Gestis ab obitu Mauricii ad Constantinum usque Copronymum, Gr et Lat ex interp et cum Notis D Petavio. Folio *Parisiis*, 1648
   Syncelli (Geor.) Chronographia, Gr. et Lat cum Notis J Goar Folio *Parisiis*, 1652
   Theophanis Chronographia, Gr et Lat ex interpret. J. Goar, cum Notis F Combehsii Folio *Parisiis*, 1655.
   Theophanis Historiæ Byzant Scriptores post Theophanem, Gr et Lat cum Notis F Combefisii Folio *Parisiis*, 1685
   Cedreni (Geo) Compendium Historiarum ab orbe condito ad Isaacum Comnenum, Gr et Lat cum Notis J Goar, et C A Fabroti Glossario 2 vols folio *Parisiis*, 1647
   Zonaræ (Jo) Annales, Gr. et Lat cum Notis C Dufresne D Ducange 2 vols. folio *Parisiis*, 1686
   Glycæ (M) Annales, Gr et Lat. cum Notis P Labbe Folio *Parisiis*, 1660
   Comnenæ (Annæ) Alexias, Gr. et Lat cum Notis D. Hoeschelii Folio *Parisiis*, 1651
   Cinnami (Jo) de Rebus Gestis à Jo. et Man. Comnenis Libri VI , Gr et Lat cum Notis C Dufresne D Ducange Folio *Parisiis*, 1670
   Acommati (N) Choniatæ Historia, Gr et Lat., edente C A. Fabroto. Folio. *Parisiis*, 1647
   Acropolitæ (Geo.) Historia Byzantina, Gr et Lat cum Notis T. Douzæ Folio *Parisiis*, 1651
   Pachymeris (Geor) Historia, Gr et Lat ex interp et cum Notis Pet Possini 2 vols. folio *Romæ*, 1666–69
   Gregoræ (Nicephori) Historia Byzant Gr et Lat cum Notis J Boivin 2 vols folio *Parisiis*, 1702
   Cantacuzeni (Jo) Historia, Gr. et Lat cum Notis Jac. Gretseri 3 vols. folio *Parisiis*, 1645
   Chalcocondylæ (L) Historia Turcarum, Gr et Lat edente C A Fabroto Folio *Parisiis*, 1650
   Genesii (Jos) Geo. Phrantzæ et aliorum Historia Byzantina, Gr et Lat Folio *Venetiis* 1733
   Phrantzæ (Geo) Chronicon Græci, edidit F C Alter Folio *Viennæ*, 1706
   Ducæ, M Ducæ Nepotis, Historia Byzant. Gr. et Lat cum Notis Ism Bullialdi Folio *Parisiis*, 1649
   Ville Hardouin (Geoffroy de), Histoire de l'Empire de Constantinople sous les Empereurs François, avec les Notes de C Dufresne Ducange Folio *Paris*, 1657

HISTORY

The Chronicle of Geoffry de Villehardouin, concerning the conquest of Constantinople by the French and Venetians, Anno M CCIV Translated [with Introductory Preface] by T. Smith. 8vo. *London,* 1829

Dufresne (C) D Ducange Historia Byzantina. Folio. *Paris* 1680.

Corporis Historiæ Byzantinæ nova Appendix, opera Geo Pisidæ, Theodosii Diaconi, et Corippi Africani complectens, Gr. et Lat ex recensione P. Γ. Foggini Folio *Romæ,* 1777.

Leonis Diaconi Caloensis Historia Scriptoresque alii ad res Byzantinas pertinentes, Gr et Lat Notis illustr. C. B Hase. Folio, *Parisiis,* 1819

Gesta Dei per Francos, sive Orientalium et Regni Francorum Hierosolymitani Historia, ex recensione J Bongarsii 2 vols. folio. *Hanoviæ,* 1611

Chronicon Paschale, Gr et Lat cum Notis Car. Dufresne D. Ducange Folio *Parisiis,* 1688

Chronicon Orientale, ex Arabico Latinè versum ab Abr. Ecchellensi. Folio *Parisiis,* 1651.

Manassis (Const.) Breviarum Historicum, Gr. et Lat. ex interp J Leunclavii, cum ejusdem et Jo Meursii Notis Folio. *Parisiis,* 1655

Banduri (Anselmi) Imperium Orientale, sive Antiquitates Constantinopolitanæ, Gr et Lat. 2 vols folio *Parisiis,* 1711

Porphyrogennetæ (Const) de Ceremoniis Aulæ Byzantinæ, Gr et Lat., curârunt J. H Leichius et Jo Ja Reiskius. 2 vols. in one, folio. *Lipsiæ,* 1751.

Theophylacti Archiep Bulgariæ Institutio Regia ad Porphyrogennitam, Gr. interprete P Possino. 4to. *Parisiis,* 1651.

Notitia Dignitatum Imperii Romani, à P Labbe. 12mo *Par.* 1651.

Dufresne (C) D Ducange de Imperatorum Constantinopolitanis Numismatibus 4to *Romæ,* 1755

Anastasii Bibliothecarii Historia Ecclesiastica [et de Vitis Romanorum Pontificum, ex divers Auct Græcis excerpta, et in Lat versa] cum Notis, &c C. A Fabroti Folio *Parisiis,* 1649

Codini Curopolatæ (Geo) de officiis Magnæ Ecclesiæ et Aulæ Constantinopolitanæ, Gr et Lat , edente Jac Goar Folio. *Parisiis,* 1648

Boschius (P) de Patriarchis Antiochenis Folio *Venetiis,* 1748.

Cuperus (Guil.) de Patriarchis Constantinopolitanis. Folio *Venet* 1751.

Gibbon's (Edw) History of the Decline and Fall of the Roman Empire, with some account of the Author's Life and Writings 12 vols 8vo. *London,* 1820

Gibbon's (E) Vindication of the 15th and 16th Chapters of his Roman History. (Misc. Works, 4to. Vol. II)

History of the Eastern and Western Empires, to the taking of Constantinople by the Turks. (An Un Hist Vols. XIV and XV)

History of the Empires of Nice and Trapezond (An Un. Hist Vol XVI)

Mahon's (Lord) Life of Belisarius 8vo. *London,* 1829.

Sect. IV.—HISTORY OF THE MIDDLE AGES.

Eccardi (J G) Corpus Historicum Medii Ævi, à temp. Caroli Magni usque ad finem Sæculi XV 2 vols folio *Lipsiæ*, 1723

Hallam's (Henry) View of Europe during the Middle Ages 2 vols 4to *London*, 1818

Fuller's (Thos) Historie of the Holy Warre. Folio. Front. by Marshall. *Cambridge*, 1639

Michaud (M), Histoire des Croisades depuis les premiers temps ; avec l'analyse de tous les chroniques d'Orient et d'Occident qui parlent des Croisades 7 vols 8vo *Paris*, 1812–22

Mills's (Charles) History of the Crusades for the possession of the Holy Land 2 vols 8vo *London*, 1822

Mills's (C.) History of Chivalry, or, Knighthood and its Times 2 vols. 8vo. *London*, 1826

Strickeri Rhythmus antiquus Germanicus de Caroli Magni Expeditione Hispanicâ, nunc primùm in luce donatus ex MS Pergam Notisque suis auctum J G. Scherzio (Schilteri Thes. Vol. II)

Anonymi Fragmentum de Bello Caroli M contra Saracenos, versibus antiquis Germanicis, edidit ex MS. Perg. et Notis illustravit J. Schilterus (Schilteri Thes. Vol. II.)

Sect. V —MODERN HISTORY.

Europe.— General History.

Butler (Charles) on the chief Revolutions of the principal States which composed the Empire of Charlemagne, from 814 to its dissolution in 1806 , on the Genealogies of the Imperial House of Hapsburgh , and of the six Secular Electors of Germany , and on Roman, German, French, and English Nobility   Royal 8vo *London*, 1807

Voltaire's (M. de) General History and State of Europe, from the time of Charlemain to the age of Louis XIV , with a Preliminary View of the Oriental Empires. 3 vols. 8vo *Lond* 1754–7

Jove, (Histoire de P), sur les choses, faictes, et advenues de son temps [1494–1547] en toutes les parties du monde, traduites de Latin en François par Denis Sauvage 2 vols. in one, folio *Par* 1581

Thuani (J. A) Historia sui temporis [ab Ann 1543 ad 1607, et ad 1610 continuavit N Rigalto] , accedit Sylloge Scriptorum varii generis et argumenti, in quâ de vitâ, scriptis, &c , amicis et inimicis Thuan scitu dignissima continentur, curâ S Buckley   7 vols folio, large paper , successively the Harley and Roxburgh copy *Londini*, 1733, &c

> The suppressed passages of Camden's Annals were communicated by the author to Thuanus, and are incorporated in his history this edition also replaces similar suppressions made in De Thou's own work

Siri (V) Memorie Recondite, dall' Anno 1601 sino al 1640. 8 vols *Ronco, Parigi, è Leone*, 1677–79 , — Il medesimo, il Mercurio, ovvero Historia de' correnti tempi [1635–55] 15 vols in 18 *Casale, Lione, Parigi, è Firenze*, 1614–82 ;—Il med Bollo nel Mercurio Vendico del Sig Dott Birago. *Modena*, 1613. 27 vols. 4to

Wraxall's (N W) View of the Civil, Political, and Social States of Europe, between the middle and the close of the XVIth Century. (History of France, Vol 1)

Parival (J N. de), Abrégé de l'Histoire de ce Siècle de Fer, contenant les misères et calamitéz des derniers tems, avec leurs causes et prétextes. Small 8vo   *Leyde*, 1653

Temple's (Sir W.) Memoirs of what passed in Christendom from 1665 to 1680   (Works, Vols I and II)

Bougeant (le P), Histoire des Guerres et des Négotiations qui précéderent et suivirent le Traité de Westphalie   6 vols 12mo.   *Paris*, 1744.

Russell s (Lord John) Memoirs of the Affairs of Europe from the Peace of Utrecht [with Introduction, on the Character of the ancient Germans, and Relations of Government to each other]   Vols I and II containing to 1742   4to.   *London*, 1824–9

[Dodsley's (J)] Annual Register ; or, a View of History, Politics, and Literature, from 1758.   *London*, 1758, &c

Georgel (l'Abbé)   Mémoires pour servir à l'Histoire des Evénemens de la fin du XVIII Siècle, depuis 1760 jusqu'en 1810.   6 vols 8vo.   *Paris*, 1818.

Paoli-Chagny (M le Comte de), Histoire de la Politique des Puissances de l'Europe, depuis le commencement de la Revolution Française, jusqu'au Congres de Vienne.   4 vols. 8vo   *Paris*, 1817

Bigland (John) on the Modern History and Political Aspect of Europe. 8vo   *London*, 1806

Schoel (Fred), Tableau des Peuples qui habitent l'Europe, classés d'après les langues qu'ils parlent, et des religions qu'ils professent 8vo   *Paris*, 1812

Lewkenor (Sam), a Discourse not altogether unprofitable nor unpleasant for such as are desirous to know the situation and customes of forraine cities without travelling to see them , containing a Discourse of all those cities wherein doe flourish at this day priviledged Universities 4to   *London, H Hooper*, 1600

Malcom's (J P) Miscellaneous Anecdotes, illustrative of the Manners and Customs of Europe, during the reigns of Charles II , James II , William III , and Queen Anne   8vo   *Lond* 1811

Froissart's (Sir John) Chronicles of England, France, and adjoining countries   (English History)

Lanquet, &c 's Epitome of Cronicles, conteyning the whole Discourse of the Histories as wel of England as al other countreys   (English History)

Chambre (David), Histoire Abrégée de tous les Roys de France, Angleterre, et Ecosse, mise en ordre par forme d'harmonie.   Small 8vo. *Paris*, 1579

Rocoles (J B de), les Imposteurs Insignes ; ou, Histoires de plusieurs hommes de néant, de toutes nations, qui ont usurpé la qualité d'Empereurs, Roys, et Princes   Small 8vo   *Amsterdam*, 1683

Miller's (Geo) History Philosophically illustrated, from the Fall of the Roman Empire to the French Revolution   4 vols 8vo   *London*, 1832

History of England.

Topography and Antiquities.

Leland's (John) Laboryouse Journey and Serche for England's Antiquities geven of hym as a newe yeare's gyfte to K. Henry the VIII, in the xxxvii yeare of his reygne; with Declaracyons enlarged by John Bale. Black letter, small 8vo. (See also Leland's Life.) *London, by Johan Bale,* 1549

[Rawlinson's (Richard)] English Topographer, or, an account of all the pieces relating to the Antiquities, Natural History, or Topography of England. 8vo. With MS Notes by Mr T. Wilson, of Leeds. *London,* 1720

Gough's (Richard) Topography, or an historical account of what has been done for illustrating the Topographical Antiquities of Great Britain and Ireland. 2 vols 4to *Lond* 1789.

Upcott's (William) Bibliographical Account of the principal works relating to English Topography. 3 vols 8vo. large paper. *Lond* 1818

Britton's (John) Catalogue of the Historical and Illustrative Works on English Topography (Appended to the several counties Beauties of England and Wales)

Adams' (John) Index Villaris, or, an Alphabetical Table of all the Cities, Towns, Parishes, Villages, and Private Seats in England and Wales Folio *London,* 1680

Lambarde's (Wm) Dictionarium Angliæ Topographicum et Historicum, an alphabetical description of the chief places in England and Wales, now first published from the Author's MSS 4to *London,* 1730

Capper's (B P) Topographical Dictionary of the United Kingdom. 8vo *London,* 1808.

Carlisle's (Nicholas) Topographical Dictionary of England, Wales, Ireland, Scotland, and the British Isles 6 vols 4to *Lond* 1808-13
England, Vols I and II Ireland, Vol III
Wales, Vol. IV Scotland and the British Isles, Vols V and VI

Roman Topography

Horsley's (John) Britannia Romana, or, the Roman Antiquities of Britain Folio *London,* 1732

Baxter (Guil) Glossarium Antiquitatum Britannicarum, sive, Syllabus Etymologicus Antiquitatum veteris Britanniæ atque Iberniæ temporibus Romanorum. Accedunt E Luidii de fluviorum, montium, urbium, &c in Britannia, nominibus adversaria. 8vo *London,* 1733

Gale (Roger) on the recovery of the Courses of the four great Roman Ways (Leland's Itinerary, Vol VI)

Roy's (Wm) Military Antiquities of the Romans in North Britain, and particularly of their ancient system of castrametation; and comprehending a treatise wherein the ancient geography of that part of the island is rectified Folio *London,* 1793

Musgrave (Guill.) Belga, Antiquitates Britanno-Belgicæ, præcipuè Romanæ [cura Guil. Musgravii filii et Samuelis Musgravii] 4 vols. 8vo. *Iscæ-Dunmoniorum (Exeter)*, 1719, 16, 11, and 20

Ecclesiastical and Monastical Topography

See also Manuscripts, and for particular accounts, &c. of cathedral churches or abbeys, vide the various counties

Willis' (Browne) Survey of the Cathedrals of York, Durham, Carlisle, Chester, Man, Litchfield, Hereford, Worcester, Gloucester, Bristol, Lincoln, Ely, Oxford, Peterborough, Canterbury, Rochester, London, Winchester, Chichester, Norwich, Salisbury, Wells, Exeter, St. David's, Llandaff, Bangor, and St. Asaph, containing an Account of the bishops, deans, prebends, &c. belonging to them. 3 vols. 4to. *London*, 1742

Willis' (B.) Parochiale Anglicanum; or, the Names of all the Churches and Chapels within the Dioceses of Canterbury, Rochester, London, Winchester, Chichester, Norwich, Salisbury, Wells, Exeter, St. David's, Llandaff, Bangor, and St. Asaph. 4to. *London*, 1733; in Vol. III of the preceding

Willis' (B.) Survey of the Cathedral of St. Asaph, considerably enlarged and brought down to the present time, with an historical Appendix and Life of the Author by E. Edwards. 2 vols. 8vo. *Wrexham*, 1801

Willis' (B.) Survey of the Cathedral of Landaff. 8vo. *London*, 1719.

Willis' (B.) Survey of the Cathedral of Bangor. 8vo. *Lond.* 1721

Willis' (B.) Survey of the Cathedral of St. David's. 8vo. *Lond.* 1717

Pegge's (Sam.) Sylloge of the remaining authentic Inscriptions relative to the erection of our English Churches. Plates. (Nichols's Bib. Top. No. 41 Vol. VI.)

Staveley's (Thomas) History of the Churches in England [containing an account of their sacred furniture, &c. from their earliest origin] 8vo. *London*, 1712

Lewis' (John) Accounts of Books, Vestments, and Utensils, used in the Churches of England before the Reformation. (Gutch's Collect Cur Vol. II.)

Bacon's (John) Liber Regis, vel Thesaurus Rerum Ecclesiasticarum [Valuations of all Ecclesiastical Benefices in England and Wales], with proper directions and precedents relating to Presentations, Institutions, Inductions, Dispensations, &c. 2 vols. 4to. *London*, 1786

Hodgson's (Christ.) Account of the Augmentation of Small Livings by the Governors of Queen Anne's Bounty. 8vo. *London*, 1826

Tanner's (Thomas) Notitia Monastica, or, an Account of all the Abbies, Priories, and Houses of Friers, formerly in England and Wales. Edited, with many additions, by J. Nasmith. Folio. *Camb* 1787

Dugdale (W.) et Rogeri Dodsworth Monasticon Anglicanum. 3 vols. folio. *Londini*, 1655, 61, and 73

Dugdale (Sir W.) and Roger Dodsworth's Monasticon Anglicanum, new edition, enlarged and improved by A. Cayley, H. Ellis, and B. Bandinel. 6 vols. folio, large paper. *London*, 1813

Dugdale (Sir W.) and Roger Dodsworth's Monasticon Anglicanum abridged and Englished, with two additional volumes, and an Appendix, containing the charters, grants, and other original writings referred to, by John Stevens   3 vols folio   *London*, 1718–23

Memoirs of the Antiquities of Great Britain relating to the Reformation [principally in answer to Stevens's Remarks on the late Bp Burnet]   Small 8vo   *London*, 1723

Willis' (Browne) View of the Mitred Abbies, with a Catalogue of their respective Abbats, with preliminary Observations by Thos Hearne, (Leland's Collect Vol VI)

Willis' (B.) History of the Mitred Parliamentary Abbies and Conventual Cathedral Churches   2 vols 8vo   *Lond* 1718–19

[Gough (R.)], Some Account of the alien Priories, and of such as they are known to have possessed in England and Wales   2 vols 8vo   *London*, 1779.

Bourget's (John) History of the Royal Abbey of Bec, near Rouen, in Normandy, which held lands in England, translated from the French [by Ducarel]   (Alien Priories)

Fosbrooke's (T D) British Monachism, or, Manners and Customs of the Monks and Nuns of England   4to   *London*, 1817

Buckler's (J) Thirty-eight Views of Cathedrals, Abbeys, Collegiate Churches, and Colleges, in England   Proofs—Sections of St Paul's, and Views of Lincoln and York Cathedrals   Folio. (Coll of Prints, Vol XVII)

Carlisle's (Nich) Concise Description of the endowed Grammar Schools in England and Wales   2 vols 8vo.   *London*, 1818

Surveys, Descriptions, Itineraries, and Tours.

Domesday Book, seu, Liber censualis Wilhelmi I Regis Angliæ, inter archivos regni in Domo Capitulari Westmonasterii asservatus, cum Indicibus et Supplementis   4 vols folio   *Londini*, 1816

Doomesday Book, so far as relates to Amounderness, Lonsdale, and Furness, in Lancashire, and such part of Westmoreland, Cumberland, Derby, Nottingham, and Rutland, as are contained in the Survey, translated by W Bawdwen   (Yorkshire)

Doomesday Book, so far as relates to the counties of Middlesex, Hertford, Buckingham, Oxford, and Gloucester, translated by W Bawdwen   *Doncaster*, 1812

Richard of Cirencester's Description of Britain, translated, with the original Treatise de Situ Britanniæ, and a Commentary on the Itinerary   8vo Maps   *Lond* 1809

John (Pauli) Descriptiones Britanniæ, Scotiæ, Hyberniæ, et Orchadum; Elogia quorundd Anglorum, et Chronicon Anglorum Regum.   (Descriptiones)

Lhuyd (Humfrey), the Breviary of Britayne, as this most noble and renowned Island was of ancient time divided into three kingdoms, England, Scotland, and Ireland   Englished by Thos Twyne.   Black letter, small 8vo.   *London, by R. Johnes*, 1573

<blockquote>Mr Thoresby's copy, with his autograph   A MS memorandum on the fly-leaf states that this edition is so scarce, that "Mr Thos Hearne could never meet with a compleat copy, but one in the Earl of Oxford's library   Dr John Moore, Bishop of Ely, offered Mr Thoresby, for this copy, its weight in gold"</blockquote>

Camden's (W) Britannia, or, a Chorographical Description of England, Scotland, Ireland, and the Islands, from the earliest antiquity translated from the edition published by the author in 1607, and enlarged with the latest discoveries, by Rich Gough 3 vols folio *Lond* 1789

Perlin (Estienne), Description des Royaulmes d'Angleterre et d Ecosse, 1558. [Reprinted from the original edition, with Introduction and Notes by Rich Gough] Large paper, 4to *London*, 1775

Harrison's (W) Description of the Iland of Brittaine, 1586 (Holinshed's Chron. Vol I)

Drayton's (Michael) Poly-Albion, a Chorographical Description of Great Britain, digested into a poem ; with the intermixture of remarkable stories, &c Both parts Folio, Maps, and port of Prince Henry *London*, 1622

Drayton's Polyalbion (Illustrations of) (Selden's Works, Vol III.)

Burton's (R) Admirable Curiosities, Rarities, and Wonders of England, Scotland, and Ireland. 4to (*Reprint*) *Westminster*, 1811

Leycester's (Sir P) Historical Antiquities of Great Britain and Ireland (Cheshire)

Nichols' (John) Bibliotheca Topographiæ Britannicæ, comprehending Antiquities in various counties of England and Wales 8 vols 4to *London*, 1789–90

Nichols' (J) Bibliotheca (Miscellaneous Antiquities, in continuation of). 2 vols 4to *London*, 1791–94

Lysons' (Daniel and Samuel) Magna Britannia, a topographical account of the several counties in Great Britain 8 vols 4to large paper *London*, 1806–21
> This copy is illustrated with plates from Grose, Hearne and Byrne, Watts, Beauties of England, Britton, Medland's Stowe, &c, inserted in Beds, Berks, Bucks, and Cambridgeshire ; and from Farington's Lakes, in Cumberland and Westmoreland

Leigh's (Ed) England described, or, the several Counties and Shires thereof briefly handled Small 8vo. *London*, 1659

[Brydges (Sir E) and Stebbing Shaw], the Topographer, containing a variety of original articles, illustrative of the local history and antiquities of England Both parts 4to. *London*, 1791

Antonini Iter Britanniarum, cum variis lectionibus T. Hearne. Accedunt R Talboti Annotationes. (Leland's Itinerary, Vol III)

Antonini Iter Britanniarum, or, that part of the Itinerary of Antoninus which relates to Britain ; with a new Commentary by T Reynolds 4to large paper *Cambridge*, 1799.

Burton's (W.) Commentary on Antoninus his Itinerary of Great Britain Folio port by Hollar. *London*, 1658

Leland (the Itinerary of John), the Antiquary, published from the original MS in the Bodleian Library, by Thomas Hearne. 9 vols *Oxford*, 1710–12

Stukeley's (Wm) Itinerarium Curiosum, or, an account of the Antiquities and Curiosities observed in travels through Great Britain, with the Itinerary of Richard of Cirencester, and an account of that author and his work 2 vols in one, folio *London*, 1776.

Plat's (D) Account of an intended Journey through England and Wales. (Leland's Itin Vol II)

Hentzner's (Paul) Journey into England in 1598 [edited by Horace Walpole] Small 8vo *Strawberry Hill,* 1758

Cosmo III, Grand Duke of Tuscany's Travels through England during the reign of Charles II, translated from the Italian MS in the Laurentian Library at Florence with a memoir of his life, and 39 views of cities, &c. as delineated at that period by artists in his suite 4to *London,* 1821.

Espriella's (Don) [Robt Southey] Letters from England, translated from the Spanish 3 vols 12mo *London,* 1808

[Simond's] Journal of a Tour and Residence in Great Britain, during the years 1810-11, by a French Traveller, with remarks on the country, its arts, literature, politics, &c 2 vols. *Edinb* 1815

Spiker's (Dr S H) Travels through England, Wales, and Scotland, in 1816, translated from the German 2 vols 12mo *Lond* 1820.

German Prince (Tour of a) in England, Ireland, and France, in 1828, with remarks on the manners and customs. 4 vols crown 8vo *London,* 1832

Hearne's (Thomas) Journeys to Reading in 1716, and to Whaddon Hall, the seat of Browne Willis, Esq. Bucks, in 1713 (Letters from the Bodleian, Vol II)

Pennant's (Thos.) Journey from Chester to London 4to *Lond* 1782

Pennant's (T.) Journey from London to Dover, and thence to the Isle of Wight 2 vols 4to. *London,* 1801

Pennant's (T) Tour from Downing to Alston Moor, and thence to Harrowgate and Brimham Crags 2 vols 4to *London,* 1801-4.

Warner's (Richard) Walks through some of the Western Counties of England 8vo *Bath,* 1800.

Warner's (R.) Tour through the Northern Counties of England, and the Borders of Scotland 2 vols 8vo *Bath,* 1802

Warner's (R) Tour through Cornwall in 1808 8vo *Bath,* 1809

Norden's (John) England, an intended Guide for English Travellers, [38 tables] shewing in generall how far one citie and many shire-towns are distant from one another with a table of those of Wales 4to *London,* 1621

Oulton's (W C) Traveller's Guide, or English Itinerary, containing accurate and original descriptions of all the counties, cities towns, villages, hamlets, &c and their exact distances from London 2 vols small 8vo *London,* 1805

Paterson s (Lieut.-Col) Description of the Roads in England, Wales, and part of Scotland, with their distances, &c., improved by Edward Mogg 8vo *London,* 1826

[West's (Thomas)] Guide to the Lakes in Cumberland, Westmoreland, and Lancashire 8vo *Kendall,* 1807

Green's (William) Tourist's Guide, containing a description of the lakes, mountains, and scenery in Cumberland Westmoreland, and Lancashire 2 vols 8vo large paper *Kendall,* 1819

Hutchinson's (William) Excursion to the Lakes in Westmoreland and Cumberland, with a Tour through the Northern Counties, in 1773-4 8vo *London,* 1776

Aust's (Mrs Murray) Useful Companion and Guide to the Beauties of Scotland and the Hebrides, to the Lakes of Westmoreland, Cumberland, and Lancashire, and to the Curiosities in the district of Craven, in the West Riding of Yorkshire   2 vols 8vo   *London*, 1810

Architectural and Sepulchral Antiquities, and Graphic Illustrations

King's (Edward) Munimenta Antiqua, or, Observations on ancient Castles, including remarks on the whole progress of architecture, ecclesiastical as well as military and on the corresponding changes of manners, laws, and customs in Great Britain, with Appendix   4 vols folio. Sir M M. Sykes's copy   *London*, 1799–1806

Vetusta Monumenta   Ancient Memorials relating to Great Britain 6 vols in five, folio   *London, by the Soc of Antiquaries* 1747–1828

Angus' (William) Seats of the Nobility and Gentry in Great Britain and Wales   Oblong 4to   *London*, 1787

Britton (John) and Ed W Brayley's Beauties of England and Wales, or, delineations, topographical, historical, and descriptive; with Introduction, comprising observations on the history and antiquities of the Britons, the Romans in Britain, the Anglo-Saxons, the Anglo-Danes, and the Anglo-Normans, together with remarks on the progress of ecclesiastical, military, and domestic architecture in succeeding ages. 19 vols in 25, large paper, royal 8vo   *Lond* 1801–18
   To each of the counties is appended a catalogue of all the historical or illustrative works connected with it

Britton's (John) Architectural Antiquities of Great Britain represented and illustrated, with historical and descriptive accounts, and chronological and historical illustrations of the ancient architecture of Great Britain   5 vols imp 4to large paper, proofs   *Lond* 1806–25

Buck's (S and N) Antiquities, or venerable Remains of Castles, Palaces, Towns, &c in England and Wales, with brief descriptions   17 collections in 4 vols oblong 4to, an original subscription copy   *Lond* 1726–42

   Vol I.—1st to 5th Collections; or, York, Lincolnshire, Nottingham, Lancashire, Cheshire, Derby, Durham, Northumberland, Oxfordshire Warwickshire, and Northampton.

   Vol II —6th to 10th Collections, or, Cambridge, Huntingdon, Bedfordshire, Buckinghamshire, Leicestershire, Rutlandshire, Shropshire, Staffordshire, Worcestershire, and Herefordshire

   Vol III —11th to 14th Collections, or, Kent, Sussex, Surrey, Middlesex, Herts, Norfolk, Suffolk, Essex, Cumberland, and Westmorland.

   Vol IV —Wales, in three collections

Fowler s (William) Illuminated Engravings from Mosaic Pavements, stained Glass, and various Antiquities in different parts of England. A complete set in 2 vols large folio   *Winterton*, V Y

Grose's (Fr.) Antiquities of England and Wales, with Supplement 8 vols 4to   *London*, [1787–97]

Hearni (Tho) Ectypa varia ad Historiam Britannicam illustrandam, ære olim insculpta; studio et curâ Thomæ Hearne   Folio   *Oxoniensis*, 1737

MODERN

Kip (Jean), Nouveau Théâtre de la Grande Bretagne; ou, description exacte des palais du roy, des églises, cathédrales, &c et des maisons les plus considérables des seigneurs et gentilshommes du dit royaume [avec le Supplément, contenant les vues d'Audley-end, gravées par Henri Winstanley] 5 vols in three, large paper, atlas folio *Londres,* 1724-28.

> The Supplement, besides containing the Audley-ende, the plates of which are considered rare, includes also the unfortunate Winstanley's engraving of the Eddystone Lighthouse, built by himself, and in the destruction of which he lost his life.

Neale's (J P) Views of the Seats of Noblemen and Gentlemen in England, Wales, Scotland, and Ireland First and second series 10 vols 4to *London,* 1818-29

Relics of Antiquity, or, Remains of ancient Structures in Great Britain: with descriptive sketches. Folio, large paper, proofs *Lond* 1811

Watts's (W) Seats of the Nobility and Gentry, in a collection of picturesque views, with descriptions Very early impressions, oblong 4to *London,* 1779

Pyne's (W H) History of the Royal Residences of Windsor Castle, St James's, Carlton House, Kensington Palace, Hampton Court, Buckingham House, and Frogmore Plates, coloured 3 vols royal 4to *London,* 1819

Ayton's (Richard) Voyage round Great Britain, undertaken in 1813, and commencing from the Land's-end, with a series of views illustrative of the character and prominent features of the coast, drawn and engraved by W Daniel 8 vols folio *London,* 1814, &c

> An original subscription copy, the plates coloured after the original drawings, under the immediate inspection of the artist

Sandby's (P) Collection of Landscapes [in Great Britain], engraved by Rooker and Angus, with descriptions Oblong 4to. *Lond* 1777

Sandby's (P) Virtuosi's Museum; containing select views in England, Scotland, and Ireland Oblong 4to *London,* 1778

Turner's (J M W) England and Wales, with descriptive and historic Illustrations by H E Lloyd 4to India proofs *London,* 1827.

Views (LIV) in England, by Woollett, Sullivan, Smith, Mason, Vivares, &c , and 11 of the Giant's Causeway, Ireland (Coll. of Prints, Vol XVI.)

Gilpin (William) on Picturesque Beauty, particularly the mountains and lakes of Cumberland and Westmorland 2 vols 8vo. *Lond* 1792

Gilpin (W) on several parts of the Counties of Cambridge, Norfolk, Suffolk, and Essex, also several parts of North Wales, relative chiefly to picturesque beauty 8vo *London,* 1809

Gilpin (W) on the Coasts of Hampshire, Sussex, and Kent, relative to the picturesque 8vo *London,* 1804

Gilpin (W) on the Western Parts of England and the Isle of Wight, relative to the picturesque. 8vo *London,* 1808

Lakes of Lancashire, Westmoreland, and Cumberland, delineated in XLIII Engravings, from drawings by J Farington, with descriptions, historical, topographical, and picturesque, the result of a tour made in the summer of 1816, by T H Horne Folio *Lond* 1806

Views in Suffolk, Norfolk, and Northamptonshire, illustrative of the works of Robert Bloomfield, accompanied with descriptions, and a memoir of the poet's life, by E W Brayley Royal 8vo *London*, 1806

Ireland's (Sam) Picturesque Views on the River Medway, from the Nore to the vicinity of its source in Sussex 8vo *Lond* 1793

Ireland's (S) Picturesque Views on the Upper or Warwickshire Avon, from its source at Naseby to its junction with the Severn at Tewkesbury. 8vo *London*, 1795

Ireland's (S) Picturesque Views on the River Wye, from its source at Plinlimmon Hill to its junction with the Severn below Chepstow. 8vo *London*, 1797

Ireland's (S) Picturesque Views on the River Thames, from its source in Gloucestershire to the Nore. 2 vols 8vo. *London*, 1801

The Thames, or, Graphic Illustrations of Seats, Villas, Public Buildings, and Picturesque Scenery on its banks, from drawings by Sam Owen, and engraved by W B Cooke, with descriptions 2 vols 4to large paper, proofs *London*, 1811

History of the River Thames, with illustrations from drawings by Farington 2 vols folio *London, Boydell* 1794

Scott's (Sir W) Border Antiquities of England and Scotland, accompanied with descriptions, together with illustrations of remarkable incidents in Border history and traditions, and original poetry 2 vols. 4to large paper, proofs *London*, 1814–17

Blore's (Edward) Monumental Remains of noble and eminent Persons, comprising the sepulchral antiquities of Britain, with historical and biographical illustrations 4to large paper, proofs *Lond* 1826

Brown's (Sir Thomas) Hydriotaphia, or Urn-burial, a discourse of the sepulchral Urns lately found in Norfolk (Brown's Works.)

Douglas's (James) Nænia Britannia, or, sepulchral history of Great Britain, from the earliest period to its general conversion to Christianity Folio, large paper, the Plates coloured *London*, 1793

Gough's (Rich) Sepulchral Monuments in Great Britain, applied to illustrate the history of families, manners, habits, and arts, at the different periods from the Norman conquest to the fifteenth century, with introduction on sepulture, habits, &c Two parts in 4 vols folio. *London*, 1786–96

Weever's (John) Ancient Funerall Monuments within the united monarchie of Great Britain, Ireland, and the Isles Folio, portrait and frontispiece *London*, 1631

Le Neve's (John) Monumenta Anglicana, or, Inscriptions on the Monuments of eminent persons, from 1600 to 1718 5 vols 8vo large paper. *London*, 1717–19

Toldervy's (Wm) Select Epitaphs. 2 vols 12mo *London*, 1775

Webb's (Thomas) Collection of Epitaphs. 2 vols 12mo *Lond* 1775

Collection of Epitaphs, with an essay on Epitaph-writing, by Dr. Sam Johnson 2 vols 12mo. *London*, 1806

Collection of Epitaphs and Monumental Inscriptions. 12mo. *London*, 1806

The Variety and Antiquity of Tombs and Monuments, and on Epitaphs (Curious Discourses, Vol I)

Miscellaneous Antiquities

Camden's (Will) Remaines concerning Britain, the languages, names, armories, monies, apparell, &c of the inhabitants, with additions by John Philipot and W D Gent 4to portrait *London*, 1657

Verstegan's (Ri) Restitution of decayed Intelligence, in Antiquities concerning the English Nation 4to *Antwerp*, 1605

On the Antiquities and Natural History of England (Leland's Itinerary, Vol 1)

On the Antiquity of Shires, the Dimensions of Land, and the Etymology, Antiquity, and Privileges of Castles, Towns, &c in England (Curious Discourses, Vol I.)

Lelandi (Jo) Collectanea de Rebus Britannicis, ex autogr descripsit ediditque T Hearne 6 vols 8vo *Oxonii*, 1715

Hearne's (Thos) Collection of Curious Discourses, written by eminent Antiquaries upon English Antiquities, now first published 8vo *Oxford*, 1720

Hearne's (T) Collection of Curious Discourses Second edition with additions 2 vols 8vo *London*, 1775

Gutch's (John) Collectanea Curiosa; or, miscellaneous tracts relating to the history and antiquities of England and Ireland, and the Universities of Oxford and Cambridge. 2 vols 8vo. *Oxford*, 1781.

Peck's (Fr) Desiderata Curiosa, a collection of pieces of English History. 4to *London*, 1779.

Antiquarian Repertory, a miscellaneous assemblage of topography, history, biography, customs, and manners, chiefly compiled by F Grose, Thos Astle, &c, with additions [by Edward Jeffery]. 4 vols 4to. large paper *London*, 1807

[Walpole's (Horace)] Miscellaneous Antiquities, or, a collection of curious papers, either republished from scarce tracts, or now printed from original MSS 4to *Strawberry Hill*, 1772

Miscellanea Antiqua Anglicana, or, a select collection of rare and curious tracts, illustrative of the history, literature, manners, and biography of the English nation during the sixteenth and part of the seventeenth centuries 4to *London*, 1814

Strutt's (Jos) Compleat View of the Manners, Customs, Arms, Habits, &c of the Inhabitants of England, from the arrival of the Saxons to the reign of Henry VIII, with a short account of the Britons during the government of the Romans 3 vols 4to *London*, 1775–76.

Strutt's (J) Complete View of the Dress and Habits of the People of England, from the establishment of the Saxons in Britain to the present time, illustrated with coloured engravings taken from the most authentic remains of antiquity Prefixed is an Introduction, containing a general description of the ancient habits in use among mankind, from the earliest period of time to the conclusion of the seventh century 2 vols 4to *London*, 1796

Jeffreys' (Thos.) Collection of the Dresses of different Nations, ancient and modern, particularly old English dresses 4 vols. 4to. *London*, 1757–72

HISTORY.

Strutt's (J.) Sports and Pastimes of the People of England, including the rural and domestic recreations, May-games, mummeries, pageants, processions, and pompous spectacles, from the earliest period to the present time, illustrated by engravings selected from ancient paintings, in which are represented most of the popular diversions. 4to *London*, 1801

Brand's (J.) Observations on Popular Antiquities, chiefly illustrating the origin of our vulgar customs, ceremonies, and superstitions, with additions by Henry Ellis. 2 vols 4to large paper. *Lond.* 1813

Hone's (Wm.) Every-day Book; or, everlasting calendar of popular amusements, sports, pastimes, ceremonies, manners, customs, events, &c incident to each day, in past and present times. 3 vols. 8vo. *London*, 1828-30.

Liber Quotidianus Contrarotulatoris Garderobæ 28 Edwardi I., A D 1299-1300. Ex Codice MS in Bibliothecâ Soc. Antiquar. Londinensis 4to *London*, 1787
> This contains the establishment, military and civil, during this year in which Edward invaded Scotland, and the daily account of every expense and proceeding

Privy Purse Expenses of Elizabeth of York, Wardrobe Accounts of Edward IV. with a memoir of Elizabeth, and Notes by N H. Nicolas. 8vo. *London*, 1831.

The Regulations and Establishment of the Household of Henry Algernon Percy, the fifth Earl of Northumberland, at his Castles of Wresil and Lekenfield in Yorkshire, begun MDXII. Edited by Bishop Thos Percy. 8vo *London*, 1827.

A Collection of Ordinances and Regulations for the Government of the Royal Household, made in divers reigns, from King Edward III to King William and Queen Mary. Also Receipts in ancient Cookery. 4to *London*, 1790

The Household Expenses for one year of Philip III Lord Wharton. [Edited by W C Trevellyan]. 4to. *Newcastle*, 1829.

Warner's (Richard) Antiquitates Culinariæ, or, curious tracts relating to the culinary affairs of the old English. With preliminary Discourse, Notes, and Illustrations 4to large paper. The Roxburgh copy *London*, 1791.

Pegge (Sam.), the Forme of Cury, a roll of ancient English Cookery, compiled about A D 1390, by the Master Cooks of King Richard II; presented afterwards to Queen Elizabeth by Edward Lord Stafford; and now in the possession of Gust Brander, Esq, illustrated with Notes and a Glossary. A Manuscript of the Editor, of the same age and subject, is subjoined. 8vo *London*, 1780

[Lewis's (John)] Dissertation on the Antiquity and Use of Seals in England 4to *London*, 1740 (Hist of Faversham)

Lethieullier's (Smart) Description of the Tapestries remaining in the Cathedral of Bayeux [illustrative of Earl Harold's Embassy to Duke William of Normandy]. Infeuditiones Militum qui debent servitia militaria Duci Normanniæ. Description of the Basso-Relievos representing the interview of Henry VIII. with Francis I; and copy of the appointments for K. Henry VIII. and his Queen at the interview (Appendix to Ducarel's Anglo Norman Antiq)

[Howell (James)], A Character of England, as it was lately presented to a nobleman in France;—a perfect Description of the People and Country of Scotland;—a brief Character of the Low Countries under the States Small 12mo *London*, 1659.

Hearne (the various Works edited by Tho) viz , Spelman's Alfred , Leland's Itinerary , Dodwell de Parmâ Equestri , Lelandi Collectanea , Rossi Hist. Ang ; T Livii Foro-Juliensis Vita Hen. V ; Aluredi Beverl Annales , Roperi Vita T Mori , Camdeni Annales , Guil Neubr. Historia, Sprotti Chronica; Curious Discourses, Textus Roffensis , Robert. de Avesbury Hist Edw. III. , Jo. de Fordun Scotichronic , Hist of Glastonbury , Hemingii Chart Wigormensis , Robert of Gloucester's Chronicle, Peter of Langtoft's Chron ; Jo. Glastoniensis Chronica , Adam de Domerham Hist. Glast , Tho. de Elmham Vita Hen V ; Liber Niger Scac ; Anonymi, &c de Comit Warwicensibus , Jo de Trokelowe Annales , Cau Vindiciæ Ant. Oxon ; Walter Hemingford Hist ; Thomæ de Otterbourne, &c Chronica ; Chronicon de Dunstaple , Benedictus de Vitâ Hen II &c. Vindication of those who took the Oath of Allegiance 62 vols 8vo. Original copies as subscribed for by Dr. Richardson, of Bierley. *Oxonii*, 1709-35

Topography of the several Counties.

BEDFORDSHIRE

Collection towards the Natural History and Antiquities of Bedfordshire (Nichols's Top Brit Vol IV Nos 8 and 26)

Lysons' Topographical Account of Bedfordshire (Magna Brit Vol I)

Cooper's (O. St. John) Historical Account of the Parishes of Wimmington and Odell, Beds (Nichols's Top Brit Vol IV No 29)

Chronicon, sive Annales Prioratûs de Dunstable, unà cum Excerptis è chart. ejusdem Prioratûs è cod MSS in Bib Harlæianæ primùmque vulgavit T Hearne. 2 vols. 8vo. *Oxonii*, 1733.

BERKSHIRE.

Ashmole's (Elias) History and Antiquities of Berkshire, with a particular account of the Castle and Town of Windsor Folio *Reading*, 1736

Lysons' Topographical Account of Berkshire. 4to. (Mag Brit Vol. I.)

Collections towards a Parochial History of Berkshire. (Nichols's Bib. Topog Vol IV No 16)

Some Account of the Parish of Great Coxwell, in the county of Berks (Nichols's Bib Topog. Vol IV No. 13.)

Coates' (Charles) History and Antiquities of Reading, with Supplement. 4to *Reading*, 1810

Pote's (Jos) History and Antiquities of Windsor Castle , with an account of the town and corporation of Windsor 4to *Eton*, 1749

Hofland's (Mrs) Descriptive Account of the Mansion and Gardens of White Knights, a seat of the Duke of Marlborough, near Reading Folio *London*, 1819

Hearne's (Tho) Account of some Antiquities between Windsor and Oxford (Leland's Itinerary, Vol. V)

Hearne's (T) Antiquities of Chilswell, near Oxford (Liber Niger, Vol II)

Extract from a book written by Fr Little, relating to Abingdon (Liber Niger, Vol II)

BRISTOL

Hooke's (And) Bristollia, or, Memoirs of the City of Bristol, civil and ecclesiastical 8vo *London*, 1748

Barrett's (Wm) History and Antiquities of the City of Bristol 4to *Bristol*, 1789

Britton s (John) Historical and Architectural Essay relating to Redcliffe Church, Bristol, illustrated with views, an account of the monuments, &c 4to *London*, 1813

Britton's (J) History and Antiquities of the Abbey and Church of Bristol. 4to. large paper *London*, 1830

BUCKINGHAMSHIRE.

Lipscomb's (Geo) History and Antiquities of the County of Buckingham. 4 vols imperial 4to large paper *London*, 1831

Lysons' Topographical Account of Buckinghamshire 4to (Mag Brit. Vol. I)

Willis' (Browne) History of the town and hundred of Buckingham. 4to 1755

Seeley's (Jos) Description of Stowe, the seat of the Marquess of Buckingham 4to. *Buckingham*, 1797

Storrer and Greig, Cowper illustrated by a series of Views in or near the Park of Weston-Underwood, Bucks (Cowper's Poems)

Kennet's (White) Parochial Antiquities attempted in the history of Ambrosden, Burcester, and other adjacent villages. (Oxfordshire)

CAMBRIDGESHIRE

Blomefield's (Francis) Collectanea Cantabrigiensia, or, collections relating to Cambridge University, town, and county 4to *Norwich*, 1750

Carter's (Edmund) History of the County of Cambridge, from the earliest account to the present time 8vo *Cambridge*, 1753

Lysons' Topographical Account of Cambridgeshire (Magna Brit Vol II)

Caius (Jo) [or Kay] de Antiquitate Cantabrigiensis Academiæ. 4to. *Londini, J Dau*, 1574.

Caii (Jo) Historia Cantabrigiensis Academiæ ab urbe condita 4to. *Londini*, 1574

Fuller's (Thomas) History of the University of Cambridge since the Conquest (Church History)

History and Antiquities of the University of Cambridge, containing its original and progress, translated from a MS published by Hearne in Sprotti Chronicon, and a Description of the present Colleges, &c by Richard Parker. 8vo *London*, [1721]

Dyer's (Geo.) History of the University and Colleges of Cambridge, including notices of the Founders, with a series of illustrative Engravings, by J Greig 2 vols royal 8vo large paper. *London*, 1814

Catalogus Cancellariæ, &c Academiæ Cantabrigiensis (Parker de Antiq Ecclesiæ Britannicæ)

Neli (Thomæ) Dialogus inter Reginam Elizabetham et Robertum Dudleium, Comit Leycest , in quo de Academiæ Ædificiis præclarè agitur (Dodwell de Parmâ Equest)

Parker (Richard) Skeletos Cantabrigiensis; sive, Collegiorum umbratilis Delineatio (Leland's Collectanea, Vol V)

Harraden's (William) Cantabrigia depicta, a series of Engravings representing the edifices in the University of Cambridge, with descriptions Folio, large paper. *Cambridge*, 1809

Masters's (Robert) History of the College of Corpus Christi and Ben'et, in the University of Cambridge, with additional matter, and continuation to the present time, by J Lamb 4to *Cambridge*, 1831

Malden's (Henry) Account of King's College Chapel, in Cambridge. 8vo *Cambridge*, 1769

[Cole's (William)] Account of Pythagoras's School in Cambridge, as in Mr Grose's Antiquities, and other Notices Folio [1768].
A severe castigation of Masters's Merton Hall.

Bentham's (James) History and Antiquities of the Conventual and Cathedral Church of Ely, to the year 1771 4to *Cambridge*, 1771

Bentham's (J) Supplement to the above, by W Stevenson. 4to *Norwich*, 1817.

Miller's (George) Description of the Cathedral Church of Ely; with some Account of the Conventual Buildings 8vo. large paper *London*, 1808

The History and Antiquities of Barnwell Abbey and Sturbridge Fair (Nichols's Top. Brit Vol V No. 38)

CHESHIRE

King's (Daniel) Vale Royal of England , or, County Palatine of Chester illustrated. with a Discourse on the Isle of Man Folio *Lond*. 1656.

Leycester's (Sir Peter) Historical Antiquities concerning Chester, whereunto is added, a transcript of Doomsday Book, so far as regards Cheshire Folio. *London*, 1673

Ormerod's (George) History of the County Palatine and City of Chester. 3 vols. folio, large paper *London*, 1819

Leigh's (Charles) Natural History and Antiquities of Cheshire. (Lancashire)

Lysons' Topographical Account of Cheshire. (Magna Brit. Vol. II)

CORNWALL.

Carew's (Richard) Survey of Cornwall; with a MS Index in a contemporary hand 4to *Lond* 1602.

Borlase's (William) Antiquities, historical and monumental, of the county of Cornwall; consisting of several essays on the first inhabitants, Druid superstition, customs, and remains of the most remote antiquity, in Britain and the British Isles, exemplified and proved by monuments now extant in Cornwall and the Scilly Islands With a Vocabulary of the Cornu-British language. Folio *London*, 1769

Polwhele's (R) General History of Cornwall   7 vols 4to   *Lond* 1816.
Lysons' Topographical Account of Cornwall   (Magna Brit. Vol III.)
Whitaker's (John) Ancient Cathedrals of Cornwall historically surveyed. 2 vols 4to   *London*, 1804
Hedgeland s (J. P) Description, accompanied by 16 coloured Plates, of the splendid decorations recently made to the Church of St Neot, Cornwall, to which are prefixed, some Translations and Collections respecting St. Neot, and the former state of this Church, by Davies Gilbert.   4to.   *Lond.* 1830
Gorham's (J. C.) History of St Neot's   (Huntingdonshire.)

CUMBERLAND

Hutchinson's (W.) History of the County of Cumberland and some places adjacent   2 vols 4to.   *Carlisle*, 1794-8
Collinson's (Thos) Essay towards a Natural History of Cumberland (Westmoreland.)
Nicholson (J.) and R. Burn's History and Antiquities of Cumberland. (Westmoreland)
Lysons' Topographical Account of Cumberland.   (Magna Brit. Vol. IV)
Warburton's (John) Vallum Romanum, or the Picts' Wall.   4to. *Lond.* 1753.
Dugdale's (Sir W.) Brief Account of the Cathedral of Carlisle.   (St. Paul's)

DERBYSHIRE

Davies's (C. P.) Historical and Descriptive View of Derbyshire.   8vo. large paper   *Belper*, 1811.
Pilkington's (J) View of the present state of Derbyshire ; with an Account of its most remarkable Antiquities   2 vols 8vo   *Lond.* 1789.
Lysons' Topographical Account of Derbyshire   (Magna Brit Vol. V)
Hutton's (W) History of Derby, from the remotest ages to 1791 ; with Additions [by J. B Nichols].   8vo.   *Lond* 1817.
Pegge's (S) Sketch of the History of Bolsover and Peak Castles. (Nichols' Top. Brit Vol. IV., No 32)
Pegge's (S) Roman Roads, Ikineld Street and Bath Way, discovered and investigated, through the county of Derby   (Nichols' Top Brit. Vol IV., No 24)
Blore's (Thos) History of the Manor and Manor House of South Winfield.   4to   *Lond* 1816.
Leigh's (C.) Natural History and Antiquities of the Peak   (Lancashire)
Cotton's (C) Wonders of the Peak, a poem   18mo   *Nottingham*, 1725
Williams' (W) Petrifactions in Derbyshire.   (Mineralogy)
Mawes' (J) Mineralogy of Derbyshire.   (Mineralogy)

DEVONSHIRE.

Polwhele's (Rich) History of Devonshire   3 vols in one, folio   *Exeter*, 1793-1806

Lysons' Topographical Account of Devonshire. (Mag. Brit Vol VI)

Izacke's (R) Remarkable Antiquities of the City of Exeter, enlarged and continued to 1723 by S Izacke 8vo *London*, 1724.

Vowell (Jo.) *alias* Hoker's Antique Description and Account of the City of Exeter [by Andrew Brice] 4to. *Exeter*, 1765.

Jenkins' (Alex) History and Description of the City of Exeter and its Environs, ancient and modern, civil and ecclesiastical 4to *Exeter*, 1806

Dunsford's (Martin) Historical Memoirs of the Town and Parish of Tiverton, in the county of Devon. Large paper, 4to *Exeter*, 1790.

Watkins' (Jo.) History of Biddeford 8vo *Exeter*, 1792

Britton's (John) History and Antiquities of the Cathedral Church of Exeter 4to large paper *Lond* 1826

Prince's (John) Worthies of Devon New edition, with notes 4to *Lond* 1810.

DORSETSHIRE.

Hutchins' (Jo) History and Antiquities of the County of Dorset [continued by Gough and Nichols]; with an Appendix of Additions and Corrections 4 vols folio *Lond* 1774–1815

Discourse on Sherborne Castell and Manor in 1620 (Leland's Collect. Vol. II)

DURHAM

Introduction to the History and Antiquities of the County Palatine and Bishoprick of Durham (Gutch's Collect Curiosa, Vol II)

Hutchinson's (Wm) History and Antiquities of the County Palatine of Durham. 3 vols 4to *Newcastle*, 1785, *and Carlisle*, 1794.

Surtees' (Robt) History and Antiquities of the County of Durham, compiled from original records. 3 vols folio *London*, 1816-23

Raine's (James) History and Antiquities of North Durham Folio *London*, 1830

Wallis' (John) Account of so much of the County of Durham as lies between the Tyne and the Tweed, commonly called the North Bishoprick (Northumberland)

Allan's (Geo) Collectanea Durhelmensia, tracts relating to the county of Durham, viz. Collections relative to St. Edmund's Hospital, at Gateshead,—Sherburn Hospital, with the Life of Bp. H Pudsey, the founder, and an account of the masters,—the Foundation Charter of the Cathedral Church of Durham,—the Legend of St Cuthberd, by Robert Spegge,—and the Recommendatory Letter of Oliver Cromwell for the erecting a College and University at Durham, and his letters patent for the same. 4to. [*Newcastle*], 1769–1773.

Symeonis Monachi Historia Ecclesiæ Durhelmensis, cui præmittitur T R. de auctore hujus libelli Edidit T. Bedford. 8vo. *Londini*, 1732

Davies' (John) Ancient Rites and Monuments of the Cathedral of Durham 12mo *Lond* 1672.

Dugdale's (Sir W) Brief Account of the Cathedral of Durham (St Paul's)

Brewster's (John) Parochial History of Stockton-upon-Tees. 4to *Stockton*, 1796

ESSEX

S[almon's] (N) History and Antiquities of Essex, from the Collections of Thos Jekyll of Barking, the Papers of Mr Ouseley of Springfield, and Mr Holman of Halstead Folio [*London*, 1740]
This copy was collected by Mr Lysons.

Morant's (Philip) History and Antiquities of Essex 2 vols folio, large paper *Lond* 1768

Cromwell's (Thos) History and Description of the ancient Town and Borough of Colchester 2 vols in one, 8vo *London*, 1825

Taylor's (Silas) History and Antiquities of Harwich and Dover Court; to which is added, the Natural History of the sea-coast and country about Harwich, by Sam Dale 4to *London*, 1732.

Gough's (R) History and Antiquities of Pleshy, in the county of Essex. 4to *Lond* 1803

Lysons' Account of such parishes in Essex as are within twelve miles of London (Environs, Vol IV.)

Fuller's (Thos) History and Antiquities of Waltham Abbey. (Church History)

Britton's (John) History and Antiquities of the Abbey and the Church of Peterborough 4to large paper. *London*, 1828.

GLOUCESTERSHIRE

Atkyns' (Sir Rob.) Ancient and Present State of Gloucestershire Folio, large paper. *London*, 1712.

[Rudder's (Sam)] History of Gloucestershire, and of the City of Gloucester, to the present time. Folio *Cirencester*, 1779

Bigland's (Ralph) Historical, Monumental, and Genealogical Collections relative to the County of Gloucester. Vol I., and Vol II to pp 252 all published Folio *Lond* 1791-2

Fosbrooke's (T. D) Abstracts of Records and MSS. respecting the County of Gloucester, formed into a History, correcting the erroneous accounts, and supplying the deficiencies of Sir R Atkyns and subsequent writers. 2 vols. 4to *Gloucester*, 1807

Britton's (John) History and Antiquities of the Abbey and Cathedral Church of Gloucester 4to. large paper. *London*, 1829.

Dyde's (W) History and Antiquities of Tewkesbury 8vo *Tewkesbury*, 1798

An Account of the Parish of Fairford, in the county of Gloucester, with a particular description of the Stained Glass in the Windows of the Church, and Engravings of ancient Monuments. 4to *Lond* 1791

Anonymi Chronicon Godstovianum, et Fenestrarum depictarum Ecclesiæ Parochialis de Fairford in agro Glocestriensi Explicatio (Roperi Vita T Mori à Hearne)

A Description of the House and Castell of Thornbury, 1582 (Leland's Collect Vol II)

Lysons's (Samuel) Account of Roman Antiquities discovered at Woodchester in the county of Gloucester Folio The Plates highly coloured as drawings, and only twelve copies thus executed. *London*, 1797

HAMPSHIRE

Warner's (Rich) Collections for the History of Hampshire, and the Bishoprick of Winchester 6 vols in three, 4to. *London*, 1795, &c

Milner's (John) History, civil and ecclesiastical, and Survey of the Antiquities of Winchester 2 vols 4to *Winchester*, 1809.

Britton's (John) History and Antiquities of the See and Cathedral Church of Winchester, including biographical anecdotes of the bishops, &c 4to large paper *London*, 1817

Gilpin's (Wm) Remarks on Forest Scenery and other Woodland Views, illustrated by scenes of the New Forest 2 vols. 8vo *Lond* 1808

Englefield's (Sir H. C.) Walk through Southampton. 4to *Southamp* 1801

White's (Gilbert) Natural History and Antiquities of Selborne. (Natural History)

[Worsley's (Sir Richard)] History of the Isle of Wight 4to large paper *London*, 1781

Englefield's (Sir H C) Description of the Picturesque Beauties, Antiquities, and Geology of the Isle of Wight, with Observations on the strata of the island, and their continuation in the adjacent parts of Dorsetshire, by Thomas Webster Folio, large paper, proofs *Lond.* 1816.

Warner's (Rich) History of the Isle of Wight, military, ecclesiastical, and civil 8vo *Southampton*, 1795

HEREFORDSHIRE.

Coningsby's (Thomas, Earl) Collections concerning the Manor of Marden, in the county of Hereford [made and privately printed in 1720; with title, preface, and index, printed in 1813] Sir M M. Sykes's copy Folio, 1720–1813

Price's (John) Historical Account of the City of Hereford; with some remarks on the river Wye 8vo *Hereford*, 1796

Price's (J.) Account of Leominster and its vicinity 8vo. *London*, 1795

Gibson's (Mat) View of the ancient and present State of the Churches of Door, Home-Lacy, and Hempsted, with memoirs of the ancient family of Scudamore 4to. *London*, 1727.

Britton's (John) History and Antiquities of the Cathedral Church of Hereford. 4to large paper *London*, 1831

HERTFORDSHIRE

Chauncy's (Sir H.) Historical Antiquities of Hertfordshire Folio. *Lond* 1700

Clutterbuck's (Robt) History and Antiquities of Hertfordshire. 3 vols. folio, large paper *London*, 1816-27

Lysons's Account of the Parishes in Herts within twelve miles of London (Environs, Vol IV)

Newcome's (Peter) History of the Abbey of St Alban 4to *Lond* 1795

The Foundation and Incorporation of Jesus College, near Chipping Barnet (Hearne's Liber Niger, Vol II)

Vallans' (W) Tale of Two Swannes, wherein is comprehended the original and increase of the river Lee, with the antiquitie of sundrie places and townes seated upon the same. (Leland's Itinerary, Vol V)

HUNTINGDONSHIRE

Gorham's (G C) History and Antiquities of Eynesbury and St Neot's, in Huntingdonshire, and of St Neot's in the county of Cornwall. 8vo *Lond* 1820.

Papers relating to the Protestant Nunnery of Little Gidding ; with historical Notes relating to the family of Ferrars. (Cau Vindiciæ Acad. Oxoniensis à Hearne, Vol II)

KENT.

Kilburne's (Rich) Topographie, or Survey of the county of Kent 4to. portrait by Crosse. *London*, 1659

Philipott's (Thomas) Villare Cantianum, or, Kent surveyed and illustrated, with a catalogue of the high sheriffs by John Philipott. Folio, map by Hollar *London*, 1659

Hasted's (Edward) History and Topographical Survey of the county of Kent 4 vols. folio, large paper *Canterbury*, 1778-99.

Henshall's (Sam) Specimens and Parts, containing a history of the county of Kent, and a dissertation on the laws from Edward the Confessor to Edward I.: a topographical, commercial, civil, and nautical history of South Britain, from authentic documents. 4to. *London*, 1798.

Lysons's Account of Parishes in Kent within twelve miles of London (Environs, Vol IV)

Thorpe's (John) Illustrations of several Antiquities in Kent. (Nichols's Top. Brit Vol I. No 6)

Somner's (Wm) Treatise on the Roman Ports and Forts in Kent, edited by W Brome 12mo *Oxford*, 1693

Newton's (W) History and Antiquities of Maidstone, the county town of Kent 8vo *London*, 1741.

Somner's (W.) Antiquities of the City and Suburbs of Canterbury, and N Battely's Cantuaria Sacra, or Antiquities of the Cathedral, and other religious places in or near Canterbury Folio *London*, 1703

Dart's (John) History and Antiquities of the Cathedral Church of Canterbury, and the once adjoining Monastery Folio, large paper. *London*, 1726

Britton's (John) History and Antiquities of the Metropolitan Church of Canterbury 4to large paper. *London*, 1821

Duncombe's (John) and N Battely's History and Antiquities of the Archiepiscopal Hospitals of St Nicholas, St John, and St. Thomas; with some account of the Priory of St Gregory, &c at or near Canterbury   (Nichols's Top Brit. Vol I No 30)

Pegge's (Sam) Historical Account of the Textus Roffensis, including memoirs of Mr Elstob and his sister, and biographical anecdotes of Mr Johnson.   (Nichols s Top Brit Vol I. No 25)

Textus Roffensis [è MS in Bib D Edwardi Dering, Baronetti], è cod. MSS descripsit ediditque T. Hearne   8vo   *Oxon.* 1720.

Thorpe's (John) Registrum Roffense, or, a Collection of ancient Records, &c to illustrate the history and antiquities of the diocese and cathedral of Rochester   Folio   *London,* 1760

Thorpe's (J) Custumale Roffense, containing an account of the foundation and endowment of churches, &c , memorials of Rochester cathedral, and antiquities in Kent within its diocese. Folio   *London,* 1788

Darell's (W , Chaplain to Queen Elizabeth) History of Dover Castle [published by F Grose]   4to   *London,* 1786

Lyons' (John) History of the Town and Port of Dover, and Dover Castle; with a short account of the Cinque Ports. 2 vols 4to   *Dover,* 1813-14

Burr s (T B) History of Tunbridge Wells. 8vo   *London,* 1766.

Amsinck's (Paul) Tunbridge Wells and its Neighbourhood illustrated by a series of Etchings, with historical descriptions   4to. large paper   *London,* 1810.

[Lewis's (J)] History and Antiquities of the Abbey and Church of Favresham, in Kent, of the adjoining Priory of Davington, and Maison Dieu of Ospringe, and parish of Bocton subtus le Bleyne   4to   *Printed* 1727

Battely's (Jo) Antiquitates Rutupinæ [Richborough]   8vo large paper.   *Oxonii,* 1711

Sketch of the History and Antiquities of Hawkhurst   (Cont. of Topog Brit Vol I)

Morres's (Rowe) History and Antiquities of Tunstall in Kent   (Nichols's Bib Topog Brit Vol I No 1)

Duncombe's (John) History and Antiquities of Reculver and Hearne, and Appendix, with observations on the archiepiscopal palace of Mayfield, in Sussex   (Nichols's Top Brit Vol I. Nos 18 and 45)

History, &c of St Radegund's, or Bradsole Abbey near Dover, Description of the Moat near Canterbury, Sketch of Hawkhurst Church, Dissertation on the Urbs Rotupiæ of Ptolemy, &c   (Nichols's Bib. Topog Brit Vol I No 42)

Lewis's (John) History and Antiquities of the Isle of Tenet, in Kent   4to   *London,* 1736

Somner s (Wm) History of Gavel Kind   (Jurisprudence)

LANCASHIRE

Leigh's (Charles) Natural History and Antiquities of Lancashire, Cheshire, and the Peak in Derbyshire   Folio.   *Orford,* 1700

Whitaker's (Jo) History of Manchester, containing the Roman, Roman-British, and Saxon periods   2 vols 4to   *London*, 1771-75

Aikin's (Jo) Description of the Country from thirty to forty miles round Manchester. 4to large paper.   *London*, 1795

History of Preston, in Lancashire, together with the Guild Merchant, and some account of the duchy and county palatine of Lancaster   4to   *London*, 1822

[Rauthmell's (Rich)] Roman Antiquities of Overborough, wherein Overborough is proved to be the Bremetonacæ of Antoninus   4to   *Lond.* 1746

West's (Thos) Antiquities of Furness, or, an account of the royal abbey of St Mary, in the Vale of Nightshade   4to   *London*, 1774

Whitaker's (T D) History of the Parish of Whalley, and Honor of Clitheroe   (Yorkshire)

LEICESTERSHIRE

Burton's (William) Description of Leicestershire, containing matters of antiquity, history, armoury, and genealogy   Folio   *Lynn*, 1777.

Nichols's (John) History and Antiquities of the County of Leicester; including Mr Burton's description of the county, and the later collections of Mr. Stanley, Mr Carte, Mr Peck, and Sir Thomas Cave   4 vols in eight, folio, large paper.   *London*, 1795-1811-15

Nichols's (John) Miscellanies on Leicestershire. (Top Brit Vol VII)

Thoresby's (John) Select Views in Leicestershire, with supplementary volume, containing a series of excursions to the villages and places of note in the county with descriptive and historical accounts, and, in notes, the most valuable parts of Burton, Nichols, &c   2 vols.   4to   *London*, 1789-90

Curtis's (J) Topographical History of the County of Leicester, the ancient part compiled from parliamentary documents, and the modern from actual survey   8vo   *London*, 1831.

LINCOLNSHIRE.

Catalogus Tenentium terras per singulas hundredas in Comitu Lincolniensis temp Henrici II   (Hearne s Liber Nigen, Vol II)

Peck's (Francis) Antiquarian Annals of Stamford, or Stamford; also a series of ecclesiastical affairs under each reign   Folio   *London*, 1727

Butcher's (Rich) Survey and Antiquity of the Town of Stamford, in the county of Lincoln, and of Tottenham High Cross, in the county of Middlesex   8vo   *London*, 1717

Peck's (Fr) Description of Burleigh   (Desiderata Curiosa)

Turner's (Edm) Collections for the History of the Town and Soke of Grantham   4to large paper   *London*, 1806

Illingworth's (C) Topographical Account of the Parish of Scampton, and of the Roman Antiquities discovered there   4to   *Lond* 1810

An Account of the Gentleman's Society at Spalding, being an Introduction to the Reliquiæ Galeanæ —Reliquiæ Galeanæ, or, miscellaneous pieces by Roger and Samuel Gale   (Nichols's Top Brit Vol. III Nos 2 and 20)

Gough's (R.) History and Antiquities of Croyland Abbey, Mr Essex's Observations on Croyland Abbey. (Nichols's Top Brit Vol III Nos 11 and 22.)

LONDON AND WESTMINSTER

Stillingfleet (Bp.) on the true Antiquity of London, and its state in the Roman times (Works, Vol III.)

Stephanidis (Gml.) Descriptio Civitatis Londini (Leland's Itinerary, Vol VIII, and Stow's Survey)

A Chronicle of London from 1089 to 1483, written in the 15th century, and for the first time printed from MSS in the British Museum. To which are added, numerous contemporary illustrations consisting of royal letters, poems, and other articles descriptive of public events, or of the manners and customs of the metropolis; [edited by Sir N H. Nicolas] 4to *London*, 1827.

Brieffe Description of the Royal Citie of London (Manuscripts)

Howell's (James) Londinapolis; an historical discourse or perlustration of the cities of London and Westminster 1 oho *London* 1657

This copy is illustrated with a unique impression of the portrait before the face was engraved, maps of London, about the commencement of Elizabeth's reign, on wood and copper, views of London, the Bridge, the Tower, the Royal Exchange, Westminster, Covent Garden, &c by Hollar and others, and the plan of the city as fortified in 1642-3

Stow's (John) Survey of the Cities of London and Westminster, brought down to the present time by John Strype, with Life of the Author, Appendix of Tracts on the state of London, and a Perambulation four or five miles round about to the parish churches 2 vols folio *London*, 1720

Maitland's (William) History of London, including the several parishes in Westminster, Middlesex Southwark, &c, within the bills of mortality, continued to 1772 by John Entick. 2 vols folio *London*, 1775

Burton's (Rich.) Historical Remarks on the ancient and present state of the Cities of London and Westminster, with an account of the most considerable occurrences therein for above nine hundred years past, till 1681 4to *Westminster, M Stace*, 1810

Pennant's (Thos.) Account of London, with the additions and corrections 4to *London*, 1790-91

Malcolm's (J. P.) Londinium redivivum, or, an ancient and modern Description of London 4 vols 4to *London*, 1803-7

Brayley's (E. W.) Londiniana, or Reminiscences of the British Metropolis, including characteristic sketches. antiquarian, topographical, descriptive, and literary 4 vols 12mo *London*, 1829

A true and faithful Account of the several Informations exhibited to the Committee appointed to inquire into the late burning of the City of London, 1667 (Somers' Tracts, Vol VII)

Observations, both historical and moral, upon the burning of London, Sept 1666 (Harleian Misc. Vol III)

Waterhouse's (E.) Short Narrative of the late dreadful Fire in London, together with certain considerations remarkable therein 8vo. *London*, 1667

The City Remembrancer, being historical Narratives of the great Plague at London, 1665, great Fire, 1666, and great Storm, 1703 To which are added, observations and reflections on the plague in general, with historical accounts of the most memorable plagues, fires, and hurricanes 2 vols 8vo. *London*, 1779

Woodward's (J) Account of the Roman and other Antiquities digged up near Bishop-gate (Leland's Itin Vol VIII)

Bagford (J) on the Antiquities of London (Leland's Coll Vol I)

Gough's (W) Londinum Triumphans, or, an historical account of the grand influence the actions of the City of London have had upon the affairs of the nation for many ages past 8vo *London*, 1682

The Customs of London, otherwise called Arnold's Chronicle, including its Charters and Privileges, with Introduction by F. Douce. 4to *London*, 1811.

Logan's (Jo) Account of the Customs, Government, Privileges, &c of the City of London (Gwillim's Heraldry)

Tables of the Bailiffs, Sheriffs, and Mayors of the Citie of London, from 1180 to 1558 inclusive (Grafton's Chronicles and Arnold's Chronicle)

The XII Worshipful Companies or Misteries of London (Manuscripts)

Malcolm's (J P) Anecdotes of the Manners and Customs of London during the 18th century 4to *London*, 1808

[Thomson's (Ri)] Chronicles of London Bridge 12mo *London*, 1827

Graunt's (John) Observations upon the Bills of Mortality, with reference to the government, diseases, &c. of London. 12mo *Oxford*, 1665.

Marshall's (J) Mortality of the Metropolis; a Statistical View of the number of persons reported to have died of each of more than 100 kinds of disease and casualties, within the bills of mortality, in each of the years 1629-1831, with a topographical arrangement of the parishes comprising the metropolis, the population thereof at different periods, and the number in each reported to have died of the Plague in 1593, 1625, 1636, and 1665, and also a circumstantial account of the still greater plague of Spasmodic Cholera, which desolated Asia and Europe between 1345 and 1362, and Great Britain in 1348-9 4to *London*, 1832

Newcourt's (Rich) Repertorium Ecclesiasticum Parochiale Londinense; an ecclesiastical parochial history of the diocese of London. 2 vols folio. *London*, 1708

Architectura Ecclesiastica Londini, being a series of Views of the cathedral, collegiate, and parochial Churches in London, Southwark, and Westminster, and the adjoining parishes with descriptional Remarks by Charles Clarke Folio India paper proofs *London*, 1819

Dugdale's (Sir Wm) History of St Paul's Cathedral. The first edition, with the original impressions of Hollar's Plates Folio. *Lond* 1658

Dugdale's History of St Paul's Cathedral, corrected and enlarged by the author's own hand, and edited by E Maynard. Folio *Lond* 1716.

Dugdale's History of St Paul's Cathedral; with Continuation and Additions by H Ellis Folio, large paper. *London*, 1818

[Holland's (Henry)] Monumenta Sepulcralia S Pauli, together with the foundation of the church, and a catalogue of the bishops. 4to *London*, 1614

Bayley's (John) History and Antiquities of the Tower of London, with memoirs of royal and distinguished persons, deduced from records, state papers, and other original and authentic sources. 2 vols in one, 4to large paper   *London*, 1821-5.

Denham's (J F) Views of the exterior and interior, and the principal Monuments, of St Dunstan's in the West   4to Proofs   *London*, 1831.

Ducarel's History of St Catherine s, near the Tower of London, from its foundation in 1273   (Nichols's Top. Brit Vol II , No 5)

Bucke's (Sir Geo) Third Universitie of England ; or, the foundations of all the colleges, schools, and houses of learning and liberal arts, within and about the Citie of London. (Stow's Annals)

The Charter House , with the last Will and Testament of Thomas Sutton, Esq   4to   Port by Elstracke   *London*, 1614

Ireland's (Sam) Views and Historical Account of the Inns of Court. 8vo.   *London*, 1800

Herbert's (W) Antiquities of the Inns of Court and Chancery. 8vo *London*, 1804

Smith's (J T) Antiquities of Westminster , containing 246 Engravings of topographical objects, of which 122 no longer remain · with Descriptions, including the duplicate print, on stone, of the Painted Chamber, and the 62 additional Plates   4to large paper   *Lond* 1807

[Cameni (Gul)] Reges, Reginæ, Nobiles, et alii in ecclesiâ collegiatâ S. Petri Westmonasteriensis sepulti usque ad annum salutis 1603 [ex collect J Skelton]   4to   *London, M Brodwood*, 1603
   Vertue's copy, with his autograph and MS collations with the first edition

Dart's (John) Westmonasterium ; or, the History and Antiquities of the Abbey Church of St Peter, Westminster   2 vols folio, large paper *London*, 1723

MIDDLESEX

Norden's (John) Speculum Britanniæ ; or, historical and chorographical description of Middlesex   Front. and Maps, 4to   *London*, 1593

Lysons's (Dan.) Environs of London , an historical account of the towns, villages, and hamlets, within twelve miles of that capital [including the whole of Middlesex], interspersed with biographical anecdotes · with Supplement   6 vols 4to large paper   *Lond* 1796-1811

Butcher's (Rich) Survey of Tottenham High Cross, in the county of Middlesex   (Stamford)

Walpole's (Hor) Description of his Villa at Strawberry-Hill , with an inventory of the furniture, &c   4to. *Strawberry-Hill*, 1784, and Works, Vol II.

Faulkner's (Thos) Historical and Topographical Account of Chelsea and its environs   8vo   *Lond* 1810

Nelson's (John) History, Topography, and Antiquities of the Parish of St Mary, Islington   4to   *London*, 1811

Park's (J J) Topography and Natural History of Hampstead   4to large paper   *London*, 1814

Brown's (James) Sketches of the History and Antiquities of Stoke-Newington, in the county of Middlesex. (Nichols's Topog. Brit. Vol II Nos 9 and 14)

Nichols's (John) History and Antiquities of Canonbury-House, at Islington   (Nichols's Top Brit Vol II , No 49)

MONMOUTHSHIRE.

Williams' (David) History of Monmouthshire, illustrated with Views by the Rev. J Gardner   4to large paper   *Lond.* 1796

Coxe's (Wm) Historical Tour in Monmouthshire   2 vols 4to   *London*, 1801

NORFOLK

Blomefield (F) and C Parkin's Topographical History of the County of Norfolk   5 vols folio   *Fersfield and Lynn*, 1739-75

Parkin's (Char) History and Antiquities of the City of Norwich. 8vo   *Lynn*, 1783

Description of the Diocese of Norwich, or, the present state of Norfolk and Suffolk, of the City of Norwich in particular, and of the several market-towns in those two counties   8vo. *Lond* 1735

Brown's (Sir T) Posthumous Works, viz . Repertorium , or, the Antiquities of the Cathedral of Norwich,—an Account of some Roman Urnes, &c. found at Brampton, near Norwich,—Antiquitates Capellæ D Joannis Evang , authore J Burton   To which is prefixed his Life   8vo   *London*, 1712

Britton's (John) History of the See and Cathedral Church of Norwich, including biographical anecdotes of the bishops, &c   4to Proofs. *Lond* 1816.

Mackrell's (B) History and Antiquities of King's Lynn   8vo   *London*, 1738.

Swinden's (H) History and Antiquities of Great Yarmouth   4to. *Norwich*, 1772

Martin's (Thomas) History of the Town of Thetford, in the counties of Norfolk and Suffolk [Edited by Rich. Gough.] 4to *London*, 1779.

NORTHAMPTONSHIRE

Morton's (John) Natural History of Northamptonshire ; with some account of the Antiquities, and a transcript from Doomsday Book as far as it relates to that county   Folio   *London*, 1712.

Bridges' (John) History and Antiquities of Northamptonshire, compiled from his manuscript collections by Peter Whalley. 2 vols. folio. *Oxford*, 1791

Baker's (Geo) History and Antiquities of the County of Northampton. 2 vols. folio, large paper. *London*, 1822-30

Hyett's (W H) Sepulchral Memorials of the County of Northampton. 4to   *London*, 1818

Gunton's (Symon) History of the Church at Peterburgh, by Bp Patrick   Folio   *London*, 1686

The History and Antiquities of Fotheringhay, in the county of Northampton , with several particulars of the execution of Mary Queen of Scots. (Nichols's Top Brit. Vol. IV., No 40)

Bonney's (H K) Historic Notices in reference to Fotheringhay   Royal 8vo large paper   *Oundle*, 1821.

NORTHUMBERLAND

Wallis' (Jo) Natural History and Antiquities of Northumberland, and part of the county of Durham between the Tyne and the Tweed, commonly called the North Bishoprick. 2 vols. in one, 4to. *London*, 1769.

Bourne's (Hen) History of Newcastle-upon-Tyne; or, the ancient and present state of that town. Folio *Newcastle*, 1736.

Brand's (Jo) History and Antiquities of the Town and County of Newcastle-upon-Tyne, including an account of the coal trade. 2 vols 4to *London*, 1789.

[Trevelyan's] Account of the Parish of Hartburn, with the History and Pedigrees of the Trevelyans, &c Lords of Wallington 4to *Newcastle*, 1827

[Trevelyan's] History of the Parish of Meldon, and of the extra-parochial Township of Rivergreen 4to *Newcastle*, 1828

Sharpe's (Sir Cuthbert) History of Hartlepool. 8vo the Wood-cuts by Bewick and Nicholson *Durham*, 1816

NOTTINGHAM

Thoroton's (Robert) Antiquities of Nottinghamshire, extracted out of records, original evidences, leiger books, MSS., and authentic authorities. Folio *London*, 1677

Thoroton's (Robert) Antiquities of Nottinghamshire, with additions by J Throsby 3 vols 4to *London*, 1797.

Deering's (Charles) Nottinghamia Vetus et Nova, or, an historical account of the Town of Nottingham 4to *Nottingham*, 1751

Rook's (H) Sketch of the ancient and present State of Sherwood Forest. 8vo *London*, 1799

Dugdale's (Sir W) History of the Collegiate Church of Suthwell (Hist of St Paul's)

OXFORDSHIRE

Plot's (Rob) Natural History of Oxfordshire, with additions and corrections, and a short account of the Author Folio *Oxford*, 1705

Wood's (Antony à) Notes relating to the History of Oxford and the places thereabouts (Hearne's Liber Niger, Vol II.)

Hutten's (L) Antiquities of Oxford, with Views of Osency and Rewley (Hearne's Textus Roffensis)

Warton's (Thomas) Companion to the Guide, and Guide to the Companion, being a complete Supplement to all accounts of Oxford hitherto published [A satire] 12mo *Oxford* [1760]

Hearne (Thomas) on King Edward the Confessor's Chapel at Islip; on Oxford Castle, Osency, &c (Curious Discourses)

Hearne (T) concerning the Stunsfield Tessellated Pavement, and the Custome of the Manor of Woodstocke (Leland's Itinerary, Vol VIII)

Hearne's (T) Account of several Antiquities in and about the University of Oxford (Leland's Itin Vol II)

Hearne (T) on St. Peter's in the East, Oxford; with three Prints   (Leland's Collectanea, Vol I)

Statuta Hospitalis de Ewelme in Agro Oxoniensis   (Hearne's Tho of Otterbourne.)

Kennet's (White) Parochial Antiquities, attempted in the History of Ambrosden, Burcester, and other adjacent parts in the counties of Oxford and Bucks. 4to. *London* 1695.

Dunkin's (John) History and Antiquities of the Hundreds of Bullington and Ploughley, in Oxfordshire. 2 vols in one, 4to. *Lond* 1823

Warton's (J) History and Antiquities of Kiddington   4to. *London*, 1815

A Discourse about Fair Rosamond and the Nunnery of Godstowe ; with occasional Notes about Binsey. (Hearne's Guil. Newbrigensis, Vol. III)

Freiberti (N) Oxoniensis Academiæ Descriptio   (Leland's Itinerary Vol. IX)

Neli (Thos) Collegiorum Scholarumque publicarum Academiæ Oxoniensis Topographica Delineatio   (Dodwell de Parmâ Equest)

Assertio Antiquitatis Oxoniensis Academiæ, incerto authore; ejusdem Gymnasii, ad illust Reginam anno 1566, cum fragmento Oxoniensis historiolæ 4to. *Londini, in ædib. J. Dau*, 1574   (Caius de Antiq Cantabr)

Cau (Thos) Vindiciæ Antiquitatis Academiæ Oxoniensis contra J Caium Cantabrigiensem, edidit T Hearne, cum Reliquiis ad familiam Relig. Ferrariorum de Gidding parvæ subnexit   2 vols. 8vo   *Oxonii*, 1730.

Wood's (Ant à) Annals of the University of Oxford   (Athenæ Oxonienses · Biography.)

Wood's (Ant à) History and Antiquities of the University of Oxford, and of its Colleges and Halls and the Fasti Oxonienses, or, a Commentary on the supreme magistrates of the University   Published from the original MSS, with Continuations to the present time, and a Life of the Author, by John Gutch 4 vols. in 5, 4to   *Oxford*, 1790–96

Tracts on the University of Oxford   (Gutch's Coll. Curiosa)

Chalmers' (Alexander) History of the Colleges, Halls, and Public Buildings, attached to the University of Oxford, including the Lives of the founders   4to large paper, India Proofs   *Oxford*, 1810.

Loggan's (David) Oxonia Illustrata, Views of the Colleges and Halls in Oxford. with an additional volume, containing XXXVII large Plates by Vertue, Basire, &c illustrative of the same subjects. 2 vols. folio   *Oxford*, 1675, &c

<small>The engravings by Vertue, in the second volume, are views of the colleges, introducing the portraits of the founders, and are not enumerated by Walpole in his catalogue of this artist's works.</small>

Skelton's (Jos.) Oxonia Antiqua Restaurata; containing numerous representations of buildings now either altered or demolished   2 vols 4to. large paper   *Oxford*, 1823

Williams (Guil) Oxonia Depicta; sive, Collegiorum, &c in inclytâ Oxoniensi delineatio Folio ——

Oxoniana [a Collection of historical, antiquarian, biographical, and miscellaneous Anecdotes, illustrative of the colleges of Oxford]. 4 vols 18mo *London,* [1807]

Berebloci (J.) Comment de Rebus Gestis Oxoniæ, ibidem commorante Elizabethâ Reginâ (Hearne's Richard II.)

Account of the Reception of King James at Oxford in 1605. (Leland's Collectanea, Vol. I.)

Smith's (William) Annals of University College, proving William of Durham to be the founder. 8vo *Newcastle,* 1728

Britton's (John) History and Antiquities of the Cathedral Church of Oxford. 4to large paper *Lond* 1821

RUTLAND.

Wright's (James) History and Antiquities of the County of Rutland Folio *Lond* 1684

SHROPSHIRE.

[Owen's (W.)] Account of the ancient and present State of Shrewsbury. Small 8vo *Shrewsbury,* 1808

Philips' (T.) History and Antiquities of Shrewsbury 4to *Shrewsbury,* 1779

Blakeway's (J B.) Sheriffs of Shropshire; with their armorial bearings, and notices, genealogical and biographical, of their families Folio *Shrewsbury,* 1831

A Description of Hawkstone, the seat of Sir John Hill, Bart, and a memoir of Lord Hill. 12mo. *Shrewsbury,* 1822

Statutes and Charters of Trinity Hospital, in Clune. (Leland's Collect Vol IV.)

SOMERSETSHIRE

Collinson's (John) History and Antiquities of the County of Somerset, collected from authentic records and an actual survey, by the late Mr. Rack 3 vols 4to large paper. *Bath,* 1791.

Wood's (John) Essay towards a Description of the City of Bath 8vo. *Bath,* 1742

Wood's (J.) Description of Bath, wherein the antiquities of the city, &c are treated of 2 vols 8vo *London,* 1765

Warner's (Rich.) Excursions from Bath 8vo. *Bath,* 1801.

[Rawlinson's (Th.)] History and Antiquities of the Abbey Church of Bath (Salisbury.)

Britton's (John) History and Antiquities of the Abbey Church of Bath. 4to large paper *London,* 1825

Toulmin's (J.) History of the Town of Taunton, enlarged and brought down to the present time by Savage Royal 8vo large paper *Taunton,* 1822

Adami de Domerham, Hist de Rebus Gestis Glastoniensibus, è Cod MS perantiquo, in Bib Col S Trinitatis Cantabr descripsit primusque in lucem protulit T Hearnius, qui et Guilielmi Malmesb lib de Ecc Glaston et E Aicheri excerpta aliquam multa è Reg Wellensibus, præmisit 2 vols 8vo *Oxonii,* 1727

Johannis Monach Glastoniensis Chronica, sive Historia de Rebus Gestis Glastoniensibus, è Cod MS membraneo antiquo descripsit ediditque T Hearne Qui et ex eodem Cod de antiquitate, &c Vet Ecclesiæ S Mariæ Glastoniensis præmisit, multaque excerpta è Iti Beere Terrarum hujus Cœnob subjecit. Accedunt de S Ignatii Epist Cod Mediceo, et de Jo Dee Vita atque Scriptis agitur. 2 vols 8vo *Oxonii*, 1726

Roll concerning Glastonbury Abbey. (Langtoft's Chronicle)

History and Antiquities of Glastonbury · to which are added, the endowments and orders of Sherington's Chantry, and Dr Plot's Letter concerning Thetford with Preface and Appendix by T. Hearne. 8vo *Oxford*, 1722

Tract on Conquest in Somersetshire (Langtoft's Chronicle.)

Britton's (John) History and Antiquities of the Cathedral Church of Wells 4to. large paper. *London*, 1824.

STAFFORDSHIRE

Plot's (Robert) Natural History of Staffordshire Folio *Oxford*, 1686.

Stebbing's (Shaw) History and Antiquities of Staffordshire. 2 vols folio, large paper *London*, 1798–1811.

Erdeswicke's (Sampson) Survey of Staffordshire; containing the Antiquities of the county, with a description of Beeston Castle, in Cheshire, to which are added, some observations upon the possessors of monastery lands in Staffordshire, by Sir Simon Degge Collated with MS. copies, and with additions and corrections by Wyrley, Chetwynd, Degge, Smith, Lyttleton, Buckendge, &c. illustrative of the history and antiquities of that county, by Thomas Harewood 8vo. large paper *Westminster*, 1820

Harwood's (Thos) History and Antiquities of the Church and City of Lichfield ; containing its ancient and present state, civil and ecclesiastical 4to *Gloucester*, 1806.

Britton's (John) History and Antiquities of the See and Cathedral Church of Lichfield 4to large paper *London*, 1820.

Sanders' (Henry) History and Antiquities of Shenstone, in the county of Stafford. 4to. *London*, 1794

Sanders' Shenstone, with the pedigrees of all the families, both ancient and modern, of that parish (Nichols's Top. Brit. Vol. IX. No. 4.)

Clifford's (Sir Thos. and Arthur) Topographical and Historical Description of the Parish of Tixall. 4to. *Paris*, 1817.

SUFFOLK.

Kirby's (Jos) Suffolk Traveller ; with many alterations and additions by several hands 8vo large paper. *London*, 1764.

Collections towards the History and Antiquities of Elmeswell and Campsey Ash, in the county of Suffolk. (Nichols's Top. Brit. Vol. V. No. 52)

Cullum's (Sir John) History and Antiquities of Hawksted and Hardwick, in the county of Suffolk , with corrections by the author, and notes by his brother, Sir T. G. Cullum. 4to. large paper. *Lond.* 1813

Gardner's (T) Historical Account of Dunwich, Blithburgh, and Southwold; with remarks on some places contiguous thereto   4to   *Lond.* 1754

Yates's (R) Monastic History and Antiquities of the Town and Abbey of St Edmund's Bury   4to.   *London*, 1805.

Gillingwater's (E) Historical Account of the ancient Town of Lowestoffe   4to   *London*, [1790]

Hawes' (R) History of Framlingham, including brief notices of the masters and fellows of Pembroke Hall, in Cambridge with considerable additions and notes by R. Loder   4to   *Woodbridge*, 1798.

History of Framlingham Castle, and Account of the principal Monuments in St Michael's Church   (Leland's Coll Vol II)

Gage's (John) History and Antiquities of Hengrave, in Suffolk. Large paper, imp. 4to   *London*, 1822

Specimens of Gothic Ornaments from Lavenham Church   (Architecture)

SURREY

Aubrey's (Jo) Natural History and Antiquities of Surrey, begun in 1673 and continued to the present time   5 vols 8vo.   *London*, 1719

Manning's (Owen) History and Antiquities of the County of Surrey, continued to the present time by William Bray; with a fac-simile copy of Doomsday   3 vols. folio   *London*, 1804-14

Lysons's Account of that part of Surrey within twelve miles of London   (Environs of London, Vol I)

Nichols's (John) History and Antiquities of the Parish of Lambeth.   (Nichols's Top. Brit Vol. II. No 39)

Ducarel's (A C) History and Antiquities of the Archiepiscopal Palace at Lambeth   4to ports and plates inserted   *London*, 1785

Ducarel's Lambeth Palace   (Nichols's Top Brit. Vol II. No. 27, and Vol X No 5)

Ducarel (A C), some Account of Croydon.   (Nichols's Top. Brit Vol II No. 12.)

The Case of the Inhabitants of Croydon, 1673, and Description of Trinity Hospital, Guildford, and of Albury House, with notes on Battersea, Chelsham, Nutfield, and Talsfield   (Nichols's Top Brit. Vol II No 46)

Ironside's (R) History and Antiquities of Twickenham   (Nichols's Top. Brit Vol IX No 6)

SUSSEX.

Dallaway's (James) History of the Western Division of the County of Sussex, including the Rapes of Chichester, Arundel, and Bramber, with the City and Diocese of Chichester, with continuation by Edward Cartwright   2 vols imp 4to.   *London*, 1825-30

Antiquities of Arundel, and the peculiar Privilege of its Castle and Lordship   8vo   *London*, 1766

Hay's (A) History of Chichester, interspersed with notes on the most remarkable places in its vicinity, and the county of Sussex generally.   8vo   *Chichester*, 1805

WARWICKSHIRE

Dugdale's (Sir W.) Antiquities of Warkwickshire   Folio.   *Lond* 1656.

Dugdale's (Sir W) Antiquities of Warwickshire, from the author's corrected copy, edited and continued by W. Thomas   2 vols folio. *London*, 1730.

Rossi (Joannis) Historialia de Comitibus Warwicensibus   (Hearne's Richard II)

Extracts from the Black Book of Warwick ; Pegge's Memoirs of Guy Earl of Warwick, Sir T More's Narrative of a Religious Frenzy at Coventry. (Nichols's Top Brit Vol IV. No 17)

Account of erecting the New Cross at Coventre. (Hearne's Liber Niger, Vol II)

Fowler's (Wm) Engravings from ancient Stained Glass in the windows of the Hall at Aston, near Birmingham   (Misc Eng. Antiquities)

Bartlett's (Benj) History and Antiquities of the Parish of Manceter, and also of the adjacent parish of Ansley   4to   *London*, 1790. (Continuation of Top Brit. Vol I)

Pegge's (Sam) History and Antiquities of Eccleshal Manor and Castle, and of Lichfield House, London   (Nichols's Top Brit Vol IV. No. 21.)

Wheeler's (R B) History and Antiquities of Stratford-upon-Avon   8vo. *Stratford*, 1730.

Fisher's (Thomas) Series of Ancient Allegorical, Historical, and Legendary Paintings, which were discovered in the summer of 1804 on the walls of the Chapel of the Trinity at Stratford-upon-Avon, in Warwickshire ; also, Views and Sections illustrative of the architecture of the Chapel · [with the legends reprinted from Caxton's Golden Legend]   Nos I –III , containing 33 plates, royal folio, coloured in imitation of paintings   *Hoxton*, 1807–21.

> The letter-press, which is necessary to complete the work, was not published, owing to the loss which would have been sustained by the claims of privileged libraries for copies when so completed.

WESTMORELAND   See also Tours in England, p 189.

Robinson's (Thos) Essay towards a Natural History of Westmoreland and Cumberland   8vo   *London*, 1709

Nicholson's (J) and R Burn's History and Antiquities of Westmoreland (Cumberland)

WILTSHIRE

Hoare's (Sir Richard Colt) History of Ancient Wiltshire · southern and northern districts   2 vols. folio, large paper.   *London*, 1812–20.

Hoare (Sir R. C), Lord Arundel, and the Rev John Offer's History of Modern Wiltshire ; comprehending the hundreds of Mere, Heytsbury, Branch, Dole, Everley, Ambresbury, Underditch, and Dunworth   2 vols folio, large paper.   *London*, 1824–31.

Hoare's (Richard) Journal of his Shrievalty, in the years 1740–41. Published from the MS in his own handwriting [by Sir R. C Hoare] Royal 4to   *Bath, printed for private distribution*, 1815.

Britton's (John) Beauties of Wiltshire, displayed in statistical, historical, and descriptive sketches, illustrated by views; with anecdotes of the arts [and memoir of the author by himself] 3 vols 8vo *Lond* 1801–25.

Jones (Inigo), the Most Notable Antiquity vulgarly called Stone-Heng, restored [Edited by J Webb] Folio, portrait by Hollar, and illustrated with additional plates *London*, 1655

Stukely's (Wm) Stone-Henge, a temple restored to the British Druids Folio *London*, 1740.

A Concise Account of Stonehenge and the Barrows around it, compiled for the use of those whose curiosity may lead them to see this famous monument of antiquity 12mo *Salisbury*, 1767

Tract on Stonehenge (Langtoft's Chronicle)

Stukely's (Wm.) Abury, a temple of the British Druids, with some others, described. Folio *London*, 1743

[Rawlinson's (T)] History and Antiquities of the Cathedral Church of Salisbury, and the Abbey Church of Bath 8vo. *London*, 1723

Britton's (John) History and Antiquities of the Cathedral Church of Salisbury, including biographical anecdotes of the bishops 4to. large paper *London*, 1814

Description of the House and Gardens at Stourhead, in the county of Wilts, the seat of Sir R. C. Hoare; with a catalogue of the pictures, &c 12mo. *Salisbury*, 1800

Rutter's (John) Illustrated History and Description of Fonthill Abbey 4to. *Shaftesbury*, 1823.

Description of Fonthill Abbey, illustrated by views, drawn and engraved by James Storrer. 4to *London*, 1812.

[Davies' (D.)] Origines Devisianæ; or, the Antiquity of the Devizes (Satirical) 8vo *London*, 1754

Bowles' (W L) Parochial History of Bremhill, in the county of Wilts, including a dissertation on the origin and designation of the vast Celtic monuments in the vicinity, and the progress of parochial establishments 8vo *London*, 1828.

WORCESTERSHIRE

Nash's (T) Collections for the History of Worcestershire [edited by R Gough], with Supplement 2 vols folio, large paper *London*, 1799

Green's (Val) History and Antiquities of the City and Suburbs of Worcester 2 vols 4to large paper *London*, 1796.

Hemmingii Chartularium Ecclesiæ Wigornensis, è Cod MS penès R Graves edidit T Hearne, qui et eam partem libri de Domesday, quæ ad ecclesiam pertinet Wigorn 2 vols 8vo *Oxonii* 1723

Abingdon's (Thomas) Antiquities of the Cathedral Church of Worcester. to which are added, the Antiquities of the Cathedral Churches of Chichester and Lichfield 8vo *London* 1723

Thomas s (William) Survey of the Cathedral Church of Worcester; with an account of the bishops thereof to the year 1600 4to *London*, 1737.

Britton's (John) History and Antiquities of the Cathedral Church of Worcester 4to large paper. *London*, 1832.

Green's (V) Account of the Discovery of the Body of King John, in the cathedral church of Worcester, 17th July, 1797   4to   *Lond* 1797

Tindal's (William) History and Antiquities of the Borough and Abbey of Evasham. 4to   *Evasham*, 1794

YORKSHIRE.

Doomsday Book for Yorkshire, transcribed ; with notes by Tho Wilson, of Leeds   (Manuscripts)

Bawdwen's (William) Translation of the Doomsday Book, as far as relates to the county of York ; with an introduction, glossary, and indexes   4to. large paper. *Doncaster*, 1809

Dugdale's (Sir W) Visitation of the County of York. (Manuscripts)

Hopkinson's various Collections relative to Family History and Antiquities of Yorkshire. (Manuscripts)

Jeffreys' (Thos) County of York surveyed in 1767–70. Large folio. *Lond* 1770.

Thoresby (Ralph) on some Antiquities found in Yorkshire. (Leland's Itinerary, Vols. I. and IV.)

Views (XLIV) in Yorkshire , including those by Dunning and Hofland, and the Lithographic Sketches by Cave, &c. Folio   (Coll of Prints, Vol XIV)

Fowler's (W) Engravings of Antiquities in Yorkshire   (Misc English Antiquities)

Burton's (Jo.) Monasticon Eboracense, and the Ecclesiastical History of Yorkshire   Folio   *York*, 1758.

Drake's (Fr) History and Antiquities of the City of York. Folio, large paper   *London*, 1736

Gent's (Thos) Ancient and Modern History of the City of York, and particularly of its magnificent Cathedral   Small 8vo   *York*, 1730.

Gent's (T.) History of the great Eastern Window in St Peter's Cathedral, York. Small 8vo   *York*, 1760.

[Torr's (Jas.)] History and Antiquities of the City of York to the present times   3 vols small 8vo   *York*, 1785

Dugdale's (Sir W) Historical Account of the Cathedral Church of York, and the Collegiate Churches at Rippon and Beverley   (St Paul's)

Britton's (John) History and Antiquities of the Metropolical Church of York ; with biographical anecdotes of the archbishops. 4to large paper   *London*, 1819

Halfpenny's (John) Etchings of Gothic Ornaments in the Cathedral Church of York. 4to large paper   *York*, 1795

Cave's (H.) Etchings of the Picturesque Buildings in York. 4to large paper.   *York*, 1800

Wellbeloved's (C) Account of St Mary's Abbey, York ; with ground-plan picturesque views, and architectural details, by F Nash   Folio *London, Soc of Antiquaries*, 1829

Poulson's (Geo) Beverlac ; or, the Antiquities and History of the Town of Beverley   2 vols in one, 4to.   *London*, 1829

Prickett's (Marm) Historical and Architectural Description of the Priory Church, Bridlington   Royal 8vo   *Cambridge*, 1831

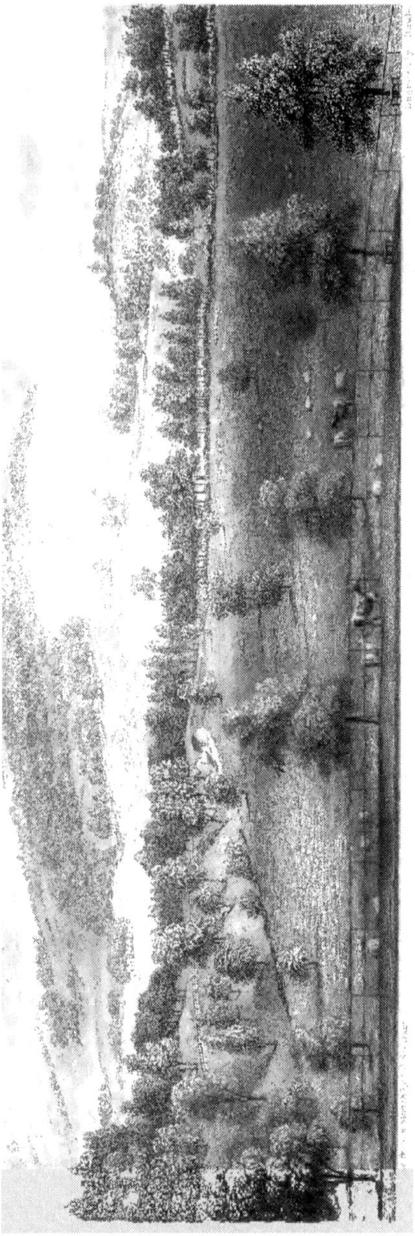

Graves' (John) History and Antiquities of Cleveland, in the North Riding 4to *Carlisle*, 1808

Whitaker's (T D) History and Antiquities of the Deanery of Craven, with additional plates, genealogical tables, and MS additions, by Mrs Dor Richardson Folio, large paper *Lond* 1812

Hofland's (J C) Sixteen original Drawings of Views in Craven Oblong folio

Hurtley's (Thos) Account of Natural Curiosities in the environs of Malham, in Craven 8vo. *London*, 1786

Eastmead's (W) Historia Rievallensis, containing the history of Kirby-Moorside, &c to which is prefixed, a dissertation on the animal remains in the cave at Kirkdale 8vo *Thisk*, 1824

Hunter's (Joseph) History and Topography of the Deanery of Doncaster 2 vols folio *London*, 1828.

Miller's (Edw) History and Antiquities of Doncaster and its vicinity 4to *Doncaster*, 1810

Wright's (Thos) Antiquities of the Town of Halifax. 12mo *Leeds*, 1738.

Watson's (Jo) History and Antiquities of the Town of Halifax 4to *London*, 1775

[Midgley's (Sam)] Halifax and its Gibbet Law placed in a true light; published by W Bently *London*, 1712

Simpson's (T) State of that part of Yorkshire adjacent to the level of Hatfield Chase 4to. *York*, 1701.

Gent's (Thos) History of the Town of Kingston-upon-Hull. 8vo *York*, 1735

Tickell's (Jo) History of the Town and County of Kingston-upon-Hull, from its foundation to the present time 4to large paper *London*, 1798

Hargrove's (E) History of the Castle, Town, and Forest of Knaresborough, with Harrowgate and its waters 12mo *York*, 1798

The Privileges of New Malton, as claimed by the Burgesses thereof, 1596 (Liber Niger, Vol II.)

Thoresby's (R) Topography of the Towne and Parish of Leedes, and parts adjacent (The Sale Catalogue of Thoresby's Museum, 8vo inserted) Folio *London*, 1715

Thoresby's (R) Vicaria Leodiensis, or the history of the Church of Leedes, containing an account of the learned men, bishops, and writers, vicars of that parish with catalogues of their works 8vo *Lond* 1724

Thoresby's (R) Ducatus Leodiensis, or the topography of Leeds and parts adjacent, with notes and additions by T D Whitaker Folio, largest paper *Leeds*, 1816

Whitaker's (T D) Leodis et Elmete, or the lower portions, Aredale and Whartedale, together with the entire vale of Calder, illustrated. Folio, largest paper. *London*, 1816.

Scatcherd's (N) History of Morley, in the parish of Botley, and West Riding of Yorkshire, and especially of the old chapel in this village; with some account of other places in the vicinity 8vo *Leeds*, 1830

HISTORY.

Boothroyd's (B.) History of the ancient Borough of Pontefract, with notes and pedigrees of some of the most distinguished royalists and parliamentarians in the civil war. 8vo *Pontefract*, 1807

[Gale (R.)] Registrum Honoris de Richmond, exhibens terrarum et villarum quæ quondam fuerunt Edwini Comitis infra Richmundshire Descriptionem Folio, large paper *London*, 1722.
> This is usually attributed to Roger Gale but his name, as well as Samuel's, appears in the list of subscribers Sir M M Sykes's copy

Whitaker's (T. D.) History of Richmondshire, in the North Riding of Yorkshire, together with the Wapentakes of Lonsdale, Ewecross, and Amunderness, in the counties of York, Lancaster, and Westmoreland. 2 vols folio, largest paper *London*, 1823.

Gent's (Thos.) Ancient and Modern History of the Town of Rippon. Small 8vo. *York*, 1733

Slacke's (John) Account of the Hospital of St Mary Magdalene near Scroby. (Langtoft's Chronicle.)

Hinderwell's (Thos.) History and Antiquities of Scarborough and the vicinity. 8vo *York*, 1811

Parker's (T. L.) Description of Browsholme Hall, and of the Parish of Waddington 4to *London, privately printed*, 1815

Whitaker's (T. D.) History of the original Parish of Whalley and Honour of Clitheroe, in the counties of York and Lancaster to which is subjoined, an Account of the Parish of Cartmell Folio, large paper *London*, 1818

Young's (George) History of Whitby and Streoneshall Abbey, with a statistical survey of its vicinity 2 vols 8vo *Whitby*, 1817

ENGLISH ISLANDS

Borlasse's (William) Ancient and present state of the Islands of Scilly 4to *Oxford*, 1756

Barry's (Wm.) History of the Island of Guernsey to the year 1814, with particulars of the neighbouring islands of Alderney, Serk, and Jersey, compiled from the Collections of Henry Budd, and other authentic sources 4to *London*, 1815

History of the Islands of Guernsey and Sarke, by D Y (Warner's Hampshire, Vol VI.)

Falle's (Ph.) and P Morant's Cæsarea; an account of Jersey in the ancient duchy of Normandy 4to. *London*, 1797 (Warner's Hampshire.)

Antiquitates Celto-Normannicæ, the Chronicles of Man and the Islands Now first published complete, by John Johnstone. 4to *Copenhagen* 1786

Sacheverell's (Wm.) Account of the Isle of Man; with a voyage to I-Columb-Kill, and a Dissertation on the Mona of Cæsar, by Thos. Brown 12mo. *Lond* 1702

Wilson's (Bp T.) History of the Isle of Man. (Works, Vol I.)

Wood's (Geo.) Account of the past and present state of the Isle of Man 8vo. *London*, 1811

History of England.

Narrative.

Introduction.

Libri Saxonici, qui ad manus J Joscelini venerunt. Nomina eorum qui scripserunt hist gentis Anglorum, et ubi extant; per J. Joscelinum (Hearne's Robert de Avesbury)

Leland (Jo) Comment de Scriptoribus Britannicis, nunc primùm edidit Antonius Hall. 2 vols. in one, 8vo *Oxonii,* 1709

Nicolson's (Bp W) English, Scotch, and Irish Historical Libraries, giving the Characters and Sources of the Historians, either in print or manuscript Folio Mr Wilson of Leeds' copy, with his MS. corrections and additions *Lond* 1736

Hoare's (Sir R. C.) Catalogue of Books relating to the History and Topography of England, Wales, Scotland, and Ireland, compiled from the Library at Stourhead, in Wiltshire 8vo *London, privately printed,* 1815

Gibbon's (Edward) Address, &c on the subject of a Collection of English Historians (Misc Works, Vol II.)

Heylin's (Peter) Help to English History, or, Catalogues of the Kings, Nobles, and Bishops with Lists of the extinct Viscounts and Barons, by P Wright *London,* 1772

Beatson's Political Index. (Parliamentary Hist)

Sammes' (Aylet) Britannia Antiqua Illustrata, or, the antiquity of ancient Britain derived from the Phœnicians, and plainly set forth and collected out of approved Greek and Latin authors. together with a chronological history of this kingdom from the first beginning until the year 800 Folio *London,* 1676.

The Light of Britayne; a Recorde of the honorable originale and antiquitie of Britaine [by Henry Lyte of Lytescane] 8vo. large paper, in 4to. [edited by W. Upcott]. *Lond reprint,* 1588

Macpherson's (James) Introduction to the History of Great Britain and Ireland, or, the origin, &c of the Britons, Scots, Irish, and Anglo-Saxons 4to *London,* 1773

Macpherson —[Leland s (Thos)] Remarks on an Introduction to the History of Great Britain 4to. *London,* 1772

Macpherson —Whitaker's (John) Remarks on an Introduction to the History of Great Britain 8vo *Lond* 1772

Ralegh's (Sir W) Introduction to a Breviary of the History of England (Works, Vol VIII)

Burke's (Edmund) Essay towards an Abridgement of the English History (Works, Vol. X)

Collections of Ancient English Historians.

Britannicarum Gentium Historiæ Antiquæ Scriptores III. recensuit, Notisque et Indice auxit C. Bertram. 8vo *Haunuæ, impensis editoris,* 1757. Vid —
    Ricardi Corinensis de Situ Britanniæ,
    Gildæ Badonici de Excidio Brit Hist
    Nennii Banchorensis Hist Brit.

Rerum Britannicarum, id est, Angliæ, Scotiæ, vicinarumque insularum ac regionum, Scriptores vetustiores ac præcipui Folio *Lugduni Bat* 1587 Vid —
    Galfridus Monumetensis,   Gildas,   Gulielmus Newbricensis,
    Ponticus Verunnius,   Beda,   Joannes Froissardus

Historiæ Anglicanæ Scriptores III, sumptibus M Parkeri Episc Cantuariensis Folio *Lond J Dau et H Binneman,* 1574 Vid —
    Jo Asseri Alfredi Regis Res Gestæ [Saxonicè, cum Præfatione S Gregorii, Sax. et Lat et Præfatione M Parkeri].
    Ypodigma Neustriæ vel Normanniæ, per Thom de Walsingham ab irruptione Normannorum usque ad annum sext regni Hen V.
    Historia Brevis Thomæ de Walsingham ab Edwardi I. ad Henricum V cum Præfat M Parkeri

Anglica, Normannica, Hibernica, et Cambrica, à veteribus scripta ex Bib. Guil Camdeni. Folio *Francof.* 1603 Vid —
    Asser Menevensis,   Thomas de la More,
    Anon de Vitâ Guil. I   Guliel. Gemiticensis,
    Thomas de Walsingham,   Giraldus Cambrensis

Duchesne (A) Historiæ Anglicanæ circa tempus Conquestûs Angliæ à G. Notho Normannorum Duce, selecta monumenta; cum Notis plurimis Anglico sermone conscriptis à F. Maseres 4to *Lond* 1807. Vid —
    Emmæ, Ang Reginæ, Richardi I Ducis Norm Filiæ, Encomium
    Gesta Guil Ducis Norm et Regis Anglorum, à Guil Pictavensi, Lexoviorum Archidiacono, contemporaneo scripta
    Excerpta ex Oderico Vitali de Guil I Rege Ang à Guil Pictavensi, scripta
    Chronica Sancti Stephani Cadomensis
    Nomina Normannorum qui floruerunt in Angliâ ante Conquestum
    Cognomina Nobilium, qui Guil Norm Ducem in Angliam sequuti sunt, ex Tab Monast vulgò Battail Abbay
    Cognomina Nobilium, &c. authore Joanne Bromptono, qui floruerunt anno 1199.
    Magnates superstites anno vicesim. regni Willelmi Conquestoris et quibus in comitatibus terras tenuerunt
    Catalogus Nobilium, qui immediatè prædia à rege Conquestore tenuerunt
    Familiæ Regum, Ducum, Comitum, et aliorum Nobilium, quæ in Volumen Scriptorum Normanniæ ab A. Duchesnio editum, deducuntur

Rerum Anglicarum Scriptores post Bedam, præcipuè ex vetust cod. MSS. in lucem editi à H Saville Folio *Londini,* 1596 Vid.:—
    Will Malmesburiensis,   Ingulph Abbas Croylandiensis, ad-
    Henr Huntingdoniensis,   jecta est Chronologia [et Fasti
    Roger de Hovedon,   Regum, et Episc Angliæ ad
    Chronicon Ethelwerdi,   Will Seniorem]

Historiæ Anglicanæ Scriptores X ex vetust MSS nunc primùm editi, Var Lect et Glossario illustrati per Roger Twysden. Folio. *Londini*, 1652. Vid —
    Simeon Monachus Dunelm   Johannes Brompton,
    Johannes Prior Hagustald.   Gervasius Monach. Dorabor.
    Ricardus Prior ejusdem,   Thomas Stubbes,
    Ailredus Abbatis Rievall   Gulielmus Thorne,
    Radulphus de Diceto,   Henricus Knyghton

Selden (Jo) Judicium de X. Hist Angl Scriptoribus. (Opera, Vol II.)

Rerum Anglicarum Scriptores Veteres, curâ [W. Fulman et] Jo Fell Folio. *Oxonn*, 1684 Vid —
    Ingulphi Hist Croylandensis,   Annales Monast. Burtonensis.
    Petri Blessensis Continuatio ejusd   Historia Croylandensis Continuatio
    Chronica de Mailros,

Historiæ Brit Sax Anglo-Sax Scriptores XV nec non Hist Ang. Scriptores V., ex vet cod MSS editi et in unam collecti operâ et studio T Gale. 2 vols folio *Oxonii*, 1687–91 Vid —
    Gildas,   Joan Walingfordensis,
    Eddius,   Rad de Diceto,
    Nennius,   Anon de Partitione Provinciæ,
    (Pseudo) Asserius,   Joannes Fordun,
    Ran Higden,   Alcuinus Flaccus,
    Guil Malmesburiensis,   Annales Marginenses,
    Anon Malmesburiensis,   Chronicon Thomæ Wikes,
    Anon Ramesensis,   Annales Waverleyenses,
    Anon Elyensis,   Galfridus Vinesalvi,
    Thomas Elyensis,   Walt de Hemmingford

Historiæ Anglicanæ Scriptores varii, è cod MSS. nunc primùm editi J Sparke Folio *Londini*, 1723.
    Chronicon Jo Abbat S. Petri de Burgo,
    Chronicon Ang per Rob de Boston,
    Hist Cœnobii Burgensis Script varii,
    Vita S Thomæ Cantuariensis à W. Stephanide

Particular Histories before the Conquest, Chronicles, and General Histories of England

Gildas de Excidio et Conquestu Britanniæ; cum Præfatione ad M. (Parker) Cant. Archiepisc J Josselin. Sm. 8vo. *Londini*, J. Daius, 1568

Gildas' Description of Great Brittain, written eleven hundred yeares since, [translated by W Habington] 18mo. *Lond*. 1652

Nennius —The Historia Brittonum, commonly attributed to Nennius, from a MS lately discovered in the Vatican, edited in the tenth century by Mark the Hermit with an English Version, Notes, and Illustrations, by W. Gunn 8vo large paper *Lond* 1819.

Thorkelin's (G J) Fragments of English and Irish History in the ninth and tenth centuries, translated from the Islandic (Nichols's Top Brit Vol. VI No 8)

Galfridus Monumetensis — Britaniæ utriusque Regum et Principum origo et gesta insignia, ab Galfrido Monumetensi. Ex antiquiss Brit. sermone in Latinum traducta, et ab Ascensio curâ et impedio Mag Luonis Cavillate in lucem edita 4to Editio princeps. [*Parisiis*] ex ædib. B Ascensio 1508

Jeffrey of Monmouth, his British History translated, with a Preface on the Author, by A. Thompson. 8vo   *London*, 1718

Virunnii (Pont.) Britannicæ Historiæ Lib VI, conscripti ad Brit Cod fidem correcti, quibus præfixus est Catalogus Regum Brit. per D Pouelum Small 8vo   *Londini, imp H Denham et R Nuberu*, 1585

Lelandi (Jo) Laus et Defensio Galfridi Monumetensis contra P. Vergilium   (Collectanea)

Twini (Jo) Comment de Rebus Albionicis, Britannicis, atque Anglicis. Sm 8vo   *Londini, ap E Bollifont*, 1590.

Johnstone (Jacobi) Antiquitates Celto-Scandicæ; sive, series rerum gestarum inter nationes Britannicarum et gentes septentrionales 4to   *Hauniæ*, 1786

Chronological Series of the British Kings before the Roman Invasion; — Index Memorabilium Brit. ante Cæsarem; — Of the coming in of the Saxons, and their Conquests in Britain; — Saxon Annals. (Manuscripts)

Langhorne's (Daniel) Introduction to the History of England; comprising the principal affairs of this land from its first planting to the coming in of the Saxons; together with a Catalogue of the British and Pictish kings. Small 8vo.   *London*, 1676

Strutt's (Joseph) Chronicle of England; or, complete history, civil, military, and ecclesiastical, of the ancient Britons and Saxons; with a view of the manners, customs, arts, habits, &c. of those people 2 vols 4to.   *London*, 1777-8.

Chronicon Saxonicum, seu, Annales Rerum in Angliâ, præcipuè gestarum ad A.D 1154. Saxonicè et Latinè ab E Gibson   4to.   *Oxon* 1692

Chronicon Saxonicum; with an English Translation and Notes, critical and explanatory to which are added, chronological, topographical, and glossarial Indices; a short Anglo-Saxon grammar; a new map of England during the Heptarchy, &c   By J Ingram. 4to   *London*, 1823.

Asserii (Jo) Annales Rerum Gestarum Ælfridi Magni, à J. Wise. 8vo. large paper.   *Oxonii*, 1722

Alfredi Magni Anglorum Regis Vita, à Jo Spelman, Henrici primùm Anglicè conscripta, dein Latinè reddita, et annotationibus illustrata   Folio   *Oxonii*, 1678

Powell's (Robt) Life of Alfred or Alured, the first institutor of subordinate government in this kingdom, and refounder of the University of Oxford   18mo   *Oxford*, 1634

Selden (Jo.) Janus Anglorum, et Analecta Anglo-Britannicæ. (Opera, Vol II and Jurisprudence)

Turner's (Sharon) History of the Anglo-Saxons, comprising the history of England to the Norman conquest. 3 vols 8vo   *London*, 1823.

Milton's (John) History of Great Britain, from the first traditional beginning to William the Conqueror (Works, 4to. Vol. II ; 8vo. Vol V.)

Florentii Wigornensis Chronicon, ex Chronicis, ab initio mundi usque ad an 1118 accessit etiam continuatio usque ad 1141, per quendam ejusdem Cœnobii eruditum Nunquam antehâc in lucem editum 4to   *Londini, excud T Dausonius*, 1592

Eadmeri Historia sui Sæculi Libri VI., res gestæ ab anno 1066 ad 1122; in lucem ex Bibl. Cott. emissit et notas adjecit J Selden Folio *Londini,* 1623

Eadmeri (J. Seldeni Notæ et Spicilegium ejusdem; Opera, Vol. II.)

Alured Beverlacensis Annales, sive historia de gestis Regum Britanniæ · è cod pervetusto in Bib. T. Rawlinson, cum præfatione, notis, &c T. Hearne. 8vo *Oxonii,* 1716.

William of Malmsbury's History of the Kings of England, translated from the Latin by John Sharp. Folio, large paper *Lond* 1815

Gulielmi Neubrigensis Historia, sive chronica rerum Anglicarum, è cod MS pervetusto in Bibl. D T. Scabright, Baronetti; studio et industriâ T. Hearne, quæ et præter J. Picardi annotationes suas etiam notas et spicilegium subjecit . accedunt homiliæ tres eidem Gulielmo à viris eruditis adscriptæ. 3 vols 8vo *Oxonii,* 1719.

Matthæi Paris Historia Major [à Guil Conq ad mortem Hen. III anno 1273], et cum Rogeri Wendoveri, Willielmi Rishangeri, &c. Historiâ Chronicisque MSS Accedunt Vita decorum affarum, mercorum, regum, et XXIII. abbatum S. Albani Edidit cum var lect , adversaria, glossarium, &c. W Watts. Folio *London,* 1640

Langtoft's (Peter) Chronicle, as illustrated by Robert of Brunne, from the death of Cadwallader to the end of Edward I 's reign Now first published from a MS. in the Inner Temple Library , with a glossary by T Hearne. 2 vols. 8vo. *Oxford,* 1725

Robert of Gloucester's Chronicle , with continuation by the author himself Now first published from two MSS in the Harleyan and Cottonian Libraries , with glossary by Thomas Hearne. 2 vols 8vo. *Oxford,* 1724

Triveti (N) Chronicon, sive annales VI. Regum Angliæ ab 1136 ad 1307, corumque continuatio; ut et Adami Muremuthensis chronicon ejusdem, continuatione, &c., edidit, &c. A Hall 8vo. *Oxonii,* 1719.

Wilhelmi Worcestri Annales Rerum Anglicarum. (Liber Niger Scac)

The Polychronicon , conteyning the berynges and dedes of many tymes [by " Ranulphus (Higden), monke of Chestre," and translated by " Johan Trevissa, chapelayn unto Lord Thomas of Barkley.] **Black letter**, folio *Westminster, imprynted by William Caxton,* M.CCCC LXXXII

> Mr. Wilson, of Leeds, whose copy this was, has added the following note. "The ingenious Mr Baker writ the above (a copy of the colophon), this having been his book, and being an imperfect copy, or rather *a former impression,* this wants the preface and the table of contents at the beginning, and Mr Caxton himself added an eighth book, which brings it down to 1482 " On the first fly-leaves are a list of the works printed by Caxton, also in Mr Wilson's hand

The Polychronicon Folio, **black letter** *Southwerke, imprented by my Peter Treveris, at ye expences of John Reynes, boke-seller,* M CCCCC.XXVII.

> With the MS notes of Mr. R Nicolson, A D 1589, and map of a survey by Norden, "impensis R Nicolson," inserted. This copy was formerly Dr Dibdin's see Typog Antiq Vol. III p 41

Matthæi Westmonasteriensis Flores Historiarum, præcipuè de rebus Britannicis ab exordio mundi usque ad A D 1307; et Chronicon et Chronicus usque ad A D 1118, deductum auctore Florentio Wigorniensi, cui accessit continuatio usque ad A D 1141 Folio *Francof* 1601

Froissart's Chronicles of England, &c. (French History.)

Thomæ Otterbourne et Jo. Wethamstede [Chronica Regum Angliæ], ab origine gentis Britannicæ usque ad Edwardum IV · è cod. MSS. antiquiss. nunc primùm eruit Tho. Hearne. Accedunt liber de Vitâ et Miraculis Henrici VI per Jo Blackmannum. 2 vols 8vo. *Oxonii*, 1732.

Diary of Events from 1221 to 1440. (Manuscripts.)

Hardyng's (John) Chronicle, containing an account of public transactions, from the earliest period of English history to the beginning of the reign of Edward IV, with continuation to the 34th Henry VIII. by Richard Grafton. With a biographical and literary preface by Henry Ellis. 4to. *London*, 1812.

The Cronicles of Englonde; with the Fruite of Timis. 𝔅lack letter, small folio, on vellum. *At St Albon's, in the 23d yeer of the reigne of Kyng Edward IV., and in the yeer of oure Lorde M.IIII^c.LXXXIII*

This copy has the first leaf of the table, commencing " Here begynnyeth a schorte and breve tabull to thes Cronicles," the half of A. viii is wanting, L. i and ii, and z i and ii, are on paper, and the last leaf is supplied by a facsimile, otherwise it is perfect. The vellum is very irregular both in texture and in purity, and the initial letters, except the commencements of the prologue and the Chronicle, are certainly *printed* in red, as described by Ames. The title, as above, is taken from the colophon, and the date from the body of the prologue.

Rossi (Jo.) Antiquarii Warwicensis Historia Regum Angliæ, è cod MS descripsit, notisque adornavit T Hearne. 8vo. portrait of Hearne. *Oxonii*, 1716.

Fabian (the Chronicle of Robert), whiche he nameth the Concordaunce of Histories newly perused. And continued from the beginnyng of Kyng Henry the Seventh to the ende of Queene Mary, 1559. 2 vols. in one, folio, 𝔅lack letter. *London, John Kingston*, 1559.

Fabian (R.), the Chronicles of England and France, in two parts, named by him, the Concordance of Histories; reprinted from Pynson's edition of 1516; to which are added, a biographical and literary preface, by Henry Ellis. 4to. *London*, 1811.

Polydori Vergilii Anglicæ Historiæ Libr XXVI ad Henricum VII. Folio. *Basileæ*, 1546.

Rastell's (John) Pastime of People; or, the Chronicles of divers realms, and most especially of the realme of England, to Richard III; briefly compiled and imprinted A.D. 1529, now reprinted and systematically arranged by T F Dibdin. 4to. *London*, 1811.

Lanquet, Cooper, and Crowley's Epitome of Cronicles, conteyninge the whole discourse of the histories, as well of this realme of England as al other countreys, with the succession of their kinges, the time of their reigne, and what notable actes they did · gathered out of most probable auctours. Firste, by Thomas Lanquet, from the beginning of the worlde to the incarnacion of Christe, secondely, to the reigne of King Edward the Sixt, by Thomas Cooper; and thirdly, to the reign of Queene Elizabeth, by Robt Crowley. 4to black letter. *London, by Thomas Marshe*, 1559.

Lillii [or Lilly] (Geo.) Chronicon; sive, brevis enumeratio regum et principum, in quos, variante fortunâ, Britanniæ imperium diversis temporibus translatum est. 4to. *Francofurti*, 1565.

MODERN.

Grafton's (Richard) Chronicle, or History of England to 1558; to which is added, his table of the bailiffs and mayors of the city of London, from the year 1189 to 1558, inclusive. 2 vols 4to *Lond.* 1809.

Holinshed (Raphael), William Harrison, and others' Chronicles, comprising the description and historie of England, Ireland, and Scotland, augmented and continued (with manifold matters of singular note and worthie memorie), to the yeare 1586, by John Hooker, *alias* Vowell, gent Finished in Januarie 1587, with the full continuation of the former yeares The castrations supplied by the reprint. 3 vols. in four, folio. *London, by H. Denham,* 1587

Holinshed's (R.), W. Harrison, and others' Chronicles of England, Scotland, and Ireland 6 vols 4to. *London,* 1807.

Stowe's (John) Summarie of our Englysh Chronicles, diligently collected in the yeare of oure Lorde 1566 𝔅𝔩𝔞𝔠𝔨 𝔩𝔢𝔱𝔱𝔢𝔯, small 8vo. *London, by Thomas Marshe,* 1566

Stowe's (J) Summarie of our Englysh Chronicles, augmented with sundry memorable antiquities, and continued with maters forein and domesticall unto this present yeare 1607, by Edmund Howes 𝔅𝔩𝔞𝔠𝔨 𝔩𝔢𝔱𝔱𝔢𝔯, small 8vo *London, for the Companie of Stationers,* 1607.

Stowe's (J) Annales, or a generall Chronicle of England, continued and augmented with matters forraigne and domestique, ancient and moderne, unto the end of this present yeere 1631. Folio. *London,* 1631.

Daniel's (Sam.) Collection of the History of England [from the time of the Romans to the end of the reign of Edward III]. Folio *Lond.* 1626. (Kennet's History, Vol 1)

Daniel —Trussell's (John) Continuation of Daniel's History to the end of the dissensions between the Houses of York and Lancaster; with the matches and issues of all the kings and nobles of this nation during these times Folio *London,* 1636.

Warner's (Wm.) Albion's England, a continued history of the same kingdome from the originals of the first inhabitants unto and in the reigne of our Lord King James [in verse]: whereunto is newly added, an epitome of the whole historie of England 4to *Lond.* 1612.

Slatyer's (W) Palæ Albion; a history of Great Britaine from the first peopling of this island to the present reigne [a poem, Latin and English, with historical notes]. Folio, portrait, large paper *Lond.* 1621

Speed's (John) History of Greate Britaine under the conquests of the Romans, Saxons, Danes, and Normans; their originals, manners, warres, coins, and seales. with the successions, lives, acts, and issues of the English monarchs, from Julius Cæsar to King James Revised, enlarged, and corrected. Folio *London,* 1632.

Baker's (Sir R) Chronicle of the Kings of England, from the time of the Romans' Government unto the death of King James: whereunto is now added, the reign of King Charles I [by Edward Phillips], and the first thirteen years of ye reign of King Charles II [by Sir T Clarges] Revised and corrected. Folio *London,* 1684

Stevenson's (Mat) Florus Britannicus, or, an exact Epitome of the History of England, from William the Conqueror to the twelfth year of the reign of Charles II illustrated with perfect portraictures Folio *London,* 1662

Whitlocke's (Sir B.) History of England; or, Memorials of English Affairs, from the supposed expedition of Brute to this island to the end of the reign of King James. Published from the original MS., with an introduction by Governor W. Penn; to which is prefixed, the author's life, and a preface by James Wellwood. Folio. *Lond.* 1713.

Kennet's Complete History of England, from the earliest account of time [to the death of James I. by various authors; edited by John Hughes and continued] to the death of William III. [by Bp. White Kennet]. 3 vols folio. *London*, 1706.

Rapin's History of England, translated from the French; with continuation to the death of George I. by N. Tindal. illustrated with maps, genealogical tables, heads, and monuments of the kings, portraits of eminent persons, and medallic history. 5 vols folio. *London*, 1743–47.

Carte's (Thos.) General History of England, from the earliest times to 1654. 4 vols folio, large paper. *London*, 1747–55.

Swift's (Jonath.) Abstract of the History of England, from the Invasion of Julius Cæsar to the reign of Henry II. (Works, Vol. X.)

Hume's (David) History of England, from the Invasion of Julius Cæsar to the Revolution in 1688; and continued by T. Smollett to the death of George II. 16 vols. 8vo. portraits, and wood-cut illustrations, large paper. *London, Wallis,* 1803.

History of Great Britain. (Mod. Univ. Hist. Vols. XVII. and XXXVII.)

History of England, to the accession of the House of Hanover. (Mod. Univ. Hist. Vols. XXXIX and XL.)

Henry's (Robert) History of Great Britain, from the Invasion of Julius Cæsar to the death of Henry VIII. [finished by M. Laing, with life of the author] 12 vols. 8vo. *London*, 1814.

Henry (R.)—Continuation of the History of Great Britain, to the accession of James I.; by J. P. Andrews. 2 vols 8vo. *London*, 1806.

Lingard's (John) History of England, from the Invasion of the Romans to the Revolution in 1688. 8 vols 4to. *London*, 1819–30.

Turner's (Sharon) History of England, from the Norman Conquest to the reign of Henry VIII. 4 vols. 4to. *London*, 1814–26.

Ayscu's (Edward) Historie; containing the warres, treaties, marriages, and other occurrents betweene England and Scotland, from William the Conqueror until the happy union of them both in King James: with briefe declaration of the first inhabitants of this island, and what severall nations have sithence settled themselves therein. 4to *London, by J. Eld,* 1607.

History of the ancient and modern State of the English Borders. (Nicolson and Burn's Westmoreland, Vol I.)

Particular Histories since the Conquest

Ralegh's (Sir W.) Reign of King William I., entitled the Conqueror. (Works, Vol VIII.)

Temple's (Sir W.) Introduction to the History of England [an account of the reign of William the Conqueror] (Works, Vol III.)

Lyttleton's (George, Lord) History of King Henry II., and of the age in which he lived; with a history of the revolutions of England, from Edward the Confessor to Henry III 4 vols. 4to. *Lond.* 1767

Berrington's (Joseph) History of the Reign of King Henry II., and of his two Sons, with a vindication of the life of Thomas à Becket from the attack of Lord Lyttleton 4to. *Birmingham*, 1790

Benedictus, Abbas Petroburgensis, de Vitâ et Gestis Henrici II et Ricardi I. è cod. MS in Bib. Harleianâ, nunc primus edidit T Hearne 2 vols 8vo *Oxonii*, 1735

Prynne's (W) History of King John, Henry III, and Edward I (English Records)

Cotton's (Sir R.) Short View of the Long Life and Reign of Henry III (Somers's Tracts, Vol IV)

The Siege of Carlaverock, in the XXVIIIth Edward I, A D M CCC; with the arms of the earls, barons, and knights, who were present on the occasion with a translation, a history of the castle, and memoirs of the personages commemorated by the poet; by N. H. Nicholas. The arms illuminated. 4to *London*, 1828.

Walter Hemingford, Canonici de Gisseburne, Historia de Rebus gestis Edwardi I. II et III. · accedunt Edwardi III historia per anonymum, excerpta historica è Tho. Gascoignii Doct. Theologico E cod MSS nunc primus publicavit Tho Hearne. 2 vols. 8vo *Oxonii*, 1731

[Halifax's (Sir Geo Sackville, Marquess of)] Historical Observations on the Reigns of Edwards I and II, and Richard I., with remarks upon their faithful counsellors and false favourites · written by a person of honour Small 8vo. *London*, 1689.

Johannis de Trokelowe Annales Edwardi II, Henrici de Blandeforde Chronica, et Edwardi II, Vita à Monacho quodam Malmesburiensi fusè enarrata è cod. MSS nunc primus devulgavit T Hearne 8vo *Oxonii*, 1729.

Roberti de Avesbury Historia de mirabilibus Gestis Edwardi III è cod. MSS. edidit T. Hearne 8vo. *Oxonii*, 1720.

Barnes' (Joshua) History of King Edward III, and Edward the Black Prince Folio *Cambridge*, 1688.

Bree's (John) Cursory Sketch of the State of the Naval, Military, and Civil Establishment, Legislative, Judicial, and Domestic Economy of this Kingdom, during the fourteenth century; with a particular account of the campaign of King Edward the Third in Normandy and France, in the years 1345 and 1346, to the taking of Calais Collected from the ancient manuscripts in the British Museum and elsewhere (Vol 1 all published) 4to. *London*, 1791.

History of the Reigns of Richard II., Henry IV V and VI (Kennet, Vol 1)

Historia Vitæ et Regni Ricardi II, Angliæ Regis, à Monacho quodam de Evesham consignata. è cod. MS nunc primus edidit T Hearne 8vo. *Oxoniæ*, 1729

Biondi's (Sir Jo Fr) History of the Civil Wars of England between the Houses of Lancaster and York, translated by Henry Earl of Monmouth Folio *London*, 1641

[Halle's (Edw.)] The Unyon of the Twoo Noble and Illustre Families of Lancastre and Yorke, beyng long in continuall Discension for the Crounne of this noble realme; with al the actes done in both the tymes of the princes, both of the one lynage and of the other, beginnyng at the tyme of Kynge Henry the Fourthe, the first aucthor of thys devision, and so successively proceeding to y* raygne of the high and prudent prince, Kynge Henry the Eyghte, the indubitate floure and very heyre of both the sayde linages Black letter, folio. *Lond. by R. Grafton*, 1550

Halle's (E.) Chronicle; containing the History of England during the reign of Henry the Fourth and the succeeding monarchs, to the end of the reign of Henry the Eighth, in which are particularly described the manners and customs of those periods. carefully collated with the editions of 1548 and 1550. 4to *London*, 1809.

Titi Livii Foro-Juliensis Vita Henrici V Regis Angliæ; accedit sylloge epist è variis Angliæ principibus scriptorum. è codicibus edidit 8vo. *Oxon* 1716.

Thomæ de Elmham Vita et Gesta Henr. V. Anglorum Regis: è cod. MS primus luci publicæ dedit T Hearne. *Oxon*. 1727.

Luders's (Alex.) Essay on the Character of Henry V when Prince of Wales 8vo. *London*, 1813

Blackmanni (J.) Vita et Miracula Henrici VI. (Hearne's Thomas of Otterbourne.)

Nicolas's (Sir Harris) Proceedings of the Privy Council in the reign of Henry VI, from the original MS in the British Museum. 2 vols 8vo *London*, 1832.

Life of Bp William Waynflete, Lord Chancellor in the reign of Henry VI and Founder of Magdalene College, Oxford, by R Chandler [edited by C Lambert]. 8vo *London*, 1811

Beckington's (Bp.) Journal of his Embassy to negotiate the Marriage between Henry VI. and a Daughter of the Count Armagnac, A.D. 1442: edited by Sir N. H. Nicholas. 8vo. *London*, 1828.

Habington's (John) Reign of King Edward IV. (Kennet, Vol. I.)

More's (Sir T.) Lives of King Edward V and Richard III. (Kennet, Vol. I.)

More's (Sir T.) History of King Richard III. (More's Life by Cayley.)

More's (Sir T.) History of King Richard III; new edition, revised and corrected [with a preface by S. W. Singer]. Large paper, royal 8vo. *London*, 1821.

Buck's (Geo.) Life of King Richard III. (Kennet, Vol. I.)

Walpole's (Horace) Historic Doubts on the Life and Reign of King Richard III.; with supplement, postscript, and remarks on some answers made to them. (Orford's Works, Vol. II.)

Hutton's (W.) Battle of Bosworth Field, between Richard III. and Henry Earl of Richmond, 1485; with its consequences, the fall, treatment, and character of Richard, and a history of his life till he assumed the regal power; with additions by John Nichols. 8vo *London*, 1813

Bacon's (Lord) Life of King Henry VII. (Kennet, Vol 1, and Works, Vol. III.)

HENRY VIII

Bacon's (Lord) Henry VIII (Works, Vol VI)

Herbert of Cherbury's (Lord) Life and Reign of King Henry VIII. Folio *London*, 1633.

Thomson's (Mrs A. T.) Memoirs of the Court of Henry VIII. 2 vols. 8vo. *London*, 1826.

Literæ perplures de Rebus gestis in partem nostris septentrionalibus, A D 1523-4. (Hearne's Tho of Otterbourne)

The Determinations of the moste famous and moaste excellent Universities of Italy and, Fraunce, that it is unlefull for a man to marie his brother's wyfe, that the Pope hath no power to dispence therewith. Small 8vo secretary type. *London, T. Berthelet*, 1531

Tyndall's (W) Practyse of Prelates. whether the Kynge's Grace maye be separated from his Quene, because she was his brother's wyfe. 𝔅𝔩𝔞𝔠𝔨 𝔩𝔢𝔱𝔱𝔢𝔯, small 8vo *Marborch, M.CCCCC XXX.*

"Take," says Strype, referring to the above, "some description of the court craft of Cardinal Wolsey from the relation of a notable man who lived in his time." (Memorials, Vol I p 189)

Wyat's (Geo.) Extracts from the Life of the virtuous, Christian, and renowned Queen Anne Boleigne; written at the close of the XVIth century, and now first printed. 4to. portraits. *London*, 1817.

An Account of Queen Anne Bullen, from a MS in the handwriting of Sir Roger Twesden, Bart 1623 8vo. *London,* ——

Flodden —Hereafter ensue the Trewe Encountre or Batayle lately don betwene Englande and Scotlande; in which batayle the Scottsshe Kynge was slayne 4to. 𝔟𝔩𝔞𝔠𝔨 𝔩𝔢𝔱𝔱𝔢𝔯, on vellum, only six copies printed. *London, imprinted by R Faques*, [*reprinted* 1809.]

Wolsey's (Cardinal) Life, by George Cavendish, with notes and illustrations by S W. Singer [together with Jos. Hunter's, who wrote Cavendish's Life of Wolsey] 2 vols. 8vo. large paper. *Chiswick*, 1825.

Wolsey's (Cardinal) Life, by Richard Fiddes. Folio, large paper *London*, 1724.

Wolsey's (C.), History of his Life and Times, collected from ancient records, MSS., and historians [by J. Grove]. 4 vols 8vo. *London*, 1742-4.

[Hunter (Joseph), who wrote] Cavendish's Life of Wolsey. 4to *Lond* 1814.

Storer's (Thos) Life and Death of Cardinal Wolsey (in verse) *London*, 1599. (Helicoma.)

[Godwin (Edwardi)] Rerum Anglicarum, Henrico VIII, Edwardo VI., et Mariâ regnantibus, Annales. 4to. *Londini*, 1628

With the autograph of Sir Edward Dering.

Godwyn's (Francis) Annales of England; containing the reigns of Henry VIII, Edward VI., and Queen Mary, translated from the Latin, corrected and enlarged with the author's consent, by Morgan Godwyn. Folio. *London*, 1630.

HISTORY

EDWARD VI.

Hayward's (Sir John) Life and Raigne of King Edward VI Folio. *London*, 1630 (Kennet, Vol. II)

King Edward VI —The Journal of his Reign, written with his own hand (Burnet's Reformation, and Walpole's Royal and Noble Authors.)

Patten's (William) Expedicion into Scotlande of the most woorthely fortunate Prince Edward, Duke of Soomerset, vncle vnto our most noble Soveieign Lord ye Kinge's Majestie Edward the VI , Govournour of hys Hyghnes' persone, and Protectour of hys Grace's realmes, dominions, and subjectes, set out by way of diarie. Small 8vo. black letter. *London, by Richard Grafton*, 1548.

Life of Sir John Cheke, first Instructor, and afterwards Secretary of State to Edward VI., by J. Strype. 8vo *Oxford*, 1821.

Howard's (Geo) Lady Jane Grey and her Times. 8vo *Lond.* 1822.

ELIZABETH.

Camden's (Wm.) Historie of Queen Elizabeth, composed by way of annals, [now translated by R. N] Folio, port *London*, 1630 (Kennet, Vol II.)

Camdeni (Guil) Annales Rerum Anglicarum et Hibernicarum regnante Elizabethâ: è cod præclaro Smithiano, propriâ auctoris manu correcti, multisque magni momenti additionibus locupletati, eruit edidit- que T Hearnius, qui et alium cod è Bib. Rawlinsonianâ adhibuit. 3 vols 8vo two ports of Queen Elizabeth. [*Oxon*] 1717

Aikin's (Lucy) Memoirs of the Court of Queen Elizabeth. 2 vols. 8vo. *London*, 1826.

Birch's (Thos.) Memoirs of the Reign of Elizabeth, from the year 1581 till her death in which the secret intrigues of her court, and the conduct of the Earl of Essex, are particulaily illustrated, from the original papers of Anthony Bacon, his particular friend, and other MSS 2 vols. 4to. *London*, 1754

Bacon's (Lord) Felicity of Queen Elizabeth and her Times. (Works, Vols. III. and XI.)

The Passage of our most drad Soveraigne Lady, Quene Elizabeth, through the citie of London to Westminster, the day before her Coronation, anno 1558. 4to. MS. A transcript of the tract printed by Tothill.

The Progresses and public Processions of Queen Elizabeth; now first printed from original MSS., or scarce pamphlets, of the times, with notes, &c. by John Nichols. 3 vols 4to *London*, 1788–1805.

Naunton's (Sir R) Fragmenta Regalia . Memoirs of Elizabeth, and her Court and Favourites A new edition, collated with the MS copies in the British Museum; with notes, and a memoir of the author. 8vo. portraits *London*, 1824.

Naunton's Fragmenta Regalia, with explanatory annotations; and Memoirs of Robert Carey, Earl of Monmouth, written by himself. 8vo. *Edinburgh*, 1808

An Epistle of Hieron. Osorius, Bp of Arcoburge, in Portugale, to Queen Elizabeth, or a Pearle for a Prynce; translated oute of Latten by Richard Shacklock Small 8vo *Antwerp, by Ægidius Diest*, 1565.
Mr Cole's copy, with his MS. notes

Norton (Thos), a Warning against the dangerous Practices of the Papistes; and especially the Partners in the late [Earls of Westmoreland and Northumberland's] Rebellion   Small 8vo 𝖇𝖑𝖆𝖈𝖐 𝖑𝖊𝖙𝖙𝖊𝖗. *London, by John Daye*, 1569.

[Lancham's (Rich.)] Letter, wherein part of the entertainment untoo the Queen's Majestie at Killingworth Castl, in Warwicksheer, in this soomer's progress, 1575, is signified; from a freend officer attendant on the court, unto his ficend, a citizen and merchant of London, 1575. 4to. MS a transcript of the printed tract

The Estate of the English Fugitives under the King of Spaine and his Ministers; containing besides, a discourse on the said king's manner of government, and the injustice of many late dishonorable practices by him contrived   [4to. *Lond*. 1595.] (Sadler's State Papers, Vol III)

[Walpole's (Richard)] Discoverie and Confutation of a Tragical Fiction, devysed and played by Edward Squyer, yeoman soldiar, hanged at Tyburne, the 23 of Nonemb. 1598, &c , written by A. M. Preest. Small 8vo   [*Abroad*], *with license*, 1599.

Chandos' (Lord) Speeches delivered to Queen Elizabeth on her visit to Giles Brydges, Lord Chandos, at Sudely Castle, in Gloucestershire; edited by Sir Egerton Brydges. 4to   *Lee Priory*, 1815

Life of Sir Thos. Smith, principal Secretary of State to Edward VI and Queen Elizabeth, by J. Strype. 8vo   *Oxford*, 1820.

Life of Sir W Cecil, Lord Burghley, Treasurer in the reign of Queen Elizabeth, by Arthur Collins   8vo, large paper. *London*, 1732.

Memoirs of the Life and Administration of William Cecil, Lord Burghley; containing an historical view of the times in which he lived, and of the eminent persons with whom he was connected; by Edward Nares. 3 vols. 4to   *London*, 1828–31.

Leycester's (Earl of) Commonwealth; conceived, spoken, and published with good will and affection towards this realm, for whose good only it is made common to many   4to.   *Printed* 1641.

Life of Robert, Earl of Leicester, the favourite of Queen Elizabeth, drawn from original writers and records [by John Jebb]   8vo large paper, portrait by Vertue   *London*, 1727.

Sidney's (Sir P) Defence of the Earl of Leicester;— Letter to Queen Elizabeth   (Misc Works)

Bacon's (Lord) Papers relative to the Earl of Essex, &c   (Works, Vol VI)

Melvil of Halhil's (Sir James) Memoirs , containing an account of the affairs of state, not mentioned by other historians, relating to England and Scotland, under Queen Elizabeth, Mary Queen of Scots, and King James, published from the original MS , by Geo Scott 8vo   *Edin* 1752

Osborne's (Fr) Traditionall Memorialls in the Reigns of Queen Elizabeth and King James I   (Secret History of King James)

Jonston (Roberti) Historia Rerum Britannicarum, ut et multarum Gallarum, Belgicarum, et Germannicarum, tàm politicarum quàm ecclesiasticarum, ab anno 1572 ad 1628. Folio. *Amstelodami*, 1655

Hopkinson's (J.) Collection of several Passages in the latter end of Elizabeth's Reign and that of James I. (Manuscripts.)

JAMES I

Camden's (Wm) Annals of King James   (Kennet, Vol. II)

Wilson's (Arthur) History of King James   (Kennet, Vol II)

Aikin's (Lucy) Memoirs of the Court of King James I. 2 vols 8vo *London*, 1822

Secret History of the Court of King James ; with notes and introductory remarks [by Sir W Scott]. 2 vols. 8vo. *Edinb* 1811

W[eldon's] (Sir A.) Court and Character of James. Small 8vo. port inserted. *London*, 1650.

[Sanderson's (W.)] Aulicus Coquinariæ ; or, the Character of him [Weldon] who satyrized King James and his Court. (Secret History of James.)

D'Israeli's (I.) Inquiry into the Literary and Political Character of James I   8vo. *Lond* 1816.

Coke's (Roger) Detection of the Court and State of England during and from the Reign of James I. to the death of Queen Anne , consisting of private memoirs, &c., wherein are many secrets not before made public; as also a more impartial account of the civil wars than has yet been given. 3 vols 8vo. *London*, 1719.

Brook's (Sir Fulke Greville, Lord) Five Yeares of King James , or, the Condition of the State of England, and the relation it had to other provinces   4to   *Lond* 1643.

Truth brought to Light and discovered by Time ; or, a Discourse and Historical Narration of the first XIV Yeares of King James's reigne. 4to front &c   *London*, 1651

The Connexion , being a choice Collection of some principal matters in King James's reign, which may serve to supply the vacancy between Townsend and Rushworth's Historical Collections 8vo. *Lond* 1681

Vicars's (John) Mischeefe's Mysterie , or, Treason's Master-piece, the Powder-Plot, invented by hellish malice, prevented by heavenly mercy, truly related · from the Latin of Dr. Herring, translated and very much dilated. 4to. *London*, 1617.

The Gunpowder Treason , with the manner of its discovery, and the proceedings against the conspirators   8vo *Lond.* 1679
   See other tracts on this subject in the Harleian Miscellany.

Cotton's (Sir R) Choice Narrative of Count Gondomar's Transactions during his Embassy in England   4to port of Gondomar *London*, 1659

Bacon's (Lord) Tracts relating to England   (Works, Vol. V)

Bacon's (Lord) Charges against Oliver St John, Earl of Somerset; Advice to Sir Geo. Villiers, &c. (Works, Vol VI)

Ralegh's (Sir W.) Discourse touching a Match propounded by the Savoyan, between the Lady Elizabeth and the Prince of Piedmont; and on the Marriage between Prince Henry and a Daughter of Savoy. (Works, Vol VIII)

Dekker (Thomas), the magnificent Entertainment given to King James, Queen Anne his wife, and the Prince Henry, upon the day of his majestie's triumphant passage through his honourable citie of London, 15th March, 1603   4to   *Lond* 1604

The Royal Entertainment of the Right Honourable the Earle of Nottingham, sent ambassador from his Maiestie to the King of Spaine 4to. black letter *London*, 1605

Relation of the late Entertainment of the Right Hon Lord Roos, his majestie's ambassador extraordinarie to the King of Spaine, his entrie into Madrid, his first audience at the court there. 4to. *London*, 1617

True Relation and Journall of the manner of the arrivall, and magnificent entertainment given to the high and mighty Prince, Charles Prince of Great Britain, by the King of Spaine in his court at Madrid Published by authority. 8vo. Ports of Charles by Delaram, and of Buckingham by Dolle, inserted *London*, 1623

Wynn (D. Rich.) Baronetti Narratio Hist de Caroli, Walliæ Principis, Famulorum in Hispaniam Itinere A D 1623 (Hearne's Rich. II)

Nichols (John), the Progresses, Processions, and magnificent Festivities of King James I, his Royal Consort, Family and Court, collected from original MSS, scarce pamphlets, &c, comprising masques and entertainments, civic pageants, original letters, and annotated lists of the peers, baronets, and knights, who received those honours during this reign 4 vols. 4to *London*, 1828

Life and Death of Henry Prince of Wales Small 8vo. *Lond*. 1641.

Benger's Memoirs of Elizabeth Stuart, Queen of Bohemia, daughter of James I. (Hist of Germany)

Life of Sir W Ralegh, by Arth Cayley 2 vols 8vo. *Lond* 1806.

CHARLES I

Sanderson's (W) History of the Life and Raigne of King Charles I [edited by James Howell] Folio, portrait of Charles by Faithorne *London*, 1658.

Warwick's (Sir Ph.) Memoirs of the Reign of Charles I.; with continuation to the Restoration 8vo *London*, 1701

D'Israeli's (I) Commentaries on the Life and Reign of Charles I. 5 vols 8vo *Lond* 1828-31.

History and Life of Charles I (Kennet, Vol III)

Rushworth's Historical Collections (Documentary History)

Nalson's (Jo) Impartial Collection of the great Affairs of State, from 1639 to the death of King Charles I 2 vols folio *London*, 1682-3

Whitelock's (Sir B) Memorials of English Affairs, from the beginning of the reign of Charles I to the Restauration; containing the publick transactions, civil and military, together with the private consultations and secrets of the cabinet. Folio. The suppressed passages restored *London*, 1732

Bulstrode's (Sir R) Memoirs and Reflections on the reign of Charles I, containing remarkable facts not mentioned by other historians of those times 8vo *London*, 1721

May's (Thos) History of the Parliament of England which began Nov 3, 1640, with a short and necessary view of some preceding years [Edited, with Preface and Appendix, containing the declarations of both houses of parliament, with the king's answers, from Husband's Collection, by Baron Mascres] 4to. *London*, 1812

Ludlow's (Edmund) Letters to Sir Edward Seymour, comparing the oppressive government of King Charles I. in the first four years of his reign, with that of the four years of the reign of King James II, and vindicating the parliament begun in 1640. [Published by Baron Maseres.] 4to. *London*, 1812.

Letters from Charles I in his confinement, and Charles II in his exile, and other papers relating to the history of that time. (Barwick's Memoirs)

Case of Charles I. and other original Papers (Ludlow's Memoirs)

Powell's (Robert) Parallel of Charles I and Alfred the Great, until 1634 (Powell's Life of Alfred)

Essay towards attaining a true State of the Character and Reign of Charles I, and the causes of the Civil War 8vo *London*, 1780

Weldon's (Sir A) Character of the Court of Charles I. unto the beginning of these unhappy times; with observations upon him, instead of a character (Secret Hist of King James)

Serre (le Sr. de la), Histoire de l'Entrée de la Reyne [Mary de Medicis] mère du Roy très Chrétien, dans la Grande Bretagne, 1639. Reprinted from the original, with Plates, Introduction, and Notes, by Richard Gough 4to large paper. *London*, 1775

Life of Archbishop Williams, Lord Keeper in the reigns of James I. and Charles I, containing some remarkable occurrences of those times, by Amb Philips 8vo *Cambr.* 1700.

The Life and Times of William Laud, Abp of Canterbury, by John Parker Lawson 2 vols 8vo *London*, 1829.

Pym's (John) Speech or Declaration to the Lords of the Upper House upon the delivery of the Articles against W Laud, Abp of Canterbury; together with a true copy of the Articles 4to. Port of Pym by Glover, and of Laud by Passe, inserted. *Lond* 1641

Mercurius Aulicus; a Diurnall communicating the Intelligence and Affairs of the Court to the rest of the kingdom, from January 1 to December 30, 1642. 4to. *Orford*, 1642

Libellus de Caroli I ab urbe Oxoniensi fugâ sive decessu, è cod. MS nunc primus publicavit T. Hearne (Hearne's Walter de Hemingford)

[Ryves (Bruno)] Mercurius Rusticus, or, the Countrie's Complaint of the barbarous outrages committed by the sectaries of this late flourishing kingdom with a chronology of the battles, sieges, and other remarkable passages of this unnatural war, to the 25th March, 1646. 8vo *Lond* 1685

Hampden.—Nugent (Lord), some Memorials of John Hampden, his party, and his times. 2 vols 8vo *London*, 1832.

Fairfax's (Thos. Lord) Short Memorialls during the War from 1642 to 1644 Small 8vo port by Worlidge inserted. *London*, 1699

Dugdale's (Sir W) Perfect Narrative of the Treaty of Uxbridge, 1644 (Troubles in Eng)

[Carter's (Mat.)] most true and exact Relation of that as honourable as unfortunate Expedition of Kent, Essex, and Colchester, by M C, a loyal actor in that engagement, anno 1648. Small 8vo *Printed* 1650

This records particulars not noticed by Clarendon or other historians.

[Birch (Thos.)] an Inquiry into the share which King Charles I had in the transactions of the Earl of Glamorgan, afterwards of Worcester, for bringing over Irish rebels to assist that king in 1645-6   8vo   *London*, 1747.

Carte's (Thos) History of the Duke of Ormond.   (Charles II)

Milton (John) on the Articles of Peace between James Earl of Ormond, for King Charles I on the one hand, and the Irish rebels and papists on the other.   (Prose Works, 4to Vol I , 8vo Vol II.)

Reliquiæ Sacræ Carolinæ; the Works of that great monarch King Charles I, both civil and sacred with a view of his life and reign, from his birth to his buriall   8vo   *Hague*, ——

Eikon Basilike, the Portraicture of his sacred Majestie in his solitude and sufferings   (Charles I.'s Works)

Eikonoklastes, in Answer to Eikon Basilike, by John Milton.   (Prose Works, 4to Vol I , 8vo Vols II and III)

Fellowes' (W D) Historical Sketches of Charles I., Cromwell, Charles II, and the principal personages of that period; including the king's trial and execution to which is annexed, an account of the sums exacted by the commonwealth from the royalists, and the names of those who compounded for their estates.   4to   *London (Paris)*, 1828

Peyton (Sir E), the Divine Catastrophe of the kingly family of the House of Stuart , or, a short history of the rise, reigne, and ruine thereof   (Secret History of King James)

COMMONWEALTH

Milton (John) pro Populo Anglicano Defensiones contra Salmasium et A. Morem   (Prose Works, 4to Vol II ; 8vo Vol V.)

Milton's (J.) pro Populo Anglicano, &c , translated by Washington   (Prose Works, 4to Vol I , 8vo Vol III)

Clarendon's (Edward Hyde, Earl of) History of the Rebellion and Civil Wars in England ; to which is added, a view of the affairs in Ireland. New edition, exhibiting a faithful collation of the original MS , with all the suppressed passages ; also, the unpublished Notes of Bp. Warburton   [Edited by Dr Bandinel.]   8 vols. 8vo   *Oxford*, 1826

Clarendon (F H Earl of), a Supplement to the History of the Grand Rebellion ; containing the tracts, speeches, letters, &c mentioned in the said history   with ports. of the great men on both sides   8vo.   *London*, 1717

Clarendon (E. H., Earl of), Life of; being a continuation of the History of the Grand Rebellion, from the Restoration to his banishment in 1667, written by himself   3 vols 8vo   *Oxford*, 1761

Ellis's (G. A) [Lord Dover] Historical Inquiries respecting the character of Edward Hyde, E of Clarendon, Lord Chancellor of England.   8vo   *London*, 1827

[Oldmixon's (John) History of England during the reign of the royal house of Stuart ; wherein the errors of late histories [Clarendon, &c] are discovered and corrected   Folio   *Lond* 1730.

Burton (John), the Genuineness of Lord Clarendon's History of the Rebellion vindicated, and Mr. Oldmixon's Slander confuted   8vo   *Oxford*, 1744

Burton's (Rich) Wars in England, Scotland, and Ireland, and other remarkable transactions, revolutions, and accidents, which happened from the beginning of the reign of Charles I to the Restoration 4to large paper *Reprint, Westminster*, 1810

Dugdale's (Sir W) View of the late Troubles in England, also, some parallel thereof with the Barons' wars in the time of Henry III , but chiefly with that in France called the Holy League, in the reign of Henry III. and IV Folio. *Oxford*, 1681

Heath's (James) Brief Chronicle of the late intestine War in England, Scotland, and Ireland ; with the intervening affairs, as also the several usurpations, foreign wars, differences, and interests depending upon it, to the happy restitution of King Charles II , with all the memorable affairs since his time 4 vols small 8vo With the portraits, &c Narcissus Lutterel's copy, with his autograph. *London*, 1663–4

Tragicum Theatrum Actorum, et Casuum Tragicorum Londini publicè celebratorum, quibus Hiberniæ Proregi, Episcopo Cantuariensi, ac tandem Regi ipsi, aliusque vita adempta, et ad Anglicanum metamorphosin via est aperta Small 8vo fine impressions of the portraits, &c. *Amst. ap Jansonum*, 1649

Winstanley (Wm), the Loyal Martyrology , or, brief Catalogues and Characters of the most eminent persons who suffered for their conscience during the late times of rebellion, by death, imprisonment, &c Small 8vo front &c and port of Cromwell by Stent, inserted *London*, 1665

Catalogue of the Lords, Knights, and Gentlemen, that have compounded for their estates Small 8vo. *London*, 1665.

Lilly's (W.) Monarchy or no Monarchy in England ;—Grebner his Prophecy concerning Charles the son of Charles ;—Passages upon the Life and Death of the late King Charles ,—Ænigmatical Types of the future state and condition of England. 4to. *London*, 1651.

Walker (Clement), the Compleat History of Independency upon the Parliament begun 1640, and continued till this present year, 1660, by T. M 4to *London*, 1661.
  " Ex libris Petri Leycester de Tabley "—*MS Note.*

Baillie's (Robt.) Letters and Journals, containing the public transactions, civil, ecclesiastical, and military, both in England and Scotland, from 1637 to 1662 [by Robert Aiken] 2 vols 8vo. The Roxburgh copy. *Edinburgh*, 1775

Whitelock's (Sir B.) Journal of the Swedish Embassy, in 1653–4, from the Commonwealth ; with an Appendix of original papers [Edited from the Whitelock papers by Dr Morton] 2 vols 4to *London*, 1772

Ludlow's (Edmund) Memoirs ; with a collection of original papers, serving to confirm and illustrate many important passages contained therein, and the case of Charles I. 4to *Lond* 1771

Original Memoirs, written during the great Civil War, with Notes, &c. [by Sir W. Scott] 8vo. *Edinb* 1806 Viz —
  Life of Sir Henry Slingsby,
  Memoirs of Captain John Hodgson,
  Relations of the Campaigns of Oliver Cromwell in Scotland in 1650, published from the originals, by order of Parliament.

MODERN. 237

Hutchinson's (Lucy) Memoirs of Col. Hutchinson, Governor of Nottingham Castle and Town, representative of the county in the long parliament, and of the town in the first parliament of Charles II.; with anecdotes of his contemporaries, and a summary view of public affairs Published from the original MSS by Julius Hutchinson To which is prefixed, a short memoir of her own life, written by herself 4to *London*, 1806.

Lilly's (W) History of his Life and Times, from 1602 to 81 Small 8vo. *London*, 1715

Life of John Milton (Works, Vol I)

Godwin's (W) Lives of Edward and John Philips, nephews and pupils of Milton , including various particulars of the literary and political history of their times. 4to *London*, 1815

Godwin's (William) History of the Commonwealth of England, from its commencement to the restoration of Charles II. 5 vols 8vo *Lond.* 1824–32

THE PROTECTORATE

[Stace's (M)] Cromwelliana; a chronological detail of events in which Oliver Cromwell was engaged, from 1642 to his death in 1658 with a continuation of other transactions to the Restoration. Folio, large paper *Westminster*, 1810.

D[awbeny's] (H) Historie and Policie reviewed, in the heroick transactions of his most Serene Highnesse Oliver, late Lord Protector, from his cradle to his tomb , declaring his steps to princely perfection, as they are drawn in parallels to the ascents of the great patriarch Moses in thirty degrees, to the height of honour. 8vo portrait of Cromwell by Glover inserted *London*, 1659

Peck's (Fr.) Memoirs of the Life and Actions of Oliver Cromwell, as delivered in three panegyrics of him written in Latin . the first, by Don Juan Roderiguez de Saa Meneses, Conde de Penaguiano, the Portugal Ambassador , the second, by a certain Jesuit, the Lord Ambassador's chaplain; yet both, as it is thought, by John Milton, as was the third   the whole illustrated with a preface, notes, and a collection of divers curious historical pieces relating to Cromwell, &c. 4to *London*, 1740

Noble's (Mark) Memoirs of the Protectoral House of Cromwell, with the lives of such persons as were distinguished by the Cromwells with honours and great employments 2 vols 8vo *London*, 1789

Cromwell (Oliver), Memoir of the Protector, and of his sons Richard and Henry, illustrated by original letters and other family papers. 4to *Lond* 1820

Burton's (Thomas) Diary of the Parliaments of Oliver and Richard Cromwell, from 1656 to 1659, published from the original MS , with an introduction containing an account of the parliament of 1654, from the journal of Gibbon Goddard, M P , also now first published. Edited and illustrated with notes, historical and biographical, by J. T Rutt   4 vols 8vo *London*, 1828

The French Charity ; written upon occasion of Prince Harcourt's coming into England Small 8vo *London*, 1655

Manifesto of the Lord Protector against the Spaniards, 1655 (Milton's Prose Works, 4to Vol II, 8vo Vols. V)

Court and Kitchen of Elizabeth, commonly called Joan Cromwell the wife of the late Usurper, truly described and represented (Secret Hist of King James)

Cowley's (Abr) Discourse, by way of vision, concerning the Government of Oliver Cromwell (Works, Vol III)

[Fiennes' (Nath)] Monarchy asserted to be the best, most ancient, and legal form of Government, in a conference held at Whitehall with Oliver Cromwell and a committee of Parliament, and made good by their arguments Small 8vo *London, printed* 1679

Titus's (Col) Killing no Murder 4to. *London, reprinted* 1689

[Hawke's (Mich)] Killing is Murder, [or an answer to the above] 4to *London*, 1657.

[Evelyn's (John)] Apology for the Royal Party; with a touch at the pretended " Plea for the Army " (Misc. Works)

May's (Thos) Epitome of English History, wherein arbitrary government is displayed to the life, in the illegal transactions of the late times under Oliver Cromwell, being a parallel to the four years' reign of the late King James [II] Small 8vo *London*, 1690

Withers' (Geo.) Fides Anglicana, or, a plea for the public faith of these nations, lately pawned, forfeited, and violated by some of their former trustees 8vo *London*, 1660.

CHARLES II

History of his sacred Majesty Charles II, begun from the murder of his royal father, and continued to the present year, 1660; by a Person of Quality. 8vo *London*, 1660.

An Account of the Preservation of King Charles II. after the Battle of Worcester [dictated by himself to Mr Sam Pepys] To which are added, his letters to several persons; [edited by D Dalrymple, Lord Hailes] 8vo *Edinburgh*, 1801

The Royal Pilgrimage; or, the progresse and travels of Charles II through the most and greatest courts of Europe 4to *London*, 1660.

England's Joy; or, a relation of the most remarkable passages from his majesty's arrival at Dover to his entrance at Whitehall 4to. 1660. (Harleian Misc. Vol III)

A Collection of his Majesty's gracious Letters, Speeches, Messages, and Declarations, since April 4, 1660. 4to *London*, 1660

History of the Reign of Charles II from the Restoration to 1667 (Life of Clarendon)

The History and Life of King Charles II (Kennet, Vol III)

History of the Reign of Charles II (Burnet's Own Times, Vols I and II)

Bulstrode's (Sir R.) Memoirs and Reflections upon the Reign and Government of Charles II. 8vo *London*, 1720.

MODERN.

The Secret History of the Court and Reign of Charles II, by a member of his privy council [from a MS belonging to the Earl of Chatham] To which are added, introductory sketches of the preceding period, from the accession of James I ; with notes, and a supplement continuing the narrative to the Revolution, by the editor 2 vols 8vo *London*, 1792

Hamilton (Ant), Mémoires du Comte de Grammont, augmentées des notes et des éclaircissemens nécessaires, par M Horace Walpole 4to *Strawberry Hill*, 1772

Hamilton's (A) Memoirs of Count Grammont, with biographical sketch of Count Hamilton [illustrated with notes by Sir W Scott, &c] and 64 portraits 2 vols 4to large paper, proofs. *London*, 1811

Carte's (Thomas) History of the Life of James Duke of Ormonde, from 1610 to 1688, with a collection of state letters. 3 vols. folio. *Lond.* 1736.

Diary of Lord Rochester during his Embassy in Poland in 1676 (Clarendon's Letters)

Dryden's (John) Translation of the Third Book of Maimbourg's History of the League, with advertisement and postscript · intended as a parallel to the Solemn League and Covenant (Works, Vol XVII.)

Letters of Lady Rachel Russell, from the MS in Woburn Abbey, [by Thomas Selwood]. to which is prefixed an introduction vindicating the character of Lord Russell against Sir John Dalrymple, and an account of the trial of Lord William Russell for high treason 8vo *London*, 1792

Life, Trial &c of Algernon Sydney (Sydney on Government)

A True Relation of the late King's [Charles II] Death to which are added, copies of two papers written by him, found in the strong box. (Somers's Tracts, Vol. VIII)

Reresby's (Sir John) Travels and Memoirs, the former during Cromwell's usurpation, the latter containing anecdotes and secret history of the courts of Charles II and James II Imp 8vo. large paper *Lond* 1813

Jones's (D) Secret History of Whitehall, from the restoration of Charles II. to the abdication of King James II Small 8vo *Lond* 1697.

North's (Roger) Life of Lord Keeper North (Biography.)

Pepys (Memoirs of S), Secretary to the Admiralty in the reigns of Charles II and James II, comprising his diary from 1659-69, and a selection from his private correspondence. edited by Lord Braybrooke. 2 vols 4to. *London*, 1825

Fox (Memoirs of the Life of Sir Stephen) [domestic servant to King Charles II during his exile, and one of the Lords of the Treasury for twenty-two years in his majestie's and the three successive reigns] Large paper, with two impressions of the portrait Folio *London, reprint,* 1807.

Wynne's (W) Life of Sir Leoline Jenkins [plenipotentiary for the peace of Nimeguen, and one of the secretaries to Charles II]. To which is added, a complete series of letters, wherein are related the most remarkable transactions of his time, both foreign and domestic 2 vols. folio *London*, 1724

Evelyn's (John) Diary from 1641 to 1705–6 , and a selection of familiar letters   (Memoirs)

Thoresby's (Ralph) Diary from 1677 to 1724, edited from the original MS by Joseph Hunter. 2 vols 8vo. *London*, 1830

Social Life in England and France from the Restoration of Charles II to July 1830, by the editor of Madame du Deffand's Letters 2 vols 8vo   *London*, 1831.

JAMES II.

History and Life of King James II. (Kennet, Vol III.)

History of the Reign of James II   (Burnet's Own Times, Vol. III.)

The Life of James II , collected out of memoirs writ of his own hand , together with the king's advice to his son, and his majesty's will. Published from the original Stuart MSS by J. S Clarke   2 vols. 4to   *London*, 1816.

Extracts from the Life of James II. as written by himself (Macpherson's original Papers)

Fox's (C. J) History of the early part of the reign of James II ; with an introductory chapter [edited by Lord Holland]. 4to. *London*, 1808

Fox's (C J) History, &c. (Sir Geo. Rose's Observations on), with a narrative of the events which occurred in the enterprise of the Earl of Argyle in 1685, by Sir Patrick Hume. 4to. *London*, 1809.

Heywood's (Samuel) Vindication of Mr Fox's History of the early part of the reign of James II. 4to. *London*, 1811

Memoires by Sir John Hinton, physician in ordinary to his Majestie's person, 1679 [of some memorable passages, wherein the Divine providence hath bin extended to a miraculous degree upon his majesty's person and affaires, wherein he was personally instrumentall]. 8vo. *London, Bensley*, 1814

Anglesey's (Arthur Earl of) State of the Government and Kingdom; with an answer to the " Memoirs of the Earl of Anglesey." 4to. *London*, 1694.

Memoirs of Arthur Earl of Anglesey, late Lord Privy-seal [by himself], published by Sir Peter Pett. 8vo   *London*, 1693.

Diary of the Earl of Clarendon from 1687 to 90; containing many minute particulars attending the Revolution. (Clarendon's Letters)

An exact Account of the Sickness and Death of the late King James II as also the proceedings at St. Germains thereupon, 1701. (Somers's Tracts, Vol XI)

WILLIAM AND MARY.

History and Life of King William and Queen Mary (Kennet, Vol. III)

Burton's (W) History of William and Mary, being an impartial account of the most remarkable passages and transactions in these Kingdoms, from their accession to 1693   (History of the House of Orange)

Mackintosh's (Sir James) History of the Revolution in 1688. 4to. *London*, 1832

Boyer's (Abel) History of the Reign of William III 3 vols 8vo *London*, 1702

Burnet's (Bp.) History of his own Time, from the Restoration to 1713, with the suppressed passages of the first volume, and notes by the Earls of Dartmouth and Hardwicke, and Speaker Onslow, hitherto unpublished. To which are added, the Cursory Remarks of Swift, and other observations, with life of the author, by Thomas Burnet 6 vols 8vo *Oxford, Clarendon Press*, 1823

Correspondence of the Duke of Shrewsbury with King William (Documentary History)

Collection of State Tracts published on occasion of the Revolution, and during the reign of William III. 3 vols folio *London*, 1705

Cunningham's (Alex) History of Great Britain, from the Revolution in 1688 to the accession of George I Translated from the Latin MS by William Thomson, with an account of the author [Edited by T Hollingbery] 2 vols 4to *London*, 1787.

ANNE

De Foe's (Daniel) History of the Union between England and Scotland [including a general History of Unions in Great Britain], with an appendix of original papers, and a life of the author [by Chalmers], and J L Delolme on the Union of Scotland and England, and on the present state of Ireland 4to *London*, 1786-7

Hamilton's (Charles) Transactions during the reign of Queen Anne, from the Union to the death of that princess 8vo *Edinburgh*, 1790

Swift's (Jonathan) Tracts Historical and Political during the reign of Queen Anne. (Works, Vols III —V and XII)

Swift's (J) History of the four last years of Queen Anne (Works, Vol V)

Wilson's (W.) Memoirs of the Life and Times of Daniel De Foe, containing an account of his writings, and his opinions upon a variety of important matters, civil and ecclesiastical 3 vols 8vo. *Lond* 1830

King's (Will) Political and Literary Anecdotes of his own Times 8vo *London*, 1818

Life of John Duke of Marlborough (Eng Military Hist)

The Opinions of Sarah Duchess-Dowager of Marlborough, published from the original MSS [by David Dalrymple, Lord Hailes] Small 8vo *Privately printed*, 1788

GEORGE I

Burnet (Bishop), A Memorial offered to the Princess Sophia, Electress of Hanover, containing a delineation of the constitution and policy of England, with anecdotes concerning remarkable persons of that time To which are added, letters from Burnet and Leibnitz, edited by J G. H. Feder 8vo. *London*, 1815

Annals of the Reign of King George I 6 vols 8vo *London*, 1716-21

History of the Rebellion in 1715 (Scottish History)

Coxe's (Wm) Memoirs of the Administration of Sir Robert Walpole, with original correspondence 3 vols 4to *London*, 1798.

Walpole's (Hor) Reminiscences of the Court of George I (Works, Vol. IV)

GEORGE II

Walpole's (Horace) Reminiscences of the Court of George II (Works, Vol IV)

Walpole's (H) Memoirs of the last Ten years of the Reign of George II from the Original MS 2 vols 4to. *London*, 1822

Walpole's (H.) Account of his own Conduct, relative to places he held under Government, and towards Ministers (Works, Vol. II)

Walpole (Memoirs of Horatio) connected with a History of his Times from 1678 to 1757; by William Coxe 4to *London*, 1802

Doddington's (G B.) Diary from March 8, 1749, to February 6, 1761, edited, with an appendix of curious papers, by H. P Wyndham. 8vo *London*, 1785.

Waldegrave's (James Earl) Memoirs, from 1754 to 58 4to. *London*, 1821

Lyttleton (Geo Lord) upon the present state of our Affairs both at home and abroad. (Misc. Works)

Chesterfield (Memoirs of the Life of Philip Dormer Stanhope, Earl of) tending to illustrate the civil, literary, and political history of his own time, by Maty. (Works, Vol. 1)

History of the Rebellion in the year 1745. (Scottish History.)

GEORGE III

Bisset's (Robert) History of the Reign of George III; to which is prefixed a view of the progressive improvement of England in prosperity and strength, to the accession of his majesty, and completed to his death 6 vols 8vo. *London*, 1820

Chatham's (Earl of) Anecdotes of his Life, and of the principal events of his time, with his speeches in Parliament, from 1736 to 1778 4 vols 8vo *London*, 1792.

Coxe's (W.) Memoirs of the Administration of the Right Hon. Henry Pelham, collected from the family papers and other authentic documents. 2 vols 4to. *London*, 1829.

Wraxall's (Sir N W) Historical Memoirs of his own Time, from 1772 to 1784 2 vols. 8vo The first and suppressed edition *London*, 1815

Wraxall's (Sir N W) Answer to the Calumnious Misrepresentations of the "Quarterly Review," the "British Critic," and the "Edinburgh Review," contained in their Observations on the Historical Memoirs. 8vo. *London*, 1815

Pitt (William), History of his Political Life, including an account of the Times in which he lived, by John Gifford [John Richard Green] 3 vols 4to largest paper *London*, 1809.

Pitt's (W), Memoirs, by Bp Geo Tomline 2 vols. 4to *Lond.* 1821.

Junius's Letters. (Parliamentary History)

GEORGE IV

MODERN

Naval and Military History of Great Britain.

Beatson's (Robt) Naval and Military Memoirs of Great Britain, from 1727 to 1783 6 vols 8vo *Lond* 1804

Ralegh (Sir W), the Strength and Defects of the Sea Forces of England, France, Spain, and Venice, with Observations on the Royal Navy and Sea Service (Works, Vol VIII)

Pine's (John) Tapestry Hangings of the House of Lords, representing the several engagements between the English and Spanish fleets, in the ever-memorable year 1588, with the portraits of the lord high admiral and other noble commanders, &c &c, and an historical account of the day's action. Folio *Lond.* 1739

Ralegh's (Sir W) Relation of the Cadiz Action, in the year 1596 (Works, Vol VIII)

Charnock's (John) Biographia Navalis, or, Memoirs of the Officers of the Navy of Great Britain, from the year 1600. 6 vols 8vo *London*, 1794–98.

Campbell's (John) Lives of the British Admirals, containing also a new and accurate Naval History. from the earliest periods Continued to the year 1779 by Dr Berkenhout, and revised, corrected, and brought down to the present time, by Henry Redhead Yorke, with Lives of the most eminent naval commanders, by Will Stevenson 8 vols. 8vo. large paper *Lond* 1812–17.

James's (Wm) Naval History of Great Britain, from the Declaration of War by France, in February 1793, to the accession of George IV. in January 1820, new edition with considerable additions and improvements, including diagrams of all the principal actions 6 vols 8vo. *London*, 1826

Ralfe's (J) Naval Chronology of Great Britain; or, an Historical Account of the Naval and Maritime Events, from 1803 to the end of 1816 3 vols imp 8vo The Duke of York's copy, plates carefully coloured *Lond* 1820

Nelson, (Life of Horatio, Viscount) from his Lordship's Manuscripts, edited by J S Clarke and J M'Arthur 2 vols. imp 4to. large paper, proof impressions of the plates *London*, 1809

Collingwood's (G L N) Selection from the Public and Private Correspondence of Vice-Admiral Lord Collingwood, interspersed with Memoirs of his Life 8vo *London*, 1829

Salamé's (Abrah) Narrative of the Expedition to Algiers in the year 1816, under the command of Admiral Lord Viscount Exmouth 8vo *London*, 1819

Grose's (Fr) Military Antiquities; or, a History of the English Army, from the Conquest to the present time 2 vols. 4to. *London*, 1801

[Cotton's (Sir Robert)] Wairs with Foreign Princes dangerous to our Commonwealth, or, Reasons for Foreign Wars answered, with a list of all the confederates from Henry I 's reign to the end of Queen Elizabeth's, proving that the Kings of England alwaies preferred unjust peace before the justest warre Small 8vo. port of Sir W Raleigh inserted *London*, 1657

This contains curious particulars of the expenses of the various wars, the mode of levying them, &c

The Field of Mars, or, an Account of the Military and Naval Engagements of Great Britain and her Allies, from the 9th century to the peace of 1801 2 vols 4to 1801

Vere's (Sir Francis) Commentaries, being diverse pieces of service wherein he had command, written by himself, and published by W Dillingham Folio, with all the portraits, by Faithorne, and maps *Cambridge*, 1657

Discipline of the Army under William Marquis of Newcastle in 1643, and Muster Roll of England and Wales, 1674 (Manuscripts)

Military History of the Prince Eugene of Savoy and John Duke of Marlborough, including a particular description of the several battles, &c, in which these generals commanded, collected from the best authors with Supplement, containing a succinct account of the remarkable events which happened in the late war wherein neither of these generals had any share Illustrated with plates by Du Bosc 2 vols folio *London*, 1735-7

Coxe's (Wm) Memoirs of John Duke of Marlborough with his Original Correspondence, collected from the family records at Blenheim, and other authentic sources. Illustrated with portraits, maps, and military plans 3 vols 4to *Lond* 1818-19

Wilson's (R. T.) History of the British Expedition to Egypt 4to *Lond* 1803

Anderson's (Æneas) Journal of the Forces on a Secret Expedition under Lieut.-Gen Pigot, in 1800, till their arrival in Minorca, and continued through the subsequent transactions of the army under Sir R Abercromby in the Mediterranean and Egypt 4to *London*, 1802

Moore's (James) Narrative of the Campaign of the British Army in Spain, commanded by Sir John Moore, authenticated by official papers and original letters 4to. *London*, 1809

Southey's (Robt) History of the Peninsular War 3 vols. 4to. *London*, 1823-32

Napier's (Col W F. P.) History of the War in the Peninsula and in the South of France, from 1807 to 14 3 vols 8vo *London*, 1828-31.

Londonderry's (Lieut.-Gen W Vane Stewart, Marquess) Narrative of the War in Germany and France 4to *London*, 1830

The Battle of Waterloo, containing the series of accounts published by authority, British and foreign with circumstantial details relative to the battle, by a Near Observer 2 vols 8vo *London*, 1817.

[Scott (Walter)], Paul's Letters to his Kinsfolk (Misc. Works, Vol. V)

Pasley's (C W) Essay on the Military Policy and Institutions of the British Empire 8vo. *London*, 1813

Political and Parliamentary History of England.

Prynne's (Will.) Exact Chronological Vindication and Historical Demonstration of our British, Roman, Saxon, Danish, Norman, English Kings' Supreme Ecclesiastical Jurisdiction, in and over all spiritual or religious affairs, causes, persons, &c as well as temporal, within their dominions, from the original planting of Christianity to the death of King Henry III 2 vols. (Vol II only) folio *London*, 1665, 66.

Prynne's (Will) History of King John, King Henry III , and King Edward I , wherein the ancient sovereign dominion of the Kings of England, Scotland, France, and Ireland, over all persons in all causes, is asserted and vindicated   Folio   *London*, 1670
> This, with the preceding, forms the " three tomes" of the celebrated work usually known as " Prynne's Records "

Palgrave's (Francis) Rise and Progress of the English Commonwealth, from the first settlement of the Anglo-Saxons in Britain, with an Appendix of unpublished documents and records, illustrating the history of the civil and criminal jurisprudence of England   2 vols 4to   *London*, 1832

Hallam's (Henry) Constitutional History of England, from the accession of Henry VII to the death of George II   2 vols 4to.   *London*, 1827

Beatson's (Rob) Political Index to the Histories of Great Britain and Ireland , or, a complete Register of the hereditary honours, public offices, and persons in office, from the earliest periods to the present time   3 vols 8vo   *London*, 1806

Beatson's (Rob) Chronological Register of both Houses of Parliament, from 1708 to 1807   3 vols 8vo   *London*, 1807

Oldfield's (T H B) Representative History of Great Britain and Ireland ; being a history of the house of commons, and of the counties, cities, and boroughs of the United Kingdom, from the earliest period.   6 vols 8vo   *London*, 1816.

Willis's (Browne) Notitia Parliamentaria ; or, an history of the counties, cities and boroughs in England and Wales , their charters, privileges, and lists of their knights, &c returned to Parliament, from the first summons to the present time   4 vols 8vo   Including both 1st and 2d edition of Volume I   *London*, 1715-50

Parliamentary History of England, from the earliest period to the year 1803 [by Cobbett and Hansard]   36 vols royal 8vo   *London*, 1807-20

Parliamentary Debates, being a continuation of the " Parliamentary History," from 1803 to 1820   41 vols royal 8vo   *Lond* 1804-21

Parliamentary Debates, new series, from the accession of Geo IV.   Royal 8vo   *Lond* 1822, &c

Speeches in Parliament in Elizabeth and James I.'s reigns   (Manuscripts)

Mackenzie's (H) Review of the principal Proceedings in the Parliament of 1784   (Works, Vol VII)

Addison's (Joseph) Whig Examiner, Freeholder, and Present State of the War, and Necessity of an Augmentation, considered   (Works, Vol IV 4to , and Vols V and VI 8vo)

Bacon's (Lord) Speeches, &c in Parliament   (Works, Vol VI)

Burke's (Edmund) Speeches in Parliament   (Works, Vols II III and V)

Burke's (E) Speeches, &c on East Indian Affairs   (Works, IV. XI to XIII)

Curran's (J P) Speeches on the late State Trials   8vo   *Dublin*, 1808

Erskine's (Thos. Lord) Speeches when at the Bar, on subjects connected with the Liberty of the Press, and against Constructive Treasons. Collected by James Ridgway   4 vols 8vo.   *London*, 1810

Fox's (Ch. James) Speeches in the House of Commons [edited by J Wright]   6 vols. 8vo   *London*, 1815

Horsley's (Bp Sam) Speeches in Parliament   8vo   *Dundee*, 1813.

Littleton's (Geo Lord) Speeches in Parliament   (Misc. Works)

Pitt (William), Earl of Chatham's Speeches   (Life.)

Pitt's (W) Speeches in the House of Commons, edited by W S Hathaway   3 vols 8vo   *London*, 1808

Selden's (John) Speeches and Arguments in the Impeachment against the Duke of Buckingham, 1626   (Works, Vol III)

Wyndham's (Wm) Speeches in Parliament, with an account of his life by Th. Amyot   3 vols 8vo   *London*, 1812.

Junius's Letters   2 vols 8vo with portraits, large paper   *Lond* 1797.

Junius's Letters, including letters by the same writer under other signatures; to which are added, his confidential correspondence with Mr Wilkes, and his private letters addressed to Mr H S Woodfall, with a preliminary essay, notes, &c   3 vols 8vo large paper *London*, 1812

Junius.—Letters on the Author of Junius by E H. Baker   12mo. *London*, 1828

Junius —A Critical Enquiry regarding the real Author of the Letters of Junius, proving them to have been written by Lord Viscount Sackville, by George Coventry.   8vo.   *London*, 1824

Junius —Tracts relative to the supposed Author; containing a discovery of the Author, Blakeway's Attempt to ascertain the Author, Girdlestones Facts to prove General Lee to be the Author. In one vol 8vo   *London*, 1813.

Junius.—Documents for the opinion that Hugh M'Auley Boyd wrote Junius's Letters; and an appendix to the supplemental apology for the believers in the supposititious Shakspeare papers, by Geo. Chalmers. 8vo.   *London*, 1800

Documentary History of England.

Cooper's (C P) Account of the most important Public Records of Great Britain, and the Publications of the Record Commissioners   2 vols 8vo   *London*, 1832

Burton's (John) Account of all the Charters, Patents, and Escheat Rolls in the archives of the Tower of London   (Manuscripts)

Strachey's Index to the Records, with directions to the several places where they are to be found , and a list of the Latin sir-names and names of places, as they are written in the old records, explained by modern names   8vo.   *London*, 1739

Liber Niger Scaccarii è cod MS nunc primùm edidit T Hearne   2 vols. 8vo   *Oxonii*, 1728

Placitorum in Domo Capitulari Westmonasteriensi asservatorum Abbreviatio, temp regum Ric. I , Joannis, Henrici III , Edwardi I et II Folio   [*London*], 1811.

 Illustrating the early history of our courts of judicature, as well as the laws and customs and the constitution of the country.

Testa de Nevill; sive liber feodorum in curiâ Scaccarii, temp Henrici III. et Edwardi I   Folio   [*London*], 1807.
: Gives a condensed and accurate view of the feudality of the 13th century

Rotuli Hundredorum, temp Henrici III et Edwardi I in Tur Lond et in curiâ Receptæ Scaccarii Westmonasteriensi asservati   2 vols folio   [*London*], 1812
: This constitutes a species of resting-point between the Anglo-Norman feudality and that order which was established when Littleton expounded.

Placita de quo Warranto, temporibus Edwardi I , II , III , in curiâ Receptæ Scaccarii Westmonasteriensi asservata   Folio   [*London*], 1818.
: Containing the boundaries of free chases, warrens, and fisheries, the allowance in eyre of various franchises and liberties and royal charters to ecclesiastical and lay corporations, not elsewhere found on record

Taxatio Ecclesiastica Angliæ et Walliæ, auctoritate P. Nicholai IV circa A D. 1291   Folio   [*London*], 1802.
: By this all taxes were regulated until the 26th of Henry VIII

Nonarum Inquisitiones in curiâ Scaccarii, temp Edwardi III   Folio   [*London*], 1807.
: Contains the value of the ninth part of the corn, &c , and by its description of the several tithes and their respective values, the want of the original endowments of vicarages is in a great measure supplied.

Calendarium Rotulorum, Chartarum, et Inquisitionum ad quod Damnum, temp reg Edwardi II. et Henrici VI   Folio   [*London*], 1803
: Containing royal grants of liberties, privileges, and possessions to religious bodies, civil corporations, and individuals

Calendarium Rotulorum Patentium in Turri Londinensi.   Folio   [*London*], 1802
: Containing grants of liberties, privileges, lands, wardships, and offices, creations of nobility, special liveries, &c.

Calendarium Inquisitionum Post Mortem, sive Esceatarum temp reg Henrici III , Edwardi I , II , III., Ricardi II , Henrici IV , V., et VI , Edwardi IV , et Ricardi III   4 vols folio   [*London*], 1806
: Exhibits not only the possessions of persons *in capite*, but the extent, survey and valuation of the manors, lands, and possessions of vacant bishoprics, &c

Ducatus Lancastriæ [Inquisitiones Post Mortem et Placitorum]   Partes tres   2 vols. folio   [*London*]

Rotulorum Originalium in curiâ Scaccarii Abbreviatio, temporibus reg Henrici III , Edwardi I , II , et III. 2 vols folio   [*London*], 1805-10
: Or the estreats of all grants of the crown, whereon any rent is reserved, any salary payable, or any service performed

Valor Ecclesiasticus temp. Henrici VIII , auctoritate regiâ institutus 5 vols folio   Maps of the dioceses.   [*London*], 1810
: Forming the register by which first-fruits and tenths are calculated, and affording a complete view of the value and description of all ecclesiastical property in this reign

Abbreviatio Inquisitionum ad capellam domini regis retornatarum, quæ in publicis archivis Scotiæ adhuc servantur   3 vols folio.   [*Lond*] 1811
: Comprehending all those proceedings by " Inquest," or the verdict of an " Assize," originating in certain writs issuing from Chancery

Calendars of Chancery Proceedings in the reign of Elizabeth.   2 vols folio   [*London*], 1827-30.

Fœdera, Conventiones, Litteræ, et cujuscunque generis acta publica, inter reges Angliæ et alios quosvis imperatores, reges, pontifices, principes, vel communitates; ab A D 1066, ad nostra usque tempora, curâ et studio T Rymer et R Sanderson, denuò aucta A. Clarke, F Holbrooke, &c vols folio [*Lond*] 1816

Collection of all the Wills now known to be extant of the Kings and Queens of England, Princes and Princesses of Wales, and every branch of the blood royal, from William I to Henry VII, with notes, a preface, and glossary [by Gough] *London, Nichols*, 1780.

Original Letters, written during the reigns of Henry VI., Edward IV and V., Richard III., and Henry VII, by various persons [of or to the family of Paston] of rank and consequence. With notes historical and explanatory, and authenticated by engravings of autographs, fac-similes, paper-marks, and seals, by Sir John Fenn; with notices of his life, by William Frere. 5 vols 4to *London*, 1787–1823.

[Croft's (John)] Excerpta Antiqua, or, a collection of original English MSS 8vo *York, privately printed*, 1797

[Bentley's (Samuel)] Excerpta Historica, or, illustrations of English history [consisting of original documents illustrative of the history, laws, and constitution, the state of the navy and army, royal household, arts, heraldry, &c from the XIIIth to the XVIth centuries] Royal 8vo *Lond* 1831

Original Letters illustrative of English history, including numerous royal letters, from autographs in the British Museum, and one or two other collections, with notes and illustrations by Henry Ellis. 3 vols 8vo *London*, 1824

Original Letters, &c. Second series 4 vols. 8vo. *London*, 1827

Transcripts of Letters from Henry VIII, Edward VI, Mary Queen of Scots, Elizabeth, James I, &c and others, relating to the family of Talbot, found in Sheffield Castle (Manuscripts)

State Papers, published under the authority of his majesty's commission. [Edited by R Lemon] Vol. I Henry VIII 1518–30 4to [*Lond*] 1830

Correspondence of Lord Dacre, Warden of the East and Middle Marches, from June 1523 to August 1524. (Manuscripts)

Copies of Seven Original Letters of King Edward VI to Barnaby Fitzpatrick [Edited by H Walpole] 4to *Strawberry Hill*, 1772.

Sadler's (Sir Ralph) State Papers and Letters [1539–84], edited by Arthur Clifford; to which is added, a memoir of the life of Sir Ralph, with historical notes by Sir Walter Scott 3 vols 4to *Edinburgh*, 1809.

Harrington's (Sir John) Nugæ Antiquæ; being a miscellaneous collection of original papers, written during the reigns of Henry VIII, Edward VI, Mary, Elizabeth, and James I; edited, with illustrative notes, by Th. Park. 2 vols 8vo *London*, 1804

Lodge's (Edmund) Illustrations of British History, Biography, and Manners, in the reigns of Henry VIII, Edward VI, Mary, Elizabeth, and James I, exhibited in a series of original papers, from the MSS of the noble families of Howard, Talbot, and Cecil 3 vols 4to *London*, 1791

Hardwicke's (Earl of) Miscellaneous State Papers, from 1501 to 1726 2 vols 4to *London*, 1778

Burleigh's (W. Cecil, Lord) Collection of State Papers relating to affairs in the reigns of Henry VIII, Edward VI, Queen Mary, and Queen Elizabeth, from 1542 to 1570 Edited from the originals in Hatfield House, by S. Haynes   Folio   *London*, 1740

Burleigh —A Collection of State Papers relating to affairs in the reign of Queen Elizabeth, from 1571 to 1596 Transcribed from the originals left by Lord Burleigh, and reposited in the library at Hatfield House, by W Murdin, [edited by Birch]   Folio   *London*, 1759

The Sydney Papers; or, collection of letters and memorials of state, in the reigns of Queen Mary, Queen Elizabeth, King James, King Charles I and II, and Oliver's usurpation; by Arthur Collins   2 vols folio *London*, 1746

Letters of Sir Philip Sydney   (Sydney's Misc Works)

Cabala, sive Scrinia Sacra, mysteries of state and government in letters of illustrious persons and great ministers in the reigns of King Henry VIII, Queen Elizabeth, King James, and King Charles. Folio. *London*, 1691.

Digges' (Sir Dudley) Compleat Ambassador; or, two treaties of the intended marriage of Queen Elizabeth; comprised in letters of negotiation of Sir F Walsingham, together with the answers of the Lord Burleigh, the Earl of Leicester, Sir T Smith, and others, relative to the marriage   Folio   *London*, 1655

Forbes (Pat.), A Full View of the Public Transactions in the reign of Queen Elizabeth, from letters and other state papers, written by herself and her principal ministers, from 1559 to 1563   2 vols. folio *London*, 1740

Winwood's (Sir R) Memorials of Affairs of State in the reigns of Queen Elizabeth and King James I; comprehending the negotiations of Sir Henry Neville, Sir Charles Cornwallis, Sir Dudley Carleton, Sir T. Edmondes, Mr Trumbull, Mr Cottington, and others, by Edmund Sawyer   3 vols folio   *London*, 1725

Bacon's (Lord) Original Letters, &c, from the Cabala, Resuscitatio, British Museum, Lambeth Library, &c (Works, Vol XII. and XIII)

Transcripts of Letters relative to Public Affairs, from 1606–34 (Manuscripts)

Carleton's (Sir Dudley) Letters to and from him, during his embassy in Holland, from January 1615 to 1620; [with a preface by the Earl of Hardwick]   4to.   *London*, 1757.

Dalrymple's (David) [Lord Hailes] Memorials and Letters relating to the history of Britain in the reigns of James and Charles I   Published from the originals [in the Advocates' Library, Edinburgh]. 2 vols. in one. 8vo   *Glasgow, Foulis*, 1766

Rushworth's (John) Historical Collections of State, Law, and Parliamentary Matters, from 1618 to the death of Charles I   8 vols folio *London*, 1721

Private Correspondence between King Charles I and his Secretary of State, Sir Edward Nicholas, also between Sir E Hyde, afterwards Earl of Clarendon, and Sir R. Browne (Evelyn's Memoirs)

Bromley's (Sir Geo.) Collection of original Royal Letters, written by King Charles I and II, King James II, and the King and Queen of Bohemia, together with those of Prince Rupert, Charles Louis Count Palatine, the Duchess of Hanover, and several other distinguished persons, from 1619 to 1665   8vo portraits   *Lond*. 1787

[Knowler's (W)] State Papers, Letters, and Dispatches of the Earl of Strafforde, with his life by Sir Geo Radcliffe. 2 vols folio portraits. *London*, 1739

Correspondence of Sir Geo Radcliffe. (Life by Whitaker)

Clarendon's (Edward, Earl of) State Papers, commencing from the year 1621, containing the materials from which his History of the Rebellion was composed, and the authorities on which the truth of his relation is founded. 3 vols folio *Oxford*, 1767–86.

Collection of Letters written by King Charles I and II, the Duke of Ormonde, the Secretaries of State, the Marquis of Clanricarde, and other great men during the troubles of Great Britain and Ireland. Folio *London*, 1735. (Life of Ormonde, Vol III)

Collection of Letters from original MSS in the reigns of Charles I and II, and James II., in the possession of T L Parker, Esq (Account of Browsholme Hall, Yorkshire)

Milton's (John) Letters of State, Latin and English, during the Commonwealth and the Protectorate (Prose Works, 4to Vol II 8vo. Vols. IV and V)

Collection of the State Papers of John Thurloe, Secretary to the Council of State, and to the two Cromwells, containing authentic memorials of the English affairs from 1638 to the restoration of Charles II, with life of Mr Thurloe, by J. Birch 7 vols. folio *Lond* 1742

Nickolls's (John) Letters and Papers of State addressed to Oliver Cromwell, from 1649 to 59 Folio *London*, 1743

Bulstrode's (Sir Rich) Original Letters from the Earl of Arlington, envoy at Brussels from Charles II. 8vo *London*, 1712

Jenkins' (Sir L.) Letters. (Life, Eng Hist Charles II)

Arlington's (Earl of) Letters to Sir W. Temple, Sir R Fanshawe, the Earl of Sandwich, Earl of Sunderland, and Sir W Godolphin, during their embassies 1664–1674, by Babington. 2 vols 8vo *Lond* 1715

Letters written by Sir W. Temple and other Ministers of State at home and abroad, from 1665 to 72 · reviewed by Sir W Temple, and published by Jonathan Swift. (Works, Vols I. and II)

Letters to the King, the Prince of Orange, &c by Sir W Temple. (Works, Vol IV)

Macpherson's (James) Original Papers from 1688 to 1714, to which are prefixed, extracts from the life of James II as written by himself 2 vols 4to *London*, 1775

Prior's (M) History of his Negotiations, 1690 to 1710 8vo *Lond* 1740.

Clarendon (Correspondence of H Earl of) and of his brother Lawrence Hyde, Earl of Rochester; with the diary of the Earl of Clarendon from 1687 to 1690: edited from the original MSS with notes by S. W. Singer 2 vols. 4to *London*, 1828

Cole's (Ch) Memoirs of Affairs of State, containing letters written by ministers employed in foreign negotiations, treaties, memorials, &c. from 1697 to 1708 Folio *London*, 1733

Private and Original Correspondence of Charles Talbot, Duke of Shrewsbury, with King William, the Leaders of the Whig Party, and other distinguished Statesmen; illustrated with narratives, historical and biographical from the family papers in the possession of the Duchess of Buccleugh, by William Coxe 4to. *London*, 1821

Rose's (Sir G. H.) Selection from the Papers of the Earls of Marchmont, illustrative of events from 1685 to 1750 3 vols 8vo. *London*, 1831

Letters to and from Henrietta, Countess of Suffolk, and her second husband the Hon Geo Berkeley, from 1712 to 1767, with biographical, historical, and explanatory notes 2 vols 8vo. *Lond* 1830

British and Foreign State Papers, 1828-9, compiled by the librarian and keeper of the papers in the Foreign Office 8vo *Lond* 1831

Ecclesiastical History of England.

Broughton's (Richard) Ecclesiastical Historie of Great Britaine during the first 400 years after the birth of Christ; whereby is manifestly declared a continuall succession of the true Catholike religion as at this day professed in the Roman Church. Folio. *Douay*, 1633.

Usserii (Jacobi) Britannicarum Ecclesiarum Antiquitates. Folio. *Londini*, 1687

Stillingfleet's (Bp Ed.) Origines Britannicæ, or, the Antiquities of the British Churches (Works, Vol III)

Bedæ (S Venerabilis) Historia Ecclesiastica gentis Anglorum. 18mo *Coloniæ Agrippæ*, 1601

Bedæ (S V) Historia Ecclesiastici Gentis Anglorum [Sax. et Lat.] unà cum reliquis ejus operibus historicis, curâ et studio Jo Smith Folio *Cantabrigiæ* 1722.

Bede's (S. V.) History of the Church of England, translated out of Latin into English by Thomas Stapleton · [with the differences betweene the primitive faithe of England continued almost these thousand yeres, and the late pretensed faith of Protestants, and the life of Bede written by Trithemius.] 4to *Antwerpe, by John Laet,* 1565

Inett's (John) Origines Anglicanæ, or, a history of the English church, [continuing Stillingfleet's Origines] from the first planting of the Christian religion amongst the English Saxons, till the Norman Conquest. Folio *Lond* 1704

Harpsfeldii (Nicolai) Historia Anglicana Ecclesiastica, à primis gentis susceptæ fidei incunabulis ad nostra fere tempora deducta Adjectâ brevi narratione de divortio Henrici VIII regis ab uxore Catherinâ et ab Ecclesiâ Catholicâ Romanâ dissensione, scripta ab Ed Campiano nunc primum in lucem producta studio et operâ Ri Gibboni Folio *Duaci*, 1622.

<small>This contains the " Historia Wicleffiana ejusdem auctoris," and " Catalogus Religiosarum Ædium "</small>

Alfordi (Mich.), alias Griffith, Annales Ecclesiastici Britannorum, Saxonum, et Anglorum, ad A.D. 1189 4 vols folio *Leodii*, 1663

Southey's (Robert) Book of the Church 2 vols 8vo *Lond* 1824

<blockquote>
Southey's (R) Vindiciæ Ecclesiæ Anglicanæ Letters to Charles Butler, Esq comprising Essays on the Romish religion, and vindicating the " Book of the Church " 8vo *London*, 1826

Townsend's (George) Accusations of History against the Church of Rome, examined in remarks on Mr Butler's " Book of the Roman Catholic Church " 8vo. *London*, 1826
</blockquote>

White's (Joseph Blanco) Practical and Internal Evidence against
Catholicism, with strictures on Mr. Butler's " Book of the
Roman Catholic Church " 8vo *London*, 1826.

Philpott's (Henry) Letters to Charles Butler on the theological
parts of his ' Book of the Roman Catholic Church " 8vo
London, 1826

Fox's (John) Acts and Monuments of Matters most special and memorable
happening in the Church; with an universal history of the same,
from the primitive age to these later times of ours. 𝕭𝖑𝖆𝖈𝖐 𝖑𝖊𝖙𝖙𝖊𝖗.
Port by Glover. 3 vols folio *Lond* 1641

Fuller's (Thos) Church History of Britain until the year 1648 ; History
of the University of Cambridge ; History of Waltham Abbey. Folio
London, 1655

Collier's (Jeremy) Ecclesiastical History of Great Britain, chiefly of England,
from the first planting of Christianity to the end of the reign of
King Charles II ; with a brief account of the affairs of religion in
Ireland. Collected from the best ancient historians. 2 vols. folio
London, 1708–14

[Gibson's (Thos)] Breve Cronycle of the Bysshope of Rome's Blessynge,
and of his Prelates' benefyciall and charitable Rewardes,
from the tyme of Kynge Heralde unto this day. Small 8vo 𝕭𝖑𝖆𝖈𝖐
𝖑𝖊𝖙𝖙𝖊𝖗 *London, by John Daye*, ——
> Both Wood and his editor, Di Bliss, cite this, but acknowledge never having seen it.

Bedœ (Ven) Martyrologium (Hist Ecc à Smith)

[Capgravii (Johannis)] Nova Legenda Angliæ [Sanctorum]. Folio, black
𝖑𝖊𝖙𝖙𝖊𝖗. *Impr. Londini, in domo Wynandi de Worde*, M CCCCC XVI.

[Porter's (Hierome)] Flowers of the Saincts of England, Scotland, and
Ireland Vol 1 January to June, all published 4to *Doway*, 1632.

Metrical Life of St Robert, of Knaresborough [edited by H. Drury]
4to *Privately printed*, 1824

Sprotti (Tho) Chronica [Archiepisc Cantuariensis] è Cod. MS. in Bib
D. Ed. Dering Baronetti, descripsit ediditque T Hearne. 8vo.
Oxonii, 1719.

[Parker (Matth)] de Antiquitate Britannicæ Ecclesiæ, et Privilegiis
Ecclesiæ Cantuariensis, cum Archiepiscopo ejusdem. Folio. [*Lambeth,
by John Day*], 1572 , — Ejusdem Catalogus Cancellariorum,
Procancellariorum, Procuratorum, ac eorum qui in Academiâ Cantabrigiensi
ad gradum Doctoratûs aspiraverunt ab 1500 ad 1571 ;—
Indulta Regum ad Acad Cantabr ,— Episcopi ex Acad Cantabr.
ab 1500 ad 1571 , — De Scholarum Collegiorumque in Acad Cantabr.
Patronis atque Fundatoribus Scholarum Pub extructio ,—
Hospitiorum, Aularum, &c situs ac mutatio Folio [*Lambeth,
by John Day*, 1572]
> Together in one volume, the Sykes copy, with the portrait of Abp Parker by Berg or Hogenberg, and one of those in which all the titles, arms, initials, &c are illuminated, as mentioned by the Abp. in his letter to Lord Burleigh, given in Strype It differs, however, from the copies described by Strype and Dibdin, possessing neither the arms of the colleges, nor the cut of Queen Elizabeth on the reverses of the title to " Catal Cancelleriæ," and plate " Variæ Scholarum ," but, in addition, containing, as a continuation of the Abp.'s life, an account of Elizabeth s progress into Kent in 1573, occupying six pages inserted between pp. 18 and 19, and " Hospitiarum, aularum, &c situs ac mutatio," nine leaves, paged 31 to 47.

Godwini (Fr.) de Præsulibus Angliæ Commentarius, omnium episcoporum necnon et cardinalium ejusdem gentis, nomina, tempora, seriem, atque actiones maximè memorabiles Ad præsens usque sæculum continuavit Gul Richardson Folio. *Cantab.* 1743.
: This copy belonged to Mr Allan, of Darlington, and is illustrated by him with MS. notes, portraits, arms, seals, and views

Edmeri (Fratris) Angli de Vitâ D Anselmi Archiepiscopi Cantuariensis libri duo, nunquam antehac editi Small 8vo *Antverpiæ, excud J Græuius,* 1551

The Life, or the Ecclesiastical History of St. Thomas à Becket [culled out of the most authentic and best authors, by A. B] 8vo *Coloniæ,* 1639

Stapletoni (Thos) Tres Thomæ, seu res gestæ S Thomæ Apostoli, S. Thomæ Archiep Cantuariensis, et Thomæ Mori Angliæ Cancellarii Small 8vo. port of Stapleton inserted *Col Agrip.* 1612

Whitaker's (John) Life of St Neot, the eldest of all the brothers of King Alfred. 8vo *London,* 1809

Bedæ Vita Sancti Cuthberti, Episc Landisfernii (Hist Ecc. à Smith)

St Cuthbert's Legend, with the antiquities of the church of Durham, by B. R Small 8vo *London,* 1663

Symonis Monachi Dunhelmensis Libellus de exordio atque procursu Dunhelmensis Ecclesiæ cui præmittitur T Rud disquisitio, in quâ probatur non Turgotum sed Symonem luisse verum hujus libelli auctorem · è Cod MS. perantiquo in Bib Episc Dunhelm descripsit ediditque T Bedford. 8vo large paper *Londini,* 1732.

Matthæi Paris Vitæ XXIII Abbatum S. Albani (Historia Ang)

Le Neve's (John) Fasti Ecclesiæ Anglicanæ a regular succession of all the Dignitaries in each Cathedral, Collegiate Church, or Chapel, in England and Wales, to this present year. Folio *London,* 1716

Lewis (John) and Sam Pegge's Account of the suffragan Bishops in England (Nichols's Bib Top Vol VI No 28)

Godwyni (F.) Catalogus, hactenus meditus, Episc Bathensium et Wellensium, Humphredi que Humphreys Comment de Decanis Bangor et Asaphiensibus (Hearne's Thos. of Otterbourne.)

Cassan's (S H) Lives of the Bishops of Bath and Wells to the present period 8vo *Frome,* 1829.

Cassan's (S. H) Lives of the Bishops of Winchester to the present time 2 vols 8vo *Frome,* 1827

Lewis's (John) History of the Life and Sufferings of John Wicliffe, with additions 8vo portrait *Orford,* 1820

Baber's (H) Memoirs of the Life, Opinions, and Writings of John Wicliffe. (Wicliffe's New Testament)

Lewis's (J) Life of Bp R Pecock, being a sequel to the Life of Wicliffe 8vo *Oxford,* 1820

Joannis Whethamstedi Narratio de Processu contra Reg Peacockum (Walter de Hemingford, Hearne)

Bale's (Jo) Brefe Chronycle concernynge the Examynacyon and Death of Syr Johan Oldecastell, the Lord Cobham [Edited by John Blackbourne] Royal 8vo. *Reprint, Lond* 1729

Knight's (S.) Life of Dr John Colet, Dean of St Paul's in the reigns of Henry VII and VIII. With an Appendix, containing his Convocation Sermon in 1511, with translation, several of his epistles, and some account of the masters and more eminent scholars of St. Paul's School   8vo   *London*, 1724

Knight's (S.) Life of Erasmus   (Biography)

[Dodd's (Chas.)] Church History of England, from 1500 to 1688, chiefly with regard to Catholicks, particularly the Lives of the most eminent Cardinals, Bishops, inferior Clergy, and Laymen, who have distinguished themselves. To which is prefixed, a general history of ecclesiastical affairs under the British, Saxon, and Norman periods.   3 vols folio   *Brussels*, [*Lond*] 1737–42

Dodd (C.) Certamen utriusque Ecclesiæ, or, a List of all the eminent Writers of Controversy, Catholics and Protestants, since the Reformation. With an historical idea of the politic attempts of both parties in every reign in order to support their respective interests   4to 1724. (Somers's Tracts, Vol XIII)

Dodd —Constable's (   ) Specimens of Amendments for Dodd's Church History   12mo.   *London*, 1741

Dodd's (C.) Apology for the Church History.   8vo   *London*, 1742

Carwithin's (J. B. S.) History of the Church of England to the restoration of church and monarchy in 1660.   2 vols 8vo   *Lond* 1829

Burnet's (Bp G.) History of the Reformation of the Church of England.   7 vols 8vo   *Oxford*, 1829.

Soames's (Henry) History of the Reformation of the Church of England.   4 vols 8vo.   *Lond.* 1826–8.

Strype's (John) Ecclesiastical Memorials, relating chiefly to religion, and the reformation of it, under King Henry VIII, King Edward VI, and Queen Mary   6 vols 8vo   *Oxford*, 1822

Strype's (J.) Annals of the Reformation, and of the establishment of Religion, and other various occurrences in the Church of England, during Queen Elizabeth's reign.   4 vols. in 7, 8vo   *Oxford*, 1824

Richmond's (L.) Memorials of the Fathers of the English Church   (Miscel Divinity)

Lives of Tyndal, Fryth, and Barnes.   (Tyndal, &c 's Works)

Ward's (Thos) England's Reformation, from the time of Henry VIII to the end of Oates's Plot, a poem, with large marginal notes   8vo   *London*, 1716.

Strype's (J.) Life and Memorials of Abp. Cranmer   2 vols 8vo   *Oxford*, 1812

Todd's (Henry John) Life of Abp. Cranmer   2 vols. 8vo   *Lond* 1831

Todd's (Henry John) Vindication of the Character of Abp. Cranmer, and therewith the Reformation in England, against the allegations of Dr Lingard, Dr. Milner, and Charles Butler.   (Cranmer on the Sacrament

Ridley's (Gloucester) Life of Bp N. Ridley, shewing the plan and progress of the Reformation   4to.   *London*, 1763

Baily's (Thos) Life and Death of John Fisher, Bishop of Rochester; comprising the highest and hidden transactions of church and state in the reign of Henry VIII   12mo   *London, printed* 1655.

Strype's (John) Life and Acts of Abp. Matt Parker. 3 vols. 8vo. *Oxford*, 1821

Strype's (J.) Life and Acts of Abp. E Grindal. 8vo *Oxford*, 1821.

Strype.—A brief and true Character of Abp. Grindal, published to rectify some errors in Strype 8vo *London*, 1713
> This pamphlet is not noticed by the editors of the new edition of Strype, nor in the Biographia Britannica

Strype's (J) Life and Acts of Abp John Whitgift. 8vo. *Oxford*, 1821.

Strype's (J) Life and Acts of Bp John Aylmer. 8vo. *Oxford*, 1821

Downes' (Sam.) Lives of the Compilers of the Liturgy. 8vo. *London*, 1722.

A Bull graunted by the Pope to Dr Harding and other, by reconcilement and assoyling of English papists, to undermyne faith and allegeance to the Quene with a true declaration of the intention and fruites thereof, and a warning of perils thereby immenent not to be neglected. Anno 1567 𝕭lack letter, small 8vo. *London, by John Daye*, ——.

An Addition declaratorie to the Bulles, with a searching of the maze. 𝕭lack letter, small 8vo *London, by John Daye*, ——

A Disclosing of the Great Bull, and certain Calves that he hath gotten, and specially the monster Bull that roared at my Lord Byshop's gate 𝕭lack letter, small 8vo. *London. by John Daye*, ——

Jewell's (Bp) View of the seditious Bull sent into England from Pius Quintus, 1569 (Works, Vol I)

Historia aliquot nostri sæculi Martyrum [Angliæ], cum pia tum lectu jucunda, nunquam antehac typis excusa [à M. Chauncey] 4to. *Moguntiæ, excud F Behem* 1550.

Lives of Abp Sancroft, Bps Walton and Taylor. (Biography)

Walker's (John) Account of the Sufferings of the Clergy who were sequestered, &c during the grand Rebellion, in answer to Calamy's Life of Baxter. Folio *London*, 1714

Bowles's (W L) Life of Bp Thos Ken, viewed in connexion with public events and the spirit of the times, political and religious, in which he lived, including some account of the fortunes of Morley, Bishop of Winchester 2 vols 8vo *London*, 1830.

Ecclesiastical Biography, or the Lives of eminent Men connected with the history of Religion in England from the commencement of the Reformation to the Revolution, selected and illustrated with Notes by Christopher Wordsworth 6 vols 8vo *London*, 1818

Brewster's (John) Secular Essay, containing a retrospective view of events connected with the ecclesiastical history of England during the eighteenth century. 8vo *London*, 1802

Buchanan's (Claudius) Colonial Ecclesiastical Establishment, being a brief view of the state of the Colonies of Great Britain in respect to religious instruction 8vo. *London*, 1813

Neal's (Daniel) History of the Puritans, or Protestant Nonconformists, from the Reformation to the death of Queen Elizabeth, with an account of their principles, their attempts for a farther reformation in the church, their sufferings, and the lives and characters of their most considerable divines revised, corrected, and enlarged by Joshua Toulmin 5 vols. 8vo *Bath*, 1793-7

HISTORY.

Neal's Puritans —Maddox's (Bp. Isa.) Vindication of the Government, Doctrine, and Worship of the Church of England, established in the reign of Elizabeth, against the reflections of Mr Neal 8vo   London, 1733.
Neal's (D) Review of the Principal Facts objected to in Vol I of his History of the Puritans by Bp Maddox   8vo   London, 1734
Grey's (Zach) Impartial Examination of Neal's History of the Puritans   4 vols 8vo   London, 1740.

Baxter's (Richard) Narrative of his Life and Times, by E Calamy; with continuation   4 vols 8vo   London, 1713

Baxter's (R) History of his Life and Times, by W Orme. (Baxter's Works, Vol I)

Journal of the Proceedings of the Assembly of Divines from Jan. 1, 1643, to Dec 31, 1644. (Lightfoot's Works, Vol XIII)

Calamy's (Edmund) Historical Account of his own Life, with reflections on the times in which he lived (1671–1731), now first printed, edited and illustrated with notes, historical and biographical, by John Towell Rutt   2 vols 8vo   London, 1829

Bogue (David) and James Bennet's History of Dissenters, from the Revolution in 1688 to the year 1808.   4 vols 8vo   Lond. 1808–20.

Southey's (Rob.) Life of Wesley, and the rise and progress of Methodism   2 vols 8vo   London, 1820

Owen's (John) History of the British and Foreign Bible Society.   3 vols 8vo.   London, 1816–20.

History of Wales.

Topography.

Giraldi Cambrensis Itinerarium Cambriæ; seu, laboriosæ Baldwini Cantuar archiepiscopi per Walliam legationis accurata descriptio : cum annotationibus Davidis Poueli   Small 8vo   Londini, H Denham, 1585.

Giraldi Cambrensis Itinerarium ; cum annotationibus Davidis Powell [edidit R. C Hoare]   4to large paper.   Londini, 1804.

Giraldus's Itinerary of Abp Baldwin through Wales in 1118; translated and illustrated with views, annotations, and a life of Gualdus, by Sir R C Hoare.   2 vols 4to large paper.   London, 1806

Prise's (Sir John) Description of Cambria, augmented by H. Lloyd. (Caradoc's History of Cambria)

Carlisle's Topographical Dictionary of Wales.   (English Topography)

[Nicholson's (George)] Cambrian Traveller's Guide   8vo   Stourport, 1814

Pennant's (Thomas) Tour in Wales, 1773.   4to.   London, 1778.

Warner's (Richard) Walks through Wales in 1797–8.   2 vols. 8vo.   Bath, 1799–1801.

Sotheby's (W) Tour through part of Wales; with engravings from drawings by Smith   4to. large paper   London, 1794

Batty's (Robt) Welsh Scenery   4to proofs   London, 1823

Hutton's (Wm.) Remarks upon North Wales, the result of sixteen tours.   8vo   Birmingham, 1803

Bingley's (W) North Wales. including its scenery, antiquities, and customs, and some sketches of its natural history; delineated from two excursions during 1789–1801 2 vols. 8vo. *London*, 1804

Buckler's (J) Thirty-six original coloured Drawings, illustrating the antiquities of North Wales, executed in 1810. In a 4to portfolio

Donovan's (E) Descriptive Excursions through South Wales and Monmouthshire, in 1804 and four preceding summers 2 vols 8vo large paper, coloured plates *London*, 1805.

Gilpin's (W) Tour to the River Wye and several parts of South Wales 8vo. *London*, 1800

Jones's (Thos) History of Brecknockshire , containing the chorography, general history, antiquities, &c of that county. 3 vols 4to *Brecon*, 1805–9

Meyrick's (S R) History and Antiquities of the County of Cardigan 4to *London*, 1808.

Smith's (Sir J E) Account of Hafod in Cardiganshire, the seat of Thomas Johnes, Esq Large folio, coloured plates *Lond* 1810

Fenton's (Richard) Historical Tour through Pembrokeshire. 4to *London*, 1810

Pennant's (Thos) History of the Parishes of Whiteford and Holywell 4to *London*, 1796.

Pennant's (Thos) Journey to Snowdon 4to *London*, 1781

State of the Town of Kidwillie in the reign of Queen Elizabeth. (Leland's Collect Vol II.)

Norris's (Charles) Etchings of Tenby: with a short account of that town, and of the principal buildings in its neighbourhood 4to. large paper *London*, 1823

Rowland's (Henry) Mona Antiqua restaurata · the Antiquities, natural and historical, of the Isle of Anglesey. 4to *Dublin*, 1723

Narrative

Davies' (Edward) Celtic Researches on the Origin, Traditions, and Language of the ancient Britons 8vo. *London*, 1804.

Chronicles of the Kings of Britain, translated from the Welsh copy attributed to Tysilio; with original dissertations on the primary population of Britain the ancient British church, &c. and copious notes ; by P Roberts 4to *London*, 1811

[Caradoc's] Historie of Cambria, now called Wales , written in the British language above 200 yeares past , translated by H. Lloyd Corrected, augmented, and continued out of records, &c. by David Powell. 4to black letter *London, by Rafe Newberrie*, 1584

Dodridge's (Sir John) History of the ancient and modern Estate of Wales, Dutchy of Cornewall, and Earledome of Chester 4to. *Lond*. 1630

Enderbie's (Percy) Cambria Triumphans, or Brittain in its perfect lustre ; shewing the origin and antiquity of that ancient nation Reprint of the edition of 1661, with an index Folio, largest paper. *London*, 1810

Warrington's (W) History of Wales 2 vols 8vo. *London*, 1788

The Myvyrian Archæology of Wales; being a collection of historical documents from ancient MSS 3 vols 8vo. *London*, 1801.

History of Scotland.

Topography and Antiquities.

Carlisle's Topographical Dictionary of Scotland. (English Topography)
Boetius' (Hector) Description of Scotland (Holinshed's Chron Vol II)
Leslæi (Jo) Nova et accurata Regionum et Insularum Scotiæ Descriptio. (De Origine, &c Scotorum)
Ubaldini (P) Descrittione del Regno di Scotia e delle Isole sue adjacenti Folio *Anversa*, 1588
Camden's (W) Description of Scotland. (Britannia, Vol III)
Chalmers (Geo) Caledonia, or, an account, historical and topographical, of North Britain, from the most ancient to the present times, with a dictionary of places chorographical and philological 3 vols 4to *London*, 1807–24.

Buchan (David, Earl of) on the Progress of the Roman Army in Scotland during the Sixth Campaign of Agricola, with a plan and description of the camp at Rae-dykes (Nichols's Top Brit Vol V No 36)
Jameson's Account of the Roman Camps of Battledykes and Haerfauds, with the Via Militaris extending between them, in the county of Forfar (Nichols's Top Brit Vol V No 36)
Roy's Military Antiquities of the Romans in North Britain (Eng Topography)
Dalyell's (J G) Monastic Antiquities, with some account of the recent search for the remains of the Scottish kings. 8vo on vellum, only 6 copies printed *Edinburgh*, 1809
Spottiswood's (Bp John) Account of all the Religious Houses that were in Scotland at the time of the Reformation. (Keith's Scottish Bishops)
Alphabetical Table of the Parishes in Scotland, and where situated. (Keith's Scottish Bishops)

Forsyth's (R) Beauties of Scotland; containing accounts of the agriculture, commerce, mines, and manufactures, the population, cities, towns, villages, &c of each county 5 vols 8vo large paper. *Edinb* 1805–8
Murray's (Mrs) Companion and Useful Guide to the Beauties of Scotland and the Hebrides 2 vols 8vo *London*, 1810.
Traveller's Guide through Scotland and its Islands. 2 vols. 12mo. *Edinburgh*, 1818
[Slezer's (Jo.)] Theatrum Scotiæ · Views of castles and palaces, and of the most considerable towns, abbeys, churches, &c. in Scotland, with short descriptions Folio *London*, 1718.
Cordiner's (Charles) Remarkable Ruins and Romantic Prospects, with ancient monuments and singular subjects in natural history in North Britain. 2 vols 4to ; plates by Mazell *London*, 1788

Grose's (Fr) Antiquities of Scotland   2 vols 4to   *London*, 1797

Scott's (Sir W.) Provincial Antiquities and Picturesque Scenery of Scotland, with descriptive illustrations   2 vols in one, imp. 4to proofs   *Lond* 1826

Landscape Illustrations of the Waverley Novels, from Drawings by Daniel, Dewint, Stothard, Stanfield, &c , engraved by W and E Finden, with descriptions   4to India proofs   *London,* 1830.

Campbell's (Alexander) Journey from Edinburgh through the Highlands, &c of Scotland. 2 vols 4to   44 aquatinta engravings by Medland, Jukes and Pickett   *London*, 1802

Carr's (Sir John) Caledonian Sketches, or Tour in Scotland, 1807   4to   *Lond* 1807

Garnett's (Thomas) Tour through the Highlands, and part of the Western Islands of Scotland particularly Staffa and Icolmkill   2 vols 4to. 52 plates after drawings by Watts.   *London*, 1800

Gilpin s (William) Observations on several parts of Great Britain, particularly the Highlands of Scotland, relative to picturesque beauty. 2 vols 8vo   *London*, 1808

Pennant's (Thomas) Tour in Scotland in 1769   4to   *London*, 1776.

Pennant's (T) Tour in Scotland, and Voyages to the Hebrides, 1772   2 vols 4to   *London*, 1776

Stoddart's (John) Remarks on Local Scenery and Manners in Scotland, in 1799 and 1800   2 vols 8vo , plates by Merigot, coloured.   *London*, 1801

Welldon s (Sir A) Perfect Description of the People and Country of Scotland   (Secret History of James I)

Letters from a Gentleman in the North of Scotland to his friend in London, containing an account of the manners and customs of the Inhabitants   2 vols. in one, 8vo   *London*, 1815

[Grant's (Mrs)] Essays on the Superstitions of the Highlanders of Scotland, with Translations from the Gaelic.   2 vols 12mo   *Lond* 1811

Stewart s (Major-Gen David) Sketches of the Character, Manners and present State of the Highlands of Scotland , with details of the military services of the Highland regiments. 2 vols. 8vo.   *Edinb* 1825

Kirk (Rob) on the Nature and Actions of Elves, Fauns, and Fairies, or the lyke, among the Low Country Scots   4to   *Edinburgh, reprint*, 1815

Extracts from the Household Book of Ladie Marie Stewart, daughter of Esmé, Duke of Lennox, and Countess of Mar, 1638-43   [With biographical notice and historical notes, by   Erskine of Mar]   4to   *Edinburgh*, ——

Sibbaldi (Rob) Scotia illustrata sive, Prodromus Historiæ Naturalis, in quo regionis natura, incolarum ingenia et mores, et medicina indigena accurate explicantur   Folio   *Edinburgh*, 1684

Kennedy's (W) Annals of Aberdeen, from the reign of King William the Lion to the end of the year 1818 , with an account of the city, cathedral, and old University of Aberdeen   2 vols 4to   *Lond.* 1818

Orem's (W) Description of the Chanonry of Old Aberdeen in the years 1724 and 5 (Nichols's Bib Topog Vol. V No. 3)

[Martine's (Geo)] Reliquiæ Divi Andreæ, or, the state of the primitial see of St Andrews; with some historicall memoirs of the most famous prelates and primates thereof [Edited from the original MS of 1683] 4to *St Andrew's*, 1797

Martin's (Geo) History and Antiquities of St Rule's Chapel in the Monastery of St Andrew's in Scotland, with remarks by Professor Brown (Nichols's Bib Top Vol V No 47)

Wood's (J. P.) Ancient and Modern State of the Parish of Cramond; to which are added, biographical and genealogical collections. 4to. *Edinburgh*, 1794

Chartulary of Dunfermline (Dalyell's Monastic Antiquities)

History of Carlaverock Castle, Dumfriesshire. (Siege of Carlaverock, History of England)

Alesu (Alex) Edinburgi regiæ Scotorum Urbis Descriptio 4to *Edin privately printed,* ——

Arnot's (Hugo) History of Edinburgh, from the earliest account to the present time 4to. plan and plates *Edin* 1779.

Maitland's (W) History of Edinburgh, from its foundation to the present time Folio *Edinburgh*, 1753

Chambers's (R) Traditions of Edinburgh 2 vols 12mo. *Edin* 1825

Crawford's (Profes Thomas) History of the University of Edinburgh, from 1580 to 1646, with the charter granted in 1583 8vo. *Edin* 1808

Sibbald's (Sir Robt) Ancient and Modern History of the Sheriffdoms of Fife and Kinross, with a description of both, and of the Firths of Forth and Tay, and the islands in them, with notes and illustrations [by A. Tullis] 8vo *Cupar*, 1803

Hamilton (W) of Wishaw's Descriptions of the Sheriffdoms of Lanark and Renfrew, compiled about 1710, with illustrative extracts from the commissary records, and an appendix of ancient charters, edited by J Dillon and J Fullarton. 4to. *Privately printed*, 1831.

Shaw's (Lach) History of the province of Moray, including part of the shire of Banff, the whole of Moray and Nairn, and the greatest part of Invernesshire 4to. *Edinburgh*, 1775

Crawford s (Thos) History of the shire of Renfrew, containing a genealogical history of the royal house of Stewart, and of the nobility and gentry of the county of Renfrew, continued to the present time by W Semple 4to *Paisley*, 1782

Nimmo's (Wm) History of Stirlingshire, brought down to the present time, by W Macgregor Stirling 8vo *Stirling*, 1817.

History of Stirling to the present time 12mo. *Stirling*, 1817

Maculloch's (J) Highlands and Western Isles of Scotland, containing descriptions of their scenery and antiquities, with an account of the political history and ancient manners, and of the origin, language, agriculture, economy, music, present condition of the people, &c founded on a series of annual journeys between the years 1811 and 1821, and forming an universal guide to that country 4 vols 8vo *London*, 1824

MODERN

Macculloch's (J) Description of the Western Islands of Scotland, including the Isle of Man, comprising an account of their geological structure, with remarks on the agriculture, scenery, and antiquities 2 vols 8vo. The plates and maps, with explanations, 4to London, 1819.

Martin's (M) Description of the Western Islands of Scotland. 8vo London, 1703

Johnson's (Samuel) Journey to the Western Isles of Scotland. (Works, Vol VIII)

Boswell's (James) Journal of a Tour with Dr Johnson to the Hebrides 8vo London 1786.

Wallace's (James) Account of the Islands of Orkney, with an essay on the Thule of the ancients 8vo, maps by Speed inserted London, 1700

Neil's (Pat) Tour through some of the islands of Orkney and Shetland, with a view chiefly to objects of natural history. 8vo Edin. 1806

Orkneyinga Saga, sive Historia Orcadensium à primâ Orcadum per Norvegos occupatione ad exitum sæculi XII., Saga Hins Helga Magnuser enjea Jarls, sive Vita S Magni Insularum Comitis Ex MSS Arna-Magnæana, cum versione Latinè, var lect, et indicibus · edidit J Jonæus 4to. *Hafniæ*, 1780

Torfæi (Ther) Orcades; seu, Rerum Orcadensium Historia. Folio *Haumæ*, 1715

Barry's (George) History of the Orkney Isles, with additions by J Headrick 4to London, 1808

Gifford's (Thos) Historical Description of the Zetland Isles. (Nichols's Top. Brit Vol. V No 37)

Edmonston's (Arthur) ancient and present state of the Zetland Isles 2 vols 8vo *Edinburgh*, 1809

Narrative

Nicholson's (Bp W) Scottish Historical Library, or, an account of most of the writers, records, registers, law books, &c of Scotland (English Hist Library)

Registrum Metellanum, [or, works worthy of being printed, illustrative of the history, &c of Scotland] 4to *Glasgow, privately printed*, 1831

Innes's (Thos) Critical Essay on the ancient Inhabitants of Scotland 2 vols 8vo London, 1729

Sibbald's (J) Observations on the Origin of the Terms Picti, Caledonii, and Scotti) (Chronicle of Scottish Poetry Vol IV)

Johnstone's (James) Accurate Catalogue of the Pictish and Scottish Kings, &c (Antiquitates Celto-Normannicæ)

Fordum (Jo de) Scoti-Chronicon, unà cum ejusdem supplemento, ac continuatione [per Walt Bowerum] è cod MSS eruit ediditque T Hearne, qui et append præfat atque indicibus adornavit 5 vols 8vo *Oxonii*, 1722

Fordum (J de) Scoti-Chronicon, cum supplementis et continuatione Walteri Boweri è cod MSS editum, cum notis et var lectionibus Præfixa est ad list Scotorum introductio cura Walt Goodall 2 vols folio *Edinb* 1759

HISTORY.

Chronicle of Perth, from 1210 to 1668. 4to. *Glasgow, privately printed,* 1831.

Wyntoun's (Androw of) Oryginale Chronykil of Scotland; now first published, with notes, a glossary [general rules for reading Wyntoun, which may serve for other Scottish writers], &c ; by David Macpherson. 2 vols 8vo. large paper. *London,* 1815.

Boece (Hector)—The History and Chronicles of Scotland, written in Latin by Hector Boece, Canon of Aberdeen, and translated by John Bellenden, Archdean of Moray and Canon of Ross. 2 vols 4to. *Edinburgh,* 1821.

Leslæi (Jo.) de Origine, Moribus, et Rebus gestis Scotorum ad nostra tempora (1561) Historia accesserunt Scotiæ descriptio [Parænesis ad nobilitatem populumque Scoticum, et de titulo et jure Mariæ Scotorum Reginæ, &c]. 4to. *Romæ,* 1675.

Holinshed's (R.) History of Scotland, from the original thereof unto the year 1571, and continued to 1586 by F. Botevile, commonly called Thin. (Holinshed's Chron. Vol II., new edition, Vol V.)

Buchanani (Georgii) Rerum Scoticarum Historia. Editio princeps. Folio. *Edinburgi, apud Alex Arbuthnetum, M D LXXXII.*

"Fra Mylles ex dono reverendissimi in Dno Patris Fdwardi Grindalli, Cantuariensis archiepiscopi, 20 Jan. 15."—MS. Note

Chambre (D.), Histoire Abrégé de tous les Rois d'Ecosse, et sur les anciennes alliances entre la France et l'Ecosse. (Eng Hist.)

Chronicle of the Kings of Scotland from Fergus I to James VI [edited by J. W M'Kenzie]. 4to *Glasgow. privately printed,* 1830.

Balfour's (Sir James) Historical Works; [containing the annales of Scotland from 1057 to 1640, and some breiffe memorialls and passages of church and state from 1641 to 1652. Edited from the original MSS in the Advocates' Library, Edinburgh, by James Haig]. 4 vols. 8vo. *Edinburgh,* 1824.

[Wallace's (James)] History of the Kingdom of Scotland from Fergus, the first king, to the Union in 1707. To which are added, an account of the Rebellion in 1715, and a description of Scotland. 4to *Dublin,* 1724.

History of Scotland to the Union of the Kingdoms. (Mod Univ. Hist. Vol XLI.)

Noble's (Mark) Historical Genealogy of the Royal House of Stuart. (Genealogical History.)

Ridpath's (Geo) Border History of England and Scotland, to the Union of the two Crowns, edited by P. Ridpath. 4to *Edin.* 1776.

Scott's (Sir W.) Illustrations of Border History and Traditions. (Border Antiquities.)

Criminal Trials before the High Court of Justiciary in Scotland, from 1369 to 1624, selected and edited by R. Pitcairne. 8 vols. 4to. *Edinburgh, privately printed,* 1829–30.

History of particular Periods.

Haco's Expedition (the Norwegian Account of) against Scotland, A.D M CC LXIII. Icelandic and English, with notes by James Johnstone. Small 8vo [*Copenhagen*], 1782.

Pinkerton's (John) Enquiry into the History of Scotland preceding the reign of Malcolm III., or the year 1056 and including the authentic history of that period. 2 vols. 8vo. *London*, 1794.

Desultory Reflections on the state of ancient Scotland [between the reign of Malcolm Canmore and the death of Alexander III, with a catalogue of the Lordes Chief Justiciars to 1643, and of all the grante constables since the 4th of Malcolm III. (Dalyell's Fragments)

Hailes's (Sir D. Dalrymple, Lord) Annals of Scotland, from the accession of Malcolm III. to that of the house of Stewart in Robert II. 2 vols 4to. *Edinburgh*, 1776–9.

Ayscu's (Ed) History of the Wars, Treaties, &c between England and Scotland, to the reign of James IV. (English History)

Henry the Minstrel's [Blind Harry] Wallace, or, the Life and Acts of Sir William Wallace, of Ellerslie. Published from a MS. dated 1488. with notes and preliminary remarks by John Jamieson 4to. *Edinburgh*, 1820.

William Wallace —[Sibbald (Sir Robt)] de Gestis illust Herois Gulielmi Vallæ, Scotiæ olim Custodis, Collectanea varia, quorum pleraque nunc primùm è MSS. in lucem prodeunt Small 8vo *Edinburgi*, 1705.

Barbour's (John) Bruce, or, a metrical history of Robert 1 King of Scots Published from a MS. dated 1489 with notes, and a life of the author by John Jamieson 4to. *Edinb* 1820.

Kerr's (Robt.) History of Scotland during the reign of Robert I., surnamed the Bruce : with a genealogical view of the origin and descent of the Bruce family. 2 vols. 8vo *Edinburgh*, 1811.

Prynne's (Historical and Critical Remarks on) History, so far as concerns the submission and fealty sworn by the Scottish nation to Edward I, commonly called the Ragman-Roll (Nesbit's Heraldry, Vol II)

Tytler (W.) on the Life of James I. (Poetical Remains)

Drummond's (Wm) History of Scotland from 1423 to 1542, containing the lives and reigns of James I. II III IV and V, with several memorials of state during the reigns of James VI and Charles I., with a prefatory introduction by W. Hall. Folio, portraits by Gaywood. *London*, 1655.

The Diarey of Robert Birrel, Burges of Edinburghe, containing divers passages of staite, and others memorable accidents, from 1532 to 1605. (Dalyell's Fragments)

Lesley's (John, Bp of Ross) History of Scotland, from 1436 to 1561 4to. *Edinb privately printed*, 1830

Flodden Field (Historical Pieces relating to the Battle of) (Poetry)

The late Expedicion into Scotlande, made by the Kynges Hyghnys Armye, under the conduit of the Earle of Hertforde, the yere of oure Lorde God, 1544. *Reprinted from the original, London, by R. Wolfe,* 1544 (Dalyell's Fragments)

[Lindsay's (Sir David)] Complaint of Scotland, written in 1548, with a preliminary dissertation and glossary, by J Leyden 4to. large paper *Edinburgh*, 1801

The Expedicion into Scotlande of Edward, Duke of Somerset, Vncle unto ye Kinges Majestie Edward the VI, &c made in the first yere of his Majestie's most prosperous reign, and set out by way of diarne by W. Patten, Londoner   *Reprinted from the original, London*, 1548 (Dalyell's Fragments)

Beague's (Mon.) History of the Campaigns 1548 and 9, by the Scots and French on the one side, and by the English and their foreign auxiliaries on the other, with an introductory preface by the translator [Dr Patrick Abercrombie]   12mo   *Printed [Edinburgh]*, 1707

Johnston (R.) Historia Rerum Scotorum.   (Eng Hist)

Robertson's (William) History of Scotland, during the reigns of Queen Mary and King James VI, till his accession to the crown of England   2 vols 4to   *London*, 1791.

Sanderson's (Will) compleat History of the Lives and Reigns of Mary Queen of Scotland, and of her son and successor James VI, reconciling several opinions in testimony of her, and confuting others in vindication of him   [With the second part, continuing the reign of James to his death]   Folio   *London*, 1646–55

Udall's (W) [W Stranguage] Historie of the Life and Death of Mary Stuart, Queene of Scotlande   12mo portrait of Mary, and front. by Marshall.   *London*, 1636

Chalmers' (Geo) Life of Mary Queen of Scots, drawn from the State Papers; with subsidiary memoirs [viz of Francis II, Henry Lord Darnley; John Stewart, Earl Bothwell; the Regent Murray; Secretary Maitland]   2 vols 4to   *Lond* 1818.

Benger's (Miss) Memoirs of the Life of Mary Queen of Scots with anecdotes of the Court of Henry II during her residence in France.   2 vols 8vo   *London*, 1823.

Melvil's (Sir James) Memoirs   (Eng History.)

Chambre (D), la Recherche des singularitéz plus remarquables concernant l'estât d'Ecosse   Small 8vo   *Paris*, 1579

[Buchanan (Geo)] de Mariâ Scotorum Reginâ, totâque ejus contra Regem conjuratione, fœdo cum Bothwellio adulterio, nefariâ in maritum crudelitate et rabie, &c —et

[Wilson (Thomæ)] Actio contra Mariam Scotorum Reginam, in quâ ream et consciam esse eam hujus parricidii necessariis argumentis euincitur   Small 8vo 2 ports of Mary inserted   [*Londini*, 1572.]

Riccio (Some particulars of the Life of David).   (Misc. Antiqua.)

Darnley —The Testament and Tragedie of umquhile King Henrie Stewart of gude memorie   Reprint from that of Lepreuik, 1572   (Dalyell's Scottish Poems)

Murray (Some incidents in the Life of James Earl of), Regent of Scotland   (Dalyell's Scottish Poems)

Chambre (D), de la légitime Succession des Femmes aux Possessions de leurs Parens, et du Gouvernement des Princesses aux Empires et Royaumes   Small 8vo   *Paris*, 1579
This was written with a view to Mary's succession to the crown of England.

Leslæus (Jo) Episc Rossensis de Titulo et Jure Ser. Principis Mariæ Scotorum Reginæ, quo Regni Angliæ successionem sibi justè vindicat; nunc verò Latino sermone in lucem editus [per Lane?]   Accessit ad Anglos et Scotos Parænesis   4to   *Rhemis*, 1580

Leslæus (Jo) de illustrium Fœminarum in repub administrandâ ac ferendis legibus authoritate , nunc verò Latino sermone in lucem editus   4to   *Rhemis*, 1580

De Vitâ Mariæ Scotorum Reginæ, quæ scriptis tradidere authores XVI. ad optim codices recens Sam Jebb. 2 vols folio. *Londini*, 1725 Vid —

    Chambre (D.) de la Succession des Femmes aux Gouvernements.
    Leslæus (J.) de Titulo et Jure Mariæ Scot Reg
    Leslæus (J.) de Rebus gestis Scotorum regnante Mariâ
    Buchanani (G) Detectio Mariæ Reg. Scot
    Buchanan (G), Histoire Tragique de Marie Royne d'Ecosse, touchant la conjuration faicte contre le roy son mari, &c
    Barnstaplii Vindicis Maria Stuarta innocens à cæde Darnleianâ
    [Belleforest (F des)], l'Innocence de la très illustre, très chaste, et débonnaire Princesse, Marie Royne d'Ecosse.
    Conœi (G.) Vita Mariæ Stuartæ Scotorum Reginæ.
    Caussin (N), l'Histoire de l incomparable Royne Marie Stuart.
    F. Strada de Mariæ Scotorum Reg. Vitâ et Morte
    Romoaldi Summarium Rationum, quibus Cancell Angliæ, prolocutor Puckering, persuaserunt occidendam esse Ser Mariam
    Blackwood (A.), Martyre de la Royne d'Ecosse
    Herrara (Ant. de), Historia de lo Succidido en Ecocia y Ingleterra, en 44 anno vivio Maria Estuardi Reyna de Ecocia
    Extrait des Mémoires de M Michel de Castlenau
    La Mort, &c. de la Royne d'Ecosse
    [Beauleu (R. de)] Oraison Funèbre de la Royne d'Ecosse.

Collections relating to the History of Mary Queen of Scotland , containing a great number of original papers never before printed also, a few scarce pieces reprinted, taken from the best copies Revised and published by James Anderson, with explanatory index of the obsolete words, and prefaces shewing the importance of these collections 4 vols 4to large paper   *Edinb* 1727, *London*, 1728   Vid. —

    Life of John Lesley, Bp of Ross, subjoined to his " Congratulatio Alberti, Archd Austriæ.' (Vol. 1. No. 1.)
    Discourse touching the pretended Match between the Duke of Norfolk and Mary   (Vol 1 No 2)
    Treatise concerning the Defence of the Honour of Mary Queen of Scotland, made by Morgan Philippes (Bp. Lesley) (Vol. I No 9)
    Ane Detectioun of the Doings of Marie Queen of Scottis, tuching the murther of hir husband , translatit out of the Latine, quilk was written by G Buchanan. (Vol II No 1)
    The Copie of a Letter written by one in London to his friend, concerning the credit of the late published Detectioun. (Vol. II. No. 17.)

        Besides these reprints, Vols I and II. chiefly relate to Darnley's murder and consist of state papers.

    A Discourse, contevning a perfect accompt given to the moste virtuous and excellent Princesse Marie Queen of Scots and her Nobility, by John Leslie, Bishop of Rosse, ambassador for her highnes toward the Queen of England , of his whole charge and proceedings during his ambassage, from his entries in England, Sept 1568, to the 26th March, 1572   From a MS in the Advocate's Library   (Vol III)

        The remaining contents of Vols. III. and IV. are letters or papers relating to the conferences held in England

Whitaker's (John) Mary Queen of Scots vindicated   3 vols 8vo. *London*, 1787.

Bothwell —Les Affaires du Conte de Boduel l'an 1568.   4to.   *Edinb. privately printed*, 1829

Bannatyne's (Rich) Journal of the Transactions in Scotland during the contest between the adherents of Mary and those of her son, 1570-73 ; edited by J. G. Dalyell   8vo   *Edinb* 1806.

The Sege of the Castel of Edinburgh, from that of Lepreuik, 1573, and biographical sketches of Sir W Kirkaldy the governor   (Dalyell's Scottish Poems)

The Historic of King James the Sext [from 1566 to 1582]   Written during the latter part of the 16th century , edited by Malcolm Laing.   8vo   *Edinburgh*, 1804

Moysie's (David) Memoires of the Affairs of Scotland, from 1577 to 1603 [edited by J Dennistoun]   4to.   *Glasgow, privately printed*, 1830

Cromarty's (George Mackenzie, Earl of) Account of the Conspiracies of the Earl of Gowry, and Robert Logan of Restalrig, against King James VI. also a Vindication of Robert III and all his descendants from the imputation of bastardy   8vo   *Edinb.* 1713

Narrative of the Battle of Strathaven and Balrinnes. (Dalyell's Scottish Poems.)

Laing's (Malc) History of Scotland, from the accession of James VI to the throne of England to the Union of the Kingdoms in 1709 , with a dissertation on the participation of Mary Queen of Scots in the murder of Darnley. 4 vols. 8vo. *London*, 1819.

Burnet's (Bp Gilbert) Memoires of the Lives and Actions of James and William, Dukes of Hamilton and Castleherald , [or, an Account of the Civil Wars in Scotland in 1625-52.] Folio, portraits. *Lond* 1677

The Riding of the Parliament in Scotland in 1606 and 81 , and the Ceremonials observed in 1685. (Nichols's Bib. Top. Vol V. No 47)

Urquhart's (Sir Thos.) Εκσκυβαλανον or Jewell, serving in this place to frontal a vindication of the honour of Scotland from that infamy whereunto the rigid presbyterian party hath involved it   12mo.   *Edinburgh, reprinted* 1774

Spalding's (John) History of the Troubles and memorable Transactions in Scotland and England, from 1624 to 45   2 vols 4to   *Edinburgh, privately printed*, 1828.

Ogilvie's (Sir Geo) Account of the Preservation of the Regalia of Scotland from falling into the hands of the English usurpers   1701. (Somers's Tracts, Vol XI.)

Chronicle of Fife, being the Diary of John Lamont from 1649 to 72. [Edited by Archibald Constable]   4to   *Edinb* 1810

Wishart's (Geo.) Memoirs of James Grahame, Marquess of Montrose ; translated from the Latin   To which are added, sundry original letters never before published. 8vo. *Edinburgh.* 1819

Hume's (Sir Patrick) Narrative of Occurrences at the Expedition of the Earl of Argyle in 1685; edited by Geo Rose   (Observations on Fox's James II)

Siege of Edinburgh Castle in 1689 [edited by R Bell]. 4to   *Edinburgh, privately printed*, 1828

Hume's (Sir David) Diary of the Proceedings in the Parliament and Privy Council of Scotland, from May 21, 1700, to March 7, 1707.   4to   *Edinburgh, privately printed*, 1828

Account of the Massacre of Glencoe   (Somers's Tracts, Vol XI)

Defoe's (Dan) History of the Union between England and Scotland   (Eng Hist)

Chambers's (Robert) History of the Rebellions in Scotland, under Montrose, Dundee, Mar, and Prince Charles Stuart.   5 vols. 12mo   *Edinburgh*, 1829

Patten's (Robert) History of the Rebellion in 1715   8vo   *Lond* 1717

Home's (John) History of the Rebellion in 1745   4to   *London*, 1802

Johnstone's (Chevalier de) Memoirs of the Rebellion in 1745 and 6, translated from a French MS originally in the Scots college at Paris [by the Chevalier Watson].   4to   *London*, 1820

Lovat (Memoirs of the Life of Simon Fraser, Lord), written by himself in the French language, and now first translated from the original MS   8vo.   *London*, 1817.

Catalogue of the Lords of Session from 1532, with historical notes, and of the Faculty of Advocates, from the institution of the College of Justice to 1688.   (Hailes's Tracts)

Miscellanea Scotica; a collection of tracts relating to the history, antiquities, topography, and literature of Scotland   4 vols   12mo   *Glasgow*, 1818.

Bacon's (Lord) Tracts relating to Scotland   (Works, Vol V)

Hailes's (Sir David Dalrymple, Lord) Tracts relative to the History and Antiquities of Scotland.   4to   *Edinburgh*, 1800.

[Dalyell's (J. G.)] Fragments of Scottish History.   4to.   *Edinburgh*, 1798

Documentary History of Scotland

Anderson (Jacobi) Selectus Diplomatum et Numismatum Scotiæ Thesaurus, auxit et locupletavit Thomas Ruddimannus   Folio, plates by Sturt   *Edinburgh*, 1739

Registrum Magni Sigilli Regum Scotorum in archivis publicis asservatum 1306-1424   Folio.   [*London*], 1814

The various charters granted by the kings of Scotland

Rotuli Scotiæ in Turri Londinensi et in Domo Capitulari Westmonasteriensi asservati, temporibus Edwardi I ad Henricum VIII   2 vols folio   [*London*], 1814-19

Consist of documents arising out of the public affairs between Scotland and England during this period

Sadler's (Sir R) State Papers.   (English Documentary History)

Baillie's (Robert) Letters and Journals   (Eng History, Commonwealth.)

Forbes's (Duncan) Culloden Papers, comprising an extensive and interesting correspondence, from the year 1625 to 1748, including numerous letters from the unfortunate Lord Lovat, and other distinguished persons of that time, with occasional state papers of much historical importance   To which is prefixed, Memoirs of the Right Hon Duncan Forbes, by Duncan Geo Forbes   4to   *Lond.* 1815

Lockhart (George, of Carnwath's) Lockhart Papers; containing memoirs and commentaries upon the affairs of Scotland, from 1702 to 1715, his secret correspondence with the son of James the Second, from 1718 to 1728, and his other political writings also journals and memoirs of the young Pretender's expedition in 1745, by Highland officers in his army. Published from original manuscripts in the possession of Ant Autrere, Esq of Hoveton, in Norfolk 2 vols. 4to. *London*, 1817.

Carstares's (Wm.) State Papers, and Letters addressed to him when confidential secretary to King William during the whole of his reign, relating to Public Affairs in Great Britain, but more particularly Scotland, during the reigns of King William and Queen Anne, with his Life, edited by Jos. M'Cormick. 4to *Edin*. 1774.

Ecclesiastical History of Scotland

Jamieson's (John) Historical Account of the Ancient Culdees of Iona, and of their settlements in Scotland, England, and Ireland 4to *Edinburgh*, 1811

Spottiswoode's (Abp John) History of the Church and State of Scotland, from A D 203 to the end of the reign of James VI With appendix, containing the succession of bishops from the Reformation to 1676. Folio, with the portraits *London*, 1677.

Skinner's (Bp John) Ecclesiastical History of Scotland, from the first appearance of Christianity to the present time; and Annals of Scottish Episcopacy 3 vols 8vo *Lond* 1788–1818

Keith's (Robt) Catalogue of the Bishops of the several Sees in Scotland to 1688, corrected and continued to the present time, with life of the author, by Russell 8vo *Edin*. 1824.

Knoxe's (John) Histoire of the Reformatioun of Religioun in Scotland; [edited from the original MS in the University library of Glasgow, by T Ruddiman] Together with the life of Knoxe [by Matthew Crawford], glossary, and several curious pieces wrote by him, viz

    Lettre to the Ladie Marie Regent of Scotland, 1556, augmented in 1558.

    Appellation from the cruel and unjust sentence pronounced against him by the false bishoppes and clergie of Scotland; with his supplication to the estates, 1558.

    First Blast of the Trumpet against the monstrous regiment of women [1558]. Folio. *Edinburgh*, 1732

Calderwood's (David) True History of the Church of Scotland, from the beginning of the Reformation unto the end of James VI.'s reign. Folio *Printed* 1678

M'Crie's (Thomas) Life of John Knox, containing illustrations of the history of the Reformation in Scotland, with biographical notices of the principal Reformers, and sketches of the progress of literature in Scotland during the greater part of the 16th century 2 vols. 8vo. *Edinburgh* 1818

M'Crie's (Thomas) Life of Andrew Melville, containing illustrations of the ecclesiastical and literary history of Scotland during the latter part of the 16th and beginning of the 17th centuries. 2 vols 8vo. *Edinburgh*, 1824.

MODERN 269

Register of Ministers, Exhorters, and Readers, and of their stipends, after the period of the Reformation in Scotland [Edited by A M'Donald] 4to *Glasgow, privately printed,* 1830.

M'Crie's (Thos) Memoirs of Mr William Veitch and Mr. Geo. Brysson, written by themselves, with other narratives illustrative of the history of Scotland from the restoration to the revolution 8vo *Edin* 1828.

Wodrow's (Robert) History of the Sufferings of the Church of Scotland, from the Restoration to the Revolution, with an original memoir of the author, extracts from his correspondence, a preliminary dissertation and notes by Robert Burns, D.D. 4 vols 8vo. *Glasgow,* 1827.

Kirkton's (James) History of the Church of Scotland from the Restoration to the year 1678 To which is added, an account of the murder of Abp Sharp, by James Russell, an actor therein Edited from the MSS by C R Sharpe 4to large paper *Edin* 1817.

History of Ireland.

Topography, Antiquities, &c

Stanihurst's (R) Description of Ireland (Holinshed, Vol II.)

Spenser's (Edmund) View of the State of Ireland. (Works, Vol VIII)
This is stated in a memorial of one of Spenser's descendants, "to have moddled the settlement of Ireland."

Rich's (Barnabe) New Description of Ireland; wherein is described the disposition of the Irish whereunto they are inclined 4to *London,* 1610

Camden's Description of Ireland (Britannia, Vol III)

Carlisle's Topographical Dictionary of Ireland. (English Topography)

Wakefield's (E) Account of Ireland, statistical and political 2 vols 4to *London,* 1812.

Ledwich (E) on the Antiquities of Ireland 4to. *Dublin,* 1790

Grose's (F) Antiquities of Ireland 2 vols 4to *London,* 1791–7

Croker's (T C) Researches in the south of Ireland, illustrative of the scenery, architectural remains, and the manners and superstitions of the peasantry. 4to *London,* 1824

Edgecumb's (Sir R) Voyage into Ireland in 1488 (Harris's Hibernica)

Carr's (Sir John) Stranger in Ireland, or a tour in 1805. 4to. *Lond* 1806

Hoare's (Sir R C) Journal of a Tour in Ireland in 1806 8vo *Lond* 1807.

Bicheno's (E) Ireland and its Economy, being observations made in a tour in 1829 8vo. *London,* 1830

Ulster —Pynnar's Survey, and other Tracts relating to the plantations in Ulster (Harris's Hibernica)

Ulster —Conditions to be observed by the British Undertakers of the escheated lands in Ulster 4to *London,* 1610

Warburton (J.) and J Whitelaw's History of the City of Dublin, from the earliest accounts to the present time To which are added, biographical notices of eminent men, [continued and completed] by Robert Walsh. 2 vols 4to *Dublin,* 1818.

Wright's (G N) Historical Guide to ancient and modern Dublin 8vo Plates after drawings by Petrie *London,* 1821

Mason's (W M) History and Antiquities of the Collegiate and Cathedral Church of St Patrick, near Dublin from its foundation in 1190 to 1819, and biographical memoirs of its deans   4to large paper. *Dublin*, 1820

Smith's (Charles) ancient and present state of the County and City of Cork, of the County and City of Waterford, and of the County of Kerry, containing their natural and civil history   4 vols 8vo. *Dublin* 1774

Hamilton's (Wm) Letters concerning the Northern Coast of Antrim in Ireland, containing a natural history of its basaltes, with an account of the antiquities, manners, and customs of that country   8vo. *London*, 1790.

[Harris's (W)] ancient and present state of the County of Down.   8vo. *Dublin*, 1744

Sampson's (Geo Vaughan) Statistical Survey of the County of Londonderry.   8vo.   1802.

Phillips (Sir T) on the Plantations of the Londoners   (Hibernica.)

Tighe's (W) Statistical Observations relative to the County of Kilkenny.   8vo   *Dublin*, 1802.

Weld's (Isaac) Illustrations of the Scenery of Killarney and the surrounding country.   4to   *London*, 1807

Croker's (T C) Legends of the Lakes, or Sayings and Doings at Killarney.   2 vols. 18mo.   *London*, 1829

Letters from the Irish Highlands   12mo   *London*, 1825

Fairy Legends and Traditions of the South of Ireland.   3 vols. 12mo *London*, 1825-29

Walker's (John) Historical Essay on the Dress of the ancient and modern Irish; with a memoir on their armour and weapons.   4to *Dublin*, 1788.

Dewar's (Daniel) Observations on the Character, Customs, and Superstitions of the Irish, and on the causes which have retarded the moral and political improvement of Ireland   8vo   *London*, 1812

Newenham's (Thos) Historical Enquiry into the Progress and Magnitude of the Population of Ireland   8vo.   *London*, 1805

Newenham's (T) View of the Natural, Political, and Commercial Circumstances of Ireland.   4to   *London*, 1809.

Clarendon's (R V) Sketch of the Revenue and Finance of Ireland; with abstracts of the principal heads of receipt and expenditure, and the various supplies since the revolution   4to.   *London*, 1791.

Lawrence's (Rich.) Interests of Ireland in its Trade and Wealth stated   Both parts, small 8vo   *Dublin*, 1682

Swift's (Jonathan) Tracts relative to Ireland, including the Drapier's Letters   (Works, Vols VI. and VII)

Temple (Sir W) on the Advancement of Trade in Ireland   (Works, Vol III)

Narrative.

Harris (Walter) on the Defects of Histories of Ireland, and Remedies proposed for the amendment and reformation thereof   (Hibernica)

Nicholson's (Bp) Irish Historical Library, pointing out most of the authors and records which may be serviceable to the compilers of a general history of Ireland   (English History)

O'Reilly's (Ed) Chronological Account of nearly 400 Irish Writers down to 1750, with a descriptive catalogue of their works. 4to *Dublin*, 1820

Waræus (Jac) de Scriptoribus Hiberniæ   4to   *Dublini*, 1639

Webb's (Wm) Analysis of the History and Antiquities of Ireland prior to the fifth century, with a review of the general history of Celtic nations   8vo   *Dublin*, 1791

[Harris's (W)] Hibernica; or, some ancient pieces relating to Ireland   8vo   *Dublin*, 1770

Vallancy's (Ch) Collectanea de Rebus Hibernicis, or, collection of papers relative to Ireland, published from original MSS   6 vols 8vo   *Dublin*, 1770–1814

Campbell's (Thomas) Strictures on the Ecclesiastical and Literary History of Ireland, also, an historical sketch of the constitution and government. 8vo   *Dublin*, 1789.

Chronicles of Eri; being the history of the Gaal Sciat Iber, or Irish people translated from the original MS in the Phœnician dialect of the Scythian language, by Arthur O Connor. 2 vols 8vo   *Lond.* 1822

Rerum Hibernicarum Scriptores, edidit [cum Prolegomenis, &c] C. O'Connor. 4 vols 4to.   *Buckinghamiæ*, 1814–26

    Prolegomena &c   Annales IV Magistrorum ex ipso
    Annales Tigernachi   O'Clerii autographo
    Annales Inisfalenses.   Annales Ultonienses.
    Annales Buellianı.   Index Generalis

Keating's (Geoffry) General History of Ireland, translated from the original Irish, with many curious amendments by Dermod O'Connor Second edition, with an appendix by Anthony Raymond, explanatory of the ancient names of mountains, places, &c   Folio   *London*, 1723, *and Westminster*, 1726.

Keating's (G) General History of Ireland; a new and correct translation as far as the Christian era, with the original Irish on opposite pages, by William Halliday   8vo   *Dublin*, 1811

Regan's (Maurice) History of Ireland from 1167 to 1173, translated from the Irish into French, and thence into English, by Sir George Carew   (Harris's Hibernica)

O'Flaherty's (R) Ogygia, or, a chronological account of Irish events, translated by J Kely   2 vols 8vo   *Dublin*, 1793

Gualdus Cambrensis' History of Ireland, by John Hooker, and the Chronicles of Ireland, compiled by P Flatsburie, &c in continuation of Gualdus to 1587   (Holinshed's Chron Vols II and VI)

History of Ireland to 1691   (Mod Univ. History, Vol XLI)

Burton's (Richard) History of Ireland, from the conquest of that nation by Henry II to the time of William III. 4to   *Westminster*, 1811.

Leland's (Thomas) History of Ireland from the invasion of Henry II to William III, with a preliminary discourse on the ancient state of that kingdom   3 vols 4to   *London*, 1773

Plowden's (Francis) Historical Review of the state of Ireland from the invasion by Henry II to its union with Great Britain in 1801 2 vols. in 3. 4to. *London*, 1803.

Gordon's (Jas) History of Ireland to the Union in 1801. 2 vols 8vo *London*, 1806.

Finglass's (Pat) Breviate of the Getting of Ireland, and of the Decaie of the same. (Harris's Hibernica.)

Story of King Richard II., his last being in Ireland, translated by George Carew Earl of Totness (Harris's Hibernica)

Waræi (Jac) Rerum Hibernicarum Annales, regnantibus Hen. VII Hen VIII Edwardo VI et Maria. Folio *Dublin* 1664.

Musgrave's (Sir Rich.) Memoirs of the different Rebellions in Ireland, from the arrival of the English; also, a particular detail of that which broke out 23d May, 1798, with the history of the conspiracy which preceded it 2 vols 8vo. *Dublin*, 1802

History of Sir John Perrot; containing an account of the Rebellion of Fitzmoriis in 1572, of the remarkable attainder of Viscount Baltinglass and his four brothers in 1586, and of Sir J. Perrot's government to 1588, now published from the original MS [by Ri. Rawlinson] 8vo *London*, 1728.

[E C S], the Government of Ireland under Sir John Peirot, Knight beginning 1584 and ending 1588 ; being the first booke of the continuation of the historie of that kingdome, formerly set forth to the year 1584, and now continued to this present. 4to *London*, 1626.

Stafford's (Sir Thomas) Pacata Hibernia Ireland appeased and reduced ; or, an historie of the late warres of Ireland, especially within the province of Mounster, under the government of Sir George Carew Folio *London*, 1633.

<small>With a contemporary MS. list of the privy council, April 7, 1596, and of all the nobility, spiritual and temporal, according to their rank, who sat in Parliament April 26, 1585, or the last of Elizabeth's reign, inserted</small>

Morysine's (F) History of Ireland from 1599 to 1603. (Itinerary.)

G[ainsforde's] (T[hos]) True, Exemplary, and Remarkable History of the Earle of Tirone, wherein the manner of his first presumption, and the means of his ensuing rejection is truly related 4to. *Lond* 1619

[Davies' (Sir John)] Discoverie of the true Causes why Ireland was never entirely subdued, nor brought under obedience of the crown of England, until the beginning of his Maiestie's happie raigne. 4to [*London*] 1612.

[Borlace's (Edmund)] History of the execrable Irish Rebellion in 1641, to the Act of Settlement in 1662. Folio *Lond* 1680.

Temple's (Sir John) Memoirs of the Rebellion in Ireland, 1641. 4to. *London*, 1646.

Memoirs of James Touchet, Earl of Castlehaven, his engagement and carriage in the Wars of Ireland, from 1642–51; written by himself. 8vo *Dublin*, 1815.

History of James Duke of Ormonde, containing a history of Ireland under his government. (English Hist Charles II.)

Story's (Geo.) Impartial History of the Wars of Ireland, 1689–92. 4to. *London*, 1693

Macartney's (Sir Geo) Account of Ireland in 1773 (Life)

Gordon's (James) History of the Rebellion in Ireland in 1798, &c. containing an account of the proceedings of the Irish revolutionists from 1782 to the suppression of the rebellion 8vo *London*, 1803.

Adams' (Jane) Private Narrative of the Rebellion in Ireland of 1798, &c. (Croker's South of Ireland.)

Life of Theobald Wolfe Tone, founder of the United Irish Society; with a complete diary of his negotiations for the liberation of Ireland, of the expeditions of Bantry Bay, the Texel, &c written by himself, and edited by his son 2 vols 8vo *London*, 1827.

Curran's (J P) Speeches on the late interesting State Trials in Ireland. 8vo. *Dublin*, 1808

Hardy's (Thos) Memoirs of the Political and Private Life of the Earl of Charlemont 4to. *Lond*. 1810.

Barrington's (Sir Jonah) original Sketches of his own Times 3 vols. 8vo. *London*, 1827-32.

Barrington's (Sir Jonah) Historic Anecdotes and Secret Memoirs relative to the Legislative Union between Great Britain and Ireland. 4to. *London*, 1809-15

Bacon's (Lord) Tracts relating to Ireland (Works, Vol. V.)

Two Treatises concerning Ireland, setting forth how and by what means the Laws and Statutes of England came to be in force in Ireland; by Sir R Bolton and Sir Sam Mayart. (Harris's Hibernica)

[Lodge's (J)] Desiderata Curiosa Hibernica, or, a select Collection of State Papers consisting of royal instructions, directions, despatches, and letters To which are added, some historical tracts The whole illustrating the political system of the chief governors and government of Ireland during the reigns of Elizabeth, James, and Charles I. 2 vols 8vo *Dublin*, 1772

Ecclesiastical History of Ireland

Lanigan's (John) Ecclesiastical History of Ireland, from the first introduction of Christianity, to the beginning of the 13th century 4 vols 8vo. *Dublin*, 1822.

Archdall's (Mervyn) Monasticon Hibernicum, or, an history of the abbies, priories, and other religious houses in Ireland 4to *Dublin*, 1786.

General History of Northern Nations.

Mallet's (M. P. H.) Northern Antiquities, or, a Description of the ancient Danes, and other northern nations, including those of our own Saxon ancestors with a translation of the Edda, &c. from the ancient Icelandic tongue Translated from the French [by John Calder], with additional notes [by Thos Percy, Bp of Dromore]. 2 vols 8vo. *London*, 1770

Illustrations of Northern Antiquities, from the earlier Teutonic and Scandinavian Romances, being an Abstract of the Book of Heroes and Nivelungen Lay, with translations of metrical tales, notes and dissertations [by H. Weber, J Jamieson, and Sir Walter Scott] 4to *Edinb*. 1814

Magno (Olao) Historia delle Genti et della Natura della Cose Settentrionali, tradotta in lingua Toscana. Folio *Vinegia, appresso 'i Giunti*, 1565

Snorronis Sturlonidis Historiæ Regum Septentrionalium ante sæculo V patrio sermone antiquo conscriptæ ex MSS. edidit notisque illustravit J Peringskiold Folio *Stockholmiæ*, 1697

Grotii (Hugonis) Historia Gothorum, Vandalorum, et Longobardorum 8vo *Amst* 1655

Gothicarum et Longobardicarum Rerum Scriptores aliquot veteres, ex Bib Bon Vulcanii et aliorum Small 8vo *Lugd Bat* 1618.

Prætorii (M) Orbis Gothicus , id est, Historica Nairatio omnium ferè Gothici nominis Populorum Four parts in one vol folio *Typis Monast Olimensis*, 1688–9

Prætorii (M) Mars Gothicus, exhibens veterum Gothorum militiam, potentiam, &c. Folio. *Typis Monast. Oliviensis*, 1691.

Krantzius (Al) de Wandalorum verâ Origine, variis Gentibus, crebris è patriâ Migrationibus, Regnis item quorum vel autores vel eversores fueiunt. Folio *Hanoviæ*, 1619

Schilten (Jo) Thesaurus Antiquitatum Teutonicarum ecclesiasticarum, civilium, et literarium. 3 vols. folio *Ulmæ*, 1728

History of several Northern Nations (Mod. Un. Hist Vol XVII)

Catteau-Calleville (J P), Tableau de la Mer Baltique, considérée sous les rapports physiques, géographiques, historiques, &c 2 vols 8vo *Paris*, 1812.

Denmark and Norway, including Greenland and Iceland.

Scriptores Rerum Danicarum medii ævi, partim hactenùs inediti, partim emendatiùs editi, J Langebek et P F. Suhm 8 vols. folio, fine papei. *Hafniæ*, 1772–92.

Saxonis Grammatici Danorum Regum Heroumque Historia, abhinc supra trecentos annos conscripta, et nunc primùm literariâ serie illustrata [edidit Christiernus Petrus] Folio Editio princeps *Parrhisorum, J B Ascensius*, M D XIIII

Saxonis Grammatici Historia Danica , summo studio notisque et prolegomenis illustravit S. J Stephanius Folio, fine paper. *Soræ*, 1644–5

Wormii (Olais) Danica Monumenta è spissis antiquitatum tenebris et in Daniâ ac Norvegiâ extantibus ruderibus eruta. Folio *Hafniæ*, 1643

Wormii (O) Regum Daniæ Series, duplex descriptio, ex vet legum Sanicanicarum literis Runicis in membr exarato codice eruta, et notis illustrata Folio *Hafniæ* 1652

Wheaton's (Henry) History of the Northmen, or Danes and Normans, from the earliest times to the conquest of England by William I 8vo *London*, 1831

History of Denmark. (Mod Un. Hist Vols. XXVIII , XXIX , and XXXVII)

Malling (Ove), Recueil de Traits mémorables, tirés de l'Histoire de Danemarc, de Norvège, et de Holstein, trad du Danois par F. M. Maurier. 8vo. *Copenhague*, 1794

MODERN.

[Molesworth's (Lord)] Account of Denmark as it was in 1692;—Account of Sweden in 1688, with several pieces relating thereto. 8vo. *London*, 1738.

Andrews' (John) History of the Revolutions of Denmark; with an Appendix of remarks on the laws and internal government. 2 vols. 8vo *London*, 1784.

Hellfried's (C F) Outlines of a Political Survey of the English Attack on Denmark in 1807; translated from the Danish   8vo. *London*, 1809

Randulphi (Env. N) Tuba Danica; hoc est, de aureo Cornu in Cimbriâ invento Small folio. *Hauniæ*, 1644

Snorrii Sturlæ Filii Historia Regum Norvegiæ, Islandicè, Danicè, et Latinè. 5 vols folio. *Hauniæ*, 1777–1818

Sturlson's (Snorro) Anecdotes of Olave, the Black King of Man, and the Hebridean Princes of the Somerlad family, with XVIII Eulogies on Haco, King of Norway. Islandic and English, with notes by James Johnstone   Small 8vo   [*Copenhagen*], 1780

Torfæi (Thor) Groenlandia antiqua   Small 8vo   *Hauniæ*, 1706.

Crantz's (David) History of Greenland; translated. 2 vols 8vo *London*, 1767

Ilands Landnambok; hoc est, Liber Originum Islandiæ, Is et Lat; lectionibus variantibus et indicibus illustratus J. Finnæus. 4to. *Hauniæ*, 1774

Ionæ (Aing) Crymogœa, sive, Rerum Islandicarum Libri III   4to. *Hamburgi*, 1610

Rymbegla, sive, Rudimentum Computi ecclesiastici et Annales veterum Islandorum, Isl et Lat; lect var, notis, et indice Steph Biornonis   Addita sunt Talbyrdingus ejusdem, notis illustratus;—Oddi Astronomi Somnia,—et Jo Arnæ et Finni Johannæi Horologia   4to *Sumptibus illust P Fr Suhm, Hauniæ*, 1780

 "Ex donatione illust Suhmii habet Wilhelmus Ernestus Christiani"

Henderson on the History, Antiquities, &c of Iceland   (Travels)

Landt's (Geo) Description of the Feroe Islands, their climate and productions, the manners. &c of the inhabitants   8vo *London*, 1810

History of Sweden, including Lapland.

Scriptores Rerum Suecicarum medii ævi, edidit E M Fant   3 vols. folio *Holmiæ et Upsaliæ*, 1818

History of Sweden   (Mod Un Hist Vols XXIX, XXX, and XXXVII)

Archenholz, Histoire de Gustave Wasa, traduit de l'Allemande par Propiac   2 vols. 8vo   *Paris*, 1803.

Harte's (W) History of the Life of Gustavus Adolphus, surnamed the Great   2 vols 8vo   *London*, 1763

Catteau-Calleville (J P), Histoire de Christine, Reine de Suède, avec un précis historique de la Suède depuis les anciens tems jusqu'à la mort de Gustave Adolphe   2 vols 8vo   *Paris*, 1815

Voltaire (M de), Histoire de Charles XII, Roi de Suède, avec les remarques de M de la Mottraye, et les reponses de M de Voltaire   2 vols 12mo   *Amst.* 1733.

Vertot (l'Abbé), Histoire des Revolutions de Suède 2 vols 12mo. *Paris*, 1722.

Leemius (Canutus) de Lappombus Finmarchiæ, earumque Linguâ, Vitâ, et Religione pristinâ, cum Notis J. E Gunneri, et E J Jessen de Finnorum Lapponumque Norvegiæ Religione paganâ. Dan et Lat. 4to. plates. *Kiopenhagé*, 1767

Scheffer's History of Lapland. (Travels)

History of Russia.

Muscoviticarum Rerum Scriptores unum in corpus congesti, quibus et gentis historia continetur et regionum accurata descriptio   Folio. *Francofurti*, 1600.

Milton's (John) Brief History of Muscovia, and other less known countries lying eastward of Russia, towards Cathay (Prose Works, 4to Vol I.; 8vo Vol IV.)

Karamsin, Histoire de l'Empire de Russie, traduit de Russe par St. Thomas et Jauffret. 11 vols. 8vo. *Paris*, 1820-26

Lévesque (Pierre Charles), Histoire de Russie, jusqu'à la mort de l'Impératrice Catherine II   8 vols. 8vo. *Hambourg*, 1800.

History of Russia. (Mod Un Hist Vols XXXI XXXII , XXXVII)

History of Great Tartary and Asiatic Russia. (Mod. Univer. Hist. Vol. XXXVII)

Tooke's (Wm) History of Russia, from the foundation of the monarchy to the accession of Catherine II   2 vols. 8vo   *London*, 1800.

Segur's (Count P) History of Russia under Peter the Great. 8vo *London*, 1829.

Whitworth's (Charles Lord) Account of Russia as it was in 1710   8vo. *Strawberry Hill*, 1758.

Rulhière (M de), Histoire, ou Anecdotes sur la Révolution de Russie en l'an 1762   8vo   *Paris*, 1797

> MS. "Note du lecteur   Une personne principale de Russie, dont la famille a joué un grand rôle dans cette revolution, assure, qu'excepté le fait du détrônement et de la mort violente de Pierre III, il n'y a dans l'histoire composée par M de Rulhiere que faussetés, erreurs, et alterations de circonstances "   The margins are filled with MS. remarks in the same hand

Tooke's (W) History of the Russian Empire during the reign of Catherine II , and to the close of the present century   3 vols 8vo *London*, 1799.

Potemkin (Memoirs of Prince), comprehending Anecdotes of Catherine II. and of the Russian Court. 8vo   *London*, 1812

Porter's (Sir R K.) Narrative of the Campaigns in Russia in 1812. 4to. *London*, 1813

Labaume's (Eugene) Circumstantial Narrative of the Campaign in Russia under Napoleon in 1812. 8vo   *London*, 1814.

Segur's (Philip de) History of the Expedition to Russia, undertaken by the Emperor Napoleon in the year 1812. 2 vols 8vo. *Lond* 1825.

Heber's (Bp Reg) History of the Cossacks   (Life, Vol I)

Wilson's (Sir Robert) Remarks on the Character and Composition of the Russian Army, and a Sketch of the Russian Campaign in Poland in 1806-7. 4to. *London*, 1810.

History of Poland.

Dlugłossi (Jo) seu Longini Historiæ Polonicæ Libri XII ; accedunt liber XIII. et alii libri rarissimi, cum præfatione et continuatione Got Krause. 4 vols. in 2, folio. *Francof* 1711.

Saliguac (P. J de la) Histoire Générale de Pologne 6 vols. 12mo. *Paris*, 1750.

History of Poland. (Mod. Univ. Hist. Vols. XXX., XXXI., XXXVII.)

Letters Patent for the Election of John III. King of Poland, May 22, 1674 (Milton's Prose Works, 4to Vol II ; 8vo Vol IV)

Coyer (l'Abbé), Histoire de J Sobieski, Roi de Pologne 3 vols. 12mo. *Paris*, 1761.

Rulhière, Histoire de l'Anarchie de Pologne et des Démembrements de cette République; avec la suite par Ferrand 7 vols. 8vo. *Paris*, 1819-20.

Oginski, Mémoires sur la Pologne et les Polonois depuis 1788 jusqu'à la fin de 1815 5 vols. 8vo *Paris*, 1826

History of Germany.

Tacitus de Situ, Moribus, et Populis Germanorum. (Classics)

Schoettgenii (Ch) et Kreisigii Diplomataria et Scriptores Historiæ Germaniæ medii ævi. 3 vols folio. *Altenberg* 1753–60

Struvii (B. G.) Corpus Historiæ Germanicæ; præmittitur C G. Buderi Bibliotheca Scriptorum rerum Germanicarum. 2 vols 4to *Jenæ*, 1753

Krantzii (Alberti) Rerum Germanicarum Historici de Saxonicæ Gentis vetustâ origine, longinquis expeditionibus susceptis, et bellis domi pro libertate diù fortiterque gestis , cum præfatione Nic Cisneri. Folio. *Franc* 1621.

History of Germany and of the German Empire (Mod Univ. Hist. Vols. XVII., XXV , XXVI , XXVII , XXXII , and XXXVII)

Butler's (Charles) History of the Geographical and Political Revolutions of the Empire of Germany. (General History of Europe)

Coxe's (Wm.) History of the House of Austria, from the foundation of the monarchy by Rhodolph, 1218, to the death of Leopold the Second, 1792 3 vols 4to *London*, 1807

Ascham's (Roger) Report and Discourse of the Affairs and State of Germany, and the Emperor Charles his court, during certain years while the said Roger was there (Works)

Robertson's (William) History of the Reign of the Emperor Charles V , with a view of the progress of society in Europe to the 16th century 3 vols 4to *London*, 1813

Schiller (Fr), Histoire de la Guerre de Trente Ans, traduit de l'Allemande [par M. Chaufeux] 2 vols 8vo *Paris*, 1803.

The Invasions of Germanie , with all the civill and bloody warres therein, since the first beginning of them in 1618, and continued to this present yeare 1638. With the pictures of the commanders on both sides. Small 8vo. *London*, 1638

A true and brief Relation of the bloudy Battle fought foure dayes and foure nights together betweene Duke Bernard von Wimeren, victour, and the Imperial Generalls, who were utterly overthroune Small 8vo. *London*, 1638.

Eugene of Savoy (Memoirs of Prince), written by himself, translated from the French 8vo. *Lond.* 1811

Retzow, Mémoires Historiques sur la Guerre de Sept Ans. 2 vols. 8vo *Paris*, 1803

Stael (Mad de), de l'Allemagne. 3 vols 8vo. *London*, 1813

History of the Archduchy of Austria. (Mod Univ Hist Vol XXXII)

Pray (Geo.) Historia Regum Hungariæ, cum notitiis præviis ad cognoscendum veterem regni statum pertinentibus. 3 vols. 8vo *Budæ*, 1801.

History of Hungary. (Mod. Univ. Hist. Vols XXXII. and XXXVII.)

History of Bohemia. (Mod. Univ Hist. Vol. XXXII.)

Benger's (Miss) Memoirs of Elizabeth Stuart, Queen of Bohemia, including sketches of the state of society in Holland and Germany in the 17th century. 2 vols. 8vo. *London*, 1825.

Gibbon's (E) Antiquities of the House of Brunswick. (Misc Works, Vol. II)

History of Prussia. (Mod Univ. Hist Vol XXXI)

[Mirabeau (M. le Comte)], Histoire secrette de la Cour de Berlin, ou, correspondance d'un voyageur François, depuis le 5me Juillet, 1786, jusqu'au 19me Janvier, 1787 Avec l'essai sur la secte des Illuminés [par M. le Marquis de Luchet]. 3 vols in one, 8vo *Paris (Alençon)*, 1789

Thebault's (Dieud) Original Anecdotes of Frederick II King of Prussia, and of his Family, his Court, his Ministers, his Academies, and his Literary Friends. Translated from the French 2 vols 8vo *Lond.* 1805

Segur's (L P) History of the principal Events of the Reign of Frederick II. King of Prussia 3 vols 8vo *London*, 1807

Dover's (Lord) Life of Frederick II King of Prussia 2 vols 8vo. *London*, 1831.

Wraxall's (N W) Memoirs of the Courts of Berlin, Dresden, Warsaw, and Vienna, in 1777, 78, and 79 2 vols. 8vo *London*, 1800.

History of the Electorates Palatine of Saxony, Hanover, Brandenburg, and of the Duchy of Mecklenberg. (Mod Univ. Hist Vols. XXXII. and XXXIII)

History of the Low Countries.

Grotii (Hugonis) Annales et Historia de Rebus Belgicis Folio *Amst* 1657.

Démez, Histoire Générale de la Belgique, depuis la Conquête de César 7 vols. 8vo *Bruxelles*, 1807

Grimestone's (Ed) General History of the Netherlands to 1608, [translated from J F Petit's Chronique d'Hollande, and continued]. Folio *London*, 1609

History of the Austrian, French, and United Netherlands, and of the Republic of Holland. (Mod Univ Hist Vols XXXVII XXXVIII.)

Lothian's (Wm) History of the United Provinces of the Netherlands, from the death of Philip II to the truce made with Albert and Isabella 8vo *Dublin*, 1780.

Stradæ (Fam) de Bello Belgico, ab 1555 ad 1589, Decades duæ. 2 vols folio Editio princeps *Romæ*, 1640-47

Dondini (Guil) Historia de Rebus in Galliâ gestis ab Alex Farnesio Parmæ Duce III Folio *Romæ*, 1673

Gallucii (Aug) de Bello Belgico, ab anno 1593 ad annum 1609, Partes duæ 2 vols folio *Romæ*, 1671.

Vere's (Sir Francis) Commentaries; being diverse pieces of service wherein he had command in the Low Countries, and containing a continuation of the Siege of Ostend. Published by W Dillingham. Folio *Cambr* 1657

Burton's (W) History of the House of Orange ; or, a Relation of the Achievements of his Majesty's renowned predecessors, and likewise of his own heroic actions till the late Revolution (1688) 4to. *London*, 1814.

A Justification or Cleering of the Prince of Orendge agaynst the false Sclaunders wherewith his Ilwillers goe about to charge him wrongfully; translated out of French by Ar Goldyng Small 8vo. 𝔟𝔩𝔞𝔠𝔨 𝔩𝔢𝔱𝔱𝔢𝔯. *London, by John Day*, 1575

[Howell's (James)] Brief Character of the Low Countries under the States , being three weeks' observations of the vices and virtues of the inhabitants Small 12mo. *Lond* 1659

Temple's (Sir W) Observations upon the United Provinces of the Netherlands. (Works, Vol I.)

Bonaparte's (Louis, ex-King of Holland) Historical Documents, and Reflections on the Government of Holland from 1806 to 1813. 3 vols 8vo *London*, 1820.

History of France.

Le Long (J.), Bibliothèque Historique de la France, contenant le catalogue des ouvrages imprimés et manuscrits qui traitent de l'histoire de ce royaume, avec des notes critiques et historiques Considérablement augmentée [par F de Fontette, L T et A P Hérissant, Rondet, Camus, B de la Bruyère, Coquereau, &c] 5 vols folio, the Le Tellier copy *Paris*, 1768-78

History of the Ancient State and History of Gaul (An Univ Hist. Vol XVI)

History of France (Mod Un. Hist Vols XIX —XXI , and XXXVII)

Gilles (Nicole), les Chroniques et Annales de France, depuis la Destruction de Troye jusqu'au Roy Louis IX, par Denis Sauvage. 2 vols in one, folio *Paris*, 1566

Belle-Forest (Fr. de), les Grandes Annales et Histoire Générale de France, dès la Venue des Francs en Gaule jusqu'au Règne du Roy Henri III 2 vols. folio *Paris*, 1579

Mezeray (Fr. Eudes de), Histoire de France depuis Faramond jusqu'au règne de Louis le Juste, enrichie de plusieurs belles et rares antiquités, de la vie des reines, et d un recueil des médailles qui ont été fabriquées sous chaque règne; et augmentée d'un volume de l'origine des Français 3 vols folio, large paper. *Paris*, 1685

Sismondi (J. C. L Sismonde de), Histoire des François jusqu'à 1514. 15 vols 8vo. *Paris*, 1821–31.

Gifford's (John) [John Richard Green] History of France, from the earliest times to the present important era From the French of Velly, Villaret, Garnier, Mezeray, Daniel, &c 5 vols. 4to *Lond* 1791–95

Chambre, Histoire Abrégée de tous les Roys de France, &c. Small 8vo *Paris*, 1579.

Recueil des Historiens des Gaules et de la France, accompagné des sommaires, des tables, et des notes, par DD. M Bouquet, J B et Ch Haudiquier, Haussean, J Precieux, Poirier, Fr Clement, M J Brial, et Druon, religieux Bénédictins. 18 vols. folio. *Paris*, 1738–1822

Contenant

Tome I Tout ce qui a été fait par les Gaulois, et qui s'est passé dans les Gaules, avant l arrivée des François, et plusieurs autres choses qui regardent les François depuis leur origine jusqu'à Clovis

Tome II et III. Ce qui s'est passé dans les Gaules, et ce que les François ont fait sous les rois de la première race.

Tome IV. Les lettres historiques, les loix, les formules, les diplomes, et plusieurs autres monumens, qui concernent les Gaules et la France sous les rois de la premiere race.

Tome V. Ce qui s'est passé sous les règnes de Pepin et de Charlemagne, c'est-à-dire, depuis l'an DCCLII jusques à l'an DCCCXIV.

Tome VI. Les gestes de Louis le Débonnaire, d'abord roi d'Aquitaine, et ensuite empereur, depuis l'an DCCLXXXI jusques à l an DCCCXL, avec les lois, les ordonnances, et les diplomes de ce prince, et autres monumens historiques.

Tome VII. Les gestes des fils et des petit-fils de Louis le Debonnaire, depuis l'an DCCCXL jusques à l'an DCCCLXXVII, avec les capitulaires de Charles le Chauve, et autres monumens historiques, les diplomes étant rejettés dans le volume suivant

Tome VIII Ce qui s'est passé depuis le commencement du règne de Louis le Bégue, fils de Charles le Chauve, jusqu'à la fin du règne de Louis V, dernier roi de la seconde race, c'est-à-dire, depuis l'an DCCCLXXVII jusqu à l'an DCCCCLXXXVII Avec les diplomes des fils et des petits-fils de Louis le Debonnaire, qui n'ont pu entrer dans le volume précédent.

Tome IX Ce qui restoit à publier des monumens de la seconde race des rois de France, depuis le commencement du règne de Louis le Bégue, fils de Charles le Chauve, jusqu'aux premières années du règne de Hugues Capet, chef de la troisième race, c'est-à-dire, depuis l'an DCCCLXXVII jusqu'à l'an DCCCCXCI.

Tome X. Surtout ce qui s'est passé depuis le commencement du regne de Hugues Capet jusqu'à celui du roi Henry I, fils de Robert le Pieux

Tome XI. Principalement ce qui s'est passé sous le règne de Henri Premier, fils du roi Robert le Pieux, c'est-à-dire, depuis l'an MXXXI jusqu'à l'an MLX.

Tome XII. Une partie de ce qui s'est passé sous les trois règnes de Philippe I, de Louis VI dit le Gros, et de Louis VII surnommé le Jeune, depuis l an MLX jusqu'en MCLXXX

Tome XIII. La suite des monumens de trois règnes de Philippe I, de Louis VI dit le Gros, et de Louis VII surnomme le Jeune, depuis l'an MLX jusqu'en MCLXXX.

Tome XIV-XVI. La suite des monumens des trois règnes de Philippe I, de Louis VI dit le Gros, et de Louis VII, depuis l an MLX jusqu'en MCLXXX

Tome XVII. Les monumens des règnes de Philippe Auguste et de Louis VIII, depuis l'an MCLXXX jusqu'en MCCXXVI.

Saint-Simon, Histoire des Révolutions du Gouvernement de la France. (Œuvres, Vol XIII.)

Froissart (Jehan), Histoire et Chronique [de France, d'Angleterre, d'Ecosse, d'Espaigne, de Bretaigne, &c. depuis 1326 jusqu'à 1400], revue et corrigée par Denis Sauvage 4 vols. in two. Folio. *Lyon, par Jan de Tournes,* 1559-61.

Froissart's (J.) Chronicles, translated at the command of King Henry VIII. by John Bourchier, Lord Berners; reprinted from Pynson's edition, with the names of places and persons carefully corrected, and a memoir of the author by E. V. Utterson 2 vols 4to *London,* 1811

Froissart's (J) Chronicles, newly translated from the best French editions; with variations and additions from many celebrated MSS and memoirs of the author, by Thomas Johnes 5 vols. 4to *Hafod,* 1803-10.

Monstrelet (Eng), Chroniques · histoire de bel exemple et de grand fruict aux François, commençant en l an M CCCC, où finist celle de Jean Froissart, et finissant en l'an M.CCCC LXVII, peu outre le commencement de celle de M Philippe de Commines · revue et corrigée, &c 3 vols in one, folio. *Paris, P. Mettayer,* 1595

Monstrelet's (E) Chronicles, beginning at the year 1400, where that of Sir John Froissart finishes, and ending at the year 1467 ; continued by others to the year 1516 : translated by Thos. Johnes. 5 vols. 4to *Hafod,* 1809.

Fabyan's (Robert) New Chronicles of England and France (English History)

James's (G P. R) History of Charlemagne. 8vo. *London,* 1831

Gervaise, Histoire de Suger, Abbé de Saint Denis, Ministre d'Etat 3 vols 12mo. *Paris,* 1721

Joinville (Jean, Seigneur de), l'Histoire et Cronique du Roy S. Loys, IX du nom, et XLIII Roy de France, maintenant mise en lumière par Antoine Pierre de Rieus. 4to. [8vo] *Poitiers,* 1561.

Joinville —Memoirs of John, Lord de Joinville, written by himself; containing a history of part of the life of Louis IX , surnamed Saint Louis, including an account of that king's expedition to Egypt in 1248, with the notes and dissertations of M. Ducange ; together with the dissertations of M le Baron de Bastie on the life of Saint Louis, M l'Evesque de la Ravalière, and M Falconet on the assasins of Syria The whole translated by Thomas Johnes 2 vols 4to *Hafod,* 1807.

Wraxall's (Sir N W) Memoirs of the Kings of France of the race of Valois 2 vols 8vo *London,* 1807

Memoirs of Jeanne d'Arc, surnamed la Pucelle d'Orléans, with the history of her times [translated from original MSS , with notes, introductory matter, &c by W H. Ireland] 2 vols. royal 8vo, large paper. *London,* 1824

Commines (Phil de), Mémoires sur les principaux Faicts et Gestes de Louis XI et Charles VIII; revues, &c. par Denis Sauvage de Fontenailles. Folio *Paris, G Du Pré,* 1561.

Life and Times of Francis I of France 2 vols 8vo *Lond.* 1829

Bayard —The light joyous and pleasant History of the Feats, Gests, and Prowesses of the Chevalier Bayard, the good knight without fear and without reproach; by the Loyal Servant. 2 vols. 8vo. *London,* 1825.

[Stephens's (Henry)] Mervelous Discourse upon the Lyfe, Dedes, and Behaviours of Katherine de Medicis, Quene Mother; wherein are displayed the meanes which she hath practised to attayne unto the usurping of the kingedome of France, and to bringing of the estate of the same unto utter ruine and destruction Small 8vo. *Heydelberge,* 1575

Thuani Historia sui temporis (History of Europe)

Hôpital (an Essay on the Life of Michael de l') Chancellor of France; by Charles Butler. 8vo. *London,* 1814.

Castlenau (Mic. de), Sr de Mauvissière, Mémoires, illustrées et augmentées par J de Laboureur. 3 vols folio. *Bruxelles,* 1731.

Varamund [Fr. Hotman] de Furoribus Gallicis, horrendâ et indignâ Amirallii Castillionei, nobilium atque illustrium virorum, cæde, scelerata ac inauditâ piorum strage, passim edita per complures Galliæ civitates, sine ullo discrimine generis, sexûs, ætatis, et conditionis hominum, vera et simplex Narratio. 4to *Edimburgi, anno* 1573.

[Goulart (Simon)], Recueil, contenant les choses plus mémorables advenues sous la Ligue 5 vols. 12mo ———, 1590–99

Maimbourg's History of the League, Book III., translated by Dryden. (Dryden's Works, Vol. XVII)

Davila (E C), Storia delle Guerre Civili di Francia dopo l' anno 1550 al 1598. 6 vols. 8vo. *Milano,* 1807

Mémoires et Correspondances de Phil. de Mornay, Sieur Duplessis, pour servir à l'histoire des guerres civiles et religieuses en France, sous les règnes de Charles IX, Henri III et IV, et de Louis XIII. 12 vols 8vo *Paris,* 1824.

Wraxall's (N W) History of France, from the accession of Henry III. to the death of Louis XIV. 3 vols 4to *London,* 1795

HENRY IV.

Péréfixe (H de), Histoire du Roy Henri le Grand. 8vo. *Paris, Renuard,* 1816.

Henry IV.—Correspondance de Henri le Grand avec Jean Roussat, Maire de Langres, rélative aux événemens qui ont précéde et suivi son avénement au trône, publiée par MM Guyot de St Michel et de Verseilles *Paris,* 1816.

Sully —Mémoires des sages et royales Economies d'Estat, domestiques, politiques, et militaires, de Henry le Grand [1570 à 1628]; et des servitudes utiles, obéissances convenables, et administrations loyales, de Maximilian de Bethune. 4 vols. in two, folio. *Amstelredam,* [*Château de Sully*], 1638, *et Paris,* 1662

The two last volumes were edited by Laboureur.

Sully —The Memoirs of the Duke of Sully, Prime Minister of Henry the Great, translated from the French by Charlotte Lennox: a new edition, revised and corrected, with additional notes, some letters of Henry IV. and a brief historical introduction. 5 vols. royal 8vo *London*, 1810.

Satyre Menippée de la Vertu du Catholicon d'Espagne [par Le Roy, Gillot, Passerat, Rapin, Florent-Chrétien, et Pithou], augmentée des notes tirées des éditions de Dupuy et Le Duchat, par Verger, et d'un commentaire historique, littéraire, et philologique, par C. Nodier. 2 vols 8vo. papier vélin. *Paris*, 1824.

Jeannin (les Négotiations de M. le Président). 4 vols. 18mo *Jouxte la copie de Paris [par les Elzevirs]*, 1659.

LOUIS XIII

Le Vasor (Michel), Histoire du Règne de Louis XIII 10 vols in 25, 12mo *Amsterdam*, 1700

[Evelyn's (John)] State of France, as it stood in the ninth year of this present monarch, Lewis XIII. (Misc. Works.)

[Arconville (Madame d')] Vie de Marie de Médicis, Princesse de Toscane, Reine de France et de Navarre. 3 vols 8vo. *Paris*, 1774

Matthieu (De), l'Entrée de la Princesse Marie de Médicis, Royne de France et de Navarre, en la ville de Lyon; avec l'histoire de l'origine et progrès de l'illust maison de Médicis Small 8vo. *Rouen*, 1601.

Bassompierre (Mémoires du Maréchal de), contenant l'histoire de sa vie, et de ce qui s'est fait de plus remarquable à la cour de la France pendant quelques années. 4 vols. 18mo. *Amsterdam*, 1723.

Aubery (Ant), Histoire du Cardinal de Richelieu; avec les mémoires pour l'histoire du Cardinal. 3 vols 12mo *Cologne [Elzevir]*, 1666-7

La Vie du véritable Père Josef, Capucin nommé au Cardinalat, contenant l'histoire anecdotique du Cardinal de Richelieu Small 8vo *Haye*, 1705

Motteville (Madame de), Mémoires pour servir à l'histoire d'Anne d'Autriche, épouse de Louis XIII 6 vols 12mo. *Maestricht*, 1782

LOUIS XIV.

Voltaire's Age of Louis XIV, translated 2 vols. 8vo *London*, 1752.

Louis XIV, ses Œuvres, accompagnées d'explications historiques, de notes, &c par Grouvelle et Grimoard 6 vols. 8vo. *Paris*, 1806

    Vol I Considerations sur sa vie et ses écrits par Grouvelle, et une chirographie ou copie figurée de l'écriture originale des hommes illustres qui ont été le plus marqué sous son règne, par le General Grimoard

    Vol I-IV Mémoires historiques, politiques, et militaires, depuis l'année 1661-94, et instructions pour le Dauphin son fils, par Louis XIV.

    Vol. V. Lettres particulières de Louis XIV, 1661-1714

    Vol VI Pièces historiques et anecdotes, servant d'éclaircissemens et de supplément aux écrits de ce monarque

Mazarin (Card.), Histoire du, par Aubery. 4 vols. 12mo. *Amst* 1751.

Mazarin (le Card.), joué par un Flamand ; ou, Relation de ce qui se passe à Ostend le 14 Mai, 1658. *Cologne* [*Amst Elzev*], 1671.

Retz (Card de), Mémoires du ; contenant ce qui s'est passé remarquable pendant les premières années du règne de Louis XIV 4 vols 12mo. *Genève*, 1777

Saint-Simon (Louis de), Œuvres complettes, pour servir à l'histoire des cours de Louis XIV, de la Régence, et de Louis XV, avec des notes, des explications, et des additions 13 vols. in 7, 8vo. best edition. *Strasbourg*, 1791.

Condé —Mémoires pour servir à l'histoire de la Maison de Condé ; contenant la vie du grand Condé, par le feu Prince de Condé, et la correspondance de l'auteur avec les souverains et princes de l'Europe. 2 vols 8vo. *Paris*, 1820

Turenne (Histoire du Vicecomte de). 4 vols 12mo *Amst* 1749.

Dangeau (Abrégé des Mémoires du Marquis de), extrait du MS. original, contenant beaucoup de particularités et d'anecdotes sur Louis XIV, sa cour, &c 1684–1720 · avec des notes historiques et critiques, et un abrégé de l'histoire de la régence, par Mad de Genlis 4 vols. 8vo. *Paris*, 1817

Beaumelle (M. de la), Mémoires et Lettres pour servir à l'histoire de Madame de Maintenon, et à celle du siècle passé ; avec les souvenirs de Mad. de Caylus pour servir de supplément augmentée des remarques critiques de M de Voltaire. 16 vols. 12mo. *Maestricht*, 1778.

Lettres inédites de Mad de Maintenon et Mad. la Princesse des Ursins. 4 vols 8vo *Paris.* 1826.

_{This illustrates the transactions of the courts of France and Spain from 1716, during the reigns of Louis XIV and Philip V.}

LOUIS XV.

[Piossens (Ch de)], Mémoires de la Régence du Duc d'Orléans durant la minorité de Louis XV ; augmentée par Lenglet du Fresnoy. 5 vols 12mo —— 1749.

Argenson (Mémoires du Marquis d'), Ministre sous Louis XV ; avec une notice sur la vie et les ouvrages de l'auteur, publiés par Réné d'Argenson 8vo *Paris*, 1815

Besanval (Mémoires du Baron de); avec une notice de sa vie, des notes, et des éclaircissemens historiques, par Berville et Barrière 2 vols 8vo. *Paris*, 1821.

Berwick (Maréchal de), Mémoires par lui-même ; publiés par le Duc de Fitz-James. 2 vols. small 8vo *Paris*, 1778

Wood's (J P) Life and Projects of John Law of Lauriston. (History of Cramond.)

Hausset (Mad. du), Femme de Chambre de Mad de Pompadour, Mémoires ; avec des notes par Quintin Crawfurd, et une notice sur sa vie, &c 8vo *Paris*, 1824.

Gibbon (Edward) on the subject of " L'homme au masque de fer " (Misc Works, Vol. II.)

Ellis (Geo Agar), the true History of the State Prisoner commonly called the Iron Mask, extracted from documents in the French archives 8vo *London*, 1826.

Pièces originales et Procédures du Procès, fait à Robert-François Damiens, [avec un précis historique de sa vie, et une relation de son exécution]. 4to *Paris*, 1757.

> To this copy are appended some MS additions, consisting of curious enigmatical papers, received during the trial, and accounts of other " crimes de lese-majeste " From the Lamoignon and Roxburgh collections

Gibbon (Mémoire justificatif pour servir de réponse à l'Exposé des Motifs de la Conduite du Roi de France relativement à l'Angleterre (Misc. Works, Vol II)

LOUIS XVI. AND THE REVOLUTION.

History of the Bastile, with a concise account of the late French Revolution, and an inquiry into the history of the prisoner with the iron mask. 8vo. *London*, 1790

Hué's (Fr) Last Years of the Reign and Life of Louis XVI ; translated by R C Dallas. 8vo *London*, 1806,

Mémoires de Weber, concernant Marie-Antoinette, Archduchesse d'Autriche et Reine de France et de Navarre ; avec des notes, &c par Breville et Barrière 2 vols 8vo *Paris*, 1822

Mémoires sur la Vie privée de Marie-Antoinette ; suivis de souvenirs et anecdotes historiques sur les règnes de Louis XIV, XV, et XVI ; par Mad. Campan. 3 vols 8vo. *Paris*, 1783.

Mémoires relatifs à la Famille Royale de France pendant la Révolution ; publiés d'après le journal, les lettres, et les entretiens de la Princesse de Lamballe. 2 vols 8vo *Paris*, 1826

Journal de ce qui s'est passé à la Tour du Temple pendant la captivité de Louis XVI, par Cléry, suivi des dernières heures de Louis XVI, par M. Edgworth de Firmont, du recit des événemens arrivés au Temple, par Madame Royale, et des éclaircissemens historiques. 8vo *Paris*, 1825

Burke's (Edmund) Reflections on the French Revolution, and on the proceedings of certain societies in London relative to that event (Works, Vol V)

Barruel's (Abbé) Memoirs, illustrating the history of Jacobinism, translated by R Clifford. 4 vols 8vo *London*, 1798.

Moleville's (Bertr. de) Annals of the French Revolution, translated from the original and unpublished MS., by R. C. Dallas. 9 vols. 8vo. *London*, 1800–9.

Stael's (Mad. de) Considerations on the principal Events of the French Revolution, edited by the Duke de Broglie and the Baron de Stael. 3 vols 8vo *London*, 1818.

Mémoires du Marquis de Bouillé sur la Révolution Française, depuis son origine jusqu'à la mort de Louis XVI, avec une notice sur sa vie, des notes, &c. par Berville et Barrière 8vo *Paris*, 1822.

Mémoires (inédits) de l'Abbé Morellet sur le XVII siècle et sur la Révolution, suivis de sa correspondance ; par M. Lemontey. 2 vols. 8vo. *Paris*, 1823.

Mémoires de Condorcet sur le règne de Louis XVI et la Révolution Française, extraits de sa correspondance et de celles de ses amis. 2 vols 8vo *Paris*, 1824.

Mémoires du Marquis de Ferrières, pour servir à l'histoire de la Révolution Française ; avec une notice sur sa vie, et des notes par Berville et Barrière. 3 vols. 8vo. *Paris*, 1822.

Mémoires Anecdotiques pour servir à l'histoire de la Révolution Française, par Lombard de Langres. 2 vols. 8vo *Paris*, 1823.

Mémoires sur divers Evénemens de la Révolution et de l'Emigration, par A H Dampmartin. 2 vols. 8vo. *Paris*, 1825.

Mémoires d'un Témoin de la Révolution, ou journal des faits qui ont préparé et fixé la Constitution Française, par J S Bailly, avec une notice sur sa vie, des notes, et des éclaircissemens historiques, par Berville et Barrière 2 vols. 8vo. *Paris*, 1821.

Mémoires pour servir à la Vie du Général la Fayette, et à l'Histoire de l'Assemblée Constituante ; rédigés par M Regnault-Warin. 2 vols. 8vo. *Paris*, 1824.

Mémoires de Rivarol ; avec des notes et des éclaircissemens historiques, par M Berville. 8vo. *Paris*, 1824

Moore's (John) Journal during a residence in France in 1792 ; with an account of the most remarkable events that happened in Paris from that time to the death of the French king. 2 vols 8vo. *Lond.* 1793.

Mémoires de la Vie du Général Dumourier ; avec son jugement sur Buonaparte, des notes, et éclaircissemens historiques, par M. Berville et Barrière. 4 vols. 8vo. *Paris*, 1822.

Mémoires de Linguet, sur la Bastile, et de Dusaulx, sur le 14 Juillet ; avec des notices, des notes, et des éclaircissemens historiques, par Berville et Barrière 8vo. *Paris*, 1822.

Relation du Depart de Louis XVI, le 20 Juin, 1790, par M. le Duc de Choiseul 8vo. *Paris*, 1822.

Mémoires de M. le Baron de Goguelat, sur les événemens relatifs au voyage de Louis XVI à Varennes ; suivis d'un précis des tentatives qui ont été faites pour arracher la reine à la captivité du Temple 8vo. *Paris*, 1823.

Mémoires sur l'Affaire de Varennes ; comprenant le mémoire inédit de M. le Marquis de Bouillé, deux relations inédites de MM. les Comtes de Raigecourt et de Damas, celle de M. le Capitaine Deslon, et le précis historique de M le Comte de Valory. 8vo *Paris*, 1823.

Histoire de la Convention Nationale, par Durande de Maillare ; suivie d'un fragment historique sur le 31 Mai (1793), par le Comte Lanjuinais. 8vo. *Paris*, 1825.

Mémoires sur les Journées de Septembre 1792, par J de Saint-Méard, Mad la Marquise de Fausse-Lendry, l'Abbé Sicard, et M Gabriel-Aimé Jourdan. 8vo *Paris*, 1823

Mémoires de Meillan, Député à la Convention Nationale ; avec des notes, &c 8vo *Paris*, 1823.

Mémoires (inédits) de Charles Barbouroux, Député à la Convention Nationale ; avec des éclaircissemens historiques de MM. Berville et Barrière. 8vo. *Paris*, 1822.

Révélations puisées dans les Cartons des Comités de Salut Public ; ou, mémoires (inédits) de Senart, agent du gouvernement révolutionnaire, publiés par A. Dumesnil. 8vo. *Paris*, 1824.

Mémoires sur la Révolution Française, par Buzot, Député à la Convention Nationale ; précédés d'un précis de sa vie et de recherches historiques sur les Girondins, par M. Guadet. 8vo. *Paris*, 1823.

Le Vieux Cordelier, journal politique, rédigé en l'an II, par C. Desmoulins, Député à la Convention Nationale Causes secrettes de la Journée du 9 au 10 Thermidor, an II, &c par Vilote. Précis historique inédit des événemens de la soirée du 9 Thermidor, an II, par C. A. Meda. 8vo. *Paris*, 1825

Mémoires de S. A. S Louis-Antoine-Philippe d'Orléans, Duc de Montpensier, prince du sang, [par lui-même] 8vo *Paris*, 1824

Mémoires sur la Convention et le Directoire, par A. C. Thibadeau 2 vols 8vo. *Paris*, 1824

Mémoires de Madame Roland ; avec une notice sur sa vie, des notices historiques sur la Révolution, des notes, et des éclaircissemens historiques, par Berville et Barrière. 2 vols 8vo *Paris*, 1821

Memoires [ou quelques notices pour l'histoire et le récit de mes périls, depuis le 31 Mai] de J. B. Louvet de Couvray; avec une notice sur sa vie, des notes, &c. 8vo. *Paris*, 1823.

Mémoires sur les Prisons. 2 vols 8vo. *Paris*, 1823. Contenant.

    Les Mémoires d'un Détenu, pour servir à l'histoire de tyrannie de Robespierre, par Riouffe

    L'Humanité Méconnue, ou les horribles souffrances d'un prisonnier, par Joseph Paris de l'Epinard

    L'Incarceration et les Terreurs paniques de Beaumarchais

    Tableau Historique de la Prison de Saint Lazare

    Maison d'Arrêt de Port-Libre, communément appelée la Bourbe.

    Le Luxembourg

    Precis Historique sur la Maison d'Arrêt de la Rue de Serres, et faits relatifs à la révolution du 9 Thermidor

    Les Madelonnettes

    La Mairie, la Force, et le Plessis

    Voyage de cent trente-deux Nantais, envoyés à Paris par le Comité révolutionnaire de Nantes.

    Les Horreurs des Prisons d'Arras, ou les crimes de Joseph Lebon et de ses agens.

    Relation de ce qu'ont souffert pour la religion les Prêtres Français insermentés, déportés en 1794 dans l'île d'Aix, près Rochefort

Mémoires d'Olivier d'Argens, et Correspondances des Généraux Charette Stofflet, Pusaye, d'Autichamp, Frotté, Cormatin, Bothérel, de l'Abbé Bernier, et de plusieurs autres chefs, officiers, ou gens royalistes ; pour servir à l'histoire de la guerre civile de 1793 à 1796. 8vo. *Paris*, 1824.

Mémoires de Madame la Marquise de Bonchamps, rédigés par Mde. la Comtesse de Genlis ; suivis des pièces justificatives 8vo. *Paris*, 1823

Guerres des Vendéens et des Chouans contre la République Française, ou, annales des départemens de l'Ouest pendant les guerres depuis l'Août 1792 jusqu'au mois d'Avril 1795 Par un Officier Supérieur des Armées de la République. 2 vols 8vo *Paris*, 1824

Mémoires sur la Vendée, comprenant les mémoires inédits d'un ancien administrateur militaire des armées républicanes, et ceux de Madame de Sopinaud. 8vo. *Paris*, 1823.

Mémoire Historique sur la Réaction Royale, et sur les Massacres du Midi, par le Citoyen Fréron, avec les pièces justificatives, et augmenté d'éclaircissemens et des documens historiques. 8vo. *Paris*, 1824.

Mémoires Historiques sur la Catastrophe de Duc d'Enghien. 8vo. *Paris*, 1824.

Mémoires Historiques et Militaires sur Carnot, rédigés d'après ses MSS., sa correspondance inédite, et ses écrits. Précedés d'une notice par P. F Tissot. 8vo. *Paris*, 1824

Mémoires Politiques et Militaires du Général Doppet, avec des notes et des éclaircissemens historiques 8vo *Paris*, 1824

Mémoires, Souvenirs, Opinions, et Ecrits du Duc de Gaeté, ancien Ministre des Finances, ex-Député, et Gouverneur de la Banque de France. 2 vols. 8vo. *Paris*, 1826.

Mémoires pour servir à l'histoire de la Ville de Lyon pendant la Révolution, par M. l'Abbé Aimé Guillor de Montléon 2 vols. 8vo. *Paris*, 1824

History of the Campaigns in 1796 to 1799, in Germany, Italy, Switzerland, &c. 4 vols 8vo. *London*, 1812

Biographie Moderne Lives of remarkable Characters who have distinguished themselves in the French Revolution 3 vols 8vo *Lond* 1811.

NAPOLEON

Life of Napoleon Buonaparte, Emperor of the French, with a preliminary view of the French Revolution; by Sir Walter Scott 9 vols. 8vo. *Edinburgh*, 1827

Rovigo, (Memoirs of the Duke of) M Savary, written by himself, illustrative of the history of the Emperor Napoleon 4 vols 8vo. *London*, 1828

Bourrienne (Mémoires de M de), sur Napoléon, le Directoire, le Consulat, l Empire, et la Restauration 10 vols. 8vo *Paris*, 1829

Abrantes' (Duchess d') Memoirs, or Historical Recollections of Napoleon, the Revolution, the Directory, the Consulate, the Empire, and the Restoration, translated   vols 8vo *London*, 1832, &c

Boyce's (Edm) Second Usurpation of Buonaparte; or, a history of the causes, progress, and termination of the Revolution in 1815. 2 vols. 8vo. *London*, 1816

Las Casas' Journal of the Private Life and Conversations of the Emperor Napoleon, at St. Helena. 4 vols. 8vo 1823

Napoléon (Derniers Momens de) par le Docteur F. Automarchi. 2 vols. 8vo *Paris*, 1825

Correspondance (inédite) Officielle et Confidentielle de Napoléon Buonaparte avec les cours étrangères, les princes, les ministres, les généraux, &c. François. 7 vols 8vo. *Paris*, 1818.

Napoleon (Fac-similes of Eight Letters in the handwriting of the Emperor) to Josephine. (Tennant's Tour)

French Ceremonials, Monuments, &c.

[Bevy (Charles)], Histoire des Inaugurations, &c. suivie d'un précis de l'état des arts et des sciences sous chaque règne, des principaux faits, mœurs, coutumes, et usages plus remarquables de François depuis Pepin jusqu'à Louis XVI   (Heraldry)

Chifletii (Jo. Jac) Lilium Francicum, veritate historicâ, botanicâ, et heraldicâ illustratum   Folio. *Antverpiæ, ex off. Plantin.* 1658.

<small>A curious work, wherein the author shews that bees, not the fleurs-de-lis, are the arms of France This copy has the autograph of Le Neve, Norroy, to whom it belonged</small>

Chifletius (J. J.) de Ampullâ Remensi, ad dirimendam litem de prærogativâ ordinis inter reges   Accessit Parergon de unctione regum. Folio   *Antverpiæ, ex off. Plant.* 1651.

<small>An exposé of the fable of the Holy Vial</small>

Feron (Jean le), Catalogue des Noms, Surnoms, Faits, et Vies, des Connestables, Chanceliers, Grands Maistres, Amiraux, et Maréchaux de France ensemble de Prévosts de Paris, depuis leur première établissement [continué] jusqu'à Henri IV [par F Morel]   The arms emblazoned   Folio   *Paris,* 1598-9

Lenoir (Alex), Musée des Monumens Français, ou, description historique des statues, bas-reliefs, et tombeaux des hommes et femmes célèbres, pour servir à l'histoire de France et à celle de l'art   8 vols royal 8vo.   *Paris,* 1800

Marchangy (M. F de), la Gaule Poétique, ou l'histoire de France considerée dans ses rapports avec la poésie, l'éloquence, et les beaux arts.   4 vols 8vo.   *Paris,* 1813-15.

Provincial History of France.

Duchesne (And) Historiæ Normannorum scriptores antiqui, res ab illis gestas explicantes, ab ann 838 ad ann 1220   Folio   *Lutetiæ,* 1619. Continens

    Gesta Normannorum ante Rollonem Ducem ;—Abbo de obsidione Lutetiæ per Normannos,—Dudo de moribus et actis primorum Normanniæ Ducum

    Emmæ Anglorum Reginæ Encomium,—Guil Pictavensis gesta Guillelmi Ducis Norman et Regis Anglorum 1

    Willelmi Gemmeticensis Historia Normannorum.

    Orderici Vitalis ecclesiastica historia.

    Gesta Stephani Regis Anglorum et Ducis Normannorum, incerto auth.;—[Robert de Monte] Chronica Normanniæ, ab 1139 ad 1159

    Nomina Normannorum qui floruerunt in Angliâ ante conquestum, &c.

Denyaldi (R) Rollo Normanno-Britannicus, continet res gestas VII Ducum Normannorum, usque ad tempus quo facti Reges Angliæ à primâ virtute degeneraiunt   Folio   *Rothomagi,* 1660

<small>See Lelong Bib Historique, No 34962 On the fly-leaves at beginning and end of this copy is written a chronological list of the Abps of Rouen to 1735</small>

Επινικιον, rhythmico Teutonico Ludovico Regi acclamatum contra Nortmannos, ann. D.CCC LXXXIII   Ex Cod MS per Jo Mabillon descriptum   Interp. Latinâ et commentat historicâ illustravit Jo. Schilter. (Schilteri Thes Vol II)

Depping (G B), Histoire des Expéditions maritimes des Normands, et de leur établissement en France au 10me siècle   2 vols 8vo. *Paris,* 1826

Histoire de Normandie, contenant les faits et gestes des ducs et princes du dit pays, depuis Aubert, premier duc [751] jusques à la dernière reduction d'iceluy pays à l'obéissance de la couronne de France [1450]   12mo.   *Rouen,* 1558
> A reprint of the earliest specimen of typography from the city of Rouen, "Les Chroniques de Normandie" (par Guil le Tilleur) 1487   That work was printed at the private hotel of its author, and it appears, from the preface to this edition, had long been suppressed

Jumiège (Guil de), Histoire des Ducs de Normandie, publiée par M Guizot, et suivie de la vie de Guillaume-Conquérant par Guillaume de Poitiers.   8vo.   *Caen,* 1826

Lobineau (G A.), Histoire de Bretagne, avec les pièces justificatives. 2 vols folio, large paper   *Paris,* 1707

Daru (M.), Histoire de Bretagne. 3 vols 8vo   *Paris,* 1826

Bouchet (Jean), les Annales d'Aquitaine ; faicts et gestes en sommaire des Roys de France et d'Angleterre, Pays de Naples et de Milan . augmentées par Mounin   Folio.   *Poitiers,* 1644

History of Switzerland.

Gibbon (E), Introduction à l'Histoire Génerale de la République des Suisses   (Misc Works, Vol III.)

Simond's (L) Historical Sketch of ancient and modern Helvetia   (Travels in Switzerland, Vol. II.)

Naylor's (Fr Hare) History of Helvetia, containing the rise and progress of the Federative Republics to the middle of the 15th century 2 vols. 8vo   *London,* 1801.

Planta's (Jos) History of the Helvetic Confederacy   3 vols 8vo *London,* 1804.

Muller (J), Histoire des Suisses, traduite de l'Allemande par Labaume. 12 vols 8vo   *Lausanne,* 1795-1803

History of the Republic of the Swiss. (Mod Un Hist Vols. XXXII and XXXVII.)

Keate's (Geo) Account of the ancient History, present Government, and Laws of the Republic of Geneva.   8vo   map   *London,* 1761.

History of Geneva. (Mod Un. Hist Vol XXXII)

History of Spain.

Rerum Hispanicarum Scriptores aliquot, ex Bib Roberti Beli   3 vols in one, folio   *Francof* 1579

Vol I	M. Aretius	Franciscus Farapha
	Jo Gerundensis	Lucius Marineus Siculus
	Rodericus Toletanus	Laurentius Valla.
	Rodericus Santius	Ælius Antonius Nebrissensis.
	Joannes Vassæus	Damianus à Goes.
Vol. II.	Alfonsus à Carthagena	Vol. III. Al. Gomerius de rebus gestis
	Michael Ritius	Fr. Ximenes Cardinalis

Garibây (Estevan de), los XL Libros del Compendio historial de las Chronicas universal y Historia de todos los Reynos de España Original edition 2 vols in three, folio *Anveres, Plantino,* 1571.

Mariana (Juan de), Historia general de España, illustrada en esta nueva impression de tablas chronologicas, notas, y observationes criticas ; con la vida del autor Best edition 9 vols small folio *Valencia,* 1783–96

History of Spain (Mod Un History, Vols XVI XVII XVIII. and XXXVII)

[Adolphus's (John)] History of Spain, from the establishment of the colony of Gades by the Phœnicians to the death of Ferdinand surnamed the Sage 3 vols. 8vo. *London,* 1793

Murphy's (J C) History of the Mahometan Empire in Spain, designed as an introduction to the Arabian Antiquities of Spain 4to. *Lond.* 1816

Conde, Historia de la Dominacion de los Arabes en España, sacada de varios Manuscritos y Memorias Arabigas. 3 vols 4to *Madrid,* 1820-21

Chronicle of the Cid, translated from the Spanish by Robert Southey 4to. *London,* 1808

[Perez (Genes di Hita)], Historia de las Guerras Civiles de Granada ; with French marginal translations of difficult words and phrases 12mo *Paris,* 1660

Mendoza (Don Diego de), Historia de la Guerra de Granada hecha por el Rey Don Filipe II contra los Moriscoes. Large 8vo *Madrid,* 1674.

Chronicle of the Conquest of Granada, from the MSS of Fray Antonio Agapida, by Washington Irving 2 vols 8vo *London,* 1829.

Baudier's (Mich) History of the Administration of Cardinal Ximenes, translated by Walt Vaughan 8vo *London,* 1671

Barrett's (B) Life of Cardinal Ximenes 8vo. *London,* 1813.

Sandoval (Prudencio de), Historia de la Vida y Hechos del Emperador Carlos V , Rey de España y de los Indias 2 vols folio *Pampl* 1614

Robertson's (Wm) History of the Emperor Charles V (Hist of Germany.)

Watson's (Robt) History of the Reign of Philip II of Spain. 2 vols 4to *London,* 1777

Watson's (R) History of the Reign of Philip III [concluded by W Thomson] 4to. *London,* 1783

Bacon's (Lord) Tracts relating to Spain (Works, Vol V)

Coxe's (Wm) Memoirs of the Kings of Spain, of the House of Bourbon, from Philip V to Charles III 3 vols 4to *London,* 1813

Moore's (Geo) Lives of Cardinal Alberoni, the Duke of Ripperda, and the Marquis of Pombal, exhibiting a view of the kingdoms of Spain and Portugal during a considerable portion of that period 8vo. *London,* 1814

Memoirs of Captain Geo. Carleton , including anecdotes of the war in Spain under the Earl of Peterborough, and particulars of the manners of the Spaniards in the beginning of the last century 8vo *Edinb.* 1809.

Pradt (M de) Memoires historiques sur la Revolution d'Espagne 8vo *Paris,* 1816

Blaquiere's (Edward) Historical Review of the Spanish Revolution; including some account of the religion, manners, and literature of Spain 8vo London, 1822.

Lopez de Ayala (Juan), Historia de Gibraltar. Small 4to. Madrid, 1782

Dameto's (Juan) and Vicente Mut's History of the Balearick Islands; or of the kingdom of Majorca, which comprehends the islands of Majorca, Minorca, Yvica, Formentera, &c, translated from the Spanish by Colin Campbell. 8vo London, 1719.

History of Portugal.

Resendius (Luc And) de Antiquitatibus Lusitaniæ à J M Vasconello recogniti. accessit liber de antiquitate Eboiensis ab eodem Vasconello conscriptus. Folio *Eboræ, excud M Burgensis*, 1593

Clede (De la), Histoire Générale de Portugal 8 vols 12mo *Paris*, 1735

History of Portugal (Mod Un Hist. Vols XVIII. XIX. and XXXVII.)

Osorio's (Jerome) History of the Portuguese during the reign of Emanuel; containing all their discoveries, and their wars with the Moors translated from the Latin by James Gibbs 2 vols. 8vo. *London*, 1752

Conestaggio (Jer) [Jo de Sylva, Comes Pontalegre], Istoria dell' Unione de Portogallo alla Corona di Castiglia Small 8vo *Venet* 1642.

Dumouriez' (Gen) Account of Portugal in 1766. 12mo. *Lond.* 1797.

History of Italy.

Hoare's (Sir R. C) Catalogue of Books relating to the History and Topography of Italy, collected during the years 1786-90 Royal 8vo *London, printed for presents only*, 1812.

Thesaurus Antiquitatum et Historiarum Italiæ, Neapolis, Siciliæ, Sardiniæ, Corsicæ, Melitæ, atque adjacentium terrarum insularumque, curâ et studio Jo. Geo. Grævii, nunc autem continuatus et ad finem perductus, cum præfationibus P Burmanni. 24 vols. in 45, folio, Dr Parr's copy. *Lugduni Bat* 1704-25

Volumen 1. Gabriel Barrius de laudibus Italiæ
Petri Leonis Casellæ de primis Italiæ colonis liber.
Jacobi Bracelli oræ Ligusticæ liber
Ejusdem de claris Genuensibus libellus
Gaud Merula de Gallorum cisalpinorum antiquitate.
Bonav Castelhonei de Gallorum Insubrum antiquis sedibus liber.
Uberti Foliotæ historia Genuensium libri 12.

Pars 2. Ejusdem clarorum Ligurum elogia
Ejusdem conjuratio Joannis Ludovici Flisci.
Ejusdem tumultus Neapolitani
Ejusdem cædes Petri Ludov Farnesii Placentiæ Ducis
Idem de sacro fœdere in Selimum libri 4
Ejusdem variæ expeditiones in Africâ, cum obsidone Melitæ
Ejusdem opuscula nonnulla varii argumenti, nempe — De vitæ et studiorum ratione homins sacris initiati — De ratione scribendæ historia, — De causis magnitudinis Turcarum imperii, — Tiburtinum Hippolyti Cardinalis Ferrariensis, — Rium inus, sive de laudibus urbis Neapolis, — De nonnullis, in quibus Plato ab Aristotele reprehenditur, — De norma Polybriana, — Oratio in festo die omnium sanctorum

MODERN.

Jacobi Bracelli de bello quod inter Hispanos et Guenenses seculo suo gestum libri 5.
Jacobi Bonfadii annalium Genuensium ab anno 1528 (in quo desinit Ubertus Folieta) recuperatæ libertatis usque ad annum 1550 libri 5
Hieronymi de marinis Genuæ, sive reipubl Genuensis compend descriptio.
Petri Bizari dissertatio de reipubl Genuensis
Ejusdem reipublicæ Genuensis leges novæ

Volumen 2 Andreæ Alciati historiæ Mediolanensis libri 4.
Tristani Calchi historiæ patriæ libri 20
Josephi Ripamontii historiæ patriæ libri 23.

Pars 2 Ejusdem historiæ patriæ continuatio, comprehensa octo libris, in quibus res quas gessit Philippus II tàm Mediolani cùm in ejus ditionem redigeretur, quàm alibi, exponuntur
Galeatii Capellæ de bello Mediolanensi, seu de rebus in Italià gestis pro restitutione Franc Sfortiæ II ab anno 1521 usque ad 1530, libri 8
Caroli à Basilicapetri de metropoli Mediolanensi libellus.

Volumen 3. Georgii Merulæ Alexandrini antiquitates vicecomitum, libri 10
Pauli Jovii vitæ duodecim vicecomitum Mediolani principum singulorum, veris imaginibus illustratæ.
Joh Ant Castellionæi Mediolanenses antiquitates, ex urbis Paroecus collectæ, ichnographicis ipsarum tabulis, recentibus rerum memoriis, variis ecclesiasticis ritibus, auctæ et illustratæ.
Bernardi Sacci historiæ Ticinensis libri 10
Joh. Chrysostomi Zanchii de Orobiorum sive Cenomanorum origine, situ ac Bergomi rebus antiquis, libri 3
Johannis Baptistæ Villanovæ Laudis Pompejæ, sive Laudæ (nunc Lodi) urbis historia.

Pars 2. Othonis Morenæ et Acerbi Othonis F historia rerum Laudensium, tempore Friderici Ænobarbi Cæsaris
Erycii Puteani historia Cisalpina libri duo, quibus continentur res potissimum circa Lacum Larium à Joh. Jacobo Mediceo gestæ.
Alexandri Dukeri Comi urbis historia et descriptio
Camilli Ghilini descriptio Lacûs Larii et Vallis Tellinæ.
Pauli Jovii descriptio Lacûs Larii, sive Comensis
Galeatii Capellæ de bello Mussiano libri adoptivus
Ludovici Cavitelli Cremonenses annales
Umberti Locati de Placentinæ urbis origine, successu, et laudibus seriosa narratio

Volumen 4. Joannis de Cermenate historia Ambrosianæ urbis.
Arnulphi historia Mediolanensis
Joannis Petri Puricelli Ambrosianæ Basilicæ ac Monasterii Monumentorum descriptio

Pars 2. Ludovici Ant Muratorii de coronâ ferreâ commentarius
Justi Fontanini dissertatio de coronâ ferreâ Longobardorum.
Benedicti Jovii historiæ patriæ, sive Novocomensis.
Octavii Rubei monumenta Brixiana.
Antonii Gatti historia gymnasii Ticinensis
Baptistæ Sacchi Platinæ historia urbis Mantuæ.

Volumen 5 Bernardi Justiniani de origine urbis Venetiarum, rebusque gestis à Venetis, libri 15
Donati Jannotti dialogus de republicâ Venetorum.
Gasparis Contareni de magistratibus et republicâ Venetorum libri 5, accesserunt Balth Bonifacii de majoribus comitiis et judiciis capitalibus duæ epistolæ
Nicolai Crassi de formâ reipublicæ Venetæ liber
Blondus Flavius de origine et gestis Venetorum
Petri Bembi historiæ Venetæ libri 12
M Ant Coccii Sabellici de situ urbis Venetæ descriptio, &c

Par 2 et 3 Splendor magnificentissimæ urbis Venetiarum clarissimus, figuris elegantiss.

Pars 4. Antonii Stellæ elogiorum Venetorum navali pugnâ illustrium liber.
Nicolai Crassi elogia patritorum Venetorum belli pacisque artibus illustrium
Bartholomæi Pacii de bello Veneto Clodiano liber.
Antonii de Ville pyctomachia Veneta, seu pugna Venetorum in ponte annui

HISTORY.

        Josephi Laurentii de desponsatione maris Adriatici.
        Joannis Valaerii spectacula Veneta, epigrammatibus aliquot celebrata.
        Andreæ Moceuici belli memorabilis Cameracensis adversus Venetos historiæ libri 6
        Bernard Arlunus de bello Veneto sæculo 16.

Volumen 6 Rolandini grammatici libri chronicorum
        Monachi Paduani chronicorum libri tres de rebus in Insubribus et Euganeis
        Gerardi Maurisii dominorum de Romano et Marchiæ Tarvisinæ historia
        Antonii Godii chronica ab anno 1194 usque ad 1260, cum supplem C Sigonii
        Nicolai Smeregi chronicon, cum scriptoris anonymi supplemento.
        Ricciardi vita S Bonificii comitis.
        Laurentii de Monacis Fzerinus tertius
        Guilhelmi et Albrigeti Cortusiorum historia de novitatibus Paduæ et Lombardiæ, cum supplemento.

    Pars 2 Albertini Mussati de gestis Henrici VII , Cæsaris, &c.
        Ejusdem tragœdiæ duæ Eccerinis et Achilleis, cum notis N Villani, ut et alia auctoris poemata

    Pars 3 Petri Pauli Vergerii de Carrariensium familiâ et ejus principum historiâ.
        Bernardini Scardeonii historia de urbis Patavii antiquitate, &c
        Idem de sepulchris insignibus exterorum Patavii jacentium
        Laurentii Pignorii origines Patavinæ et Antenor
        Ejusdem epistola de ritu nuptiarum.
        Ejusdem vita, bibliotheca, et musæum.
        Octavii Ferrarii oratio de laudibus urbis Patavii

    Pars 4. Ant Riccoboni de gymnasio Patavino commentariorum libri 6.
        Henr Palladii de olivis rerum Foro-Iuliensium libri 11.
        Ejusdem de oppugnatione Gradiscanâ libri 5.
        Basilii Zancaroli antiquitatum civitatis Foru Julii libri 4
        Joannis Candidi commentariorum Aquilejensium libri 8.
        Philippi a Turre dissertationes de Beleno, &c
        Joannis Bapt Goynæi de situ Istriæ libellus
        Marc Ant Sabellici de vetustate Aquilejæ et Foru Julii libri 6
        Ejusdem carmen, Vincentinus Crater.
        Pauli Pincii de Timavo fluvio dissertatio
        Pauli Jovitæ Rapiini descriptio balneorum ad Timavi ostium
        Joh Piei Valeriani antiquitatum Bellunensium sermones quatuor.
        Antonii de Ville antiquitates portûs et urbis Polæ antiquitat.

Volumen 7. Barth Dulcini de Bononiæ vario statu libri 6.
        Joan Bapt Agocchi fundatio et dominium antiquum urbis Bononiæ
        Descriptio Bononiæ antiquæ et hodiernæ
        Cynthii Ioh Bap Gyraldi de Ferrariâ et Atestinis principibus commentariolum
        Laurentii Schraderi urbis Ferrariæ descriptio et monumenta.
        Alphonsi Cagnacini antiquitates urbis Ferrariæ
        Hippolyti Angeleni antiquitates urbis Atestinæ liber
        Desiderii Spreti de urbis Ravennæ amplitudine, &c libri 3
        Laurentii Schroederi urbis Ravennæ descriptio et antiquitates
        Hieronymi Rubei Italicarum et Ravennatum historiarum libri 11

    Pars 2 Petri Mariæ Kavinæ Faventia rediviva
        Scipionis Claramontii Cæsenæ urbis historiarum libri 16
        Jacobi Villani Ariminensis Rubicon in Cæsenam Scipionis Claramontii
        Vincentii de Rubicone antiquo adversus Ariminenses scriptores dissertatio
        Jacobi Villani de Rubicone antiquo Ariminensi in Pisciatellum Cæsenæ responsa
        Gabrielis Naudæi exercitatio, quod nomen Senæ non Cæsenæ Senogalliæ conveniat.
        Fortunii Liceti pro urbis Cæsenæ antiquitate apologia contra Scip. Claramontium.
        Simeonis Claramontii contentio apologetica de Cæsenâ triumphante
        Philippi Antonini Sassina antiqua.
        Jos Malatestæ Garuffi lucerna lapidaria
        Joan Angelitæ urbis Recineti origines, historia, et descriptio
        Fr Adami de rebus gestis in civitate Firmana fragmentorum libri 2
        Cæsaris Ottinelli de Firmo elogium.

MODERN.

Volumen 8. Guil Postelli de Etruriâ regione commentatio
Francisci Dyni antiquitates Etruriæ.
Ejusdem antiquitates Umbriæ
Barth Scalæ historiæ Florentinorum libri 5.
Ejusdem vita Vitaliani Borrhomæi.
Pogii Bracciolini historiæ Florentinæ libri 8
Joan Michaelis Bruti historiæ Florentinæ libri 8

Pars 2 Francisci Contereri historia Hetruriæ.
Benedetto e Giovan Filipo Varchi istoria delle guerre della republica Florentina, aggiunt. la vita de Filipo Strozzi.
Matthæi Palmeri de captivitate Pisarum historia

Pars 3 F Hen Noris cenotaphia Pisana
Dominicus Angelus de depredatione Castrensium
Justi Fontanini de antiquitatibus Hortæ, coloniæ Etruscorum, libri 2.
Andreæ Mugnoti Eremi Camaldulensis descriptio
Cæsar Orlandius de urbis Senæ ejusque episcopatûs antiquitate.
Antonii Massæ de origine et rebus Faliscorum liber.
Petri Cursii civitatem Castellanam Faliscorum non Vejentum oppidum esse.
Jacobi Mazocchii Veji defensi
Famiani Nardini Veji antiqui
Dom Mazocchii, Vejorum defensoris, epistola apologetica
Pomp Angelotti descriptio et antiquitates urbis Reatæ.

Pars 4 Dom Barn Mathæi memoriæ historicæ Tusculi antiqui.
Jacobi Manilli descriptio villæ Burghesiæ
Pyrrhi Ligorii descriptio villæ Tiburtinæ Hadrianæ.
Franc Martii historia Tiburtina amplificata
Annonii del Re antiquitates Tiburtinæ
Jos Mariæ Suaresii Prænestes antiquæ libri 2
Philippi a Turre monumenta veteris Antii
Nicolaus Alemannus de Lateranensibus Parietinis

Volumen 9 Benedicti di Falco antiquitates Neapolis
Henrici Bacci descriptio regni Neapolitani.
Ant Sanfelicius de situ ac origine Campaniæ.
Camilli Peregrini historia principum Longobardorum.

Pars 2 Ejusdem dissertationes de veteri significatu vocis portæ
Ejusdem dissertationes de Campania Felice
Julii Cæsaris Capacii antiquitates et historiæ Neapolitanæ

Pars 3 Ejusdem antiquitates et historia Campaniæ Felicis
Marci Antonii Surgentis Neapolis illustrata.
Barthol Facii de rebus gestis ab Alphonso I Neapolitanorum rege commentariolus
Johan Joviani Pontani historia Neapolitanæ libri 6
Angeli Fonticulani belli Braccini, Aquilæ gesti, fidelis narratio.

Pars 4 Ferrantis Loffredi antiquitas Puteolorum descriptionibus
Scipionis Mazellæ Puteolorum et Cumarum descriptio
Joan. Fr Lombardi, eorum quæ de balneis aliisque miraculis Puteolanis scripta sunt synopsis
Antonii Ferri apparatus statuarum in destructis Cumis inventarum.
Julii Cæsaris Capacii de balneis liber
Ambrosii Leonis antiquitatum nec non historiarum urbis ac Nolæ descriptio.
Hen Brenemanni dissertationes de republicâ Amalphitinâ
Antonii Mazza urbis Salernitanæ historia et antiquitates
Mutii Phæbonii historiæ Marsorum libri 3

Pars 5 Lucii Camarræ de Teate antiquo libri 3
Us redivivum Cimisiorum per Abbatem Damadenum
D Pauli Antonii de Tarsi historiarum Cupersmensium libri 3.
Gabrielis Barrii de Calabriæ antiquitate et situ libri 5
Joan Juvenis de antiquitate et varia fortuna Tarentinorum libri 8
Antonii Galatei de situ Iapygiæ liber

Pars 6 Philiberti Pingonii Augusta Taurinorum chronica et antiquitatum inscriptionis
R D Petri Joffredi Nicæa civitas sacris monumentis illustrata
Benedicti Accolti de præstantia virorum sui ævi dialogus
Petri Azarii chronicon gestorum in Lombardiâ.
Fr Andreæ Bilii historia patria libri 9.

HISTORY.

Georgii Flori de bello Italico et rebus Gallorum libri 6.
Pet. Pauli Boschæ de origine et statu bibliothecæ Ambrosianæ libri 5.
P D Christ. Guirdæ liberalium disciplinarum icones symbolicæ bibliothecæ Alexandrinæ, illust

Pars 7. Dominici Macanei Verbani Lacûs lacorumque adjacentium chronographica descriptio
Franc Bellafini de origine et temporibus urbis Bergomi liber.
M. Ant Michaelis agri et urbis Bergomatis descriptio
Vincentii Coronelli rerum ac temporum Bergomensis ecclesiæ synopsis.
Barth Farinæ de Bergomi origine et fatis commentarius.
Antonii Cornazzani de vita et gestis Bartholomæi Colæi commentariorum libri 6
Heliæ Capreoli chronicorum de rebus Brixianorum libri 14
Alex Squadrom fasciculus laudum regu Lepidi.
Laurentii Schrœderi descriptio regu Lepidi
Torelli Sarayıæ de civitatis Veronæ origine libri 6.
Ejusdem historiarum et gestorum Veronensium temporibus Scaligeri libri 3
Jos Just Scaligeri epistola de vetustate et splendore gentis Scaligeriæ.

Pars 8. Andreæ Chiocci de collegii Veronensis illustribus medicis et philosophis, &c.
Pauli Cigalini de C Plinii secundi natur hist scriptoris vera patria.
Polycarpi Palermi de vera C. Plinii secundi superioris patria atque eâ Veronâ, libri 3
Joan Nicolai Doglioni dissertatio de origine et antiquitate civitatis Belluni, &c.
Laur Marucini Bassanum, sive dissertatio de urbis antiquitate et de viris ejusdem illustribus.
Hieron Baruffaldi de poetis Ferrariensibus dissertatio
Jos. Lanzoni de jatrophysicis Ferrariensibus dissertatio.
Cæsaris Brixii urbis Cæsena descriptio
Fr Bern Mansoni Cæsenæ chronologia
Geo Marchesii Foro-Livii, civitatis celeberrimæ, compendium historicum.
Alphonsi Ciccarelli de Clitumno Umbriæ flumine celeberrimo opusculum.
Gab Naudæi tibulari majoris templi Reatini instauratio.
Naldi Naldii vita Jannoctii Manetti
Martini Manfredi monumentorum historicorum urbis Lucæ libri 5
Gauges de Gozze de inscriptione columnæ rostratæ, olim in foro Romano, dissertatio
Francisci Mariæ de Aste de memorabilibus Hydruntinæ ecclesiæ epitome.

Siciliæ.

Volumen 1. Philippi Cluverii Sicilia antiqua.
Cl Marii Aretii Siciliæ chorographia accuratissima.
Dominici Marii Nigri Siciliæ descriptio
Placidi Carafæ Sicanæ descriptio et delineatio.
Antonini Mongitoris regni Siciliæ delineatio

Volumen 2. P Octavii Cajetani isagoge ad historiam sacram Siculæ.
Alberti Piccoli de antiquo jure ecclesiæ Siculæ dissertatio.
Antonini de Amico de urbis Syracusarum antiquo archiepiscopatu
D D Francisci Baronii ac Manfredi judicium in Anton. de Amico de antiquo Syracusarum episcopatu, &c.
D. Rocchi Pirri disquisitiones de patriarchâ Siciliæ, de metropolità Siciliæ, et de præsulum Siciliensium electione.

Volumen 3 D Rocchi Pirri Siciliæ sacræ.
Ejusdem notitia capellæ Sancti Petri in Panormo.
Cæsaris Boronii cardinalis de monarchiâ Siciliæ.

Volumen 4. Thomæ Fazelli de rebus Siculis decades duæ.
Francisci Maurolyci Sicanicarum rerum compendium, sive Sicanicæ historiæ, libri 6.

Volumen 5. Michaelis Ritii de regibus Siciliæ, eorumque origine et successione, libri 4
Felini Sandei de regibus Siciliæ et Apuliæ liber
Rocchi Pirri chronologia regum Siciliæ.
Gaufredus Malaterra de rebus gestis Roberti Guiscardi Ducis Calabriæ, et Rogerii Comitis Siciliæ
Ejusdem, Alexandri Abbatis, Rogerii Siciliæ Regis rerum gestarum, libri 4.

Gaufredi Malaterræ historia brevis liberationis Messinæ à Saracenorum dominatu per Comitem Rogerium
Ejusdem Ptolomei Lucensis, Roberti Guiscardi, et eorum principum qui Siciliæ regnum adepti sunt, genealogia
Hugonis Falcandi de rebus gestis in Siciliæ regno historia.
Descriptio victoriæ per Carolum contra Manfredum Siciliæ regem
Sabas Malispini rerum Sicularum libri 6
Nicolai Specialis rerum Sicularum libri 8.
Anonymi chronicon Siciliæ, complectens accuratam regni Siciliæ historiam
Conradi Vecerii historia de duabus seditionibus Siciliæ, sub imperio Caroli V

Volum 6, 7, 8. Phil. Parutæ, Leon Augustini, Hub. Goltzii, et Sig. Havercampi Sicilia numismatica
Georg Gualterii Siciliæ et adjacentium insularum atque Bruttiorum tabulæ antiquæ.

Volumen 9. Josephi Bonfilii et Constantii Messanæ urbis nobilissimæ descriptio
Placidi Reynæ urbis Messanæ notitia historica
Antonii Philothei de Homodeis Ftnæ topographia, atque ejus incendiorum historia.
Petri Carreræ descriptio Ætnæ, libri 3
Alex. Burgos descriptio terræmotûs Siculi

Volumen 10. D. Petri Carreræ monumentorum historicorum urbis Catanæ libri 4
Ep.stolæ Diodori cum annotationibus D. Petri Carreræ
D. Petri Carrera disquisitio de vero significatu numismatum quorumdam Messanensium seu Mamertinorum Catanensium.
Joannis Baptistæ de grossis Catanensis decachordum, sive novissima sacræ ecclesiæ Catanensis notitia.

Volumen 11. Joannis Bapt. Guarnerii dissertationes historicæ Catanenses.
Vincentii Mirabellæ et Alagonæ ichnographia Syracusarum antiquarum explicatio
Jacobi Bonanni et Columnæ Syracusarum antiquarum illustratarum libri 2.

Volumen 12. Joannis Pauli Chiarandæ Plutia sive Platia, civitas Siciliæ, antiqua et nova.
P. Mario Pace antiquitates Caltageronis, urbis pulcherrimæ Siciliæ.
Mariani Perelli antiquitas Scicli, quam olim vocarunt Casmenas
Vincentii Littaræ de rebus Netinis libri 2
Placidi Carrafæ Motucæ descriptio seu delineatio
Augustini Inveges Carthago Sicula

Volumen 13. Mariani Valguarneræ de origine et antiquitate Panormi dissertatio
Francisci Baronii ac Manfredis de Panormitana majestate libri 4

Volumen 14. Augustini Inveges Panormus antiqua.
Antonii Mongitoris sacræ domus mansionis S. S. Trinitatis, militaris ordinis Theutonicorum urbis Panormi
Josephi Vincentii Auriæ notitia historica originis et antiquitatis Cephaledis.
Hieron. Ragusæ elogia Siculorum qui veteri memoriâ literis floruerunt
Benedicti Coeborellæ Trennitane olim Diomedæ insulæ accuratissima descriptio
Palladii Fusci de situ oræ Illyrici libri 2
Joannis Lucii de regno Illyrici liber.
Ejusdem inscriptiones Dalmaticæ

Volumen 15. Philippi Cluverii Sardinia et Corsica antiquæ
Ioannis Francisci Faræ de rebus Sardois historia.
Salvatoris Vitalis annales Sardiniæ
Quintini Haedui descriptio insulæ Melitæ.
Coelii secundi Curionis de bello Mehtensi historia.
Commendatoris Fr. Joh. Francisci Abelæ descriptio Melitæ, libri 4
Johan Henr. Maii duo specimina linguæ Punicæ

Muratori (L. A.), Annali d'Italia dal principio dell' era volgare sino all' anno 1750, colle prefazioni critiche di Gieuseppi Catalani, e col proseguimento di detti annali fino agli anni presenti (1762) 14 vols. 4to. *Lucca*, 1762–70.

Oggeri Vincenti (Ab.), Continuazione degli Annali d'Italia dall' anno 1750 all' anno 1786. 5 vols. 8vo. *Roma*, 1790

Guicciardini (Fr.), Istoria d' Italia [reveduti dopo un MS del autor, da B P. Bonsi]. 10 vols 8vo *Milano*, 1803

History of the Ostrogoths in Italy, the Exarchs of Ravenna, and the Lombards in Italy. (Mod Un Hist Vol XVII)

Naudet (J.), Essai sur l'Etat civil et politique des Peuples d'Italie sous le Gouvernement des Goths 8vo *Paris*, 1811.

History of Italy (Mod Un Hist Vols XXII XXIII. and XXXVII.)

Denina (Carlo), delle Revoluzioni d' Italia, con Continuazione. 3 vols. 8vo. *Milano*, 1820

Denina (Carlo), Istoria della Italia occidentale. 6 vols 8vo. *Torino*, 1809-10.

Perceval's (Geo.) History of Italy, from the fall of the Western Empire to the commencement of the wars of the French Revolution 2 vols 8vo. *London*, 1825.

Récit historique de la Campagne de Buonaparte en Italie dans les années 1796-7, par un Temoin oculaire 8vo *Londres*, 1808

Botta's (Carlo) History of Italy during the Consulate and Empire of Napoleon, translated from the Italian 2 vols 8vo *London*, 1828.

Vieusseux's (A.) Italy and the Italians in the XIXth Century. a view of the civil, military, political, and moral state of that country, with a sketch of the history of Italy under the French, and a treatise on modern Italian literature 2 vols small 8vo *London*, 1824.

Sismonde de Sismondi (J C L), Histoire des Républiques Italiennes du Moyen Age 11 vols 8vo. *Paris*, 1809-15.

History of the House of Savoy (Mod Un Hist Vol. XXXIV)

History of Genoa. (Mod Un Hist Vols XXV and XXXVII.)

History of Milan (Mod Un Hist Vols XXXIII and XXXIV)

Daru (P.), Hist. de la République de Vénise. 8 vols 8vo. *Paris*, 1821

History of Venice. (Mod Un Hist. Vols XXIII. XXIV and XXXVI.)

Ceremony of the Coronation of the Doge, by Brustola. (Coll. of Prints, Vol XV)

Castlemaine's (Roger Palmer, E. of) Account of the War between the Venetians and the Turks, with the state of Candia Small 8vo map of Candia by Hollar, and Portrait. *London*, 1666

Panvinii (O.) de Antiquitatibus Veronensium Lib XIII.; nunc in lucem editæ [M. A Clodio]. Folio [*Veronæ*] 1647.

Varchi (Bened.), Istoria della Republica Fiorentina, nella quale principalemente si contengo e ultime revoluzzione della republica e lo stabilimento del principato nella casa de Medici. Folio *Colonia*, 1721.

Boyd's (Henry) Historical Essay on the State of Affairs in the 13th and 14th centuries as it respects the history of Florence (Dante)

Pignotti (Lor.), Storia della Toscana sino al principato, con diversi saggi sulle Scienze, Lettere, ed Arti. 6 vols 8vo *Firenze*, 1824

History of the Tuscan States (Mod. Un Hist Vol XXXIII)

Galluzzi (Rig.), Histoire du Grand Duché de Toscane, sous le Gouvernement des Medicis; traduite de l'Italien 9 vols 12mo *Paris*, 1782.

Noble's (Mark) Memoirs of the House of Medici, from Giovanni, the founder of their greatness, to 1737. 8vo *Lond* 1797

Tenhove's (Nich) Memoirs of the House of Medici, from its origin to the death of Francesco, the second Grand Duke of Tuscany, and of the great men who flourished in Italy within that period, translated, with notes and observations, by Sir R. Clayton 2 vols 4to large paper *Bath*, 1797

Roscoe's (W) Life of Lorenzo di Medici, called the Magnificent 2 vols. 4to *London*, 1796

Memoir of the Life of Cosmo III, Grand Duke of Tuscany (Travels in England)

Roscoe's (W), Life and Pontificate of Leo X. 4 vols 4to *Liverpool*, 1805

Torriano (Geo), a New Relation of Rome, as to the government of the city, the noble families thereof, the revenue and expenses of the Pope, &c Small 8vo port of P. Alexander VII by Chantry. *London*, 1664

This copy has a duplicate title, by which the work is better known,—"Rome exactly described as to the present state of it under P Alexander VII,"&c

Corraro's (Angelo) Relation of the State of the Court of Rome, made in the year 1661 at the Council of Pregadi; translated out of Italian by J[ohn] B[ulteel] Small 8vo. *London*, 1664

Giannone (P), Istoria Civile del Regno di Napoli, con accrescimento di note, riflessione, medaglie, &c all' aja 1753 4 vols. 4to *Napoli*, 1762

Giannone (P), Opere posthume in difesa della sua Storia del Regno di Napoli, con la di lui Professione di Fide 4to *Palmyra*, 1760.

History of Naples. (Mod. Univ. History, Vols XXIV, XXV, and XXXVII)

Historical Life of Joanna of Sicily, Queen of Naples and Countess of Provence, with co-relative details of the literature and manners of Italy and Provence in the 13th and 14th centuries 2 vols 8vo *London*, 1824

D'Egly, Histoire des Rois des deux Siciles de la Maison de France; contenant ce qu'il y a de plus intéressant dans l'histoire de Naples depuis la fondation de la monarchie jusqu'à présent 4 vols 12mo. *Paris*, 1741

History of European Islands (Mod. Un Hist Vol XXXVII)

Boisgelins' (L de) Account of Ancient and Modern Malta; with a history of the Knights of St John 2 vols 4to *London*, 1805

History of the Island and Order of the Knights of Malta, to 1725 (Mod. Un Hist Vol XV)

Anderson's (Æneas) Particular Account of Malta during the time it was subject to the British Government (Journal of the Forces under Pigot)

History of the Ottoman Empire.

Mouradja d'Ohsson, Tableau Générale de l'Empire Ottoman [comprenant la législation, les mœurs, et coutumes, avec les détails les plus exacts sur l'organisation et l'administration de l'empire Ottoman 8 vols 8vo *Paris*, 1788–1824

Georgieviz (Barth) de Origine Imperii Turcorum, eorumque administratione et disciplinâ, cui adjectus est de Turcorum moribus, cum præfatione D Phil Melancthonis Sm 8vo *Wittbergæ*, 1560.

History of the Othman Empire to the peace of Carlowitz and deposition of Mostafa (Mod Un Hist Vols IX and X)

History of Turkey in Europe (Mod Un Hist Vol XXXVII)

Jovius' (Paulus) Shorte Treatise upon the Turke's Chronicles ; translated oute of Latyne by Peter Ashton Small 8vo **black letter** London, by E. *Whitchurche*, 1546
> Mr. Thoresby's copy, with his autograph

Alix (P), Précis de l'Histoire de l'Empire Ottoman depuis son origine jusqu'à nos jours, avec une introduction 3 vols. 8vo *Paris*, 1824.

Tott (Mémoires du Baron de) sur les Turcs et les Tartares 3 parts in 2 vols 12mo *Maestricht*, 1782.

Thornton's (Thomas) Present State of Turkey, together with Moldavia and Wallachia ; from observations made during 15 years' residence [including an introductory history from the origin of the Turkish nation to Selim III] 2 vols 8vo. *London*, 1809

Dallaway's (James) Constantinople, ancient and modern, with excursions to the shores and islands of the Archipelago 4to. plates. *London*, 1797.

[Evelyn's (John)] History of the Three late famous Impostors: viz. Padre Ottomano, Mahomed Bei, and Sabatai Sevi ; with a brief account of the ground and occasion of the present war between the Turk and the Venetian, together with the cause of the final extirpation, destruction, and exile of the Jews out of the empire of Persia (Misc Works)

Haji Khalifeh's History of the Maritime Wars of the Turks ; translated from the Turkish by James Mitchell 4to *London*, 1831

History of the War in Bosnia, during the years 1737, 8, and 9 , translated from the Turkish by C Fraser 8vo. *Lond* 1830

Emerson's (James) History of Modern Greece, from its conquest by the Romans, B C 146, to the present time 2 vols 8vo *Lond* 1830.

Leake's (W M) Historical Outline of the Greek Revolution, with remarks on the present state of affairs in that country Small 8vo. *London*, 1826

History of the Gipsies.

Grellman (H M G), Histoire des Bohémians ; ou, Tableau des Mœurs, Usages, et Coutumes de ce Peuple nomade, suivie de recherches historiques sur leur origine, leur langage, et leur première origine en Europe ; traduite de l'Allemande 8vo *Paris*, 1809.

Asia.—General History, &c.

D'Herbelot (Bart), Bibliothèque Orientale, ou Dictionnaire Universel ; contenant tout ce qui fait connoitre les peuples de l'Orient, continuée par C Visdelou et A. Galand 4 vols 4to *La Haye*, 1777–79

Jones's (Sir W.) Miscellaneous Pieces on the Language, Literature, and History of Eastern Nations   (Works, Vol I, and Suppl. Vols I and II.)

Richardson (John) on the Languages, Literature, and Manners of Eastern Nations   (Pers and Arabic Dict Vol I)

Asiatic Researches; or, Transactions of the Society instituted in Bengal, for inquiring into the history and antiquities, the arts, sciences, and literature of Asia.   8vo. *Lond.* 1806, &c

History of Asia in general. (Mod Un Hist Vol XXXVI.)

Guignes (Jos de), Histoire Générale des Huns, des Turcs, des Mogoles, et des Tartares. 5 vols. 4to   *Paris*, 1756.

History of the Turks till the destruction of their empire in Tartary   (Mod Un Hist. Vol III)

History of the Turkmâns and Usbecks. (Mod. Univ. Hist. Vol V.)

History of the Turks, Tartars, and Moguls (Modern Universal History, Vol XVIII)

History of the Dispersion of the Jews, or, an account of their distressed state from the destruction of Jerusalem to the end of the 17th century.   (Mod Un Hist Vols X and XI)

History of Asia Minor, Syria, Arabia, and Asiatic Turkey. (Mod Un Hist Vol XXXVI)

Dissertations on the Assassins of Syria, by M l'Evesque de Ravalière and M Falconet   (Joinville's Memoirs by Johnes)

Puget de St. Pierre, Histoire des Druses, peuples de Liban   12mo   *Paris,* 1762

[Rousseau], Description du Pachalik de Bagdad; suivie d'une notice historique sur les Wahabis, et de quelques autres pièces relatives à l'histoire et à la littérature de l'Orient, publiée par De Sacy.   8vo. *Paris,* 1809

Arriani Historia Indica, et Expeditio Alexandri   (Classics)

History of the Arabs and Saracens.

Murphy's (J C) General History of the Arabs, their institutions, conquests, literature, arts, sciences, and manners. (Mahometan Empire in Spain)

Price's (David) Essay towards the History of Arabia antecedent to the birth of Mohammed, arranged from the Tarikh Tebry and other authentic sources   4to   *London*, 1824

History of the Arabs and their Ancient State to Mohammed   (An Un Hist Vol XVI)

Ockley's (Simon) History of the Saracens, containing the lives of Mahomet and his immediate successors; an account of their most remarkable battles, sieges, &c.; and illustrating the religion, rites, customs, and manner of living of that warlike people, collected from authentic Arabic authors   [Edited by Dr. Roger Long] 2 vols 8vo   *London,* 1757

History of the Empire of the Arabs to the taking of Constantinople by the Turks   (Mod Un Hist Vols I to III)

Price's (David) Memoirs of the principal Events in Mohammedan History, from the death of the Arabian legislator to the accession of the Emperor Akbar, and the establishment of the Mogul empire. 4 vols. 4to. *Lond* 1812, &c.

History of Persia and Armenia.

Sacy (Silvestre de), Mémoires sur divers Antiquités de la Perse, et sur les Médailles des Rois de la dynastie de Sassanides, suivis de l'histoire de cette dynastie, traduite du Persan de Mirkhond 4to *Paris*, 1793.

The Shah Nameh of the Persian Poet Ferdousi, translated and abridged, in prose and verse, with notes and illustrations, by James Atkinson. 8vo. *London*, 1832

Jones's (Sir W.) Short History of Persia. (Works, Vol V)

Malcolm's (Sir John) History of Persia, from the most early period to the present time; with an account of the present state of that kingdom, and remarks on the religion, government, science, manners, and usages of its ancient and modern inhabitants 2 vols. 4to. *London*, 1815

History of Persia at large, and Kermân (Mod Un. Hist Vols III, IV, and XXXVI)

History of the Kingdom of Karazm [Khorasan] (Mod Univ History, Vol V)

History of the Shahs reigning in Persia, to Nadir Shah, and of the Arab Kings of Ormuz in Persia (Mod Univ. Hist Vol. V)

Histoire de Nadir Chah, connu sous le nom de Thammas Kuli Khan, Empereur de Perse traduite d'un MS Persan avec des notes, &c. par W. Jones (Sir W Jones's Works, Vol. V)

History and Literature of Persia (Waring's Tour to Shiraz)

Mosis Chorenensis Historia Armeniaca, ejusdem Epitome Geographiæ Arm ediderunt et Lat verterunt, notisque illustrav Guil et Georg Whiston 4to *Londini*, 1736.

Mosis Choronensis Historia abbreviata Armenicè 18mo *Venice*, 1827

Elisæus, Bp of Amadunians', History of the Vartan, and of the Battle of the Armenians; containing an account of the religious wars between the Persians and Armenians: translated from the Armenian by C F Neumann 4to *London*, 1830

Vahram's Chronicle of the Armenian Kingdom of Cilicia during the time of the Crusades; translated from the original Armenian, with notes and illustrations by C F Neumann 8vo *London*, 1831

History of India.

Robertson's (William) Historical Disquisition concerning the Knowledge which the Ancients had of India 4to. *London*, 1791

Maurice's (Thos) Indian Antiquities; or, dissertations relative to the ancient geography, theology, laws, government, commerce, and literature of Hindoostan, compared throughout with those of Persia, Egypt, and Greece 7 vols 8vo *London*, 1800

MODERN.

Maurice's (T.) History of Hindostan, its Arts and Sciences, during the most ancient periods of the world. 2 vols 4to *Lond* 1795-8

Maurice's (Thomas) Modern History of Hindostan, comprehending that of the Greek empire of Bactria, and other great Asiatic kingdoms bordering on its western frontier, from the death of Alexander to the 18th century, including a history of the East India Company. 2 vols 4to *London*, 1802-9

Ward's (William) View of the History, Literature, and Religion of the Hindoos; including a minute description of their manners and customs, and translations of their principal works 4 vols 8vo. *Lond.* 1817-20

History of the Religion of the Hindûs (Mod. Univ. Hist Vol VI.)

[Ferishta's (Moham Casim)] History of Hindostan, translated from the Persian by Alex Dow 3 vols 8vo *London*, 1803

Stewart's (Charles) History of Bengal, from the first Mohammedan invasion until the virtual conquest of that country by the English in 1757 [principally from Persian historians]. 4to *London*, 1813

History of the Moguls and Tartars, from Jenghiz Khân to the reign of the Sultan Bâbi. (Mod Univ. Hist. Vols IV and V.)

History of Hindûstân, or, the Empire of the Great Mogul to the Massacre at Delhi, and what passed there till Nâdir Shâh's return. (Mod Univ Hist Vol V.)

Memoirs of Zehir-eddin Muhammed Baber, Emperor of Hindostan, written by himself in the Jaghatai Turki, and translated partly by the late John Leyden, partly by W. Erskine, with notes, and geographical and historical introduction, by Charles Waddington. 4to. map of the countries between the Oxus and Jaxtartes. 4to *Lond* 1826.

Mulfuzat Timury; or, autobiographical Memoirs of the Mogul Emperor Timur, written in the Jagtay-Turky language, turned into Persian by Abu Talib Hussyng, and translated into English by Charles Stewart 4to *London*, 1830

Jahanguen (Memoirs of the Emperor) written by himself, and translated from the Persian MS by David Price 4to *London*, 1829

Shah Jehan (Rules observed during the reign of) (Gladwin's P. Moonshee.)

Orme's (Robt.) Historical Fragments of the Mogul Empire, of the Marattoes, and of the English concerns in Indostan, from 1659, with an account of the author's life and writings 4to *London*, 1805

Francklin's (Wm.) History of the Reign of Shah-Aulum, the present Emperor of Hindostan, containing the transactions of the court of Delhi, &c for thirty-six years 4to *London*, 1798

Mill's (James) History of British India, [from the commencement of the trade with that country to 1805] 6 vols. 8vo *Lond* 1820

Malcolm's (Sir John) Political History of India, from 1784 to 1823 2 vols 8vo. *London*, 1826

Orme's (Robt.) History of the Military Transactions of the British Nation in Indostan from the year 1745 to 61, to which is prefixed, a dissertation on the establishments made by the Mohamedan conquerors in Indostan. 3 vols 4to *London*, 1803.

HISTORY

Wilks's (Mark) Historical Sketch of the South of India, in an attempt to trace the history of Mysore from the origin of the Hindoo government of that state to the extinction of the Mohammedan dynasty in 1799, founded chiefly on Indian authorities 3 vols. 4to *London*, 1810–17.

Stewart's (C J) Memoirs of Hyder Ali Khan and his son Tippoo Sultaun. (Cat. of Tippoo's Library.)

Ferishta's History of Dekkan, from the first Mahummedan conquest, and continued from other native writers to the present day, and the history of Bengal from the accession of Aliverdee Khan to 1780, by Jonath Scott 2 vols 4to *Shrewsbury*, 1794

Malcolm's (Sir J.) Memoir of Central India, including Malwa and adjoining provinces, with the history, and copious illustrations of the past and present condition, of that country 2 vols 8vo. *London*, 1824

Tod's (James) Annals and Antiquities of Rajast'han, or the central and western Rajpoot states of India. 2 vols. 4to. *London*, 1829–32.

Cambridge's (Rich. Owen) Account of the War in India between the English and French on the coast of Coromandel, from 1750 to 1760. 4to *London*, 1761.

Munro (Life of Major-General Sir Thos), late Governor of Madras, with extracts from his correspondence and private papers, by the Rev. G R Gleig. 2 vols 8vo *London*, 1830.

History of the Countries contained in the hither Peninsula of India (Mod Un Hist Vol VI)

Duff's (James Grant) History of the Mahrattas, [from A D. 1000 to 1819] 3 vols 8vo *London*, 1826.

Elphinstone's (Mount-Stuart) Account of the Kingdom of Caubal and its dependencies in Persia, Tartary, and India; comprising a history of the Afghann nation, and a history of the Dooraunee monarchy. 4to *London*, 1815

Neamet Ullah's History of the Afghans, translated from the Persian by Richard Dorn. 4to. *London*, 1829

Hamilton's (Charles) Historical Relation of the Origin, Progress, and final Dissolution of the Rohilla Afgans, in the northern provinces of Hindoostan, compiled from a Persian MS and other original papers. 8vo. *London*, 1787.

Kirkpatrick's (William) Account of the Kingdom of Nepaul, being the substance of observations made during a mission in that country. 4to *London*, 1811

Malcolm s (Sir John) Sketch of the Sikhs, a singular nation in the provinces of Peryab in India, situated between the rivers Jumna and Indus. 8vo. *London*, 1812.

History of the Commerce to, and Settlement in, the East Indies by the several European nations (Mod Univ. Hist Vols VII and VIII)

History of the English East India Company. (Mod Univ History, Vol VIII)

History of the Dutch East India Company (Mod. Univ History, Vols VIII and IX)

History of the Danish, French, Ostend, and Swedish East India Companies   (Mod Univ Hist Vol IX)

Macpherson's (David) History of the European Commerce with India. (Commerce)

Bruce's (John) Annals of the Honourable East India Company, from their Establishment in 1600 to the Union of the London and English East India Companies, 1708   3 vols. 4to   *London*, 1810

Clive's (Robert, Lord) Speech in the House of Commons on a Motion made for an Inquiry into the Nature, State, and Condition of the East India Company, and the British Affairs in the East Indies in 1772   4to   *Privately printed*, 1772.

Burke's (Edmund) Speeches, &c. on Indian Affairs   (Political Hist)

Jones's (Sir W) Works, containing all his publications on the manners, customs, &c. of India, on oriental literature in general, and including those published in the Asiatic Researches.   8 vols. 4to.   *London*, 1798–1801.

Forbes's (James) Oriental Memoirs, selected and abridged from a series of Letters written during seventeen years' residence in India.   4 vols. 4to   *London*, 1813–15.

Dubois' (Abbé J A) Description of the Character, Manners, and Customs of the People of India, translated.   4to.   *London*, 1817.

Buchanan's (Claudius) Memoir of the Expediency of an Ecclesiastical Establishment for India   8vo.   *London*, 1812

History of China, Tartary, and Siam.

[Castillon (J)], Anecdotes des Mœurs, Usages, Coutumes, et Religions des Tonquinoises, Chinoises, Japonoises, Siamoises.   One vol. in 2, 12mo.   *Paris*, 1774

Halde's (J. B. du) [Geographical and Historical] Description of the Empire of China and Chinese Tartary, together with the Kingdoms of Corea and Tibet   From the French, with notes and other improvements by the translator.   2 vols. folio   *London*, 1738–41.

Couplet (Ph.) Tabula Chronologica Monarchiæ Sinicæ, juxta cyclos annorum LX, ab anno ante Christum 2952, ad annum post Christum 1683   Folio   *Parisiis*, 1686   (Confucius, Sm. Philosophus)

Tong-Kien-Kangmou, Histoire Générale de la Chine, traduite par Mayriac de Mailla, et publiée, avec la description de la Chine, par l'Abbé Grosier   7 vols. 8vo.   *Paris*, 1818.

History of the Eastern Tartars   (Modern Universal History, Vol VII.)

History of the Empire of China   (Modern Universal History, Vols VII. and XVIII)

History of the Pirates who infested the Chinese Sea from 1807 to 1810, translated from the original Chinese, with notes and illustrations by C F Neumann   8vo.   *London*, 1831

History of the farther Peninsula of India, Assam, Arrakan, Pegu, Ava, Siam, Kochin-China, and Tong-King.   (Modern Universal History, Vol VI.)

History of the Asiatic Isles.

Kœmpfer's (Engelbert) History of Japan, together with a description of the kingdom of Siam: translated from the original in High Dutch [in the library of Sir Hans Sloane], never before printed, by J G. Scheuchzer, with the life of the author, and an introduction [containing a list of authors who have previously written on this subject, and of Japanese writers] 2 vols. folio. *London, for the translator*, 1726.

History of Japan (Mod Univ Hist Vol. VII)

Titsingh, Mémoires et Anecdotes sur la Dynastie régnante des Djogouns souverains du Japon; avec des notes par A Rémusat. 8vo. *Paris*, 1820

Crawfurd's (John) History of the Indian Archipelago. 3 vols. 8vo *Edinburgh*, 1820

Knox's (Robt) Historical Relation of the Island Ceylon, with an account of the detaining in captivity the author and others, and of the author's miraculous escape Folio. *London*, 1681

Percival's (Robt) Account of the Island of Ceylon, containing its history, geography, customs, manners, &c.; with the journal of an embassy to the court of Candy 4to. *London*, 1805.

Cordiner's (James) Description of Ceylon; containing an account of the country, inhabitants, and natural productions; with an account of the Candian campaign of 1803. 2 vols. 4to. *London*, 1807.

Marsden's (William) History of Sumatra, an account of the government, &c of the native inhabitants, with a description of the natural productions, and a relation of the ancient political state of the country 4to, with plates in folio *London*, 1811.

Raffles's (Sir Thomas Stamford) History of Java 2 vols 4to. *Lond*. 1817.

Raffles (Memoirs of the Life and Public Services of Sir T S), particularly in the government of Java, 1811–16, and of Bencoleen and its dependencies, 1817–24, with details of the commerce and resources of the eastern Archipelago. by his Widow. 4to *London*, 1830

Zuniga's (Mart de) Historical View of the Philippine Islands, translated by J Mayer 2 vols 8vo *London*, 1814.

Leith's (Sir G) Short Account of the Settlement, Produce, and Commerce of Prince of Wales's Island, in the Straits of Malacca. 8vo *London*, 1805.

Africa.—General History.

Leonis (Joan) Descriptio Africæ (Travels)

Leo's (J.) Geographical History of Africa, before which, out of the best ancient and modern writers, is prefixed a general description of Africa, and also a particular treatise of all maine lands and isles undescribed by Leo, and a relation of the great princes and the manifold religions in that part of the world translated and collected by John Pory Folio *London*, 1600

History of Africa, and all the principal Nations and States which inhabit it. (Mod Univ Hist. Vols XI. and XXXVII.)

History of Egypt and Abyssinia.

See also page 178

Wilford (Francis) on Egypt and other Countries adjacent to the Calf River, or Nile of Ethiopia; from the ancient books of the Hindus (Jones's Works, Supplement, Vol II.)

Abd-Allatif, Relation de l'Egypte, suivie de divers extraits d'Ecrivains Orientaux, et d'un état des provinces et des villages de l'Egypte dans le XIV siècle; le tout trad et enrichi de notes, par De Sacy. 4to *Paris*, 1810.

Quatremère (E.), Mémoires Géographiques et Historiques sur l'Egypte, et sur quelques contrées voisines, recueillis et extraits des MSS Coptes, Arabes, &c 2 vols 8vo *Paris*, 1810

Champollion (J. F.), Lettres à M le Duc de Blacas d'Aulps, relatives au Musée Royal Egyptien de Turin, qui renferment la restoration chronologique, par les monuments, de la XV dynastie Egyptienne de Manéthon, et des suivantes, jusqu'aux Romains. 8vo plates in 4to. *Paris*, 1824–6.

History of Modern Egypt. (Mod Univ Hist. Vols XI and XXXVII)

Martin (P.), Histoire de l'Expédition Française en Egypte. 2 vols 8vo *Paris*, 1815

Mengin, Histoire de l'Egypte sous le Gouvernement de Mohammed-Aly jusqu'en 1823 Enrichi de notes par Langles et Jomard, et d'une introduction historique par Agoub 2 vols 8vo. *Paris*, 1824

Wilson's (R T) Moral and Physical State of Egypt. (Campaign in Egypt)

Burckhardt's (J L) Manners and Customs of the Modern Egyptians illustrated (Arabic Proverbs)

Ludolfi (John) Historia Æthiopica, sive descriptio regni Habessinorum quod vulgò malè Presbyteri Joannis vocatur, cum commentario 2 vols folio. *Francf* 1681–91

Ludolphi Relatio nova de hodierno Habessinæ statu, ex India nuper allata. Appendix secunda ad Historiam Æthiop, continens dissert de locustis folio *Francof*. 1693–4

Bruce's (James) Annals and Natural History of Abyssinia (Travels.)

Lobo (Jerome), Relation Historique d'Abyssinie, traduit du Portugais, continuée et augmentée de plusieurs dissertations, lettres, et mémoires, par M le Grand 4to *Paris*, 1728

History of Abyssinia (Mod Univ. Hist Vol XII and XXXVII)

History of Barbary and other parts of Africa.

History of Barbary, Morocco, Fez, Algiers, Tunis, Tripoli, &c (Mod Univ Hist Vols XIV and XV)

Chenier, Recherches Historiques sur les Maures, et Histoire de l'Empire de Maroc. 3 vols 8vo. *Paris*, 1787.

Morgan's (John) History of Algiers from the earliest to the present times 2 vols 4to. *London*, 1728–29

History of the Interior Countries of Africa. (Mod. Univ. Hist Vols XIV and XXXVII)

Norris's (Rob) Memoirs of the reign of Bossa Ahàdee, King of Dahomy; to which are added the author's Journey to Abomey, the capital, and an account of the Slave-trade. 8vo. *Lond.* 1789.

History of the Western Coast of Africa (Mod Univ. Hist Vols. XIII and XXXVII.)

Beaver's (Capt. Ph) African Memoranda relative to an attempt to establish a British Settlement on the Island of Bulama, on the Western Coast of Africa, in 1792. 4to. *London*, 1805.

History of the Southern Coast of Africa (Mod Univ Hist. Vols. XII. and XXXVII)

Percival's (Robert) Account of the Cape of Good Hope. 4to. *Lond.* 1804.

History of the Coast of Zanguebar (Mod. Univ. Hist Vols. XII and XXXVII)

History of the African Islands. (Mod. Univ Hist Vols XI, XII, and XXXVII)

Grant (Charles), Viscount de Vaux's, History of Mauritius, or the Isle of France, and the neighbouring Islands, from their discovery to the present time. 4to. *London*, 1801.

Brooke's (T. H.) History of the Island of St. Helena, from its discovery to 1806. 8vo. *London*, 1808.

Beatson's (Alex) Tracts relative to the Island of St Helena, written during a residence of five years. 4to *London*, 1816.

America.—General History.

Bibliotheca Americana : a Catalogue of Books, State Papers, &c. upon the subject of North and South America 4to *London*, 1789

Catalogue of Spanish Books and Manuscripts on America. (Robertson's America.)

Alcedo (Antonio de), Geographical and Historical Dictionary of America and the West Indies, translated, with large additions, by G. A Thompson. 5 vols 4to, and atlas in folio. *Lond* 1812–15

Barton's (B S) New Views of the origin of the Tribes and Nations of America 8vo *Philadelphia*, 1796

Humboldt (Alex de), Monumens des Peuples indigènes de l'Amérique. (Vues de Cordilleras, Travels)

Herrera (Ant de), Historia General de los Hechos de los Castellanos en los Islas y Terra Firma del Mar Oceano 8 vols in 4, folio. *En Madrid*, 1730.

Herrera (A de), Descripcion de las Indias Occidentales. Folio *En Madrid*, 1725.
> Forming the Supplement to the "Historia General," and containing the General Index.

History of America. (Mod Univ Hist. Vols XXXIV. and XXXVIII.)

Robertson's (Wm) History of America. 2 vols 4to *London*, 1778

Holmes's (George) American Annals; or, a chronological history of America from its first discovery in 1492 to 1806. 2 vols. 8vo. *Cambridge (New England)*, 1808.

Burney's (J.) History of the Buccaneers of America. (Discoveries in the South Sea.)

History of South America.

History of South America (Mod Univ Hist Vol. XXXVIII.)

Southey's (Robt) Expedition of Orsua, and the Crimes of Aguirre. 12mo. *Lond.* 1821

Cieza (Pietro), Historie del Peru, dove se tratta l'ordine delle provincie, delle città nuove en quel paese edificate, i riti e costumi degli Indiani — *La Seconda Parte* si tratta particolarmente della presa del Re Atabalippa, delle perle, dell' oro, delle spetierie, retrovate alle Malucche, et delle guerre civili tra gli Spagnuoli ; tradotte di Spagnuolo per And Arrivabene — *La Terza Parte*, nella quale particolarmente si tratta della conquista della grande et maravigliosa città di Messico, et delle altre provincie ad essa sottoposte ; trad. da ling. Spagnuola di F. Lopez de Gommara, da Lucio Mauro. 3 vols small 8vo *In Venetia, Giorg. Zilletti*, 1557, 1560, and 1566

> Neither Dr. Robertson nor Meusselius (Bib Hist) seem to have been aware that more than the First Part of this was published. The latter particularly regrets that it is not finished Richarderie also only specifies the First Part, but gives it as 2 vols. including, perhaps, the second.

Molina's (Don J Ignatius) Geographical, Natural, and Civil History of Chili. Translated, with notes, from the French and Spanish versions, with two historical appendixes. 2 vols 8vo. *London*, 1809.

Charlevoix's (P F Xavier de) History of Paraguay, translated. 2 vols. 8vo. *London*, 1769

Dobrizhoffer's (Martin) Account of the Abipones, an equestrian people of Paraguay, translated from the Latin [by R. Southey]. 3 vols. 8vo. *London*, 1822

Southey's (Robert) History of Brazil. 3 vols. 4to. *London*, 1809-19

Bancroft's (E) Guiana. (Nat. History)

History of North America.

History of North America (Mod. Univ. Hist. Vol XXXVIII)

Clavigero's (Fran. Sav) History of Mexico, compiled from the Spanish and Mexican Historians, and translated by Ch. Cullen 2 vols 4to. *London*, 1807

[Gomara (Lopez de)], The Pleasant Historie of the Conquest of the Weast India, now called New Spayne, atchieved by the worthy Prince Hernando Cortez. Translated out of the Spanish tongue by T[homas] N[icholas]. 𝔅𝔩𝔞𝔠𝔨 𝔩𝔢𝔱𝔱𝔢𝔯 4to *London, Hen. Bynneman* [1578]

Cortez (Hernan), Historia de Nueva Espana, aumentada por D. Fr Ant Lorenzana. Folio *En Mexico*, 1770

Solis (Ant de), Historia de la Conquista de Mexico, Poblacion y progressos de la Nueva Espana Folio *Amberes*, 1704

Ward's (H G) Mexico ; with an account of the political events of that Republic to the present day (Travels)

Humboldt (Alex de), Essai Politique sur la Nouvelle Espagne (Voyage)

Venegas' Natural and Civil History of California, translated from the Spanish. 2 vols 8vo *London*, 1759

Cardenas (G de), Ensayo por la Historia de la Florida Folio *Madrid*, 1723.

History of the British Settlements in America (Mod. Univ Hist Vols. XXXV, XXXVI, and XXXVII)

Hinton's (J. H.) History and Topography of the United States of North America, from the earliest period to the present time Proof plates. 2 vols 4to *London*, 1830-32.

Adair's (James) History of the American Indians, particularly those nations adjoining to the Mississippi, East and West Florida, Georgia, North Carolina, and Virginia 4to *London*, 1775.

Washington's (George) Life by John Marshall, corrected under the inspection of the Hon. B Washington. With a compendious view of the colonies planted by the English in North America. 5 vols. 8vo *London*, 1804-7.

Franklin's (Benj) Public Negotiations and American Politics. (Works, Vols IV. and V.)

Witherspoon's (John) Speeches in Congress, &c. (Works, Vol. IX.)

Jefferson's (President, Thos) Memoirs, Correspondence, and Private Papers, from the original MSS, edited by Thos. Jefferson Randolph. 4 vols 8vo. *London*, 1829

Stedman's (C) History of the Origin, Progress, and Termination of the American War. 2 vols. 4to. *London*, 1794.

Smith's (Capt. John) Generall Historie of Virginia, New England, and the Summer Islands; with the names of the adventurers, planters, and governours, from their first beginning, 1584. Folio The Hardwicke copy, with the rare pott. of the Duchess of Richmond, by Passe *London*, 1624

Neal's (Daniel) History of New England, containing an account of the civil and ecclesiastical affairs of that country to 1700 To which is added, their character, ecclesiastical discipline, and municipal laws. 2 vols. 8vo. *London*, 1720

Macgregor's (John) British America. 2 vols 8vo. *Lond* 1832.

Catesby's (M) Carolina, Florida, and the Bahama Islands. (Nat. Hist.)

History of the West India Islands.

History of the West India Islands (Mod Univ Hist. Vols XXXVI and XXXVIII)

Edward's (Bryan) History, Civil and Commercial, of the British West Indies; with continuation to the present time 5 vols. 8vo. Maps and plates in 4to *London*, 1819

[Rochefort (M. de)], Histoire Naturelle et Morale des Iles Antilles de l'Amérique. 4to *Rotterdam*, 1665

Hughes's (G) Barbadoes. (Nat Hist)

Poyer's (John) History of Barbadoes, from the discovery of the Island in 1605 to 1801 4to *London*, 1808

Histoire de l'Ile de S Domingue, depuis l'epoque de sa découverte jusqu'en 1818 8vo. *Paris*, 1819.

Long's (Edw) History of Jamaica, or, a general survey of the ancient and modern state of that island, with reflections on its situation, settlements, inhabitants, climate, laws, government, &c 3 vols. 4to *London*, 1774

Dallas's (R C) History of the Maroons, from their origin to the establishment of their chief tribe at Sierra Leone With a succinct history of the Island of Jamaica, and its state for the last ten years. 2 vols. 8vo *London*, 1803.

Fowler's (John) Account of the Colony of Tobago 8vo. *London*, 1774.

Smith's (W) History of Nevis, &c (Nat. Hist)

Sect. VI.—BIOGRAPHICAL AND MONUMENTAL HISTORY.

Biographical History.

General Biography.

Moreri (Louis), le Grand Dictionnaire Historique ; ou, le mélange curieux de l'histoire, sacrée et prophane nouvelle édition, dans laquelle on a refondu des supplémens de M l'Abbé Gouget ; le tout corrigée et augmentée par M Drouet 10 vols folio. *Paris*, 1759

A General Dictionary, historical and critical, including that of Bayle ; by J P. Bernard, T. Birch, J. Lockman, and other hands The articles relating to oriental history by Geo Sale. 10 vols. folio. *London*, 1734–41.

Chaufepie (J. G de), Nouveau Dictionnaire, historique et critique, pour servir de supplément à celui de Bayle 4 vols folio *Amsterdam*, 1750–56

Bayle —Marchand (Pr), Remarques Critiques sur le Dictionnaire de Bayle. 2 vols in one, folio *Paris*, 1748–52

The General Biographical Dictionary ; containing an historical and critical account of the lives and writings of the most eminent persons in every nation, particularly the British and Irish, from the earliest to the present time revised and enlarged by Alex. Chalmers 32 vols. *London*, 1812–17.

General Biography ; or, lives, critical and historical, of the most eminent persons, by J. Aikin, W. Enfield, — Nicholson, T Morgan, and W. Johnston 10 vols 4to. *London*, 1799–1815.

Chaudon (L M) et F A Delandine, Nouveau Dictionnaire Historique ; ou, histoire abrégé de tous les hommes qui se sont fait un nom par des talens, &c. avec des tables chronologiques, pour réduire en corps d'histoire les articles répandus dans ce Dictionnaire. 13 vols. 8vo *Caen et Lyon*, 1804

Galerie Historique des Hommes les plus célèbres de tous siècles et de toutes les nations, contenant leurs portraits, gravés au trait, avec l'abrégé de leurs vies, et des observations sur leurs caractères, ou sur leurs ouvrages, par une Société de Gens de Lettres Publiée par Landon 13 vols 12mo *Paris*, 1805–11

[Barbier], Examen Critique et Complément des Dictionnaires Historiques les plus repandus, depuis le Dictionnaire de Moreri jusqu'à la Biographie Universelle inclusivement, Vol I *A to F*. 8vo *Paris*, 1820.

Biographium Fœmineum; or, memoirs of the most illustrious ladies of all ages and nations. 2 vols small 8vo *London*, 1767

[Heywood's (Thos.)] Exemplary Lives and Memorable Acts of Nine of the most worthy Women of the world—three Jewes, three Gentiles, and three Christians. 4to. *London*, 1640.

Ecclesiastical Biography.

See also History of the Christian Religion, and Lives of the Saints, Popes, &c page 64

Gilpin's (W) Lives of the Reformers 2 vols. 8vo. *London*, 1809.

Middleton's (Erasmus) Evangelical Biography; or, an historical account of the lives and deaths of the most eminent authors or preachers, both British and foreign, in the several denominations of Protestants. 4 vols. 8vo *London*, 1816

Wordsworth's Ecclesiastical Biography. (English Ecclesiastical History.)

Ancient Biography

Lempriere's (J) Classical Dictionary; containing an account of all the persons mentioned in ancient authors. (Antiquities.)

Plutarch's Lives. (Classics)

Seran de la Tour's (Abbé) Life of Scipio Africanus and of Epaminondas, intended as a supplement to Plutarch's Lives, with notes and observations on the battle of Zama, and on the principal battles of Epaminondas, by M de Folard · with a dissertation on the distinction between a great and an illustrious or eminent man, by the Abbé St Pierre. Translated by R. Parry. 2 vols in one, 8vo. *London*, 1787

C Nepotis Vitæ Imperatorum. (Classics.)

Suetonii Vitæ XV Cæsarum. (Classics)

Diogenis Laertii Vitæ Philosophorum (Classics)

Berwick's (Edward) Lives of Marcus Valerius, Messala Corvinus, and Titus Pomponius Atticus; with notes and illustrations To which is added, an account of the families of the first five Cæsars 8vo. *Edinburgh*, 1813.

Berwick's (E) Lives of Caius Asinus Pollio, Marcus Terentius Varro, and Cneius Cornelius Gallus; with notes and illustrations. 8vo. *London*, 1814

Modern Biography

BRITISH BIOGRAPHY.

Biographia Britannica, or, the lives of the most eminent persons of Great Britain and Ireland. 6 vols in 7, folio *Lond*. 1744–66.

Biographia Britannica; with corrections and additions by Andrew Kippis and others Vols. I to V, *A to Fas* Folio *London*, 1778–93

Wilford's (John) Memorials and Characters; together with the lives of divers worthy and eminent persons, natives of Great Britain, from 1600 to 1740. Folio. *London*, 1741

Fuller's (Thos) History of the Worthies of England; with notes by John Nichols   2 vols 4to   *London*, 1811.

Winstanley's (Will) England's Worthies, select lives of the most eminent persons of the English nation, from Constantine the Great to the present time   8vo   *London*, 1684.

Walpole's Catalogue of Royal and Noble Authors   (Literary History)

Lloyd's (David) State Worthies, or, the statesmen and favourites of England, from the Reformation to the Revolution; with the characters of the kings and queens during that period, by Ch Whitworth   2 vols 8vo.   *London*, 1766.

Macdiarmid's (John) Lives of British Statesmen   4to   *Lond* 1807.

Wood's (Anthony) Athenæ Oxonienses   an exact history of all the writers and bishops who have had their education in the University of Oxford, to which are added, the Fasti, or annals of the said university   with additions and a continuation by Philip Bliss   5 vols 4to   *London*, 1813-20

Aubrey's (John) Lives of eminent Men   (Letters from the Bodleian Collection, Vol III)

Biographical Dictionary of Living Authors   (Literary History)

Biographical Memoirs of eminent Persons of the 18th century   (Nichols's Literary Anecdotes)

Ballard's (George) Lives of several Ladies of Great Britain who have been celebrated for their writings, or skill in the learned languages, &c.   4to.   *Oxford*, 1752

Memoirs of eminently Pious Women of the British Empire, by [Thos Gibbons, Geo Jerment, and] Samuel Burder   3 vols 8vo, portraits   *London*, 1815

Charnock's Biographia Navalis   (Eng Naval History)

Campbell's (A) Lives of the Admirals.   (Eng Naval History)

Noble's (Mark) Lives of Kings Heralds, and Pursuivants-at-Arms, since Richard III   (College of Arms.)

Johnson's (Sam) Lives of the English Poets   (Works, Vols. IX to XI, and Chalmers's British Poets)

Walker's (J. C) Historical Memoirs of the Irish Bards   (Irish Poetry)

Irving's (David) Lives of the Scottish Poets, with preliminary dissertations on the literary history of Scotland, and the early Scottish drama   2 vols 8vo   *Edinburgh*, 1804

Scott's (Sir W) Biographical and Critical Notices of eminent Novelists   (Misc Works, Vols III and IV)

Baker's Biographia Dramatica   (Drama.)

Johnson's (Capt Ch) Lives and Adventures of Highwaymen, &c &c from 1399 to 1733   Folio, best edition   *London*, 1736

Walton's (Isaak) Lives of Dr J Donne, Sir H Wotton, Mr R Hooker, Geo. Herbert, and Dr Robt Saunderson, with index and illustrative notes   Plates, small 8vo   *London, J. Major*, 1825.

Ward's (John) Lives of the Professors of Gresham College, with the life of the founder, Sir Th Gresham   Folio   *London*, 1740

Churton's (Ralph) Lives of William Smyth, Bishop of Lincoln, and Sir Richard Sutton, Knt, founders of Brasennose College, with an appendix of letters and papers never before printed. 8vo *Oxford*, 1800

Aikin's (John) Lives of John Selden and Abp Usher, with notices of the principal men of letters with whom they were connected 8vo. *London*, 1812.

Lives of those eminent Antiquaries, John Leland, Thomas Hearne, and Anthony à Wood, from original papers, in which are inserted memoirs relating to many eminent persons and various parts of literature [By W Huddesford, with the assistance of Dr. Ducarel, Mr. Warton, &c] 2 vols 8vo *Oxford*, 1772

Johnson's (Samuel) Lives of eminent Persons, [viz Blake, Sir F Drake, Sydenham, Cheynell, Cave, Browne, and Ascham] (Works, Vol XII)

Prince's (John) Worthies of Devon, wherein the lives and fortunes of the most famous divines, statesmen, &c of that province are memorized. 4to *London*, 1810

Chambers's (John) Biographical Illustrations of Worcestershire. 8vo *Worcester*, 1820.

Zouch's (Thos.) Lives of John Lord Lonsdale, Dean Sudbury, Sir G Wheeler, and Sketches of Yorkshire Biography. (Works, Vol II)

Ryan's (Rich) Biographical Dictionary of the Worthies of Ireland. 2 vols. 8vo. *London*, 1819

FOREIGN BIOGRAPHY.

Greswell's (W P.) Memoirs of Politianus, Picus of Mirandula, Sannazarius, Bembus, Francastorius, Flamminius, and the Amalthæi, with notes and observations concerning other literary characters of the 16th and 17th centuries 8vo *Manchester*, 1805

Johnson's (Samuel) Lives of sundry eminent Persons [viz Paolo Sarpi, Boerhaave, Barretier, Morin, Burman, and the King of Prussia]. (Works, Vol XII)

Moore's (George) Lives of the Cardinal Alberoni, the Duc de Ripperda, and the Marquis of Pombal (Spanish History.)

Perrault (M.) les Hommes Illustres qui ont paru en France pendant ce siècle; avec leurs portraits Including the suppressed portraits of Pascal and Arnauld 2 vols. in one, folio. *Paris*, 1696–1700.

Biographie Moderne. Lives of remarkable Characters who have distinguished themselves from the commencement of the French Revolution to the present time. 3 vols 8vo *London*, 1811.

LIVES OF ARTISTS

See History of the Fine Arts, Painting, and Engraving.

BIOGRAPHICAL ANECDOTES

[Seward's (W.)] Anecdotes of distinguished Persons, chiefly of the present and two preceding centuries, with Supplement 5 vols. 8vo *London*, 1795–97

[Seward's (W)] Biographiana 2 vols 8vo *London*, 1799.

Biographical, Literary, and Political Anecdotes of the most eminent persons of the present age. 3 vols. 8vo. *London*, 1797

Peter's Letters to his Kinsfolk [descriptive of literary characters, &c in Scotland]. 3 vols 8vo. *Lond* 1819.

PORTRAITS.

Physiognomical Portraits of One Hundred distinguished Characters, from undoubted originals, engraved by the most eminent British artists. [Edited with biographical notices in English and French, by Edward Walmsley.] Proofs, 2 vols. 4to. *London*, 1824.

Bezæ (Theo) Icones; id est, veræ Imagines Virorum doctrinâ et pietate illustrium; additis eorundem vitæ et operæ descriptionibus, quibus adjectæ sunt nonnullæ picturæ quas emblemata vocant 4to Dedicated to James VI of Scotland, with his port Large paper. *Genevæ, ap Io. Laonium*, 1580

Portraits illustrative of the Novels, Tales, and Romances, of the Author of Waverley [with biographical notices] Large paper, proofs, 8vo *London*, 1824

Iconographie des Contemporains depuis 1789 jusqu'à 1820. 2 vols folio. *Paris*, ——

Granger's (James) Biographical History of England, from Egbert the Great to the Revolution, with a continuation to the end of the reign of George I by Mark Noble Large paper, 7 vols. royal 8vo. *London*, 1804–6.

The Regal and Ecclesiastical Antiquities of England, containing the representations of all the English monarchs, from Edward the Confessor to Henry VIII, and many eminent persons; collected from ancient illuminated MSS, and engraved on copper-plates by the author, with Supplement. 4to *Lond* 1793

[Holland (Henry)] Basileωlogia, a Booke of Kings, beeing the true and lively effigies of all our English Kings, from the Conquest untill this present. With their severall coats of armes, impresses, and devises, and a briefe chronologie of their lives and deaths Elegantly graven in copper [by Elstracke, Passe, &c] Folio [*London*], *printed for H Holland*, 1618.

H[olland] (H) Herωologia Anglica hoc est, clariss et doctiss. aliquot Anglorum qui floruerunt ab anno M D usque ad presentem annum M DC XX. vivæ effigies [65]. vitæ, et elogia 2 vols. in one Folio *Londini, impensis Crispini Passæi*, [1620].

Birch's (Thomas) Heads of illustrious Persons of Great Britain, engraved by Houbraken and Vertue, with their lives, &c by Thomas Birch 2 vols in one, folio, large paper. *Lond* 1743–52

Adolphus's (John) British Cabinet, containing portraits of illustrious Personages, with biographical memoirs, Vol. 1 (all published) Folio, large paper *London, Harding*, 1799

Portraits of illustrious Personages of Great Britain, from authentic pictures in the galleries of the nobility, &c , with biographical and historical memoirs of their lives and actions, by Edmund Lodge, Norroy King at Arms 4 vols. folio, large paper, proofs on India paper. *London*, 1821, &c

Holbein's (Hans) Original Drawings of the Portraits of illustrious Persons of the Court of Henry VIII, with biographical notices by E Lodge, published by J Chamberlayne. Folio, large paper *Lond* 1792

Pinkerton's (John) Iconographia Scotica; or, Portraits of illustrious Persons of Scotland, with biographical notices. 4to *Lond* 1797

Pinkerton's (J) Scottish Gallery, or, Portraits of eminent Persons of Scotland, with brief accounts of the characters represented, and an introduction on the use and progress of painting in Scotland. 4to. *London*, 1799.

Separate Biographical Memoirs.

Abercrombie (Life of Alexander, Lord) (Mackenzie's Works, Vol. VII)
Adam (Life of Tho) of Wintringham (Works, Vol. II)
Æsop (Life of) by De Meziriac, translated, with notes, by R Dodsley. (Fables.)
Æsop (la Vie d'), par Fontaine (Œuvres de Fontaine, Vol. I.)
Alexander the Great (Life of) (Q Curtius.)
Alfieri (Memoirs of the Life and Writings of Victor), by himself, translated. 2 vols. 8vo *Lond* 1810.
Allan (Life of David), the Scottish Hogarth. (Ramsay's Gentle Shepherd)
Anglesey's (Arthur Earl of) Memoirs. (Eng Hist, James II)
Anstey (Life of Christopher) (Poetical Works)
Anville (Eloge de M d') (Bibliography)
Apollonius of Tyana (Life of), translated from the Greek of Philostratus, with notes and illustrations by E Berwick 8vo *London*, 1809
Argenson (Mémoires du Marquis d') (French History)
Aristotle (Life of) (Aristotle's Ethics)
Arminius (Life of James). (Works by Nichols, Vol 1)
Ascham (Life of Roger). (Works.)
Atterbury (Memoirs of Bp. Fr) (Correspondence)
Aylmer (Life of Abp) (Eng Ecc Hist)
Bacon (History of Fryer) (Miscellanea Antiqua)
Bacon (Memoirs of Antony) (Birch's Elizabeth)
Bacon's (John) Memoirs (Cecil's Works, Vol I)
Baker (Life of the Rev Tho), by Horatio Walpole (Orford's Works, Vol. II)
Barnes' (Life of Robert). (Tyndal, &c 's Works.)
Barrington (Life of Shute, Viscount) (Works, Vol. I)
Barrington (Memoir of Bp Shute) (Works, Vol I)
Barrow (Account of Isaac) (Works, Vol I.)
Barry (Life of J.) (Works, Fine Arts)
Barthélemy (Mémoires sur la Vie de J J) (Voyage d'Anacharse, Vol. I.)
Bannatyne's (George) Memorials, with the contents of the Bannatyne MSS 4to *Edinburgh, privately printed*, 1829.

BIOGRAPHY

Barwick (Life of Dr. John), by P. Barwick 8vo large paper, port by Vertue *London*, 1724

Basire (Memoirs of Isaac). (Basire's Correspondence.)

Bassompière (Mém du Mareschal de) (French History.)

Baxter (Life and Times of Richard). (Eng Ecc. History.)

Beattie (Account of the Life and Writings of Dr James), by Sir W Forbes, including many of his original letters 3 vols. 8vo *Edinburgh*, 1807

Becket (Life of Thomas à) (Eng Ecc. Hist.)

Bentley (The Life of Richard), with an account of his writings, and anecdotes of distinguished characters during the period in which he flourished, by J. H. Monk. 4to *Lond* 1830

Berkely (Life of Bp Geo.) (Works, Vol I.)

Berwick (Mémoires du Mareschal de) (French History.)

Besanval (Mémoires du Baron de) (French History.)

Beveridge (Life of Bp W), by T H Horne (Works, Vol. I)

Bewick (Memoirs of Messrs). (Select Fables)

Blacklock (Some account of the Life and Writings of Dr Thomas). (Mackenzie's Works, Vol VII)

Bois (Life of Mr. John), one of the Translators of the Bible, by Anthony Walker. (Peck's Desiderata Curiosa)

Bolingbroke (Life of Henry, Lord Visc). (Goldsmith's Works, Vol IV)

Bourgoing (Memoirs of General) (Works)

Bourrienne (Mémoires de). (French History)

Boyle (Life of the Hon. Robt), by Birch (Works, Vol. I)

Bramhall (Life of Abp), by Bp John Vesey (Works)

Brathwait (Life of Richard), by Haslewood (Barnabee's Journal)

Britton (Memoir of John) (Beauties of Wiltshire, Vol III)

Brown (Memorial Sketches of the Rev David) [by his Widow, and edited by Charles Simeon] 8vo *London*, 1816.

Brown (Life of Sir Thos) (Posthumous Works)

Bruce (James)—Account of the Life and Writings of the Author of the Travels to discover the Source of the Nile, by Alexander Murray 4to *Edinburgh*, 1808.

Brysson (Memoirs of W) (Scottish Ecc Hist)

Buchanan (Memoirs of the Life and Writings of Dr Claudius), by Hugh Pearson 2 vols 8vo *London*, 1819

Buchanan (Memoirs of the Life and Writings of George), by David Irving 8vo *Edinburgh*, 1807

Buchanan (New Anecdotes of George) (Life of Ruddiman)

Bunyan (Memoirs of the Life of John), by Rob Southey (Pilgrim's Progress.)

Buonarotti (Life of Michael Angelo), with his Poetry and Letters, by R Duppa 4to, large paper *London*, 1807.

Burghley (Life of William Cecil, Lord) Secretary of State and Lord High Treasurer to Queen Elizabeth, published from the original MSS. in the library of the Earl of Exeter With memoirs of the family of Cecil, by Arthur Collins 8vo *London*, 1732

HISTORY.

Burghley (Life and Actions of Sir W. Cecil, Lord) (Peck's Desiderata Curiosa.)

Burghley (Life and Actions of Sir W. Cecil, Lord), by Nares. (Eng Hist., Eliz.)

Burns (Life of Robert), by J. G. Lockhart. 8vo *Edinburgh*, 1828.

Byron (Letters and Journals of Lord), with notices of his Life by Thomas Moore. 2 vols 4to *London*, 1830

Cabot (Memoir of Sebast.). (Travels, America.)

Cadogan (W. B.) Memoirs of (Cecil's Works, Vol I.)

Calamy (Life of Edmund) (Eng Eccl Hist)

Cambridge (Memoirs of R. O.). (Works)

Camoens (Memoirs of the Life and Writings of Luis de), by John Adamson. 2 vols small 8vo. *Newcastle*, 1820.

Campbell (Life of Geo.) (Lect. on Ecc. Hist.)

Carleton (Memoirs of Capt. George) (Spanish History.)

Carnot (Mémoires sur). (French History.)

Carstares (Life of William) (State Papers.)

Caxton (Life of William) (Bibliography)

Cecil (Life, Character, and Remains of the Rev Thos.), collected and revised by Josiah Pratt. 8vo. *London*, 1812.

Cellini (Vita del Benvenuto), scritta da lui. 4to. *Colonia*, [1730].

Cellini (Memoirs of Benvenuto), a Florentine Artist, written by himself. Containing a variety of information respecting the arts, and the history of the 16th century Corrected and enlarged from the last Milan edition, with the notes and observations of G P. Carpani, now first translated by Thomas Roscoe, Esq. 2 vols. 8vo. *London*, 1822.

Cervantes (Life of). (Don Quixote.)

Charlemont (Memoirs of James Caulfield Earl of) (Irish History.)

Chatterton (Life of Thomas). (Works, Vol I)

Chaucer (Life of Geoffry), by W. Godwin, including memoirs of his near friend and kinsman, John of Gaunt, Duke of Lancaster With sketches of the manners, opinions, arts, and literature in England during the 14th century 2 vols 4to *London*, 1803.

Chaucer (Illustrations of the Life of), by Todd. (*See* Gower)

Cheke (Life of Sir John) (English History, Edward VI)

Chesterfield (Memoirs of Philip Dormer Stanhope, Earl of), by Maty (Misc Works, Vol I.)

Chillingworth (Life of W) (Works, Vol I)

Cicero (Life of M T.), by C. Middleton. 2 vols 8vo. *London*, 1819

Clarendon (The Life of Edward, Earl of), to his banishment in 1667, published from his original MSS. 2 vols 8vo. large paper *Oxford*, 1760

Clarke (The Life and Remains of Dr. E. D.), by William Otter. 4to. *London*, 1824.

Clement XIV. (Anecdotes of) (Ganganelli's Letters)

Colet (Life of Dr John), by Samuel Knight. 8vo *London*, 1724.

BIOGRAPHY.

Collingwood (Memoirs of Lord)   (Eng Naval Hist)
Columbus (Life of Christ)   (Travels, America.)
Cook (Memoirs of Capt James), by Andrew Kippis   4to   *Lond* 1788.
Corbet (Life of Bp R)   (Poems)
Corneille (la Vie de P), par B. le Bovier de Fontenelle.   (Œuvres.)
Coucy (Memoires Historiques sur Raoul de), par M. de la Borde   2 vols. in one, small 8vo   *Paris*, 1781
Cowley (Life of Abr)   (Works.)
Cowper's (Wm) Life and Posthumous Writings, by Wm Hayley   3 vols 4to   *Chichester*, 1803
Cranmer (Life of Abp).   (Eng Ecc Hist)
Creichton (Memoirs of Capt John), by Jonath Swift   (Works, Vol III)
Crichton (Life of James), of Cluny, commonly called the Admirable Crichton, with an appendix [of notes and illustrations, and of testimonia of various authors regarding him], by Pat Fr Tytler   8vo. *Edinburgh*, 1819.
Cromwell (Life of Oliver)   (Eng. Hist., Protectorate)
Cumberland (Memoirs of Richard), by himself; interspersed with anecdotes and characters of the most distinguished men of his time. 2 vols 8vo   *London*, 1807.
Cumberland (Life of Richard), embracing a critical examination of his writings with an occasional literary inquiry into the age in which he lived, and the contemporaries with whom he flourished, by William Mudford   8vo   *London*, 1812.
Currie (James), Memoirs of his Life, Writings, and Correspondence, edited by his Son   2 vols 8vo.   *London*, 1831.
Cullen (Account of the Life, Lectures, and Writings of William), by John Thomson   2 vols 8vo   *Edinb* 1832
Dante (Life of), translated from Brum by Boyd.   (Poetry)
Darnley (Memoir of Henry, Lord).   (Chalmers's Mary Queen of Scots)
Darwin (Memoirs of the Life of Dr. Erasmus), with anecdotes of his friends, and criticisms on his writings, by Anna Seward   8vo *London*, 1804.
Davy (Life of Sir Humphry), by J A Paris   2 vols. 8vo   *London*, 1831.
De Foe (Life of Daniel), by Chalmers   (History of the Union with Scotland, and Novels, and by Wilson, English History, Anne)
Dermody (Life and Correspondence of Thomas), by J G Raymond 2 vols 8vo.   *London*, 1806
Doddridge (Life of Philip), by Job Orton   (Family Expositor, Vol I)
Doppet (Mémoires du Général)   (French History.)
Drake's (Memoirs of Capt. Peter), by himself, containing an account of many strange and surprising events which happened to him through a series of sixty years, and several anecdotes regarding King William's and Queene Anne's War with Louis XIV   8vo   *Dublin, printed for the author*, 1755
  This was carefully suppressed by Capt. Drake's family.
Drake (Life and Death of Sir F.), by Charles Fitz-Geffrey   Small 8vo *Lee Priory*, 1819

HISTORY

Dryden (Life of John), by Sir Walter Scott. (Dryden's Works, Vol I, and Scott's Prose Works, Vol. I)

Dugdale (Life, Diary, and Correspondence of Sir W), by Hamper   4to large paper. *London*, 1827

Dudgale (Life of Sir W.), by himself   (Hist of St Paul's, 2d edition, and Dallaway's Heraldry)

Dumourier (Mémoires du Général de).   (French History)

Dunton (Life and Errors of John), with the lives and characters of more than one thousand contemporary divines and persons of literary eminence   2 vols 8vo   *London*, 1818

Dwight (Memoirs of Tim.)   (System of Theology)

Edgeworth (Memoirs of Rich Lovell), begun by himself, and concluded by his daughter   2 vols. 8vo.   *London*, 1820

Epicurus (Life of)   (Lucretius de Rerum Naturâ)

Erasmus (Life of), more particularly that part of it spent in England, wherein an account is given of his learned friends, and of the state of religion and learning at that time in both our universities, by Sam Knight   8vo large paper, portrait, &c   *Cambridge*, 1726.

Erasmus (Life of), by J Jortin.   3 vols 8vo   *London*, 1808

Evelyn (Memoirs illustrative of the Life and Writings of John), Esq edited by Wm Bray   2 vols 4to   *London*, 1819

Falconer (Life of William), by J S Clarke   (Shipwreck)

Falkland's (Letice, Vicountess) Returns of Spiritual Comfort and Grief in a devout Soul, exemplified in the life and death of the said honourable ladie, by John Duncon, portrait by Marshall   Small 8vo   *London*, 1649

Fanshawe (Memoirs of Lady), wife of Sir Richard Fanshawe, Bart. Ambassador from Charles II. to the Court of Madrid in 1665, written by herself, with extracts from the correspondence of Sir Richard, [by Charles Robert Fanshawe.]   8vo   *London*, 1829

Fayette (Mémoires du Général La)   (French History.)

Fenelon (Life of), Abp of Cambray, by Charles Butler   8vo.   *London*, 1810

Ferrar (Memoirs of the Life of Nicholas), [Founder of the Arminian Nunnery at Little Gidding, Huntingdonshire], by P Peckard.   8vo.   *Cambridge*, 1790

Fielding (Murphy on the Life, &c. of Henry)   (Works, Vol I)

Finlayson (Life of Geo)   (Mission to Siam.)

Fisher (Life and Death of Bp John), by Thomas Baily.   12mo   *Lond* 1655.

Forbes (Memoirs of Duncan, Lord President)   (Culloden Papers)

Fourmont (Vie de M) l'Ainé.   (Origine des Nations)

Fox (C J.), Memoirs of the latter Years of, by J. Ber Trotter, [with the postscript]   8vo   *London*, 1811

Fox (Character of the late Charles James), selected, and in part written by Philopatris Varvicensis [Dr Parr, with notes, principally on the English penal laws]   2 vols 8vo   *London*, 1809

Fox (Memoirs of the Life of Sir Stephen)   (History of England, Charles II)

BIOGRAPHY.

Franklin (Memoirs of the Life and Writings of Benj.) (Works)
Fryth (Life of John). (Tyndal, &c 's Works)
Gaete (Mémoires du Duc de) (French History)
Garcilasso de la Vega (Life of). (Works, by Wiffen)
Garrick (Life of David). (Correspondence.)
Gibbon (Memoirs of Ed.), by himself (Roman History, Vol I, and Misc Works, Vol I)
Giraldus de Barri (Life of), by Sir R. C Hoare. (Itinerary)
Goethe (Memoirs of), written by himself; with biographical notices of the principal persons mentioned in the memoirs 2 vols. 8vo London, 1824
Goldoni (Memorie del Signor) (Commedie, Vol 1.)
Goldsmith (an Account of the Life and Writings of Oliver), by Washington Irving. (Works, Vol I)
Gower and Chaucer (Illustrations of the Lives and Writings of), collected from authentic documents by H. J. Todd). 4to London, 1810
Grammont (Memoirs of) (English History, Charles II.)
Gray (Life of Thomas) (Works, by Mason, Mitford, and Mathias.)
Grey (Life and Literary Remains of Lady Jane). (Eng. History.)
Grindal (Life of Abp) (Eng Ecc Hist.)
Hafiz-ool-Moolk, Hafiz Rehmut Khan (Life of), written by his Son, the Nuwab Moostujah Khan Buhadoor, and entitled Goolistan-i-Rehmut; abridged and translated from the Persian by Charles Elliott. 8vo London, 1831
Hale (Life of Sir M.), by Bp Burnet; with additional notes by R Baxter. (Works, Vol I)
Hall (Account of some Specialties in the Life of Bp. Joseph), by himself. (Works, Vol I)
Hall (Life of Robert) (Works)
Hamilton (Memoirs of Count) (*See* Grammont)
Hamilton (Memoirs of James and William, Dukes of) (Scottish Hist)
Hampden (Memorials of John) (Eng. Hist, Charles I.)
Harrington (Life of James), by Toland (Works)
Harris (Life of James), by the Earl of Malmesbury (Works, Vol. I.)
Hausset (Mémoires de Madame de). (French History)
Hayley (Memoirs of the Life and Writings of W), the Friend and Biographer of Cowper, written by himself; with extracts from his private correspondence and unpublished poetry, and memoirs of his son T A. Hayley, the young sculptor Edited by J. Johnson 2 vols. 4to London, 1823.
Hazin (Life of Sheikh Mohammed Ali), written by himself, translated from two Persian MSS, and illustrated with notes explanatory of the history, poetry, geography, &c which therein occur, by F. C. Belfour. 8vo London, 1830.
Heber (the last days of Bp), by Thomas Robinson, Archdeacon of Madras 8vo London, 1831

Heber (The Life of Reginald), Bp of Calcutta, by his Widow, with selections from his correspondence, unpublished poems, and private papers : together with a journal of his tour in Norway, Sweden, Russia, Hungary, and Germany, and a history of the Cossacks 2 vols 4to *London*, 1830

Herbert (Life of Edward, Lord), of Cherbury, by himself, with prefatory memoir [by Sir W. Scott]. 8vo *Edinburgh*, 1809

Hill (Memoir of Lord) (Description of Hawkstone)

Hill (Life of Robert) (*See* Maghabechi)

Hinton's (Sir John) Memoirs. (Eng History, James II)

Hodgson (Life of Capt John) (Eng History, Commonwealth.)

Hollis (Memoirs of Thos); [including anecdotes of Sidney, Milton, Locke, Ludlow, Hutchison, &c], by [Francis Blackburne]   2 vols 4to. *London*, 1780.

<small>Printed only for private distribution, by Thomas Brand Hollis This copy has the additional pages of remarks on Johnson's Life of Milton, inserted after page 531, the index, which did not appear until after 1804, and all the plates, including that of Sir I Newton.</small>

Hôpital (Butler on the Life of M. de l'). (French History)

Hopkins (Life of Bp Ez), by Josiah Pratt   (Works, Vol I)

Horne (Life of Bp. Thos.), by Jones (Works, Vol. VI)

Hough (Life of Bp John), containing many of his letters, and biographical notices of several persons with whom he was connected, by John Wilmot 4to *London*, 1812

Howard (Memoirs of Henry), Earl of Surrey, by C. F Nott (Works of Surrey and Wyatt)

Howard (Memoirs of Henry), Earl of Northampton, by C F. Nott (Works of Surrey and Wyatt)

Howard (Memoirs of the Public and Private Life of John), the Philanthropist, compiled from his own diary, his confidential letters, &c. by J. B. Brown. 4to. *London*, 1818.

Hutchinson (Life of Mrs. Lucy) } (Eng. Hist. Commonwealth)
Hutchinson (Memoir of Col.).

Jackson (Life of Thomas) (Works, Vol I.)

Jefferson (Memoirs of the President Thos.) (American History.)

Jenkins (Life of Sir Leoline) (Eng. Hist., Charles II)

Jewell (Life of Bp. John). (Works.)

Joan of Arc (Memoirs of). (French History)

John of Gaunt, Duke of Lancaster (Memoirs of). (Godwin's Life of Chaucer)

Johnson (Life of Samuel), including a Journal of a Tour to the Hebrides, by James Boswell, with numerous additions and notes by J. W Croker 5 vols. 8vo *Lond*. 1831.

Johnson (Murphy on the Life and Genius of) (Works, Vol. I.)

Jones (Sir W.) Memoirs of his Life, Writings, &c. by Lord Teignmouth. 4to. *London*, 1806.

Jones (Life of W.) of Nayland, by W. Stevens. (Works, Vol. I.)

Jonson (Memoirs of Ben), by W Gifford. (Works, Vol I)

Josef (Vie du Père)   (French History)

Kaimes (Memoirs of the Life and Writings of Henry Home, Lord), by A F. Tytler [Lord Woodhouselee]. 2 vols 4to   Edin 1807

Kemble (Memoirs of the Life of John), by James Boaden. (English Dramatic History)

Ken (Life of Bishop Thos), by Bowles   (Eng Ecc History)

King (Life of Gregory) from his own MSS. (Dallaway's Heraldry)

Kirkaldy (Biog. Sketch of Sir W) of Grange. (Dalyell's Scottish Poems)

Knox (Life of John); by M'Crie. (Scottish Ecc. Hist.)

Kotzbue (Aug von), the most remarkable year of his life; containing an account of his exile to Siberia, written by himself, and translated by Benj Beresford. 3 vols 12mo. *London*, 1806.

Lake (Life of Bp. A.) (Works.)

Lardner (Life of Nath); by And Kippis   (Works, Vol. V.)

Laud (Life of Abp. W), by Parker. (Eng Hist , Charles I.)

Law (Life of John), of Lauriston, Comptroller-General of the Finances in France, by Wood   (History of Cramond)

Lawrence (Life and Correspondence of Sir Thos), by D. E. Williams. 2 vols 8vo   *London*, 1831

Lightfoot (Memoirs relative to Dr John)   (Works, Vol. I)

Leighton (Memoirs of Abp. R.), by Jerment   (Works, Vol. I.)

Leo X. (Life of)   (Italian History.)

Lesley (Life of Bp. John)   (Anderson's Collections)

Leyden (Memoirs of Dr John), by Morton   (Remains, Poetry)

Lilly (Life of W), by himself. (Occult Philosophy)

Locke (Life of John). (Works, Vol. I.)

Locke (Life of John), with extracts from his correspondence, journals, and common-place books, by Lord King. 4to   *London*, 1829.

Longinus (Life and Character of Dionysius), by Smith.   (Longinus on the Sublime)

Lope de la Vega (Account of the Life and Writings of Carpio), by Lord Holland. 8vo   *London*, 1806

Lovat (Memoirs of Simon Fraser, Lord), written by himself (Scot Hist)

Lucian (Life of), by John Dryden   (Dryden's Works, Vol. XVIII)

Lucretius (Life of). (De Rerum Naturâ)

Ludlow's (Ed) Memoirs. (Eng Hist , Commonwealth)

Luther (Life of Martin). (Hist. of the Christian Religion)

Lindsay (Life of Sir David)   (Poetical Works)

Macartney (some Account of the Public Life, and a Selection from the unpublished Writings, of the Earl of), by John Barrow. 2 vols. 4to. *London*, 1807.

Maghabechi (a Parallel, in the manner of Plutarch, between) and Robert Hill, by Joseph Spence   8vo   *Strawberry Hill*, 1758

Malayan Family (Memoirs of a), written by themselves, and translated from the original by W Marsden   8vo   *London*, 1830.

HISTORY.

Maintenon (Mémoires de Madame de). (French History.)
Marlborough (Life of John Duke of). (English Military History.)
Marmontel (Mémoires de), par lui-même. 4 vols. 12mo. *Lond.* 1806.
Mazarin (Histoire du Cardinal). (French History.)
Mede (Life of Joseph), by J Worthington. (Works.)
Medici (Memoirs of Lorenzo de) (Italian History.)
Meillan (Mémoires de) (French History.)
Melancthon (Life of P.) (Hist. of the Christian Religion.)
Melville (Life of Andrew), by M'Crie. (Scottish Eccles. Hist.)
Metastasio (Memoirs of the Life and Writings of Pietro); with translations of his principal Letters; by Charles Burney. 3 vols. 8vo. *London*, 1796.
Millar (Life of Professor John), by John Craig (Origin of Ranks.)
Milton (Collections for the Life of), by John Aubrey, from the MS copy in the Ashmolean Library, and Life by Edward Philips [from the printed copy, 8vo 1685]. (Godwin's Lives of E. and J Philips.)
Milton (New Memoirs of the Life and Poetical Works of John), by Francis Peck 4to *Lond.* 1740
Milton (Historical and Critical Account of the Life of J.), by T. Birch. (Prose Works, 4to Vol. I.)
Milton (Life of J.), by J Richardson. (Notes, &c. on Milton.)
Milton (Life of John), by Symons. (Prose Works, 8vo Vol. VII.)
Milton (Life of J.), by Todd (Poetical Works, 8vo. Vol. I.)
Molière (la Vie de), par Voltaire, avec un Supplément par Bret (Œuvres de Molière.)
Montague (Memoirs of Lady Wortley), by Dallaway (Works, Vol. I.)
Montrose (Memoirs of James Graham, Marquis of) (Scottish Hist.)
More (Life of Dr. Henry), with divers of his letters, by Richard Ward. 8vo. *Lond.* 1710.
More (Memoirs of Sir Thomas); with a new translation of his Utopia, his Richard III., and his Latin Poems, by Art. Cayley, jun. 2 vols. 4to *Lond* 1808
More (History of Sir T.), by J Hoddesdon Small 8vo port. by Wierx *Lond* 1652
Mori (Gul Roperi Vita Thomæ), accedunt Mori Epistolæ et Orationes aliquam multæ. Ediditque è cod. MS. vet. descripsit T Hearne. 8vo. *Oxonii,* 1716.
More (Life of Sir T.), by W Roper 8vo. *Lond* 1818.
More.—The Life and Death of Sir Thomas More, Lord High Chancellouie of England, written by M. T[homas] M[ore], and dedicated to the Queen's most gracious majesty 4to. *No date, but supposed to be printed abroad about* 1627.
Mori (Vita del T.), per Domenico Regi 12mo *Milano,* 1675
Munro (Life of Sir Thomas), by Gleig. (Indian History.)
Murillo (Life of Bart e), compiled from various authors; translated by Thos Davies Small 8vo. *London,* 1819
Neot (Life of St.), by Whitaker. (Eng. Ecc Hist.)

BIOGRAPHY

Nelson (Life of Horatio, Lord Visc.), by J. S. Clarke and J. M'Arthur. (English Naval History.)

Newton (Memoirs of Sir I.), sent by M. Conduitt to M Fontenelle, now first published from the Newtonian MSS. (Turner's History of Grantham)

Newton (Memoirs of John). (Cecil's Works, Vol. I)

Newton (Life of Bp T.), by himself; with Anecdotes of his Friends. (Works, Vol I.)

North (Fr Lord Guildford), Life of, Lord Keeper under Charles I and James II, wherein are inserted, the characters of Sir Matthew Hale, Sir Geo Jefferies, Sir Leol Jenkins, and other eminent lawyers and statesmen of that time; by the Hon. Roger North. 2 vols 8vo *London*, 1808

Nowell, Dean of St Paul's (Life of Alexander), by Ralph Churton 8vo *Oxford*, 1809.

Oberlin (Memoirs of John Fred), Pastor of Waldbach, in the Ban de la Roche. 12mo *Lond* 1831

Oppiani (Vita). (Oppian de Piscatu)

Orleans (Mémoires du Duc d') (French Hist)

Orme (Life of Robert). (Fragments, Indian History)

Otway (Life of Thomas). (Dramatic Works)

Paley (Wm.) Memoirs of, by Geo W. Meadley. 8vo *Edin.* 1810.

Park (Life of Mungo) (Travels, Vol. II)

Parker (Life of Abp.) (Eng. Ecc Hist.)

Parnel (Life of Dr. Thos) (Goldsmith's Works, Vol IV.)

Pascal (Vie de M), par Mad Perier, sa Sœur (Pensées)

Pascal (Memoirs of the Life of Blaise) (Thoughts)

Pearce (Life of Nath) (Travels in Abyssinia)

Pecock (Life of Bp.) (Eng Ecc Hist)

Pennant's (Thos) Literary Life, by himself (Literary History)

Pepys (Life of Samuel), by Lord Braybrooke (Memoirs, English History, Charles II)

Perrott (the History of Sir John), Lord Lieutenant of Ireland. (Irish History)

Petrarque, (Mémoires pour la Vie de Fr) tires de ses œuvres et des auteurs contemporains, avec des notes ou dissertations [par l'Abbé de Sadé] 3 vols. 4to *Amst* [*Avignon*], 1764-67.

Petrarch (Life of), collected from " Mémoires pour sa Vie," by Mrs Dobson 2 vols 8vo. *London*, 1797

Petrarch, Historical and Critical Essay on the Life and Character of [by Lord Woodhouselee] 8vo *Edin* 1810

Philip of Macedon (Life of). (Grecian History)

Phillips (Lives of Edw. and John), Nephews and Pupils of Milton; by Wm. Godwin (English Hist Commonwealth)

Pitt (Wm Earl of Chatham), Anecdotes of his Life 4 vols 8vo *London*, 1792.

Pitt (Political Life of the Right Hon Wm), by John Gifford. (English Hist., Geo. III)

HISTORY.

Pitt (Memoirs of the Life of the Right Hon. Wm), by Geo Tomline. (Eng Hist., Geo III)

Pliny (Life of) (Pliny's Letters)

Plot (Life of Dr. Robt) (Oxfordshire)

Plutarch (Life of) (Dryden's Works, Vol XVII.)

Poggio Bracciolini (Life of), by Wm Shepherd 4to *Liverpool*, 1802.

Polwhele's (R.) Traditions and Recollections (Literary History)

Pomponius Atticus (Life of) (Hale's Works, Vol. I)

Pope (Life of Sir Thos.), Founder of Trinity College, Oxford, by Thomas Warton. 8vo *London*, 1780.

Pope (Life of Alex), compiled from original MSS; with an Essay on his writings and genius, by Owen Ruffhead. 8vo *London*, 1769.

Pope (Life of Alex), by W L Bowles (Works, Vol. I)

Potemkin (Memoirs of Prince) (Russian History)

Prideaux (Life of Dean Humphrey). (Old and New Test. connected, Vol I)

Quarles (Life and Death of Francis), by T F. Dibdin (Manual of Devotion)

Racine (Mémoires sur la Vie de Jean) (Œuvres, Vol. I)

Radcliffe's (Sir Geo) Life and Original Correspondence, by T D. Whitaker. 4to. *London*, 1810.

Raffles (Memoir of the Life and Public Service of Sir Thos. S.) (East Indian History.)

Ralegh (Sir W) Life of, by Arth Cayley. 2 vols. 8vo. *Lond* 1806.

Ralegh (Sir W), Life of, by T Birch. (Works, Vol I)

Ralegh (Sir W.), Life of, by Wm Oldys (Works, Vol. I.)

Rami (Vita Petri), ex J T. Freigio descripta. (Milton's Prose Works, 4to. Vol. II, 8vo Vol VI)

Ramsay (Life of Allan). (Gentle Shepherd)

Reid (Thomas), Memoirs of the Life and Writings of, by Dugald Stewart. 4to *Edinburgh*, 1811

Reresby's (Sir John) Memoirs (Eng Hist., Charles II.)

Reynold's (Sir Josh) Memoirs of, with original anecdotes of many distinguished persons, and a brief analysis of his discourses, by J Northcote. 4to *London*, 1813.

Reynolds (Life of Sir Joshua), by E. Malone. (Works, Vol I)

Riccio (some Particulars of the Life of David). (Miscellanea Antiqua)

Richelieu (Histoire du Cardinal). (French History)

Ridley (Life of Bp) (Eng. Ecc. Hist)

Robertson (Wm), Memoirs of the Life and Writings of, by Dug. Stewart. 4to. *Edin* 1811. (Robertson's Scotland, Vol 1)

Robinson (Life of Thomas), of Leicester, by Ed Th Vaughan. 8vo. *London*, 1816.

Rochester (some Passages in the Life and Death of the Earl of), by Gilb Burnet 12mo *London*, 1805

Roland (Vie de Madame)   (French History)
Rollin (Life of C), by Lynman.   (Ancient History.)
Romney (Life of Geo), with Illustrations from his Works, by W Hayley   4to   *London*, 1809
Rovigo (Memoirs of the Duke of)   (French History)
Ruddiman (Life of Thomas), Librarian to the Faculty of Advocates of Edinburgh, with new anecdotes of Buchanan, by George Chalmers. 8vo port by Bartolozzi   *London*, 1794.
Ruggle (Life of George)   (Ignoramus, Latin Drama)
Sadler (Memoirs of Sir Ralph)   (State Papers)
Sancroft (Life of William), Abp of Canterbury. With an appendix; life of the learned Henry Wharton, and two letters of Dr Sanderson, from the archiepiscopal library, Lambeth. by Geo D'Oyly   2 vols. 8vo   *London*, 1821
Sandwich (Life of John Montague, 1st Earl of), by Cooke.   (Sandwich's Voyage)
Sandys (Life of Abp E), by Whitaker.   (Sermons)
Savigny (Précis de la Vie de Mad de)   (Lettres)
Schilteri (B J.) Vita et Memoria Meritorum Operumque Catalogus.   (Schilteri Thes. Vol II)
Scott (Life of Thomas), including a narrative drawn up by himself, and copious extracts from his letters, by John Scott   8vo.   *Lond* 1822
Secker (Life of Abp. Thomas)   (Works, Vol I)
Selden (Life of John), by Aikin   (Lives of Selden and Usher)
Seldeni (Vita Joannis) à D Wilkins.   (Seldeni Opera Vol I)
Servetus (History of)   (History of Sects.)
Seward (Biographical Sketch of Anna), by Sir W Scott   (Seward's Works)
Shaftesbury (Memoirs relative to the Life of Anthony, 1st Earl of).   (Locke's Works, Vol IX)
Shakespeare (Life of W), by N Drake   (Dramatic History)
Shakespeare (Life of), by Malone   (Works)
Sharp (Life of Abp. John), collected from his diary, letters, &c by his son, and edited by Thomas Newcome.   2 vols 8vo   *Lond* 1825.
Sheridan (Memoirs of the Life of Richard Brinsley), by Thomas Moore. 4to.   *London*, 1825
Siddons (Memoirs of Mrs), by Boaden.   (English Dramatic History)
Slingsby (Life of Sir Henry)   (English Hist , Commonwealth)
Smellie (Memoirs of the Life and Writings of Wm), by Robert Kerr. 2 vols   8vo   *Edinburgh*, 1811
Smith (Memoirs of the Life and Writings of Adam), by Dugald Stewart.   4to   *Edinburgh*, 1811.
Smith (Life of Sir Thomas)   (Eng. Hist., Elizabeth)
Smollett (Memoirs of the Life and Writings of Tobias)   (Works, Vol I.)
Somner (Life of W.), by White Kennet.   (Treatise on Gavelkind)
Spence (Life of Joseph), by Singer   (Spence's Anecdotes)
Spenser (Life of Edmund), by Todd   (Works)

Sterne (Life of Lawrence), by himself. (Works, Vol. I.)
Stillingfleet (Life of Bp. Edward). (Works, Vol. I.)
Stillingfleet (The Literary Life of Benjamin), by Coxe. (Works, Vol. I)
Stow (Life of John), by Strype (Survey of London, Vol. I)
Strafforde (Life of the Earl of). (Strafford Papers.)
Suger (Histoire de l'Abbé) (French History.)
Sutton (Thomas), his last Will and Testament, taken out of the Prerogative Court 4to *London*, 1614
Swift (Memoirs of Jonathan), by Sir W Scott (Works Vol I, and Scott's Misc Works, Vol. II.)
Sydneys (Memoirs of the Lives and Actions of the), by A. Collins. (Sydney Papers)
Sydney (Life of Sir Philip), by Thos. Zouch 4to *York*, 1808.
Sydney (Life of Sir P.), by Lord Brooke, with an introduction by Sir E. Brydges. 8vo *Lee Priory*, 1817.
Sydney (Life of Sir P), by W. Gray. (Gray's Misc Works.)
Sydney (Life of Algernon). (Sydney on Government)
Tasso (Life of Torquato), by Wiffen. (Jerusalem Delivered)
Tasso (Life of T.), with an historical and critical account of his writings, by John Black. 2 vols 4to *Edinb* 1810
Tassoni (Memoirs of Alexandro), interspersed with occasional notices of his literary contemporaries With an appendix, containing biographical sketches of Renuccini, Galilei, Chiabrera, Guarini, and an inedited poem of Tasso, by Joseph Cooper Walker, and edited by Sam. Walker. Small 8vo. *London*, 1815.
Taylor (Life of Bp Jeremy), and critical examination of his writings, by Bp Reg Heber. (Works, Vol. I)
Temple (Life of Sir W). (Works, Vol I)
Thomson (Life of James) (Poetical Works.)
Thuanus (Life of), with some account of his writings, and a translation of the preface to his history, by J. Collinson. 8vo *London*, 1807.
Tillotson (Life of Abp.), by Birch (Works, Vol. I.)
Titian (Life of), with anecdotes of the distinguished persons of his time, by J. Northcote, Esq 2 vols 8vo *Lond.* 1830
Tone (Life of Theobald Wolfe), Founder of the United Irish Society, edited by his son William T W Tone; with a brief account of his own education, and campaigns under the Emperor Napoleon 2 vols. 8vo. *Washington, U S.* 1827.
Tournefort (Life of), by Begon. (Travels.)
Townson (Life of Thomas) (Works, Vol. I)
Turenne (Histoire du Vicecomte de) (French History)
Tweddel (Memoir of John), by Robert Tweddel (Remains.)
Tyndall (Life of William) (Works)
Tytler (Account of the Life and Writings of William). (Mackenzie's Works, Vol. VII)
Veitch (Memoirs of W.) (Scottish Ecc. Hist.)

Virgil (Life of P.), by K. Chetwood   (Dryden's Works, Vol XIII.)
Virgil (Life of P.), by Martyn.   (Virgil's Bucolics.)
Waldegrave (Memoirs of the Earl of)   (Eng. Hist., Geo. II.)
Walker (Life and Ministry of Sam.) of Truro.   (Sermons, Vol. I.)
Wallace (Life of Sir W.)   (Scottish Hist.)
Walpole (Memoirs of Horace).   (Eng. Hist., Geo. II.)
Walton (Memoirs of the Life and Writings of Brian), Bp. of Chester, editor of the London Polyglot Bible. With notices of his coadjutors in that work, of the cultivation of Oriental learning in this country preceding and during their time; and of the Authorised English Version of the Bible. To which is added, Dr. Walton's own vindication of the Polyglot. By Henry John Todd. 2 vols 8vo London, 1821.
Warburton (Life of Bp. W.), by Hurd   (Works, Vol. I.)
Warton (Memoirs of the Life and Writings of Thomas), by Richard Mant.   (Poetical Works.)
Warton (Biographical Memoirs of Dr Joseph), by John Wooll.   4to. London, 1806.
Washington (Life of Geo.), by Marshall   (American Hist.)
Waterland (Life of Daniel).   (Works, Vol. I.)
Waynflete (Life of Bp. William).   (English History, Henry VI.)
Wesley (Life of John).   (Eng. Ecc. Hist.)
Wharton (Life of Henry)   (D'Oyly's Life of Sancroft.)
White (Life of Henry Kirke), by Robert Southey.   (Remains.)
Whitgift (Life of Abp.)   (Eng. Ecc. Hist.)
Whitlocke (Life of Sir B.)   (English History, Charles II.)
Wicliff (Memoirs of the Life, Opinions, and Writings of John), by H. Baber.   (Wicliff's New Testament.)
Wicliff (Life of), by Lewis.   (Eng. Ecc. Hist.)
Williams (Life of Abp. John), by A. Philips.   (Eng. Hist., Charles I.)
Wilson (Life of Arthur) the Historian, written by himself   (Peck's Desiderata Curiosa.)
Wilson (Life of Bp. Thos.).   (Works, Vol. I.)
Winklemann (Vie de J. J.), par Huber   (Hist. de l'Art.)
Witherspoon (Life of John)   (Works, Vol. I.)
Wolsey (Life of Cardinal)   (Eng. Hist., Henry VIII.)
Wood (Life of Anthony), by himself   (Athenæ Oxon., Vol. I.)
Wyatt (Memoirs of Sir Thomas) the elder, by C. F. Nott   (Works of Surrey and Wyatt.)
Wyndham (Life of the Right Hon. William), by T. Amyot   (Speeches.)
Xavier (Bohours' Life of St. Francis), of the Society of Jesus and Apostle of the Indies and Japan, translated   (Dryden's Works, Vol XVI.)
Ximenes (The Life of Cardinal), by B. Barrett.   8vo. London, 1813.
Zouch (Life of T.)   (Works, Vol. I.)
Zwingle (Life of Ulrich), by Hess   (Hist. of the Christian Religion.)

HISTORY.

Heraldic and Genealogical History.
⁎* See also Manuscripts.

Heraldry, History of Knighthood and Nobility, &c.

Gore (Thomæ) Catalogus omnium Auctorum qui de re heraldicâ scripserunt   4to.   *Oxon* 1674

Moule's (Thomas) Bibliotheca Heraldica Magnæ Britanniæ, an analytical catalogue of books on genealogy, heraldry, nobility, knighthood, and ceremonies; with a list of provincial visitations, pedigrees, collections of arms, and other manuscripts, and a Supplement enumerating the principal foreign works   Royal 8vo.   *London*, 1822

[Nicolas' (Sir N H)] Catalogue of the Heralds' Visitations, with references to many other valuable genealogical and topographical manuscripts in the British Museum.   8vo large paper.   *Lond* 1825

Ansus' Account of the Visitation Books of the several Counties   (Gutch's Coll. Curiosa, Vol II)

Dallaway's (James) Origin and Progress of the Science of Heraldry in England; with explanatory observations on armorial ensigns, [and including, Catalogue of all the Officers at Arms, from their first establishment to the present time,—Editions of books published in England on the science of Heraldry, or connected with Genealogy;—and a copy of the third part of the Book of St. Albans, from the original edition of 1486   4to.   *Gloucester,* 1793

Noble's (Mark) History of the College of Arms, and the Lives of all the kings, heralds, and pursuivants, from the reign of Richard III. until the present time; with a dissertation relative to the different orders in England since the Conquest.   4to   *London,* 1804.

The Antiquity, Authority, Office, and Priviledges of Heralds in England. (Curious Discourses, Vol I)

Thynne's (Francis) Office and Duty of an Herald   (Gwillim's Heraldry)

The Antiquity of Arms in England   (Curious Discourses, Vol. I.)

The Manner of Judicial Proceedings in the Court of Constable and Marshall, touching the use and bearing of Coats   (Curious Discourses, Vol 1)

The Antiquity, Variety, and Reason of Mottos with Arms in England. (Curious Discourses, Vol 1)

The Office of Earl Marshall of England, taken from a MS. in the possession of Joseph Edmonson, Esq, and edited by Charles Howard, 10th Duke of Norfolk   (Anecdotes of the Howards.)

Segar (Sir W), The Earl Marshall's Power, both in Peace and War; with observations on the office and officers of arms   (Gwillim's Heraldry)

[Segar's (Sir W)] Booke of Honor and Armes; wherein is discovered the causes of quarrel, and the nature of injuries, with their repulses also, the means of satisfaction and pacification, with divers other things necessarie to be knowne of all gentlemen and others, possessing armes and honor.   4to wants title   *Lond. by Richard Jhones,* 1590

> It is to this rare work that Shakspeare is thought to refer in *As you like it,* Act v. Scene 4—" O, sir, we quarrel in print, by the book " It is sometimes attributed to the printer Jhones, who has prefixed a dedication to Sir C. Hatton.

BIOGRAPHY.

Selden's Duello; or single combat, from antiquity derived into England, with the forms and ceremonies thereof. (Works, Vol. III.)

Cook's (E) Duello Foiled, or, the whole proceedings for a single fight, by occasion whereof the unlawfulness and wickedness of a Duello is preparatively disputed. (Curious Discourses, Vol. II)

Duells (several Tracts on). (Gutch's Collect Curiosa, Vol I)

The Antiquity Rise, and Ceremony of Lawful Combats in England. (Curious Discourses, Vol. II)

Wyrley's (Wm) True Use of Armorie, shewed by Historie, and plainly proved by example. 4to Lond by J. Jackson, 1592

Berry's (William) Encyclopædia Heraldica; or, complete Dictionary of Heraldry 3 vols 4to London, [1829].

Kent's (W) New Dictionary of Heraldry, edited by James Coates. 8vo London, 1739

Bolton's (Edm) Elements of Armories 4to London, 1610

Upton (Nic) de Studio Militari ;—Jo de Bado Aureo de Armis ;—Hen Spelmanni Aspilogia. Ed. Bissæus è cod MSS primus publici fecit notisque illustravit Folio. Londini, 1654
> This has the rare port of Spelmann, and the set of plates illustrative of the creation of a Knight of the Bath

Leigh's (Gerard) Accedence of Armorie; newly corrected and augmented [by Richard Argoll]. The cuts blazoned 4to. London, 1612.

Bossewell's (John) Workes of Armorie, in three bookes ;—the Concordes of Armorie, the Armories of Honour, and of coates and creastes. 4to black letter London, R Tottell, 1572

Gwillim's (John) Display of Heraldry, with large additions, and a Dictionary of Terms, [by James Coates]. Folio, large paper London, 1724.

Nesbet's (Alex) System of Heraldry, with the true Art of Blazon 2 vols folio. Edinburgh, 1804

Edmondson's (Joseph) [and Sir Joseph Ayloffe] Complete Body of Heraldry, with an alphabet of arms, and a copious glossary. 2 vols. folio Lond. 1780

Abbildungen der Wappen Sæmmtlicher Europæischen Souveraine, der Republiken und Freien Staedte Nebst Erklarung der einzelnen Wappenfelder und Titel der Regenten. Oblong folio. Berlin, 1831
> This splendid work exhibits the arms of the various European kingdoms, &c beautifully emblazoned in their proper metals and colours, with blank shields containing explanations of the various quarterings, &c

Heraldry of Crests, accompanied by remarks, historical and explanatory, and a dictionary of terms Small 8vo London, 1829

Heraldic Anomalies, or, rank confusion in our orders of precedence. with disquisitions, moral, philosophical, and historical, on all the existing orders of society 2 vols small 8vo London, 1823.

Mill's (Charles) History of Chivalry, or Knighthood and its Times 2 vols 8vo London, 1826

Viton de St Alais, Histoire générale des Ordres de Chivalerie, civiles et militaires, existant en Europe 4to Paris, 1811

HISTORY.

Ashmole's (Elias) Institution, Laws, and Ceremonies, of the most noble Order of the Garter. Folio. *London*, 1672.

Pote's (Joseph) Institutions, Laws, and Ceremonies of the Order of the Garter. (Hist. of Windsor Castle.)

Anstis' (John) Register of the most noble Order of the Garter, from the Black-book; with notes, an introduction [a specimen of the lives of the members of the order, and an appendix to Ashmole's History]. 2 vols folio, large paper *London*, 1744.

Salmon's (Tho) Historical Account of St George, and the original of the noble order of the Garter. Small 8vo. *London*, 1704.

Anstis' (John) Observations introductory to a History of the Knighthood of the Bath. 4to. *London*, 1725

The Statutes and Fees of the Order of the Thistle; the suspension of Lyon king at arms, and particular description of the regalia of Scotland. (Nichols's Bib. Top. Vol V No 47)

Of Knights made by Abbots. (Curious Discourses, Vol. I)

Hozier (Pierre), les Noms, Surnoms, Qualités, Armes, et Blasons, des Chevaliers de l'Ordre du Sainct Esprit, créez par Louis le Juste [XIII] le 14 Mai, 1633 Folio. *Paris*, 1634

Ferne (John), the Blazon of Gentrie, wherein is treated of the beginning, parts, and degrees of gentlenesse. 4to. *London, by John Windet*, 1586.

Bird's (John) Magazine of Honour; or, a treatise of the severall degrees of the nobility, with their rights and priviledges; perused and enlarged by Sir John Doderidge 8vo *London*, 1642

Mackenzie (Sir Geo.) on the Laws and Customs of Nations as to Precedency. (Gwillim's Heraldry)

Humfrey (Lawr) the Nobles, or of Nobilitye the original nature, dutyes, right, and Christian institution thereof whereunto is coupled a small treatise of Philo, a Jewe, concernynge nobilitye, done out of Greeke. **Black letter**, small 8vo. *Lond by T Marsh*, 1563.

An Historical and Critical Essay on the true Rise of Nobility, political and civil 2 vols 8vo. large paper. *London, printed for the author*, 1720.

Logan's (Capt John) Analogia Honorum; or, a treatise of honour and nobility, according to the laws and customs of England. With the customs, government, privileges, armorial ensigns of the city of London, and of other cities and chief corporate towns in England (Gwillim's Heraldry)

Lowthen's (Baron Von) Analysis of Nobility in its origin, translated from the German. 8vo. *Lond* 1754

Vulson (Marc de), Sieur de la Colombiere, le vray Théâtre d'Honeur et de Chevalrie; ou, le miroir héroique de la noblesse. Folio, large paper. *Paris*, 1648

Selden's (John) Titles of Honour (Works, Vol III)

The Antiquity of the Title of Duke in England. (Curious Discourses, Vol I)

Anstis (J) de Baronus (Manuscripts.)

Collins's (Arth) Proceedings, Precedents, and Arguments of Claims and Controversies concerning Baronies by Writ, and other Honours. Folio London, 1734.

[Bevy (Charles)], Histoire des Inaugurations des Rois, Empereurs, et autres Souverains de l'univers, depuis leur origine jusqu'au présent. 8vo Paris, 1776.

The Antiquity of Ceremonies used at funerals. (Curious Discourses, Vol I)

Sandford (Francis) [and Gregory King's] History of the Coronation of James II, and of his Royal Consort, Queen Mary, on the 23d April, 1685; with an exact account of the several preparations, processions, and the magnificent feast in Westminster Hall. Folio. *In the Savoy*, 1687.

> "Jacobus Smyth Miles liber ejus pretium 9lb 6s , Lord Mayor of London, at ye coronation of King James and Queen Marie, 1685" On page 32 is a correction and formal attestation, signed by Sir James, of the place, as Lord Mayor, which he occupied in the procession to the abbey, "next before ye king, none going between."

Genealogical History.

*** See also Topography of the separate English Counties.

Burke's (John) General and Heraldic Dictionary of the Peerage of England, extinct, dormant, and in abeyance. 8vo London, 1831

[Milles's (Thos.)] Catalogue of Honor, or treasury of true nobility ; that is to say, a collection historical of all the free monarches, as well kings of England as Scotland, with the princes of Wales, dukes, marquisses, and erles; their wives, children, alliances, families, descentes, and achievements of honour· with a treatise of nobility, politicall and civill. Folio, large paper London, 1610

Rolls of Arms of the Peers and Knights in the reigns of Henry III, Edwards II and III, edited by Sir N. H Nicolas. 2 vols in one, 8vo. London, 1829.

Segar's (Sir William) Baronagium Genealogicum ; or, the pedigrees of our English peers · continued to the present time by [Sir J Aylofte and] Joseph Edmondson 6 vols folio London, 1764-84

[Lodge's (Edmund)] English Peerage , or, a view of the ancient and present state of the English nobility with the arms, after designs by C. Cotton, R A. 3 vols in 2, 4to London, 1790

Collins's (Arthur) Peerage of England, greatly augmented, and continued to the present time, by Sir E Brydges 9 vols 8vo Lond 1812.

Lodge's (E) Peerage of the British Empire as at present existing 8vo London, 1832

Dugdale's (Sir William) Baronage of England ; or, an historical account of the lives of our English nobility in the Saxon's time to the Norman conquest, and from thence of those who had their rise before the 11th of Richard II. 2 vols folio London, 1675-6

Dugdale's (Sir W) Perfect Copy of all Summons of the Nobility to the great Councils and Parliament of England (But Const Law)

Banks (T C.) Dormant and Extinct Baronage of England, from the Norman conquest to 1809 3 vols 4to. London, 1807-9.

Betham's (Sir Wm.) Baronetage of England ; or, the history of English Baronets, and of such Scottish Baronets as are of English families 5 vols 4to. *Ipswich and London*, 1801–5

Townsend's (Fi) Calendar of Knights; being the names of persons upon whom the honour of knighthood has been conferred, from 1760 to 1828, in alphabetical order, together with the names of such British subjects as have received the Orders of the Garter, Bath, Guelph, the Ionian Order of St Michael and St. George, and any foreign order. 8vo. *London*, 1828.

Douglas's (Sir Robt.) Peerage of Scotland ; containing an historical and genealogical account of the nobility of that kingdom · with continuation to the present period by J P Wood. 2 vols folio, large paper *Edinburgh*, 1813

Douglas's (Sir R) Baronage of Scotland Vol I all published, folio. *Edinburgh*, 1798

Lodge's (John) Peerage of Ireland, revised, enlarged, and continued by Mervyn Archdall. 7 vols. 8vo *Dublin*, 1789.

Anderson's (James) Royal Genealogies ; or, the genealogical tables of emperors, kings, and princes, to these times Folio *Lond* 1732.

Garibay (E. de), Illustraciones Genealogicos de los Catholicos Reyes de las Espagnas, y de los Christianissimos Reyes de Francia, y de los Emperadores de Constantinopola, hasta el Catholico Reye nuestro, Señor Philippe el II Folio. portrait of Philip II , engraved by Perret *Madrid*, 1596

Sandford's (Francis) Genealogical History of all the Kings and Queens of England and Monarchs of Great Britain from the Conquest, continued to this time by Sam. Stebbing. Folio. *London*, 1707

Reden (F Baron de), Tableaux Généalogiques et Historiques de l'Empire Britannique, accompagné des notes critiques, et des quatre dissertations historiques et critiques Folio *Hannovre*, 1830

Leslæi (Jo) Tabulæ Genealogicæ Regum Scotorum. (De Moribus, &c)

Noble's (Mark) Historical Genealogy of the Royal House of Stuart, from their origin in the reign of Malcolm to that of King James VI. 4to. *London*, 1795

Crawford's (Geo) Genealogical History of the House of Stewart, and of the illustrious House of Hanover, from the intermarriage with the Stewart family (Hist of Renfrew.)

Harry's (Geo Owen) Genealogy of the High and Mighty Monarch James ; with his lineall descent from Noah, by divers direct lynes to Brutus, and from him to Cadwalader, and from thence sundry wayes to his majesty . where also is handled the worthy descent of Owen Tudyr. Gathered at the request of Mr Robert Holland. Small 4to. with the plates Sir E. Dering's copy *London*, 1604

Slayter (William) Genethliacon, sive stemma Jacobi, genealogia scilicet regia Catholica Anglo-Scoto-Cambro-Britannica ; wherein, besides the pedigree of King James and King Charles, the descent of the Emperor, the Kings of Spaine, France, and Denmark, with many of the princes and nobility, and most part of Christendome, derived in direct line from Noah, may be discerned Folio. *London*, 1630.

Gibbon's (Edward) Antiquities of the House of Brunswick. (Misc. Works, Vols II and III)

Noble's (Mark) Memoirs of the House of Medici; illustrated with genealogical Tables. (Italian History.)

Memoirs of the Peers and Knights present at the Siege of Carlaverock Castle, A.D. 1300. (Hist of the Siege)

Lodge's (E) Genealogy of the existing British Peerage; with brief sketches of the family histories of the nobility 8vo Lond 1832.

Collins' (Arthur) Historical Collections of the Noble Families of Cavendishe, Holles, Vere, Harley, and Ogle, with the lives of the most remarkable persons, and containing curious private memoirs not hitherto published Folio, portraits by Vertue London, 1752.

Watson's (John) Memoirs of the Ancient Earls of Warren and Surrey, and their descendants to the present time, for the purpose of proving the right of Sir Geo Warren, of Paynton, to the title of Lord Warren. 2 vols 4to plates by Basire Warrington, 1782.

Noble's (Mark) Memoirs of the Protectoral House of Cromwell, and also the families allied to or descended from them 2 vols 8vo. Lond. 1788.

> Namely, the Cromwells, Earls of Essex, and Lords Cromwell, the St Johns, Neales, Barringtons, Mashams, Hampdens, Knightleys, Pyes, Trevors, Hobarts, Whalleys, Dunches, Flemings, Palavicini, Ingoldsbys, Stewards, Whitstones, John Jones, Valentine Wauton, the Sewsters, Lockharts, Disbrowes, Abp Tillotson, Lord Deputy Ireton, Mrs. Bendysh, Fleetwoods, Claypooles, Earl Fauconberg, Robt Rich, Russells, General Reynolds, Earl of Thomond, the Franklands, and Hewlings

Dugdale's (Sir W) Visitation of Yorkshire in 1665. (Manuscripts)

Hopkinson's (John) Pedigrees and Descents of Yorkshire and Lancashire Families (Manuscripts)

[Buchanan's (W)] Brief Inquiry into the Genealogy and present state of ancient Scottish Surnames 4to Glasg. 1723.

Genealogical Accounts of many Families in Scotland, communicated to Mr Nesbit (Heraldry, Vol II)

Clifford's Genealogy and Historical Memorials of the Family of Aston of Tixall. (Description of Tixall)

Ker's (R.) Genealogy of the Bruce Family (Hist of Scotland)

[Carlisle's (N.)] Collections from the History of the ancient Family of Carlisle. 4to Presentation copy London, privately printed, 1822

[Buckler's (Benj)] Stemmata Chicheleana, or, a Genealogical Account of the families derived from Thomas Chichele, of Higham Ferrars, all whose descendants are held to be entitled to Fellowships in All-Souls' College, Oxford, by virtue of their consanguinity to the founder; with the Supplement. 4to. Oxford, 1765-75

Cleaveland's (Ezra) Genealogical History of the Noble and most Illustrious Family of Courtenay Folio, uncut Exeter, 1735

Dobie's (J.) Examination of the Claim of John Lindsay Crawford to the Titles and Estates of Crawford and Lindsay. 4to Edinburgh, privately printed, 1831.

Gordon's (Sir Robert, of Gordonstoune) Genealogical History of the Earldom of Sutherland, with Continuation [by Gilbert Gordon, of Sallagh] to 1651 [Edited by H Weber] Folio. Edin 1813

[Edmondson's (Jos)] Historical and Genealogical Account of the Noble Family of Greville, to the present time 8vo. London, 1766

Selden's (Jo) Argument concerning the Baronies of Grey and Ruthen (Works, Vol III)

Wynne's (Sir John) History of the Gwedir Family. (Barrington's Miscellanies)

Howard's (Charles, Xth Duke of Norfolk) Historical Anecdotes of some of the Howard Family. 8vo. *London*, 1769.

Bell's (Henry Nugent) Huntingdon Peerage; comprising the evidence and proceedings connected with the recent restoration of the earldom, and the report of the attorney-general on that occasion to which is prefixed, a genealogical and biographical history of the House of Hastings, including a Memoir of the present earl. 4to *Lond* 1820

Laciesms' Nobility [a Genealogical Detail of the Earls of Lincoln]; with MS. additions by Thos Wilson of Leeds, forming 18 pages. (Ferne's Blazon of Gentrie)

Genealogy of the Mackenzies preceding the year 1661, written in 1669, by a person of quality 4to *Edin privately printed*, 1829

Maitland's (Sir R) History of the House of Seton, with continuation by Viscount Kingston 4to ports and view of Seton chapel *Glasgow, privately printed*, 1829

Urquhart's (Sir T) Pedigree and Descent of the Family of Urquharts to 1652. 12mo *Edin* 1774

Andersons (James) Genealogical History of the House of Yvery, in its different branches of Yvery, Luvel, Percival, and Gournay. 2 vols. royal 8vo *London, privately printed*, 1742.

Gambrivii (H. C) Genealogia Ranzoviana, ad annum 1585 4to *Antverpiæ*, 1585.

CLASS VI.—LITERATURE.

Sect I.—HISTORY OF LITERATURE AND BIBLIOGRAPHY.

History of Literature.

Mancy (A Jarry de), Atlas Historique et Chronologique des Littératures anciennes et modernes, des Sciences et des Beaux Arts, d'après la Méthode de l'Atlas du Comte de Las Casas Large folio. *Paris*, 1831

Schoell (F), Histoire Abrégée de la Littérature Grecque et Romaine jusqu'au VIme siècle; avec une appendix de l'influence de la littérature des peuples de l'Orient sui celles de Grecs et Romains; par Fred Schlegel 6 vols 8vo. *Paris*, 1813-15.

Matter (Jacques), Essai Historique sur l'Ecole d'Alexandrie, et coup-d'œil comparatif sur la littérature Grecque, depuis le temps d'Alexandre le Grand jusqu'à celui d'Alexandre Sévère 2 vols 8vo *Strasbourg*, 1820.

Berrington's (Joseph) Literary History of the Middle Ages, comprehending the state of learning from the close of the reign of Augustus to its revival in the 15th century 4to *London*, 1814.

[Millot (l'Abbé)], Histoire Littéraire des Troubadours ; contenant leurs vies, les extraits de leurs pièces, et plusieurs particularités sur les mœurs, les usages et l'histoire du XII et XIII siècles [sur les MSS de M St. Palaye] 3 vols 12mo *Paris*, 1774.

Literary History of the Troubadours, containing their lives, extracts from their works, and many particulars relative to the customs, morals, and history of the 12th and 13th centuries, collected and abridged by Mrs Dobson from Saint Pelaye 8vo *London*, 1779

Introduction to the Literary History of the 14th and 15th centuries. 8vo. *London*, 1798.

D'Israeli's (I) Curiosities of Literature, consisting of anecdotes, characters, sketches, and observations, literary and historical 3 vols 8vo *London*, 1807-17

D'Israeli's (I) Second Series of Curiosities of Literature ; consisting of researches in literary, biographical, and political history; of critical and philosophical inquiries, and of secret history. 3 vols 8vo. *London*, 1823.

D'Israeli's (I) Literary Character illustrated by the History of Men of Genius. 8vo. *London*, 1818

[Irailh (l'Abbé)], Querelles Littéraires, ou mémoires pour servir à l'histoire des révolutions de la République des Lettres, depuis Homère jusqu'à nos jours 4 vols 12mo *Paris*, 1761.

D'Israeli's (I) Quarrels of Authors, or, some memoirs for our literary history, including specimens of controversy to the reign of Elizabeth 3 vols 8vo *Lond* 1814

Rousseau (Narrative of what passed relative to the Quarrel of David Hume and J J), as far as Mr Walpole was concerned in it (Orford's Memoirs, Vol IV)

Proceedings on the Trial of Rob Faulder, bookseller, for publishing a Libel on John Williams, alias Anthony Pasquin, Esq. (Gifford's Baviad)

D Israeli's (I) Calamities of Authors, including some inquiry into their moral and literary character. 2 vols 8vo *London*, 1812

Turner (S) on Anglo-Saxon Literature. (Anglo-Saxon Hist)

Walpole's (Horace) Catalogue of Royal and Noble Authors of England, Scotland, and Ireland, with a list of their works enlarged and continued to the present time, by Thomas Park 5 vols. 8vo. large paper *London*, 1806 (Orford's Works, Vol I)

Nichols's (John) Literary Anecdotes of the 18th Century, comprising biographical memoirs of William Bowyer and many of his learned friends, an incidental view of the progress and advancement of literature in this kingdom during the last century, and biographical anecdotes of a considerable number of eminent writers and ingenious artists 9 vols 8vo *Lond* 1812-15

The indexes are contained in Vols VII, and XI

Nichols's (J) Illustrations of the Literary History of the 18th century; consisting of authentic memoirs and original letters of eminent persons, and intended as a sequel to the Literary Anecdotes Vols I to VI 8vo London, 1817-31

[Beloe (Wm)], the Sexagenarian, or, recollections of a literary life 2 vols. 8vo. London, 1817.

Brydges' (Sir E) Desultoria, or, comments of a South Briton on books and men Crown 8vo. Lee Priory, 1816

Coleridge's (T S.) Biographia Literaria; or, biographical sketches of my literary life and opinions 2 vols in one, 8vo London, 1817.

[Pegge's (F)] Anonymiana, or, ten centuries of observations on various authors and subjects 8vo London, 1809

Pennant (the Literary Life of Thomas), by himself. 4to London, 1793

Spence's (Joseph) Anecdotes, Observations, and Characters, of Books and Men, collected from the conversation of Mr. Pope and other eminent persons of his time, with notes and life of the author by S. W. Singer. 8vo London, 1820

Polwhele's (R.) Traditions and Recollections, domestic, clerical, and literary; in which are included, letters of Charles II, Cromwell, Fairfax, Edgecumbe, Macaulay, Wolcot, Opie, Whitaker, Gibbon, Buller, and other distinguished characters 2 vols 8vo. London, 1826

Biographical Dictionary of Living Authors of Great Britain and Ireland, comprising literary memoirs and anecdotes of their lives, and a chronological register of their publications 8vo London, 1816.

Irving (D) on the Literary History of Scotland (Lives of Scottish Poets.)

Leyden (J.) on Early Scottish Literature (Complaint of Scotland)

Literary History of Scotland during the 16th and 17th centuries (M'Crie's Lives of Knox and Melville.)

Tytler s (J. F.) Sketches of the Progress of Literature and general Improvement in Scotland during the greater part of the 18th century (Life of Lord Kaimes)

Memoirs of William Smellie [the compiler of the first edition of the Encyclopædia Britannica], containing his literary correspondence. (Biography)

Sismonde (J D L) de Sismondi de la Littérature du Midi de l'Europe 4 vols. 8vo. Paris, 1813

Sismonde de Sismondi on the Literature of the South of Europe, translated, with notes, by T. Roscoe 4 vols. 8vo London, 1823

[Sade (l'Abbé)], les Trois Siècles de la Littérature Française, ou tableau de l'esprit de nos écrivains depuis François I jusqu'à 1773 5 vols. 12mo Amst 1774

Genlis (Memoirs of the Countess de), illustrative of the [Literary] History of the 18th and 19th centuries, written by herself, and translated 6 vols 8vo. London, 1825.

Grimm (le Baron de) et Diderot, Mémoires Historiques, Littéraires, et Anecdotiques tirees de la correspondance philosophique et critique addressée au Duc de Saxe-Gotha. 4 vols, 8vo. London, 1813

Genlis (Mad de), de l'Influence des Femmes sur la Littérature Française, ou, précis de l'histoire des femmes Françaises le plus célèbres 8vo *Paris*, 1811

Hobhouse's (John) Essay on Italian Literature (Illustrations of Byron)

Tiraboschi (Giolamo), Storia della Litteratura Italiana all' anno 1700, con Indice. 9 vols in 13, 4to *Modena*, 1787-94

Guinguené (P. L.), Histoire Littéraire d'Italie 6 vols 8vo *Paris*, 1811-13

Twiss's (R.) Account of Spanish and Portuguese Literature, and a Catalogue of the books which describe those countries (Travels in Spain)

Bouterwek (M.), Histoire de la Littérature Espagnole 2 vols. 8vo. *Paris*, 1812

Loève-Veimars (A.), Résumé de l'Histoire de la Littérature Allemande. 12mo *Paris*, 1824.

Kohlu (J. P.) Introductio in Historiam et Rem Litterariam Slavonum. Small 8vo *Altonæ*, 1729.

[Du Bois (J. B.)], Essai sur l'Histoire Littéraire de Pologne. 8vo. *Berlin*, 1778

Harris's (James) Account of Literature in Russia (Works, Vol II.)

Jones (Sir W.) sur la Littérature Orientale (Works, Vol V.)

Littérature Orientale. (D'Herbelot, Bib. Orient)

Toderini (Giamb.) Litteratura Turchesca. 3 vols 8vo. *Venet.* 1787.

History of Writing and Diplomatics.

Astle's (Thos.) Origin and Progress of Writing, as well hieroglyphical as elementary, also some account of the origin and progress of Printing 4to *London*, 1803

Montfaucon (Bern de) Palæographia Græca, sive de ortu et progressu literarum Græcarum, et de variis omnium sæculorum scriptionis Græcæ generibus, itemque de abbrevationibus et de notis variarum artium ac disciplinarum Folio. *Parisiis*, 1708

Waltheri (J. L.) Lexicon Diplomaticum, cum præfatione J. D. Koelen 2 vols in one, folio *Gottingæ*, 1745

Autographs of Royal, Noble, Learned, and Remarkable Personages conspicuous in English history, from the reign of Richard II. to that of Charles II, including some illustrious foreigners. Engraved under the direction of C. J. Smith, and accompanied by biographical memoirs, &c by J. G. Nichols Imp 4to *London*, 1829

Peignot (Gab.), Essai sur l'Histoire du Parchemin et du Vélin 8vo *Paris*, 1812

History of Literary and Philosophical Societies, Literary Journals, &c.

For History of British Universities, see Topography

Birch's (Th.) History of the Royal Society of London for improving of Natural Knowledge 4 vols 4to *London*, 1756-7

LITERATURE

Thomson's (Th) History of the Royal Society of London, to the end of the 18th century. 4to *London*, 1812

Philosophical Transactions of the Royal Society of London, from their commencement in 1665 to 1800, abridged, with notes and biographic illustrations, by C Hutton, G. Shaw, and R Pearson 18 vols 4to *London*, 1809

Memoirs of the Literary and Philosophical Society of Manchester 5 vols 8vo *Warrington*, 1785-98

Essays, by a Society of Gentlemen at Exeter. 8vo *Exeter*, 1796

Mémoires de l'Institut National des Sciences et des Arts; viz sciences mathématiques et physiques, 1792-1806, 7 vols, sciences morales et politiques 1792-1803, 5 vols, littérature et beaux arts, et mémoires présentées à l'Institut par divers savans, et lus dans ses assemblées, 1792-1805, 5 vols 17 vols 4to. *Paris*, 1792-1810

Mémoires Littéraires, et l'Histoire de l'Academie des Inscriptions et Belles Lettres, depuis son établissement jusqu'à 1793. avec le tableau général des ouvrages contenus dans ce recueil. 50 vols 4to *Paris*, 1736, &c

Mémoires Littéraires, et l'Histoire de l'Academie des Inscriptions et Belles Lettres ; nouvelle série, publiée par l'Institut Vols I to VIII 4to *Paris*, 1815-28.

Transactions of the Asiatic Society instituted in Bengal. (Asiatic Researches, Indian History)

Edinburgh Review, or Critical Journal, with index. 8vo. *Edinburgh*, 1802, &c

Quarterly Review; with index. 8vo *London*, 1809, &c.

Gentleman's Magazine (a selection of curious articles from the), classed under their proper heads, by P Bliss 4 vols. 8vo. *Lond* 1809

Blackwood's Edinburgh Magazine 8vo *Edinb* 1817, &c.

Foreign Quarterly Review 8vo *London*, 1828, &c

Giornale de' Letterati d' Italia 8 vols. 12mo *Venezia*, 1710-11.

Bibliography.

Achard (C F), Cours Elémentaire de Bibliographie 3 vols. 8vo *Marseille*, 1806-7

Horne's (T H) Introduction to the Study of Bibliography, to which is prefixed, a memoir on the public libraries of the ancients 2 vols. 8vo *London*, 1814

History of Printing.

Cotton's (Henry) Typographical Gazetteer 8vo *Oxford*, 1825.

Astle's (Thos) Account of the Origin and Progress of Printing (Hist. of Writing)

Dibdin (T F) on the Origin of Printing. (Ames's Typog Antiq Vol I)

Lambinet (P), Origine de l'Imprimerie, d'après les titres authentiques. 2 vols 8vo. *Paris*, 1810

Lichtenberger (J Frid.) Initia Typographica illustr 4to *Argent*, 1811

LITERATURE

Meerman (G.), de l'Invention de l'Imprimerie, ou, analyse de deux ouvrages publiées sur cette matière par M. Jansen, suivi d'une notice chronologique et raisonnée des livres, avec et sans date, avant l'année 1501, dans les Pays Bas, par M. Visier, augmentée par l'éditeur 8vo *Paris*, 1809.

Schoepflin (J. D.) Vindiciæ Typographicæ. 4to. *Argent* 1760.

Fischer (Gott.), Essai sur les Monumens Typographiques de Jean Guttenberg 4to *Mayence*, 1802

Née de la Rochelle (J. F.), Eloge Historique de Jean Guttenberg, premier inventeur de l'art typographique à Mayence. 8vo *Paris*, 1811.

Camus (A. G.), Notice d'un Livre imprimé à Bamberg en 1462 4to *Paris*, 1799

Maittaire (M.) Annales Typographici, ab artis inventæ origine ad annum 1664; cum indice 5 vols. in 9, 4to *Hagæ Comit et Londini*, 1719-51

Maittaire (M.) Annales Typographici; supplementum adornavit M. Denis 2 vols 4to. *Viennæ*, 1789

Panzer (G. W.) Annales Typographici, ab artis inventæ origine ad annum 1536, continuati post Maittairii, Denisu, aliorumque doctiss virorum curas 11 vols 4to *Norimbergæ*, 1793-1803

Santander (C. de la Serna), Mémoire sur l'Origine et le premier Usage des Signatures et des Chiffres dans l'art Typographique. 8vo. *Bruxel.* 1806 (Catalogue de Santander, Vol V)

Santander (C. de la Serna), Observations sur le Filigrane du Papier des Livres imprimés dans le 15ème siècle. (Cat de Santander, Vol V.)

Singer's (S. W.) Researches into the History of Playing Cards; with illustrations on the origin of printing and engraving on wood 4to. *London*, 1816

Ged (Biographical Memoirs of W.), including an account of his progress in the art of block-printing [compiled by J. Nichols] 8vo. *Lond.* 1781.
An account of the first attempt at stereotype printing

Caxton (Wyllyam), Life of, in which is given an account of the rise and progress of the art of pryntyng in England till 1493, by John Lewis. 8vo *London*, 1737

Typographical Antiquities, or the history of printing in England, Scotland, and Ireland, containing memoirs of our ancient printers, and a register of the books printed by them begun by Joseph Ames, considerably augmented by W. Herbert, and now greatly enlarged, with copious notes, &c. by T. F. Dibdin. 4 vols 4to. largest paper. *London*, 1809-19.

Decree of the Starre-Chamber concerning Printing, 11th July, 1637 4to. *London*, 1637
This famous decree is an epoch in English literary history, being that on which all others were founded until 1662

Milton's (John) Areopagitica, a speech for the liberty of unlicensed printing to the Parliament of England (Prose Works, 4to and 8vo Vol I)

Greswell's (W Pari) Annals of Parisian Typography; containing an account of the earliest typographical establishments in Paris, and notes and illustrations of the most remarkable productions of the Parisian Gothic press   8vo   *London*, 1818.

[Audefndi (J. B.)] Catalogus Historico-Criticus Romanarum editionum sæculi XV   4to.   *Romæ*, 1783.

Federici (Fortunato), Annali della Tipografia Volpi-Cominiana, colle Notizie intorno la vita e gli studj de' Fratelli Volpi   8vo   *Padova, nel Seminario*, 1809

Renouard (Ant Aug), Annales de l'Imprimerie des Aldes   3 vols 8vo   *Paris*, 1803–12

[Adry], Notice sur les Imprimeurs de la Famille des Elzeviers.   8vo.   *Paris*, 1806.

Thomas's (J) History of Printing in America, with a biography of printers, and an account of newspapers to which is prefixed a concise view of the discovery and progress of the art in other parts of the world.   2 vols 8vo   *Worcester (America)*, 1810

General Bibliographers

Barbier (A. A) et N. L. M. Desessarts, Nouvelle Bibliothèque d'un Homme de Goût, contenant des jugemens tires des journaux et des critiques sur les meilleurs ouvrages   5 vols 8vo.   *Paris*, 1808–10.

Beloe's (William) Anecdotes of Literature and scarce Books   6 vols 8vo   *London*, 1807–12.

Brunet (J C.), Manuel du Libraire et de l'Amateur de Livres, contenant un nouveau dictionnaire bibliographique et catalogue raisonné, re-imprimé, augmenté de plus de deux mille articles et d'un grand nombre de notes   4 vols. 8vo.   *Bruxelles*, 1821

Clement (D), Bibliothèque Curieuse, historique et critique, ou, catalogue raisonné des livres difficile à trouver   A to H, all published   9 vols.   4to   *Gottingen et Leipsic*, 1750–60.

Debure (Guil Fr), Bibliographie Instructive, ou traité de la connoissance des livres rares et singuliers   7 vols 8vo   *Paris*, 1763–68

Dibdin's (T. F.) Library Companion, or the young man's guide and the old man's comfort in the choice of a library   2 vols in one, royal 8vo.   *London*, 1824.

Dibdin's (T. F) Bibliomania, or book-madness, containing the history, symptoms, and cure of this fatal disease. 8vo first edition   *Lond* 1809.

Dibdin's (T. F) Bibliomania, a bibliographical romance.   8vo   *Lond* 1811.

Dibdin's (T. F.) Bibliographical Decameron; or, ten days' pleasant discourse upon illuminated manuscripts and subjects connected with early engraving, typography, and bibliography.   3 vols. imp. 8vo.   *London*, 1817.

Dibdin's (T F) Bibliographical, Antiquarian, and Picturesque Tour in France and Germany   3 vols in 4, imp. 8vo.   *Lond* 1821.

[Dibdin's (T. F)] Bibliophobia   8vo.   A presentation copy from the author   *London*, 1832

Fommer (Fr Ing), Dictionnaire portatif de Bibliographie   8vo   *Paris*, 1809

Peignot (G), Dictionnaire Raisonné de Bibliologie. 3 vols 8vo *Paris*, 1802.

Peignot (G.), Dictionnaire Critique, Littéraire, et Bibliographique, des Livres condamnées au feu, supprimés, ou censurés 2 vols 8vo. *Paris*, 1806

Peignot (G), Répertoire Bibliographique Universel, contenant la notice raisonnée des bibliographies speciales. 8vo *Paris*, 1812

National and Professional Bibliographers.

Watt's (Robt.) Bibliotheca Britannica; or, a general index to British and foreign literature [both according to authors and subjects]. 4 vols 4to *Edinburgh*, 1824

Lowndes' (W T) Bibliographer's Manual; being an account of rare, curious, and useful books, published in or relating to Great Britain and Ireland with bibliographical and critical notices, collations of the rarer works, &c 4 vols 8vo *London*, 1828–32

Brydges' (Sir E) Censura Literaria; containing titles, abstracts, and opinions of old English books 10 vols 8vo *London*, 1806–9

Brydges' (Sir E) and Joseph Haslewood's British Bibliographer. 4 vols. 8vo *London*, 1810–13

Brydges' (Sir E) Restituta , or, titles, extracts, and characters of old books in English literature revived 4 vols. 8vo. *London*, 1814.

Oldy's (Wm) British Librarian ; or, abstract of old English books in all sciences, as well in MS. as in print 8vo *London*, 1738.

Reuss's (J D) Alphabetical Register of all the Living Authors in Great Britain, Ireland, and the United States of North America, with a catalogue of their publications, from 1770 to 1803 2 vols 8vo *Berlin*, 1804

Savage's (James) Librarian , [being an account of libraries, MSS , scarce, valuable, and useful books, &c] 3 vols 8vo. *London*, 1808–9

Juvigny (M Rigoley de), les Bibliothèques Françoises de la Croix du Maine, et de Du Verdier, nouvelle édition, augmentée d un discours sur les progrès des lettres en France et des remarques historiques, critiques, et littéraires, de M de la Monnaye, et de M. le Pres. Bouhier, et de M Falconet 6 vols 4to *Paris*, 1772–3

Queraid (J M), la France Littéraire, ou, dictionnaire bibliographique des savants, historiens, et gens de lettres de la France, ainsi que des littéraires étrangères qui ont écrit en François A to *L*. 4 vols 8vo *Paris*, 1830

Haym (Nic. Fr), Biblioteca Italiana, ossia Notizia de' Libri rari Italiani. 4 vols in 2, 8vo *Milano*, 1803

Fontanini (Giusto), Biblioteca dell' Eloquenza Italiana, con le Annotaz del Signor Apost Zeno [distribuiti in varie classi] 2 vols 4to *Venezia*, 1753

Antonio (Nic) Bibliotheca Hispana Vetus et Nova ad annum 1684, curante P Bayerio, qui prologum, &c adjecit 4 vols. folio *Matriti*, 1783–88

Le Long (J) Bibliotheca Sacra   (Sacred Philology)

Orme's (W) Bibliotheca Biblica. (Sacred Philology)
Trittenhem (J. de) de Scriptoribus Ecclesiasticis   (Hist of Religion)
Dupin's (L E) History of Ecclesiastical Writers. (Hist of Religion)
Camus, Bibliothèque Choisie des Livres de Droit. (Jurisprudence)
Dryander (Jonæ) Catalogus Bibliothecæ Historico-Naturalis Josephi Banks, Baronetti   5 vols. 8vo   *London*, 1798–1800
Gronovii (L T) Bibliotheca Regni Animalis atque Lapidei (Nat Hist.)
[Bocage (Barbie du)], Notice [Bibliographique] des Ouvrages de M. d'Anville, précédée de son éloge [par Dacier]   8vo   *Paris*, 1802
Richarderie (G B de la), Bibliothèque Universelle de Voyages (Travels)
Struvii (B G) Bibliotheca Historica, aucta à C J Budero et J. G. Meuselio. (Universal History)

Rawlinson's (T) English Topographer
Gough's (R) British Topography
Upcott's (W) English Topography.
Britton's (J) English Topography
} (English Topography)

Nicolson s (Bp) Historical Libraries (English History.)
Lhuyd (E) Antiquâ Britanniæ Linguâ Scriptorum, qui non impressi sunt, Catalogus (Archæologia.)
Wanlen (Hump) Librorum Vet Septent qui in Angliæ Bibliothecis extant, nec non multorum vet. cod septent alibi extantium Catalogus historico-criticus. (Hickesii Thesaurus, Vol II)
M'Arthur's (John) Brief Notices of Books which treat of the Celtic, Gaelic, Irish, and Welsh Languages, Antiquities, Manners, and Customs , also, of Gaelic and Irish MSS still existing in Great Britain and Ireland   (Translation of Cæsarotte on Ossian.)
O'Reilly's Chronological Account of Irish Writers , with a catalogue of their works   (Irish History)
Le Long (J), Bibliothèque Historique de la France. (French Hist)
Hoare's (Sir R. C.) Catalogue of Italian History and Topography. (Italian History)
Bibliotheca Americana   (American History)
Robertson's (W.) Catalogue of Spanish Works illustrative of America. (History of America)
Moule s (T) Bibliotheca Heraldica Magnæ Britanniæ   (Heraldry)
Marsden's (W) Catalogue of Dictionaries, Vocabularies, Grammars, and Alphabets   4to   *London, privately printed*, 1796
[Ritson's (Jos)] Bibliographica Poetica ; a catalogue of English poets of the 12th to the 16th centuries : with a short account of their works 8vo. *London*, 1802
[Griffith's (A F)] Bibliotheca Anglo-Poetica ; or, a descriptive catalogue of early English poetry in the possession of Longman and Co   illustrated by occasional extracts, and remarks critical and biographical. Royal 8vo. *London*, 1815
Dibdin's (T F) Introduction to the Knowledge of rare and valuable Editions of Greek and Roman Classics; together with an account of Polyglot, Hebrew, and Greek Bibles, and the Greek and Latin Fathers   Large paper, 2 vols imp 8vo   *Lond* 1827

Fabricii (J A) Bibliotheca Græca; sive, Notitia Scriptorum veterum Græcorum, quorumcumque monumenta integra aut fragmenta edita extant, tum plerorumque è MSS ac deperditis Curante G C. Harles: accedunt B. J A Fabricii et C A Heumanni supplementa inedita 12 vols 4to. *Hamburgi*, 1790–1809.

Fabricii (J A) Bibliotheca Latina, nunc meliùs dilecta, rectiùs digesta, et aucta diligentiâ J A. Ernesti 3 vols 8vo. *Lipsiæ*, 1773–4.

Anonymous and Pseudonymous Works.

[Baillet (Ad)], Auteurs déguisez sous des noms étrangers, empruntéz, supposéz, feints à plaisir, chiffréz, renverséz, retournéz, ou changéz d'une langue en une autre Small 8vo. *Paris*, 1690.

Barbier (Ant. Alex), Dictionnaire des Ouvrages Anonymes et Pseudonymes, composés, traduits, ou publiés en Français; avec les noms des auteurs, traducteurs, et éditeurs 4 vols. 8vo *Paris*, 1806.

On Libraries, and their Arrangement

Petit-Radel (L C. F.), Recherches sur les Bibliothèques, anciennes et modernes, jusqu'à la fondation de la Bibliothèque Mazarine, et sur les causes qui ont favorisé l'accroissement du nombre des livres 8vo. *Paris*, 1819

[Horne's (T H)] Outlines of the Classification of a Library submitted to the Trustees of the British Museum [as a plan for the new catalogue of that collection]. 4to. *London* (*not published*), 1825

Catalogues of Public and Private Libraries.

Hunter's (Joseph) Catalogue of the Library of Bretton, in Yorkshire; and notices of the libraries belonging to other religious houses. Small 4to *London*, 1831

Catalogue of the MSS in the Cottonian Library deposited in the British Museum, by J Planta. Folio *London*, 1802.

Catalogue of the Harleian MSS in the British Museum [edited by R. Nares and H Ellis], with Indexes of persons, places, and matters [by T. H Horne] 4 vols in two, folio *London*, 1808–12.

Catalogue of the Lansdowne MSS. in the British Museum, with Indexes of persons, places, and matters 2 vols folio [*London*], 1812.

Catalogue of the Library [MS. and printed] belonging to the Faculty of Advocates, Edinburgh [by Thomas Ruddiman, W Goodall, Alex Brown, &c] 3 vols folio *Edin* 1742–1807

Catalogue of the Library of the Royal Institution, including a complete list of all the Greek writers, by Dr Charles Burney, methodically arranged, with an alphabetical index by W Harris Royal 8vo *London*, 1821

Catalogue of the Library of the London Institution, by Wm Upcott 8vo *London*, 1813

Catalogue of Sanscrit MSS presented to the Royal Society by Sir W and Lady Jones (Jones's Works, Vol. VI)

Bibliotheca Chethamensis; sive Bibliothecæ Publicæ Mancuniensis (Manchester) Catalogus, contexuit, indices adjecit, atque edidit G P Greswell. 3 vols 8vo *Mancunii*, 1791–1826.

Account and Extracts of the Manuscripts in the Library of the King of France, translated. 2 vols 8vo *London*, 1789.
Harris (James) on the Arabic MSS., and those of Livy, in the Escurial; and of the MSS of Cebes in the King of France's library (Works, Vol II)
Delandine (Ant. Fr.), Manuscrits de la Bibliothèque de Lyon, ou notices sur leur ancienneté, leurs auteurs, &c., précédées d'une histoire des anciennes bibliothèques de Lyon 3 vols 8vo. *Paris*, 1789
Stewart's (C. J.) Descriptive Catalogue of the Oriental Library of the late Tippoo, Sultan of Mysore 4to *Cambr* 1809

Pettigrew's (T. J.) Bibliotheca Sussexiana; a descriptive catalogue, accompanied by historical and biographical notices, of the MSS and printed books contained in the library of his Royal Highness the Duke of Sussex, in Kensington Palace. Vol. I Parts I and II. Imperial 8vo. *Lond* 1827
Dibdin's (T. F.) Bibliotheca Spenceriana, or, a descriptive catalogue of the books printed in the 15th century, and of many valuable first editions in the library of Earl Spencer — Ædes Althorpianæ, or an account of the mansion, books, and pictures at Althorp. — Supplement to the Bibliotheca 7 vols in 6, impl 8vo *Lond* 1814–22.
[Revicksky (Count Charles)], Catalogue de mes Livres, avec des remarques tirées de différens ouvrages bibliographiques, souvent éclaircies, quelquefois redressées 8vo *Berolini*, 1784.
This collection now forms part of Earl Spencer's.
Catalogus Librorum qui in Bibliothecâ Blandfordiense reperiuntur 1812. 4to.
Bibliotheca Parriana, a catalogue of the library of the late Samuel Parr. 8vo *London*, 1827
Thoresby's Catalogue of the MSS. and various editions of the Bible in his Museum (Whitaker's Leeds.)
Bunau (le Comte) Catalogus Bibliothecæ Bunavianæ, edente J. M. Franckio. Vols I. to III in 4 vols 4to all published *Lipsiæ*, 1750–55.
Crevenna (A. B.), Catalogue des Livres de sa Bibliothèque 5 vols. in 3, 8vo. with the prices. *Amst* 1789.
Mac Carthy (le Comte), Catalogue des Livres de sa Bibliothèque, par G. de Bure 2 vols 8vo *Paris*, 1815.
Renouard (Ant Aug.), Catalogue de la Bibliothèque d'un Amateur; avec des notes bibliographiques, &c 4 vols 8vo. *Paris*, 1819.
Santander (C de la Serna), Catalogue de ses Livres, rédigé par lui-même; avec des notes bibliographiques et littéraires, et un supplément 5 vols 8vo. *Bruxelles*, 1803.

Askew (Ant) Catalogus Librorum rarissimorum, with prices 8vo. large paper *London*, 1775
Beauclerk (Topham), Catalogue of his Library, by S Paterson Both Parts, with prices. 8vo. *London*, 1781
Bindley (James), Catalogue of his Library 4 parts, 8vo. *Lond.* 1820
Bridges (John) Catalogus Librorum. 8vo. large paper. *London*, 1725.

Crofts (Catalogue of the Library of T), by S Paterson 8vo large paper, with prices *London*, 1783

Hibbert (Catalogue of the Library of Geo), sold by R. H Evans 8vo with prices. *London*, 1829.

Roscoe (Wm), Catalogue of the Library of. 8vo. *Liverpool*, 1816.

Roxburghe (Duke of), Catalogue of his Library, arranged by G and W Nicol, and sold by R H. Evans. 8vo. with prices *Lond* 1812

Stanleiana (Bibliotheca), Catalogue of a Selection from the Library of Col Stanley 8vo inlaid in 4to, with prices. *London*, 1813

Steevens (Catalogue of the Library of Geo) 8vo large paper, with prices. *London*, 1800

Sykes (Sir M M), Catalogue of his Library, sold by Evans. 8vo port with prices *London*, 1824

Taylor (G W), Catalogue of the Books, Pictures, and Furniture, at Erlestoke Mansion, sold by Robins 4to. 1832.

West (James), Catalogue of his Library, by S Paterson. 8vo. with prices *London*, 1773.

Sect. II.—POLITE LITERATURE

Introductions to the Study, and Courses of Polite Literature.

Addison's (Jos) Discourse on Ancient and Modern Learning (Works, Vol VI)

Barrington (Daines) on the French and English Writers (Miscellanies)

Blair's (Hugh) Lectures on Rhetoric and Belles Lettres 2 vols 4to. *London*, 1783.

Gibbon (Edward), Essai sur l'Etude de la Littérature (Misc. Works, Vol II)

Gibbon (E) Abstract of his Reading, with Reflections (Misc Works, Vol II)

Goldsmith's (O) Enquiry into the present state of Polite Learning in Europe (Works, Vol I)

Rollin's (M) Method of Teaching and Studying the Belles Lettres 3 vols. 8vo *London*, 1804.

Waterhouse's (Ed) Humble Apologie for Learning and Learned Men, [shewing the antiquity of letters and learned men in our nation, and the advantages we have obtained thereby] 8vo *London*, 1653

[Goldsmith's (O)] Anecdotes of Polite Literature 5 vols. 18mo *London*, 1764

Laharpe (J. F.), Lycée, ou Cours de Littérature Ancienne et Moderne, [avec la dernière partie Philosophie du XVIII Siècle, et la table analytique] 17 vols in 20, 8vo *Paris*, 1799–1810

Laharpe (J. F), Mélanges Inédits de Littérature, recueillis par J B Salgues, pouvant servir de suite au cours de littérature 8vo *Paris*, 1810

Grammar.

On the Origin and Formation of Language, and Universal Grammar.

Nicholson (Gul) de universis totius Orbis Linguis. (Oratio Dominica)

Wotton (Guil) de Confusione Linguarum Babylonicâ. (Oratio Dominica)

Beattie's (James) Theory of Language 8vo *London*, 1788

Monboddo (James Burnet, Lord), of the Origin and Progress of Language 6 vols 8vo *Edinb* 1774–92

Gébélin (Count de), le Monde Primitif analysé et comparé avec le Monde Moderne, considéré dans l'histoire naturelle de la parole , ou, grammaire universelle et comparative. 9 vols. 4to *Paris*, 1773–82.

Townsend's (Jos) Veracity of Moses established from the History of Languages (Character of Moses, Vol 1)

Murray's (Alex) History of the European Languages , or, researches into the affinities of the Teutonic, Greek, Celtic, Sclavonic, and Indian nations 2 vols 8vo *Edinb.* 1823

Kennedy's (Lieut -Col Vans) Researches into the Origin and Affinity of the principal Languages of Asia and Europe 4to *Lond* 1827.

Harris's (James) Hermes ; or, a philosophical enquiry concerning universal grammar (Works, Vol 1)

Urquhart's (Sir Thos) Introduction to the Universal Language. (Tracts.)

Grammars and Dictionaries.

VARIOUS LANGUAGES

Leibnitz de Variis Linguis (Oratio Dominica)

Lacroze (Matur) de Variis Linguis (Oratio Dominica)

Tooke's (J Horne) Επια Πτεροντα, or the Diversions of Purley new edition, edited, with numerous additions, from the copy prepared by the author for publication, [by Richard Taylor] 2 vols. 8vo *London*, 1829.

Fry's (Edmund) Pantographia; containing accurate copies of all the known alphabets in the world ; together with an English explanation of the peculiar force of each letter Royal 8vo, with the original prospectus appended Mr Brand's copy *London*, 1799.

Whiter's (W) Etymologicon Universale; or, Universal Etymological Dictionary, on a new plan , shewing that consonants alone are to be regarded in discovering the affinities of words, with illustrations from various languages 3 vols 4to. *Cambridge*, 1822-25

Calepini (Amb) Septem Linguarum, hoc est Lexicon Latinum, variarum linguarum interpretatione adjectâ, [post edit. J. Facciolati]. 2 vols folio *Patavii*, 1772.

Macdonnel's (D E) Dictionary of Quotations in most frequent use, from the Latin, French, Greek, Spanish, and Italian languages, with translations 12mo. *London*, 1811.

LITERATURE

Hamilton's (Walter) Hand-Book, or, short, convenient, and intelligent dictionary of terms used in the arts and sciences, tracing their derivation Small 8vo *London*, 1825

ORIENTAL LANGUAGES

Waltoni (B) Introductio ad Lectionem Linguarum Orientalium. 12mo *Londini*, 1655.

Castelli (Edmundi) Lexicon Heptaglotton, Hebraicum, Samaritanum, Chaldaicum, Æthiopicum, Syriacum, Arabicum conjunctim, et Persicum separatim. Cui accessit brevis et harmonica grammaticæ omnium præcedentium linguarum delineatio. 2 vols folio *Lond.* 1669

Jennings (David) on the Hebrew Language (Jewish Antiq., Vol II)

Lee's (Prof Sam) Grammar of the Hebrew Language, in a series of Lectures 8vo *London*, 1827

Gesenius's (W) Hebrew and English Lexicon to the Old Testament [with points], including the Biblical Chaldee, translated from the German [and collated with the author's other works], by Josiah Gibbs 8vo *London*, 1827.

Parkhurst's (John) Hebrew and English Lexicon, without points, with a Hebrew and Chaldee Grammar. 8vo *London*, 1807

Sacy (Silv de), Grammaire Arabe, à l'usage des Elèves de l'Ecole des Langues Orientales 2 vols 8vo *Paris*, 1810

Ruphy (J. F.), Dictionnaire Abrégé François-Arabe [Vulgaire] 4to *Paris*, 1802

Richardson's (J) Arabic Dictionary. (Persian.)

Wilkins (David) de Linguâ Copticâ (Oratio Dominica)

Reland (Hadr) de Veteris Linguâ Ægyptiæ. (Oratio Dominica)

Tattam's (Henry) Grammar of the Egyptian Language as contained in the Coptic and Sahidic Dialects, with observations on the Bashmuric together with Alphabets and Numerals in the Hieroglyphic and Enchorial characters, and a few explanatory observations. With an appendix, consisting of the rudiments of a Dictionary of the ancient Egyptian language, in the Enchorial character, by Thomas Young 8vo. *London*, 1829.

Ludolphi (J) Grammatica Linguæ Amharicæ, vel Æthiopicæ, quæ vernacula est Habessinorum Folio *Francof* 1702.

Ludolphi (J) Lexicon Amharico-Latinum Folio. *Francof* 1698

Ludolphi (J) Lexicon Æthiopico-Latinum. Folio. *Francof* 1698

Jones's (Sir W) Grammar of the Persian Language. (Works, Vol II)

Gladwin's (Francis) Persian Moonshee [containing a Persian grammar, the Pund Nameh, select stories, lives of philosophers, dialogues, &c Persian and English] 4to. *Calcutta*, 1795

Ouseley's (Sir W) Persian Miscellanies, an essay to facilitate the reading of Persian MSS, with engraved specimens, philological observations, &c 4to *London*, 1795

Richardson's (John) Dictionary of the Persian, Arabic, and English Languages; with additions and improvements by Charles Wilkins. 2 vols. 4to. *London*, 1806–10.

Ferhang Chaouri ; a Dictionary Persian and Turkish, with dissertation on the Persian language, and an alphabetical collection of the proverbial and obscure phraseology, by Ibrahim Effendi Monteferrica (in Turkish) 2 vols. folio *Constantinople, an Heg* 1155 [1742]

> This copy belonged to the well-known French orientalist Le Grand, who, for the facility of reference, has indexed it throughout in red ink, with the initial and final letters of the words contained in each page, and for the same purpose has also underlined in red all the Persian words

Schrœderus (Jo) de Rebus Armenicis   (Oratio Dominica)

Aucher's (Paschal) Grammar, Armenian and English. 8vo   *Venice*, 1819

Aucher (P) and John Brand's Dictionary, Armenian and English, and English and Armenian. 2 vols. 4to   *Venice*, 1821–25

[Holderman (le Père)], Grammaire Turque , avec un recueil des noms, des verbes, et des manières de parler. 4to. *Constantinople*, 1730

Jones (Jezieel) de Linguâ Shilhensi [Chinese]   (Oratio Dominica.)

Morrison's (Robert) Grammar of the Chinese Language   4to   *Scrampore*, 1815

Basile de Glemona, Dictionnaire Chinois, François, et Latin, par De Guignes   Folio. *Paris*, 1813.

Basile de Glemona (Supplément au) par Klaproth   Folio   *Paris*, 1819.

Clifford's (H. J) Vocabulary of the Loo-Choo Language   (Hall's Voyage to Loo-Choo.)

Raffles' (Sir T S) Comparative Vocabulary of the Languages of the Eastern Archipelago. (Java)

Dictionary of the English and Malabar Languages 4to   *Vepery*, 1786.

GREEK LANGUAGE

Knight's (R. P.) Analytical Essay on the Greek Alphabet. 4to. *Lond* 1791.

Matthiæ (Augustus) copious Greek Grammar, translated by E V Blomfield [and edited by Bp. C. J. Blomfield]. 2 vols. 8vo. *Cambridge*, 1818.

Budæi (Gulid.) Commentarii Linguæ Græcæ, ab auctore accuratè recogniti atque aucti. Folio   *Basiliæ, ap N Episcopum*, 1556.

Bos Ellipses Græcæ, edidit Schæfer; quibus adduntur Pleonasmi Græci, sive Comment de Vocibus, auctore B Weiske ; unà cum Hermanni Diss de Ellipsi et Pleonasmo in Græcâ linguâ 8vo   *Londini*, 1825

[Caius (Jo)] de Pronuntiatione Græcæ et Latinæ Linguæ. 4to   *Londini, T Daius*, 1574.

Booth (John) Medullæ, seu Radices insigniores Linguæ Græcæ; or the principal Greek primitives, with a Latin and English interpretation. 4to   *Huddersfield*, ——

Hesychii Lexicon Græcè, cum notis variorum, ex recensione et cum animad , prolegomenis, et apparatu Jo. Alberti. 2 vols folio, large paper. *Lugd Bat* 1746–66.

Suidæ Lexicon Græcè, et versio Latina Æmili Porti ; notisque perpetuis illustravit, indicibus adjecit L. Kusterus. 3 vols. folio, large paper. *Cantabrigiæ*, 1705

Suidæ Lexicon Græcè (Toupii Emendationes in). 4 vols 8vo *Oxonii*, 1790

Labbæi (Car.) Cyrilli, Philoxeni, aliorumque Veterum Glossaria, Latino-Græca et Græco-Latina, cum aliis opusculis   (Stephani Thes. Vol VII.)

[Stephani (Hen.)] Glossaria [Latino-Græca et Græco-Latina Vetera] ad cog. utriusque linguæ perutilia Item de Atticæ linguæ seu dialecti idiomatibus   Folio *Excud H Stephanus*, 1573.

Stephani (H.) Thesaurus Græcæ Linguæ; editio nova, auctior et emendatior [editus E H Barker]   8 vols. folio. *Londini*, 1816–18

Morelli (Th.) Lexicon Græco-Prosodiacum, correxit, animadversionibus illustravit, verbis plurimis auxit, &c. Ed. Maltby   Large 4to. *Cantabr.* 1815

Hederici (Benj) Græcum Lexicon Manuale, curâ S Patricii, J. A Ernesti, et T. Morell: cui accedit magnus verborum et exemplorum numerus ex schedis P. H. Larcheri   4to. *Londini*, 1821.

Damm (Christ Tab) Novum Lexicon Græcum Etymologicum et Reale; cui pro basi substratæ sunt concordantiæ et elucidationes Homericæ et Pindaricæ, curâ J. M Duncan   4to. *Glasguæ*, 1824

Schleusneri (J F) Novus Thesaurus Philologo-Criticus; sive, Lexicon in LXX et reliquos Interpretes Græcos ac Scriptores Apocryphos Veteris Testamenti, post Biehum et alios. 3 vols. 8vo. *Glasguæ*, 1822

Schleusneri (J F) Lexicon Græco-Latinum in Novum Testamentum, recens J Smith, J Strauchon, et A. Dickinson. 2 vols in 4, 8vo. *Glasguæ*, 1817.

Parkhurst's (John) Greek and English Lexicon to the New Testament, with the more valuable parts of the works of later writers, by Hugh James Rose to which is added a plain and easy Greek grammar. 8vo. *London*, 1829

Walker's (John) Key to the Classical Pronunciation of Greek and Latin Proper Names, with a complete vocabulary of Scripture proper names   8vo *London*, 1798.

Robertson's (H) Grammar of the Modern Greek Language, with extracts from Romaic Authors. 12mo *London*, 1818.

Lowndes' (T) Lexicon of the Modern Greek and English Languages. 2 vols 8vo. *Corfu*, 1827

Meursii (Joan.) Glossarium Græco-Barbarum. 4to *Lugd Bat. ap. Elzev.* 1614.

Leake's (W Martin) Researches in Greece, being remarks on the modern Greek dialect, the Albanian, Wallachian, and Bulgarian languages. 4to *London*, 1814

LATIN LANGUAGE.

Milton's (John) Accidence, supplied with sufficient rules for the use of such as are desirous without more trouble than needs to acquire the Latin tongue   (Prose Works, 4to Vol 1 and 8vo. Vol III)

Ascham's (Roger) Schoolmaster, or, a plain and perfect way of teaching children to understand, write, and speak the Latin tongue with notes by J Upton   (Works.)

Scheller's (I J. G) copious Latin Grammar, translated from the German, with alterations, notes, and additions, by Geo. Walker. 2 vols 8vo. *London*, 1825.

Doleti (Steph) Commentarii Linguæ Latinæ. 2 vols. folio. *Lugd ap. Seb. Gryphium*, 1536–38

Forcellini (Ægidii) totius Latinitatis Lexicon, consilio et curâ J Facciolati. 4 vols. in 2, folio, large paper *Patavii*, 1771.

Gesneri (Jo Math) Novus Linguæ et Eruditionis Romanæ Thesaurus, post R Stephani et aliorum curas digestus, locupletatus, emendatus. 4 vols. in 2, folio *Lipsiæ*, 1749.

Ainsworth's (R) Latin and English Dictionary, improved by T Morell, with considerable additions by R. Carey 4to *London*, 1823

Nizolii (Marii) Lexicon Ciceronianum, ex recensione Alex Scoti Accedunt phrases et formulæ linguæ Latinæ, ex commentariis S. Doleti. 3 vols. 8vo *London*, 1820

Hill's (John) Synonyms of the Latin Language, with dissertations on its prepositions. 4to *Edinburgh*, 1804

Dufresne (Car.) Dom du Cange Glossarium ad Scriptores Mediæ et Infimæ Latinitatis Editio locupletior et auctior, et studio Monachorum Ordinis S. Benedicti 6 vols. folio. *Parisiis*, 1733–36.

Spelmanni (Hen) Glossarium Archaiologicum; continens Latino-barbara, peregrina, obsoleta, et novatæ significationis vocabula, scholiis et commentariis illustrata. Folio. *London*, 1687

ANGLO-SAXON LANGUAGE

Brown (Sir T), of Languages, and particularly of the Saxon Tongue. (Works)

Turner (S) on the Anglo-Saxon Language. (Anglo-Saxon History)

Ingram's Anglo-Saxon Grammar (Chronicle)

Elstob's (Eliz.) Rudiments of Grammar for the English-Saxon Tongue. 4to. *London*, 1715

Thwaites (Ed.) Grammatica Anglo-Saxonica, ex Hickesiano Ling. Septent excerpta. 8vo *Oxoniæ*, 1711

Hickesii (Geo) Institutiones Grammaticæ Anglo-Saxonicæ et Mœso-Gothicæ (Thesaurus, Vol I Part I)

Somneri (Gul) Dictionarium Saxonico-Latino-Anglicum accessit Ælfrici Abbatis Grammatica Latino-Saxonica, cum Glossario suo. Folio *Oxonii*, 1659.

Junii (Fr.) Etymologicon Anglicanum, permultis auctum, edidit E Lye, præmit grammatica Anglo-Saxonica, et vita auctoris. Folio, large paper *Oxonii*, 1743

Gibsoni (Ed) Regulæ ad investigandas Nominum Locorum Origines. (Chronicon Saxonicum)

ENGLISH LANGUAGE, INCLUDING PROVINCIAL DIALECTS AND LOWLAND SCOTCH

Booth's (David) Introduction to an Analytical Dictionary of the English Language. 8vo *London*, 1814.

Jodrell's (R P) Philology of the English Language. 4to. *Lond.* 1820.

LITERATURE

Richardson's (Ch) Illustrations of English Philology; containing a critical examination of Johnson's Dictionary   4to   *Lond* 1815

Maittaire's (Mich) English Grammar, or, an essay on the art of grammar applied to the English tongue   8vo   *London*, 1712

Murray's (Lindley) English Grammar, with exercises and key. 2 vols 8vo   *York*, 1809

Kersey's (John) Dictionarium Anglo-Britannicum, or, a general English Dictionary   8vo   *London*, 1715

Ash's (John) Dictionary of the English Language   2 vols 8vo   *Lond* 1775

Johnson's (Sam) Dictionary of the English Language, together with a history of the language, and an English grammar   With numerous corrections and additions by H J Todd   5 vols 4to   *Lond* 1818

Booth's (David) Analytical Dictionary of the English Language   4to   *London*, 1822-24

Crabb's (Geo) English Synonymes explained, with copious illustrations and examples   8vo   *London*, 1816

Jones's (Stephen) Sheridan improved; a dictionary of the English language   8vo.   *London*, 1804

Walker's (John) Critical Pronouncing Dictionary, and Expositor of the English language   4to   *London*, 1806

Murdoch's (John) Dictionary of Distinctions in the Sound of Words 8vo   *London*, 1811

Boucher's (J) Glossary of Archaic and Provincial Words, edited by J. Hunter and J Stevenson   4to   *London*, 1832

Nares' (Robt) Glossary, or, collection of words, phrases, and names, allusions to customs, proverbs, &c in the works of English authors, particularly Shakespeare and his contemporaries   4to   *Lond* 1822

Toone's (William) Glossary and Etymological Dictionary of Obsolete and Uncommon Words, Antiquated Phrases, Proverbial Expressions, &c 12mo   *London*, 1832

Grose's (Francis) Classical Dictionary of the Vulgar Tongue   8vo. *London*, 1796

Grose's (F) Provincial Glossary, with a Collection of Local Proverbs and Popular Superstitions   8vo   *London*, 1787

Grose's Provincial Glossary (Supplement to)   (Pegge's Anecdotes)

Ray's (John) Collection of English Words not generally used, proper to the Northern and Southern Counties   (Ray's Proverbs)

[Pegge's (Sam)] Anecdotes of the English Language, chiefly regarding the local dialect of London and its environs.   8vo   *London*, 1814

Wilbraham's (Roger) Attempt at a Glossary of some Words used in Cheshire   Small 8vo   *London*, 1826

Forby's (Robert) Vocabulary of East Anglia, an attempt to record the Vulgar Tongue of the twin sister counties of Norfolk and Suffolk, as it existed in the last twenty years of the 18th century, and still exists Edited by G Turner   2 vols 8vo   *London*, 1830

Brockett's (J T) Glossary of North Country Words in use, with their etymology and affinity to other languages   and occasional notices of local customs and popular superstitions   Small 8vo   *London*, 1829

LITERATURE.

Hunter (Joseph), the Hallamshire Glossary. Small 8vo. *Lond* 1829

[Carr's (William)] Horæ Momenta Cravenæ, or, the Craven dialect exemplified in two dialogues between farmer Giles and his neighbour Bridget to which is annexed a copious glossary. 8vo *Lond* 1824

Works of Tim Bobbin, containing his view of the Lancashire dialect, a glossary of Lancashire words and phrases 12mo *Manchester*, 1793

Jamieson's (John) Etymological Dictionary of the Scottish Language, illustrated with examples from ancient and modern writers To which is prefixed, a dissertation on the origin of the Scottish language With the Supplement 4 vols 4to *Edinburgh*, 1808-25

CELTIC, INCLUDING CORNISH, WELSH, GAELIC, AND IRISH

Bullet (J B) Mémoires sur la Langue Celtique, contenant l'histoire de cette langue, une description etymologique des villes, rivières, &c et un dictionnaire Celtique. 3 vols folio large paper *Besançon*, 1754-60

Manoir's (Julian) Armoric Grammar and Vocabulary, translated from the French by M Williams (Lhuyd's Archæologia)

Lhuyd's (Edward) Archæologia Britannica, giving some account of the languages of the original inhabitants of Great Britain. Vol I (all published) Folio *Oxford*, 1707

Lhuyd's (E) Comparative Etymology and Vocabulary of the original Languages of Britain and Ireland (Archæologia)

Parry's (David) British Etymologicon, or, the Welsh collated with the Greek, Latin, and some other European languages (Lhuyd's Archæol)

Richards' (Thos) British or Welsh-English Dictionary, with a compendious Welsh grammar and a collection of proverbs 8vo. *Dolgelly*, 1815

Owen's (Wm) Welsh and English Dictionary 2 vols 8vo *London*, 1793

Lhuyd's (F) Cornish Grammar (Archæologia)

Borlase's (William) Vocabulary of the Cornu-British Language (Hist. of Cornwall)

Armstrong's (R A) Gaelic and English Dictionary, with an appendix of ancient names to which is prefixed, a new Gaelic grammar. 4to *London*, 1825

Brief Introduction to the Irish, or ancient Scottish, Language, out of Molloy's Grammar (Lhuyd's Archæologia)

Marcel (J J) Alphabet Irlandais, précédé d'une notice historique, littéraire, et typographique. 4to *Paris*, 1804.

Vallancey's (Charles) Grammar of the Iberno-Celtic, or Irish Language 4to *Dublin*, 1773

Lhuyd's (E) Irish-English Dictionary. (Archæologia)

M'Curtin's (James) English-Irish Dictionary 4to *Paris*, 1732

FRENCH LANGUAGE

Dissertation sur l'Origine de la Langue Françoise, sur ses Variations et sur ses Richesses, avec un projet de dictionnaire étymologique (Barbazan, Fabliaux)

Roquefort (J B B), Glossaire de la Langue Romane; précédé d'un discours sur l'origine, les progrès, et les variations de la langue Françoise 2 vols 8vo *Paris*, 1808

Lacombe (M), Dictionnaire du Vieux Langage François, nécessaire pour l'intelligence des loix d'Angleterre, depuis Guillaume II jusqu'à Edouard III, &c 8vo *Paris*, 1766

Wodroephe's (John) Grammar of the French Language Folio. *Lond.* 1616

Du Vivier (C P), Grammaire des Grammaires, ou analyse raisonnée des meilleurs traités sur la langue Françoise 2 vols 8vo *Paris*, 1827

Cotgrave's (Randle) French-English Dictionary, and Robt Sherwood's English-French Dictionary, with additions by James Howell Folio *London*, 1650

Dictionnaire de l'Académie Françoise [la dernière édition publiée par l'Académie elle-même] 2 vols folio *Paris*, 1762

Dictionnaire de l'Académie Françoise, augmenté de plus de 20,000 articles [par Lavaux] 2 vols 4to. *Paris*, 1802

Dictionnaire de l'Académie Françoise (Supplément au), contenant les termes appropriés aux arts et aux sciences, et les mots nouveaux consacrés par l'usage 4to *Paris*, 1824

Chambaud (Louis), Dictionnaire François-Anglois et Anglois-François, par J. Th Des Carrières 2 vols 4to *London*, 1805

Guizot, Dictionnaire Universel des Synonymes de la Langue Françoise. 2 vols 8vo. *Paris*, 1829.

Planché Dictionnaire Françoise de la Langue Oratoire et Poétique, suivi d'un vocabulaire de tous les mots qui appartiennent au langage vulgaire. 3 vols 8vo *Paris*, 1819–22.

Le Roux (P. J.), Dictionnaire Comique, Satirique, Critique, Burlesque, Libre, et Proverbial 2 vols 8vo *Pamprelune [Paris]*, 1786.

Dictionnaire Languedocien François. 2 vols 8vo *Nismes*, 1785

ITALIAN LANGUAGE

Veneroni (J), le Maître Italien, ou, la Grammaire Françoise et Italienne, révu sur les éditions par Minagio, Placardi, et Rastilli 8vo *Lyon*, 1789.

Barberi, Grammaire des Grammaires Italiennes, ou cours complet de la langue Italienne 2 vols. 8vo *Paris*, 1819

Florio's (John) Worlde of Wordes, or, most copious and exact Dictionarie in Italian and English Folio *London, by Arnold Hatfield*, 1598.

Vocabolario degli Accademici della Crusca, quarta impressione. 6 vols in 5, folio *Firenze*, 1729–38.

Vocabolario —Giunta de' Vocabuli raccolti dalle Opere degli Autori approvati dall' Acad della Crusca, apposta nell' edizione Napolitana. Folio *Napoli*, 1751

Baretti's (Jos) Dictionary of the Italian and English Languages, with a grammar prefixed 2 vols 8vo *London*, 1824

Capello (L), Comte de San Franco, Dictionnaire Piemontais-Français 2 vols 8vo *Turin*, 1814.

LITERATURE

SPANISH AND PORTUGUESE LANGUAGES.

Fernandez (Don Felipe), Practical Grammar of the Spanish Language
8vo London, 1808

Orozco (Sebast Cobarruvias) Tesoro della Lingua Castellana, o Española
Folio En Madrid, 1611

Diccionario de la Lengua Castellana, compuesto par la Real Academia Española, reducido a uno tomo 4to Madrid, 1823

Connelly (F Thomas) and Thos Higgins's Dictionary of the Spanish and English Languages 4 vols 4to. Madrid, 1797–8.

Neuman and Baretti's Dictionary of the Spanish and English Languages
2 vols 8vo London, 1823.

Vieyra's (Ant) Portuguese Grammar 8vo London, 1820.

Vieyra's (Ant) Dictionary of the Portuguese and English Languages
2 vols 4to London, 1773.

DUTCH LANGUAGE.

Van der Pyl's (R) Practical Grammar of the Dutch Language 8vo
Rotterdam, 1819

Sewell's (W) Dictionary of the Dutch and English Languages 2 vols
4to Amsterdam, 1766.

GERMAN LANGUAGE.

Killiani Dufflœi (C.) Etymologicum Teutonicæ Linguæ, sive Dictionarium Teutonico-Latinum, curante G Hasselto. 2 vols. 4to Traj. 1777

Hickesii (Geo) Institutiones Grammaticæ Franco-Theotiscæ (Thesaurus, Vol I , Part II)

Glossarium ad Scriptores Linguæ Francicæ et Alemanicæ Veteris [sive Teutonico-Latinæ], cum præfatione de origine et const linguæ Alemanicæ J Schilteri (Schilteri Thes Antiq Vol III)

Becker's (C. F) Grammar of the German Language, 8vo Lond 1830.

Kuttner (C G) and M Nicholson's Dictionary of the German Language, according to that of J C Adelung 3 vols roy 8vo Leipsic, 1805–13

Poetevin (E L), Dictionnaire Suisse-Français-Allemand 2 vols
4to Basle, 1754.

Bowring (J) on the Language of Hungary and Transylvania (Poetry of the Magyars)

NORTHERN LANGUAGES, ANCIENT AND MODERN.

Hickesii (Georgii) Antiquæ Literaturæ Septentrionalis Libri Duo, Linguarum Vet Septentrionalium Thesaurum Grammatico-Criticum et Archæologicum, ejusdem de Antiquæ Literaturæ Septent Utilitate Dissertationem epistolarem, et A Fountaine Numismata Saxonica et Dano-Saxonica, complectentes 2 vols folio, large paper, ruled with red lines Oxoniæ è Theatro Sheldoniano, 1705

Wotton's (W) View of Hickes's Archæological Treasure of the Ancient Northern Languages, translated, with notes, by M Shelton 4to large paper. London, 1735

Ihre (Jo) Glossarium Suio-gothicum, in quo hodierno usu frequentia vocabula explicantur, et ex dialectis cognatis origines illustrantur 2 vols in one, folio *Upsaliæ*, 1769

Jamieson's (John) Hermes Scythicus , or, the radical affinity of the Greek and Latin Languages to the Gothic illustrated , with a dissertation on the historical proofs of the Scythian origin of the Greeks 8vo *Edinburgh*, 1814

Lye (E) Grammatica Gothica (Evangelia Gothica.)

Glossarium Eddæ Sæmundinæ (Edda, Mythology)

Jonæ (Runalphi) Grammaticæ Islandicæ Rudimenta et Dictionariolum Islandico-Latinum , cum G Hickesii additamentis aucta et illustrata (Hickesii Thesaurus, Vol I , Part III)

Haldersonii (B) Lexicon Islandico-Latino-Danicum, ex MSS Legati Arnæ-Magnæani, curâ R K Raskii editum , præfatus est P E Muller 4to *Haunæ*, 1814.

Egede (Pauli) Grammatica Groenlandico-Danico-Latina. 8vo. *Hauniæ*, 1760.

Egede (P) Dictionarium Groenlandico-Danico-Latinum 8vo. *Hauniæ*, 1750

Lindahl (Erici) et Joh Ohrling Lexicon Lapponicum , cum interp vocab. Sueco-Latinâ et Indice Suecano-Lapponico, illust præfatione Joa Ihre, nec non auctum Grammaticâ Lapponicâ 4to *Holmiæ*, 1780

Grammaire Polonaise et Françoise 8vo *Breslau*, 1803.

Heard's (James) Practical Grammar of the Russian Language ; with exercises, key, vocabulary, and reading lessons 2 vols 12mo. *Petersburg*, 1827

Dictionnaire Russe-Allemand-François 2 vols 8vo *Petersbourg*, 1816

Brunnmark's (Gust) Introduction to Swedish Grammar, by Wahlin 12mo *London*, 1825

Brisman (Sven) Svensk och Engelskt Hand-Lexicon 4to *Upsalia*, 1801.

Raske's (Eras) Grammar of the Danish Language 12mo *Copenhagen*, 1830

Bay's (C F) Danish and English Dictionary 2 vols. 8vo *Copenhagen*, 1824

AFRICAN AND AMERICAN LANGUAGES

Salt's (Henry) Vocabularies of the Dialects of the different Nations of the Coast of Africa, from Mosambique to the borders of Egypt (Abyssinia)

Drury's (Rob) Vocabulary of the Madagascar Language (Adventures)

Jackson on the Languages of Africa (Morocco)

Adair's Vocabulary of American Indian Language (American Indians)

Heriot's Vocabulary of the Algonquin Tongue (Travels in America)

Grammar and Vocabulary of the Language of the Natives of the Tonga Islands (Mariner's Tonga Islands Vol II.)

LITERATURE

Criticism.

*** See also Literary History, and under the respective authors subjects of criticism

Athenæi Deipnasophistæ,
Aulu Gelii Noctes Atticæ,
Hierocles in Aurea Carmina Pythagoræ,
Macrobius in Somnium Scipionis, &c } (Classics)

Coleridge's (H. N.) Introduction to the Study of the Greek Classics [containing Homer] Small 8vo *London*, 1830

Holdsworth's (Edw) Remarks and Dissertations on Virgil, with other classical observations Published, with notes and additional remarks by Mr Spence 4to. *London*, 1768

Luzac (Jo) Lectiones Atticæ, de Διγαμία Socratis Dissertatio edidit et præfatus est J O Sluiter 4to *Lugd Bat* 1809.

Porsoni (Ric) Adversaria, notas et emendationes in poetas Græcos ex schedis MSS deprompserunt J H Monk et C J Blomfield. 8vo. *Cantabr.* 1812.

Ruhnkenii (Dav) Opuscula; præfationem et indices addidit Th Kidd 8vo. *London*, 1807.

Sluiter (J O) Lectiones Andocideæ, interjectæ sunt L C. Valckenærii et J O. Luzacii animadversiones 8vo *Lugd Bat* 1804

Blount (T. P.) Censura celebrium Authorum, sive, tractatus, in quo varia virorum doctorum de clarissimis cujusque sæculi scriptoribus judicia traduntur Folio *Londini*, 1690

Kames' (Henry Home, Lord) Elements of Criticism. 2 vols. 8vo *London*, 1805.

Pope's (Alex) Essay on Criticism. (Works, Vol I)

Beattie's (James) Essays on Poetry and Music, as they affect the mind; on Laughter and Ludicrous Composition, and on the Utility of Classical Learning. 8vo. *Edin* 1788.

Burnett's (Geo) Specimens of English Prose Writers to the close of the 17th century, with biographical and literary sketches, including an account of books as well as of their authors 3 vols 8vo *London*, 1807

Drake's (N.) Biographical, Critical, and Historical Illustrations of the British Classics. (B Classics)

Goldsmith's (O) Prefaces and Criticisms (Works, Vol II)

Gray's (Thos)'Extracts, Philological, Poetical, and Critical, selected and arranged from his original MSS., by Matthias (Works, Vol. II)

Hall's (Robt.) Reviews and Miscellaneous Pieces (Works, Vol IV)

Harris's (James) Three Treatises :—Art, Music, Painting, and Poetry, and Happiness and Philosophical Arrangements. (Works, Vol I)

Johnson s (Dr Sam) Philological Tracts. (Works, Vol II)

[Jortin (John)] Miscellaneous Observations upon Authors, ancient and modern 2 vols 8vo *London*, 1731

Longinus on the Sublime (Classics)

Boileau, Traité du Sublime   (Œuvres, Vol III)

Burke's (Edmund) Philosophical Inquiry into the Origin of our Ideas of the Sublime and Beautiful, with an introductory discourse concerning Taste   (Works, Vol I)

Knight's (Rd Payne) Analytical Inquiry into the Principles of Taste. 8vo. *London*, 1808.

Hume (D) on the Standard of Taste   (Essays, Vol. I)

Alison's (Arch) Essays on the Nature and Principles of Taste   2 vols 8vo. *Edin* 1811

[D'Israeli's (I)] Essays on the Sources of the Pleasures derived from Literary Compositions   8vo   *London*, 1809

Young's (Ed) Conjectures on Original Composition   (Works, Vol V.)

[Tytler's (A F.)] Essay on the Principles of Translation   8vo. *London*, 1813.

Rhetoric and Oratory.

Aristotelis Ars Rhetorica   (Opera, Vol II , Classics.)

Cicero de Rhetoricâ,
Cicero de Oratore et claris Oratoribus. } (Classics)

Quintilian de Institutione Oratoriæ   (Classics)

Campbell's (Geo) Philosophy of Rhetoric. 2 vols 8vo   *Lond* 1815

Blair's (Hugh) Lectures on Rhetoric.   (Polite Literature)

Milton (Jo) Prolusiones Oratoriæ   (Prose Works. 4to Vol II., 8vo Vol VI)

Witherspoon's (John) Lectures on Eloquence   (Works, Vol VII)

Ciceronis
Demosthenis
Isocratis
Quintiliani
Senecæ
Rhetorum antiquorum selectorum
} Orationes   (Classics)

Orations of Arsanes against Philip, the treacherous Kyng of Macedon ; and of the Embassadors of Venice against the Prince that, under crafty league with Scanderbeg, layd snares for Christendome , and of Scanderbeg prayeng ayde of Christian princes agaynst perjurious, murderyng Mahomet. Black letter, small 8vo   *London, by John Daye,* ——

Trésor de tous les Livres d'Amadis de Gaule ; contenant les plus belles harangues faictes aux roys epistres concions lettres missives, &c pour l'instruction de la noblesse de France à bien haranguer et escrire lettres missives   1 vol in 2, 18mo   *à Paris*, 1573

Poetry.

On the Art of Poetry.

Aristotelis de Arte Poeticâ   (Op Vol II , Classics)

Horatii Ars Poetica , with notes and critical dissertations by Bp Hurd. (Hurd's Works, Vols I and II)

Metastasio, Estratti dell' Arte Poetica d' Aristotile e di Q Orazio Flacco, con considerazioni sur le medisima (Opere, Vol XII)

Beattie (James) on Poetry and Music. (Criticism)

Dryden's (John) Art of Poetry (Works, Vol XV)

Harris (James) on Poetry. (Works, Vol I)

Hurdis's (James) Lectures, shewing the several sources of that pleasure which the mind receives from poetry 4to *Bishopstone, Sussex, at the Author's own Press,* 1797.

Ritson (Joseph) on Romance and Minstrelsy (Metrical Romances)

Boileau, l'Art Poétique (Œuvres, Vol. II.)

Fabre-d'Olivet, Discours sur l'Essence et la Forme de la Poésie. (Pythagoras, Classics)

Greek Poets

Gnomici Poetæ Græcæ
Poetæ Græci Principes, Stephani } (Classics)
Miscellanea Græcorum Carmina, Maittaire

Analecta Græcorum Poetarum Vet, Brunck·

Anacreon.	Lycophron
Apollonius Rhodius	Moschus
Aratus	Musæus
Bion	Oppianus.
Callimachus.	Orpheus
Hesiodus	Pindarus
Homerus	Quintus Smyrnæus.
Heraclidis Allegoriæ	Theocritus

} (Classics)

Chants Populaires de la Grèce Moderne, recueillis et publiés, avec une traduction Française, des éclaircissements et des notes, par C Fauriel 2 vols. 8vo. *Paris,* 1824.

Latin Poets.

Baker Medulla Poet Rom.
Opera et Fragmenta Vet Poet Lat, Maittaire } (Classics)

Poetæ Latini Minores, Burmanni

Ausonius.	Phædrus
Catullus	Propertius
Claudianus.	Prudentius
Horatius	Silius Italicus.
Juvenalis	Statius
Lucretius.	Tibullus
Martialis	Virgilius
Ovidius	Valerius Flaccus
Persius	

} (Classics)

Musarum Anglicanum Analecta, sive poemata quædam melioris notæ seu hactenùs inedita, seu sparsim edita 2 vols 8vo large paper *Oxonii,* 1699

Musarum Anglicanarum Analecta. 3 vols. 12mo Lond 1721, et Oxon. 1717.

Musæ Etonensis sive Poemata. 2 vols. 12mo Londini, 1755.

Delitiæ Poetarum Scotorum hujus ævi illustrium, Art Jonstono collectore. 2 vols. 12mo Amstelodami, 1637.

Selecta Poemata Italorum qui Latinè scripserunt, iterum in lucem data, unà cum aliorum Italorum operibus, accurante Alex. Pope. 2 vols small 8vo Londini, 1740.

Delitiæ C. Poetarum Gallorum, collectore Ranutio Gherio [J Grutero] 3 vols 12mo Francofurti, 1609.

Delitiæ Poetarum Germannorum, collectore A [Antwerpiano] F[ilio] G[uil.] G[rutero] 6 vols. 12mo. Francofurti, 1612.

Delitiæ Poetarum Belgicorum, collectore G. Grutero 4 vols 12mo. Francofurti, 1614

Delitiæ Poetarum Hungaricorum, à J. P Pera. 12mo Francofurti, 1619.

Delitiæ quorumdam Poetarum Danorum, collectore F Rostgaard. 2 vols 12mo. Lugduni Bat 1693.

Poetarum Polonorum Carmina Pastoralia, ex Bib. Zaluscianâ iterum edita 8vo. Altenburgi, 1779

Carminum rariorum Maccaronicorum Delectus in usum ludorum Appolinarium. 8vo. Edinb 1801

Paræneses Antiquæ Germannicæ Tyrolis Regis Scotorum ad Filium Fridebrantum, ut et Winsbeckii ad Filium et Winsbeckiæ ad Filiam ab hinc annos D et quod excurrit, scriptæ: cum notis edidit M H. Goldastus; ac notis J G Scherzii. (Schilteri Thes)

Addison (Jos.) Poemata (Works, Vol I. 8vo, and Vol. I 4to)

Crashaw (Rich) Poemata et Epigrammata Small 8vo. Cantab 1670.

Heinsii (Nic) Poemata· accedunt Jo Rutgersii quæ quidem colligi potuerunt. 32mo. Lugd Bat ex off. Elzev 1653

Johnsoni (Sam.) Poemata. (Works, Vol I)

Lelandi (J.) Genethliacon illust Edwardi Principis Cambriæ. Londini, 1543. (Itinerarium, Vol IX.)

Lelandi Cygnea Cantio, cum comment., &c. Londini, 1545. (Itinerarium, Vol IX.)

Kinschottii (Casparis) Poemata, omnia ex chirographo auctoris diligenter edita [à J Gronovio] Small 8vo Three portraits of Kinschotius, by Hollar, in various states Hagæ Comitis, 1685

Markham (Rev Guil) Carmina Quadragesimalia, &c, edente Rev F Wrangham 4to Privately printed, 1820

More (Sir T.) Poemata. (Life by Cowley.)

Murphy (A) Poemata (Works, Vol. VII)

Owen's (John) Latin Epigrams, rendered into English by Th Harvey The three books in one vol 12mo. London, 1677

Sarbievii (Mat. Casimeri) Carmina; studiis Soc Biponti. 8vo. Argent. 1803.

Seldeni (Jo) Poemata, Gr. et Lat (Opera, Vol II)

English Poetry.

HISTORY OF AND DISSERTATIONS ON ENGLISH POETRY.

Warton's (Thomas) History of English Poetry, from the close of the 11th to the commencement of the 18th century, to which are added, dissertations on the origin of romantic fiction in Europe, the introduction of learning into England, and on the Gesta Romanorum: with numerous additional notes by the late Mr. Ritson and Dr. Ashby, Mr. Dance, Mr Park, and other eminent antiquaries; and a preface by the editor. 4 vols. 8vo. *London*, 1824.

Gray's (Thos.) Collections for a History of English Poetry (Works by Mathias, Vol. II.)

Phillips's (Edward) Theatrum Poetarum Anglicorum, containing the names and characters of all the English poets, from the reign of Henry III. to the close of the reign of Elizabeth; enlarged with additions to every article [by Sir Egerton Brydges]. 8vo. *Canterbury*, 1800.

Sidney's (Sir P.) Defence of English Poesie. (Misc. Works.)

Ancient Critical Essays upon English Poets and Poesy, edited by Joseph Haslewood. 2 vols. 4to *London*, 1815

    Viz. The Arte of English Poesie, by Geo. Puttenham.
        Certayne Notes of Instruction concerning the Making of Verse or Rhyme in English, by Geo. Gascoigne
        A Discourse of English Poetrie, by William Webbe.
        A Treatis of the Airt of Scottis Poesie by King James II.
        An Apologie of Poetrie, by Sir John Harrington.
        A Comparative Discourse of our English Poets with the Greek, Latin, and Italian poets, by Francis Meres.
        Observations on the Art of English Poesie, by Thomas Campion.
        A Defense of Rhyme, by Samuel Daniel.
        Hypercritica, by Edward Bolton.
        Three proper and wittie familiar Letters, lately passed between two universitie men, Edmund Spenser and Gabriel Harvey.
        Two other very commendable Letters of the same men's writing.

Nott's (G F) Dissertation on the state of English Poetry before the sixteenth century. (Surrey and Wyat's Works, Vol. I.)

Collyer's (J. P.) Poetical Decameron, or, ten days' conversations on English poets and poetry, particularly of the reigns of Elizabeth and James I. 2 vols. 8vo. *Edinburgh*, 1820.

Neve's (Philip) Cursory Remarks on some of the ancient English Poets, particularly Milton. 8vo. *London, printed for presents only*, 1789.

Conybeare's (J. J.) Illustrations of Anglo-Saxon Poetry; edited, with additional notes and introductory notices, by W D. Conybeare. 4to. *London*, 1826

COLLECTIONS AND EXTRACTS OF ENGLISH POETRY.

The Works of the English Poets, from Chaucer to Cowper; including the series edited with prefaces, biographical and critical, by Dr. Johnson with the most approved translations and additional lives, by Alex. Chalmers 21 vols. roy. 8vo *London*, 1810

LITERATURE.

[Allot's (Robt)] England's Parnassus; or, the choysest flowers of our moderne poets, with their poeticall comparisons. Small 8vo. *Lond* 1600.
> This copy has successively belonged to W. Oldys and T. Warton, and autograph memoranda in both their hands are on the fly leaves Warton describes this work as the first selection of English poetry published.

Campbell's (Thos.) Specimens of the British Poets, with biographical and critical notices, and an essay on English poetry. 7 vols. 8vo. *London*, 1819

[Capell's (Ed)] Prolusions; or, select pieces of ancient poetry; containing the Nutbrowne Mayde, Mr. Sackville's Induction, Overbury's Wife, Edward III., a Play, and Nosce Teipsum, by Sir John Davies. Small 8vo. *London*, 1760

Cooper's (E.) Muse's Library; or, a series of English Poetry, from the Saxons to Charles II. Vol I. 8vo all published. *London*, 1737.

Ellis's (Geo) Specimens of early English Poets; with an historical sketch of the rise and progress of English Poetry and language. 3 vols 8vo *London*, 1811

Ellis's (Geo) Specimens of early English Metrical Romances, chiefly written during the early part of the 14th century; with an historical introduction, intended to illustrate the rise and progress of romantic composition in France and England. 3 vols. 8vo. *London*, 1811

Evans's (Thomas) Old Ballads, historical and narrative, collected from rare copies and MSS. edited by R. H. Evans. 4 vols. 8vo. *Lond.* 1810.

Fry's (J) Legend of Mary Queen of Scots, and other ancient poems; now first published from MSS. of the 16th century. 4to large paper. [*Bristol*], 1810.

Headley's (Henry) Select Beauties of ancient English Poetry, with remarks, and a biographical sketch of the author, by H. Kett. 2 vols. in one, 8vo. *London*, 1810.

Jamieson's (Robt) Popular Ballads and Songs, from traditions, MSS., and scarce editions, with translations from the ancient Danish language 2 vols 8vo *Edinb.* 1806.

Marston's (John) Miscellaneous Pieces of ancient English Poesie, viz the Troublesome Raigne of King John, by Shakspeare; the Metamorphosis of Pigmalion's Image, and Scourge of Villanie. 12mo. *London*, 1764

[Percy's (Bp Thos)] Reliques of ancient English Poetry; consisting of old heroic ballads, songs, and other pieces, of our earlier poets [with an essay on the ancient English minstrels and metrical romances, notes, and glossaries.] 3 vols. small 8vo. *London*, 1775

Percy's (Bp. Thos) Reliques of ancient English Poetry; containing a collection of ballads, songs, and other pieces, of our earlier English poets edited by Thos Percy. 3 vols 8vo. *London*, 1812.

[Phillips's (Ambrose)] Collection of old Ballads, with introductions, historical, critical, and humorous 3 vols 12mo *Lond* 1727–25

[Ritson's (Jos)] English Anthology. 3 vols. 8vo *London*, 1793

[Ritson's (J) Pieces of ancient popular Poetry from authentic MSS 8vo *London*, 1791

[Ritson's (J.)] Selection of ancient English Metrical Romances 3 vols. 8vo. *London*, 1802.

LITERATURE.

Southey's (Robt.) Specimens of the later English Poets [in continuation of Ellis's]; with preliminary notices. 3 vols 8vo. Sir M M. Sykes's copy   *London*, 1807.

[Utterson's (E V.)] Select Pieces of early popular Poetry; republished principally from early printed copies in the black letter. 2 vols. in one, 8vo.   *London*, 1817

Weber's (Henry) Metrical Romances of the 13th, 14th, and 15th centuries, published from ancient MSS, with an introduction, notes, and a glossary. 3 vols 8vo   Sir M M. Sykes's copy   *Edinb.* 1810.

Mirror for Magistrates, Part I. by John Higgins, Part II. by Thomas Blenerhaset, Part III by William Baldwin and others, and Parts IV. and V. by Richard Niccols, collated with various editions, with historical notes, &c by Joseph Haslewood. 3 vols 4to.   *London*, 1815

> For an analysis of the legends forming this work, see Warton's Eng Poetry, Vol. IV.

Heliconia, a selection of English poetry of the Elizabethan age, written or published between 1575 and 1604: edited by Thomas Park. 3 vols. 4to.   *London*, 1815.

England's Helicon; a collection of pastoral and lyric poems, first published at the close of the reign of Queen Elizabeth edited by Sir Egerton Brydges and J. Haslewood. 4to.   *London*, 1812.

Lee Priory (Poetical Works from the private Press at). 4to. and 8vo.

Poems by various Authors, written between 1540 and 1612. (Harrington's Nugæ Antiquæ, Vol. II.)

Collection of Poems, by several hands [edited, with notes, by R. Dodsley]. 6 vols 8vo.   *London*, 1782.

Collection of Poems, by several hands [edited, with notes, by G. Pearch, as a supplement to Dodsley's]. 4 vols. 8vo.   *London*, 1783.

Collection of the most esteemed Poetry; with a variety of originals and other contributions to Dodsley's collection   8vo.   *London*, 1767.

Miscellanies in Verse, by Pope, Arbuthnot, Gay, &c.; collated by Swift and Pope. (Swift's Works, Vol XIII.)

Elegant Extracts, in Verse, edited by V. Knox. 2 vols. 8vo   *London*, 1791

Fugitive Poetry (Bell's Classical Arrangement of). 18 vols. 12mo. fine paper.   *London*, 1790–97

Poetry of the Anti-Jacobin [by Gifford, Canning, Frere, &c.]. 4to.   *London*, 1801

Poems, containing the Retrospect, &c, by Robert Lovell and Robert Southey. 8vo   *Bath*, 1795.

Dyce's (Alex) Specimens of British Poetesses, chronologically arranged 8vo   *London*, 1827.

Kettell's (Sam.) Specimens of American Poetry; with critical and biographical notices [and catalogue of American poetical works]   3 vols. small 8vo   *Boston, U. S.* 1829

ENGLISH SONGS.

[Ritson's (Jos)] Ancient Songs, from the time of Henry III to the Revolution 8vo. *London,* 1790

[Ritson's (Jos)] Robin Hood; being a collection of all the songs, ballads &c. now extant, relative to that English Outlaw 2 vols. 8vo. *London,* 1795.

Ritson's (Jos) Select Collection of English Songs, with additions and occasional notes by Th Park 3 vols 8vo *London,* 1813

[Dalrymple's (Alex)] Collection of English Songs, with an appendix of original pieces. 8vo *London,* 1796.

A Collection of Loyal Songs, written against the Rump Parliament, between the years 1639 and 1661; with an historical introduction. 2 vols 12mo *London,* 1731.

Plumptree's (James) Letters to Dr. Aikin, on his Essays on Songwriting; with a collection of such English songs as are most eminent for their poetic merit, revised and altered by R. H. Evans. Small 8vo *Camb* 1811

Plumptree's (J.) Collection of Songs, with introductory letter on songwriting. 2 vols 12mo. *London,* 1806

Simes' (D.) Musical Miscellany, a collection of songs set to music 12mo. *Edin.* 1792.

The Musical Miscellany; being a collection of choice songs, set to the violin and flute. 6 vols in 3, 12mo. *London,* 1729.

SEPARATE ENGLISH POETS.

Addison's (Joseph) Poems. (Works, Vol I, 4to. and 8vo)

Anstey's (Christ) Poetical Works; with an account of his life and writings by John Anstey. 4to *London,* 1808.

Anstey's (J) Pleader's Guide, a didactic poem 8vo *London,* 1808

Baillie's (Joanna) Metrical Legends of exalted Characters. 8vo *London,* 1821

Barnard's (E W) Fifty Select Poems of Marc Antonio Flaminio imitated, with a short memoir of the author Edited by Francis Wrangham 8vo Presentation copy from the editor *Chester,* 1829.

Bayly's (T H) Psyche, or, songs on butterflies, attempted in Latin rhyme, with a few additional trifles, by Francis Wrangham. 8vo. Presentation copy from the translator *Malton,* 1828.

Beattie's (James) Minstrel; or, the Progress of Genius · with other poems. 4to *Edin* 1803.

Blair's (Robert) Grave, illustrated with etchings by Schiavonetti, from the designs of W Blake 4to *London,* 1808

Bloomfield's (Robert) Rural Tales, Ballads, and Songs; the Farmer's Boy, and Wild Flowers, or Pastoral and Local Poetry 3 vols 12mo. *London,* 1805-6

Bowles' (W L) Poems 4 vols 12mo. *Bath,* 1802-9

Brathwait's (Richard) Barnabæ Itinerarium; or, Barnabee's Journal, with a life of the author, a bibliographical introduction to the Itinerary, and a catalogue of his works. Edited, from the first edition, by Joseph Haslewood 2 vols 18mo *London,* 1820

LITERATURE.

Brathwayte's (Rich) Odes; or, Philomel's Tears. 8vo. *Lee Priory*, 1815.
Breton's (N) Melancholike Humours. Royal 4to. *Lee Priory*, 1815.
Breton's (N) Ravished Soule and Blessed Weeper Royal 8vo. *Lee Priory*, ——.
Browne's (William) Poems, never before published Royal 4to. *Lee Priory*, 1813–17.
Brydges' (Sir E) Select Poems. Royal 4to. *Lee Priory*, 1814.
Brydges' (Sir E) Occasional Poems. Royal 4to. *Lee Priory*, 1814.
Brydges' (Sir E) Select Funeral Memorials 4to *Lee Priory*, 1818.
Butler's (Sam) Hudibras; with large annotations and a preface by Z. Grey. Plates by Hogarth. 2 vols 8vo *Cambridge*, 1744.
Butler's (S) Hudibras; with Dr Grey's annotations, new edition, corrected and enlarged, with illustrative cuts and portraits 3 vols 8vo. *London*, 1819.
Butler's (S) Hudibras; avec traduction en vers François [par Jo Townley], et des Remarques [par Larcher] Plates after Hogarth, and port of Mr Townley by Skelton 3 vols. 12mo *Londres* [*Paris*], 1757.
Buchanan's (Geo) Baptistes, a sacred and dramatic Poem, in defence of liberty, translated into English by John Milton (Peck's Life of Milton.)
Byron's (Lord) Works; with Werner, Heaven and Earth, Vision of Judgment, &c not in the regular edition of his works. 8 vols. 8vo. *London*, 1823–25.
Byron's Works (Illustrations of), from designs by Westall and Stothard. 8vo *London*, 1814–19
Byron (Lord) —Historical Illustrations of the Fourth Canto of Childe Harold, by John Hobhouse. 8vo *London*, 1818.
Byron's (Lord) English Bards and Scotch Reviewers; a Satire. The first edition, small 8vo *London*, ——.
Cambridge's (Owen) Poetical Works. (Works.)
Campbell's (T) Pleasures of Hope; with other Poems. Small 8vo. *Lond.* 1826.
Campbell's (T) Gertrude of Wyoming, and other Poems. Small 8vo. *London*, 1825
Campbell's (T.) Theodoric; a Domestic Tale. and other Poems Small 8vo. *London*, 1824.
Carysfort's (John Joshua, Earl of) Poems. 2 vols in one, 8vo *London*, 1810.
Cavendish's (Geo.) Metrical Visions concerning the Fortunes and Fall of the most eminent persons of his time. (Life of Wolsey)
Chalkhill's (John) Thealma and Clearchus, a Pastoral Romance: edited by S W Singer. Small 8vo *Lond* 1820
Chatterton's (Thos) Poems (Works, and under Rowley.)
Chatterton (Papers of Horatio Walpole, relative to). (Orford's Works, Vol IV)
Chaucer (Geoff) The Works of our ancient and learned Poet; edited, with additions, by Th Speght. Folio. W Herbert's copy. *London*, 1602.
Chaucer's (Geoff) Canterbury Tales; with an Essay on his Language and Versification, notes, and a glossary, by T. Tyrwhitt. 2 vols. 4to. *Oxford*, 1798

Chaucer's Canterbury Tales ; to which are added, an Essay on his language and versification, an introductory discourse, notes, and a glossary [edited by T. Tyrwhitt]. 5 vols 8vo large paper. Sir M. M. Sykes's copy *London*, 1775–8,

Chaucer (Todd's Illustrations of the Life and Writings of). (Biography.)

Chudleigh's (Lady Mary) Poems on several occasions Small 8vo. *London*, 1722.

Corbet's (Bp Rich) Poems, with notes and a life of the author, by Oct Gilchrist 8vo. *London*, 1807.

Cowley's (Abr) Poems. (Works)

Cowper's (Wm) Poems, edited by Jo Newton ; with Storer and Greig's illustrations. 4to *London*, 1806

Crabbe's (Geo) Works ; with Westall's illustrations. 5 vols. 8vo *London*, 1823

Crashaw's (Rich) Steps to the Temple, the Delights of the Muses, and Carmen pro Nostro. Small 8vo *London*, 1670

[Cutts' (John, Lord)] Poetical Exercises upon several occasions. Small 8vo. *London*, 1687.

Darwin's (Erasmus) Botanic Garden (Botany)

Darwin's (E) Temple of Nature ; or, the origin of society ; a poem : with philosophical notes. 4to. *Lond* 1803.

Davison's (Francis) Poetical Rhapsody, edited by Sir Egerton Brydges. 3 vols in two, 8vo. *Lee Priory*, 1814.

Denham's (Sir John) Poems and Translations, with the Sophy, a tragedy. 12mo bound by Roger Payne. *London*, 1719

Dermody's (Thomas) Poetical Works, edited by J G Raymond 2 vols. 8vo. *Lond.* 1807.

Drayton's (Mich) Poly-Albion (English Topography)

Dryden's (John) Poems, historical and political. (Works, Vols IX. and X)

Dryden's (J) Poetical Epistles, Odes, Songs, and Lyrical Pieces. (Works, Vol XI)

Dryden's (J) Fables. (Works, Vols. XI. and XII)

Falconer's (Wm.) Shipwreck, a poem, with notes and life of the author, by James S Clarke and illustrative plates after Pococke. 8vo. largest paper, proofs *London*, 1804

Flodden Field (the Battle of), a poem of the 16th century, with various readings, historical notes, a glossary, and an appendix containing ancient poems and historical matter relating to the same event ; by Henry Weber. 8vo. *Edinburgh*, 1808.

Ford's (John) Fame's Memorial ; or, Elegy on the Earl of Devonshire, 1606 Royal 8vo. *Lee Priory*, 1819

Garrick's (David) Poetical Works, with explanatory notes. 2 vols. 18mo *London*, 1785

Gifford's (Wm) Baviad and Mœviad 8vo. *London*, 1810.

[Gillies' (R P.)] Childe Alarique, a Poet's Reverie. 4to. *Edinburgh*, 1813

Gisborne's (Thomas) Walks in a Forest 12mo. *London*, 1797.

[Gisborne's (T.)] Rothley Temple, a Poem. 8vo. Presentation copy from the author *London*, 1815.

Goldsmith's (O) Miscellaneous Poems. (Works, Vol II.)

Gower's (Jo) de Confessione Amantis [or, the Lover's Confession] 𝔅𝔩𝔞𝔠𝔨 𝔩𝔢𝔱𝔱𝔢𝔯, folio *London, by T. Berthelette, M.D.LIIII.*

Gower (Todd's Illustrations of the Life and Writings of) (Biography)

Grahame's (James) Poems, viz. Birds of Scotland, Sabbath and Sabbath Walk 2 vols. 12mo. *London*, 1807

Grahame's (J) British Georgics, with notes illustrative of Scottish agriculture. 4to. *London*, 1809

Gray's (Thos.) Poetical Works. (Works. 4to. and 8vo , Vol. I.)

Gray's (Thos.) Poems, with critical notes, a life of the author, and an essay on his poetry, by J. Mitford. 8vo *London*, 1814.

Grevill (Sir Fulke) Lord Brooke's Remains; being poems of monarchy and religion. Small 8vo *London*, 1670

Griffin's (B.) Fidessa; a collection of sonnets [edited, from the edition of 1596, by Ph. Bliss]. 8vo. *Chiswick*, 1815.

Habington's (Wm) Castara. Best edition, 12mo. *London*, 1640

Habington's (Wm) Castara; with a preface and notes by C. A. Elton. Small 8vo. *Bristol*, 1812.

Hall's (Bp) VI Books of Satyrs. (Works.)

Harrington's (Sir John) most Elegant and Wittie Epigrams. *London*, 1633.

Haygarth's (Wm.) Greece, with notes, classical illustrations, and sketches of the scenery. 4to. *London*, 1814.

Hayley's (W) Triumphs of Temper. Small 8vo *Chichester*, 1817.

Heber's (Reg.) Palestine, a Poem. 8vo. Presentation copy. *Oxford, privately printed*, 1803.

Heber's (R.) Palestine; a poem, recited in the theatre, Oxford, 1803; with the Passage of the Red Sea, a fragment. 4to. Presentation copy from Reginald Heber. *London*, 1809.

Heber's (Reg) Poems and Translations. 12mo. *London*, 1812.

Herbert's (George) Temple, Sacred Poems, and Private Ejaculations, 12mo *Camb* 1633.

Herbert's (William) Miscellaneous Poetry [principally translations from the Danish and Icelandic] 2 vols. 8vo *London*, 1806.

Herbert's (W) Helga 8vo. *Lond.* 1815.

Herrick's (Rob) Select Poems from his Hesperides; or, works both human and divine. with remarks by J Nott 8vo. *Bristol*, 1810.

Horace in London, in imitation of the first and second book of Horace. 12mo. *Lond* 1813

Hoyland's (Rev Mr.) Poems. 8vo. *Strawberry Hill*, 1769.

Hurdis's (James) Village Curate, Favourite Village, and other Poems. 2 vols. 8vo. *Lond.* 1810

Ingram's (H) Flowers of Wye. 8vo. *London*, 1815

Johnson's (Samuel) Poems. (Works, Vol. I)

Leyden's (Dr. John) Poetical Remains; with memoirs of his life by James Morton. 8vo. *Edinburgh*, 1819.

Lodge's (Thos) Glaucus and Silla; with other poems [and a preface by S. W Singer] Small 8vo *London*, 1819

[Longland's (Thos)] Vissio Willi͡ de Petro Ploughman, item Visiones ejusdem de Dowel, Dobet, et Dobest; or, the Vision of William concerning Piers Ploughmar, and the visions of the same concerning the origin, progress, and perfection of the Christian life Ascribed to Robert Longland, a secular priest, and written in, or immediately after, 1362. Printed from a contemporary MS., collated with others, and exhibiting the original text, together with an introductory discourse, a perpetual commentary, annotations, and a glossary; by T. D. Whitaker 4to black letter. *London*, 1813.

[Longland's (Thos.)] Pierce the Ploughman's Crede Black letter Edited from the edition of R. Wolfe, 1553, by J. Haslewood. 4to. large paper *London*, 1814

Lovelace's (Rich) Lucasta, Epodes, Odes, Sonnets, Songs, &c , edited by S W Singer 2 vols small 8vo *Lond.* 1817–18

Lyttleton's (George, Lord) Poems (Misc Works)

Mackenzie's (Henry) Poems. (Works, Vol. VIII.)

Marlow (Chr.) and Geo Chapman's Hero and Leander, a poem; with a critical preface by S. W. Singer Small 8vo. *Lond* 1821.

Marmyon's (Shakerly) Cupid and Psyche, a legend, edited by S W. Singer. Small 8vo. *Lond* 1820

Mason's (Wm.) Poetical Works (Works, Vol. I)

Milman's (H. H) Martyr of Antioch, a dramatic poem. 8vo. *London*, 1822

Milman's (H H) Anne Boleyn, a dramatic poem. 8vo. *Lond* 1826.

Milman's (H. H) Belshazzar, a dramatic poem 8vo. *Lond.* 1822

Milman's (H H) Fall of Jerusalem. 8vo. *Lond* 1822.

Milton's (John) Poetical Works ; with notes of various authors, by (Bp) Thos Newton. 3 vols 4to. *London*, 1749–52

<blockquote>The plates to this edition were executed at the expense of the Earl of Bath, as was also a portion of the printing.</blockquote>

Milton's (J) Poetical Works, with notes of various authors, and some account of his life and writings, by H J. Todd : to which are added, illustrations, with a verbal index to the whole of Milton's poetry. 7 vols 8vo *Lond.* 1809.

Milton, Memoirs of his Poetical Works (Peck's Life of Milton)

Milton's (John) Paradise Lost, a poem in ten books. 4to FIRST EDITION *London*, 1668.

Milton's (J) Paradise Regained, with Samson Agonistes 8vo FIRST EDITION *London*, 1671.

Milton's (J) Paradise Lost ; with illustrations designed and engraved by John Martin. Large paper, proofs, 2 vols imp 4to *London*, 1827.

Milton —Explanatory Notes and Remarks on Milton's Paradise Lost, by J. Richardson, Father and Son, with life of the author, and a discourse on the poem, by J R senior. 8vo *London*, 1734.

Milton's (J) Poems on several occasions, English, Italian, and Latin ; with notes and other illustrations, by Th Warton 8vo *Lond* 1791.

3 B

Minot's (Laurence) Poems on interesting events in the reign of Edward III, written in 1352; edited, with preface, dissertation, notes, and a glossary, by J. Ritson. 8vo. *London*, 1795.

Mitford's (Mary R.) Christina, or, the Maid of the South Seas. 8vo. *London*, 1811.

Montgomery's (James) Poetical Works. 4 vols. small 8vo. *London*, 1831

Montgomery's (Robert) Oxford, a poem. Small 8vo. *Oxford*, 1831.

Moore's (Thomas) Lalla Rookh, an oriental romance. 4to. *London*, 1817.

Moore's (T.) Loves of the Angels, with illustrations by Westall. 8vo. *London*, 1823.

Murphy's (Arth.) Poems. (Works, Vol. VII.)

Nut-brown Maid (the Original of the) (Arnold's Chronicle)

Orleans —Poems, written in English, by Charles Duke of Orleans, during his captivity in England, after the battle of Agincourt [edited by G. W. Taylor] 4to. *Privately printed*, 1827.

Peele's (F.) Poetical Works. (Works, Vol. II)

Percy's (W.) Cælia, containing twenty sonnets. 4to. *Lee Priory*, 1818.

Pollok's (R.) Course of Time, a poem. 12mo. *Edinburgh*, 1832.

Pope's (Alex.) Pastorals, Odes, Imitations, Miscellanies, and Epitaphs. (Works, Vols I. and II)

Pope's (A.) Essay on Man, Moral Essays. (Works, Vols. III and IV.)

Quilman's (E.) Dunluce Castle. Royal 4to. *Lee Priory*, 1814.

Quilman's (E.) Stanzas Royal 4to *Lee Priory*, 1814.

Ralegh's (Sir Walter) Poems; with a biographical and critical introduction by Sir Egerton Brydges. 4to. *Lee Priory*, 1813

Ralegh's (Sir W.) Poems (Works, Vol VIII)

Rejected Addresses, or, the New Theatrum Poetarum. 12mo 1812.

Rogers' (Sam.) Poems Small 8vo *London*, 1812.

Rogers' (S.) Italy, a poem, with plates after Stothard 8vo. large paper. *London*, 1830

Rogers' (S.) Human Life, a poem Small 8vo *London*, 1819.

Rowlands (S.), the Letting of Humours Blood in the Head-vaine; with a new morisseo, daunced by seven satyrs uppon the bottome of Diogenes' tubbe *Imprinted*, 1611 Fac-simile reprint, with introduction by Sir Walter Scott Small 4to. *Edinburgh*, 1815.

Rowley (Poems, supposed to have been written at Bristol, by Thomas), priest, &c; with a commentary, in which the antiquity of them is considered and defended. by Jeremiah Miles. 4to *London*, 1782.
    "R. Gough, from the editor, Dec. 12, 1781." with MS. marginal notes by Mr. Gough.

Rowley's Poems. (Chatterton's Works, Vol. II)

Rowley (Observations on the Poems of), in which their authenticity is ascertained, by Jacob Bryant. 8vo. *Lond.* 1781.

Rowley —An Inquiry into the Authenticity of the Poems attributed to Th. Rowley, in which the arguments of the Dean of Exeter and Mr. Bryant are examined, by Th Warton 8vo *Lond* 1782

Scott's (Sir W.) Lay of the Last Minstrel, Marmion, Lady of the Lake, Rokeby, Don Roderick, Lord of the Isles, Ballads, and Miscellaneous Poems. 8 vols 8vo *Edin* 1806, &c

Scott.—Illustrations of, by Westall and Stothard. 4to proofs on India paper. *London*, 1809-12

Scott (Sir W), the Bridal of Triermain ; or, Vale of St. John. Small 8vo *Edin*. 1813.

Scott's (Sir W) Harold the Dauntless 12mo. *Edin* 1817

Seward's (Anna) Poetical Works, edited [with biographical preface and extracts from her literary correspondence] by Sir Walter Scott 3 vols 8vo *Edin*. 1810.

Shakspeare's (W) Poems (Works, by Boswell.)

Shirley's (James) Poems, &c Small 8vo port by Marshall *Lond*. 1646

Shirley's (J) Poems (Dramatic Works)

Sidney's (Sir Philip) Miscellaneous Poems (Works)

Skelton (the Workes of Maister John), poete laureate to K Henry VIII. 12mo. *London*, 1736

Sotheby's (Wm) Tour through part of Wales, Sonnets, and other Poems. 4to *London*, 1794

Southey's (Dr Robert) Poetical Works. 14 vols. small 8vo. *Lond* ——.

Spenser's (Edmund) Works, with the principal illustrations of various commentators ; to which are added, notes, some account of the life of Spenser, and a glossary, &c. by H. J. Todd. 8 vols 8vo. large paper *London*, 1805

Spenser.—Warton's (T) Observations on the Fairie Queen. 2 vols. 8vo. *Lond.* 1808.

Stillingfleet's (Benj) Poetical Works (Works, Vol II)

Suckling's (Sir John) Poems. (Works)

Surrey (Henry Howard, Earl of) and Sir Thomas Wyat's Poetical Works (Works)

Swift's (Jonath.) Poems (Works, Vols X. XII XIV XV)

Sylvester's (Jos) Posthumi, or Remains ; containing divers sonnets, epistles, elegies, &c never till now printed (Appendix to Du Bartas)

Taylor's (John) Water-Poets, poems (Works)

Thomson's (James) Works ; with a Life of the author by Patrick Murdoch 3 vols 8vo *London*, 1788

Throckmorton's (Sir T) Legend of Sir N Throckmorton, who died of poison 1570, an historical poem (Peck's Milton)

Tighe's (Mrs. H) Psyche, with other poems 4to *London*, 1811

Tixall Poetry [or poems collected by the Hon. H Aston, 1658, &c found at Tixall] ; with notes and illustrations by Arthur Clifford 4to. *Edinburgh*, 1813

Trumpet of Fame , or, Sir F Drake and Sir John Hawkins's farewell Small 8vo *Lee Priory*, 1818

Vicars's (John) Mischeefe's Mysterie, the Powder Plot , a poem (English History.)

Walpole's (Horatio) Miscellaneous Verses and Epigrams (Orford's Works, Vol IV.)

LITERATURE.

Walpole's (H) Fugitive Pieces in verse. (Orford's Works, Vol. I)

[Walter's (William)] Certaine Worthye MS Poems of great Antiquitie, reserved long in the studie of a Northfolke gentleman, and now first published by J. S Small 8vo *London, imprinted by R Robinson, 1597, fac-simile reprint, Edinburgh, 1812*

Warner's (W) Albion's England. (English History.)

Warton's (Thomas) Poetical Works, together with memoirs of his life and writings, and notes, critical and explanatory, by Richard Mant. 2 vols. 8vo. *Oxford*, 1802

Warton's Poetical Works (Selections from) (Life, Biography)

[Way's (Lewis)] Palingenesia, the World to Come ; a poem. Royal 8vo. *Paris*, 1824.

White's (Kirke) Poems. (Works)

Wilson's (Professor John) Isle of Palms, and other Poems 8vo. *Edinburgh*, 1812

Withers's (George) Abuses Stript and Whipt ; or, satirical essays. Small 8vo. first edition *London*, 1613

Withers's (G.) Shepherd's Hunting, eclogues. 12mo. *London, Bensley*, 1814.

Withers's (G) Fidelia, a love epistle. 12mo *London, Bensley*, 1815.

Withers's (G.) Select Lyrical Poems. Small 4to. *Lee Priory*, 1815.

Withers's (G.) Hymns and Songs of the Church , with preface by Sir E. Brydges. 12mo. *London, Bensley*, 1815.

Witt's Recreations, refined and augmented; with ingenious conceits for the wittie, and merrie medicine for the melancholie Small 8vo. front by Marshall. *London*, 1654.

Wordsworth's (Wm.) Lyrical Ballads and Pastorals 2 vols. 12mo. *London*, 1805

Wordsworth's (W) Poems. 2 vols. 12mo *London*, 1807

Wordsworth's (W.) Excursion, being a portion of the Recluse, a poem. 4to. *London*, 1814

Wordsworth's (W.) White Doe of Rylstone , or, the fate of the Nortons. 4to *London*, 1815

Wrangham's (Francis) Poetical Translations. (Works, Vol III.)

Wyat's (Sir Thos) Poetical Works. (Works of Surrey and Wyat)

Wyerley's (W) glorious Life and honorable Death of Sir John Chandos, Lord of Salviour, &c. , Capital de Buz, the honourable Life and languishing Death of Sir John de Gralpy , two Knights of the Garter elected by the founder, Edward III (Use of Armoury)

Zouche's (Richard, Lord) Dove, or passages of cosmography ; transcribed from the edition of 1613, by Mrs Dor. Richardson. A MS. in 4to.

Scottish Poetry

Campbell's (Alex) Introduction to the History of Poetry in Scotland, from the beginning of the 13th century; with a conversation on Scottish song. 4to. *Edinburgh*, 1798

LITERATURE.

Pinkerton's (John) Essay on the Origin of Scottish Poetry, and a list of all the Scottish poets, with brief remarks. (Ancient Scottish Poems, Vol. I)

Sibbald's (J) Chronicle of Scottish Poetry, from the 13th century to the union of the crowns; with a glossary   4 vols 8vo   *Edinb* 1802

Maitland's (Sir Richard) Collection of ancient Scottish Poems, comprising pieces written from about 1420 till 1586, with large notes and a glossary [edited by John Pinkerton]. 2 vols. 8vo. *London*, 1786.

Bannatyne's (Geo.) ancient Scottish Poems, published from his MS. collection, 1586 [edited by Lord Hailes]. Small 8vo. *Edinburgh*, 1770.

[Dalyell's (J. G.)] Scottish Poems of the 16th Century; with introduction, notes, and glossary   2 vols. 12mo   *Edinburgh*, 1801.

Findlay's (John) Scottish Historical and Romantic Ballads, chiefly ancient, with explanatory notes, glossary, &c. 2 vols. 8vo. *Edinb.* 1808

[Pinkerton's (John)] Select Tragic and Comic Scottish Ballads; with dissertations, notes, and glossaries. 2 vols. in one, 8vo   *London*, 1781-3

Scott's (Sir W) Minstrelsy of the Scottish Border, consisting of historical ballads, collected in the southern counties of Scotland; with a few of modern date, founded on local tradition · also an introduction and notes by the editor   3 vols 8vo.   *Edinb* 1815

[Ritson's (Jos)] Scottish Songs; [with an historical essay on Scottish song]. 2 vols 12mo. *London*, 1794.

[Campbell's Alex)] Songs of the Lowlands of Scotland; with characteristic designs by D. Allan. 4to   *Edinb* 1799

Cromek's (R H.) Remains of Nithsdale and Galloway Song; with historical and traditional notices relative to the manners and customs of the peasantry   8vo   *London*, 1810.

Hogg's (James) Jacobite Relics of Scotland, being the songs, airs, and legends of the adherents to the house of Stuart collected and illustrated with an appendix of Whig songs   2 vols 8vo.   *Edinburgh*, 1819-21

Ramsay's (Allan) Tea-Table Miscellany; or, collection of Scots songs   18mo   *London*, 1730

Burns's (Robert) Works; with an account of his life, and a criticism on his writings, by J Currie   4 vols 8vo.   *Liverpool*, 1800

Burns's (R) Reliques, consisting chiefly of original letters, poems, and critical observations on Scottish songs · collected and published by R H Cromek   8vo   *London*, 1808

Drummond (William), of Hawthornden's, Poems; [with preface by Ed. Philips, Milton's nephew]   Small 8vo portrait by Gaywood   *London*, 1656

Hogg's (James) Poetical Works. 4 vols. small 8vo.   *Edinb* 1822

James I (Poetical Remains of) King of Scotland, [edited, with dissertations on his life and writings, and on Scottish music, by Wm. Tytler]. 8vo Edinburgh, 1783

Lyndsay's (Sir David) Poetical Works; with life of the author, prefatory dissertations, and glossary, by George Chalmers. 3 vols. 8vo London, 1806.

Macneil's (Hector) Poetical Works. 2 vols small 8vo. Edinb. 1806.

Maitland's (Sir R.) Poems, with an appendix of selections from the poems of Sir John and Thomas Maitland: illustrated with biographical notices by J Bain. 4to. Glasgow, privately printed, 1831.

Ossian's Poems, translated by Ja. M'Pherson. 2 vols. 8vo London, 1784.

Ossian.—Cesarotti's (Abbé) Historical and Critical Dissertation respecting the controversy on the authenticity of Ossian's Poems, translated from the Italian, with notes and supplemental observations on the same subject, by J M'Arthur. 8vo. London [privately printed], 1806.
Horne Tooke's copy, with his MS notes.

Ossian.—Laing (M.) on the supposed Authenticity of Ossian's Poems (History of Scotland, Vol IV)

Ramsay's (Allan) Poems 2 vols. 18mo. London, 1731.

[Tennant's (W)] Anster Fair, and other Poems. Small 8vo. Edinb. 1814.

Welsh and Irish Poetry.

Davies's (Ed.) Ancient British Poems. (Druidical Rites)

Turner's (Sharon) Vindication of the Genuineness of the ancient British Poems of Aneurin, Taleisin, Llywarch, Hen, and Merdhin; with specimens of their poems. 8vo. London, 1803.

Walker's (Jos C) Historical Memoirs of the Irish Bards, with anecdotes of, and observations on, the music in Ireland: also, an historical and descriptive account of the musical instruments of the ancient Irish. 4to Dublin, 1776.

Brooke's (Miss) Reliques of Irish Poetry, with translations into English verse, and notes explanatory and historical. 4to. Dublin, 1789.

French Poetry.

Barbazan (Estienne), Fabliaux et Contes des Poètes François des XI, XII, XIII, XIV, et XVème Siècles; nouvelle édition, augmentée par M. Méon 4 vols. 8vo Paris, 1808.

Le Grand (M), Fabliaux, or, tales of the XIIth and XIIIth centuries, selected and translated into English verse by G S Way and G Ellis. 2 vols in one, 8vo. large paper London, 1796.

[Lorris (Guil) et Jean de Meung], le Rommant de la Rose, nouvellement revu et corrigé oultre les précédentes impressions. 8vo woodcuts, a very fine copy. Paris, par P Vidoue pour G du Pré, M D XXIX.

Lorris (Guil) et Jean de Meung, le Roman de la Rose, avec des notes, un glossaire, &c. 5 vols 8vo. Paris, 1798.

Richard I, Chansons (La Tour Ténébreuse, Romances)

LITERATURE.

Bibliothèque des Ecrivains François, ou, choix de meilleurs morceaux en vers, extraits par MM. Moysant et De Lévizac. 2 vols. in one, 8vo   *Londres*, 1803

Bartas' (Will de Salluste du) Complete Collection of his Workes, translated by Joshua Sylvester. Folio, portrait by Vicars, and front   *London*, 1641

Boileau, Le Lutrin, et Poésies diverses   (Œuvres, Vol. II.)

Bonaparte (Lucien), Charlemagne; ou, l'Eglise delivré, poème épique. 2 vols. 4to.   *London*, 1814.

Coquillart (Guill.), les Poésies. Small 8vo.   *Lond* 1723.

Coucy (Chansons du Chatelain Raoul de), avec la traduction et l'ancienne musique. (Mémoires de Coucy, Vol II.)

Cretin (Guill), les Poésies. Small 8vo.   *Paris, Coustellier*, 1723.

Faifeu (la Legende de Pierre), mis en vers par Ch. Bourdigne. Small 8vo.   *Paris, Coustellier*, 1723

Fontaine (La), Contes et Nouvelles en vers.   (Œuvres, Vol. III)

Fontaine (La), Adonis, poème; la Captivité de St. Malo, le Quinquina; Songe du Vaux, et autres opuscules poétiques. (Œuvres, Vols. V et VI)

Gresset (J. B. I..), Œuvres Poétiques   (Œuvres, Vol. I.)

Jouy (E), Poésies Légères. (Œuvres, Vol XLVI.)

Malherbe (Poésies de), [avec une notice sur sa vie et ses ouvrages]. 8vo   *Paris. Didot*, 1815

Marivaux, Homère Travestie; ou, l'Iliade en vers burlesques   (Œuvres, Vol. X.)

Marot (Jean), Œuvres   Small 8vo   *Paris, Coustellier*, 1723.

Martial de Paris, dit d'Auvergne, Poésies. 2 vols. small 8vo.   *Paris*, 1724

Racan (H de Bueil, Sieur de), Œuvres   2 vols small 8vo.   *Paris, Coustellier*, 1724.

Villon (Fr), Œuvres. Small 8vo.   *Paris*, 1723.

Italian Poetry.

Muratori (L. A), della perfetta Poesia Italiana spiegata e demonstrata, con le annotazioni dell' Abate A M Salvini   2 vols 4to   *Venez* 1748

Rime de più illustri Poeti Italiani, scelte dell' Abate Antonini   2 vols. 12mo   *Parigi*, 1733.

Rime degli Academici Occulti   4to.   *Brescia*, 1568.

Ariosto (Lod), Orlando Furioso, con la vita del autore scritta dal Dottore G A. Barotti, e le figure di Bartolozzi, &c. 4 vols. 8vo   *Birmingham, du' Torchi di G Baskerville*, 1773

Ariosto, Orlando Furioso, in heroical English verse, by Sir John Harrington. Folio   *London*, 1634.

Ariosto, Orlando Furioso, translated, with notes, by John Hoole   6 vols 12mo   *London*, 1807

Ariosto (the Orlando Furioso of Ludovico), translated into English verse, with notes, by W Stewart Rose.   7 vols small 8vo   *Lond* 1823-29

376   LITERATURE.

Bojardo (Mat Maria), Orlando Innamorato; rifatto tutto di nuovo da M Franc Berni. Small 4to.   *In Milano, dal And. Calvo*, 1542.

Buonarroti (M. Angelo), Rime. (Life, Biography)

Casa (le Terze Rime piacevoli di M. Giovanni della); con una scelta delle migliori rime burlesche del Berni, Mauro, Dolce, ed altri autori incerti   Small 8vo. *In Benevento*, 1727

Dante Alighieri, Opere, con l' esposizione di C Landino, e d' Ales Vellutello, tavole, argomenti, &c per Fr. Sansovino. Folio. *Venetia*, 1564

Dante, (the Divina Commedia of) translated, with preliminary essays, notes, and illustrations, by Henry Boyd. 3 vols. 8vo   *London*, 1802

Dante (the Inferno of), Cantos XVIII. to XXXIV ; with a translation into English blank verse, notes, and a life of the author, by Henry F Cary   2 vols. small 8vo. *London*, 1806.

Medici (Lorenzo de), Poesie, e di altri suoi amici contemporani [per L. Nardini e S. Buonaiuti]. 2 parts in one vol 4to   *Londra*, 1801.

Petrarca (le Rime del), brevemente sposte per L. Castelvetro. 4to. *Basilea, P. Sadabonis*, 1582.

Petrarca (le Rime del), con l' Esposizione d' Alesand Vellutello. 4to. *Venegia, Gioloto*, 1545.

Petrarch (Ugo Foscolo's Essays on), with appendix of Petrarch's Latin poetry, translations of his Italian by Lady Dacre, and unpublished letters in Italian   8vo   *London*, 1823.

Petrarch (Historical and Critical Essay on the Life and Character of); with a translation of a few of his sonnets [by Lord Woodhouslee]. Small 8vo   *Edinburgh*, 1810

Petrarch (Translations, chiefly from the Italian of) and Metastasio, by *****, M A   8vo   *Oxford*, 1795

Pindemonte (Poesie d' Ippolito)   Small 8vo.   *Parma, Bodini*, 1800.

Pulci (Luigi) Morgante Maggiore   3 vols 8vo.   *Milano*, 1806

Scherzi Poetici e Pittorici [sopra Amore, da Giov Gher. de Rossi, e incisi da Gius Tekena]   4to   The plates coloured in the Etruscan style   *Parma, co' tipi Bodoniani*, 1795

> Printed for presents only. This was Sir William Hamilton's copy, and the plates coloured by Lady H.

Tansillo (Luigi), Nurse, translated by W. Roscoe   Small 8vo.   *Liverpool*, 1804

Tasso (Torquato), la Gierusalemme Liberata, con le figure di Bernardo Castello, e le annotazioni di Scipio Gentili e di Giulio Guastini   4to. *Genova, appresso Girol Bartoli*, 1590

Tasso (T.), la Gierusalemme Liberata, con le figure di Seb. Clerc. 2 vols. small 8vo large paper   *Glasgua, Foulis*, 1763

Tasso (T), stampate d' ordine di Monsieur. 2 vols. 4to. large paper. *Parigi, Didot*, 1784

> Illustrated with 115 original designs by Ant P. Novelli.

Tasso's (T) Godfrey of Bulloigne, or Jerusalem Delivered, translated by Edward Fairfax; [edited by S W. Singer]   2 vols large paper, royal 8vo. *London, Bensley*, 1817.

Tasso's (T) Godfrey of Bulloigne, or the Recoverie of Hierusalem ; an heroical poeme written in Italian, and translated by R[obert] C[arew], Esq , and now the first part, containing five cantos, imprinted in both languages   4to   *London, by John Windet*, 1594.

<small>The earliest translation of Tasso into English</small>

Tasso's (T) Jerusalem Delivered, with notes and occasional illustrations translated by J. H Hunt   2 vols 8vo   *London*, 1818

Tasso's Jerusalem Delivered, an epic poem, translated into Spenserian verse, together with a life of the author and a list of the English crusaders, by J. H Wiffen   2 vols royal 8vo large paper.   *Lond* 1824

Tasso, Aminta, favola boscherecccia, con le annotazioni d' Egidio Menagio   4to   *Parigi*, 1655

Trissino (Gian. G.), l' Italia liberata da Gotti, inveduta e corretta per l' Abate Antonini   3 vols 8vo   *Parigi*, 1729

Spanish and Portuguese Poetry

Ancient Spanish Ballads, historical and romantic , translated, with introductions, by J C Lockhart   4to   *Edinburgh*, 1823

History of Charles the Great and Orlando, ascribed to Abp Turpin ; together with the most celebrated ancient Spanish ballads relating to the twelve peers of France mentioned in Don Quixote, with English metrical versions, by Thomas Rodd.   2 vols 8vo   *London*, 1812.

Ancient Poetry and Romances of Spain, selected and translated by John Bowring.   12mo   *London*, 1824

Parnasso Español; coleccion de poesias escogidas de los mos celebres poetas Castellanos, por J. J Lopez de Sedano   9 vols 8vo.   *Madrid*, 1768

Boscan, sus Obras, y algunas Garcilasso de la Vega   12mo.   *Anvers*, P Ballero, 1576

Garcilasso de la Vega's (surnamed the Prince of Castilian poets) Works ; translated into English verse, with a critical and historical essay on Spanish poetry, and a life of the author, by J H. Wiffen   12mo   *London*, 1823

Lope de Vega, Poesias.   (Obras Sueltas)

Parnasso Lusitano, ó poesias selectos dos autores Portuguesos antigos e modernos, illustrados con notas, precido de una historia da lingua e poesia Portugueza [por Al. Garrett]   5 vols 24mo   *Paris*, 1826.

Camoens' (Luis de) Poems, from the Portuguese, with notes, remarks on his life, &c by Lord Strangford   Small 8vo   *Lond.* 1804.

German, Dutch, and Northern Poetry

Minnesingers (Lays of the); or. German Troubadours of the 12th and 13th centuries   with historical and critical notices   Small 8vo   *London*, 1825

Burger's (G A) Leonora , with translations by W R Spencer, and engravings from designs by Lady Diana Beauclerc   Folio   *London*, 1809

Wieland s (C M) Oberon, translated by W Sotheby.   2 vols. 8vo   *London*, 1798

Bowring (John) and H S Van Dyk's Batavian Anthology, or specimens of the Dutch poets with remarks on the poetical literature and language of the Netherlands Small 8vo *London*, 1824

Bowring's (J) Servian Popular Poetry, translated. Small 8vo *Lond.* 1827.

Bowring's (J) Poetry of the Magyars; preceded by a sketch of the language and literature of Hungary and Transylvania Small 8vo. *London*, 1830.

Poetæ Anonymi Teutonici Rhythmus de S. Annone Archiep. Coloniensi, à M Opitio ex memb cod primùm editus et notis illustratus; accedunt versio Latina et notæ B J Schilteri, &c (Schilteri Thes. Vol I)

Translations of Teutonic and Scandinavian Metrical Tales (Illust of Northern Antiquities)

Lodbroker-Quida, or, the Death-song of Lodbroc, Islandic and English · with various readings, a Latin version, and an Islando-Latino glossary and explanatory notes; by James Johnstone Small 8vo. [*Copenhagen*], 1782

Bowring's (John) Specimens of the Polish Poets; with notes and observations on the literature of Poland Small 8vo. *London*, 1827.

Bowring's (J.) Specimens of the Russian Poets, with introductory remarks Small 8vo *London*, 1823.

Oriental Poetry.

Jones (Sir W), Traité sur la Poésie Orientale (Works, Vol V)

Jones (Sir W) Poeseos Asiaticæ Commentarii. (Works, Vol II)

Jones (Sir W.) on the Mystical Poetry of the Hindus (Works, Vol. I.)

The Moallakat, or, seven Arabian poems which were suspended on the Temple of Mecca, with translations. (Sir W Jones's Works, Vol IV)

Haphyzi (Muham Schems-eddini agnomine) Ghazelæ, sive Odæ Persicè, cùm vers Lat, metaphrasi, paraphrasi, notis, ac proœmio [Reviczku] Small 8vo *Vindobonæ*, 1771.

Kuliat Hakim Khakani, the Poetical Works of the eminent Persian poet Khakani · an early MS. very beautifully written in two columns, the titles or commencements of the various portions richly ornamented with gold and ultramarine Small folio

Persian Poems, written in India, and in the Shekistah hand, but in excellent condition Small folio

Jones's (Sir W) Poems, consisting chiefly of translations from the Asiatic languages (Works, Vol. IV)

Jones's (Sir W) Hymns, &c translated from the Sanscrit (Works, Vol VI)

Yakstun Nattannawā, a Cingalese poem descriptive of the Ceylon system of demonology; to which is appended, the practices of a Capua or devil-priest, as described by a Budhist. and Kolan Nattannawā, a Cingalese poem descriptive of the characters assumed by natives of Ceylon in a masquerade Translated by John Callaway, and illustrated with plates from Cingalese designs 8vo *London*, 1829

LITERATURE.

Romances and Novels.

History of Romance

Dunlop's (John) History of Fiction; being a critical account of the most celebrated prose works of fiction, from the earliest Greek romances to the novels of the present age   3 vols 12mo   *lond* 1814.

Huet's (P D) History of Romances , an inquiry into their original, instructions for composing them, &c. translated by Stephen Lewis   12mo   *London*, 1715

Warton (T) on the Origin of Romantic Fiction   (History of Poetry, Vol. I)

Scott (Sir W) on Chivalry and Romance   (Misc. Works, Vol. V)

Hole (Ric.) on the Origin of Oriental Fiction   (On Arabian Nights)

Greek, Latin, and Chivalric Romances.

Achilles Tatius, Apuleius, Heliodorus, Longus, Xenophon.   (Classics)

Gesta Romanorum ; or, entertaining moral stories, invented by the monks as a fireside recreation, and commonly applied in their discourses from the pulpit whence the most celebrated of our own poets, and others, from the earliest times, have extracted their plots   translated from the Latin, with preliminary observations and copious notes, by Charles Swan.   2 vols. 12mo.   *London*, 1824.

The Byrth, Lyf, and Actes of Kynge Arthur, of his noble Knights of the Round Table, theyr merveyllous Enquestes and Adventures, Thacheuynge Sanc Greal, and, in the end, le Morte d'Arthur, with the dolourous deth and departyng out of thys worlde of them al   with an introduction and notes by Robert Southey   2 vols 4to. large paper   (*From Caxton's edition of* 1485) *London*, 1817

The History of the valiant Knight Arthur of Little Britain, originally translated from the French by John Bourchier, Lord Berners, edited by E V Utterson   4to   *London*, 1814

The most ancient and famous History of the renowned Prince Arthur, King of Britain, and of the Deeds of the Knights of the Round Table   4to 𝔟𝔩𝔞𝔠𝔨 𝔩𝔢𝔱𝔱𝔢𝔯, with frontispiece   *Lond* 1634

La très-plaisante Hystoire de Maugist-Daygremont et de Vivian son frère, en laquelle est contenue comment Maugist, à l'aide d'Oriande la fáee sa mye, alla en l'isle de Boucault, &c.   𝔏𝔢𝔱 𝔊𝔬𝔱𝔥. 4to.   *Paris, par Alain Lutrain*, [15]25

Le Triumphe des Neuf Preux, auquel sont contenus tous les faitz et prouesses quilz ont achevéz durant leurs vies ; avec l'hystoire d'Bertran de Gueschn   Small folio, 𝔏𝔢𝔱. 𝔊𝔬𝔱𝔥𝔦𝔮𝔲𝔢𝔰.   *Imprimé à Paris, par M le Noir, M D VII*

> This edition, unknown to Panzer or Maittaire, is noticed by Brunet as a reprint of the first , but if the contents of that edition, as given in Greswell, be correct, this differs from it materially   The Roxburgh copy, in morocco, in very fine preservation

Histoire du noble et très-vaillant Roy Alexandre le Grand, et des grandes proesses qu'il a faicts en son temps.   4to   *à Paris, N. Bonfons*, ——

Amadis de Gaule (les XXIV Livres d') mis en François par le Seig des Essars, N de Herberay, C Colet, J. Gohory, G Aubert de Poitiers, Gal Chappuys, et autres, avec le double du 14ème livre, trad par A Tyron 22 vols 32mo in 19, and 3 vols 8vo *Lyon, François Didier*, 1577, 1578 *et* 81; *Paris*, 1615, *et Anvers*, 1574

Amadis de Gaul, Discours des XII Livres 2 vols 16mo *Paris, par O De Hansy*, 1573.

Amadis de Gaul, translated from the Spanish version of Parceordonez de Montalvo, by R Southey 4 vols. 12mo. *Lond* 1803

Amadis de Gaul, a poem, translated from the French version of N de Herberay, with notes, by W S Rose Small 8vo. *Lond* 1803

Honour of Chivalry, or, the famous and delectable history of Don Bellianis of Greece, containing his valiant exploits, &c translated out of Italian 𝕭𝖑𝖆𝖈𝖐 𝖑𝖊𝖙𝖙𝖊𝖗 4to *Lond* 1678.

Palermino d'Inghilterra, tradotto in Italiana per Lucio Spineda 3 vols. small 8vo *Venet* 1609

Palmerin of England, by Francisco de Moraes, translated from the Portuguese by R Southey 4 vols 12mo *London*, 1807

Primaleone, nel quale si narra a pieno l'historia de suoi valorosi fatti, et di Polendo suo fratello, tradotto della lingua Spagnola nella nostra buona Italiano 8vo *In Venegia, per M Tramezzino*, 1548

The Destruction of Troy, in three books. 𝕭𝖑𝖆𝖈𝖐 𝖑𝖊𝖙𝖙𝖊𝖗, best edition, 4to *London*, 1670.

Le Livre des trois Filz de Roys, cest a ssavoir de France, d'Angleterre, et d'Escosse; lesquels, en leurs jeunesse, pour la foy Crestienne, eurent de glorieuses victoires sur les Turcs, au service du Roy de Cicile, lequel fut faict après ung des lecteurs de l'empire 𝕷𝖊𝖙𝖙𝖗𝖊𝖘 𝕲𝖔𝖙𝖍𝖎𝖖𝖚𝖊𝖘, 4to *Paris, par la veufue feu Jehan Treperel*, [MD]XXXI.
Hearne's copy, with his autograph.

Histoire et Cronique du petit Jehan de Sainctre, et de la jeune dame des belles cousines sans aultre nom nommer avecques deux autres petites histories de Messire Floridan et la belle Ellinde, et l'extrait des cronicques de Flandres. 𝕷𝖊𝖙𝖙𝖗𝖊𝖘 𝕲𝖔𝖙𝖍𝖎𝖖𝖚𝖊𝖘, small 4to *Paris, par Jehan Treperel*, [MD]XXVIII.

Famous History of Montelion, Knight of the Oracle, Son to the True Mirrour of Princes, Pericles, King of Assyria; translated and interlaced by E. Foord 𝕭𝖑𝖆𝖈𝖐 𝖑𝖊𝖙𝖙𝖊𝖗, 4to *London*, 1680.

The most famous, delectable, and pleasant Historie of Parsimus, the renowned Prince of Bohemia, by E Foord. 𝕭𝖑𝖆𝖈𝖐 𝖑𝖊𝖙𝖙𝖊𝖗. *London*, 1630

Roberte the Devyll, a metrical romance, edited from an ancient illuminated MS [by J Herbert] Small 4to coloured plates *London*, 1798.

Richard, surnommé Cœur de Lion, la Tour ténébreuse, et les Jours lumineux, contes Anglois, accompagnéz d'historiettes, et tiréz d'une ancienne chronique composée par Richard, avec le récit de diverses avantures de ce roy [par Mad l'Heritier de Villandon] 12mo *Paris*, 1705
This contains two pieces of poetry by Richard I, hitherto unpublished

LITERATURE. 381

Le Grand (M), Partenopex de Bloix, a romance; translated from the French, with notes, by W S Rose, and illustrated from designs by Smirke. 4to *London*, 1807.

Mayer (M de), Avantures et plaisante Education du Chev. Charles-le-Bon, Sire d'Armagnac; avec des observations sur le vieil langage. *Amst*. 1786.

Barclaii (Jo) Argenis, cum Clave. 24mo. *Lugd Bat Elzev.* 1630

English Novels.

Adam Blair (some Passages in the Life of), of Crossmeikle. 8vo *Edinburgh*, 1822

Almack's, a novel. 3 vols. 12mo   *London*, 1826.

Amelia   (Fielding's Works, Vols. VIII and IX.)

Anastasius, or, Memoirs of a Greek written at the close of the 18th century, by Thos Hope   3 vols 8vo   *London*, 1819.

Annals of the Parish [by John Galt] 12mo   *Edinb* 1822

Arlington, a novel, by the Author of Granby. 3 vols 8vo *London*, 1832

Atlantis (the New) by Lord Bacon   (Works, Vol. II.)

Atom (Adventures of an)   (Smollett's Works, Vol. VI)

Aurelio (the Historie of) and Isabell, daughter of the King of Scotts; French, Italian, Spanish, and English   Small 8vo   *Anvers, en casa de Juan Steelsio*, 1556

> Shakspeare is said to have founded his Tempest on this romance. This edition is unnoticed by Ames, Herbert, Warton, or Mr Park

Barony (the), by Anna Maria Porter   3 vols 12mo. *London*, 1830

Bayly's (Thos) Herba Parietas, or, the Wall Flower, as it grew out of the stone chamber of the metropolitan prison of London, called Newgate, being a history which is partly true, partly romantic, morally divine. Folio, front. *London*, 1650

> Dr Bayly, the author, wrote this whilst imprisoned for his work entitled "Royal Charter granted unto Kings by God himself, &c"

Bracebridge Hall, or, the Humorist, [by Washington Irving]. 2 vols 8vo   *London*, 1822

Brambletye House, or, the Cavaliers and Roundheads   3 vols 12mo *London*, 1826

Caleb Williams, or, Times as they are, by Wm Godwin   3 vols 12mo. *London*, 1817.

Camilla; or, a Picture of Youth; by Mrs D'Arblay   5 vols 12mo *London*, 1802.

Captain Singleton (Adventures of)   (De Foe's Novels, Vols VIII. and IX)

Castles of Athlin and Dunbayne, by Anne Radcliffe. 12mo   *London*, 1799

Castle of Otranto, a Gothic story; translated by W. Marshall from the original Italian of Onuphrio Muralto [Horace Walpole]   Edwards's edition, large paper, 8vo   *Parma, Bodoni*, 1791

Castle of Otranto   (Orford's Works, Vol IV)

Cavalier (Memoirs of a) (De Foe's Novels, Vols. IV and V)
Cecilia, or, Memoirs of an Heiress, by Mrs D'Arblay 4 vols 12mo *London*, 1809
Citizen of the World (Goldsmith's Works, Vol. III.)
Clarissa Harlowe; or, the History of a Young Lady; by Sam Richardson 7 vols 12mo. *London*, 1748.
Cœlebs in search of a Wife, by Han More 2 vols. 8vo. *Lond* 1809
Collegians (the). 3 vols 12mo. *London*, 1829
Colonel Jack (Life of). (De Foe's Novels, Vols VI and VII)
Cottagers of Glenburnie, by Eliz Hamilton. 8vo *Edin* 1808
Contrast (the), by the Author of Matilda 3 vols. crown 8vo *London*, 1832
Croppy (the), a Tale of 1798. 3 vols. 12mo. *London*, 1828.
Cyril Thornton (the Youth and Manhood of) 3 vols 8vo. *Lond* 1827.
De Foe's (Daniel) Novels, [with memoir of the author by Sir Walter Scott] 12 vols small 8vo *Edinburgh*, 1810.
Denounced (the). 3 vols. 12mo. *London*, 1830.
Destiny; or, the Chief's Daughter 3 vols. crown 8vo *Edin* 1831
De Vere, or, the Man of Independence · by the author of Tremaine. 4 vols. 12mo *London*, 1827
Devereux, a tale 3 vols 12mo. *London*, 1829.
Discipline, by Mary Brunton 3 vols 8vo *Edin* 1814.
Disowned (the). 3 vols 12mo. *London*, 1829
Edgeworth's (Maria) Tales and Novels 18 vols. 12mo *London*, 1832.
Edgeworth's (M) Harrington and Ormond, tales 3 vols 12mo *London*, 1817.
Emmeline, by Mary Brunton; with memoirs of the author by her husband. 8vo *Edinburgh*, 1819
Entail (the), or, the Lairds of Grippy [by John Galt] 3 vols. 12mo. *Edinburgh*, 1823.
Eugene Aram, by E L. Bulwer 3 vols crown 8vo. *London*, 1832
Euphues, the Anatomy of Wit, wherein are contained, the delights that wit followeth in his youth by the pleasantness of love and happinesse, he reapeth in age by the perfectnesse of wisdome, by John Lyle 𝕭𝖑𝖆𝖈𝖐 𝖑𝖊𝖙𝖙𝖊𝖗, 4to *London*, 1631.
Euphues and his England, containing his voyage and adventures, the description of the country, the court, and the manners of the isle, by John Lyle 𝕭𝖑𝖆𝖈𝖐 𝖑𝖊𝖙𝖙𝖊𝖗, 4to *London*. 1631
Evelina, or, the History of a Young Lady's Introduction to the World by Mad D'Arblay 2 vols 12mo *Lond* 1808
Fathom (Adventures of Ferdinand, Count) (Smollett's Works, Vol. IV.)
Granby, a novel. 3 vols. 12mo *London*, 1826
Grandison (the History of Sir Charles), in a series of letters. 7 vols. 12mo. *London*, 1770
Grandmother's Guests and their Tales, by Henry Slingsby 2 vols. 8vo *London*, 1825.
Gulliver's Travels (Swift's Works, Vol. XI)

LITERATURE

Hajji Baba (Adventures of) of Ispahan. 3 vols small 8vo. *London*, 1824.

Heiress of Bruges, a Tale of the year 1600, by T C Grattan 4 vols 12mo *London*, 1830

Hieroglyphic Tales, by Horace Walpole (Orford's Works, Vol IV)

High-Ways and By-Ways; or, Tales of the Roadside, picked up in the French provinces First and second series. [By T C Grattan.] 5 vols small 8vo *London*, 1824–5

Humphrey Clinker (the Expedition of). (Smollett's Works, Vol. VI)

Inheritance (the), by the Author of " Marriage " 3 vols. 12mo. *Edin* 1824

Italian, or, the Confessional of the Black Penitents, by Anne Radcliffe. 3 vols 12mo. *London*, 1811.

Jonathan Wild the Great (Fielding's Works, Vol. IV)

Joseph Andrews (Adventures of) (Fielding's Works, Vol. V)

Journey from this World to the next. (Fielding's Works, Vol IV.)

Julia de Roubigné (Mackenzie's Works, Vol. III.)

Knickerbocker's (Diedrich) History of New York, from the beginning of the world to the end of the Dutch dynasty, [by W Irving]. 2 vols. 8vo. *London*, 1812

Last of the Lairds, or, the Life and Opinions of Malachi Mailings, [by John Galt]. 8vo *Edinburgh*, 1826.

Launcelot Greaves (Adventures of Sir) (Smollett's Works, Vol. V.)

Lights and Shadows of Scottish Life Small 8vo. *Edinburgh*, 1824.

Man of Feeling (Mackenzie's Works, Vol. 1)

Man of the World. (Mackenzie's Works, Vols I. and II.)

Mandeville, a tale of the 17th century in England, by Wm Godwin. 3 vols 12mo *Edinburgh*, 1817.

Margaret Lindsay (Trials of), by the Author of " Lights and Shadows of Scottish Life " 8vo *Edinburgh*, 1823.

Marriage, a Novel. 3 vols. 12mo. *Edinburgh*, 1819.

Matthew Wald (History of) Small 8vo *Edinburgh*, 1824.

Memoirs of Modern Philosophers, by Eliz. Hamilton 3 vols 12mo *Bath*, 1804

Mohicans (the Last of the), a narrative of 1757 3 vols 12mo. *Lond.* 1826

Mysteries of Udolpho, by Anne Radcliffe. 4 vols. 12mo *Lond* 1816

Nights (the Five) of St. Albans. 3 vols 12mo *Edinburgh*, 1829.

O Hara Family (Tales by the). First and second series 6 vols 12mo. *London*, 1825–6

Our Village, sketches of rural character and scenery, by Mary Russell Mitford. 12mo *London*, 1830.

Palace of Pleasure, beautified, adorned, and well furnished with pleasant histories and excellent novels, by W Painter · edited from the edition printed in 1575 by T Marsh; by J Haslewood. 2 vols 4to *London*, 1813

LITERATURE.

Pamela, or, Virtue rewarded, in a series of letters, by S Richardson 4 vols 12mo *London*, 1771.

Pelham, or, the Adventures of a Gentleman 3 vols. 12mo. *London*, 1828

Peregrine Pickle. (Smollett's Works, Vols II and III)

Persian (Letters from a) in England to his Friend at Ispahan. (Lyttleton's Misc. Works)

Plague (History of the) (De Foe's Novels, Vol. XII)

Provost (the), by John Galt. 12mo. *Edinburgh*, 1822.

Queenhoo Hall, a romance, and Ancient Times, a drama, by Joseph Strutt [edited by Sir W Scott] 4 vols 12mo. *London*, 1808

Roby's (J) Traditions of Lancashire, both series. 4 vols royal 8vo. large paper *London*, 1829–31.

Rasselas, Prince of Abyssinia, and the Vision of Theodore, the Hermit of Teneriffe (Johnson's Works, Vols. II and III)

Rasselas, Prince of Abyssinia; with engravings by Raimbach, from pictures by Smirke. 4to. *London*, 1805

Reginald Dalton, by the Author of "Valerius" [J. C. Lockhart]. 3 vols crown 8vo. *Edinburgh*, 1823

Reynard the Fox (the most delectable History of); newly corrected, augmented, and enlarged, with sundry excellent morals, and expositions upon every several chapter *London*, 1694,—The Second Part, containing much of pleasure and content; to which is added many excellent morals *London*, 1681;— The Shifts of Reynardine, the son of Reynard the Fox; or, a history of his life and death. full of variety, &c which may be applied to the late times. *London*, 1684. Black letter, in one vol. 4to

Robinson Crusoe by Daniel Defoe, with introductory verses by B. Barton, and illustrated with engravings from drawings by Cruickshank. 2 vols small 8vo large paper *London*, 1831

Robinson Crusoe (Defoe's Novels, Vols. I II and III.)

Roderick Random (Adventures of) (Smollett's Works, Vol I)

Romance of the Forest, by Anne Radcliffe 3 vols 12mo *Lond* 1806.

Rush (the Historie of Friar), how he came to a house of religion to seek service, and being entertained by the priour, was made under-cooke. Full of pleasant mirth and delight for young people. Inlaid in 4to. *London, imprinted by Edw All-de*, 1620

Salathiel; a story of the past, the present, and the future, [by George Croly]. 3 vols 12mo *London*, 1828.

Sayings and Doings, a series of sketches from life First, second, and third series 9 vols small 8vo *London*, 1824.

Self-Control, by Mary Brunton. 3 vols. 8vo *Edinburgh*, 1811.

Sentimental Journey through France and Italy. (Sterne's Works, Vol V)

Sicilian Romance, by Anne Radcliffe 2 vols 12mo. *London*, 1796

Spy (the); a tale of the neutral ground. 3 vols 12mo. *London*, 1822

Sydney Biddulph (Memoirs of Miss), [by Mrs Sheridan]   5 vols
   12mo   *London*, 1796
Tales of a Traveller, [by Washington Irving]   2 vols 8vo   *Lond* 1824
Tale of a Tub, by Jonathan Swift   (Works, Vol X.)
Tales of the Wars of our Times   2 vols crown 8vo   *London*, 1829.
Tales round a Winter Hearth, by Jane and Anna Maria Porter.   2 vols
   12mo   *London*, 1826.
To-day in Ireland.   3 vols. 12mo   *London*, 1825
Tom Jones (History of)   (Fielding's Works, Vols. VI and VII.)
Tremaine, or, the Man of Refinement, by Ward.   3 vols crown 8vo
   London, 1831
Tristram Shandy (Life and Opinions of).   (Sterne's Works, Vols I —IV)
Valerius; a Roman story, [by J. C. Lockhart].   3 vols 12mo   *Edinb*
   1821.
Vicar of Wakefield.   (Goldsmith's Works, Vol I)
Vivian Grey   3 vols 12mo   *London*, 1826–7
Voyage (New) round the World   (Defoe's Novels, Vols X and XI)
Wanderer, or, Female Difficulties, by Charlotte Burney [Mad D'Arblay]
   5 vols. 12mo.   *London*, 1814.
Waverley Novels, with historical introductions and notes by Sir W
   Scott   48 vols small 8vo   *Edinburgh*, 1829
Waverley Novels —Letters to Richard Heber, Esq , containing critical
   remarks on the series of novels beginning with ' Waverley,' and an
   attempt to ascertain their author   8vo   *London*, 1821
Yesterday in Ireland   3 vols. 12mo.   *London*, 1829.
Zeluco, or various views of Human Nature taken from life and manners,
   by John Moore   2 vols. 8vo   *London*, 1780.

French Novels

Beroalde (Sieur de), Aventures de Floride   2 vols 12mo.   *Tours,
   par Mettayer*, 1593
[Bodin de Boismontier (Madlle Suzanne)], Mémoires Historiques de la
   Comtesse de Marienberg.   2 vols in one   Small 8vo   *Amsterdam
   [Paris]*, 1751
Cottin (Madame), Mathilde; ou, Mémoires tirés de l'Histoire des Croi-
   sades   4 vols 12mo   *Londres*, 1809
Cottin (M), Elisabeth; ou, les Exiles de Sibérie   12mo   *Lond* 1803
Florian (J P de), Numa Pompilius, second Roi de Rome.   2 vols
   18mo   *Paris, Didot*, 1786
Florian (J P de), Gonzalve de Cordoue, ou, Grenade reconquise
   3 vols 18mo   *Paris*, 1810
Florian (J P de), Galatee, Roman pastoral, imité de Cervantes.
   18mo   *Paris, Didot*, 1785
[Force (Mad de Caumont de la), les Fées, Contes des Contes, Nouveaux Contes Fées, Contes moins Contes que des autres, Contes
   de M Perrault, avec des moralitéz   4 vols small 8vo.   *Paris*,
   1724–5

Force (Madlle de la), Histoire secrète de Bourgogne [publiée, avec des notices sur les personnages de l'histoire secrète, par De la Borde]. 3 vols 12mo   Pap d'Hollande   *Paris, Didot*, 1782

Gaudence de Lucques (Mémoires de), enrichis des remarques de M Rhedi. 4 vols. in two, small 8vo.   *Amst* 1777

Gombauld's (M) Endymion; an excellent fancy elegantly illustrated by Richard Hurst   12mo   *London*, 1639.

Jouy (E) Cécile, ou, les Passions. (Œuvres, Vols. XXXIV—VI)

Le Sage, Histoire de Gil Blas de Santillane, ornée de figures. 4 vols 8vo   *Paris*, 1795

Le Sage's Adventures of Gil Blas of Santillane translated by Benj H. Malkin   Illustrated with engravings from pictures by Smirke   4 vols. 4to large paper, proofs   *London*, 1809

Marguerite de Valois, Reine de Navarre, Contes et Nouvelles, mis en beau langage, et accommodé au gout de ce tems   2 vols 18mo   *Haye*, 1777.

Marivaux (M de), les Effets surprenants de la Sympathie, ou, les Aventures de **   (Œuvres, Vols. V and VI)

Marivaux (M. de), la Vie de Marianne; ou les Aventures de Madame la Comtesse de ****. (Œuvres, Vols VI and VII)

Marivaux (M de), le Paysan Parvenu, ou, les Mémoires de M ***. (Œuvres, Vol VIII)

Marivaux (M de), le Don Quichotte Moderne   (Œuvres, Vol XI.)

Marmontel (M), les Incas, ou, la Destruction de l'Empire du Pérou. 2 vols 12mo   *Amst* 1777

Marmontel (M), Contes Moraux   3 vols 12mo   *Paris*, 1803.

Marmontel (M), Nouveaux Contes Moraux. 4 vols. 12mo   *Paris*, 1801

Martial d'Auvergne, dit de Paris, les Arrêts d'Amours, avec l'Amant rendu Cordelier à l'observance d'Amours   accompagnez des commentaires juridiques et joyeux de Bénoist de Com   Revue, corrigée, et augmentée de plusieurs arrêts, de notes, et d'un glossaire des anciens termes [par Lenglet du Fresnoy]   12mo.   *Amst* 1731

Montesquieu (Baron de), le Temple de Gnide, Céphise et l'Amour, et Arsace et Isménie   18mo.   *Paris, Didot*, 1795

Rabelais (Fr), Œuvres, contenant cinq livres de la vie, faicts, et dicts héroiques de Gargantua et de son fils Pantagruel   Small 8vo. *Imprimés sur les premières éditions*, 1626

Ramsay (M A), les Voyages de Cyrus, avec un discours sur la mythologie   2 vols 12mo   *Paris*, 1727.

Scarron (Paul), le Roman Comique; ornée de figures par Le Barbier 3 vols. 8vo   *Paris*, 1796.

Stael Holstein (Mad de), Corinne, ou l'Italie   3 vols 12mo   *Londres*, 1809.

[Utterson's (Mrs)] Tales of the Dead, principally from the French. 8vo. *London*, 1813

LITERATURE. 387

Italian Novels.

Libro di Novelle et di bel parlar gentile, nel qual si contengono cento novelle altra volta mandate fuori da Carlo Gualteruzzi da Fano, di nuovo ricorrette, con aggiunta di quattro altre nel fine, et con una dichiarazione d'alcune delle voci più antiche [di Vincenzo Borghini]. 4to *In Fiorenza, nella stamp de i Giunti,* 1582

Novelle Scelte rarissime, stampate a spese di XL amatori [cont Lionora di Bardi ed Hippolyto Buondelmonte, le amorose novelle di Giust. Nelli, Gianfiore e Filomena, novelle tre dell' ingratitudine, dell' avarizia, e dell' eloquenza, creduto di M. Marco di Mantova, S. W. Singer editore] 8vo *Londra,* 1814.

The Italian Novelists, selected from the most approved authors in that language, from the earliest period down to the close of the 18th century: arranged in an historical and chronological series Translated from the original Italian, accompanied with notes, critical and biographical, by Thomas Roscoe. 4 vols 8vo. *London,* 1825.

Arnalt and Lucinda (the pretie and wittie Historie of), [Italian and English]; with certaine rules and dialogues, set foorth for the learner of the Italian tong; by Claudius Holliband. Small 8vo. *London, by Thos. Purfoote,* 1575

Bandello (Mat), Novelle. 9 vols 8vo large paper *London [Livorno],* 1791–3

Boccacio (Giovanni), Il Decamerone, nuovamente corretti et con diligenza stampato 4to. *In Firenze, per li heredi di Phil. di Giunta,* 1527, [*Ed. contrafatto Venezia,* 1739]

Boccacio (G), Il Decamerone, nuovamente alla sua vera lezione ridotto da M Lod Dolce, con annotazioni, tavoli, &c Small 8vo. *Venegia, Giolito,* 1552

Boccacio (Istoria del Decamerone di), da Dom Mu Manni. 4to *Firenze,* 1742

Boccacio —Salviati (Leonardo), Avvertimenti della Lingua sopra il Decamerone. 2 vols. in one 4to *In Napoli,* 1712

Boccacio, le Nymphal Fiessolan, trad de Tuscan par Ant Guercin du Crest 16mo *Lyon, G. Collier,* 1556

Doni (Ant Fr), La Zucca Small 8vo *In Venegia, per F Marcolini,* 1551.
This work contains the original of the Portrait which usually passes for Caxton's

Erasto (i Compassionevoli Avvertimenti di), opera dotta e morale, di Græco ridotta in volgare. Small 8vo. *In Venegia, per C. di Trino,* 1563

Erasto —History of Prince Erastus, son to the Emperour Dioclesian, and the VII Wise Masters of Rome, written originally in Italian, then translated into French, and now rendered into English by F Kirkman. Small 8vo. *London,* 1674

Giovanni Fiorentino, il Pecorone, nel quale si contengono cinquante novelle antiche 2 vols. 8vo *Milano,* 1804

Grazzini (A F), detto il Lasca, Novelle. 8vo *London [Livorno],* 1756.

Sacchetti (F), Novelle [con prefazione, &c. P Umberti]. 2 vols 8vo. *Firenze [Napoli],* 1724

Sansovino (F), Cento Novelle. scelte da' più nobili scrittori della lingua volgare. 4to. *Venegia*, 1610

Spanish Novels

Historia VII Infantum de Lara. (Vænius, under Engraving, ante, p 120.)

Cervantes, Don Quixote de la Mancha; corregida, con el prologo, por la Real Academia Espanola [la vida del autor y análisis del Obra]. 4 vols. 4to. *En Madrid*, 1780

Cervantes' Don Quixote de la Mancha, translated from the original Spanish by Charles Jarvis, [with life of Cervantes, translated from the Spanish MS of Don Greg Mayáns y Siscar by Ozell, supplement to the translator's preface on the origin of chivalric romances, by Bp Warburton, and an advertisement concerning the prints by Vandergucht, by J Oldfield] 2 vols. 4to. *London*, 1742

Cervantes' Don Quixote, translated by Mary Smirke; with life of the author, and illustrated with engravings from pictures by R. Smirke. 4 vols. 4to Large paper, India proofs. *London*, 1818.

Cervantes —The Life and Exploits of Don Quixote, containing his fourth sally, and fifth part of his adventures, by F Alonso de Avellaneda 3 vols 12mo *Swaffham*, 1805

Fiori (Giov de), Amorosa Historia di Isabella et Aurelio, di lingua Castigliana in Italico idiomá tradotta da M Lelio Alatiphilo Small 8vo. *Venegia, Gregori*, 1526. (See also ante, p 381)

Lamarca (Fr Loubayssin de), Historia Tragicomica de Don Henrique de Castro 8vo. *Paris*, 1617.

[Mendoza (Diego de)], The pleasant History of Lazarillo de Tormes; wherein is contained his marvellous deeds and life, and strange adventures. with the pursuit of the historie, gathered out of the ancient chronicles of Toledo, by Jean de Luna Done into English and set forth by David Rowland 2 vols small 8vo. *London*, 1639

German and Northern Novels

German Novelists. Tales selected from ancient and modern authors in that language, from the earliest period down to the close of the 18th century; translated from the originals, with critical and biographical notices, by Thomas Roscoe 4 vols. 8vo *London*, 1826

Popular Tales and Romances of Northern Nations 3 vols 8vo. *Lond.* 1823.

Oriental Romances

Arabian Nights, translated [from the French of Galland] by Edward Foster, with engravings from pictures by R. Smirke. 5 vols 4to Large paper, India proofs. *London*, 1802

Arabian Nights' Entertainments (Remarks upon the); in which the origin of Sinbad's Voyages, and other oriental fictions, is particularly considered, by R Hole. 8vo *London*, 1793.

Antar (Life and Adventures of), a celebrated Bedowen, translated from the original Arabic by T Hamilton 4 vols small 8vo *Lond.* 1819

An Arabian Tale [the History of the Caliph Vathek], from an unpublished MS [by William Beckford], with notes, critical and explanatory [by Dr Stephen Henley] 8vo first edition, large paper, printed only for presents. *London*, 1786.
> See Nichols's Anecdotes, vol iv p 674, for a letter of Dr Henley's to Mr Weston, in which he affirms that this work is really a translation

Bahar-danush, or, Garden of Knowledge translated from the Persian of Emaut-Oollah, by Jonathan Scott 3 vols small 8vo *Shrewsbury*, 1799

Hatim Tai (Adventures of), a Romance, translated from the Persian by Duncan Forbes 4to *London*, 1830.

Fortunate Union (the), a Romance; translated from the Chinese original, with notes and illustrations, by J. F. Davis. 2 vols in one, 8vo *London*, 1829

Dramatic Poetry.

Treatises on Dramatic Poetry, &c.

Schlegel's (Aug Will) Course of Lectures on Dramatic Art and Literature; translated by John Black. 2 vols 8vo *London*, 1815

Adams' (Geo) Defence of Tragic Poetry, an historical account of its rise and progress, and a comparison of the ancient tragedians with each other (Translation of Sophocles Vol I)

Barrington (Daines) on the Ancient Tragedies (Miscellanies.)

[Cumberland's (Rich)] History of the Athenian Stage (Observer)

Dryden (John) on Dramatic Poesy (Works, Vol. XV)

Hume (D) on Tragedy (Essays, Vol I)

Walpole's (H) Thoughts on Tragedy and Comedy. (Orford's Works, Vol II)

Greek and Latin Drama

Tragœdiæ Æschyli, Euripidis, Sophoclis, et Senecæ.
Comœdiæ Aristophanis, Plauti, et Terentii } (Classics).

Ignoramus, Comœdia, scriptore Georgio Ruggle, nunc denuò edita, cum notis historicis et criticis · quibus præponitur vita autoris et glossarium [Anglicè], accurante J S Hawkins. 8vo *Londini*, 1787.

English Drama.

HISTORY OF THE ENGLISH THEATRE AND DRAMA

Scott's (Sir W.) Essay on the Drama (Prose Works, Vol VI)

Hawkins's (Thos) Origin of the English Drama illustrated, in its various species—mystery, morality, tragedy, and comedy—by specimens from our earliest writers, with notes. 3 vols 12mo *Oxford*, 1773

Collier's (J P) History of English Dramatic Poetry to the time of Shakspeare, and Annals of the Stage to the Restoration 3 vols. small 8vo *London*, 1831

Langbaine's (Gerard) Account of the English Dramatic Poets Small 8vo *Oxford*, 1691.

Baker's (D. Erskine) Biographia Dramatica, or, companion to the playhouse containing historical and critical memoirs of British and Irish dramatic writers, and an alphabetical account of their works, together with an introductory view of the rise and progress of the British stage; originally compiled to the year 1764, and continued to 1811 by Isaac Reed and Stephen Jones 3 vols. in 4, 8vo *Lond.* 1812

Goffe's (T) Exact and Perfect Catalogue of all our Playes that are printed. (Careless Shepherdess)

[Wright's (James)] Historia Histrionica, an historical account of the English stage *London*, 1699: *reprinted* (Dodsley's Old Plays, Vol I)

Malone's (E.) History of the English Stage (Shakspeare's Works)

Dibdin's (C) Complete History of the English Stage; introduced by a review of the ancient and modern theatres. 5 vols. 8vo. *London*, 1800.

Drake's (N.) Shakspeare and his Times (Shakspeare.)

Davies' (Thos.) Memoirs of the Life of David Garrick; forming a history of the stage during a period of thirty-six years. 2 vols. 8vo *London*, 1784

Boaden's (James) Memoirs of the Life of John Kemble, including a history of the English stage from the time of Garrick to the present period. 2 vols 8vo *London*, 1825

Boaden's (J.) Memoirs of Mrs Siddons, interspersed with anecdotes of authors and actors 2 vols. 8vo. *London*, 1827.

Kelly's (Michael) Reminiscences, including a period of nearly half a century; with original anecdotes of many distinguished persons, political, literary, and musical. 2 vols 8vo *London*, 1826.

Prynne's (Will.) Histrio-Mastix, the Player's Scourge; wherein is largely evidenced, by the concurring authorities of Scripture, the primitive church, the fathers, and Christian writers, heathen philosophers, historians, poets, &c &c that popular stage-playes are sinfull, heathenish, and pernicious corruptions 4to *London*, 1633

<small>The first English work publicly burnt in this country, and that for which the author lost his ears, and suffered a long imprisonment</small>

ENGLISH DRAMATIC WORKS.

British Drama, ancient and modern, comprehending the best plays in the English language [edited by Sir W Scott] 6 vols in 8, royal 8vo. *London*, 1810 and 1804

Dodsley's (R) Select Collection of Old Plays, a new edition, with additional notes and corrections by Isaac Reed, Octavius Gilchrist, and the editor [Together with Mr Dodsley's preface to the first edition, and Mr Reed's supplement and his preface to the second edition] 12 vols. 8vo *London*, 1825

Specimens of English Dramatic Poets who lived about the time of Shakspeare, with notes by C. Lamb Small 8vo. *London*, 1808

The British Theatre, printed from the prompt-books, with biographical and critical remarks by Mrs Inchbald 25 vols. 18mo *London*, 1808

The Modern British Theatre, selected by Mrs Inchbald 10 vols. 18mo *London*, 1811.

Collection of Farces and other After-pieces, selected by Mrs Inchbald 7 vols 18mo *London*, 1809

Addison's (Jo) Cato, Rosamond, and Drummer (Works, Vols I and VI 8vo , and VI 4to.)

Baillie's (Joanna) Series of Plays on the Passions, Family Legend, a tragedy; and Miscellaneous Plays. 4 vols 8vo *London*, 1802–12

Beaumont and Fletcher's Works; with commendatory poems, Seward's preface, and biographical and critical introduction and notes, by Henry Weber. 14 vols 8vo *Edinburgh*, 1812.

Beaumont and Fletcher's Works (Comments on), by J M. Mason. 8vo *London*, 1798.

[Brewer's (Ant)] Lingua, or, the Combat of the Tongue and the Five Senses for Superiority · a pleasant comedie. 4to. *London*, 1617.

Brother-in-Law, a comedy. Crown 8vo *Lee Priory*, 1817

Burgoyne's (Gen J.) Dramatic and Poetical Works; with memoirs of the author. 2 vols 12mo *London*, 1807

Centlivre's (Mrs.) Works 3 vols. 12mo *London*, 1741

Congreve's (Wm) Works, containing his plays and poems. 3 vols 12mo *London*, 1725

Cowley's (Abr.) Plays (Works.)

Cowley's (Mrs) Works, dramas and poems 3 vols 8vo. *Lond* 1813.

Cumberland's (Rich) Posthumous Dramatic Works [edited by his daughter, Mrs. Jansen]. 2 vols 8vo *London*, 1813.

Dryden's (John) Plays. (Works, Vols. II to VIII)

Edgeworth's (Maria) Comic Dramas 12mo *London*, 1817

Etherige's (Sir Geo) Works, containing his plays and poems 12mo. *London*, 1735

Farquhar's (Geo) Works. 8vo *London*, 1711.

Fielding's (Henry) Dramatic Pieces (Works, Vols I to IV)

Foote's (Sam) Dramatic Works 4 vols. 8vo *London*, 1781

Ford's (John) Dramatic Works; with introduction, and notes critical and explanatory, by W Gifford 2 vols 8vo. *London*, 1827

Goffe (Thos.), the Raging Turke, or Baiazet II , Courageous Turke, or Amurath I ; Tragedy of Orestes; and the Careless Shepherdess 4to *London*, 1631–56

Goldsmith's (O) Dramatic Pieces (Works, Vol II)

Jonson's (Ben) Works, with notes and a biographical memoir by W Gifford 9 vols 8vo. *London*, 1816

Kemble's (F A) Francis I , an historical drama 8vo *London*, 1832.

LITERATURE

[Knevet's (Ralph)] Rhodon and Iris, a pastoral, as it was presented at the Florists' feast in Norwich, May 3, 1631. 4to *London*, 1631

Mackenzie's (H) Dramatic Pieces (Works, Vol VIII)

Marston's (John) Dramatic and Poetical Works. 4 vols crown 8vo. *London*, 1826

Mason's (W) Dramatic Pieces (Works, Vol II)

Massinger's (P) Plays, with introduction, and notes critical and explanatory, by W Gifford. 4 vols 8vo *London*, 1805

Murphy's (A) Dramatic Works (Works, Vols I to IV)

Otway's (Thomas) Works, with notes, and a life of the author, by Th Thornton 3 vols royal 8vo large paper *London*, 1813.

Peele's (Geo) Works, with some account of his life and writings, and notes, by Alexander Dyce. 2 vols. 8vo. *London*, 1828

Ramsay's (Allan) Gentle Shepherd, a pastoral comedy, with illustrations of the scenery, life of the author, &c 2 vols royal 8vo, large paper. *Edin.* 1808.

Shakspeare s (W) Comedies, Histories, and Tragedies, published according to the true original copies, the *third* impression; and unto this is added sevene plays, never before printed in folio Folio *London*, printed for P C. 1654.
<small>The greater part of this edition was destroyed in the fire of London.</small>

Shakspeare's Plays and Poems; with the corrections and illustrations of various commentators · comprehending a life of the poet, and an enlarged history of the stage, by E Malone. [Edited from Malone s MSS by James Boswell, with prolegomena, including the prefaces to the various preceding editions, Dr Farmer on the learning of Shakspeare, Steevens on Shakspeare, Ford, and Jonson; Rowe's life of Shakspeare, [Boswell ?] on the phraseology and metre of Shakspeare, additions to Malone's history of the stage; and a further account of the early English stage by Geo. Chalmers, &c] 21 vols 8vo. *London*, 1821.

Shakspeare's Plays (Supplement to the edition of) published in 1798 by Johnson and Steevens, containing additional observations by several of the former commentators to which are subjoined, the genuine poems of the same author, and seven plays that have been ascribed to him, with notes by the editor and others 2 vols 8vo *Lond* 1780

Shakspeare's Plays, Index to all the editions, by Sam Ayscough 8vo *Dublin*, 1780

Shakspeare Himself again; or, the language of the poet asserted, by And. Beckett 2 vols in one, 8vo *London*, 1815.

Shakspeare s Plays (Notes and various Readings to); and the School of Shakspeare, or authentic extracts from divers English books that were in print in his time, by Ed Capell 3 vols. 4to. *London*, 1779

Shakspeare —Notes on some of the obscure Passages in Shakspeare's Plays, with remarks on the editions of 1785, 1790, 1793, by Lord Chedworth. 8vo *London*, 1805

Shakspeare.—Dramatic Miscellanies, consisting of critical observations on several plays of Shakspeare; with a review of his principal characters as represented by Mr Garrick, &c , by Th Davies. 3 vols. 8vo *London*, 1784

Shakspeare.—Illustrations of Shakspeare and of Ancient Manners, by Fr Douce, with dissertations on the clowns of Shakspeare, on the collection of popular tales entitled Gesta Gravorum, and on the English morrice-dance 2 vols 8vo *London*, 1807

Shakspeare.—Canons of Criticism, and Glossary [being a supplement to Warburton's edition], by Th Edwards 8vo *London*, 1758

Shakspeare.—Essay on the Learning of Shakspeare, by Rich Farmer 8vo. *Camb* 1767

Shakspeare.—Critical, Historical, and Explanatory Notes on Shakspeare, with emendations of the text and metre, by Zach. Grey 2 vols 8vo *London*, 1754

Shakspeare.—Observations on Macbeth, by Sam. Johnson (Works, Vol III)

Shakspeare's Macbeth and Richard the Third, an essay in answer to Remarks on some of the Characters of Shakspeare, by J P. Kemble 12mo *London*, 1817

Shakspeare.—Comments on the several Editions of Shakspeare, extended to those of Malone and Steevens, by J. Monck Mason 8vo *Dublin*, 1807

Shakspeare (Some further Observations on), extended to the late editions of Malone and Steevens, by J Monck Mason (Comments on Beaumont and Fletcher)

Shakspeare.—Essay on the Writings and Genius of Shakspeare, compared with the Greek and French dramatic poets, by Mrs. Montague 8vo *London*, 1770

Shakspeare.—Essays on some of the Dramatic Characters, with an Essay on the Faults of Shakspeare, by Wm Richardson 8vo *London*, 1798

Shakspeare.—Remarks on the Text and Notes of the last Edition of Shakspeare, with the Quip Modest, or supplement, by J Ritson 2 vols. in one, 8vo *London*, 1783–88

Shakspeare.—Critical Observations on Shakspeare, by John Upton 8vo *London*, 1746

Shakspeare.—Cursory Criticisms on the edition of Shakspeare published by Mr Malone 8vo *London*, 1792

Shakspeare.—Six old Plays, on which Shakspeare founded six of his, by J Nichols 2 vols 8vo *London*, 1779

Shakspeare's Hamlet and As You like It, a specimen of a new edition of Shakspeare [edited by Mr Caldecot] 8vo 1819

Shakspeare's King Lear, a tragedy, collated with the old and modern editions [by Charles Jennens] 8vo *London*, 1770

Shakspeare Illustrated, or the novels and histories on which the plays of Shakspeare are founded, collected and translated from the original authors, with critical remarks 2 vols 12mo *London*, 1753.

Shakspeare.—Letter to D Garrick, concerning a glossary to the plays of [by Rich Warner] 8vo *Lond* 1768

Shakspeare.—Copies of several unpublished documents relating to him and his family, and an account of the jubilee (Wheeler's Hist of Stratford)

Shakspeare and his Times, including a biography of the poet, criticisms on his genius and writings, and a history of the manners, customs, amusements, superstitions, poetry, and elegant literature of his age, by Nathan Drake 2 vols 4to *Lond* 1817.

Shakspeare —An Inquiry into the Authenticity of various Pictures and Prints which, from the decease of the poet to our own times, have been offered to the public as portraits of Shakspeare, by James Boaden. 4to. *London*, 1824

Pseudo-Shakspeare —Miscellaneous Papers and Legal Instruments under the hand and seal of W Shakspeare, from the original MSS in the possession of Sam Ireland Folio *London*, 1796.

The original forgeries of this collection were sold at Mr Dent's sale for 46*l*

Pseudo-Shakspeare —Malone's (E) Inquiry into the Authenticity of certain Papers and Legal Instruments published in 1795, and attributed to W. Shakspeare, Queen Elizabeth, and the Earl of Southampton 8vo. *London*, 1796

Pseudo-Shakspeare —Chalmer's (Geo) Apology, and Supplemental Apology, with appendix for the believers of the Shakespeare Papers which were exhibited in Norfolk Street 2 vols 8vo *London*, 1797–1800

Pseudo-Shakspeare —Confessions of W Ireland; containing the particulars of his fabrication of the Shakspeare MSS together with anecdotes and opinions of many distinguished persons. 8vo *Lond* 1805

Sheridan (the Works of Richard Brinsley) [edited by Thomas Moore] 2 vols. 8vo *London*, 1821

Shirley's (W.) Plays and Poems, now first collected and chronologically arranged, and the text carefully collated and restored; with occasional notes, and a biographical and critical essay, by W Gifford. 6 vols 8vo *London*, 1832

Smollett's (Tobias) Plays (Works, Vol. III)

Southern's (Thos) Plays, now first collected, with life of the author [by T Evans] 3 vols 12mo *London*, 1774

Suckling's (Sir John) Plays. (Works)

Taylor (G W), the Profligate, a comedy 4to. *London, privately printed*, 1820

Thomson's (James) Plays (Works, Vols I and II)

Vanbrugh's (Sir John) Plays 2 vols 12mo *London* 1735

Walpole's (Horace) Mysterious Mother, a tragedy (Orford's Works, Vol I)

Webster's (John) Works, with some account of the author by Alex Dyce 4 vols crown 8vo. *London*, 1830

Wilson's (Arthur) Inconstant Lady, a play [edited], with an appendix [by P Bliss] 4to. *Oxford*, 1814

Wycherley's (Wm) Plays 2 vols 12mo. *London*, 1720

French Drama.

Le Mystère des Actes des Apostres, translaté fidellement à la vérité historiale, escripté par Saint Luc, et illustré des légendes et vies des saincts recues par l'Eglise, [par A et S Greban] 2 vols in one, 4to 𝕷𝖊𝖙𝖙𝖗𝖊𝖘 𝕲𝖔𝖙𝖍𝖎𝖖𝖚𝖊𝖘. The Roxburgh copy. *Paris, A. and C Angeliers*, 1540

Campistron (M de), Œuvres, augmentées de plusieurs pièces 2 vols 18mo *Amst* 1722
Champmesle (M de), Œuvres 2 vols 12mo *Paris* 1742
Corneille (Pierre), Œuvres de, avec les commentaires de Voltaire [sa vie par B le Bovier de Fontenelle, et les trois meilleures pièces de son Frère] Figures par Moreau 12 vols 8vo *Paris*, 1817.
Crébillon (P. J de) Œuvres; ornées des figures par Peyron 2 vols 8vo. Proofs and etchings. *Paris*, 1799
Catherine of Cleves, and Hernani, tragedies, from the French of Alex. Dumas and Victor Hugo, by Lord Leveson Gower 8vo. *London*, 1832.
Fontaine (De la), Théâtre (Œuvres, Vol IV)
Fosse (M. de la), Théâtre 18mo *Amst* 1745.
Gresset (J B L), Œuvres Dramatiques (Œuvres, Vol II)
[Henault (M le Président)], Cornelie, Vestale, tragédie Small 8vo *Imprimée à Strawberry Hill*, 1768.
Jouy (E), Théâtre (Œuvres, Vols XL to XLV)
Marivaux (M de), Œuvres Dramatiques (Œuvres, Vols I to V)
Molière (Œuvres de J B de), avec des remarques grammaticales, des avertissemens, et des observations, sur chaque pièce, par M Bret [et la vie de Molière par Voltaire, avec un supplément par l'Editeur]. 6 vols. 8vo *Paris*, 1804
> Besides the plates, after Moreau, belonging to this edition, which were originally engraved for that of 1773, this copy has those published separately by Rénouard in 1813, after new and superior designs by the same artist

Pathelin (la Farce de P), avec son testament à IV personnages. Small 8vo *Paris, Coustellier*, 1722
Racine (Jean), Œuvres Dramatiques (Œuvres, Vols I. to III)
Sleep-Walker, a Comedy, translated from the French [by Horace Walpole] 8vo. *Strawberry Hill*, 1778

Italian Drama.

Walker's (J C) Historical Memoir on Italian Tragedy, from the earliest period, illustrated with specimens of the most celebrated tragedies, biographical notices, &c 4to *London*, 1799
Walker's (J. C) Historical and Critical Essay on the Revival of the Drama in Italy 8vo. *Edinburgh*, 1805

Alfieri (Vittorio), Tragedie. 5 vols 8vo *Milano*, 1822.
Goldoni (Carlo), Scelte Commedie [con un memorie del' autor] 12 vols 8vo *Padova*, 1811–17
Maffei (Scipio), Teatro 8vo. *Verona*, 1730
Metastasio (Pietro), Opere Drammatiche (Opere Compito)
Metastasio's (P) Works, translated by John Hoole. 2 vols 12mo *London*, 1767
Monti (Vicenzo), Tragedie 12mo. *Firenze*, 1827.

396 LITERATURE

Spanish Drama.

Teatro Español, ó collecion de dramas escogidos de celebres escritores precedida de una breve noticia de la Escena Española, y de los autores que la han illustrado. 4 vols. 4to *Londra*, 1817

German Drama

Goethe's Goetze, of Berlichengen, with the Iron Hand a tragedy; translated from the German by Sir Walter Scott Small 8vo. *Paris*, 1826
 Sir W Scott's first production, originally published in 1799

Goethe's Faust, a drama, and Schiller's Song of the Bell, translated by Lord Francis Leveson Gower 8vo. *London*, 1823

Oriental Drama

Sacontalá, or the Fatal Ring; an Indian drama, translated (Sir W. Jones's Works, Vol VI)

Han Koong Tsew, or the Sorrows of Han, a Chinese tragedy, translated from the original, with notes, by J F Davis 4to *London*, 1829

Polygraphy in all Languages.

Hic liber intitulatur de Nugis Curialium et Vestigiis Philosophorum, cujus Johannes Salesberiensis Carnotensis Epūs fuit actor Folio, black letter *Sine anno, loco, &c.*
 The editio princeps It is without either signatures, catch-words, or paging, and Brunet and Dibdin (see Bib Spencer.) agree in ascribing it to the press of Ther Hoernen, about 1472, but Santander, whose copy this appears to have been, attributes it to the Brussels press. "apud fratres Vitum communis, circa annum 1476." As described in the Catalogue de Santander, there is at the end, in MS of a contemporary hand, " Relatio brevis de vitâ et passione Thoma Cant p D Jo Salsburiensis " A large and fine copy

Addison's (Joseph) Works. 4 vols 4to plates after Gignon *Birmingham, Baskerville*, 1761

Addison's (J) Works, with notes by Bp Richard Hurd 6 vols 8vo large paper *London*, 1811

Ascham's (Roger) English Works, with Life by Dr Johnson. 8vo *London*, 1815

Atterbury's (Bp Fr) Epistolary Correspondence, Visitation Charges, Speeches, and Miscellanies; with historical notes by J Nichols. 4 vols. 8vo. *London*, 1783

Bacon's (Francis, Lord Verulam) Works, edited [with translations of the Latin portions] by Basil Montagu 16 vols 8vo *London*, 1825–32

Barrington's (Daines) Miscellanies. 4to *London*, 1781

Boileau Despréaux (N), Œuvres; avec un nouveau commentaire par M Amar 4 vols 8vo *Paris*, 1821

Bocharti (Sam.) Opera Omnia 3 vols folio. *Lugd Bat* 1712

Boyle's (Robt) Works, with life of the author by Thos. Buch 6 vols 4to *London*, 1772

Browne (Sir Thos) Works Folio. *London*, 1686

LITERATURE. 397

Bruyère's (M. de la) Works, with an original chapter of the manner of living with great men written after his method by Nicholas Rowe 2 vols 8vo *London*, 1713

Burke's (Edmund) Works. 16 vols 8vo *London*, 1815–27

Butler's (Sam) Genuine Remains in verse and prose, with notes by R. Thyer. 2 vols 8vo *London*, 1759

Cambridge's (R Owen) Works; with an account of his life by his Son. 4to. *London*, 1803.

Chatterton's (Thos.) Works, with Life by Dr. Gregory, edited by R Southey 3 vols 8vo *London*, 1803

Chesterfield's (Lord) Miscellaneous Works, with memoirs of his life by Dr Maty 3 vols 4to *London*, 1787–8

Cowley's (Abraham) Works, in prose and verse; with notes by Bp Hurd, and life by Dr Johnson 3 vols 8vo *London*, 1809

Della Casa (Giov), Prose e Rime, rivedute per Annab. Antonini. Small 8vo *Parigi* 1727

Dryden's (John) Works, illustrated with notes, critical, historical, and explanatory, and a life of the author, by Sir Walter Scott. 18 vols royal 8vo *Edinburgh*, 1808.

Evelyn's (John) Miscellaneous Writings, now first collected, with occasional notes, by W Upcott 4to *London*, 1825.

Fielding's (Henry) Works, with an essay on his life and genius by Arth Murphy 10 vols 8vo. *London*, 1806.

Firenzuola (Prose di M Agnola) Small 8vo. *Firenze, appresso Lor. Torrentino*, 1552.

Fontaine (J de la), Œuvres accompagnées de préfaces, de notes, l'éloge de l'auteur, et essai sur la fable et sur les fabulistes avant la Fontaine, par C. A Walckenaer 6 vols. 8vo pap vélin, with proof plates before the letters *Paris*, 1822.

Franklin's (Benj) Works, comprising private correspondence, public negotiations, political, philosophical, and miscellaneous works, and memoirs of his life and writings written by himself, and continued to the time of his death by his grandson, William Temple Franklin. 6 vols 8vo *London*, 1818. 19.

Gibbon's (Edward) Miscellaneous Works, with memoirs of his life and writings composed by himself, and illustrated with occasional notes and narrative by Lord Sheffield 3 vols 4to *Lond.* 1796–1815.

Goldsmith's (Oliver) Miscellaneous Works, edited. with an account of his life and writings, by Washington Irving 4 vols 8vo *Paris*, 1825

Grafigny (Mad de), Œuvres Choisies, augmentées des lettres d'Aza. 2 vols 18mo *Londres [Paris]*, 1783

Gray's (Thos) Works, with memoirs by Mason to which are subjoined extracts from the author's original MSS, edited and selected by T J Mathias 2 vols 4to *London*, 1814

Gray's (T) Works, containing his poems and correspondence, with memoirs of his life and writings a new edition, containing some additions not before printed, with notes of the various editors 2 vols 8vo large paper *London*, 1825

Gresset (Œuvres de), [avec les principaux traits de la vie privée et littéraire de l auteur, par A A Rénouard] 2 vols 8vo *Paris*, 1811

Grey (the Literary Remains of Lady Jane), with a memoir of her life by Sir N H. Nicolas Large paper, royal 8vo *London*, 1825

Hale's (Sir Matt) Works, moral and religious, with life by Bp Burnet including the additional notes of Baxter, by T Thirlwall 2 vols 8vo *London*, 1805

Hamilton's (Bp Hugh) Works, collected by his son Alex Hamilton. 2 vols. royal 8vo. *London*, 1809

Harris's (James) Works, with an account of his life, by his son the Earl of Malmesbury. 2 vols 4to *London*, 1801

Harrington's (James) Oceana, and other Works, with his life by John Toland. and an appendix containing all the political tracts wrote by this author, omitted in Toland's edition [edited by T. Birch]. Folio *London*, 1737

Heyne (C G.) Opuscula Academica collecta, et animadversionibus locupleta 5 vols 8vo. *Gottingæ*, 1785-1802

Hurd's (Bp Richard) Works 8 vols 8vo *London*, 1811

Johnson's (Sam) Works; with an essay on his life, &c by A Murphy 12 vols 8vo. *London*, 1806

Jones's (Sir W) Works, edited by his lady, with Supplement 8 vols 4to *Lond.* 1799-1801

Jouy (Estienne), Œuvres complètes 46 vols. 12mo *Paris et Bruxelles*, 1824-27

Knox's (Vicesimus) Works, with a biographical preface 7 vols 8vo *London*, 1824

Locke's (John) Works [by Bp E Law]. 10 vols 8vo *London*, 1801.

Lope Felix de Vega Carpio, Colecciones de los Obras Sueltos, assi en prosa como en verso 21 vols small 4to *Madrid*, 1776-9

Lyttleton's (George, Lord) Miscellaneous Works, published by G. E. Ayscough 4to *London*, 1775

Mackenzie's (Henry) Works 8 vols. 8vo *Edinburgh*, 1808

Mauvaux (P C de), ses Œuvres complètes 12 vols. 8vo. *Paris*, 1781

Mason's (Wm) Works 4 vols 8vo *London*, 1811.

Metastasio (Pietro), Opere [edizioni data dell' Abate Pezzana]. 12 vols 4to. papier d'Hollande. *Parigi, Herissant*, 1780-82.

Milton's (John) Works, historical, political, and miscellaneous; to which is prefixed an account of his life and writings by Thos. Birch [edited by Richard Baron] 2 vols 4to *London*, 1753

Milton's (John) Prose Works, with a life of the author by Ch Symmons 7 vols 8vo. *London*, 1806

Montagu's (Lady Mary Wortley) Works; including her correspondence, poems, and essays with memoirs by J Dallaway 5 vols. 8vo *London* 1803.

Murphy's (Arthur) Works 7 vols 8vo *London*. 1786.

Newton (Is) Opera quæ extant omnia, commentariis illustrabat S Horsley 3 vols 4to *Londini*, 1779-85.

LITERATURE.

Orford's (Horace Walpole, Earl of) Works, with Edwards's Supplement 7 vols 4to *Lond* 1799–1819.

Pope's (Alex) Works; containing the principal notes of Warburton and Warton, with remarks by Johnson, Wakefield, and Chalmers to which are added, some original letters, with additional observations, and memoirs of the life of the author, edited by W L. Bowles. 10 vols 8vo. *London*, 1806

Racine (Œuvres de Jean), avec les variantes et les imitations des auteurs Grecs et Latins, publiées par M Petitot 5 vols 8vo *Paris*, 1815

Ralegh's (Sir Walter) Collected Works; to which are prefixed the lives of the author by Oldys and Birch 8 vols. 8vo *Oxford University press*, 1829.

Reynolds's (Sir Joshua) Works; with an account of his life and writings by E. Malone 3 vols 8vo *London*, 1809

Scott's (Sir Walter) Miscellaneous Prose Works 6 vols. 8vo *Edinburgh*, 1827

Seldeni (Joannis) Opera Omnia, tàm edita quàm inedita, collegit ac recensuit, vitam auctoris præfationes, &c adjecit D Wilkins. 3 vols in 6, folio *London*, 1726

Sidney's (Sir Philip) Miscellaneous Works, with life and illustrative notes by W Gray 8vo. large paper. *Oxford*, 1829

Smollett's (Tobias) Miscellaneous Works, with memoirs of his life and writings, by Robt. Anderson. 6 vols 8vo *Edinb* 1806

Sterne's (Laurence) Works, with life by himself. 10 vols 8vo. *London*, 1788

Sterne (Illustrations of), by John Ferriar, with other essays and verses 2 vols. in one, 8vo *Warrington*, 1812.

Stillingfleet's (Benj) Literary Life and Select Works, edited by W. Coxe 3 vols 8vo. *London*, 1811

Swift's (Jonathan) Works, containing additional letters, tracts, and poems, not hitherto published; with notes, and a life of the author by Sir Walter Scott. 19 vols 8vo *Edinburgh*, 1814

Suckling's (Sir John) Fragmenta Aurea, a collection of all his incomparable pieces, printed by his own copies First edition, with a brilliant impression of the portrait by Marshall. Sir M M Sykes's copy 8vo *London*, 1646

Surrey's (Henry Howard, Earl of) Works, [including his poems and letters, with notes, a memoir of the author, and of his son, the Earl of Northampton], and of Sir Thos. Wyatt, the elder [consisting of his poems and letters to his son, with notes and memoirs of the author], by C F Nott 2 vols 4to *Lond* 1815–16

Talbot's (Mrs Cath) Works, by Mrs Carter, with additional papers, notes, and illustrations, and an account of her life, by Montague Pennington 8vo *London*, 1809

Taylor (all the Works of John), the Water-Poet, collected into one volume by the author Folio *London*, 1630

Hearne's copy, with his autograph

Temple's (Sir Wm) Works, with a life and character of the author 4 vols 8vo *London*, 1757

Tweddell's (John) Remains, being a selection of his letters; together with his Prolusiones Juveniles: to which is added, some account of the author's journals, MSS, collections of drawings, &c, and prefixed is a biographical memoir by the editor, Robert Tweddell. 4to. *London*, 1815.

White's (H K) Remains, with an account of his life by Robt Southey 3 vols 8vo *London*, 1808–22.

Witherspoon's (John) Works, with life 9 vols. 12mo. *Edinburgh*, 1815

Wotton's (Sir H) Reliquiæ Wottonianæ, or a collection of lives, letters, and poems, with characters of sundry personages, [edited by Isaac Walton] 8vo *London*, 1672.

Wrangham's (Fr) Works: sermons, dissertations, and translations 3 vols 8vo. *London*, 1816

Wyatt's (Sir Tho.) Works. (Surrey.)

Young's (Edward) Works. 5 vols 12mo *London*, 1767

Zouch's (Thos) Works, with memoir of his life by F Wrangham 2 vols. 8vo. *York*, 1820

Fables.

Pilpay's Fables. 12mo *London*, 1818

Hitopodesa of Vishnusarum, or amicable instruction, [the fables of Pilpay], translated by Sir W Jones (Works, Vol VI.)

Æsopi Fabulæ (Classics.)

Æsop's Fables: with his life in English, French, and Latin; the English by Th Philipot, the French and Latin by R Codrington with 112 sculptures by Francis Barlow Folio *London*, 1665

Select Fables of Æsop and other Fabulists, with life of Æsop, and an essay on fable, by R. Dodsley. Small 8vo *Birmingham, Baskerville*, 1764.

The Dialogues of Creatures moralysed, applyably and edificatably to every mery and jocunde mater, of late translated out of Latyn into our Englyshe tonge, right profitable to the governaunce of man Reprinted in black letter; edited by Joseph Haslewood 4to *Lond* 1816

Dryden's (John) Fables (Works.)

Fontaine (Fables de la) (Œuvres, Vols I and II)

Fontaine, Etudes sur la, ou, notes et excursions littéraires sur ses Fables [par Solvet], précédées de son éloge inédit, par Gaillard 8vo *Paris*, 1812

Gay's (John) Fables 2 vols 8vo. *London, Stockdale*, 1797

Select Fables, with cuts, designed and engraved by Thomas and John Bewick and others, previous to 1784 together with a memoir, and a descriptive catalogue of the works of Messrs. Bewick Royal 8vo *Newcastle*, 1820

Satirical Works

Dryden's (John) Essay on Satire (Works, Vols. XIII. and XV)

LITERATURE.

Petronii Arbitri Satyricon. (Classics)

[Arbuthnot (Dr)], Law is a Bottomless Pit , or, the history of John Bull [A satire on the war under Marlborough] (Swift's Works, Vol. VI)

Barclaii (Jo) Satyricon, accessit conspiratio Anglicana. 24mo *Elz Lugd Bat* 1637

Erasme, Eloge de la Folie, trad par M Guedeville ; avec les notes de G Lister 12mo *Amsterdam,* 1745

<small>Besides the illustrations from Holbein, this edition has the very spirited woodcuts of Le Sueur the younger worked with the letter-press.</small>

[Evelyn (John)], Mundus Muliebris ; or, the ladye's dressing-room unlocked, and her toilette spread, in burlesque : together with the Fop-Dictionary, compiled for the use of the fair sex (Misc Works)

[Matthias's (T J)] Pursuits of Literature, a satirical poem , with explanatory notes, &c. 8vo *London,* 1806

Pope's (Alex.) Dunciad , with the Prolegomena of Scriblerus, the Hypercritics of Aristarchus, and Notes variorum. (Works, Vol V)

Swift's (Jonathan) True Account of the Battle fought between the ancient and the modern Books in St James's Library. (Works, Vol X)

<small>✱✱✱ For other satirical writings, see Poetry and Novels</small>

Proverbs, Apothegms, Ana, &c.

Plutarchus et Diogenes Laertius. (Classics)

Sentences of Ali, the Son-in-law of Mahomet, translated from the Arabic (Ockley's History of the Saracens, Vol. II)

Bacon's (Lord) Collection of Apothegmes, new and old 18mo *Lond* 1626 (Works, Vol. I)

Burckhardt's (J L) Arabic Proverbs ; or, the manners and customs of the modern Egyptians illustrated from their proverbial sayings current at Cairo, translated and explained 4to *London,* 1830

Erasme (les Apothegmes d'), cest à dire, promptz, sublitz et senténtieulx, ditz de plusieurs royz, chefz darmez, philosophes, et autres, tant Grecz que Latins, translatez de Latin par Ant Macault Small 8vo *Paris,* 1539.

Kett's (Henry) Flowers of Wit ; or, a collection of bon mots, both ancient and modern · with biographical and critical remarks. 2 vols 12mo. *London,* 1814.

Leigh's (E) Choice French Proverbs. (Observ. on Rom. Emp)

Nunez (C H), Refranes o Proverbios en Romance y Glossò, y la filosofia vulgar de Juan de Mal-lara, I Parte, que contient mil refranes glossados 4to *Madrid,* 1619

Oudin (Cesar), Refranes o Proverbios Castellanos Small 8vo *Paris,* 1609.

[Panoucke (J)], Dictionnaire Portatif des Proverbes François , avec une explication des étymologies les plus avénées. 8vo *Amst* 1751

[Pancoucke], Encyclopediana , ou, dictionnaire encyclopédique des anas 4to *Paris,* 1791.

Peele's (Geo) Merrie conceited Jests , wherein is shewed the course of his life, how he lived 4to *London* [1607]

Ray's (J) Collection of Proverbs 8vo *London*, 1738.

Rochefoucauld (Duc de la), Maximes et Réflexions morales; [avec une notice sur le caractère et les écrites de l'auteur, par M Suard] 8vo. *Paris, de l'Imp Royale*, 1788

Selden's (John) Table Talk. (Works, Vol. III.)

[Southey's (Robert)] Omniana, or, Horæ Otiosiores. 2 vols 18mo *London*, 1812

[Jenkinson's (Robert)?] Wit's Theatre of the Little World. Small 8vo *London, by J R* 1599

Politeuphuia, Wit's Commonwealth, newly corrected and amended Small 8vo *London*, ——

Wit's Commonwealth, the II Part, a treasure of divine, morall, and philosophicall similes and sentences, generally useful, by Francis Meres. Small 8vo *London*, 1634

Emblems.

Alciati (Andr.) Emblematum Libellus. Small 8vo Editio piinceps *Parisiis, ei offic C Wecheli*, 1535

Bezæ (Theo) Emblemata (Icones)

Latour (Charlotte de), le Langage des Fleurs 18mo. *Paris*, ——

Peacham's (Henry) Minerva Britannia; or, a garden of heroical devises, furnished and adorned with emblemes and impreses of sundry natures 4to *Lond* 1612

Phillips' (Henry) Floral Emblems 8vo *London*, 1825.

Whitney's (Geffrey) Choice of Emblemes and other Devices, Englished and moralized, and divers newly devised Dedicated to the Earl of Leicester Both parts, 4to. cuts *Imprinted at Leyden, by F Raphelingus*, 1586

Epistolary Writings.

*** See also English Documentary History.

Ciceronis, Phalaridis, Plinii, et Senecæ Epistolæ. (Classics)

Hayley's (W) Desultory Remarks on the Letters of eminent Persons (Life of Cowper, Vol III.)

Letters by eminent Persons in the 17th and 18th centuries, from the originals in the Bodleian and Ashmolean libraries; with biographical and literary illustrations [by P Bliss] 3 vols 8vo. *Lond* 1813

Ascham's (Roger) Letters, from the originals, formerly in the custody of Mr Strype (Works)

Atterbury's (Bp F) Epistolary Correspondence. (Polygraphy.)

Atterbury's Private Correspondence with his Friends, in 1725. (Hailes' Scottish Tracts.)

Basire, (the Correspondence of Isaac), Archdeacon of Northumberland, in the Reigns of Charles I and II.; with a memoir of his life by W N Darnell 8vo *London*, 1831

Bentlen (Ric) et doctorum Virorum Epistolæ, partim mutuæ · accedit R Dawesii ad J. Taylorem epistola singularis [edidit C Burney]. 4to. *London* [*privately printed*], 1807.

LITERATURE.

Boyle (Letters from several Persons to the Hon. Robert) (Works, Vol VI.)

Boileau, Lettres (Œuvres, Vol. IV.)

Burns (Letters to and from Robert). (Works, Vol. II.)

Carter (Mrs Eliz), a Series of Letters between her and Miss Talbot, 1741-1770, also her letters to Mrs. Vesey, 1763-1787 edited by Montgomery Pennington 2 vols 4to. *London*, 1808

Chesterfield's (Lord) Letters to his Friends (Misc Works, Vol II)

Cowper's (William) Private Correspondence with several of his most intimate friends; now first published from the originals, in the possession of his kinsman John Johnson 2 vols 8vo *Lond*. 1824

Deffand's (Marquise du) Letters to Horace Walpole, from 1766 to 1780, to which are added, her letters to Voltaire, 1759 to 1775 4 vols. 12mo *Lond* 1810

Dryden's (John) Letters. (Works, Vol XVIII)

Dugdale (Letters between Sir W) and Sir T. Browne (Browne's Posthumous Works)

Fontaine (La), Lettres (Œuvres, Vol VI)

Franklin's (Benjamin) Private Correspondence, edited by W. Temple Franklin (Works, Vols. III. and IV)

Ganganelli's (Pope Clement XIV) Letters; to which are prefixed, anecdotes of his life. 4 vols. 12mo *London*, 1777

Garrick's (David) Private Correspondence with the most celebrated Persons of his time, illustrated with notes and a new biographical memoir of Garrick 2 vols imp. 4to *London*, 1831.

Gibbon (Letters to and from Edward). (Misc Works, Vols I and II)

[Grant's (Mrs)] Letters from the Mountains, being the real correspondence of a Lady, between 1773 and 1807. 3 vols 12mo *London*, 1807

Gray (Letters to and from Thos.) (Works, 8vo. Vol. II.)

Grey's (Lady Jane) Letters (Remains)

Hartford (Correspondence between Frances, Countess of) and Henrietta Louisa, Countess of Pomfret, 1738 to 41 3 vols 8vo *Lond* 1806.

Johnson (Letters to and from Dr Sam), with some poems, edited by H L Piozzi 2 vols 8vo. *London*, 1788.

Johnson's (Sam) Selected Letters (Works, Vol XII.)

Locke's (John) Familiar Letters between him and several of his Friends. (Works, Vols. IX. and X)

Maintenon (Lettres de Mde. de) (Memoires, Vols VII to XV)

Maintenon (Lettres inédités de Mde de) et Mde la Princesse d Ursins 4 vols 8vo *Paris*, 1826

Milton (Jo) Epistolæ Familiares (Prose Works, 4to Vol II, 8vo Vol VI)

Montagu's (Lady Mary Wortley) Letters (Works, Vols I to V)

Montagu's (Eliz) Letters, with some of those of her Correspondents, edited by Matth Montagu. 4 vols 8vo *London*, 1809

Nicolson (Letters, on various subjects, to and from Abp. W); including the correspondence of several eminent prelates, from 1683 to 1726–7 inclusive ; illustrated with literary and historical anecdotes by John Nichols   2 vols 8vo   *London*, 1809

Paul's Letters to his Kinsfolk.   (Sir W Scott's Misc. Works)

Peter's Letters to his Kinsfolk   (Biographical Anecdotes)

Pinkerton's (John) Literary Correspondence, edited from the originals, by Dawson Turner   2 vols 8vo.   *London*, 1830.

Pope's (Alex.) Literary Correspondence, 1704 to 43   (Works, Vols VII to X.)

Racine (Jean), Lettres à ses Amis   (Œuvres, Vol V.)

Ralegh's (Sir W.) Letters   (Works, Vol VIII)

Russell's (Lady R.) Letters, to which is added, the trial of Lord William Russell   8vo.   *London*, 1792

Selden (Jo) Epistolæ Variæ   (Opera, Vol. II.)

Sevigné (Recueil des Lettres de Mad de), augmentée d'un précis de la vie de cette femme célèbre, et des réflexions sur ses lettres, par S J. B de Vauxcelles [et des nouvelles lettres]   10 vols 12mo   *Paris*, 1801.

Seward's (Anna) Letters, from 1784 to 1807.   6 vols. 12mo.   *Edin*. 1811.

Smith's (Sir J E) Correspondence of Linnæus, &c   (Nat History.)

Steele's (Sir Rich) Epistolary Correspondence, including his familiar letters to his wife and daughters, and fragments of his plays, edited by J. Nichols.   2 vols. 8vo   *London*, 1809

Sterne's (Laur) Letters.   (Works, Vols IX. and X)

Suckling's (Sir John) Letters to eminent Persons.   (Works)

Surrey's (Earl of) Letters.   (Works)

Swift's (Jonathan) Journal to Stella, in Letters   (Works, Vols. II. and III)

Swift's (Jon) Epistolary Correspondence, 1691 to 1741   (Works, Vols. XV to XIX)

Talbot's (Mrs.) Letters.   (Works)

Tweddel's (John) Letters.   (Remains)

Wakefield's (Gilbert) Correspondence with the late C. J. Fox, in 1796–1801, chiefly on subjects of classical literature   8vo   *Lond*. 1813

Walpole's (Horatio) Letters to Richard West, 1735–42.   (Orford's Works, Vol. IV.)

Walpole's (H.) Letters to the Hon. H S Conway, Ri Bentley, Tho Gray, John Chute, Earl of Strafford, Lady Mary Lepell Hervey, Caroline Campbell, Countess Dowager of Ailesbury, and to Mrs. H. Moore.   (Orford's Works, Vol V)

Walpole's (H) Letters to George Montagu, Esq , from 1736 to 1770 ; now first published from the originals   4to.   *London*, 1818. (Orford's Works, Vol. VI.)

Warton's (Dr J.) Letters of eminent Persons   (Life)

White's (Kirke) Letters   (Works.)

Wyat's (Sir Thos) Letters to his Son.   (Surrey and Wyat's Works)

Essayists.

British Essayists, viz. the Tatler, Spectator, Guardian, Rambler, Adventurer, and Idler, with Drake's Essays, biographical, critical, and historical, illustrative of them and of the various periodical papers which, in imitation of the writings of Steele and Addison, have been published, to the commencement of 1809 29 vols. small 8vo. fine paper, and proof plates *London, Sharpe*, 1808-10.

British Essayists —The Mottos of the Spectator, Tatler, Guardian, and Freeholder, translated into English 12mo. *London*, 1737.

Bee (Papers in the) by O Goldsmith (Works, Vol IV)

Gray's-Inn Journal, by Arthur Murphy. (Works, Vols V and VI.)

Looker-on, by Roberts, Alex Chalmers, Mrs Opie, &c 4 vols 12mo *London*, 1794

Lounger, by Henry Mackenzie, &c 3 vols 12mo *Edin* 1787.

Lounger and Mirror (Papers by H. Mackenzie in the) (Works, Vols. V. to VII)

Microcosm, by Geo Canning, J. and R. Smith, and J Frere, whilst at Eton. 8vo. *Windsor*, 1788

Observer, by Richard Cumberland. 5 vols 8vo. *London*, 1787-91.

Olla Podrida, by T. Munro, Bp Horne, Kett, Graves, Pott, Mavor, and Francis Grose 8vo. *London*, 1788.

Projector. 3 vols 8vo. *London*, 1811.

Ruminator, by Sir E. Bridges, R. P. Gillies, &c. 2 vols. 12mo. *London*, 1813.

World, by Moore, Chesterfield, Walpole, Jenyns, Hailes, Dodsley, Burgess, Warton, Ridley, &c. 4 vols. 12mo. *London*, 1782.

Jouy (E), l'Hermite de la Chaussée d'Antin, ou, observations sur les mœurs et les usages Français, au commencement du XIX siècle. (Œuvres, Vols. I to V.)

Jouy (E), Guillaume, le Franc-parleur, ou, observations sur les mœurs et les usages Français, au commencement du XIX siècle. 2 vols. (Œuvres, Vols VI and VII)

Jouy (E.), l'Hermite de la Guiane. (Œuvres, Vols. VIII IX and X)

Jouy, (E.) l'Hermite en Provence (Œuvres, Vols XI to XX)

Jouy et A. Jay, les Hermites en Prison , ou, consolations de Sainte-Pelagie (Œuvres, Vols XXI. and XXII)

Jouy et A. Jay, les Hermites en Liberté. (Œuvres, Vols XXIII and XXIV)

Jouy et A Jay, l'Hermite de Londres; ou, observations sur les mœurs et usages des Anglais au commencement du XIX siècle. (Œuvres, Vols XXV. to XXVII)

Jouy et A Jay, l'Hermite en Ecosse; ou, observations sur les mœurs, &c. des Ecossais au commencement du XIX siècle. (Œuvres, Vols XXVIII. and XXIX.)

Jouy et A Jay, l'Hermite en Italie; ou, observations sur les mœurs, &c. des Italiens (Œuvres, Vols XXX. to XXXIII.)

Marivaux, le Spectateur François (Œuvres, Vol IX)
Marivaux, l'Indigent Philosophe (Œuvres, Vol IX.)
Marivaux, le Cabinet du Philosophe. (Œuvres, Vols. IX. and X)

Miscellanies.

Aikin's (J) Essays, literary and miscellaneous. 8vo. *London.* 1811.
Bacon's (Lord) Essayes, Religious Meditations, Places of Persuasion and Dissuasion, of Colours good and evil 16mo *London*, 1606 (Works, Vol. I)
Beattie's (J) Dissertations, moral and critical. 4to *London*, 1783
Bibliothèque Portative des Ecrivains Français; ou, choix des meilleurs morceaux en prose, extraits par Moysant et De Lévizac 4 vols in 2, 8vo. *London*, 1803
Brydges' (Sir E) Sylvan Wanderer, a series of moral, sentimental, and critical essays 8vo. *Lee Priory*, 1813
Brydges' (Sir E.) Excerpta Tudoriana, or, extracts from Elizabethan literature Royal 8vo. *Lee Priory*, 1814-18
Creech's (W) Edinburgh Fugitive Pieces; with letters, containing a comparative view of the modes of living, arts, commerce, literature, manners, &c of Edinburgh, at different periods 8vo *Edin.* 1815
[Collier (Jane)] on the Art of Ingeniously Tormenting with proper rules for the exercise of that pleasant art 8vo *London*, 1757.
Cowley's (Abr) Essays, in prose and verse. (Works, Vol. III.)
Decker's (T) Gull's Horn-Book [edited from the edition of 1609 by G. F Nott) 4to *Bristol*, 1802.
D'Israeli's (I) Miscellanies; or, Literary Recreation *London*, 1796.
Dodsley's (R) Miscellanies. 2 vols. 8vo. *London*, 1745.
Drake's (N) Literary Hours; or, sketches, critical, narrative, and poetical. 3 vols. 8vo. *London*, 1804.
Drake's (N.) Gleaner; a series of periodical essays, selected and arranged from neglected works; with an introduction and notes 4 vols. 8vo. *London*, 1811.
Erasmi (D.) Colloquia 24mo. *Lugd Bat Elzev.* 1643
Erasmi (D) Selecta Colloquiorum Fragmenta. Small 8vo. grand papier vélin *Paris, Barbou*, 1784
Feyjoo's (F B) Essays or Discourses, selected from his works, and translated by J. Brett 4 vols 8vo *London*, 1780.
Fielding's (H) Miscellaneous Essays (Works, Vol II.)
Foster's (J) Essays on Decision of Character, &c. 2 vols. 12mo. *London*, 1806.
Franklin's (Benj) Miscellanies (Works, Vol. V)
Goldsmith's (O) Essays. (Works, Vol. IV.)
Johnson's (S) Miscellaneous Pieces. (Works, Vol. II.)
Jouy (E), Mélanges ; ou, variétés littéraires, philosophiques, et des beaux arts. (Œuvres, Vols. XXXVII. to XXXIX)

LITERATURE

Knox's (V) Essays, moral and literary   (Works, Vols. I. and II.)

Knox's (V) Winter Evenings, or, lucubrations on life and letters. (Works, Vols II. and III)

Knox's (V) Elegant Extracts, in prose. 2 vols. 8vo   *Lond.* 1790

Lyttleton's (Geo. Lord) Dialogues of the Dead.   (Misc. Works.)

Marottes à Vendre, ou, triboulet tabletier   12mo on coloured paper.   *Londres*, 1812

Miscellanies, in prose and verse, by Pope, Arbuthnot, and Gay, collected by Swift and Pope   (Swift's Works, Vol XIII.)

Miseries of Human Life   2 vols. 12mo.   *London*, 1807

North Georgia Gazette; or, Winter Chronicle, written by the officers on board the ships employed for the discovery of the north-west passage   4to.   *London*, 1821

Prose e Verse per onorare la memoria di Livia Doria Caraffa, principessa del S R Imp e della Rocella, di alcuni renomati autori   4to   [*Privately printed*] *nella Reale Stamperia di Parma*, 1784

Racine (J.), Œuvres diverses en prose.   (Œuvres, Vol IV.)

Southey's (R) Essays, moral and political   2 vols. small 8vo.   *London*, 1832

Suard (J. B A.), Mélanges de Littérature [les deux séries].   5 vols. 8vo   *Paris*, 1806,

Swan's (John) Speculum Mundi; or, a glasse representing the face of the world whereunto is added, a discourse on the creation   4to, front. by Marshall   *Cambridge*, 1635.

Swift's (J) Essays, periodical and miscellaneous.   (Works, Vols. VIII. and IX)

Talbot's (Cath) Essays and Dialogues.   (Works.)

Temple's (Sir W.) Essays   (Works, Vol III)

Urquhart's (Sir T.) Tracts [edited by G P]   12mo.   *Edinb* 1774.

Walpole's (H) Fugitive Pieces, in prose.   (Orford's Works, Vol I)

Wolfii (Jo) Lectionum Memorabilium et Reconditarum Centenarii XVI   2 vols folio   *Lavingæ*, 1600

Wortley's (F) Characters and Elegies   4to   *Printed* 1646
    A duplicate from the king's library, with the autographs of W. Cole and J Brand

---

Keepsake (the), for 1828, &c   Royal 8vo large paper, proofs   *London*, 1828, &c

Landscape Annual, for 1830, &c edited by T Roscoe   Royal 8vo large paper, proofs   *Lond* 1830, &c

Literary Souvenir for 1825, &c., edited by Alaric Watts.   8vo large paper, proofs   *Lond* 1825, &c

Picturesque Annual for 1832, &c edited by L Ritchie.   Royal 8vo large paper, proofs   *London*, 1832, &c.

Archaica, a reprint of scarce old English prose tracts · with prefaces, critical and biographical, by Sir E. Brydges   2 vols 4to   *Lond* 1815

Bibliographical Miscellanies, a selection of curious pieces in prose and verse [edited by P Bliss]   4to   *Oxford, privately printed*, 1803

Miscellanea Antiqua Anglicana. (Misc English Antiquities)

Harleian Miscellany, a collection of scarce and curious pamphlets and tracts, selected from the library of E Harley, second Earl of Oxford; interspersed with historical, political, and critical annotations by W. Oldys, and edited, with some additional notes, by T Park. 10 vols 4to   *Lond* 1808-13.

Somers's Tracts; a collection of scarce and valuable tracts on the most interesting and entertaining subjects but chiefly such as relate to the history and constitution of these kingdoms [to the reign of Geo I], selected from the Royal, Cotton, Sion, and other public and private libraries, particularly from that of the late Lord Somers: edited by Sir W Scott   13 vols. 4to   *London*, 1809-15.

AUCTORES CLASSICI.

Dibdin's (T F) Introduction to the Classics   (Bibliography.)

Rhetores Selecti. Demetrius Phalerius, Tiberius Rhetor, Anonymus Sophista, Severus Alexandrinus, Gr. et Lat. [edidit, notis illustravit Th Gale]. 8vo large paper. *Oxonii*, 1676.

Gnomici Poetæ Græci, ad opt. exemp. emendavit R. F. P. Brunck   8vo. large paper   *Argent*. 1784.

Poëtæ Græci Principes Heroici Carminis Homerus, Hesiodus, Orphæus, Callimachus, Aratus, Nicander, Theocritus, Moschus, Bion, Dionysius, Coluthus, Tryphiodorus, Musæus, Theognis, Pythagoras, fragmenta aliorum · studio notis illust. Hen. Stephani. Folio. *Excud. H. Stephanus*, 1566.

Miscellanea Græcorum aliquot Scriptorum Carmina, cum versione Lat. et notis [collect Mich Maittaire]   4to. *Londini*, 1722

Analecta Græcorum Veterum Poetarum, editore R. Fr. Ph. Brunck. 3 vols. 8vo   *Argentorati*, 1776

Ανθολογια Florilegium diversorum Epigrammatum, Græcè. 8vo interleaved with Latin translations from eminent authors. in a very neat old hand. *Venetiis, ap. Aldi Filios*, 1550.

Collections from the Greek Anthology, and from the pastoral, elegiac, and dramatic Poets of Greece, by Robert Bland, and others. 8vo. *Lond* 1813

Scriptores Veteres de Re Militari · Vegetius, Frontinus, Ælianus, Modestus, Polybius, Æneus; incerti auctoris de re militari opusculum, cum comment God Stewechii et F Modii   2 vols in one, 8vo   *Vesaliæ Clivorum*, 1670

Γεωπονικα de Re Rusticâ Selectorum, Libri XX Græcè [Cassiano Basso collectore] J A. Brassicani operâ in lucem edita; item Aristolelis de Plantis, libri II Græcè   8vo   Editio princeps. *Basiliæ* [1539].

Scriptores de Re Rusticâ per Pet Victorum ad vet exemp. suæ integritati restituti   4 vols. 8vo.   *Parisiis, R Stephanus*, 1543

Scriptores Rei Rusticæ Veteres Latini. Cato, Varro, Columella, Palladius, Vegetius, Gargalius Martialis, &c, è recens J. M. Gesneri, cum ejusd præfatione et lexico rei rusticæ, studio Soc. Bipont. 4 vols 8vo.   *Biponti*, 1787-8

AUCTORES CLASSICI

Geoponicorum, sive de Re Rusticâ libri XX, Cassiano Basso Scholastico collectore, antea Constantino adscripta Gr. et Lat. prolegomena, notulas, et indices adjecit P Needham 8vo. *Cantab.* 1704

Scriptores Rei Rusticæ Vet — Ursini (F) Notæ ad Catonem, Varronem, et Columellam de Re Rusticâ, et in Bucolica et Georgica Virgilii 8vo *Romæ ap. G Ferrarium,* 1587

Rei Accipitrariæ Scriptores, nunc primùm editi, accessit Κυνοσύφιον, liber de curâ canum, Gr et Lat [edidit Nicolaus Regaltius] 3 vols in one 4to *Lutetiæ,* 1612

Historiæ Romanæ Scriptores; Suetonius, Sextus Aurelius, Eutropius, Ælius Spartianus, &c [cum indice rerum et annotationibus J B Egnatii] 2 vols 8vo. *Venet in æd Aldi et A Soceri, M D XIX.-XXI*

Historiæ Romanæ Scriptores, Trebellius Pollio, F Vopiscus, S Aurelius Victor, P Lætus, J B Egnatius 8vo *Parisiis, ex off R Stephani,* 1544

Historiæ Romanæ Scriptores Minores; Sex. Aur. Victor, Sex Rufus, Eutropius, Messala Corvinus studio Soc Bipont 8vo. *Biponti,* 1789

Historiæ Augustæ Scriptores VI, Ælius Spartianus. Julius Capitolinus, Ælius Lampridius, Vulcatius Gallicanus, Trebellius Pollio, Flavius Vospiscus studio Societatis Bipontinæ 2 vols 8vo *Bipont* 1787

Baker's (Henry) Medulla Poetarum Romanorum; or, the most beautiful and instructive passages of the Roman poets, disposed under proper heads, with translations 2 vols royal 8vo large paper *London,* 1737

Opera et Fragmenta Veterum Poetarum Latinorum profanorum et ecclesiasticorum [curante Mich Maittaire] 2 vols folio *Lond.* 1713

Poetæ Latini Minores, sive Gratius Faliscus, M. Aurelius Olympius, T Calpurnius Siculus, Claudius Rutilius, Q Serenus Samonicus, Q Rhemnius, et Sulpiciæ Satyra ° cum notis var curante P. Burmanno. 2 vols. 4to. *Leidæ,* 1731.

Scriptores Erotici Græci Achilles Tatius, Heliodorus, Longus, et Xenophon Gr. et Lat, edente C. G Mitscherlich. 4 vols 8vo *Biponti,* 1792–4.

Achilles Tatius (Erotici Script)

Æliani Varia Historia, Gr ad MSS cod nunc primùm recognita, cum versione J. Vulteii ad Græcam auctoris contextum emendata et perpetuo commentario J Perizonii. 2 vols in one, 8vo *Lugd Bat* 1701

Ælianus (Scr. de Re Milit)

Æneas Poliorceticus (Scr de Re Milit)

Æschinis Orationes (Demosthenes)

Æschyli Tragœdiæ cum scholiis, P Victorii curâ et diligentiâ, Græcè 4to. *Parisiis, H. Stephanus,* 1557

Æschyli Tragœdiæ, Gr et Lat recensuit, varietate lectionis et commentario perpetuo illustravit C G Schutz 2 vols 8vo *Oxonii,* 1810.

Æschylus' Tragedies, translated, with notes, by R. Potter. 8vo *London,* 1819

AUCTORES CLASSICI

Æsopi Phrygis Vita et Fabulæ, plures et emendatiores, Gr ex vet codice Bib. Regiæ   4to.   *Lutetiæ, R. Stephani,* 1546.

Æsopus —Fabularum Æsopicarum Delectus, Gr. et Lat , item Fabulæ Hebraicæ et Arabicæ · ex recens A. Alsop   8vo.   *Oxonii,* 1698

Ammiani Marcellini Rerum gestarum libri XXXI   Small 8vo.   *Parisiis, R. Stephani,* 1544

Ammiani Marcellini Rerum gestarum. studio Soc. Bipontinæ   8vo.   *Bipont.* 1786

Anacreontis Carmina, Gr et Lat , cum notis et indice [edente M. Maittaire]   4to   *Londini, Bouyer,* 1725

Anacreontis Carmina, Græcè præfixo comment quo poetæ genius traditur et bibliotheca Anacreontica adumbratur, addit variæ lectiones 16mo   Literæ majusc , thick paper   *Parmæ [Bodoni],* 1791

Anacreon's Odes ; Greek and English, with notes explanatory and poetical to which are added, the Odes, &c. of Sappho, by J Addison Small 8vo   *London,* 1735

Anacreon's Odes, translated into English verse by Thos Moore   2 vols small 8vo   *London,* 1806.

Antonini (M) Imperat eorum quæ ad seipsum libri XII. Gr et Lat post Gatakerum, &c recogniti et notis illustrati à R I Oxoniensi. Small 8vo fine paper   *Glasguæ, excud Foulis,* 1744

Antonini Imperat eorum quæ ad seipsum libri XII Gr et Lat · notis illustravit.   8vo   Large paper   *Oxonii,* 1704

Antoninus's Meditations, newly translated out of the Greek, with notes, by R Graves   8vo   *Bath,* 1792

Antonini Liberalis Transformationum Congeries, Gr et Lat , interp G. Xylandro , cum T Muncken notis, quibus suas adjecit H. Verheyk   8vo large paper   *Lugd. Bat.* 1774.

Apollonii Rhodii Argonauticon Libri IV. Græcè , cum scholiis Græcis 4to   Editio princeps, litt capital   *Florentiæ, L F de Alopa, M CCCC XCVI*
    "Collegii Lemovicensis S Jesu, 1672 "—*MS. Note*

Apollonii Rhodii Argonautica , cum scholiis Græcis   Small 8vo. *Francofurti, P Brubachius* 1546

Apollonii Rhodii Argonautica, nunc primùm Latinitate donata J Hartungo. Small 8vo   *Basiliæ, J Oporinus,* 1550.

Apollonii Rhodii Argonautica, Græcè scholia vetusta in eosdem libros , cum annot H Stephani   4to.   *Excud H Stephanus,* 1574

Apollonius' Argonautics, translated into English verse, with notes and dissertations, by W. Preston. 3 vols. 12mo   *Dublin,* 1803

Appiani Alexandrini Romana Historia, Gr et Lat , cum annotationibus H Stephani   Folio   *Excud H. Stephanus,* 1592

Appian's History, translated by J D[ryden]   Folio   *London,* 1703

Apuleii (L.) Metamorphoseos Floridorum Lib III , de Deo Socratis Lib. I ; de Philosophià Lib I , &c , cum Isagogico libro Platonicæ Philosophiæ per Alcinoum   Græcè   8vo   *Venetiis, in ædib Aldi et Andr Soceri, M.D XXI*

Apuleii (L) Opera , studiis Societatis Bipont   2 vols. 8vo.   *Biponti.* 1788.

AUCTORES CLASSICI.

Apuleius' (L.) Metamorphosis, or Golden Ass, and Philosophical Works, translated by Thomas Taylor 8vo *London*, 1822

Arati Phænomena et Prognostica, Theonis scholia et Leontii mechanica, Græcè. 4to large paper. *Parisiis, ap G. Morellium* 1559

Arati Opera, Græcè access annotationes in Eratosthenem et Hymnos Dionysii 8vo. large paper *Oxonii*, 1672

Arati Phænomena et Diosemeia, Gr. et Lat. cum scholiis, edidit J. T. Buhle 2 vols 8vo. *Lipsiæ*, 1801

Archimedis Opera quæ extant Gr. et Lat., novis demonstrationibus commentariisque illustrata per Dav. Rivaltum. Folio *Parisiis*, 1615

Aristophanis Comœdia, Græcè, cum novâ versione Latinâ et notis criticis R. F. P. Brunck 4 vols 8vo *Argent* 1781-83

Aristophanes' Comedies, translated, with notes, by R. Cumberland, W. Young, C. Dunster, and H. Fielding. 8vo. *London*, 1812.

Aristophanes Clouds, by Cumberland (Observer)

Aristotelis Opera Omnia, Gr. et Lat. vet. ac recent interpretationibus studio emendat ac brevi comment illustravit Guil Duval 2 vols folio *Lutetiæ Paris* 1629.

Aristotelis Opera, Gr. recensuit, annotationem criticam, et nov. versionem Lat. adjecit J. T. Buhle 5 vols. 8vo. *Bipont* 1791-1800
    All that is published of this edition, viz. the Organum, Rhetorica, and Poetica

Aristotelis Ethicorum Paraphrasis, incerto auctore antiquo, nunc primùm Græcè edita, emendata, et Latinè reddita à D. Heinsio 4to *Lugd. Bat* 1607

Aristotelis de Poeticâ Liber, Gr. et Lat. cum notis 8vo. large paper *Oxonii*, 1760

Aristoteles de Poeticâ Gr. et Lat., animadversionibus illustravit Th. Tyrwhitt 8vo *Oxonii*, 1806

Aristotle's Ethics and Politics, comprising his practical philosophy, translated and illustrated by introductions and notes, the critical history of his life, and a new analysis of his speculative works with a Supplement, containing an account of the interpreters and corrupters of his philosophy, in connexion with the history of the times in which they respectively flourished, by John Gillies 2 vols 8vo *London* 1804

Arriani de Rebus gestis Alexandri Magni lib. VIII, interpretatione B. Facio 16mo *Lugduni, ap Seb Gryphium*, 1552

Arriani Historia de Expeditione Alexandri Magni, Gr. cum Lat interp B Vulcanii, et Alexandri vitâ ex Plutarcho, ejusdem de fortunâ vel virtute Alexandri Folio *Paris excud H Stephanus*, 1575

Arrian's History of Alexander's Expedition, translated, with notes historical, geographical, and critical, by John Rooke 2 vols 8vo *London*, 1814

Arrian's Periplus, &c by Vincent (Ancient Voyages)

Artemidori Oneirocritica, ex cod MSS recensuit notis N Rigaltii et J J Reiskii illust, indices adjecit J G Reiff 2 vols 8vo large paper *Lipsiæ*, 1805

Artemidorus' Interpretation of Dreams, digested into five books, with life of the author 12mo *London*, 1690

Athenæi Deipnosophistarum Libri XV Gr et Lat., cum adnotationibus, &c. Ja. Dalechampii et Is. Casauboni. Is Casauboni Animadversiones in Athenæum. 2 vols in one, folio. *Lugduni*, 1657-64.

Athenæi Deipnosophistarum Lib. XV Gr. et Lat., cum animadversionibus Is. Casauboni aliorumque edidit Jo. Schweighauser. 14 vols 8vo. *Argent.* 1801.

Athénée, Banquet des Savans, trad. en François par Lefebvre et Villebrune. 5 vols. 4to grand pap. vélin. *Paris* [*Didot*], 1789-91.

Aurelii Victoris Historia Romana, accedunt de vitâ et moribus imperatorum Romanorum excerpta, cum notis variorum, integris curante J. Arntzenio. 4to. *Amst.* 1733.

Ausonii Opera, studio Societatis Bipontinæ. 8vo. *Biponti*, 1785.

Ausonii Opuscula Varia. 8vo. *Lugduni, ap. Gryphium*, 1540.

Aviani Fabulæ (Phædrus.)

Bionis et Moschi quæ supersunt, Gr. et Lat., notis Johannis Heskin. 8vo. large paper. *Oxonii*, 1748.

Bion and Moschus, translated. (Theocritus.)

Cæsaris (C. J.) Commentarii, ex emendatione J. Scaligeri. 24mo. *Lugd. Bat.* 1635.

Cæsaris quæ extant, cum libris editis et MSS optimis collata, recognita, et correcta accesserunt annotationes S. Clarke. Folio, plates, including that of the Bison, large paper. *Londini*, 1712.

Cæsar. 2 vols 18mo. *Lond. typ. Brindley*, 1744.

Cæsaris Commentarii [edente cum nomenclaturâ geographicâ et indice H. Homer]. 2 vols 8vo large paper. *Lond.* 1790.

Cæsaris de Bello Gallico et Civili, necnon aliarum de Bello Alexandrini Africano et Hispaniensi, Commentarii. 2 vols. 8vo. *Argent. ex typ. Soc. Bipont.* 1803.

Cæsar (the Commentaries of), translated, with a discourse on the Roman art of war, by Wm Duncan. 2 vols 8vo. *London*, 1806.

Callimachi Hymni et Epigrammata Græcè, ejusd. Poematium de Comâ Berenices, à Catullo versum; N. Frischlini et H. Stephani interpretationes annotationes, &c. 4to. *Excud. H. Stephanus*, 1577.

Callimachi Ύμνοι τε και Επιγραμματα. 4to. *Glasguæ, R. et A. Foulis*, 1755.

Callimachi Hymni et Epigrammata, Gr. et Lat. cum notis variorum; textum recensuit, notis adjecit J. A. Ernestus. 2 vols 8vo. *Lugd. Bat.* 1761.

Callimachus (the Hymns, select Epigrams, and the Coma Berenices of) six Hymns of Orpheus, and the Encomium of Ptolemy by Theocritus, translated into English verse, with notes, by W. Dodd. 4to. *Lond.* 1755.

Calphurnius Siculus (Poetæ Lat. Minores.)

Capitolinus, Julius (Hist. Aug. Scriptores.)

Cato (M. Porcius) de Agriculturâ, sive de Re Rusticâ post A. Popmæ editionem, studio atque operâ J. Meursii. Small 8vo. [*Antverp.*] *ex offic. Plantinianâ* 1598.

Catullus, Tibullus, et Propertius. 8vo. *Venet. in æd. Aldi, MDII*

Catullus, Tibullus, et Propertius. 18mo. *Lond. typis Brindley* 1749

AUCTORES CLASSICI.

Catulli, Tibulli, et Propertii Opera. 4to *Birming Baskerville*, 1772

Catullus, Tibullus, Propertius, cum Galli Fragmentis, et Pervigilio Veneris, incerto auth ; studiis Soc. Bipont 8vo *Bipont* 1794

Catullus (the Poems of), translated, with notes, by the Hon. Geo. Lamb 2 vols small 8vo *London*, 1821

Cebetis Tabulæ (Epictetus)

Censorini Liber de Die Natali, cum perpetuo comment. H. Lindenborgii, nec non notis variorum ut et C Lucilii Satyræ, cum notis et animad. F J. F. Douzæ, ex recens. S Havercampii 8vo large paper *Lugd. Bat.* 1671

Ciceronis Opera Omnia, Manucciorum commentariis illustrata, antiquæque lectioni restituta. 10 vols in 4, folio *Venetiis, ap Aldum*, M D.LXXXII –III

Ciceronis Opera, cum optimis exemplaribus accuratè collata 10 vols. 24mo *Lugd Bat. Elzev* 1642

Ciceronis Opera, præmittitur vita ex Plutarchi Græco Lat. reddita, cum notitiâ literariâ, &c. studiis Soc. Bipontinæ. 13 vols. 8vo. *Biponti* 1780–88

Cicero de claris Oratoribus, qui dicitur Brutus , cum præfatione, ac notis in usum Delphini, edidit J Proust 8vo large paper *Oxon* 1716

Cicero de Oratore, ex MSS. recensuit Thos Cockman 8vo large paper *Oxoniæ*, 1696

Ciceronis de Officiis Libri III , Cato Major, Lælius, Paradoxa. Somnium Scipionis , ex opt. exemp recensuit selectisque variorum notis adjecit T Tooly 8vo large paper. *Oxoniæ*, 1717.

Ciceronis Tusculanarum Disputationum Libri V , cum commentario J Davisii, et R. Bentlei emendationibus 8vo large paper. *Oxonii, è typ Clar.* 1805.

Ciceronis de Finibus Bonorum et Malorum Lib V , ex recens J Davisii, cum ejusd. animad et notis variorum. 8vo large paper *Oxonii, è typ. Clar* 1809.

Cicero de Naturâ Deorum , cum notis var recensuit animad illustravit J Davisius 8vo large paper *Oxonii, è typ Clar* 1801

Ciceronis de Officiis ad Marcum Filium Lib III Small 8vo. fine paper *Glasguæ, excud Foulis*, 1757

Ciceronis de Republicâ quæ supersunt, è cod Vaticano descripsit A Maius 8vo *Londini*, 1823

Cicero on Oratory and Orators , translated, with notes historical and explanatory, by W Guthrie and E Jones. 2 vols 8vo *London*, 1808

Cicero (those Fyve Questions which Marke Tullye) disputed in his manor of Tusculanum written afterwardes by him, in as manye bookes, to his frende and familiar, Brutus, in the Latin toungs , and now out of the same translated and Englished by John Dolman 𝔅𝔩𝔞𝔠𝔨 𝔩𝔢𝔱𝔱𝔢𝔯, small 8vo *London, by Thomas Marshe*, 1561.

Cicero's Tusculan Disputations, translated by W H. Main 8vo. *Lond*. 1824

Cicero's Morals, Conferences de Finibus, and Academics , translated by W Guthrie 8vo *London*, 1744

Cicero on the Nature of the Gods, translated, with critical, philosophical, and explanatory notes [by T. Francklin] 8vo *Lond* 1775

AUCTORES CLASSICI

Cicero's Offices, Cato Major, Paradoxes Vision of Scipio, and Letter on the Duties of a Magistrate, translated, with notes, critical and explanatory, by W Guthrie 8vo *London*, 1820

Cicero's Orations, translated, with notes, historical and critical, and arguments to each, by W Guthrie 2 vols 8vo *London*, 1820

Cicero's Two Last Pleadings against Verres, translated and illustrated with notes by C Kelsall 8vo *London*, 1812.

Cicero's Letters to several of his Friends, translated, with remarks, by W Melmoth 2 vols 8vo *London*, 1804.

Cicero's Epistles to Atticus translated, with notes, historical, explanatory, and critical, by W Guthrie 3 vols 8vo *Lond* 1806.

Cicero's Epistles to Brutus, and of Brutus to Cicero, translated, with notes, by C. Middleton 8vo *London*, 1743.

Claudiani (C) Opera, N Heinsius recensuit ac notas addidit 2 vols. in one, 24mo. *Lugd Bat Elzev* 1653

Claudiani Opera, studiis Soc Bipontinæ 8vo *Bipont* 1784

Claudian's whole Works, translated into English rhyme by A Hawkins. 2 vols. 8vo *London*, 1817

Cleanthis Hymn (Epictetus)

Columella (Scriptores Rei Rust.)

Coluthi Raptus Helenæ, recensuit ac var lect et notas adjecit J Daniel à Lennep, accedunt ejusd animad Libri III., tum in Coluthum, tum in nonnullos alios auctores 8vo large paper *Leovardiæ*, 1747

Coluthus' Rape of Helen, translated (Apollonius Rhodius)

Curtius (Q) de Rebus gestis Alexandri Magni. 16mo *Lugdun. ap Seb. Gryphium*, 1551

Curtius de Rebus gestis Alexandri Magni 24mo *Lugd Bat Elz* 1633

Curtius Quintus. 2 vols. 18mo *Londini, typis Brindley*, 1746.

Curtius de Rebus gestis Alexandri Magni; cum supplemento J. Freinshemii, studio Soc. Bipontinæ 2 vols 8vo *Argent* 1801

Curtius, (Le Clerc's Criticism upon Q.), and some remarks upon Perizonius' Vindication of that author, by Rooke (Translation of Arrian)

Curtius's (Q.) History of Alexander the Great, translated, with notes, by Pratt 2 vols 8vo *London*, 1821

Demetrius Phalereus (Rhetores Selecti)

Demosthenis Orationes Philippicæ XII Græcè, subjectæ sunt lectiones var editionis apud Benenatum Small 8vo *Glasguæ Foulis*, 1762.

Demosthenis et Æschinis, quæ extant omnia, Gr et Lat, varietate lectionis, scholiis, annotationibus variorum, illust. Gul. Steph. Dobson Accedunt animad variorum, et nunc primùm publicæ Thos Stanlei vel potiùs J Duporti 10 vols 8vo *Londini* 1827.

Demosthenes' Orations, pronounced to excite the Athenians against Philip of Macedon, translated by T Leland. 2 vols 8vo. *London*, 1806

Diodori Siculi Bibliotheca Historica; quorum priores Libri V Ægypti, Asiæ, Africæ, Insularum, et Europæ Antiquitates continent, reliqui à Persis, Græcis, &c. orbis terrarum populis, ab exped inde Xerxis in Græciam usque ad successorum Alexandri Magni in Phrygiâ prœlium, gestas exponunt, Gr et Lat annotatione illustrata studio et labore L Rhodomani 2 vols in one, folio *Hanoviæ, typis Wechelianis*, 1604

AUCTORES CLASSICI

Diodori Siculi Bibliotheca Historica, Gr et Lat.; cum adnotationibus variorum 12 vols 8vo *Bipont et Argent* 1793-98

Diodorus Siculus' Historical Library, to which are added the Fragments of Diodorus, made English by G Booth Folio. *Lond* 1721

Diogenes Laertius de Vitis, Dogmatibus, &c. clarorum Philosophorum, Gr et Lat , cum annot diversorum , emendavit M Meibomius, accedunt observationes Æg. Menagii, et notæ Joach Kuhnii 2 vols. 4to *Amst* 1692.

Diogenes Laertius' Lives, Opinions, and remarkable Sayings of the most ancient Philosophers, made English by several hands 2 vols 8vo *London*, 1696.

Dionis Cassii Historia Romana, Gr. et Lat , Xylandri interp studio J Leunclavii, notis ejusd et variorum Folio *Hanoviæ*, 1606

Dion Cassius' History abridged from Xiphilin, done from the Greek by F Manning 2 vols 8vo *London*, 1704

Dionysii Alex et Pomponii Melæ Situs Orbis Descriptio, C J Solini Polyhistor, in Dionysii Poemata Comment Eustathii, Gr et Lat · scholiis, interp. et annotat. illust H Stephanus 4to *Excud. H Steph* 1577

Dionysii Halicarnassi Opera Omnia, Gr et Lat , curante J J Reiske. 6 vols 8vo *Lipsiæ*, 1774-7

Dionysius of Halicarnassus' Roman Antiquities; translated, with notes and dissertations, by E Spelman 4 vols 4to *London*, 1758

Dionysii Hymni (Poetæ Gr. Stephani)

Epicteti Philosophiæ Monumenta, Gr et Lat , recensuit, adnotationibus illustravit J Schweighauser 6 vols 8vo *Lipsiæ*, 1799

Epicteti Enchiridion, Cebetis Tabulæ, Prodici Hercules, et Cleanthis Hymni, Græcè et Latmè 24mo large paper *Glasguæ, excud. R Foulis*, 1744

Επικτητου Εγχειριδιον, Græcè, ex editione J Upton Small 8vo fine paper. *Glasguæ excud Foulis*, 1775

Epictetus' Enchiridion, translated by Lady Mary Pierrepoint, afterwards Montagu. (Lady M W. Montagu's Works, Vol I.)

Epictetus' Enchiridion , translated, with introduction and notes, by Eliz Carter, edited by M Pennington 2 vols 8vo *London*, 1807

Epictète (Nouveau Manuel d'), extrait des commentaires d'Arien [traduit par St Fauxben]. 2 vols. 18mo grand papier *Paris*, 1784

Euclidis Elementorum Lib XV , accessit unus de Solidorum Regulis , omnes scholiis illustr , editi Clavio 2 vols 8vo *Romæ, apud Bart Grassium*, 1589

Euripidis Opera Omnia, Gr et Lat , cum scholiis Græcis, notis variorum, et indicibus locupletissimis 9 vols 8vo *Glasguæ*, 1821

Euripidis Tragœdiæ Medea et Phœnissæ, Græco-Latinè, cum scholiis Græcis, comment , variis lectionibus, atque indice accessit ejusdem vita, studio et operà W. Piers. 8vo large paper *Cantabr* 1703

Euripidis Tragœdiæ Hecuba, Orestes, Phœnissæ, et Medea, edidit R Porson 4 vols 8vo large paper *Lipsiæ*, 1824

Euripides' Tragedies, translated [with prefaces] by R Potter 2 vols. 8vo. *London*, 1808.

Eutropii Breviarium Historiæ Romanæ, cum Pæanii Metaphrasi Græcâ; Messala Corvinus de Augusti Progenie, Julius Obsequens de Prodigiis, et Anon Oratio Funebris, Gr et Lat in Imp Constantini M. Filii Cum variis lect. et annot [Th Hearnii] 8vo *Oxonii*, 1703.

Eutropii Brev. Hist. Romanæ, cum Metaphrasi Græcâ Pæanii, notis variorum recens S Havercampius. 8vo. large paper. *Lugd Bat* 1729

Florus (L Ann) Cl Salmasii, addidit Lucium Ampelium, nunquam antehac editum 24mo *Lugd Bat Elzev* 1638

Flori (L A) Epitome Rerum Romanarum, notis variorum, recensuit C A. Dukerus. 2 vols. 8vo *Lugd Bat* 1744.

Flori (L A) Epitome Rerum Romanarum, et L Ampelii Liber Memorialis, studio Soc Bipontinæ 8vo *Bipont* 1783.

Frontinum (S Julii) Opera, studiis Soc. Bipont. 8vo *Bipont* 1788.

Gallicanus Vulcatius. (Hist Aug Ser)

Gargilius Martialis. (Ser Rei Rust)

Gellii (Auli) Noctes Atticæ [ex recens Car Aldobrandi] Small 8vo *Florent di Giunti, M D XIII*

Gellii (A) Noctes Atticæ 24mo *Amst Elzev* 1665

Gellii (A) Noctium Atticarum Libri XX, studio Soc Bipontinæ 2 vols. 8vo *Bipont* 1784

Gellius' (A) Attic Nights, translated by W Beloe [with preface by Sam Parr] 3 vols 8vo *London*, 1795

Gratius Faliscus. (Poetæ Lat Min)

Heliodorus (Erotici Script)

Heraclidis Pontici Allegoriæ in Homeri Fabulas de Diis, Gr et Lat. interpret Gesneri. 8vo. *Basiliæ, J. Oporinus*, 1544.

Herodiani Historiarum Libri VIII, Græcè pariter et Latinè. 8vo. *Venetiis, in æd Aldi. et A Ausulani, M D.XXIV.*

Herodiani Historiarum Libri VIII Gr, cum A. Politiani interp ex emend H Stephani, Zosimi Hist. Novæ Lib. II. Gr et Lat 4to *Parisiis, H Stephanus*, 1581

This copy belonged to Sutton, the founder of the Charterhouse, and has his autograph

Herodiani Historiarum Libri VIII Gr et Lat. recogniti et notis illustrati. 8vo *Oxonii*, 1704

Herodian's History of his own Times, translated, with notes, by J Hart. 8vo *London*, 1749.

Herodoti Historiarum Libri IX Gr et Lat ex recensione Jac Gronovii, notis variorum, &c Folio *Lugd Bat* 1715

Herodoti Historia, Gr et Lat ad editionem J Wesselingii · ex recensione et cum emendationibus et adnotationibus J Schweighauseri 6 parts in 12 vols 8vo. *Argentorati*, 1816

Herodoti Historia, Gr et Lat, textus Wesselingianus, operâ F W Reizii accedunt index rerum, nec non editionis Wesselingianæ cum edit. Reizii et Schæferi collatio. 3 vols. 8vo *Oxonii*, 1809

Herodotus' History, translated, with notes and a life of the author, by Wm Beloe 4 vols 8vo. *London*, 1806

Hesiodi Opera et Dies, Theogonia, Scutum Herculis, omnia vero cum multis optimisque expositionibus Gr edente V. Trincavello 4to *Venet in æd B Zanetti*, 1537

Hesiodi Opera et Dies, Gr et Lat., ex recensione J Robinson, accesserunt variæ lectiones, D Rhunkenii animadversiones, curante C. F. Loesnero 8vo *Lipsiæ*, 1778

Hesiod's Remains, translated into English verse by L A Elton, with preliminary dissertations and notes Small 8vo *London*, 1809

Hesychii Lexicon (Grammar)

Hieroclis Philosophi in Aurea Carmina [Pythagoræ] Commentarius, Gr et Lat recognita, unà cum notis, edidit R Warren. 8vo large paper *Londini*, 1742

Hierocles, translated, with notes and illustrations, by W Rayner 8vo *Norwich*, 1797

Hippocratis Opera Omnia, Gr et Lat., edita industriâ et diligentiâ J A Van der Linden 2 vols 8vo *Lugd Bat* 1665

Homeri Opera, id est, Ilias et Odyssea, cum Batrachomyomachiâ et Hymnis, Græcè, cum prefationibus Gr et Lat Editio primaria princeps 2 vols folio *Florentiæ, labore et industriâ Demetrii Mediolanensis Cretensis, sumptibus Bernardi et Nerii Tanaidis Nevilii, Florentinorum, M CCCC LXXXVIII*

A large and fine copy

Homeri Opera, cum Eustathii Archiepisc Thessalon in Homeri Iliadis et Odysseæ libros Παρεκβολαῖς, Græcè 3 vols folio *Basiliæ, Froben.* 1560-59

Also a large copy, the leaves in many cases rough. The plates from Ogilby's Homer inserted

Homeri Opera, cum scholiis veterum, notis perpetuis in textum et scholia, necnon variis lectionibus operâ et studio Jos Barnes 2 vols. 4to *Cantabr* 1711.

Homeri Ilias et Odyssea, Græcè 8 vols 8vo *Oxon* 1714

Ruled with red lines "These Desenueil hath bound"—*Pope's MS Note.*

Homeri et Homeridarum Opera et Reliquiæ, Græcè, ex recensione F A Wolfii folio, Vol I all published *Lipsiæ, apud Goschen*, 1806

Homeri Ilias, Gr et Lat., cum brevi annotatione Accedunt variæ lectiones et observationes veterum grammaticorum, curante C. G Heyne 8 vols 8vo *Lipsiæ*, 1802

Homeri Batrachomyomachia, Græcè, ad vet exemp fidem recusa, glossâ Gr var lectionibus, versionibus Lat, commentariis et indicibus illustrata [M Maittaire] Royal 8vo *Londini, typis Bowyer*, 1721

Homeri Hymnus in Cererem, editus à D Ruhnkenio accedunt duæ epistolæ criticæ, et C G Mitscherlichii adnotationes in Hymnum 8vo large paper *Lugdum Bat* 1808

Homer's Iliads and Odysses, translated [in verse], according to ye Greeke, by Geo Chapman Folio *London*, 1616

Homer's Iliad and Odyssey, translated into blank verse, with notes, by Wm. Cowper, with preface by J Johnson 4 vols 8vo *Lond* 1802

Homer's Iliad, translated by W Sotheby 2 vols 8vo *Lond* 1831

Homer's Hymns, the Batrachomyomachia, translated into verse by Geo Chapman, with introductory preface by S. W Singer Small 8vo *London*, 1817

Homer (Translations from), by Dryden (Works, Vol XII.)

AUCTORES CLASSICI

Homer —Hole's (Rich) Essay on the Character of Ulysses, as delineated by Homer. 8vo. *Exeter*, 1807

Horatii Opera, cum notis J Rutgersii 12mo. *Lutet. R Stephanus*, 1613

Horatii Opera, cum novis argumentis. 64mo *Sedani, ex typog et typis novissimis J Jannoni*, 1627.

Horatii Opera, accedunt D Heinsius de Satyrâ Horatianâ, cum ejusdem in omnia poetæ animad 3 vols in 2, 24mo *Lugd Bat. Elzev* 1629

Horatii Opera Folio. *Parisus, è typog. regiâ*, 1642

Horatii Opera, in usum Delphini, recens T Faber. 12mo *Salmurii*, 1671

Horatii Opera, ex recensione et cum notis, atque emendationibus R Bentleii 4to. *Amstelod Wetstein*, 1728.

Horatii Opera 2 vols royal 8vo The first impression. *Londini, æneis tabulis incidit J Pine*, 1733-7

Horatii Opera 18mo *Lond typis Brindley*, 1744

Horatius, ad lectiones probatiores diligenter emendatus, et interpretatione novâ sæpiùs illustrantur Small 8vo *Glasguæ, Foulis*, 1756

Horatii Opera. 12mo *Birminghamiæ, Baskerville*, 1762.

Horatii Opera 4to *Birminghamiæ, Baskerville*, 1770

Horatius, cum var lectionibus et notis variorum [edentibus H. Homer] et Car Combe] 2 vols 4to *Londini*, 1792

Horatii Opera, studiis Societatis Bipontinæ. 8vo *Biponti*, 1792.

Horatii Opera Small 8vo gr. papier vélin *Parisus, Didot*, 1800

Horatius.—R Johnson Aristarchus anti-Bentleianus, Bentleii Errores super Q Horatii Odarum libros spissos, nonullos et erubescendos, tam per notas universas in Lat. lapsus fœdissimos, ostendens 8vo *Nottinghamiæ*, 1717.

Horace, translated into English verse, with prose interpretations and occasional notes, by C Smart 4 vols. 8vo *London*, 1767

Horace's Satires, Epistles, and Art of Poetry, done into English, with notes, by S Dunster 8vo large paper. *London*, 1719

Horace (Dryden's Translations from) (Works, Vol XII)

Horace.—Specimen of a Version of Horace's first four books of Odes, attempted in octosyllabic verse, by Francis Wrangham 8vo *Privately printed*, 1820

Iamblichus de Vitâ Pythagoricâ, Gr. et Lat ex emend et cum notis L Kusteri accedunt Malchus, sive Porphyrius de vitâ Pythagoræ, Gr. et Lat ; cum notis Holstenii et C. Ritterhusii itemque Anonymus apud Photium de vitâ Pythagoræ Small 4to *Amst* 1707

Isæus's Speeches translated (Sir W Jones's Works, Vol. IV.)

Isocratis Orationes et Epistolæ, Gr et Lat , interpret H Wolfii, Aristidis et Georgiæ Orationes, Gr et Lat , G Cantero interp , H Stephani in Isocratem diatribæ VII Folio. *Typis H Stephani*, 1593

Isocrates' Orations translated (Lysias)

Julian (select Works of the Emperor), and some pieces of the sophist Libanius, translated from the Greek , with notes from La Bleterie, Gibbon, &c to which is added, the history of Jovian, by De la Bleterie , by John Duncombe 2 vols 8vo *London*, 1784

Justini Historia, cum notis Is Vossii. 24mo *Lugd Bat Elzev* 1640.

Justinus de Historiâ Philippicâ et totius Mundi Originibus, interpretatione, notis illust P J Cantel, ad usum Delphini 4to *Paris* 1677

Justini Historiæ Philippicæ 8vo *Argent ex typ Soc Bipont.* 1802.

Justiniani Institutiones (Jurisprudence)

Justinian's Institutes, translated, with notes, by J Harris 4to *Oxford*, 1811

Juvenalis et Persii Satiræ 8vo *Venetus, apud Aldvm, MDL*

Juvenalis, Persii, et Sulpiciæ Satiræ, curâ N. Rigaltii. 12mo. *Lutetiæ, R Stephanus*, 1616

Juvenalis et Persii Satiræ Folio *Parisiis è typog regiâ*, 1644.

Juvenalis Satiræ, cum scholiis vet et commentariis variorum, cui ante H C. Henninis, accedit Persii Satiræ, commentariis illustravit J Casaubon, curâ et operâ M Casauboni 4to *Lugd Bat* 1695.

Juvenalis et Persius 18mo. *Lond. typis Brindley*, 1744.

Juvenalis et Persii Satiræ 4to. *Birminghamiæ, typis Baskerville*, 1761

Juvenalis et Persii Satiræ, studio Soc Bipontinæ 8vo *Biponti*, 1785

Juvenal (Persius)

Juvenal's Satires, translated into English verse, with notes and illustrations by W Gifford 4to *London*, 1802.

Juvenal's Satires, literally translated, with copious explanatory notes, by M Madan 2 vols. 8vo *Oxford*, 1807

Juvenal and Persius (Dryden's Translations from) (Works, Vol. XIII)

Lampridius, Ælius (Hist Aug Scriptores)

Leontii Mechanica (Aratus)

Libanius (Duncombe's Julian)

Livii Historiæ, ex recensione et cum notis J F Gronovii: accessit Ism Bullialdus de solis defectu, cujus Livius lib 37 meminit. 4 vols 24mo *Lugd Bat Elzev* 1644-5

Livii Historiæ, MSS Cod collatione recognitæ annotationibusque illustratæ à T Hearne 6 vols 8vo *Oxoniæ*, 1708

Livii Historiæ, cum omnium epitomis ac deperditorum fragmentis, ad optimas editiones castigatæ, accurante Tho Ruddimanno 4 vols. small 8vo fine paper, bound by Kalthoeber. *Edinburgi, in æd F et W Ruddiman*, 1751.

Livii Historiæ, cum integris J Freinshemii supplementis, præmittitur vita a J P Tomasino conscripta, studio Soc. Bipontinæ. 13 vols 8vo. *Biponti*, 1784-6

Livii Historiæ [et epitome librorum deperditorum], ex recens Drakenborchii [edidit cum indice, gloss et var lect ex edit Ernesti, H Homer] 8 vols 8vo large paper *Londini, sumpt editoris*, 1794

Livii Historiæ, ex recensione A Drakenborchii accessit varietas lectionum Gronovianæ et Crevierianæ, glossarium Livianum, curante A G. Ernesto, emendatæ ab J T Kreyssigio 3 vols 8vo large paper *Lipsiæ*, 1823.

Livy's History of Rome, translated, with notes and illustrations by Geo Baker 6 vols 8vo *London*, 1797

Longinus (Dio) de Sublimitate, Gr et nova versio Lat., notis illustravit Z Pearce 4to *Londini*, 1724

Longinus (Dio) de Sublimitate, recensuit, notasque suas atque animadversiones adjecit J. Toupius . accedit emendationes Ruhnkenii 8vo *Oxonii*, 1806

Longinus on the Sublime, translated from the Greek, with notes and observations, and life of the author, by W. Smith 8vo *Lond* 1770

Longus (Erotici Scriptores)

Lucanus 8vo *Venetiis, apud Aldum, M.D II*

Lucanus de Bello Civili, cum variis lectionibus 8vo *Lutetiæ, ex off R Stephani*, 1545

Lucani Pharsalia, cum commentario P Burmanni 4to. *Leidæ*, 1740

Lucani Pharsalia 18mo. *Lond. typis Brindley*, 1751

Lucani Pharsalia, cum notis Grotii et Bentlei. 4to. large paper. *Strawberry Hill*, 1760.

Lucani Pharsalia ; ejusdem ad Calpurnium Pisonem Poemation : studiis Soc Bipontinæ 8vo *Argent*. 1807

Lucan's Pharsalia, translated into English verse by Nicholas Rowe (Chalmers s English Poets Vol XX)

Luciani Opera, Gr cum Lat. doctor virorum interpretatione, curâ J Bourdelotii, cum ejusd. et T Marcili ac G Cognati notis Folio *Lutetiæ*, 1615.

Luciani Opera, Gr et Lat , ad editionem T Hemsterhusii et J. F Reitzii. 10 vols 8vo. *Biponti*, 1789-93

Lucian's Works, translated from the Greek by Th. Francklin. 2 vols. 4to portrait by Fairthorne, inserted *London*, 1780

Luciani Opuscula Erasmo Rotterdamo et Thomâ Moro interpretibus 8vo. *Venetiis, in ædib Aldi et Andr. Asulani Soceri, M D.XVI*

Lucilii Satyræ (Censorinus and Persius.)

Lucius Ampelus (Florus.)

Lucretius de Rerum Naturâ, [è recensione A Naugerii]. 8vo *Venet. in ædib Aldi, M D X V*

Lucretius de Rerum Naturâ, cum notis variorum, curante S Havercampo accedunt interpret T Creech, variæ lectiones, &c I. Vossii 2 vols 4to. *Lugd. Bat* 1725

Lucretius de Rerum Naturâ 18mo *Lond typis Brindley*, 1749

Lucretius de Rerum Naturâ. 4to. *Birming typis Baskerville*, 1772

Lucretius de Rerum Natura , studiis Soc Bipontinæ. 8vo *Argent* 1808.

Lucretius de Rerum Naturâ ; with English translation in verse, notes philological and explanatory [and life of the poet], by John Mason Good 2 vols 4to *London*, 1805

Lucretius ; translated, and accompanied with commentaries, comparative, illustrative, and scientific, and the life of Epicurus, by Th Busby 2 vols in one, 4to large paper *London*, 1813

Lucretius (Dryden s Translations from) (Works, Vol XII)

Lycophronis Alexandra, poema, Gr et Lat., cum Græco Isaacii, seu potiùs J. Tzetzæ commentario, ex recens. J. Potteri. Folio *Oxon* 1702

AUCTORES CLASSICI

Lycophron's Cassandra, translated by Lord Royston   4to   *Cambridge, privately printed*, 1806

Lysiæ Orationes et Fragmenta, Gr et Lat ex interpret et cum notis J. Taylor   8vo.   *Cantab* 1740

Lysias' Orations, and those of Isocrates, translated from the Greek, with some account of their lives, and a discourse on the history, manners, and character of the Greeks, from the conclusion of the Peloponnesian war to the battle of Chæronea, by J Gillies   4to   *London*, 1778

Macrobius in Somnium Scipionis [ex recensione Donati Veronensis]; ejusdem Saturnaliorum Libri VII, Censorinus de Die Natali. Small 8vo   *Venet in æd Aldi et A Asulani*, M D XXVIII

Macrobii Opera, studiis Soc. Bipontinæ. 2 vols 8vo   *Biponti*, 1788

Martialis (M. Val) Epigrammata, paraphrasi et notis variorum selectissimis, numismata, historias, atque ritus illustrantibus, exornavit L Smids   Ruled red lines, the Numismata in their places   2 vols 8vo   *Amstelod* 1701

Martialis Epigrammata, studiis Soc Bipontinæ   8vo   *Bipont* 1784.

Martial —Analecta Epigrammatum Martialis, Græcum vertit J Scaliger, publicavit P Scriverius   24mo   *Typis Raphelingianis*, 1603.

Maximi Tyrii Dissertationes, Gr et Lat ex recensione J Davisii, editio altera emendata, cui accesserunt J Marcklandi annotationes; curavit et annot. addidit J J Reiske   2 vols. 8vo   *Lipsiæ*, 1774

Maximus Tyrius (the Dissertations of), translated from the Greek by Thomas Taylor   2 vols 8vo   *London*, 1804

Messala Corvinus. (Hist. Rom. Scriptores, and Eutropius, Hearne.)

Modestus   (Scriptores de Re Milit)

Moschus.   (Theocritus.)

Musæi de Herone et Leandro Poema, Gr et Lat., cum conjecturis inedit. P. Francii, ex recensione J Schraderi, qui variantes lectiones, notas, et animadversiones adjecit. 8vo   *Leovardiæ*, 1742

Musæus' Hero and Leander, translated by Fawkes   (Chalmers' English Poets, Vol XX.)

Naumachius   (Poetæ Lat Min)

Nepotis (Corn) excellentium Imperatorum Vitæ   accessit Aristomenis Messenii Vita ex Pausaniâ, Gr et Lat. 8vo. large paper. *Oxon* 1697

Nepos (C)   18mo. *Londini, typis Brindley*, 1744.

Nepotis (C) exc. Imperatorum Vitæ, notis variorum et Van Stavern. 2 vols 8vo   *Lugd Bat* 1773.

Nepotis (C) Vitæ excellentium Imperatorum, præmittitur vita à G J Vossio scripta, studiis Soc. Bipontinæ. 8vo   *Bipont*. 1788

Nepos's (C) Life of Pomponius Atticus, translated, with observations. (Sir M. Hale's Works, Vol I)

Nicander. (Poetæ Gr., Stephani)

Obsequentis (Julii) Prodigiorum Liber. (Plinii Epist , *Aldus* , Valerius Max , et Eutropius, Hearne)

Olympius (M. Aur.)   (Poetæ Lat. Min)

Oppiani Anazarbei de Piscatu Libri V , de Venatione Libri IV Gr. et Lat   4to. *Parisiis, ap And Turnebum*, 1555

AUCTORES CLASSICI

Oppianus Anazarbeus on the Nature of Fishes and Fishing of the Ancients, translated, with an account of the life and writings of the author, and a catalogue of his fishes [by Draper and Jones]. 8vo. *Oxford*, 1722

Orphei Argonautica, Hymni, et [Poema] de Lapidibus, Gr et Lat ; cum notis var. et curâ A. C Eschenbachio 12mo *Traj ad Rhen*. 1689.

Orphæus's Mystical Hymns, translated from the Greek, with a preliminary dissertation on the life and theology of the author, by Thomas Taylor 8vo. *London*, 1792.

Orphæus (Six Hymns of) translated. (Callimachus.)

Ovidii Opera, D. Heinsius textum recensuit, accedunt notæ ex collat cod J Scaligeri et P. J Gruteri 3 vols 24mo. *Lugd. Bat Elzev.* 1629

Ovidii Opera Omnia, cum notis variorum, curâ et studio P Burmanni. 4 vols 4to *Amstelod.* 1727.

Ovidii Opera. 3 vols. 18mo. *Londini, typis Brindley*, 1749.

Ovidii Opera, præmittitur vita ab Aldo Pio Manutio collecto; studio Soc. Bipont. 3 vols 8vo. *Bipont* 1783

Ovidii Opera, ex textu Burmanni, cum notis Bentleii hactenùs ineditis, necnon Harlesii, Gierigii, et aliorum selectis 5 vols. royal 8vo. large paper *Oronii*, 1825-6

Ovid's Metamorphoses; translated into English by several hands, revised by Garth (Chalmers' Brit. Poets, Vol XX)

Ovid (Dryden's Translations from the Epistles, Metamorphoses, and Art of Love, of). (Works, Vol XII)

Palladius. (Scr Rei Rust.)

Paterculus, *see* Velleius

Pausaniæ Græciæ Descriptio, Gr cum Lat interp. R. Amasæi, accesserunt G. Xylandri et F. F. Sylburgii annotationes, ac notæ J. Kuhnii Folio. *Lipsiæ*, 1696

Pausanias' Description of Greece, translated by T Taylor 3 vols 8vo *Lond.* 1794.

Persii Flacci Satyræ; cum ejus vitâ, vet. scholiaste, et Is. Casauboni notis, &c · unà cum ejusdem Persianâ Horatii imitatione; curâ et operâ M. Casauboni. 4to. *Lugd Bat.* 1695

Persii Flacci, Juvenalis, Sulpiciæ, et Lucilii Satyrographorum principis, Fragmenta, studiis Soc. Bipontinæ. 8vo *Bipont*. 1785.

Persius. (Juvenal.)

Persius's Satires; translated, with notes, by Wm. Drummond. 8vo. *London*, 1803

Petronii Arbitri Satyricon, cum notis variorum, adjiciuntur variæ dissertationes, præfationes, et indices, curante P. Burmanni 2 vols 4to *Traj. ad Rhen* 1709.

Petronii Satyricon, Burmanni. Editio altera 2 vols 4to. *Amst.* 1743

Petronii Arbitri Satyricon, cum supplementis Nodationis acced veterum poetarum catalecta; studiis Soc. Bipont 8vo *Biponti*, 1790.

Petronius Arbiter's Satirical Works, translated by several hands, with a key. 8vo *London*, 1708.

AUCTORES CLASSICI

Phædri Fabulæ Æsopicæ, cum novo commentario P Burmanni et epistola critica in Bentleium 4to *Lugd Bat* 1727.

Phædri Fabularum Æsopiarum Lib V, ex recens P Burmanni Small 8vo. fine paper. *Glasguæ, excud Foulis,* 1741

Phædri Fabulæ Æsopicæ, accedunt Publii Syri Sententiæ, Aviani et anonymi veteris Fabulæ studiis Soc. Bipontinæ. 8vo. *Bipont.* 1784

Phædri Fabulæ. 18mo. *Londini, typis Brindley,* 1750.

Phædri, Publii Syri, et aliorum Vet. Sententiæ, recensuit et notas adjecit R Bentleius. (Terentius.)

Phalaridis Epistolæ, ex MSS. recensuit, versionem, annotat. et vitam insuper authoris donavit C. Boyle Royal 8vo. large paper. *Oxonii,* 1718.

Phalaris's Epistles, with select epistles of the most eminent Greek writers, translated by T. Franklin 8vo. *London,* 1749.

Phocylides. (Poetæ Gr., Stephani)

Pindari Olympia, Pythia, Nemea, Isthmia, Græcè. 4to. *Parisiis, ap. G Morel,* 1558

Pindari Carmina, juxta exemplar Heynianum access. notæ Heynianæ, paraphrasis Benedictina, et lexicon Pindaricum Dammii, digessit et edidit H Huntingford. 8vo. *London,* 1814.

Pindar's Odes, with other pieces, translated from the Greek, with a dissertation on the Olympic Games, by Gilbert West. 4to. *London,* 1749.

Platonis Opera, Gr et Lat., ad edit. H. Stephani, cum M. Ficini interpretatione, access var lectiones. 12 vols. 8vo. *Biponti,* 1781–6.

Platonis Scripta Græcè omnia, recensuit variasque inde lectiones enotans Im Bekker, annotationibus variorum, et cum interpretatione Latinâ Ficini aliorumque 11 vols. 8vo *London,* 1826.

Plato's Works, translated, with notes, by F Sydenham and T. Taylor. 5 vols. royal 4to *London,* 1804.

Plato's Republic, translated from the Greek by H Spens, with a preliminary discourse concerning the philosophy of the ancients 4to. large paper. *Glasgow, R. and A Foulis,* 1763.

Plato (some Account of the Dialogues and of the Epistles of), by Thos. Gray. (Works by Matthias, Vol II)

Plauti Comœdiæ XX. 2 vols 16mo. *Lugd ap Seb Gryphium,* 1549.

Plauti Comœdiæ omnes. 8vo. *Florent. per Herides B Juntæ,* 1554

Plauti Comœdiæ, ex recognitione Jani Gruteri, accedunt commentarii Frid Taubmanni 4to. [*Wittebergæ*], 1621.

Plauti Comœdiæ, ex editione J F Gronovii. 2 vols small 8vo. fine paper *Glasguæ, excud Foulis,* 1763

Plauti Comœdiæ superstites XX. [recognitæ à R F P Brunck] 3 vols 8vo. *Biponti,* 1788.

Plautus's Comedies, translated by B Thornton, G Colman, and R Warner 5 vols 8vo. *London,* 1769

Plinii Caii Secundi Naturalis Historiæ Libri Folio, the initials illuminated *Impressi Venetiis per Nic Jenson, M CCCC LXXII.*

Plinii Historia Naturalis 3 vols 24mo. *Lugd Bat. Elzevir* 1635

Plinii Historiæ Naturalis Lib. XXXVII., quos interpretatione et notis illustravit Jo Harduinus. 3 vols. folio. *Paris* 1723.

Plinii Secundi Historiæ Naturalis libri XXXVII., ex recens Joannis Harduini; studiis Soc. Bipont. 5 vols. 8vo *Biponti*, 1783-4.

Pliny's Natural History, translated by Philemon Holland 2 vols folio *London, Adam Islip*, 1601

Plinio Historia Naturale, tradocta in lingua Fiorentina per Christ. Landino. Folio. *Venetus, Opus Jansonis, M CCCC.LXXVI.*
    The editio princeps of the Italian translation This has been successively the Harley and Roxburgh copy

Plinii Epistolæ et Panegyricus, Suetonius de claris Gram ; et Julii Obseq de Prodigiis Liber *Venetus, in æd. Aldi et A Asulani, MDXVIII*

Plinii Epistolæ et Panegyricus, accedunt variæ lectiones. 24mo. *Lugd. Bat. Elzevir* 1640.

Plinii Secundi Epistolæ et Panegyricus, accedunt alii panegyrici veteres; studiis Soc. Bipont. 8vo. *Biponti*, 1789.

Pliny's Letters, translated, with observations, and an essay on Pliny's life, by the Earl of Orrery. 2 vols. 8vo. large paper. The earl's own copy, with some MS. corrections. *Dublin*, 1751.

Pliny's Letters, translated, with remarks, by W. Melmoth 2 vols. 8vo *London*, 1805

Plutarchi Opera omnia, Gr. et Lat castigavit, virorumque doctorum suisque annotationibus instruxit J J Reiske 12 vols 8vo *Lipsiæ*, 1774-82.

Plutarch's Lives, translated from the Greek, with critical and historical notes by J. and W. Langhorne. 6 vols. 8vo. large paper. *London*, 1801

Pollio Trebellius. (Hist. Aug. Scr)

Polybii Historia, Gr et Lat., cum comment. et notis I. Casauboni. Folio. *Typis Wechelianis [Parisiis]*, 1609.

Polybius' General History, translated by James Hampton 3 vols 8vo *London*, 1809.

Polybe, Histoire, traduite par Vinc Thuillier, avec un commentaire, enrichis de notes critiques et historiques [et un supplément], par M. de Folard 7 vols 4to. *Amsterdam*, 1774

Polybius (Character of) and his Writings (Dryden's Works, Vol. XVIII.)

Pomponii Melæ de Situ Orbis, Lib. III , ex recens Jacobi Gronovii. Small 8vo fine paper *Glasguæ, excud. Foulis*, 1752

Pomponii Melæ de Situ Orbis, Libri III , R. Festi Avieni Descriptio Orbis Terræ et Oræ Maritimæ, Prisciani Periegesis è Dionysio ; Cl. Rutulii Numatiani Itinerarium ; Vibius Sequester de Fluminibus, Fontibus, Lacubus, Nemoribus, Paludibus, Montibus, Gentibus, quorum apud poetas mentio fit 8vo. *Argent ex typ Soc. Bipontinæ*, 1809.

Pomponius Mela   (Dionysius Alexandr.)

Porphyrius de Vitâ Pythagoræ   (Iamblicus.)

Prisciani Periegesis   (Pomp. Melæ, *Bipont.*)

Prudentii Opera, recensita, notisque, &c illustrata à Jo. Weitzio. 8vo large paper *Hanoviæ, typis Wechel* 1613.

Prudentii Opera, ex recensione et cum animadversionibus D Heinsii 24mo *Amst Elzev* 1667

Publii Syri Sententiæ   (Terentius, Bentleii)

Pythagoræ Aurea Carmina, Gr et Lat adjectis vocibus qui ibidem occurrunt, analysi grammaticâ, &c. curâ C Knauthii. 8vo. *Dresdæ*. 1720

Pythagore, les Vers Dorés, Gr. et Français, expliqués et précédés d'un discours sur l'essence et la forme de poesie, par Fabre d'Olivet. 8vo. *Paris*, 1813

Quintiliani Opera, studiis Soc Bipontinæ. 4 vols. 8vo.   *Biponti*, 1784.

Quintilian de Institutione Oratoriæ, ad cod vet fidem recensuit et annotatione explanavit Geo Lud. Spalding   4 vols 8vo. large paper. *Lipsiæ*, 1798-1816.

Quintiliani Declamationes   Folio. *Parmæ, per Augustum Ugoletum, M CCCC XCIIII*

Quintilian's Institutes of the Orator, translated by W Guthrie   2 vols 8vo   *London*, 1805

Quinti Smyrnæi, post Homericum Lib XIV ad MSS. fidem recensuit, T Tychsen, accesserunt observationes C G Heynii   8vo finest paper   *Argentor* 1807

Rufus, Sextus   (Hist Rom Scriptores.)

Rutilii Numat Itinerarium   (Pomp. Mela, *Bipont*)

Sallustii Opera, cum vet historiarum fragmentis. 24mo   *Lugd. Bat Elzev* 1634

Sallustii Opera. 18mo. *Lond. typis Brindley*, 1744

Sallustius et L Annæus Florus   4to   *Birmingham, Baskerville*, 1773.

Sallustii Opera Omnia, excusa ad edit Cortii, cum editionibus Havercampi et Antonii collata [H Homer]. 8vo large paper. *Londini*, 1789.

Sallustii Opera ; præmittitur vita à Jo. Clerico scripta   studiis Soc Bipont   Editio tertia auctior   8vo.   *Argent* 1807

Sallustii Opera , cod scriptis simul impressisque quadraginta amplius collatis, recensuit, atque adnotationibus illustravit H E Allen   12mo. *Londini*, 1832

Sallust's Works, translated by Arth. Murphy   8vo.   *London*, 1807

Salluste, Histoire de la République Romaine, dans le cours du VIIme siècle , en partie traduite du Latin sur l'original , en partie rétablie et composée sur les Fragmens qui sont restés de ses libres perdus [Avec une Introduction et des Notes, par Ch de Brosses , Histoire de la Conjuration de Catiline ; Discours Politiques de Salluste à Jules-César sur le Gouvernement de l'Etat ; Vie de Salluste , Discours sur l'Art Historique et les Ouvrages de Salluste, par l'Abbé Cassagne] 3 vols 4to   *Dijon*, 1777.

Salustio, la Conjuracion de Catilina, y la Guerra de Jugurta, Lat y Esp [por il Enfanta D Gabriel, con la vida y principales escritos de Salustio, y notas para la mejor intelligencia y justificacion de la version Española]   Folio, plates   *Madrid, por J Ibarra*, 1772

Senecæ (L A) Philosophi Opera , ex ult J Lipsii et J Gronovii emendat Et M Ann Senecæ Rhetores que extant, ex And Schotti recensuit ; cum notis J. F Gronovii 4 vols. 24mo   *Lugd. Bat. ap Elzevirios*, 1649

Senecæ Philosophi Opera, studiis Soc. Bipontinæ. 4 vols. 8vo *Biponti*, 1782.
Senecæ Tragœdiæ, ex recensione H Avantii 8vo *Venetiis, in ædib. Aldi et A Soceri, M D XVIII*
Senecæ Tragœdiæ, studiis Soc Bipont 8vo *Biponti*, 1785
Senecæ (M A) Opera Rhetorica, studiis Soc. Bipontinæ. 8vo *Biponti*, 1783
Seneca his Tenne Tragedies, translated into Englysh by Jasper Heywood, Alex Neville, John Studley, T Nuce, and Tho Newton. 4to. black letter *London, by Thos Marshe*, 1581
Seneca's Epistles, translated, with large annotations, by T Morell. 2 vols in one, 4to *London*, 1786
Seneca's Morals, translated by Sir R. L'Estrange 12mo *London, Dodsley*, 1762
Serenius Samonicus (Poetæ Lat Minores.)
Severus Alexandrinus (Rhetores Selecti.)
Sextus Aurelius (Hist Rom Scriptores)
Silii Italici de Bello Punico Secundo XVII Libri, nuper diligentissimè castigati. 8vo *Venetiis, in æd Aldi et A Asulani, M D XXIII*.
Silii Italici de Bello Punico Secundo XVII Libri, cum notis variorum, curante A Drackenborchi 4to *Trajecti*, 1717
Silii Italici Punicorum Libri XVII, studiis Soc Bipont 8vo *Bipont* 1784
Solini Polyhistor, studiis Soc. Bipont 8vo *Bipont* 1794
Sophoclis Tragœdiæ VII Græcè [et Ajax atque Electra, Latinè], una cum omnibus Græcis scholiis, et annotationibus H Stephani 4to *H Stephanus*, 1568
Sophoclis Tragœdiæ, cum vet grammaticorum scholiis, versione, et notis illustravit R. F P Brunck 2 vols 4to *Argent* 1786
Sophocles' Tragedies, translated, with notes, historical, moral, and critical, by Geo Adams 2 vols small 8vo *London*, 1729
Sophocles' Tragedies, translated by R Potter. 4to *London*, 1788
Spartianus Ælius. (Hist Rom Scriptores.)
Statii Opera. 8vo *Parisiis, ap S Colinæum*, 1530
Statii Opera, studiis Soc Bipontinæ 8vo *Biponti*, 1785
Statius' Thebaid, translated into English verse, with notes and observations, by W. L Lewis 2 vols. 8vo *Oxford*, 1767
Strabonis Geographiæ, Gr et Lat, cum variorum, præcipuè Casauboni animadversionibus; cod MSS collationem, annotationes et tabulas geographicas adjecit T. Falconer, subjiciuntur Chrestomathiæ, Gr et Lat 2 vols in one, folio *Oxonii, è typ Clarend* 1807.
Suidæ Lexicon (Grammar)
Suetonii Opera, et in illa Commentarius S. Pitisci, et notis variorum 2 vols 4to *Leovardiæ*, 1714
Suetonii Opera; cum notis variorum, curâ et cum notis P Burmanni. 2 vols 4to *Amstelodami*, 1736
Suetonii Opera, studiis Soc Bipontinæ 8vo *Argent* 1800
Suetonii de claris Grammaticis et Rhetoribus Libellus (Plinii Epist, *Aldi*)

Suetonius's Lives of the first XII Cæsars, translated, with annotations and a review of the government and literature of the different periods, by A Thomson 8vo *London*, 1796.

Sulpicius Severus (Poetæ Lat Minores)

Tacitus, exactâ curâ recognitus et emendatus [ex recens Rhenani], variis lectionibus Small 4to large paper, old mor Grolier style *Venetiis, in ædibus Aldi Manutii et And Asulani Soceri, M D XXXIV.*

Tacitus, ex ed J Lipsii, cum notis et emendationibus H Grotii 2 vols 24mo. *Lugd Bat Elzev* 1640

Taciti Opera, Brotieri, [cum indice M Freinshemii, edente H Homer] 4 vols 8vo large paper *Lond. sumpt. autoris*, 1790.

Taciti Opera, ad edit Th Ryckii 4 vols 12mo. *Lond typis Brindley*, 1754.

Taciti Opera, ex recensione G. C Crollii, curante F C Exter 8vo. *Biponti*, 1792

Tacitus, Brotieri, curante A J Valpy 5 vols 8vo large paper *Lond* 1812

Tacitus, translated, with an essay on his life and genius, notes, supplements, and maps, by A Murphy. 4 vols. 4to large paper *London*, 1793

Terentii Comœdiæ [ex recog Fr Asulani]. 8vo. *Venetiis, in ædib. Aldi et A. Soceri, M D XVII.*

Terentii Comœdiæ, ex recensione D. Heinsii 24mo *Lugd Bat Elzev* 1642.

Terentii Comœdiæ Folio *Parisiis, è typog regiô*, 1642

Terentii Comœdiæ, recensuit, notasque suas et G Fœrni addidit R Bentleius,—Phædri Fabulæ, et Publii Syri, et aliorum veterum Sententiæ, ex recens et cum notis R Bentleii. 4to *Amstelod* 1727.

Terentii Comœdiæ 18mo *Lond typis Brindley*, 1744

Terentii Comœdiæ. 4to *Birminghamiæ, Baskerville*, 1772.

Terentii Comœdiæ VI, cum selectâ varietate lectionum et perpetuâ annotatione, accedit index Latinitatis, cum interpretatione · studiis Soc Bipont 2 vols 8vo. *Biponti*, 1779-80

Terence's Comedies, translated into familiar blank verse by George Colman 8vo *London*, 1810

Theocriti, quæ extant, Græcè, ex editione D Heinsii expressa 4to *Glasguæ, ap Foulis.* 1746

Theocriti, Moschi, et Bionis Idyllia, Gr et Lat., poetis ex Latinis illustrata, notulis quibusdam interjectis, operâ et studio T Martin 8vo large paper *Londini.* 1760

Theocritus, Bion, et Moschus, Gr et Lat accedunt animadversiones, scholia, indices, et Porti Lexicon Doricum 2 vols 8vo *Lond.* 1826

Theocritus, Bion, and Moschus, with the Elegies of Tyrtæus, translated into English blank verse, with notes by R Polwhele 2 vols 8vo. *London*, 1811

Theocritus' Encomium of Ptolemy, translated, (Callimachus)

Theocritus (Dryden's Translations from) (Works, Vol XII)

Theodosii Sphæricorum Libri III 8vo large paper *Oromæ,* 1707

Theognis (Poetæ Gr, Stephani)

Theophrasti Characteres Ethici, Gr et Lat, cum notis ac emendationibus J Casauboni et aliorum, accedunt J. Duporti prælectiones recensuit et notas adjecit P Needham. 2 vols 8vo large paper. *Cantab* 1712

Theophrasti Characterum Ethicorum Capita duo, hactenùs inedita, quæ ex cod MS Vat. Sæc XI, Græcè, edidit, Latinè vertit, præfatione et annotat illustravit J C Amadutius 4to The Roxburgh copy *Parmæ, ex reg typog [Bodoni]* 1786

Theophrastus's Characters, translated from the Greek, and illustrated with physiognomical sketches: to which are added, the Greek text, with notes and hints on the individual varieties of human nature; by F Howell Imperial 8vo large paper, proofs *London*, 1824

Theophrastus's History of Stones, with an English version, and critical and philosophical notes, including the modern history of the gems, &c described by that author, by John Hill; to which are added, two letters on the colours of the sapphire and turquoise, and upon the effects of the different menstruums on copper 8vo *Lond* 1746

Thucydides de Bello Peloponnesiaco, Gr et Lat ex interp L Vallæ, ab H Stephano recognita. Folio *Paris. H Stephanus*, 1588

Thucydides de Bello Peloponnesiaco, Gr et Lat, recens J Wasse, cum adnotationibus var, editionem curavit C Dukerus Folio *Amst apud J Wetstein*, 1731

Thucydidis Bellum Peloponnesiacum, Gr. et Lat; ex editione Wasii et Dukeri 8 vols small 8vo. fine paper *Glasguæ, excud Foulis*, 1759.

Thucydides de Bello Peloponnesiaco, Gr et Lat ad editionem J. Wasse et C A Dukeri, cum var lectionis et annot. studiis Soc Bipont. 6 vols 8vo *Biponti*, 1788-9

Thucydides' History of the Warre whiche was betweene the Peloponesians and the Athenyans; translated out of Frenche by Th Nicolls Folio **black letter** *Newely imprinted in the citye of London [by Th Wayland]*, M D L

Thucydides' History of the Peloponnesian Warre, translated by Th. Hobbes. Folio. *London*, 1676

Thucydides' History of the Peloponnesian War, translated, with discourses on the life of Thucydides, his qualifications as a historian, and a survey of the history, by W. Smith 2 vols 8vo *London*, 1805

Tiberius Rhetor (Rhetores Selecti)

Tibullus (Catullus)

Tryphiodori Ilii Excidium, cum metricâ N Frischlini versione, et selectis vii doct notis, lacunas aliquot explevit, et suas annot adjecit J Merrick 8vo *Oxonu*, 1741

Tryphiodorus's Destruction of Troy, being a sequel of the Iliad; translated, with notes, by J. Merrick 8vo *Oxford*, 1739

Valerii Flacci Argonautica Jo Baptistæ Pii Carmen, ex quarto Argonauticon, Apollonii Orphei Argonautica, innominato interprete 8vo. *Venetiis, in ædib Aldi et A Asulani*, M D XXIII

Valerii Flacci Argonautica, N. Heinsii ex vet exemp recensuit et animadversiones adjecit edente P Burmanno Small 8vo *Traj. Bat.* 1702

Valerii Flacci Argonautica, cum notis variorum, curante P. Burmanno. 4to *Leidæ*, 1724

Valerii Flacci Argonauticon Lib. VIII., studiis Soc Bipontinæ 8vo *Biponti*, 1786

Valerii Maximi Dictorum et Factorum memorabilium Libri IX. 8vo *Venetiis, in ædib Aldi et A Soceri, M D XIIII*

Valerii Maximi Dictorum Factorumque memorabilium Libri IX, accedunt Julius Obsequens de Prodigiis, cum supplement C. Lycosthenis, studiis Soc Bipont. 2 vols 8vo *Argent* 1806

Varro (M. Ter) de Linguâ Latinâ · accedunt notæ A Augustini, A Turnebii, J. Scaligeri, et A Popmæ 2 vols. 8vo *Bipont*. 1788

Varro de Agriculturâ. (Scriptores Rei Rust)

Vegetius (Fl.) de Re Militari, ex recens. N. Schwebelii, cum integris ejusdem et selectis G Stewichii, P Scriveri, F. Oudendorpii, et F. Besselii notis, acced. indices. 8vo *Argent ex typ. Bipont.* 1806

Vegetius de Arte Veterinariâ (Scriptores Rei Rust)

Velleii Paterculi Historia Romana, cum notis Ger Vossii. 24mo *Lugd. Bat Elzev* 1639.

Velleii Paterculi Historia Romana, ex editione Pet Burmanni Small 8vo large paper. *Glasguæ. Foulis*, 1752

Velleii Paterculi Historia Romana, cum notis variorum, curante D. Ruhnkenio. 2 vols 8vo *Lugd Bat* 1779

Velleius Paterculus præmittuntur H Dodwelli Annales Velleianæ; studiis Soc. Bipontinæ 8vo *Biponti*, 1780

Vellius Paterculus, translated by T. Baker. 8vo *London*, 1814

Vibius Sequester de Fluminibus, &c (Pomp. Mela, *Bipont*)

Victor Sext. Aurelius (Hist Rom Scriptores)

Virgilii Opera, ad doctiss J Pontani castigationes excusa 64mo. *Sedani, ex typog et typis noviss J Jannoni*, 1628

Virgilii Opera, ex recensione D. Heinsii 24mo. Editio vera. *Lugd. Bat. Elzev.* 1636

Virgilii Opera Folio *Parisiis, è typog regiâ*, 1641.

Virgilii Opera, recensuit cum comment. variorum, notis, &c P Masvicii. 2 vols 4to. *Leovardiæ*, 1717

Virgilii Opera, in usum Delphini, editio accuratior 4to. *Parisiis, Barbou*, 1726

Virgilii Opera 18mo *Lond Brindley*, 1744

Virgilii Opera, cum commentariis et notis variorum et P Burmanni; curâ P Burmanni secundi. 4 vols 4to *Amst* 1746

Virgilii Opera 4to *Birminghamiæ, Baskerville*, 1757

Virgilii Opera 8vo *Birminghamiæ, Baskerville*, 1766

Virgilii Opera. Small 8vo Gr papier vélin. *Parisiis, Didôt*, 1799.

Virgilii Opera, varietate lectionis et perpetuâ adnotatione illustrata à C G Heyne, accedunt indices. editio novis curis emendata et aucta 6 vols royal 8vo vellum paper. *Lipsiæ*, 1800

Virgilii Opera præmittitur notitia literaria, studiis Soc Bipontinæ 2 vols 8vo *Argent* 1808.

Virgil's Works; translated, adorned with sculptures, and illustrated with annotations, by John Ogilby. Large folio. Brilliant impressions of the plates by Hollar and Lombard, and of the portrait by Faithorne. *London*, 1654

Virgil's Works, translated into English verse by John Dryden. (Works, Vols XIII. XIV and XV.)

Virgil.—The XIII Bukes of Eneados of the famose Poete Virgill, translated out of Latyne verses into Scottish metir, bi Mayster Gawin Douglas, Bishop of Dunkel, and unkil to the Erle of Angus. every buke having hys perticular prologe. 𝔅lack letter, 4to *Imprinted at London [by W. Copland]*, 1553

<blockquote>The first English metrical version of a classic, the Scottish and English languages at this time being very similar.</blockquote>

Virgil, Eneis, avec une traduction en vers Français, et des remarques, par Jacques Delille. 4 vols 8vo *Paris*, 1804

Virgilii Georgica et Bucolica; with an English translation, notes, [and life of Virgil], by John Martyn. 2 vols 4to *London*, 1741-9

Vitruvius de Architecturâ. (Architecture.)

Vopiscus Flavius. (Hist Aug Scriptores.)

Xenophontis Opera quæ extant, Gr. et Lat, operâ J. Leunclavii; accesserunt notæ, &c Æm. et Fr Porti. Folio. *Parisiis*, 1625.

Xenophontis de Socrate Commentarii; item, Socratis Apologia, Græcè 4to *Glasguæ, Foulis*, 1761

Xenophon's Cyropædia, or, the Institution of Cyrus, translated by M. Ashley 8vo *London*, 1811.

Xenophon's Anabasis, or, the Expedition of Cyrus into Persia, and the Retreat of the Ten Thousand Greeks with critical and historical notes by Henry Spelman 2 vols 8vo *Cambridge*, 1776

Xenophon's Hellenics, or, the History of the affairs of Greece, translated by W. Smith. 8vo *London*, 1812

Xenophon's Minor Works; viz Memoires of Socrates, the Banquet, Hiero, and Economics; translated by Fielding, Welwood, Graves, and Bradley. 8vo *London*, 1813

MANUSCRIPTS.

Brief Diary of Events, from A D 1221 to 1440; with a List of the Lords Mayor, continued to the 8th of Elizabeth, and of the Convents, Monasteries, Priories, and Chapelries, in London   4to.

    On vellum the diary is in the hand of Henry the Sixth's time, and contains much curious information of minor circumstances occurring in London, not noticed by historians On the last leaf of the diary, which is misplaced at the end of the volume, is, " Iste liber constat Ricō Hedley, Clerico Come Guyhalde Civitate Londinj."

A MS. Volume, of the time of Edward IV or Richard III, on paper, in small 4to, containing.

    The Travels of Sir John Mandeville, which concludes at p 99 thus: " I John Maudewylle, Knyt, went owt of my cuntrie and passyd ye se in ye zere of o^r Lord M III C XXX and II, and hav passyd thorow many landys, cuntreys, and ilys, and now cum to rest me in ye zeie of or Lord M III C sixty and syx, or ye XXXIII zere after my depaityng from my cuntrie; for I was in travell XXXIII zere."

    The Invencion of ye glorious Confessor Scynt Antony, the whiche Seynt Jerome, the noble doctor, compownyd, and translate owt of Grec into Latten, and out of Latten into Fnglysch, the whyche invencion was made by the holy Bysschop Teophile, in the tyme of Constantyne   (Pp 100 to 118.)

    Hou an Erle was brought yn thral, thorou treason and wyckednys, and other poetical tales.   (Pp. 119 to 130.)

    A Lamentable of Kyng Edward ye IIII., by the Chronicler Fabyan   (See Warton's English Poetry, Vol III p 26.)   This occupies pp. 131 and 2

    On the fly-leaf, in a hand of Charles the First's time, is a list of the contents, and also " out of the collect of Lord Somers, sum E. Umfreville 1738 " From Mich Tutet's collection.

The Correspondence of Thomas Lord Dacre, Warden of the East and Middle Marches from June 3d, 1523, to August 4th, 1524; including original letters of the Earl of Surrey, Cardinal Wolsey, Earl of Northumberland, Maud Lady Parr, Sir W Parr, Lord Compton, Earl of Shrewsbury, Sir Wm and Sir John Heron, Sir W. Ellerker, Sir John Bulmer, Margaret Queen of Scotland, Duke of Albany, Earl of Angus, Lord Maxwell, &c &c   and also Lord Dacre's copies of his own letters, forming together 334 curious original documents, illustrative of Border History.   Contained in a case bound as a book

    From this collection, which belonged to R Richardson, Esq. of Bierley, Hearne extracted the letters which were appended to his Chronicles of Otterburne and Wethamstede, and those there published are so marked on a chronological list contained in the case

A Breffe Description of the Royall Citie of London, capital citie of this realme of England, wrytten by me William Smythe citizen and haberdasher of London, 1575   A small 4to volume of 85 leaves

    This contains a list of the Bishops of London continued to 1611, of the mayors and sheriffs, which is interspersed with remarkable occurrences, to 1633, and of the aldermen living in 1590, 1602, 5, 11, and 16, with the arms of the various corporations emblazoned, and those of the trading companies and lords mayor tricked   In Moule's Bib Heraldica, No 121, are noticed two MSS of a similar description, one by an author of the same name   " Wm Smith, Rouge Dragon, 1605"

The XII Worshipful Companies or Misteries of London, with the armes of all of them that have bin Lord Maiors for the space of almost 300 yeares, of every company particularly also, most part of the Sheriffs and Aldermen Anno 1605 A vol in sm 4to of 50 leaves, with additions and continuations, in some places, to 1616

Dugdale (Sir W.)—Visitation of the County of Yorke, begun anno Domini 1665 and finished 1666, by William Dugdale, Esq, Norroy King at Armes A stout volume in folio

> Apparently the original of this Visitation, written by H. Johnston, and illustrated with the arms in trick By the inscription on the fly-leaf preceding the title, it appears to have been intended by Sir William as a bequest to Henry St George, his immediate successor as Norroy, and to all others holding the same office From Sir M M Sykes's collection

THE HOPKINSON MSS. In 41 vols. folio and 4to.

> John Hopkinson, Esq of Lofthouse, near Leeds, attended Sir W Dugdale in his visitation of the county of York as his secretary His MSS contain many transcripts of Sir William's, with additions, and they are still farther enlarged by Mr Thomas Wilson of Leeds, a relative of Thoresby the antiquary, and in Thoresby's Diary they are more than once alluded to The following extract is from the MS correspondence of Mr Wilson to Mr Richardson of Bierley, dated June 1733 —" I have sent you your ancestor Hopkinson's MSS. Out of respect to Mr Hopkinson, I took a walk to Rothwell, and in the church choir, on the left hand of the door, pretty high on the wall, is a neat white marble monument, with a Latin inscription, being an encomium of his learning in history, antiquities, and heraldry.'

CONTENTS

Vol I —Nomina Nobilium qui seisit fuerunt de Terris et Tenementis in West Riding Comitat Ebor A fol vol of nearly 500 pages

Vol II —A Miscellanye or Collection of old Evidences and other Antiquities, as Records, Decrees, Inquisitions, &c with some other observances, with 2 indexes J H. 1660 A folio volume of nearly 800 pages

Vol III —Collections of Arms, by Robert Glover, Somerset Herald, with additions by Mr Hopkinson A folio volume of upwards of 500 pages

Vol IV.—A Collection of Coate Armors belonging to several Familyes in England, putt into alphabett John Hopkinson, 1654 A folio of nearly 400 pages

Vol V —Legis Anglicanæ Epitome, methodicè digesta Jn Hopkinson hospicii Lincoln A folio of 1137 closely written pages

Vol VI —A Collection of some Antiquityes, with several Pedigrees, written 1660 and 61, by J H A folio of nearly 600 pages

Vol VII —Lists of Shires and Counties in England and Wales, of Bishopricks and their Dioceses, Justicers itinerants their circuits, Revenues of the Principalitye of Wales, Dukedome of Cornwall, Earldom of Chester, and Dutchye of Lancaster, Benefices and Spiritual Livings, and the Forests, Chases, and Parks, in the Dutchye of Lancaster, Fees to Officers and Ministers of Justice in England, and at Court, in King James's raigne, Townes of Warr, Castles, and Bulwarkes, &c , Keepers of Castles, Houses, Forests, Chases, &c and a Collection of Auncient Fees, due and usually taken by the several officers of the countye of Yorke; with a Treatise of Weights and Measures; by J H 1663 A folio of upwards of 500 pages

Vol VIII.—Collections touching the Kings and Princes as have raigned and governed in Englande, of the Nobilitye of England since the Conquest,—Claim of Peregrine Bertie for the Stile and the Barronyes of Willoughbye and Eresbye, with the answers thereto, temp. Eliz ;—the Quartering of Armes of the Nobilitye of England A folio volume of about 400 pages

Vol IX —A Collection of the Descents of severall of the Nobilitye and Gentrye of the Counties of Cumberland and Westmoreland, with Memorialls of some other Antiquities transcribed out of Mr Dugdale his last visitation in 1664 and 5, and out of other MSS belonging Mr Christopher Townley, and of his owne, in the yeare 1669, by J H of L, in Yorkshire A folio volume of upwards of 600 pages.

Vol X —Genealogical Collections relative to the Nobility of England, Scotland, and Ireland. In Mr H.'s hand A folio volume of upwards of 500 pages

Vol. XI —A Collection of the Descents of severall Northerne Familyes who have beene active against the Scotts; with other Memorialls relating to them, and an Alphabetical Table of their Names 1668 A folio volume of more than 700 pages

This contains a great deal of curious matter relative to the Border transactions, the various expeditions into Scotland, &c, including "the Accompte for the Garrison at Barwicke-upon-Tweed, for 1606," and "severall moderne battells fought betwixt the English and the Scotts, and inroads made by the English into Scotland'

Vol XII —Pedigrees of the Northern Gentry, by Mr H. A folio volume of upwards of 500 pages

Vol XIII —The Discipline of Warr, both of Horse and Foote, used in his Majesty's Army in the north, 1643, under the command of his Excellencye William, Earle and Marquesse of Newcastle, and Prince Regent, with the order and manner of marchinge, exercising, &c. · including also Armes assessed in England from Henry II's time A folio of 220 pages.

Vol XIV.—Collections relative to the Local Divisions, Degrees of States (Titles), Laws, Courts of England, Scotland, Ireland, France, the Low Countries, Spain, and Portugal, &c That of England includes the K. Matie's offices and fees, and those of keepers of castles, &c &c A folio, upwards of 200 pages

Vol XV —Of Duells and Combates, with the proceedings therein in the Earle Marshall's Court of England with some observations relating to appeales, written anno 1664, by J H. A folio of 200 pages.

Vol XVI —Collections relative to the Titles of Lord Willoughby of Eresby, Latimer of Danby Latimer of Brooke, Powis Baronye claimed by H Vernon, of Barons by Tenure, Writ, and Patent, of the Revenues of Nobility, Precedence of Nobility, Nobility in reputation, Honors conferred by foreign Princes; Degrees of Gentry; Division of Lands amongst Sonnes, &c, by J H, 1652. A folio of 500 pages

Vol. XVII.—A Transcript or Collection of severall passages in the latter end of the raigne of Queen Elizabeth, of famous memorye, and Kynge James his raigne, out of the papers and memorialls of the late Right Hon John Lord Saville, Baron of Pontefract, and Edward Taylor, formerly of Furnival's Inne, Holborne, London, and my late father, all of them deceased many years since, with some others in the raigne of the late King Charles I. Collected and transcribed in 1674, by J H of L, with a Defense and Vindication of Titles by Edward Bagshaw, Esq 1646. A folio of about 600 pages.

Vol XVIII —Speeches in Parliament, and other Speeches, with severall Letters of concernment, being of great antiquitie, and some other Speeches and Letters relating to these late distracted tymes Collected and written oute by J H, anno 1660.

Among the letters are several from Roger Ascham, Queen Elizabeth, the Duke of Norfolk, Bp Hall, Bp Sanderson, &c

Vol. XIX —Transcripts of Letters from Henry VIII, his Queens, Edward VI, Lady Jane Grey, Queen Elizabeth, Mary Queen of Scots, King James, Charles I, Pope Pius, Abps. Grindall, Whitgift, Sir W Raleigh, Sir T Saville, Sir R Sadler, &c 1513–1666, in Mr H's hand A folio of 300 pages.

Vol XX —Transcripts of Letters in the reigns of Henry VIII, Edward VI, and Queen Mary, relating more particularly to Border and local matters Transcribed, 1677, by J. H A folio of 270 pages

Vol XXI —Letters of Lords, and other persons of great qualitie, found in Sheffield Castle, county of Yorke, in the year 1676, and relating to the great and then flourishing familye of the Lords Talbot, Earles of Shrewsbury, 1550–1606 Transcribed out of the originalls in 1677, by J H A folio of 120 pages

The letters forming the three preceding volumes appear to be unpublished, and those in the last are not contained in Mr Lodge's selections from the Talbot Papers

Vol XXII.—A Collection of the Coates of Armes and Descents of severall familyes of nobilitie and gentrye of the East Rideing of Yorkshire, collected and transcribed in the yeare 1672, by J. H, of L A folio of nearly 500 pages

Vol. XXIII.—A similar Collection for the North Riding; collected and transcribed 1672, by J H A folio of nearly 600 pages

Vol XXIV —A Catalogue or Abstracte of the Pedigrees of severall Families of Gentrye in the counties of York, Durham, and Lincolne, with tables to find out their names, 1652, by J Hopkinson. A folio of nearly 500 pages

Vol XXV —A Collection of the Pedigrees of severall Familyes of Nobilitye and Gentrye of the countyes of Yorke, Lancaster, Lincolne, &c. 1657 J. H. A folio of nearly 600 pages

Vol. XXVI —An Abstracte of the Ancient Coynes, Monies, Measures, Years, &c of the Hebrews, Grecians, and Romanes, collected of Mr. H. Bunting his Itinerary, Godwin's Jewish Antiquities, Burton's Leicestershire. and of those more moderne out of Leigh's Diatribe, Chamberlayne's Angliæ Notitia Transcribed 1671, for my own private use. J. H. A folio of nearly 200 pages

Vol. XXVII —A Collection of Poems; consisting of epigrams, odes, epitaphs, &c chiefly relative to parties or transactions of the times of Elizabeth, James, and Charles I, in Mr. H.'s hand A folio of nearly 700 pages

MANUSCRIPTS

Vol XXVIII —Transcripts of Letters relative to Publie Affairs from 1606–34 In Mr. H.'s hand, 1650 A folio of about 200 pages.

Vol XXIX —A Collection of the Antiquities and other Proceedings in the Parliaments of England, with a Project for Fishing and Navigation: transcribed anno 1662 by J. Hopkinson A folio of 224 pages

Vol XXX —Collections on Ecclesiasticall Matters. Councils, Religious Houses, Spiritual Promotions, Abps of Yorke, Jewells, Plates, &c in the Cathedral, Colleges, Houses of Religion, and Churches in the City of Yorke, Order of Preaching in the Minster, Rentall of the Abp's Tenths, and Subsidies of the Clergy in the Diocese, Buildings, Manors, Sheriffs of the Citye, and Chauntreys in the Shire of York and their Founders, Fundatio Abathie de Stanlawe et Translatio ejusdem ad Whalley, Donationes Ecclesiarum de Rotshdale, Blackborne, and Whalley; State of the Benefices in Lancashire belonging to the Abp of Canterburye; Founders of Religious Houses A highly curious volume, in Mr H's hand, and forming 440 pages

Vol XXXI.—Memorialls of Countrye (Public) Business for these Northern Counties, both military and civile, towards the latter end of Queene Elizabeth and King James's theire reignes Collected and transcribed by J H., 1674 A folio of nearly 300 pages

Vol. XXXII —Greene Sleeves, or Leicester Commonwealth, transcripts of letters from the Council in the north, 1575, &c : and the Muster-Roll of England and Wales, taken about this time, 1674, by J H. A folio of about 400 pages

Vol XXXIII —Letters relating to the late noble and auncient Familye of the Lords Talbotts, Earles of Shrewsburie, of Sheffield Castle, in the countie of Yorke, in the latter end of the reigne of Q Elizabeth, and the reigne of Kinge James, found at Sheffield Castle in 1676, and transcribed out of the said originalls that yeare and the yeare 1677, by J H of L

Like volume XXI the contents of this form no part of Lodge's illustrations. It occupies more than 500 pages.

Vol XXXIV —A miscellaneous Collection, principally Poems of the time of Elizabeth and James I ; transcribed by Mr H A folio of more than 500 pages

Vol XXXV —A Catalogue of all the Sheriffes of Yorkshire, from 1155, with their severall coats of armes, by Mr H A thin folio volume

Vol XXXVI —A Collection of Proceedings in the Sessions, by Indictement and Presentment of Bridges, Highways, Felonies, and other nuisances in the West Riding of Yorkshire, in the raignes of Queen Elizabeth, King James, and King Charles I ; with others of the same kind within the honor of Pontefract, collected out of ancient rolls of that honor in the custody of Mr Edward Ashton of Methley J H A folio of nearly 500 pages

Vol XXXVII —Assesses and Rates of the whole Countye of Yorke ; with the Hundreds, or Wapentaikes, the names of the Castells, and the Nobilitye of the North Riding and East Riding, collected by J H of L. 1672 A folio of nearly 300 pages

Vol XXXVIII —Transactions and Passages of Countrye (Public) Busines for this West Riding of the Countye of Yorke, in the latter end of the raigne of Elizabeth, beginning of Kinge James, and the late Kinge Charles collected and gathered in the year of our Lord 1658, out of my father's old scattered papers, and some of my owne which were preserved and have comed to my hands since this late warr J H With Peticions and their severall Answeares This valuable volume occupies nearly 700 pages.

Vol XXXIX —Dutchy Busines in the County of Yorke, viz Collection of Suitors and Fines paid for respiting of Corte for Pontefracte, Proceedings in the Honor Courte of P., Knights' Fees in the Honor of P, Receivers and Feodarys Accompts in the Honor for Reliefes, &c ; Knights' Fees in the said Honor in the tyme of Edward II, Survey of the whole Dutchye in Yorkshire, Fines et Homagus repretandi anno 19 Th7th Honores Pontefracti With an alphabet (index) J Hopkinson, 1659

Vol XL —The auncient Rates of the West Riding of the Countye of Yorke, agreed upon by the Justices of Peace there in anno XLIV to Regine Elizabethe Jo Hopkinson, 1684 A 4to of about 100 pages.

Vol. XLI.—Hopkinson's (J.) Collection of the Pedigrees and Descents of the Yorkshire and Lancashire Gentry, with additions by Rich Thornton and Ralph Thoresby of Leedes, Esqrs ; with a catalogue of the antient Gentry of Lancashire, collected by Capt Booth of Stockport A folio volume, in the almost typographical hand of Mr Thomas Wilson of Leeds, with his own additions, and occupying upwards of 500 pages.

A Selection of Letters, Papers, &c transcribed from the Hopkinson MSS for Dr Richardson, who has prefixed the contents in his own hand A small and thick 4to volume.

A Collection of the Pedigrees and Descents of severall of the Gentrye of the West Riding of the county of Yorke, Auncient Rates of the West Riding, &c. (a copy of Vol XL above), on Sirnames, &c Apparently in Dr Richardson's hand, and probably extracted from several of the preceding MSS A 4to volume

An Account of all the Charters, Patents, and Escheat-Rolls, in the Archives of the Tower of London, collected by John Burton, M.D. 1746, with compleat indexes of persons and places Transcribed by T. Wilson M DCC XLVII

> "I herewith send your copy of Dr Burton's MS the numbers are the same with those writ upon the original charters, &c The copy is valuable upon many respects to such as delight in antiquities "—*Mr Wilson's Letter to Dr Richardson*, Dec 1747 This forms a folio volume of 151 pages, and includes those documents only which relate to the diocese of York It never was published, being evidently compiled by Dr. Burton with a view to his History of York Mr Wilson is alluded to by Dr Whitaker, in his History of Leeds, as annotating a copy of Thoresby's Ducatus Leodensis, then in the possession of Sir M M Sykes.

Liber Judicaris; or, Doomsday Book for the County of York [beautifully] transcribed by Thomas Wilson of Leedes, 1747 with notes extracted from copies in the hands of Dr Brooke, in Field Head, and Mr. Franks of Pontefract, in 1745. Folio

> "But your copy of Domesday is the principal flower you are yet master of, and I am persuaded you think so. I beg you will keep it to yourselt, and not

suffer it to be lent out of your hands so long that it may again be transcribed, for in it I rectified several mistakes, that I discovered in my own copy, and I can justly say it is the best copy of that noble record . . . I believe there are not half a dozen copies of it in the world."—*Mr Wilson's Letter to Dr Richardson, Dec 1747* Mr Wilson collated this with every copy he could obtain access to

Adversaria, in MS. by Thomas Wilson, of Leeds, containing, Collectiones ad Historiam famosissimi Cœnobii Glastomensi concinnandum, of St Dunstan; Writers of the Life of Thomas à Becket, Life of Thomas à Becket, of the Time of the Coming in of the Saxons, and of their Conquests in Britain, de Studiis Britannicis, Chronological Series of the British Kings before the Roman Invasion; Index Memorabilium Britanniæ ante Cæsarem, Saxon Annals, Orders and Rules to be practised by the Monks and Nuns of England, translated out of Saxon and Latin; Greek Vocabulary, Saxon and English Dictionary Folio

Richardson Correspondence; consisting of the original autograph Letters on Botanical and other Scientific Subjects, addressed to Dr. R. Richardson and R Richardson, Esq of Bierley Hall, by Her. Boerhaave, Dr Bedford, J Blackstone, Prof Bobart, Dr. W Chambers, J. J Dillenius, the Earl of Derby, Dr Drake, John Fothergill, R Foulkes, R Frewen, J. F Gronovius, Thomas Hearne, Hugh Jones, Mr Knowlton, Charles Leigh, Ed Lhuyd, Mr La Trobe, Peter Miller, Lord Petre, James Petiver, Mr Rauthmell, Dr Sherard, Prof. Sutherland, Sir H. Sloane, R Thoresby, Van Swieten, F Willoughby, &c &c from 1691 to 1775 In 13 vols folio

A[nstis] (J.) de Baronus, MS. Collections on this subject, by the Historian of the Order of the Garter A 4to volume of 70 pages.

This is unnoticed by Moule, and has never been published.

Sharpe's (Abp John) Historical Account of the Silver and the Gold Coins of England, Scotland, and Ireland In folio, with tables of the Coins in 4to

> Accompanying this is a transcript of Mr Thoresby's copy, similar to that published in Nichols's Topog Brit vol vi, with the chronology of the coins from the Earl of Pembroke's MS enlarged by Thoresby —a short sketch of the Abp's Life, in the handwriting of Mr 1 Wilson —a letter from Mr. Bartlet, returning this MS to Dr Richardson, and some notes on it —a memorandum by John Bedford of Hartburn, on a collation of a copy of this MS in possession of a grandson of Dr Sharpe —and 11 plates of coins On collating this with the printed copy, besides frequent verbal differences, the latter is deficient in pp 82 to 85, and all after p 98.

APPENDIX

Benson's (R) Sketches of Corsica 8vo. *London*, 1825

Botta (C), Continuazione de Guicciardini Storia d' Italia dal 1534 sino al 1814 14 vols 8vo. *Parigi*, 1832.

Brockedon's (W.) Illustrations of the Passes of the Alps, by which Italy communicates with France, Switzerland, and Germany 2 vols royal 4to India proofs *London*, 1828–9

Craven's (Hon R Keppel) Tour through the Southern Provinces of the Kingdom of Naples; to which is subjoined, a sketch of the immediate circumstances attending the late Revolution 4to *London*, 1821

Earle's (A) Narrative of a Nine Months' Residence in New Zealand 8vo. *London*, 1832

Fountain's Abbey (Eight Views of), intended to illustrate the architectural and picturesque Scenery of that celebrated Ruin; from original drawings by J. Metcalf and J W. Carmichael · with a historical and architectural description, by T Sopwith Folio *Newcastle-upon-Tyne*, ——

Gent (Life of T), Printer at York, written by himself 8vo. *London*, 1832

Gentoo Laws (Code of), or Ordinations of the Pundits; from a Persian translation made from the original Shanscrit, by N. B Halhed. 8vo. *London*, 1781.

Gilly's (W S) Memoir of Felix Neff, Pastor of the High Alps 8vo *London*, 1832

[Irving's (Washington)] Alhambra 2 vols 8vo *London* 1832.

Kennedy's (Vans) Researches into the Nature and Affinity of Ancient and Hindu Mythology 4to. *London*, 1831.

Latrobe's (C. J) Pedestrian, a Summer's Ramble in the Tyrol and adjacent Provinces in 1830 8vo *London*, 1832

Lesson (R P), Histoire Naturelle des Colibris, suivie d'un Supplément à l'histoire des Oiseaux Mouches Royal 8vo *Paris*, 1832.

Lesson (R P.), Histoire Naturelle des Trochilidées Royal 8vo. *Paris*, 1833.

Mahon's (Lord) History of the War of the Succession in Spain 8vo. *London*, 1832

Newcastle ——His Majestie's passing through the Scots Armie, as also his entertainment by General Lesly · together with the manner of the Scots marching out of Newcastle Related by the best intelligence *Printed* 1641 8vo. *Newcastle, privately reprinted* 1820

APPENDIX. 439

Newcastle —Wm. Lithgow's experimentall and exact Relation upon that famous and renowned Siege of Newcastle *Edinb* 1645. 8vo. *Newcastle, privately reprinted* 1820

Newcastle —A particular Relation of the Taking of Newcastle *London*, 1644. 8vo. *Newcastle, privately reprinted* 1825

Pavia (La Certosa di) Large folio. *Milano*, 1825

Rammohun Roy's (Rajah) Translation of several principal Books, Passages, and Texts of the Veds, &c 8vo *London*, 1832

Rantzovii (H) Epigrammatum Historicus Liber 4to. *Antverpiæ*, 1581.

Selby's (P J.) Illustrations of British Ornithology 2 vols. 8vo, and plates in 2 vols folio *Edinburgh*, 1825, &c.

Smyth's (W H) Sketch of the Present State of the Island of Sardinia 8vo. *London*, 1828.

Spanish Novelists, a series of National Tales, translated from the originals, with biographical and critical notices, by T Roscoe 3 vols. 8vo *London*, 1832

Shurreef (J) Qanoon-e-Islam , or, the Customs of the Moosulmans of India, translated by G A Herklots. 8vo *London*, 1832.

[White's (Blanco)] Doblado's Letters from Spain 8vo. *London*, 1822

INDEX.

⁎ All Anonymous works, Translations (except of portions of the Scripture), and Memoirs, are placed under their respective subjects only. The various heads of the Catalogue are in Italics.

ABARBANEL de Statu et Jure Regio, 21.
—— de Judicium et Regum different 21
Abbo de Obsidione Lutetiæ, 289.
Abbot's Lepidopterous Insects, 100
Abd-Allatif de l'Egypt, 307
Abel's China, 151
Abelæ Descriptio Mehtæ, 297
Abercrombie (J.) on Intellectual Powers, 76
—— (Life of Lord), 316
——'s Gardener's Calendar, 126
Abicht de Lapsu Murorum Iherich 24
Abingdon's Worcester Cathedral, 215
Abrantes' (Duchesse d') Memoirs, 288
Abu Taleb Khan's Travels, 133
Abyssinia (Travels in), 146
Abyssinian History, 307
Accoltus de Vitiorum sui ævi, 295.
Accum's Mineralogy, 91
Acerbi's Travels, 136
Achard, Cours de Bibliographie, 340
Acherley's Britannic Constitution, 71.
Achilles Tatius, 409
Acominati Choniatæ Historia, 181
Acropolitæ Historia Byzantina, 181
Actes des Apôtres (le Mystere des), 394
Adair's American Indians, 310
Adam Blair, 381
Adam's Roman Antiquities, 170
Adams (G.) on the Microscope, 100
—— Geometrical Essays, 103.
—— Astronomical Essays 104
—— Defence of Tragic Poetry, 389
—— (Jane) Irish Rebellion, 273
—— (J.) History of Republics, 68
—— Brazils, 156
—— Index Villaris, 185
—— (R.) Timbuctoo, 144
—— Palace of Diocletian, 172
—— (T.) on the Romans, 13
—— Works, 35
—— (Life of), 35
Adami de Lirman's Fragmenta, 294
Addison's Works, 396
Adolphus's Spain, 291
—— British Cabinet, 315
Adry sur les Elzeviers, 342
Adventurer, 405
Advocates' Library Catalogue, 345
Æliani Tactica, 408
—— Historia, 409
Ælfrici Abbatis Gram. et Gloss. Anglo-Saxonica, 352
Æneus Polioreeticus, 408

Æschinis Orationes, 414
Æschyli Tragœdiæ, 409
—— Tragedies translated, 409
Esopi Fabulæ, 410
—— Fables, 100
—— (Life of), 400
Africa (Travels in), 144
African History, 306
—— *Languages,* 357
Agapida's Conquest of Grenada, 291
Agathias de Imperio Justiniani 181
Agocchi Urbs Bononiæ, 294
Agriculture, 123
Agricultural Surveys, 124
Agrippa's Occult Philosophy, 78.
Ahmud ben Abubekr's Ancient Alphabets, 107
Aicher de Comitiis Vet. Rom 168.
Aikin's (A. and R.) Dict. of Chemistry, 87
—— (J.) Woodland Companion, 125
—— Manchester, 204
—— General Biography, 311.
—— Selden and Usher 314.
—— Essays, 406.
—— (L.) Elizabeth, 230
—— James I 232
Ailredi Ab Rieval Historia, 221
Ainsworth's Latin Dictionary, 352
Aiton's Hortus Kewensis, 94
Alagonæ Ichonographia Syracusæ, 297.
Alban's (Saint) Chronicle, 224
—— (Five Nights of), 383
Albani Sancti Abbatum Vitæ, 253
Alberoni (Life of Card.), 291
Albertus de Pictura Veterum, 108.
Albigensian Confession of Faith, 32.
Albin's Esculent Fish, 98
Alcedo's America, 306
Alciatus de Magistratibus, 167
—— Hist. Mediolanensis, 293
—— Emblemata, 402
Alcuini Flacci Historia, 221.
Aldes (Annales des), 342
Aldrovandi Opera Hist Nat. 88
Aldus See Manutius
—— (M. et P.) de Tibus Vet 24
Alemannus de Laterinensibus Parietinis, 295
Aleandri Tab. Marmoreæ Solis Effigie, 164
Alesii Edinburgi Descriptio, 260.
Alexandri Rogerii Siciliæ Regis Gesta, 296

3 L

Alexander the Great, 414.
Alexandre (Hist. d') le Grand, 379
Alexander's Costume of China, 121
Ἀλεξ-ερφανιας Evangelicæ Significatio, 22
Alfieri (Life of V), 316
—— Tragedie, 395
Alfonsus à Carthagenâ de Rebus Hispanicis, 290
Alfordi Annales Ecc. Brit. 251
Alfredi Magni Res Gestæ, 220 and 222
—— Vita à Spelman, 222
Ali's Sentences, 401
Ali Bey's Travels, 133
Alison on Taste, 359
Alix, l'Histoire Ottoman, 300
Allan's Collectanea Dunhelmensia, 199
Allatius de Patriâ, &c. Homeri, 163
Allen's Modern Judaism, 60
Allix on the Books of the Bible, 11
—— against Unitarians, 37
—— on the Piedmontese Churches, 62
—— on the Albigenses, 62
Allot's England's Parnassus, 363
Almack's, 381
Alpinus de Balsamo, 18
Alsarius de Invidiâ et Fascino, 167
Altmann de Gallicinio Hieros audito, 22.
—— de Lydiâ Thyatirensi, 23
Aluredi Beverlacensis Annales, 223
Alwood on the Prophecies, 15
Amadis de Gaule, 380.
—— translated, 380
—— (Tresor de l'), 309
Amalthæi (Memoirs of the), 314
Ameer Khoawend's Account of Philosophers, 76
America (Travels in), 132–4
American History, 307.
Americana Bibliotheca, 308
American Languages, 357
Ames's Typographical Antiquities, 341
Amico de Archiepisc. Syracusarum, 296
Ammianus Marcellinus, 410.
Amos on Agriculture, 124
Amsinck's Tunbridge Wells, 203.
Ana, 401
Anacreontis Carmina, 410
Anacreon's Odes translated, 410
Anatomy, 101.
Anastasii Historia Ecclesiastica, 182
Ancient Navigation, 131.
—— History, 177.
—— Biography, 312
Anderson's (A.) Origin of Commerce, 85
—— (Æ.) Journal of the Forces under Pigot, 244
—— (J.) Agricultural Recreations, 124
—— Mary Queen of Scots, 265
—— Diplomata Scotiæ, 267
—— Royal Genealogies, 134.
—— House of Yvery, 336
Andrews' (J.) Buenos Ayres, 157
—— Revolutions of Denmark, 275.
—— (J P.) Great Britain, 226.
—— (Lanc.) Sermons, 55.
Angelorum Antiq. Atestinæ, 294
Angelitæ Recineti Origines, &c. 294.
Angelotti Urbis Retæ Desc. 295
Angelus de Depredit Castrensium, 295
Angerstein Gallery of Pictures, 116

Anglesey's (Earl of) State of the Government, 240
—— Memoirs, 240
Anglicanæ Ecclesiæ Reformatio Legum, 27
Anglicanum Musarum Analecta, 360, 361.
Anglo-Saxon Scriptures, 3
—— Chronicle and History, 222.
Anglo-Saxon Language, 352
—— Poetry, 362
Angus's Seats of the Nobility, &c. 190
Anne Boleyn, 229
Anne d'Autriche, 283
Annuals, 407
Annual Register, 184.
Anquetil, l'Histoire Universelle, 176
Ansaldus de Forensi Jud. Buccinâ, 22
Anselmi Arch. Cant. Vita, 253
Anstey's Poetical Works, 365
—— Pleader's Guide, 365.
—— (Life of), 365
Ansus' (Jo.) Visitation Books, 330
—— Register of the Garter, 332.
—— Order of the Bath, 332.
—— de Baronus, 437
Anthologia Epigrammatum Græce, 408
Anti-Jacobin Poetry, 364
Antiquarian Repertory, 193
Antiquities, 159.
Antonini Iter Britannicum, 188
—— by Reynolds, 188
Antonini Imp. Meditationes, 410
—— Meditations translated, 410
—— Liberalis Transformationes, 410
—— (P.) Sassima Antiqua, 294
—— (Abate) Poeti Italiani, 375
Antonio Bibliotheca Hispana, 343
Apocryphal Books, 9.
Apollonii Rhodii Argonautica, 410
—— translated, 410
—— of Tyana (Life of), 316.
Apothegms, 401
Appiani Historia, 410.
—— translated, 410
Apthorp on Prophecy, 15
Apuleii Opera, 410.
—— Golden Ass translated, 411
Arabia (Travels in), 148.
Arabian History, 301.
Arabian Nights, 388
Arabic Language, 349
Arati Opera, 411
Arbuthnot (J.) Tables of Coins, Weights, and Measures, 85
—— Law, a Bottomless Pit, 401.
Archaia, 407
Archdall's Monasticon Hibernicum, 273
Archery, 127.
Archimedis Opera, 411
Archenholz, Hist. de Gustave Wasa, 275
Architecture, 122
Aretæi Stubæ Chorographia, 296
Aretinus de Rebus Græcorum, 160
Aretius de Reb. Hispanicis. 290.
Argens (Memoires d'Olivier d'), 287
Argenson (Mém. du Marq. d'), 261
Argyle's (Marq. of) Instructions to a Son, 80
Ariosto, Orlando Furioso, 375
—— translated, 375

INDEX

Ariosto (Vita di), 375
Aristophanis Comœdiæ, 411
—— Comedies translated, 411
Aristotle's Philosophy 76
—— Life, 76
Aristotelis Opera, 411
—— Ethica 411
—— Poetica, 411
—— Ethics and Politics translated, 411
Arlington, 381
—'s (Earl of) Letters, 250
Arlunus de Bello Veneto 294
Armenia (Travels in), 149
Armenian Bible, 3
—— Liturgy, 29
—— History, 302
Armignac (Aventures du Sire), 381
Arminius's Works, 35
—— Life, 63
Arms (Antiquity of), 330
Armstrong's Gaelic Dictionary, 354
Arnald on the Apocrypha, 11
—— and Lucinda, 387
Arnold's Chronicle, 206
Arnot's (G A W) Botany, 95
—— (H) Edinburgh, 260
Arnulphi Hist Mediolanensis, 293
Arriani Expeditio Alexandri, 411
—— translated, 411
Arnaud (G. d') de Dns Parediis, 169
Arrowsmith's American Atlas 130
Arthur's (King) Adventures, 379
Artaria, il Duomo di Milano, 139
Artemidori Oneirocritica, 411
—— on Dreams translated, 411
Artists, (Lives of), 314
Arts, 106
Arundel (Antiquities of), 213
Arundel's (Lord) Wiltshire, 214
Arundelhana Marmora, 168
Ascham's Works, 396
—— (Life of), 314
Ash's English Dictionary, 353
Ashmole's Berkshire, 195
—— Order of the Garter, 332
Asia, (Travels in) 147
Asiatic History, 300
Asiatic Isles (Hist of the), 306
Asiatic Researches, 301
—— Languages, 350
Askew Catalogus Librorum 346
Assembly's Confession of Faith, 33
Asserii Alfredi Res Gestæ, 220, 222
Aste Hydruntinæ Ecclesia, 296
Astle's Origin and Progress of Writing, 349
Aston Genealogy, 335
Astorius de Deo Brutonte, 167
—— de Alcmanis Poetæ Monum 168
—— de Diis Cabiris, 169
Astrology, 78
Astronomy, 101
Athenæi Deipnophistæ, 412
—— trad en Françoise, 411
Athenian Letters, 179
Atkinson's Costume of Russia, 121
Atkyns' Gloucestershire, 200
Atlases, 130
Atterbury (Life of Bp), 316
—— Works, 396

Attica (Unedited Antiquities of), 171
Atticæ Leges, 69
Aubrey's Surrey, 213.
—— Lives of Eminent Men, 313
Aucher's Armenian Grammar, 350
—— Armenian Dictionary, 350.
Audebert, Oiseaux Dorés, 97
—— les Mollusques, 100
Audefridi Cat Editionum Rom 342
Audubon's Birds of America, 98
—— American Ornithol Biog 98
Augustana Confessio, 32
Augustinus (A) de Familiis Rom 165
—— de Legibus Rom 164
—— (L) Sicilia Numismatica, 297
Aulisius de Gymnasii Constructione, 168
—— de Colo Mayerano, 168
Aulum (Hist. of the Emperor Shah), 303
Aurelii Victoris Hist Romana, 412
Aurelio and Isabell, 381
Aureo (J de Bado) de Armis, 331
Auriæ Notitia Hist Cephaledis, 297
Ausonii Opera, 412
—— Opuscula, 412
Aust's (Mrs) Beauties of Scotland, 190
Australian Voyages, 157
Austrian Costumes, 121
Authors (Dict of Living), 338
Autographs of Royal and Distinguished Persons, 339
Automarchi, Derniers Momens de Napoléon, 288
Avellaneda's Don Quixote, 386
Aviani Fabulæ, 423
Aylmer's (Bp) Life, 255
Ayscough's Index to Shakespeare, 392
Avscue's Warres of Eng and Scot 226
Ayton's Voyage round Great Britain, 191
Azarii Chronicon Lombardicæ, 295
Azuni, Législation Maritime, 69

Baber on the Saxon Scriptures, 10.
Baber (Memoirs of the Emperor), 303
Bacchinus de Sistris, 165
Bacci Desc Regni Neapolitani, 295
Baccius de Couviviis Ant 162
—— de Thermis Vet 166
Bach on the Icelandic Edda, 135
Bacon's (A) Elizabeth, 230
—— (Memoirs of A), 316
—— (Lord) Henry VII 228
—— Henry VIII 229
—— Works, 396
—— Apothegmes, 401
—— Essayes, 406
—— (J) Liber Regis, 186
—— (Memoirs of J), 316
—— (J.) Francis I 282
—— (R.) Opus Majus, 86
—— (History of Friyer), 316
Badiah v Leblech See Ali Bey
Bagford's Antiq of London, 206
Bagot on the Prophecies, 15
Bailey's Agriculture of Durham, 124
Baillet, Auteurs déguisez, 345
Baillie's (J) Metrical Legends, 365
—— Plays on the Passions, 391
—— (M) Lisbon, 142
—— (R) Letters and Journals, 236
—— (Capt) Prints, 120

Baily (F) on Annuities, 103
—— on Leases, 103
—— (J S) sur la Revolution Fr 286
Baker's (D E) Biographia Dramatica, 390
—— (G) Northamptonshire, 208
—— (H) Medulla Poet Rom 409
—— (Life of T), 316
Balbus de Nummis, &c 166
Baldwyn's (Abp) Itinerary, 256
Bale's Syr Johan Oldecastell, 253
Balfour's Historical Works, 262
Bilguy's Divine Benevolence, 37.
Ballard's British Ladies, 313
Balsamo's Sicily, 139
Bampton Lectures, 53
Bancroft on Permanent Colours, 87
—— Nat Hist of Guiana, 89
Bandello, Novelle, 387.
Bandinel on Christian Faith, 53
Banduri Imperium Orientale 182
Banier, la Mythologie, 66
Banks' (Sir J) Voyage to Iceland, 135
—— (T C) Dormant and Extinct Baronage, 333
Bannatyne's (G) Memorials, 316
—— Ancient Scottish Poems, 373
—— (R) Journal, 266
Baptistæ Notitia Eccles Catanensis, 297
Barbary States (Hist of the). 307
Barbati Antiquæ Inscriptiones, 164.
Barbazan, Fabliaux, 374
Barberi, Grammaire Italienne, 355
Barberius de Miseria Poet Gr 163
Barbier (A A), Examen des Dict Historiques, 312.
—— Biblioth d'un Homme de Goût, 342
—— Dictionnaire des Anonymes et Pseudonymes, 343
—— 's (J) Chesse Play, 128.
Barbouroux (Memoires de), 286
Barbour's Bruce, 263
Barclau (J) Argenis, 381
—— Satyricon, 101
—— Conspiratio Anglicana, 401
—— (R) Apology for the Quakers, 33
Baretti's Italian Dictionary, 355
—— Spanish Dictionary, 356
Bargaeus de Ædificiorum Rom evers. 164
—— de Obelisco, 164
Barisonius de Archivis, 168
Barker [misprinted Baker] on Junius, 246
Barclay s Agriculture of Northumberland, 125
Barnabæ Apostoli Opera, 34
Barnes' (J) Edward III 227
—— on Hawking, &c 127.
—— (R) Works, 36
—— (Life of), 316
Barnstaple Vindiciæ Mariæ Reg Scot 265.
Barnwell Abbey (Hist of), 197
Baronius de Monarchia Siciliæ, 296
—— de Archiep Syracus 296
—— de Panormitana Majestate, 297
Barrett's Bristol, 196
Barretier (Life of), 314
Barrington's (D) Miscellanies, 396
—— (Sir J) Own Times, 273
—— Irish Union, 273

Barrington's (Viscount S) Theological Works, 35
—— (Life of) 35
—— (Life of Bp), 35
Barrius de Laudibus Italiæ, 292
—— de Calabriæ Ant 295
Barrow's (I) English Works, 35
—— (Life of Isaac), 35
—— (J) South Africa 145
—— China, 151
—— Cochin China, 151
—— (W) on Opinions of Christianity, 55.
Barruel's History of Jacobinism, 285
Barry's (G) Orkney Isles, 261
—— (J) Works, 108.
—— (Life of J), 316.
—— (W) Guernsey, 218
Bartas' (Du) Workes, 375
Bartch, le Peintre Gravure, 120
Barthel de Sadduceis, 20
Barthelemey s Italy, 137
—— le Jeune Anacharsis, 179.
—— (Mem de), 179
Bartholini Paralytica N T illust 24
—— de Morbis Biblicis, 24
Bartholomens de Proprietatibus Rerum, 76
Bartlett's (R) Manceter, 214
Bartoli (P St) Veterum Sepulchra, 163
—— Lucernæ Sepulchrales, 163
—— Picturæ Sepulch Nasonorum, 167
—— Columna Antoniniana, 171
—— Rom Antiq Vestigia, 172
Bartolocius (J) de Voce בבב, 24
—— de Musicis Inst Hebr 24
Barton's (B S) American Tribes, 308
—— (W P C) Flora Philadelphica, 95
Baruffaldus de Armis Conviviatibus, 168
—— de Piaheus, 168
—— de Poëtis Ferrariensibus, 296
Barwick (Life of J), 517
Basilicapetrius de Metrop Mediol 293
Basilikon Doron, 70
Basire's (I) Correspondence and Life, 402
Basnage, Histoire des Juifs, 60
Bassompierre (Memoires de) 283
Bastile (History of the), 285
Batchelor's Agriculture of Beds, 124
Bates's Christian Politics 37
—— Rural Philosophy, 79.
Battely's (J.) Richborough, 203
—— (N) Canterbury Cathedral, 202
—— Archiepiscopal Hospitals in Canterbury, 203
Batuta's (Ibn) Travels, 132
Batty's (R) Cities of Europe 134
—— Scenery of the Rhine, 135.
—— Danish Scenery, 136
—— German Scenery, 137.
—— Hanoverian and Saxon Scenery, 137
—— French Scenery, 140.
—— Welsh Scenery, 256
—— (Miss) Italian Scenery, 137
Baudier's Card Ximenes, 291
Bawdwen's Domesday Book, 187, 216
Baxter (A) on the Soul, 77
—— (R) New Testament, 12
—— Works, 35

Baxter's (R) Life and Times, 256
—— (T.) Costumes of the Ancients. 121
—— (W) Glossarium Antiq Brit 185
Bay's Danish Dictionary 357
Bayard (History of the Chev), 282
Bayeux Tapestries, 194.
Bayfius de Vasculis, 162
—— de Re Navali, 163
—— de Re Vestiaria, 163
Bayle's Dictionary, 311
Bayley's (J.) Tower of London, 207
—— (F W N) West Indies, 154
Bayly's (T) Herba Parietas, 381
—— (T H) Psyche, 365
Beamblock on Tythes 75
Beatson's (A) St Helena, 308
—— (R) Naval and Military Hist 243
—— Political Index 245
—— Chronological Register, 245
Beattie (J) on Truth, 77
—— (Life of), 317
—— Theory of Language, 348
—— Essays, 358
—— Minstrel, 365
—— Dissertations, 406
Beauclerk's Catalogue, 346
Beaugue's Scottish Campaigns of 1548-9, 264
Beaulieu, Oraison Funebre de la Royne d'Ecosse, 265
Beaumarchois (l'Incarceration de), 287
Beaumelle (Memoires de M de la), 284
Beaumont's (A) Rhætian Alps, 138
—— Maritime Alps, 138
—— Leopontine Alps, 138
—— on the Rhone, 138
—— South of France, 140
—— (F) and Fletcher's Works, 391
Beauties of England and Wales, 190
—— Scotland, 258
Beaver's African Memoranda, 308
Bebelius de Sacerdotibus Rom 168
Beccaria on Crimes and Punishments, 71
Beck's Universal Character, 107
Becke's Bible, 5
Becker's German Grammar, 356
Beckett's (A) Shakespeare himself again, 392
Becket's (Thomas à) Life, 253
Beckford (P) on Hunting, 127
—— (W) Caliph Vathek, 389
—— Memoirs of Painters, 109
Beckington's (Bp) Journal, 228
Becku Monumenta Ant Judaica, 25
Beckmann's Hist of Inventions 106
Bedæ (Ven) de Nummis, &c 166
—— Historia Anglicana, 220
—— Hist. Ecclesiastica Anglicana, 251
—— Church History, 251
Bedford on Christ's Incarnation, 53
Bedfordshire Topography, 195
Bee (the), 405
Beechey's (F W) Voyage, 132
—— (and H W) Northern Africa, 144
Beere de Terr Glastoniensis, 212
Belgic Bible, 7
Belgic History, 278
Belgicarum Eccles Doctrina, &c 33
—— Poetarum Delicie, 361
Beli Rerum Hispanicarum Scriptores, 290

Bell's (C.) Anatomy of Expression, 109
—— (G J) Scottish Law, 75
—— (H N) Huntingdon Peerage, 336
—— (J) New Pantheon, 66
—— Surgery, 101
—— Travels through Siberia 152
—— Fugitive Poetry, 364
Bellahnus de Urbe Bergomi, 296.
Bellarmini Doctrina Christiana, 32
Belleforest, l'Innocence de Marie Royne d'Ecosse 265
—— Annales de la France, 279
Bellenden's Chronicles, 262
Belhamis (History of Don), 380
Bellonius de Operum Ant præstantia, 161
Bellorius in Num Apibus, 161
—— Symb Dea Syria, 161
—— Veterum Sepulchra, 163
—— Lucernæ Sepulchrales, 163
—— Vestigia Vet Rom 164
—— Pictura Sepulchri Nasoniorum 167
—— Arcus Augusti, 171
—— Rom Antiq &c Vestigia, 172
Belli de Templo Angurali, 164
—— de Pharsalici Confl. 165
Beloe's sexagenarian, 338
—— Anecdotes of Literature, 342
Belzoni's (G) Egypt, 146.
—— (Mrs) Women of Egypt, 146
Bembi Historiæ Venetæ, 293
—— (Memoirs of), 314
Ben David de Templo, 18
—— de Suffitu, 18
—— de Vestitu Sacerd 19
Benedictus Ab Petrob de Vitâ Henrici II 227
Benger's Mary Q of Scots, 264
—— Elizabeth Q of Bohemia, 276
Ben Musa's Algebra, 102
Bennet's (B) Christian Oratory, 38
—— (J) Dissenters, 256
Benson (C) on Scripture Difficulties, 55
—— (R) Corsica, 438
Bentham's (James) Ely Cathedral, 197.
—— (Jer.) Morals and Legislation, 68
—— on Government, 81
Bentley (R) on Free-thinking, 38
—— Confutation of Atheism, 51
—— Epistolæ, 402
—— (Life of), 317
—— (S) Excerpta Historica 248
Berebloc de Rebus gestis Oxon 211
Bergierus de Viis Imp Rom 166
Berkely's Works, 35
—— Life, 35
Berkshire Topography, 195
Bermuder on the School of Seville, 109
Bernard's Flaminio's Poems imitated, 365
Bernier, les Etats du Grand Mogul, 150
Beroalde, Aventures de Floride 385
Berriman (J) on I Timothy, 52
—— (W) on the Gospel, 52
—— Trinitarian Controversy, 52
Berrington's (J) Henry II 227
—— Middle Ages, 337
Berry's Encyclope dia Heraldica, 331
Berthaldus de Aris, 165
Bertius de Aggeribus et Pontibus, 168
Bertram (B C) de Repub Heb 17

Bertram (C.) Brit Ant Scriptores, 220
Berwick's (E) Lives, 312
Berwick (Maréchal de) Mémoires, 284
Besantinoi Chrestomathia. 163
Besanval (Mem du Baion de), 284
Besleri Hortus Eystettensis, 94.
Betham on Dignities, 72
—'s Baronetcage, 334
Beveridge's Works, 35
—— Life, 35.
—— Pandectæ Canonum 26
Beverinus de Ponderibus, &c 22
Beverlacensis (Alured) Annales 223
Bevy, Hist des Inaugurations, 333
Bewick's (T) Quadrupeds, 96
—— History of Birds, 97.
—— (T and J) Select Fables, 400
—— (Lives of T and J), 400
Beyer Add ad Selden de Diis Syriis, 21
—— Siclus Sacer, 22
Bezæ Nov Test Latinum, 4
—— Icones Virorum, 315
Bibles, 1
Biblical Harmonies, 1
—— *Philology,* 9
—— *Antiquities,* 16
Bibliography, 310
Bibliographical Miscellanies, 407
Bicheno's Ireland, and its Economy, 269
Bickersteth's Christian Student, 10
Biddulph on the Spirit, 38
—— on the Liturgy, 31
Bidlake on Revelation, 54
Bidpai See Pilpay
Biel de Purpurâ Lydiâ, 19 and 23
—— de Gallicimo Hieros audito, 22
Bierling de Viculam decollandam Rit Hebr 22
Bigland (J) on History, 129
—— History of Europe. 184
—— (R) Gloucestershire, 200
Bihi Historia Patriæ, 295
Billingsley's Agriculture of Somerset, 125
Bindley's Catalogue, 346
Bindrim de Gradibus Excom Hebr 22
Bingham's Christian Antiquities, 62
Bingley's Useful Knowledge, 88
—— Animal Biography, 96
—— North Wales, 257
Binning's Works, 55
Biographical History, 311
—— *Memoirs (separate),* 310
—— *Anecdotes,* 314
Biographia Britannica, 312
Biographie Moderne, 288
Biographium Fœmineum, 312
Bionis Opera 412 and 27
—— translated, 427
Biondi's Civil Wars of England, 227
Birch's Elizabeth, 230
—— Glamorgan's Transactions, 235
—— Illustrious Persons, 315
—— Royal Society, 339
Bird's Magazine of Honour, 332
Birrel's Diary 263
Biscoe on the Actes, 13 and 52
Bishop on the Arian Scheme, 52
Bishops' (the) Bible, 5
Bisset's George III 242.
Bizarus de Republ Genuensi, 293.

Blackhall on Revelation, 51
—— [misprinted Blackall] Sermons, 55.
Blacklock (Life of T), 317
Blackmanni Vita et Mirac Hen VI 224 and 228
Blackstone's Commentaries, 73
Blackwood (A), Martyre de la Royne d Ecosse, 265
—— (W) Magazine 340.
Blair's (H) Sermons 53
—— Rhetoric and Belles Lettres, 317
—— (J) Sermons, 55
—— (R) Grave 365
Blakeway's Sheriffs of Shropshire, 211.
Bland's Greek Anthology, 408
Blandforde (Henry de) Chronica, 227
Blandford ensis Bibliotheca, 346
Blaquiere s Letters from the Mediterranean, 133.
—— Spanish Revolution, 292
Blayney's Bible, 5
—— Jeremiah and Lamentations, 6
—— Zechariah, 6
Blechschmid de Theocratiâ in populo sanct 21
Blenheim Gallery, 116.
Blessensis (Petri) Historia, 221
Bligh s English Improver, 124
Bliss's Selections from Gent's Mag 340
—— Bibhog Miscellanies, 407
Blomefield's (F) Collect Cantabrigiensis, 196
—— Norfolk, 208
Bloomfield's (R) Works, 365
—— (Illustrations of), 192
—— (Life of), 192
—— (S T) Recensio Synoptica, 11
Blore's (E) Monumental Remains, 192.
—— (T) South Winfield, 198
Blount's (T) Ancient Tenures 74
—— (T P) Censura Authorum, 358
Blundell's (H.) Ince-Blundell Antiquities, 170, 171
Blunt on the V Books of Moses, 12
—— on the Gospels and Acts, 13
—— 's Ancient Manners in Italy, 138
Boaden on Shakespeare's Portraits, 394
Bocage, sur les Ouvrages de D'Anville, 344
Boccacio, il Decamerone 387
—— le Nymphal Fiesolano, 387
Bochart de Paradisi Situ, 17.
—— Geographia Sacra, 25
—— de Animalibus, &c. 8 8 25
—— Opera, 396
Bocrisus de Musicâ Hebræorum, 24
Bode, les Astres, 101.
Bodleian (Letters from the), 402
Boece's Description of Scotland, 258
—— Chronicles, 262
Boeckh's Economy of Athens, 170
—— on the Mines of Laurion, 170.
Boeclerus de Scriptoribus Gr et Lat 163
—— de Legione Romanâ, 166.
Boerhaave (Life of), 314
Boeticâ, Interp Inscrip &c. reperiuntur in Hispaniâ de, 168.
Boetius. See Boece.
Bogue's Dissenters, 256
Bohemian Bible, 7
—— Confession of Faith, 32

Boileau, Œuvres, 396
Bos (Life of J), 317
Borgelin's Denmark and Sweden, 136
—— Malta, 299
Boismontier, Mém de Marienberg, 385.
Bojardo, Orlando Innamorato, 376
Boldich Pontifex M Hebr 18.
Bolingbroke (Life of), 317
Bolton's (E) Armories, 331.
—— Hypercritica, 362
—— (Sir R) on Ireland, 273
Bombardin de Carcere, 169.
Bonanni Syracusa Antiqua, 297
Bonaparte (Louis) on Holland, 279.
—— (Galerie de Lucien), 117
—— (Luc) Charlemagne 375
—— (Campagnes de Napoleon) en Italie, 298
—— See Napoleon
Bouchamps (Mém de la Marquise de), 287
Bonfadii Annales Genuensium, 293
Bonfilii Messanæ Descriptio, 297
Bonfrerii in promissæ Terræ Chorographiam, 17
Bongarsii Gesta Dei per Francos, 182
Bonifacius de Archivis, 168
—— (Sti) Martyris Historia, 64
—— Vita, 294
Bonnani, Instrumens Harmoniques, 105.
Bonner's Profetable and necessarye Doctrine, 38
Bonney's Fotheringhay, 208
Bononiæ Descriptio Ant et Hod 294
Bonpland, les Plantes Equinoxiales, 155
—— les Melastoma, 155
Boone's Book of Churches and Sects, 34
Boot, le Perfaict Joailler 92
Booth's (D) Introd to Eng Dict 352
—— Analytical English Dictionary, 353
—— (J) Greek Primitives, 350.
Boothroyd's Pentateuch, 218
Borde's (A) Boke of Knowledge, 76
Borde (De la), Tableaux de la Suisse, 137
—— Description de la France, 140
—— Voyage d'Espagne, 141.
—— Spain, 141
—— Mem de R de Coucy, 319
Borhomia (Vital) Vita, 295
Borlace's Irish Rebellion, 272
Borlasse's Scilly Islands, 218
—— Cornwall, 197
—— Cornish Vocabulary, 354
Bormius de Igne Gentil Sac. 18
Bornitius de Synagoga Vet Hebræorum, 20
Borrichius de Antiqui Urbis Romæ Facie, 164
Bos Ellipses Græcæ, 350
Boscan Obras, 377
Boscha de Bibliotheca Ambrosiana, 296
Boschius de Patr Antiochenis, 182
Bosio, Roma Sotterranea, 139
Bosii (H) Isiacus et Janotarius, 168
—— de Toga Romana, 168
—— de Senatorum Lato Clavo, 168
—— (J A) de Pontificatu Max Rom Vet 164
—— de Pontificatu Max Imp Rom 164
Bosnia (Hist. of the War in), 300.

Bossuet, Sermons, 55
Bossuet sur l'Histoire Universelle, 176
Bossewell's Armorie, 331
Boston (Rob de) Chronicon 221
Boswell's Tour to the Hebrides, 261.
Bothwell (Mem of Earl), 264
—— (Les Affaires de Conte), 266.
Botta, Storia d'Italia, 438
—— s Italy under Napoleon, 298.
Boucher's Archaic Glossary, 353
Bouchet, Annales d'Aquitaine, 290
Bougeant, Hist de Traité de Westphalie, 184
Bouillé (Mémoires du Marquis de), 285
Bouilliet, Sermons, 55.
Boudaloue, Sermons, 55.
Bouriget s Abbey of Bec, 187
Bourgoing, l'Espagne, 141
Bourne's Newcastle, 209
Bourrienne (M de), Memoires, 288.
Bourrit s Glaciers in Savoy, 137
Boutcher on Forest-trees, 125
Bouterwek de la Literat Espagnole, 339
Bowen's (A) History of the Popes, 64.
—— Escape from Inquisition, 65
—— (W) Continuacio Scoto - Chronici, 261
Bowles's Bremhill, 213.
—— Poems, 365
Bowring on the Hung and Transylv Languages, 356
—— Lays of the Minnesingers, 377
—— Spanish Poetry, 377
—— Batavian Anthology, 378.
—— Servian Poetry, 378.
—— Poetry of the Magyars, 378.
—— Polish Poets, 378
—— Russian Poets, 378
Bowyer's Critical Conjectures on the New Testament, 14
—— (Memoirs of), 337
Boxhorni Quæstiones Romanæ, 165.
Boyce's Usurpation of Bonaparte, 288
Boyd's Florence in the 13th and 14th Centuries, 298.
Boydell's River Thames, 192
Boyer's William III 241
Boyle Lectures 51.
Boyle's (R) Works, 396
—— Life, 396
Boys' (J) Agriculture of Kent, 121
—— (T) Key to the Psalms, 12
Bracelli Orae Ligusticæ, 292.
—— de Claris Genuensibus, 292
—— de Bello inter Hispanicos et Genuenses, 293
Bradford (S) on Revelation, 51
—— (W) Portugal and Spain, 141
Bradley's Sermons, 55
Bradsole Abbey (Description of), 203
Brady's Clavis Calendaria, 159
Brambletye House, 381
Bramhall [misprinted Bramball], 28
—— Works, 15
—— (Life of Bp), 35
Brand's Popular Antiquities, 194.
—— Newcastle, 209
—— Armenian Dictionary, 350.
Brande's Journal of Science, 86.

448 INDEX

Brande's Manual of Chemistry, 87
—— Pharmacy, 101.
Brandes Fossilia, 91.
Brandt's Reformation in the Low Countries, 63
Brathwait's Barnabæ Itinerarium, 365
—— Life, 365
—— Odes, 366
Braun de Adolitione Suffitus, 18.
—— de Sanctitate Pont M 18
Bray's Surrey, 213
Brayley's Beauties of England and Wales, 190
—— Londiniana, 205
Brazil (Travels in), 156
Bree's England during the 11th century, 227
Brencmann de Legum Inscrip 70
—— de Repub Amalphitana, 295
Breton's Melancholike Humours, 366
—— Ravished Soule, 366
Brett's Collection of Liturgies, 29
Bretus de Ordine Judiciorum Rom 168
Breviarium Romanum, 30
Brewer's Lingua, 391.
Brewster (D) on Philosophical Instruments, 103
—— (J) Meditations of a Recluse 39.
—— Lectures on the Acts 35
—— Stockton-upon-Tees, 200
—— Secular Essay, 255
Bridges (B) Algebra, 102
—— (C) Christian Ministry, 38
—— (J) Northamptonshire, 208
—— Catalogus Librorum 346.
—— (N) Stenographie. 107.
Bught's Hungary, 137.
Brightwell's Revelation of Antichrist, 38.
—— Antithesis, 38
Brisman's Swedish Dictionary, 357
Brisseau-Mirbel, Hist des Plantes, 88
—— Physiologie Végétale, 92
Brissonius de Adulteriis, 161
—— de Spectaculis, 161.
—— de Ritu Nuptiarum, 165
Bristol Topography, 196
British Law 71
—— *Biography*, 312
—— Gallery of Engravings, 116
—— Gallery of Pictures, 116
—— Costumes, 121
—— Atlas, 136
—— and Foreign State Papers, 251
—— Drama, 390
—— Essayists, 405
Britton's (J) Memoir of himself, 215
—— Fine Arts of the English School, 115
—— Architectural Antiquities, 190
—— Anc Architecture of Britain, 122
—— Cat of Eng Topography, 185
—— Beauties of England and Wales, 190
—— Bath Abbey 211
—— Bristol Abbey and Church, 196
—— Canterbury Cathedral 202
—— Exeter Cathedral, 199.
—— Gloucester Cathedral, 200
—— Hereford Cathedral 201
—— Lichfield Cathedral 212.

Britton's Norwich Cathedral 208
—— Oxford Cathedral, 211
—— Peterborough Abbey, 200.
—— Redcliffe Church, 196.
—— Salisbury Cathedral, 215
—— Wells Cathedral, 212
—— Wiltshire, 215
—— Winchester Cathedral, 201
—— Worcester Cathedral, 215
—— York Cathedral, 216
Brixii Urbis Cesenæ Descriptio, 296
Brochardi Descriptio Terra Sanctæ, 17
Brockedon's Road-Book, 135
—— Passes of the Alps, 438
Brockett's North Country Words, 353
—— Newcastle Tracts, 438
Brocquiere's (B de la) Palestine, 147
Broguiart, Mineralogie, 91
Bromley's (Sir G) Royal Letters, 249
—— (H) Cat of Portraits, 120
Brompton (Jo) Historia, 221
Brooke's (A de Capell) Winter in Lapland 136
—— (J) on the Rise of Nobility, 332
—— (Lord) Five Years of James I 232
—— Life of Sydney, 328
—— (T H) St Helena, 308
—— (Miss) Reliques of Irish Poetry, 374.
Brother in-Law (the), 391.
Brouer de Niédese, 169
Brougham's (Lord) Colonial Policy, 86
Broughton's (J D) Mahratta Camp, 150.
—— (R) Ecclesiastical Historie, 251.
—— (T) Dictionary of Religions, 60
Brown's (D) Sermons, 55
—— (Memoirs of D), 317
—— (J) Dictionary of the Bible, 16
—— Stoke Newington, 207
—— (R) Agriculture of Yorkshire, 125.
—— (Sir T) Posthumous Works, 208.
—— (Life of Sir T), 208
—— Works, 396
—— (W) Christianity among the Heathen 65
Browne's (E) Travels, 134
—— (J) Moral Lectures, 52.
—— on Revelation, 34
—— (W) Poems, 366.
Bruce (the), 263
—— Genealogy, 335
—— 's (J) Travels, 147
—— Life, 317
—— (Jo) East India Company, 305.
Bruckeri Historia Philosophiæ, 76.
Brun See Le Brun
Brunckii Analecta Græc Poet 408.
Brunet, Manuel du Libraire, 312
Brunnmark's Swedish Grammar, 357
Brunton's Novels, 382 and 383
—— Life, 382
Bruti Historia Florentina, 295
Bruyere's (De la) Works, 397
Bryant's Philo Judaus, 34
—— Mythology, 66
—— on the Fall of Troy, 143
—— on Rowley's Poems, 370
Brydge's Letters from the Cont 134
—— Topographer, 188
—— Desultoria, 338
—— Censura Literaria, 313

Brydge's British Bibliographer, 343
—— Restituta, 343
—— Select Poems, 366
—— Occasional Poems 366
—— England's Helicon, 364
—— Sylvan Wanderer, 406
—— Excerpta Tudoriana, 406
—— Archaica, 407
Brydone's Sicily and Malta, 140
Brysson (Life of Geo) 269
Buch's (L Von) Norway and Lapland, 136
Buchan (Day Earl of) on the Roman Army in Scotland, 258
—— (W) Domestic Medicine, 101
Buchanan's (C) Sermons, 55
—— Christianity in India, 64
—— Colonial Eec Establishment, 255.
—— Indian Ecc Estab 305
—— (Memoirs of C), 317
—— (F) Mysore, 150
—— (G) Historia Scotica, 262
—— de Mariâ Scot Reg 264-5
—— Detection of Mary, 265
—— Histoire de la Royne d'Ecosse, 265
—— (Memoirs of), 317
—— (Anecdotes of) 317
—— Baptistes translated, 366
—— (W) Memoirs of Painting, 109
—— Scottish Surnames, 335
Bucher (F) de Velato Hebr Gynæceo, 23
—— (S F) Synedrium Magnum, 22
—— de Unctione in Bethaniâ 24
Buchoz, les Tulipes 93
—— les Jacinthes 93
Buck s (C) Philosophy of Nature, 77
—— (G) Richard III 228
—— Thirde University of Eng 207
—— (S and N) Antiquities in Eng and Wales, 190
Buckingham's (J S) Palestine, 147
—— Mesopotamia, 147
—— Arab Tribes, 148
—— Assyria, &c 148
—— (Duke of) Impeachment in 1626, 246
Buckinghamshire Topography, 196
Buckland's Reliquia Diluviana, 90
Buckler's (B) Stemmata Chichelana, 335
—— (J) Views of Cathedrals, &c 187
—— North Wales 257
Budæus de Lingua Græca, 350
Buddhist Catechism, 67
Buderi Bibliotheca Script Germ 277
Buelianı Annales 271
Buffon Histoire Naturelle, 88
—— Ornithology (Index to) 97
Buhle, Hist de la Philosophie Moderne, 76
Bulenger de Ludis Vet 161
—— de Oraculis 161
—— de Templis Ethnicorum, 161
—— de Pictura 162
—— de Triumphis, &c 163
—— de Sortibus, Auguriis, &c 164
—— de Circo Rom 165
—— de Tributis, &c Rom 165
—— de Conviviis 166
Bullu Opera, 15
Bullet, Desc Etymol des Villes, &c 131

Bullet sur la Langue Celtique, 354
Bulleaddus de Populis fundis, 164
Bullock's Mexico, 154
Bulstrode's Charles I. 233
—— Charles II 238
—— Arlington's Letters, 250.
Bulwer s Eugene Aram, 382
Bunaviana Bibliotheca, 346
Bunyan's Pilgrim's Progress, 39
—— (Life of), 39
Buonarotti (Life of Mich Ang), 317
—— Rime, 376
Burchell's South Africa, 116.
Burckhardt s Nubia, 146
—— Syria, 147
—— Bedouins and Wahabys, 148
—— Hedjaz 148
—— Arabic Proverbs, 401
Burder's Oriental Customs and Literature 26
—— Pious Women, 313
Burettus de Vet Symphoniâ, 24
Burgensis (Hist Cœnobii), 221
Burger's Leonora, 377
Burghley's (Lord) Life, 231, 317, 318
—— See also Burleigh
Burgo (J Abbatis de) Chronicon, 221
Burgos Terræmotus Siculi Descriptio, 297
Burgoyne s Works, 391
—— (Life of), 391
Burke's (E) Works, 397
—— (J) English Peerage, 333
Burlamaqui, Principes du Droit, 68
Burleigh Papers, 249
—— See also Burghley.
Burmanni (J) Flora Malabarica 94
—— (P) de Vectigalibus Rom 168
—— Poetæ Latini Minores, 409
—— (Life of), 314
Burn s Justice of the Peace, 74
—— Ecclesiastical Law, 75
—— Cumberland, 198
Burnet's (Gilb) Pastoral Care, 39
—— Own Time, 241
—— Memorial, 241
—— English Reformation, 254
—— Mem. of the Dukes of Hamilton, 266
—— (Geo) Poland, 136
—— English Prose Writers 358
—— (J) on Composition, &c in Painting 109,
—— (T) on True Religion, 52
—— Theory of the Earth, 90
Burney (Miss) See D Arblay
—— (C) History of Music 165
—— State of Music in Germany &c 165
—— List of Greek Writers 315
—— (J) Discoveries in the South Sea, 131
—— Buccaneers 131
Burns (R) Works, 377
—— Relics, 373
—— (Life of R) 318 373
Burr s Tunbridge Wells, 203
Buried in Coll Vel Cinonum Ecc Hisp 27
Buitonensis Monast Annales 221
Burton (E) on the Heresies of the Apostolic Age, 54

3 M

Burton's (E.) Rome, 139.
——— (J.) Capellæ D. Johannis Norvicia, 208.
——— Yorkshire, 216
——— Genuineness of Clarendon, 235
——— Charters, &c in the Tower, 436
——— (R.) Anatomy of Melancholy, 77
——— Curiosities of England, &c 188
——— London and Westminster, 205.
——— Wars of England, &c 236
——— Ireland, 271
——— (T.) Diary, 237
——— (W.) on Antoninus's Itinerary, 188.
——— Leicestershire, 204
——— House of Orange, 279
Busby's Dictionary of Music, 105
Busbequius's Turkey, 142
Butcher's Stamford. 204
——— Tottenham, 207
Butler's (A.) Lives of the Saints, 64
——— (C.) Horæ Biblicæ, 9 66
——— Horæ Juridicæ, 67
——— on the Revolutions of Europe, 183
——— (J.) Analogy of Religion, 39
——— (L.) on Religion, 52
——— (S.) Hudibras, 366
——— in French, by Townley, 366
——— Remains, 397
Butius de Cabdo, &c Antiq Potu, 168
Buxtorfii Concordantiæ Bibliorum, 16
——— Synogoga Judaica, 17
——— Hist Arcæ Fœderis, 18
——— Hist Ignis Sacri, 18
——— de Manna, 18
——— Hist Urim et Thummim, 19
——— de Literis Hebræorum, 23
——— de Sponsalibus et Divortiis, 23.
——— de Conviviis Hebr. 23
Buzot sur la Revolution Franc 287
Bynæus de Calceis Hebr 23.
Byron's Voyage, 132.
——— (Lord) Letters and Journals, 318
——— Works, 366
——— (Illustrations of), 366
——— English Bards, 366
Bythneister de נסכ, 24
Byzantine History, 181
Byzantius de Orbis Spectac 161

Cabala, or Mysteries of State, 249
Cabot's Memoirs, 152
Cadogan (Life of W. B.), 318
Cæsaris Commentarii, 412
——— Commentaries translated, 412
Caffin's Visit to Gondar. 147
Cagnacini Ant Urbis Ferrariæ, 294
Caius (J.) de Ant Cantabr Acad 196.
——— Historia Cantabr Acad 196
——— de Pronunciatione Græcæ et Latinæ, 350
——— (T.) Vind Ant Acad Oxon 210
Caillie's Travels in Africa, 144
Cajetani Hist Sacra Siciliæ, 296
Calaber See Quintus Smyrnæus
Calamy's Life and Times, 256
Calcagnius de Talorum, &c Ludis, 161
——— de Re Nautica, 163
Calchi Hist Mediolanensis, 293
Calcott's Musical Grammar, 105

Caldecot's Hamlet, and As you like it, 393
Caldcleugh's South America, 156
Calendarium See Kalendarium
Calepini Septem Linguarum Dict 348
Callaway on Passages of Scripture, 14
Calhachius de Osiride, 169
——— de Eleusinis Mysteriis, 169
——— de Ludis Scenicis, 167 and 169
——— de Circensibus Ludis, 169
——— de Gladiatoribus, 169
Calhmachi Hymni, &c 412.
——— translated 412
Calmet's Dictionary of the Bible, 16
——— de Psalmis Graduum, 24
——— de נסכ, 24
——— de Musica, 24
——— de Musicâ Instr Hebr. 24.
——— de נסכ, 24
Calovius de Statu Judæor Eccles 21
Calpurnius Siculus, 409
Calvini Opera, 35
——— Institutes translated, 39
——— Christian dwelling among Papists, 39
Camara de Teate Ant 295
Cambridge University (Hist of), 196
Cambridgeshire Topography, 196
Cambridge's (O.) Works, 397
——— Lite, 397
——— (R. O.) Coromandel War, 304
Camden's Britannia, 188
——— Remains, 193
——— Reges, &c. in Eccl Westmonasteriensi sepulti, 207
——— Anglici, &c Scriptores, 220
——— Elizabeth, 230
——— James I 232
Camerarii Hist Rei Nummariæ, 162
——— Hippocomicus, 163
Camoens (Mem of L. de), 318
——— Poems, 377
Campan (Mad. de) sur Marie Antoinette, 285
Campbell's (A.) Journey through Scotland, 259
——— History of Scottish Poetry 372
——— Songs of the Lowlands, 373
——— (C.) Vitruvius Britannicus, 123
——— Balearic Isles, 292
——— (G.) Four Gospels, 6
——— on the Miracles, 39
——— on Ecclesiastical History, 61
——— Life, 61
——— Philosophy of Rhetoric, 359
——— (J.) on Falconry, 127
——— (J.) Great Britain, 83
——— British Admirals, 243
——— Military History, 244
——— (J.) South Africa, 146
——— (T.) on the History of Ireland, 271
——— British Poets, 363
——— Pleasures of Hope, 366
——— Gertrude of Wyoming, 366
——— Theodoric, 366
Campion's Art of English Poesie 362.
Campistron Œuvres, 395
Campsey Ash (Hist of), 212
Camus sur la Profession d'Avocat, 68
——— sur un Livre imp a Bamberg, 341.
Candidi Comment Aquilejensium, 294.

Canon Law, 71
Canova s Works, 120
—— (Memoir of), 120
Cantacuzeni Historia Byzantina, 181
Capacii Ant &c Nicopolitanæ 295
—— Ant &c Campaniæ Felicis, 295.
—— de Balneis, 295
Capell's Prolusions, 363
—— Notes on Shakespeare, 392
Capella de Bello Mediolanensi, 293
—— de Bello Mussiano, 293
Capello, Diction Piedmontaise, 355
Capgrav ii Legenda Sanctorum, 252
Capitolinus Julius, 409
Capmartin de Chaupy, Maison d Horace, 172
Cappelli Critica Sacr., 10
—— in Lyram Davidis Gomarı, 24
Capper s Topographical Dictionary, 185
Capreoli Chronica Brixianorum, 296
Caradoc s Wales, 257
Carafæ Sicanæ Descriptio, 296
—— Montiev Descriptio, 297
Caraffa (Prose e Verse per onorare Livia Doria), 407
Cardanus's Comforte, 78
Cardenas, Hist de la Florida, 310
Cardwell on Greek and Roman Coins, 174
Carew's Cornwall, 107
Carey's Atlas, 130
Carlaverock (Seige of), 227
Carleton's (Sir D) Letters, 249
—— (Capt G) Memoirs, 291
Carlisle s Topographical Dictionary, 185
—— Grammar Schools, 187
—— Family of Carlisle 336
Carne's Letters from the East, 134
—— Recollections, 134
Carnot (Memoires sur) 288.
Caroli Biblia Hungarica, 7
Caroli Magni (Anon de Bello) contra Saracenos, 183
—— Victoria contra Manfredum, 297.
Carpzov (B D) de Pontif Hebr Vestitu, 19
—— (J B) de Crethi et Plethi, 22
—— de Nummis, Effig Moysis exhib 23
—— de Chuppa Hebr 23
—— de Sepultura Josephi, 25
—— (J G) Discalceatio Religiosa, 23
Carr's (Sir J) Holland, 141
—— Stranger in Ireland, 269
—— Caledonian Sketches, 259
—— (W) Craven Dialect, 354
Carracci's Cries of Bologna, 112
—— Galeria Farnese 112
Carradori dell Sculptura, 122
Carreræ Descriptio Ætna, 297
—— Monumenta Cataniæ, 297
—— de Signif Num Catanensium, 297
Carstare's State Papers, 268
—— Life, 268
Cartes' History of England, 226.
—— Duke of Ormond, 239
Carter's (L.) Cambridgeshire, 196
—— (Mrs F) Letters, 403
—— (M) Expedition into Kent and Essex, 244
Cartwright s Sussex, 213

Carver's Travels in N America, 154
Carwithen's View of the Brahminical Religion, 54
—— Church of England, 254
Cary's Law of Juries, 74
Carysfort's (Earl of) Poems, 366
Casa, le Terze Rime, 376
Casalius de Ritu Nuptiarum Vet 161
—— de Tragediâ et Comœdiâ, 161
—— de Trichnis, &c 162
—— de Thermis, 162
—— de Insignibus, 162
Casas, la Grèce, 143
—— la Syrie, &c 148
Casellæ de Primis Italiæ Coloniis, 292
Cassagne sur l'Art Historique, 129
Cassan's Bps of Bath and Wells, 253.
—— Bps of Winchester, 253
Castalionis (J) Varia de Antiq Rom 164
—— (S) Biblia Latina, 4
Castell's Villas of the Ancients, 122.
Castellani Heortologium, 161
—— de Menabus Atticis, 162
—— Kreophagia, 162
—— Vitæ Vet Medicorum, 163
Castellioneus (B) de Gallor Insubrum Ant Sedibus, 292
—— (J A) Mediolanensis Ant 293
Castelli Lexicon Heptaglotton, 349.
Castillon, Anecdotes Tonquinaises, &c 305
Castlehaven's (E of) Memoirs, 272
Castlemaine's (E of) Venetian War, 208
Castlenau (M de), Memoires, 282
Catalogue of those who compounded for their Estates, 236
Catechisms, 31
Catechismus Romanus 31
—— Edwardi VI 32
Catecheticæ Versiones variæ, 34
Cateret's Voyage 132
Catesby's Carolina, Florida, &c 89
Catherine II 276
—— de Medicis, 282
Cato de Agricultura 412
Catteau-Calleville, la Mer Baltique, 274
—— Hist de Christine, 275
Catullus, 412
—— translated, 413
Causeus de Insign Pont Max 164
—— Deorum Simulacra, 165
—— de Signis Milit 166
—— de Vasis, Bullis, &c 167
Coussin, la Royne d Ecosse, 265
Caxton (Memoirs of W), 341
Cavallo on Electricity, 87.
—— on Magnetism, 87
—— Medical Electricity, 101
Cave's (H) Buildings of York, 216
—— (W) Apostolici et Ecclesiastici, 61
Cavendish's Wolsey, 229
—— Metrical Visions, 366.
Cavendish Family History, 335
Cavitelli Cremoneses Annales, 293
Cavlus (Mad de) Souvenirs, 264
Caylus (Count) Method of Painting, 110.
—— Recueil d'Antiquités, 170
Cebetis Tabula 413
Cecil (Memoirs of the Family of), 317
—— See Burghley and Burleigh.

Cecil's (R) Works, 35
—— [misprinted T] Life and Remains, 318
Cedreni Compend Historiarum 181
Cellarius de Itinerario S Pauli, 18
—— de Excidio Sodomæ, 18
—— Historia Samaritana, 20
—— de Pompeii Expedi Judaicâ. 22
—— de Herodibus Hist 22
—— de Studiis Roman 168
Cellini (Vita del B) 318
—— (Memoirs of B) 318
Celsus de Medicinâ, 101
Celtic Language 354
Cenalis de vera Mensur &c Ratione 166
Censorinus de Die Natali, 413
Centlivre's (Mrs) Works, 391
Cermenati Hist Ambrosii Urbis, 293
Cervantes' Don Quixote, 388
—— Life 388
Cesarotti on Ossian's Poems, 374
Chalcocondylæ Hist Turcarum, 181
Chaldaica Paraphrasis Chronicorum, 2
Clalkhill s Thealma and Clearchus 366
Chalmers' (A) Oxford University, 210
—— Biographical Dictionary, 311
—— English Poets, 362.
—— (G) on Junius, 216
—— Caledonia, 258
—— Mary Queen of Scots, 264
—— on Shakespeare Papers, 394
—— English Stage, 392
—— (T) Evidences of Christianity, 39
—— Astronomical Sermons, 55
—— Sermons, 55.
—— Political Economy, 83
—— Civic Economy, 84
Chambaud's French Dictionary, 355.
Chambers' (J) Worcestershire Biography, 314
—— (R) Traditions of Edinburgh, 260
—— Rebellions in Scotland 267
Chambre (D), Hist des Rois, 181
—— Hist d'Ecosse, 262
—— sur l'Estat d Ecosse, 261
—— de la Succession des Femmes, 261, 265.
Champmesle, Œuvres, 395
Champollion, Pantheon Egyptienne, 66
—— Système Hieroglyphique, 107
—— l'Egypte sous les Pharaons, 178
—— Annales des Lagides, 178
—— Lettres à Blacas, 307
Chancery Proceedings in Elizabeth's reign 217
Chandler's (A) Camellia Japonica 93
—— (G) Connexion of Revelation with Society, 54
—— (R) Ilium, 143
—— Asia Minor, 148
—— Ionian Antiquities, 171
—— Inscriptiones Asiaticæ, 176
Chandos' (Lord) Speeches at Sudely Castle, 231.
—— (Life, &c of Sir John), 372
Chapman's (G) Hero and Leander, 369
—— (T) on the Roman Senate, 69
Chapone's Letters, 80
Chappe d Auteroche, Voyage en Siberie, 152

Chappel s Hudson's Bay, 152
Chardin, la Perse, 148
Charlemont (Life of the Earl of), 273.
Charles I 233
—— Entertainment in Spain 233
—— Works, 235
—— Private Correspondence, 249
Charles II 238
Charles II s Letters and Speeches, 238
—— Secret History, 239
Charlemagne, 280
Charles V 291
Charles XII 275
Charlevoix's Paraguay, 309
Charnock's (J) Marine Architecture, 105
—— Biographia Navalis, 213
—— (S) Works, 35
Chatelet's (Duc de) Portugal, 141
Chateaubriand, Itineraire à Jerusalem, 140
Chatham (Anecdotes of the Earl of) 242
—— Speeches, 246
Chatterton (Walpole's Papers relative to), 366
—— Works, 397.
—— Life, 397
Chaucer (Life of) 318
—— (Illustrations of), 321
—— Works, 366
—— Canterbury Tales, 366, 367
Chauchard's Map of Germany, &c 130.
—— Desc of Germany, &c 134
Chaudon Dictionnaire Historique, 311
Chaulepié Dict Historique, 311
Chauncey Historia Maritima, 255
Chauncy's Hertfordshire, 201
Chaussard, le Pausanias Francais, 108
Chausse (M A de la) See Causeus
Chedworth (Lord) on Shakespeare, 392
Cheke on Superstition 39
—— (Life of Sir J), 230
Chemical Philosophy, 87
Chenier sur les Maures, 307.
Cheshire Topography, 197
Chess, 123
Chesterfield's Memoirs 242
—— Miscellaneous Works, 397
Chevalier's Troy, 143
Cheyne on Health, 101
Cheynell (Life of), 311
Chiarandæ Pluti, sive Platea, 207
Chicheliana Stemmata, 316
Chifletius (C) de Antiquorum Numismate, 167
—— (H T) de Othonibus æreis, 167
—— (J J) de Linteis Sepulchri Christi, 25
—— Aqua Virgo, 164
—— Geminæ Mains Sac. Titulus Sepulch explicatus, 167
—— Portus Icius, 172
—— Lilium Francicum, 289.
—— Ampulla Remensi, 289
Chija (R) de Die Expiationis, 16
Chillingworth's Works, 35.
—— Life, 35.
Chimentelli Marmor Pisanum, 165
China (Travels in), 151.
Chinese Harmony of the Gospels, 8
—— Costumes, 121

Chinese History, 305
—— Pirates (Hist of the), 305
—— Language, 550
Chiocci de Collegio Veronensi 296
Chipping Barnet (Jesus Coll &c), 202
Chishull Inscriptiones Sigeæ, 176
—— Antiquitates Asiaticæ, 176
Chivalry, 330
Chivalric Romances, 379
Cid (Chronicle of the), 291
Choiseul-Gouffier, la Grèce 142
Choiseul, le Depart de Louis XVI, 286
Choisy, le Siam 150.
Cholera (the Spasmodic) of 1343, &c 206
Christ, Dict de Monogrammes, &c 109
Christian Religion (Hist of) 61
Christiana, Q of Sweden, 275
Christie on Elementary Worship, 66
—— on the Game of Palmedes, 128
—— on Etruscan Vases, 173
—— on Greek Vases, 173
Christmannus de Calendario Roman 165
Chronicon Paschale, 182.
—— Orientale, 182
Chronology, 158
Chrysostom (St) on Education, 80
Chudleigh's Poems, 367
Church Discipline and Government, 27
Churton's Destruction of Jerusalem, 53
—— Founders of Brasennose, 314.
Chytræi Tabula Philosophica, 162
Ciacone (A), Colonna Trajana, 171
Ciarconius (P) in Colum Rostrita Insc 164
—— in Vet Rom Kalendarium, 165
Ciccarellius de Clitumno Umbriæ Flumine, 296
Cicero (Life of) 318.
Ciceronis Opera, 413
Cicero de claris Oratoribus, 413
—— de Oratore, 413
—— translated, 413
—— de Finibus, 413
—— translated, 413
—— de Natura Deorum, 413
—— translated, 413
—— de Officiis, 413
—— translated, 414
—— de Republica, 413
—— Tusculan Disputationes, 413
—— translated, 413
—— Morals &c translated, 413
—— Orations translated, 414
—— Pleadings translated, 414
—— Letters translated, 414
—— Epistles translated, 414
Cieza, Historia del Peru, 309
Cigalini de C Plinii vera Patria, 296
Cinnamus de Reb Gestis Historia, 181
Cirino de Urbe Roma, 167
City Remembrancer, 206
Civil Law, 69
Civil War, Original Memoirs during the, 236
Clapperton's Travels in Africa, 144
—— Second Journey into Africa, 145
Claramontius de Cesenâ, 294
Clarendon's (E Earl of) Religion and Policy, 27
—— Hist of the Rebellion, 235

Clarendon's (E Earl of) Life, 235, 318
—— Charles II 238
—— State Papers, 250
—— (H Earl of), Correspondence, 250.
—— Diary, 250
—— (R N) Revenue, &c of Ireland, 270
Clarges' Charles II. 225
Clark's Body of Divinity, 40
Clarke's Voyage, 132
—— (C) on Eng Architecture, 123
—— (E D) Travels, 143
—— on Alexander's Sarcophagus, 171
—— Greek Marbles, 173
—— Life and Remains, 318
—— (J) Origin of Evil, 52
—— (J B B) Sacred Literature, 10
—— (J S) James II 240
—— Late of Nelson, 243
—— (S) on the Attributes, 51
—— on Religion, 51
—— (W) Roman, Saxon and English Coins 175
Clasenii Theologia Gentilis, 161
Classics, 408
Clater's Farrier, 127
Claudiani Opera, 114
—— Works translated, 414
Claudius de Nutricibus, &c 169
Claveringius de Maimonide, 18
Clavigero's Mexico, 309
Cleanthis Hymn, 415.
Cleaveland's Courtenay Family 335
Clede (De la), Hist de Portugal, 292
Clemencet, Histoire de Port Royal, 65
Clemens de Labro Æneo, 20
Clementis Apost Opera, 34
Clement XIV's Letters, 403
—— (Anecdotes of) 403
—— (D) Bibliotheque Curieuse, 342
—— &c l'Art de Verifier les Dates, 159
Clement's (W) Moyer Lectures, 53
Clergyman's Assistant, 27
Clericus de Poesi Hebræorum, 24
—— de Stylis et Chartis Vet 169
Clerk's Naval Tactics, 105
Clerke Archit Eccles Londini, 206
Clery, Captivité de Louis XVI 285
Clifford's (A) Tixall Poetry, 371
—— (H J) Loo Choo Vocabulary, 550
—— (Sir T et A.) Tixall, 212
—— Aston Genealogy, 335
Clinton's Fasti Hellenici, 158
Clive's (Lord) Speech, 305
Clodius de Magnâ Sagittariûm, 21
Clune Trinity Hospital, 211
Clutterbuck's Hertfordshire, 201
Cluverii Sicilia Antiqua, 296
—— Sardinia et Corsica Antiq 297
Coates (C) History of Reading, 195.
—— (J) Heraldic Terms, 334
Cobb on Christian Happiness 53
Cochorelle Tunnitaniæ Insulæ Desc 297
Cochrane's Travels in Russia and Siberia, 152
Cockburn's Swiss Scenery, 137
Codini Curop de Officiis Eccles 182
Cogan's Rhine, 135.
Coins, 173
Coke's (Sir E) Institutes, 73
—— (R) Court and State of England, 232

454   INDEX

Colæ (Barth) Vita, &c 296
Cole's (C) Affairs of State, 250.
―― (W) Pythagoras's School, Cambr. 197
Coleridge's (H N) Introd to the Greek Classics, 338
―― (T S) Biographia Literaria, 338
Colet's (Dean) Life 254
―― Convocation Sermon, &c 254
Collegians (the) 382
Collier's (J.) Ecclesiastical History, 252
―― (Jane) Ingeniously Tormenting, 406.
Collingwood's (Lord) Correspondence, 243.
Collins (A) on the xxxix Articles, 32
―― Sydney Papers, 249
―― Baronies by Writ, 333
―― Peerage of England, 333
―― Families of Cavendishe, &c 335.
―― (D) New South Wales, 158
Collinson's (J) Key to the Fathers, 54
―― Somersetshire 211
―― (T) Cumberland, 198
Collyer s (J P) Poetical Decameron, 362
―― Eng Dramatic History, 390
Colonial Policy, 85
Colquhoun on the Resources of the Brit Empire, 83
―― on Indigence, 84
―― on the Police, 84
Columbus's Life, 152
Columella de Re Rusticâ, 408
Columnæ Syracusa Antiqua, 297
Coluthi Raptus Helenæ, 414
Combe (C) Nummi Vet in Mus G Hunter 174
―― Nummi Vet in Mus Brit 174
―― Index Num Augustorum et Cæsarum, 174
―― (T) Terra-Cottas, &c in B Museum, 172
―― Anglo-Gallic Coins, 175
Commelini Flora Malabarica, 94
Commentators and Expositors of Scripture, 11.
Commerce, 85
Commines (Mémoires de), 282
Commodiani Opera, 34
Common-place Books to the Bible, 16
Common Prayer (Book of), 30
Commonwealth (English), 234
Comnenæ Alexias, 181
Comyn's Digest, 73
Conchology, 100
Concordances of the Scriptures, 16
Comet Vita Mariæ Reg Scot 265
Condamine (De la), l'Amérique Merid 155
Conde, los Arabes en España, 291.
Conde (Mém des Princes de). 284
Conestaggio, el Unione de Portugal alla Castiglia, 292
Confectionary, 126
Confessions of Faith, 31
Confucius Sinarum Philosophus, 67
Congregational Churches' Conf of Faith, 34
Congreve's Works 391

Coningsby's Manor of Marden, 201.
Connelly's Spanish Dictionary, 356
Connexions of Sacred and Profane History, 16
Connexion (the), or Matters in James's Reign, 232
Conquest in Somersetshire 212
Conringius de Politia Hebr 21.
―― de Nummis Hebr 22
―― de Studiis Liberal Rom et Const 168
Constable on Dodd's Church History, 254
Constitutiones Vet Imperatorum, 70
Consularis Epistola, 166
Consulares Fasti Anonymi, 166
Contareni (F) Historia Hetruriæ, 295
―― (G) de Mag et Repub. Venet 293
―― (V) de Frumentaria Rom 165
―― de Re Milit Stipendio, 166
Contelorius (F.) de Præfecto Urbis, 167
Contrast (the) 382
Conybeare's (Bp J) Sermons, 56
―― (J J) Secondary Interp of Sc 54
―― Anglo-Saxon Poetry, 362
―― (W D) Geology, 90
Cook's (E) Duello Foiled, 330
―― (Capt J) Voyages, 132
―― (Life of), 319
Cookes (J) Preacher s Assistant, 51
―― (W B) River Thames, 192
Cookery, 126
Cooper's (C P) Public Records, 246
―― (E) Sermons, 56
―― Muses' Library, 363
―― (J F) Notions of Americans, 154
―― Novels, 383, 384
―― (O St J) Parishes of Wemmington and Odell, 195
―― (S) Surgical Dictionary, 101
―― (T) Chronicle, 224
Coote's Law of Mortgage, 74.
Copleston on Predestination, 40
Coptic Pentateuch and New Test 5.
―― Language 349
Coquillart Poësies, 375
Coras (J de), Arrest Memorable, 75
Corbet's Poems, 367.
―― Life, 367
Cordiner's (C) Scottish Marine Animals, 98
―― North Britain, 258
―― (J) Ceylon, 306
Corippi Africani Hist Byz 182
Cornarius de Conviviis Gr 162
Cornazvanus de Vita, &c Bart Colai, 296
Corneille, Œuvres, 395
―― (Vie de), 395.
Cornish Language, 354
Cornwall (Topography of), 197
Cornewallys's Essayes, 79
Coronelli Burgomensis Ecclesia, 296
Corriano's Court of Rome, 299
Cortez, Nueva Espana, 309.
Cortusiorum (Gul et Alb) Hist Paduæ, &c 294
Coryat's Crudities, 132
Cosmo III D of Tuscany's Travels in England, 189
―― (Life of), 189.

Costumes, 121
Cotgrave's French Dictionary, 355
Cotman's Normandy, 140
Cotton (Mad.), Mathilde, 385
—— Elisabeth, 385
Cotton's (H.) Typographical Gazetteer, 340
—— (Sir R.) Henry III. 227
—— Gondomar's Transactions, 232
—— Wars with Forreign Princes, 243
Cottonian Library Catalogue, 315
Cotton's (W.) Wonders of the Peak, 198
Coucy (Mem. de Raoul de), 319
—— Chansons, 375
Couché, Galerie du Palais Royal, 117
Councils, 26
Couplet, Monarchiæ Sinicæ, 305
Courtenay Genealogy, 335
Coventry on Junius, 246
Couveras, Histoire de ses Perils, 287
Coventry New Cross, 214
Coverdale's Bible, 4
Covert's Travels in India, 150
Cowley's Voyages, 132
—— (A.) Works, 397
—— Life, 397
—— (J. L.) Solid Geometry, 102
—— (Mrs.) Works, 391
Cowper's Poems, 367
—— (Illustrations of), 196.
—— Life, 319.
—— Private Correspondence, 103
Coxe's Anecdotes of Musicians, 105
—— Travels in Russia, &c. 136
—— Switzerland, 137
—— Russian Discoveries, 152.
—— Monmouthshire, 208
—— Sir R. Walpole, 241
—— H. Walpole, 242
—— Memoirs of H. Pelham, 242
—— Duke of Marlborough, 214
—— Shrewsbury Correspondence, 250
—— House of Austria, 277
—— Bourbon Kings of Spain, 291
Coxwell (Parish of Great), 195
Crabb's English Synonymes, 353
Crabbe's Works, 367
—— (Illustrations of), 367
Craig de Repub. Lacedæmon. 160
Cramer's (J. A.) Ancient Greece, 179
—— (J. J.) de Ari ext. Triumph Secundi, 18
—— (P.) Papillons Exotiques, 99
Cranmer's Bible, 4
—— on Unwritten Verities, 40
—— on the Sacrament, 40
—— Life, 254
Crantz's Unitas Fratrum, 65
—— Greenland Mission, 65.
—— Greenland, 275
Crashaw Poemata, 361
—— Steps to the Temple, 367
Crassi Elogia Patriciorum Venet. 293.
—— de Forma Repub. Venetæ, 293.
Crausius de Succoth Benoth, 21
Craven's Tour in Naples, 4 38
Crawford's (T.) Edinburgh University, 260
—— Renfrew, 260
—— House of Stewart, 334

Crawford and Lindsay Genealogy, 335
Crawfurd's Indian Archipelago, 306
Creech's Fugitive Pieces, 406
Creichton (Memoir of Capt.), 319.
Cresolii Theatrum Vet. Rhetorum, &c. 162
Cresy's Antiquities of Rome, 171
Crests (Heraldry of), 331.
Cretin, Poésies, 375
Crevenna, Cat. de sa Bibliothèque, 346
Crevier's Roman Emperors, 180
Crichton (Life of the Admirable), 319.
Criminal Law, 74
Critici Sacri, 11
Criticism, 358
Crœsius de Velando Capite Muliebris, 23
Crofts (G.) Defence of the Church of England, 53
—— (J.) Excerpta Antiqua, 248
—— (T.) Catalogue, 347
Croker's (T. C.) South of Ireland, 269
—— Legends of the Lake, 270
—— Fairy Legends, 270.
Croly's Salathiel, 384
Cromarty's (Earl of) Gowry Conspiracies, 266
Cromek's Nithsdale and Galloway Song, 373
Cromwell's (O.) Campaigns, 236
—— (Memoirs of), 237.
—— (Court and Kitchen of Elizabeth), 238
—— (O.) Memoirs of the Cromwells, 237.
—— (Memoirs of the House of), 335
—— (T.) Colchester, 200
Crophii Antiquitates Macedoniæ, 160.
Croppy (the), 382
Crosthwaite's Maps of the Lakes, 130
Crotch, the Musician (Account of), 105
Croydon (Case of the Inhabitants of), 213
Crowley's Chronicle. 224
Croze (De la), Christianisme des Indes, 64
Cruden's Concordance, 16
Cruise's (R. A.) New Zealand, 158
—— (W.) on Dignities, 72
—— Laws of Real Property, 74
Crux In Facie Var. Loc. Rom. 164
Crusius de Nocte et Noct. Officiis, 168
Cruttwell on English Translations of the Scriptures, 10
—— Concordance of Parallels, 16
Cudworth Systema Intellectuale, 77.
Cullen (Life of W.), 319
Culley's Agriculture of Northumberland, 125
Culloden Papers, 267
Cullum's Hawksted and Hardwick, 212
Cumberland Topography, 198
Cumberland's (Bp.) Origines Gentium, 177
—— Sanchoniathon, 178
—— (R.) Spanish Painters, 109
—— (Life of Richard), 319.
—— Dramatic Works, 391
—— Observer, 405
Cunæus de Repub. Hebraeorum, 17
Cunningham's (A.) Great Britain, 241.
—— (J. W.) Sermons, 56
—— (P.) New South Wales, 158

Cunninghame on the Apocalypse, 14
—— Constitutions of Governments, 81.
Cuperi (G) Varia de Antiquitatibus Romanorum, 168
—— Monumenta Ant medita, 169
—— de Ant Græcis et Romanis, 169
—— de Patriarchâ Constant 182
Curioms de Bello Melitensi Hist 297
Curran's Speeches, 245 and 273
Currie's Memoirs and Correspondence, 319
Cursius de Civitate Castellanum Faliscorum, 295
Curtis' (J) British Entomology, 99
—— Leicestershire, 204
—— (W) Botanical Magazine, 92
—— Flora Londinensis, 94
Curtius (Q) de Rebus Alexandri M. 414
—— translated, 414
Customary Law, 71
Cuthberti (Sancti) Vita, 253
—— Legend 253
Cutt's (Lord) Poetical Exercises, 367.
Cuvier, Supplement au Hist Nat de Buffon, 88
—— Theory of the Earth, 90
—— sur les Ossemens Fossiles, 91.
—— Animal Kingdom 96
— — Fossil Mammalia 96
—— Histoire des Mammiferes, 96
—— Hist Nat des Poissons, 98
Cyrilli Confessio Fidei, 32
—— Glossarium, 351

Dacre (MS Correspondence of Lord), 431
Dalbe, Carte de Naples, &c 130
Dallas's Maroons, 311
Dallaway's (J) Anecdotes of the Arts in England, 109
—— Sussex, 213
—— Constantinople 300
—— Progress of Heraldry, 330
Dalrymple's (A) English Songs, 365
—— (D) Memorials and Letters, 249
—— Preservation of Charles II 238
—— Annals of Scotland, 263
—— Scottish Tracts 267
—— (Sir J) on Feudal Property, 74
Dalyell's Monastic Antiquities, 258
—— Ancient State of Scotland 263
—— Fragments of Scottish History, 267.
—— Scottish Poems, 373
Damadeni (Abbatis) Æs Rediv. Canusiorum 295
Damas sur l'Affaire de Varennes, 286
Damascenus de Moribus Græc 161
Dameto's Balearick Isles, 292
Damiens (Procès fait à R F), 285
Dammii Lexicon Græcum, 351
Dampier's Voyages, 132
Damponartin sur la Révolution Franc 286
Dancing, 127
Dandolo on Silk-worms, 100
D'Angeau (Memoires du Marq de), 264.
Danhaveri Pohtica Biblica, 21
—— de S S Spiritûs S Pocsi, 21
Daniel's (S) So African Scenery, 146
—— Ceylon, 150
—— History of England, 225

Daniel's (S) Defense of Rhyme, 362
—— (T) Oriental Scenery, 150
—— (T and W) Voyage to India, 150
—— (W) Voyage round Great Brit 191.
—— (W B) Rural Sports, 127
Danish History, 274
Danish Language, 357
Danorum Poetarum Delitiæ, 361
Dante, Opere 376
—— translated, 376
—— Life, 376
D'Anville's (J. B B) Ancient Geography, 129
—— Atlas, 130
—— (Notice des Ouvrages de), 344
Danzii Baptismus Proselyt Jud 21
—— de Re Militari Hebr 22
D'Arblay's (Mrs) Novels, 381, 2, and 5
Darnley (Memoirs of Henry Lord), 264
—— (the Testament, &c of Lord), 264
Darrell's Dover Castle, 203
Dart's Canterbury Cathedral, 202.
—— Westminster Abbey, 207
Daru, Histoire de Bretagne, 290
—— Histoire de Venise, 298
Darwin's Temple of Nature, 77 and 367
—— Botanic Garden, 94
—— Zoonomia, 101.
—— Phytologia, 124
—— (Memoirs of), 319
Dassovii Imagines Hebr Rerum, 18
—— de Ritibus Mezuzæ 20
—— Vidua Hebræa 23
Dates (l'Art de Vérifier les) 159
Daubeny's Vindictæ Eccles Anglicanæ 28
—— Sermons, 56
Daubuz on the Revelations, 14
Daudin. Hist des Reptiles, 88
Daulby's Cat of Rembrandt's Works, 120
Davenant on the Colossians, 13
Davies's (C P) Derbyshire, 198
—— (E) Druidical Mythology, 67
—— Celtic Researches, 257
—— Ancient British Poems, 374
—— (G) Devizes, 215
—— (J) Durham Cathedral, 199
—— (sir J) Causes why Ireland was never subdued, 272
—— Nosce Teipsum 363
—— (S) Sermons 56
—— (T.) Agriculture of Wilts, 125
—— Life of Garrick, 390
—— Dramatic Miscellanies 392
—— (W) Agriculture of N Wales 125
Davila, Guerre Civile de Francia, 282
Davison's (F) Poetical Rhapsody, 367
—— (J) on Prophecy 15
Davy's Consolations in Travel, 10
—— Chemical Philosophy, 87
—— Agricultural Chemistry, 87.
—— Salmonia, 128
—— (Life of), 319
Dawbeny's Oliver Cromwell, 237
Dawes's Sermons, 56
Dawson on the Logos, 53
De Brosses sur le Gouvernement des Romains, 81
De Bure, Bibliographie Instructive, 342.
Decker's Gull's Horn-book, 406
De Courcy's Sermons, 56

INDEX. 457

Dee's Arte of Navigation, 85.
—— (de Vitâ Jo), 212
Deering's Nottingham, 209
Deffand's Letters to Walpole, 403
De Foe's History of the Union, 241
—— Memoirs, 241
—— Novels, 382
—— Life, 382
D'Egly, Hist des Rois des Siciles, 299
Dehon's [misprinted Debon] Sermons, 56
Dekker's London's Entertainment to James I 232
De la Beche's Geology, 90
De la Fond, Dict des Merveilles, 88
Delambre, Tables Astronomiques, 104
Delandine, Dict Historique, 311
—— MSS du Bib de Lyon. 340
Deleuze, Musée d'Histoire Naturelle, 83
Della Casa, Prose e Rime, 397
Dellon's Inquisition at Goa, 65
De Loire on Spectres, 79
De Luc's Geological Travels, 90
Demetrius Phalerius, 408
Demez, Histoire Belgique, 278
Demontiosius de Sculptura 162
Demosthenis Orationes, 414
—— translated, 414
Dempsteri Kalendarium Rom 165
Denham's (D) Travels in Africa, 141
—— (Sir J) Poems, 367
—— (J F) St Dunstan's Church, 207
Denina, Revoluzione d' Italia, 298
—— Istoria d' Italia Occidentale, 298
Denis Supplementum Annalium Typog 341
Denmark (Travels in), 140
Denon's Sicily and Malta, 140
—— Egypt, 146
Denounced (the), 382
Denyaldi Rollo Normanno-Brit 289
Denys-Montfort, Hist des Mollusques, 88
De Pons's South America. 156
Depping, Expeditions des Normands, 290
Derby Gallery 116.
Derbyshire Topography, 198.
Derham s Physico-Theology, 52
Dermody's Poetical Works, 367
—— (Life of), 319
Deslon sur l'Affaire de Varennes, 286
Desmarets les Tangaras, &c 97
Desmoulins, le Vieux Cordelier, 287
Desessarts, Biblioth d'un Homme de Gout, 342
Destiny, 382
De Tott sur les Turcs, 300
De Veil Præf in Op Maimonidis, 18
Devereux, 382
De Voisin ad Prœmium Pugionis Fidei, 16
Devonshire Topography, 198
Dewar on the Atonement, 40
—— on Family Religion, 40
—— on Irish Character, &c 270
Deylingii Varia de Rebus Hebr 21 and 22
Dialogues of Creatures, 400
Dicæarchus de Vita Græcia, 163
Dibdin's (C.) English Stage, 390
—— (T I) on Engraving, 119
—— Origin of Printing, 340

Dibdin's (T I) Typographical Antiquities, 341
—— Library Companion, 342
—— Bibliomania, 342
—— Bibliographical Decameron, 342
—— Bibliographical Tour, 342
—— Bibliophobia, 342
—— Introduction to the Classics, 344
—— Bibliotheca Spenceriana, 346
Diceto (R de) Historia 221
Dickson's Agriculture, 123
Dieterici Spaisio Florum, 24
Dictionaries of the Bible, 16
Diderot (Memoires de), 338
Dietzshus de Cultu Molochi, 21
Digges' Compleat Ambassador, 249
Dilettante Society's Specimens of Sculpture 172
Dillon's Voyage, 132
Dillwyn's (L W) Botanist's Guide, 93
—— Catalogue of Shells, 100
Diodati, Biblia Italiana, 7
Diodorus Siculus de Urbe Catanæ, 297
—— Bib Historica, 414, 415
—— translated, 415
Diogenes Laertius de Vitis, &c Philosophorum, 415
—— translated, 415
Dionis Cassii Historia Romana, 415
—— translated 415
Dionysii Hymni, 408
—— Alex Orbis Descriptio, 415
—— Halicarnassi Opera, 415
—— Roman Ant translated, 415
Dioscorides, 101
Diplomatics (History of), 339
Directory for Publique Worship, 31
D'Israeli's (I) James I 232
—— Charles I 233
—— Curiosities of Literature, 337
—— Literary Character, 337
—— Quarrels of Authors, 337
—— Calamities of Authors, 337
—— on Literary Compositions, 359
—— Miscellanies, 406
Disowned (the), 382
Ditche's Drawings of Flowers, 92.
Ditton on the Resurrection, 40
Divinity (Miscellaneous), 35
Dlugossi Historia Polonica, 277
Dobie's Crawford and Lindsay, 335
Dobrizhoffer's Abipones, 309
Dobson's History of the Troubadours, 317
D'Obsonville on Asiatic Animals 96
Dods's Cookery, 126
Dodd's Church History, 254
—— Apology for his Ch Hist 254
—— Certamen Ecclesiæ 254
Doddington s Diary, 242
Doddridge's Harmony of the Gospels, 8
—— Family Expositor, 12
—— Life, 12
—— Sermons 56
Dodridge's (Sir J) Wales, 257
Dodsley's Annual Register, 184
—— Collection of Poems, 364
—— Old Plays 390
—— Fables, 400
—— Miscellanies, 406

3 N

Dodsworth's Monasticon Angl 186
Dodwell's (E) Views in Greece, 142.
—— Tour in Greece, 143
—— (H) de Parma Equestri, 172
Doederlin de Candelabris Jud 18
Doghom de Civit Bellum, 296
D'Ohsson, l'Empire Ottoman, 299
Doletus de Re Navali, 163
—— Comment Linguæ Latinæ, 352
Domerham (A de) de Rebus Glastoniensibus, 211.
Domesday Book, 187
—— for Yorkshire, in MS 436
Domestic Economy, 126
Domingue (Hist de l'Ile de St), 311
Dominis (A de) de Repub Eccles 27
Donatus de Tragœdia et Comœdiâ, 161.
—— Roma Vetus ac Recens, 164
—— Vet Inscriptiones, 176
Doudim de Rebus in Gallia, 279
Done, la Zucca, 387
Donius de utrâque Pænulâ, 165
—— de Salubritate Agri Rom 167.
Donne (Life of Dr J), 313
Donovan's British Birds, 97.
—— British Fishes, 98
—— British Insects, 99
—— Indian Insects, 99
—— Chinese Insects 99
—— Insects of New Holland, &c 99
—— British Shells, 101
—— South Wales, &c 257
Doppet (Mém du Général), 288
Dorffer de Sepulchro Christi, 25.
Dorien de Cherubims, 18
Dorsetshire Topography, 199
Dort (Account of the Synod of), 63
Douce [misprinted *Dance*], 362
Douce's Illust of Shakespeare, 393
Douglas (Ja) on the Advancement of Society, 81
—— Nænia Britannica, 192
—— (Jo) on the Miracles, 40
—— (R) Agriculture of Roxburgh and Selkirkshire, 125
—— (Sir R) Scottish Peerage, 334
—— Scottish Baronage, 334
—— (T S. N) on the Greeks, 142
D'Outrein de Velando Capite Muliebri, 23.
—— de Instr. אבלם, &c. 24.
Douza de Itinere Constantinopoli 160
Dover's (Lord) Character of Clarendon, 235
—— Frederick I 278
—— See Ellis
Downes' Lives of the Compilers of the Liturgy, 31.
Doway (the) Bible, 6
Drake's (F) Yorkshire, 216
—— (Life of Sir F), 314, 319
—— (N.) Illustrations of the British Classics, 358
—— Shakespeare and his Times, 394
—— Literary Hours, 406
—— Gleaner, 406
—— (Capt P.) Memoirs, 319.
Dramatic Poetry, 389
Drant's Sermons, 56.
Drawings, 116.

Drayton's Poly-Albion, 188
Dreschler de Citharâ Davidis, 24.
Dresden Gallery, 117
Druids, 67
Drummond's (W) Cypresse Grove, 40.
—— Poems, 373
—— Hist of Scotland, 263
—— (Sir W) Herculaneum, 171
—— Origines, 177
Drury's Adventures, 147
Drusius de Hassidais, 20
Dryander Bibliothera Josephi Banks, 344
Dryden's (J) Works, 397
—— Life, 320
Dubois' People of India, 305
—— sur la Littérature de Pologne, 339
Duca. Historia Byzantina, 181.
Ducange See Dufresne
Ducarel's Norman Antiquities, 140
—— St. Catherine's, 207.
—— Lambeth Palace, 213.
—— Croydon, 213
Duchesne Hist. Anglicanæ Scriptores à Maseres, 220
—— Hist Normannorum 289.
Dudo de Ducum Norm. Moribus, &c 289
Duels (Tracts on), 331, 433
Duff's Mahrattas, 304
Dufresne (C) Glossarium, 352.
—— Numismata Constantinop 182
—— Historia Byzantina, 182
—— (R F) de Charondæ Effigie, 162
Du Fresnoy's (C A) Art of Painting, 110
—— (J) Chronological Tables 159.
Dugdale's (Sir W) Origines Juridicales, 72
—— on Imbanking, 123
—— Monasticon Anglicanum, 186
—— Monasticon, by Stevens, 186
—— St Paul's, 206
—— Warwickshire, 214
—— Troubles in England, 236
—— (Life of), 320
—— Baronage, 333
—— Letters, 403
—— Visitation of Yorke, 432
Du Halde's China, 305
Du Hamel du Monceau, Arbres Fruitiers, 95
Duke (on the Title of), 332.
Dukeri Comi Urbis Historia, 293.
Dulcinius de Bononiâ, 294
Dumourier (Mémoires du Général), 286
—— 's Portugal, 292.
Duncan's (J M) America, 153.
—— (W.) Roman Art of War, 106.
Duncomb's Agriculture of Hereford, 124
—— Reculver and Hearne, 203
—— Archiep. Hospitals of Canterbury, 203
Dunkin's Bullington and Ploughley, 209
Dunlop's (J) History of Fiction, 379
—— (W) Confessions of Faith, &c of the Church of Scotland, 33.
Dunsford's Tiverton, 199
Dunstable Chronicle, 195.
Dunton's (J) Life and Errors, 320.
Duperron, Oupnek hat, 67
Du Piles's Art of Painting, 110

Du Piles's Principles of Painting, 110.
Dupin's Ecclesiastical Writers, 61.
Duppa on Raphael's Last Judgment, 112
Dupuis's Ashantee, 145
Durham (Topography of), 199
Dusaulx sur le 14 Juillet, 286
Dusseldorf Gallery, 117.
Dutch Bible, 3
—— *School of Painting*, 114
—— *History* 278
—— *Language*, 356
—— *Poetry*, 377
Dutens, Origine des Decouverts, 106
Duty (New) of Man, 46
Du Vivier, Grammaire Françoise, 355
Dwight's Theology, 40
—— Life, 40
—— Sermons, 56
—— N England and N York, 154
Dyce's British Poetesses, 364
Dyde's Tewkesbury, 200
Dyer s Cambridge University, 196.
Dym Antiquitates Etruriæ, 295
—— Antiquitates Umbriæ, 295

Eadmeri Historia, 223
Earle's New Zealand, 438
East India Company's History, 304, 305
Lastmead's Kirby-moorside, 217.
Eberti Poëtica Hebraica, &c 24
—— Tetrasticha Heb. in Evang 24
Eccardi Corpus Hist Medii Ævi, 184
Ecchelensi Chronicon Orientale, 182
Ecclesiastical Rites, 29.
—— *Law*, 74
—— *History*, 61
Economic Arts, 123
Edda, 67
Eddii Historia, 221
Eden's State of the Poor, 84
Edgcumb's Voyage into Ireland, 269
Edgworth de Fumont, Derniers Heures de Louis XVI, 285
—— (R L) on Professional Education, 80
—— (M and R L) Practical Education, 81
—— (Life of R L). 320
—— (M) Tales and Novels, 382
—— Comic Dramas, 391.
Edinburgh Castle (Sieges of), 266
—— Gazetteer, 130
—— Review, 140
Edmerus de Vita Anselmi, 253.
Edmondson's Heraldry, 331
—— Baronagium, 335
—— Family of Greville, 335
Edmonston's Zetland Isles, 261
Edmoustone's Upper Egypt, 146
Education, 80
Edwardi I Liber Quotidianus, 194
Edward I II and III 227
Edward II Vita à Monacho anon 227
Edward IV and V 228
Edward VI 230
Edward VI 's Journal 230
Edwards's (B) West Indies, 310
—— (G) Natural History of Birds, 97
—— Anecdotes of Painters in Eng 109

Edwards's (G) Suppl to Orford's Works, 399
—— (J) on Redemption, 40
—— on Religious Affections, 40
—— on Freedom of the Will, 40
—— on Original Sin, 41
—— (T) Canons of Criticism, 393
Effigies Virorum et Mulierum illustr 160.
Egede Grammatica Groenlandica, 357
—— Diction Groenlandicum, 357
Eggelingii Mysteria Cereris, &c 161
Egypt (Travels in), 146
Egyptian History, 307
—— Language, 349
Lhret's Jessamines, 93
Eikon Basilike et Iconoclastes, 235
Einaut-Oollah's Bahui Danush, 389.
Eisenschid de Ponderibus, &c 22
Electricity, 86
Elisæus's History of the Vartan, 302
Elizabeth of York's Privy Purse Expenses, 194
—— (Memoir of), 194
Elizabeth, 230
—— Progress through London 230.
—— Progresses 230
—— Queen of Bohemia, 233
Elliot's American New Testament, 8
Ellis's (G) Early English Poets, 363
—— English Metrical Romances, 363
—— (G A) Character of Clarendon, 235
—— Iron Mask, 285
—— (H) China, 151
—— North-west Passage, 152.
—— Original Letters 248
—— (J) History of Zoophytes, 95
—— Corallines, 101
—— (W) Hawan, &c 157
—— Polynesian Researches, 157.
Elmham (Tho de) Vita Henrici V. 228
Elmswell (History of), 212
Elphinstone's Caubal, 304
—— Afghauns, 304
Elsley on the Gospels and Acts, 13
Elstob (Memoirs of Mr and Miss), 203
—— (E) Saxon Grammar, 352
Elvenus Anon Historia, 221.
—— (Thomæ) Historia, 221.
Elzeviers (Notice des), 342
Emblems, 102
Emerson's (J) Modern Greece, 300
—— (W) Mechanics, 103
Emmii Vetus Grecia, 160
—— Aug Regina Encom 220 and 289.
Encyclopædia Britannica, 76
Enderbie's Cambria, 237
Enfield's Hist of Philosophy, 76
Enghien (Mem sur le Duc d), 286
Engineering (Civil), 123
England (Church of) Canons and Constitutions, 27
—— Articles, 32
—— See also Anglicana Ecclesia
—— Toy, 248
—— Hebrew, 164
Englcheld's (Sir H C) Vases, 173.
—— Southampton, 204
—— Isle of Wight, 204
English Bibles, 4
—— *School of Painting*, 115

460 INDEX

English Topography and Antiquities, 185
—— *County History*, 195
—— *Islands*, 218
—— *History*, 219
—— Fugitives in Spain, 231.
—— *Naval and Military History*, 244
—— *Documentary History* 246
—— *Ecclesiastical History*, 251
—— *Language*. 353
—— *Poetry* 362
—— *Songs*. 365
—— *Novels*, 381
—— *Drama*, 389
Engravings (*Collections of*), 111 and 120.
Engraving (*Art of*), 119
Enthusiasm (Nat Hist of) 41
Entomology, 98
Epicteti Opera, 415
—— Enchiridion, 415
—— translated, 415
—— (Nouv Mannel d'), 415
Epinard. l'Humanité Méconnue, 287.
Epiphanius de Ponderibus, &c 22
Epistolary Writings, 402.
Epitaphs (Collections of), 192.
Erasmus's Preparation to Death, 41
—— against War, 41
—— (Life of) 320
—— (les Apothegmes d'), 401
—— Eloge de la Folie, 401
—— Colloquia, 406
Erasto (Avvertimente di), 387.
Erastus (Hist of Prince) 387
Erdeswicke's Staffordshire, 212
Eri (Chronicles of) 271
Ernest, Papillons de l'Europe, 99.
Erskine's (Lord) Speeches, 245
Eschenbachius de Scribis Rom 109
Espriella's Letters from England, 189
Essex (Agriculture of), 124
Essex (*Topography of*), 200
Esser's Obs on Crovland Abbey, 205
Essayists, 504
Ethelwerdi Chronicon, 221
Etherige s Works, 391
Ethics, 79
Ethiopic Language, 349
Eton's Turkish Empire, 142.
Etonenses Musæ, 261
Eucheru Epist ad Faustum, 18.
Euchdis Opera, 415
Eugene of Savoy's Military History, 244.
—— Memoirs, 278
Euripidis Opera, 415.
—— Tragœdiæ, 415.
—— Tragedies translated, 415
Europe (*Travels in*), 134.
Europe (*History of*), 183.
European Kingdoms (Arms of the), 331.
Eusebii Onomasticon, 17
—— Chronicon, 61
—— Historia Ecclesiastica, 61.
Eustace's Italy, 138
Eustathii Scholia in Homerum, 417
Eutropii Historia Romanæ, 416.
Eutychii Ecclesiæ Origines, 63
Evans (J) on Christian Temper, 56
—— Life, 56
—— (T) Old Ballads, 363
Evanthius de Tragœdia et Comœdia, 161

Eveleigh's Christian Theology, 53
Evelyn's Silva, 95
—— Sculptura, 119.
—— (Life of), 320
—— Miscellaneous Works, 397
Evragm Historia Ecclesiastica, 61
Ewelme (Statuta Hospitalis), 209
Exmouth's (Lord) Expedition to Algiers, 243
Eybenius de Ordine Equestri Rom 167.

Faber's (G. S) Calendar of Prophecy, 15.
—— on the Restoration of Israel, 15.
—— on the 1260 Years, 15
—— on the Seventy Weeks, 15.
—— on Infidelity, 41
—— Apostolicity of Trinitarianism, 41.
—— on Expiatory Sacrifice, 41
—— on the Three Dispensations, 41
—— Horæ Mosaicæ, 53
—— on the Cabiri, 66.
—— Pagan Idolatry, 66
—— (R) de Re Athletica, 161
Fabian's Chronicle, 221
—— Lamentable of Edward III 431.
Fables, 400.
Fabre-d Olivet sur la Poésie, 360
Fabrettus de Aquis et Aquad Rom 164
Fabricii (G) Desc Urbis Romæ, 164.
—— (J A) Collectiones Canonum Vet Ecc et Concil 26
—— Bibliotheca Græca, 345.
—— Bibliotheca Latina, 345
—— (J L) de Ludis Scenicis, 161
Fabri Vitæ Poetarum Græcorum, 163.
Fabrotti Vers Lat. Basilikon Libri, 70.
Fabrus de Magistratibus Rom 168.
Fabularum (de Consuet) Antiquarum, 161.
Faccius de Rebus, &c. Neapolitanarum, 295
—— de Bello Veneto, 293.
Facciolati Lexicon Latinitatis, 352.
Faden's General Atlas, 109.
Fuchsius de Nummo Pylamensi, 162.
Faifeu (la Légende de P), 375.
Fairfax's (Lord) Memorials, 234
Fairford (Account of the Parish of), 200
Faith (Formularies of), 32
Falcandi Historia Siciliæ, 297
Falco Antiquitates Neapolis, 295.
Falconeri (O) Inscript Athleticæ, 161.
—— de Nummo Apamensi, 163
—— de Pyramide C. Cestii, 164
—— de Latere. 164
—— (T) on the Dissonance of the Evangelists, 54
—— (W) on the Influence of Climate, &c 82
—— Marine Dictionary, 106
—— Shipwreck, 367.
—— Life, 367
Falconet on the Assassins of Syria, 301.
Falconry, 127
Falkland (Life of Lady), 320
Falle's Jersey, 218
Family Lecturer, 56
Fanshawe (Mem. of Lady), 320
Fant Scriptores Suecici 275.
Farapha de Rebus Hispanicis, 290.

INDEX. 461

Faræ Sardois Historia, 297.
Farinæ de Bergomi Origine, 296
Farington's Delineations of the Lakes, 191.
—— River Thames, 192
Farmer on the Learning of Shakespeare, 392 and 393
Farquhar's Works, 391.
Farrer on the Character, &c of Christ, 53.
Farnerv, 127
Fathers, 34
—— of the English Church, 37
Faulder's Trial, 337
Faulkner's Chelsea, 207
Faunus de Ant Urbis Romæ, 167
Fauriel, Chants Popul de la Grece, 360
Fausset's Claims of the Established Church, 54
Fausse-Landry. les Journées de Septembre, 286.
Faux's America, 154
Fayette (Memoires sur La), 286
Fazellus de Rebus Siculis, 296
Fazoldi Græcorum Vet. Hierologia, 161
Tea, Description de Rome, 139
Federici Tipografia Volpi Cominiana, 342.
Feithin Antiq Homericæ, 161
Felibien, Principes de l'Architecture, 122
Fell Rerum Anglicarum Scriptores, 221.
Fellowss's Historical Sketches, 235
Felton on Christian Faith 52
Fenelon (Life of Bp), 320
Fenn's Paston Letters, 248
Fenton's Pembrokeshire, 257
Ferdousee's Shah Nameh, 302.
Ferguson's (A) Roman Commonwealth, 180.
—— (J.) Astronomy, 104
Ferhang Chaouri, 350.
Ferishta's Hindostan, 303
—— History of Dekkan, 304
Fermin, Description de Surinam, 156
Fernandez's Spanish Grammar, 356
Ferne's Blazon of Gentrie, 332
Feron, Connestables, &c de France, 289
Ferrar (Life of N), 320
—— See also Gidding
Ferrarius (F B) de Vet Acclamationibus, 165
—— (J B) Hesperides, 95
—— (O) de Origine Romanorum, 163.
—— de Re Vestiaria, 163
—— de Lucernis Sepulch 167
—— de Pantomimis, 167
—— de Balneis, 169
—— de Gladiatoribus, 169.
—— de Laudibus Urbis Patavii, 294.
Ferrerio Palazzi di Roma, 139
Ferri Apparatus Statuarum in Cumis, 295
Ferriar's Illustrations of Sterne, 399
Ferrieres (Mémoires du Marquis de), 286.
Feudal Law, 69.
Feijoo's Essays, 406
Field's New South Wales, 158
Fielding's Works, 397.
—— Life, 397
Fiennes's Monarchy asserted, 238
Fierberti Oxon. Acad Descriptio, 210
Fife (Chronicle of), 266.

Filangieri, Sienza della Legislatione, 68.
Filz de Roys (le Livre de trois), 380.
Finance, 85.
Finati's Life and Adventures, 146.
Finch on Christianity, 53
Findlay's Scottish Ballads, 373.
Fine Arts, 107
Finett on Ambassadors, 83
Finlayson's Siam and Hué, 151
—— Life, 151.
Fiori Hist di Isabella et Aurelio, 388.
Fire of London, 205 and 206
Firenzuola, Prose, 397
Fischer sur Guttenberg, 341.
Fisher's (A) Arctic Regions, 153
—— (Life of Bp John), 254
—— (T) Paintings in Stratford Trinity Chapel, 214.
Fishing, 128
Fitz-Geffrey's Sir F Drake, 319
Flaminus (Memoirs of M A) 314
Flavel's Works 33
Flavius de Origine Venetorum, 293.
Flaxman's Compositions, 120
Flecknoe's Characters, 80
Fleetwood Chronicon Preciosum, 85
—— English Coins, 175
Flemish School of Painting, 114.
Fletcher. See Beaumont
Fleury in Poesin Hebræorum, 24.
—— Manners of the Israelites, 25.
Flinders' Terra Australis, 158
Flodden Field (Battle of), 229.
—— a Poem, 367
Florence Gallery, 117.
Florentii Wigorn Chronicon, 222.
Florentinum Museum, 170
Florian, Numa Pompilius, 385
—— Gonsalve de Cordoue, 385
—— Galatee, 385
Florio's World of Words, 355.
Flori Historia Romana, 116.
—— de Bello Italico, 296
Folard, Cours de Science Militaire, 106.
Folietæ Varia de Historia Italiæ, 292
Folkes's English Coins, 175
Fontaine (De la), Œuvres, 397
Fontanini (G) Biblioteca Italiana, 343
—— (J.) de Corona Ferrea, 293
—— de Horta Coloniæ Etrusc 295.
Fonticulani Bellum Biaccianii, 295
Foote's Works, 391
Forbes' (D) Culloden Papers, 267
—— Memoirs, 267
—— (J) Oriental Memoirs, 305
—— (P) Letters and State Papers, 249
Forbin (le Comte de), le Levant, 144
Forby's Last Anglian Vocabulary, 353
Force (Mad de la), les Fees, &c 385.
—— Hist de Bourgogne, 386
Forcellini Lexicon Latinitatis, 352
Ford's Fame's Memorial, 367
—— Dramatic Works, 391
Forduni Historia, 221
—— Scoti-Chronicon, 261
Foreign Law, 75
—— *Biography*, 314
—— Quarterly Review, 340
Forster's (E) British Gallery, 116.
—— (J R) on India, 149.

Forster (T) on Atmospheric Phenomena 86
Forsyth's (J) Italy, 138.
—— (R.) Beauties of Scotland, 258
—— (W) on Fruit-trees, 126
Fortunate Union, 389.
Fosbrooke's Ency of Antiquities, 159.
—— Foreign Topography, 159
—— British Monachism, 187
—— Gloucestershire, 200
Foscolo (Ugo) on Petrarch, 376
Fosse (De la), Théâtre, 395.
Fossils, 91.
Foster's History of Enthusiasm, 41
—— Saturday Night, 41
—— Essays, 406
Fotheringhay (Hist of), 208.
Fountain's Abbey (Views of), 438
Fourmont, l Origine des Anciennes Peuples, 177
Fournier, Dict de Bibliographie, 342
Fowlers (J) Tobago, 311
—— (W) Mosaic Pavements, Stained Glass, &c 190
Fox's (C J) James II 240
—— Speeches, 246
—— (Character of), 320
—— (Memoirs of), 320
—— (J) Martyrs, 252
—— (Memoirs of Sir S), 239.
Framlingham Castle (Hist of), 213
Francastorius (Memoirs of H), 314.
France (Discipline des Eglises Reformées de), 33
France (Travels in), 140.
Frances's (King of) Manuscripts, 346.
Francica Evangelia 4
Francis I's Life, 282
—— II (Memoirs of), 264
Francklin's Shah Aulum, 303
Françoise (Dict de l'Académie), 355.
—— (Bibliothèque), 406
Frank's Cat Bibliothecæ Bunavianæ, 346
Frankland's Constantinople, 142
Franklin's (B) Works, 397
—— Life. 397
—— (Sir J) Journeys to the Polar Sea, 153
—— (W) Persia, 149
Franks on our Lord's Discourses, 55
—— Apostolical Preaching, 55
Frann's Insurrections of Protestants, 63
Fraser's Khorasan, 149
—— Himala Mountains, 150
Frederick II (Late of), 278 and 314
Freheri Decisionum Areopag Sylvula, 160
—— Cecropistromachia, 166
—— de Re Monetaria Rom. 166.
Frehnshem de Calido Potu, 162
French Bibles, 7
—— School of Painting, 113
—— Gallery of Pictures, 117.
—— Costumes, 121.
—— Charity, 237
—— History, 279
—— Revolution, 285
—— Campaigns (Hist. of the) 288
—— Provincial History, 289
—— Language, 354
—— Poetry, 374

French Novels, 385
—— Drama, 394
Freron, de la Réaction Royale, 288.
Fresnoy See Du Fresnoy
Friar Rush, 384.
Frisch, les Oiseaux d'Allemagne, 97
Froissardi Historia, 220.
Froissart, Chronique, 281
Frontinus de Aquæductibus Rom. 164
—— Opera, 416
Fry's (E) Pantographia, 348
—— (J) Legend of Mary Queen of Scots, &c 363
Fryth's Works, 36.
—— Life, 36
Fuller's Pisgah Sight of Palestine, 6
—— Holy and Profane States, 41.
—— Holie Warre, 183
—— University of Cambr 196.
—— Church History, 252
—— Worthies, 313
Fulman Rerum Anglicarum Scrip 221.
Funeral Ceremonies, 333.
Funnel's Voyages, 132
Furneaux's Voyage, 132
Fuscus de Situ Ora. Illyrici, 297.
Fuseli's Lectures on Painting, 110

G (A) de Armis Romanis, 168.
Gabriel on White's Bampton Lect 53.
Gaelic Bible, 7
Gaelic Language, 354
Gnetc (Mémoires, &c du Duc de), 288
Gage's Hengrave, 214
Gagnier de Nummis Samaritanis, 23
Gainsforde's Earl of Tirone, 272.
Galateus de Situ Japygiæ, 295.
Gale (R.) on the Roman Ways, 185
—— Honor de Richmond 218
—— (T) Court of the Gentiles, 41
—— Hist Britannicarum Scriptores, 221.
Galeanæ (Reliquiæ), 204
Galfredus Monumetensis, 220
Galland, Pelerinage de la Mecque, 66
Gallatin, Sermons, 56
Galleries of Paintings, 116.
Gallicanus Vulcatius 409
Gallorum Poetarum Delitiæ, 361
Gallucius de Bello Belgico, 279
Galli Fragmenta, 413
Galluzzi, Histoire de Toscane, 293
Galt's Voyages, 133
—— Novels, 381-4.
Galvanism, 87
Gambrini Geneal. Ranzoviana, 336
Gandy's Pompeiana, 171
Ganganelli's Letters, 403
Ganilh, sur l'Économie Politique, 83.
Garcilaso de la Vega, Obras, 377.
—— translated, 377.
—— (Life of), 377.
Gardening, 123
Gardiner on the Beatitudes, 13
Gardner's Dunwich, 213.
Gargilius Martialis, 408
Garibay, Historia de Espana, 291
—— Illustraciones Genealogicos, 334
Garmann de Panc Lugentium, 25
Garnet's Tour through the Highlands 259

INDEX. 463

Garrett, de la Poesia Portugueza, 377
Garrick's Poetical Works, 367
—— Life, 390.
—— Private Correspondence, 403
Garufii Lucerna Lapidaria, 294
Gascoigne on English Verse, 362.
Gassendi Kalendarium Rom expositum, 163
Gastrell on the Trinity, 41.
—— on Revelation, 51
Gatti Hist. Gymnasii Ticenensis, 293
Gaudence de Lucques, 386
Gaudin, les Finances, &c de la France, 85
Gaunt (Life of J. Duke of), 318
Gauntlett on the Revelation, 14
Gauricus de Sculpturâ, 162
Gay's Fables 400
Gaza de Mensibus Atticis, 162
Gebelin, le Monde Primitif, 348
Ged (Memoirs of W), 341
Gedæus de Instr Circums à Zipporâ et Josuâ adhibito, 21
Geddes's Church of Malabar, 64
—— Church of Ethiopia, 64
Geiger de Hillele et Sammai, 20.
Gejer de Hebræorum Luctu, 24
Gell's (W) Itinerary of Greece, 143.
—— Troy, 143
—— Pompeiana, 171
Gelli (A) Noctes Atticæ, 416
—— translated, 416
Gemiticensis (Gul) Hist Angl 220
—— Hist Normannorum, 289
Gemmæ Antiquæ ex Thes Mediceo, 173.
Gems, 173
Genealogical History, 333
General Dictionary, 311
Genes di Hita, las Guerras de Grenada, 291
Genesii Historia Byzant 181.
Genevan Bible, 5
Genlis' (Mad de) Memoirs, 338
—— l'Influence des Femmes Littéraires, 339
Gent's (T) York, 216
—— E Window of York Cathed 216
—— Kingston upon Hull, 217
—— Rippon, 218.
—— Life, 438
Gentilis (A) de Actoribus, 161
—— de Jure Publico Romano, 168
Gentleman's Magazine (Selections from), 340
Geoffroi S. Hilaire, Hist. des Mammiferes, 96
Geography, 129
Geology, 90
Geoponica, 409
George I II III 241-2
Georgel, Histoire du xviii. Siècle, 184
Georgiviez de Imp Turcarum, 300
Gerarde's Herball, 92
Gerbelii Græciæ Descriptio, 160
Gerdesii Historia Reformationis, 63
—— Scrinium Antiquarium, 63
—— Reformatio Italiæ, 63
German Bible, 7
—— *School of Painting*, 115
—— Prince's Tour of England, 189
—— *History*, 277

German Language, 356
—— *Poetry*, 377.
—— *Novels*, 388
—— *Drama*, 396.
Germanorum Poetarum Delitiæ, 361.
Germany (Travels in), 137
—— (Notes on), 137.
—— (Invasions of), 277.
Gerundensis de Rebus Hispanicis, 290
Gervasii Dorab Historia, 221
Gesenius's Hebrew Lexicon, 349
Gesneri Thesaurus Linguæ Romanæ, 352.
Gesta Romanorum, 379
Ghemarâ Hierosolymitanica Tractatus varii, 19, 20, 22, 23
—— Babylonica Tract varii, 20
Ghilini Descriptio Lacûs Larii, 293
Giannone, Istoria di Napoli, 299.
—— Opere Posthume, 299
Giardæ Icones Symb. Bib. Alexandr 296
Gibbon's Roman Empire 182
—— Miscellaneous Works, 397
—— Life, 397
Gibson's (E) Pastoral Letters, 42
—— Codex Juris Eccles Anglicanæ, 74
—— Chronicon Saxonicum, 222
—— (M) Churches of Door, Home-Lacy, &c 201.
—— (T) Bp of Rome's Blessynge, 232
Gidding (Protestant Nunnery at Little), 202
Gifford's (J) History of France, 279
—— (T) Zetland Isles, 261
—— (W) Baviad and Mæviad, 367
Gilbert's St Neot's Church, 198
Gildas de Excidio Britanniæ, 220, 221
Gill's Exposition of the Bible, 11
Gilles, Annales de France, 279
Gillies's (J) Ancient Greece, 179
—— Hist of the World, 179
—— (R P) Childe Alarique, 367
Gillingwater's Lowestoffe, 213
Gilly's Waldensian Researches, 62
Gilpin's Exposition of the New Test 12.
—— Sermons, 56
—— on the Picturesque, 110
—— Lakes of Cumberland, &c 191
—— Cambridge, Norfolk, &c 191
—— Coasts of Hampshire, &c 191.
—— Western Parts of England, 191
—— Isle of Wight, 191.
—— New Forest, 201
—— River Wye, 257
—— Highlands of Scotland, 259
—— Lives of the Reformers, 312.
Giovanni, il Pecorone, 387
Gipsies (History of the), 400
Giraldi Cambrensis Historia, 220.
—— Itinerarium, 256
—— (Life of), 256
—— Ireland, 271.
Gisborne's Christian Religion, 42
—— Sermons, 56
—— Duties of Men, 80
—— Duties of Females, 80
—— Walks in a Forest, 367
—— Rothley Temple, 368
Giuli Romani Adventus Sigismundi, 112
Gladwin's Persian Moonshee, 349
Glacser de Instrument Hebr Musicis, 24

Glamorgan's (E of) Transactions, 235
Glanvil's Sadducismus Triumphans, 78
Glanvilla (Barth de) de Proprietatibus Rerum, 76
Glastoniensis (Jo) Chronica Glaston 212
Glastonbury (History of) 211, 212
Glemona (de), Dictionnaire Chinoise, 350
Glencoe (Massacre of), 267
Glover's Collection of Arms, 431
Gloucestershire Topography, 200
Gloucester's (Robert of) Chronicle, 223
Glycæ Annales, 181
Gnomici Poetæ Græci, 408
Goar Rituale Græcum, 29
Goddard (C) on Religious Evidence, 54
—— (G) Journal, 237
Godn Chronica, 294
Godstowe Nunnery, 210
Godstovianum Chronicon Anon 200
Godwin (E) Regni Henrici VIII Ed. VI et Mariæ, 229
—— (F) de Præsulibus, &c Angliæ, 253
—— Episc. Bathensium, &c 253.
—— (T) Moses and Aaron, 25.
—— Roman Antiquities, 170
—— (W) on Population, 84
—— English Commonwealth, 237
—— Novels, 381, 383
Goes (Dam à), de Rebus Hispanicis, 290.
Goethe (Memoirs of), 321
—— Goëtze, 396
—— Faust, 396
Goetz de Molis et Pistrinus, 23
Goezius de Osculo, 23
Goffe's Plays, 391
Goguelat (Mémoires du Baron de), 286
Gold-headed Cane, 101
Goldoni Commedie, 395
Goldsmith's Works, 397.
—— Life 397
Goltzii Sicilia Numismatica, 297
Gomari Davidis Lyra, 24.
Gombauld's Endymion, 386
Gomerius de Gestis Ximinii Cardinalis, 290.
Gommara (Lopez de) Conquista de Mesico, 309
—— Conquest of the West India, 309
Gooch's Agric of Cambridgeshire, 121
Good's Book of Job, 6
—— Song of Songs, 6
—— Book of Nature 88
—— Study of Medicine, 101
Goodall Introd ad Hist Scotorum, 261
Goodwini Moses et Aaron, 17
—— de Theocratià Israelis, 21
Gordon's (J.) Ireland, 272
—— Irish Rebellion, 273
—— (Sir R) Earldom of Sutherland, 335
Gore's Voyage, 132
—— (T) Catalogus Script. Herald 330
Gorham's Eynesbury and St Neot's 202
Gorii Monument Lava, Angustæ, &c 169
—— Nummi in Thes Ducis Etruriæ, 174
Gothica Evangelia, 3
Gothicarum, &c Scriptores, 274
Gothic Language, 357
Gothofredi Fontes Juris Civilis, 69
Gough's Topography, 185
—— Alien Priories, 187
—— Sepulchral Monuments, 192

Gough's History of Pleshy, 200
—— Croyland Abbey, 205
—— Londinium Triumphans, 206
Goulart, Hist. de la Ligue, 282
Gould's Birds of Europe 97
—— Himalayan Birds, 93
Gower (Jo) de Confessione Amantis 368
—— (Todd's Illustrations of), 321
—— (Lord L) Catherine of Cleves, 395
Gowrie Conspiracies, 266
Goynæus, de Situ Istriæ, 294.
Gozze de Inscript Columnæ Rostratæ, 298
Graberg de Uncturâ Christi 24
Gradonicus de Siclo Argenteo, 22
Grævii Thesaurus Antiquitatum Græcarum, 160
—— Thesaurus Antiquitatum Romanarum, 163
—— Thesaurus Antiq Italiæ, &c 292
Grahgny, Œuvres, 397.
Grafton's Chronicle, 225
Graham's (M) India, 150
—— (T J) Domestic Medicine, 101.
Grahame's (J) Poems, 368.
Gralpy (Life, &c of Sir J. de), 372
Grammar, 348
Grammont (Memoires de), 239
Granby 382
Grand (le) Partenopex de Blois, 381
Granger's Biographical History of England, 315
Grant's (C) Mauritius, 308
—— (Mrs) Highland Superstitions, 259
—— Letters from the Mountains, 403
Granville's St Petersburgh 134
Grapius de Percussione Sepuli 23
Grasseri Antiquitates Nemausenses, 167
Gratarolus on the Health of Magistrates, 101
Gratius Faliscus, 409
Grattan's Novels, 383
Graunt on the Bills of Mortality 206
Graves (R) on the Pentateuch, 12
—— Antoninus, 410
—— (T) Cleveland, 217
Gravinæ Origines Juris Civilis, 69
Gray (A) on the Parables, 13
—— (J E) Indian Zoology, 96
—— (R) Key to the Bible, 9
—— Jewish and Heathen Authors, 26
—— Principles of the English Reformation 53
—— (T) Poems, 368
—— Works 397
—— Life, 368, 397
Gray's Inn Journal 403
Grazzini il Lasco, 387
Grebner his Prophecy 78
Greece (Travels in), 142
Grecian History 179
Greek Testaments, 1
—— Bibles, 2
Greek Language 350
—— *Romancers* 379
Green's (V) Worcester, 215
—— Disc of King John's Body 216
—— (W) Guide to the Lakes, 169
Greenhouse Companion, 92
Greenland (History of), 274

Greenland (Language of), 357.
Gregorii Historia Byzantini, 181
Grellman, Histoire de Bohemians, 300
Grenius de Rusticatione Rom 167
—— de Villarum Rom Structura, 167
Gresham (Life of Sir T), 313.
Gresset, Œuvres, 398
Greswell (G P) Bibliotheca Chethamensis, 345
—— Biographical Memoirs, 314
—— Parisian Typography, 342
Greville (Sir F) Lord Brooke's Remains, 368
—— (R K) Icones Filicum, 93
—— Scottish Cryptogamic Flora, 93
—— Algæ Britannica, 93
Greville Genealogy, 335
Grey's (Lady Jane) Remains and Life, 398
—— Life and Times, 230
—— (R) Memoria Technica, 107
—— (Z) on Neal's Puritans, 256
—— Notes on Shakespeare, 393
Grey and Ruthen Baronies, 336
Gribalde on Francis Spira, 42
Grier's Councils of the Church, 26
Griffin's Fidessa, 368
Griffith's (A F) Bibliotheca Anglo-Poetica, 344.
—— (E) Cuvier's Animal Kingdom, 96
—— (M) See Alford
Grimstone's History of the Netherlands, 278
Grimm (Memoires du Baron de), 338
Grindal (Abp) Life, 255
Groddek de Cæremoniâ Palmarum, 19
—— de Judæis Præputium attrah 21
—— de Heb. Purgationibus Castitatis, 23
Gronovius (J F) de Museo Alexand. 162
—— (J G) Thesaurus Antiquit Græca-rum, 160
—— (L A) Bibliotheca Regni Animalis, 87
—— (L T) Colossus Tib Cæsaris, 161
Grose's Antiquities of Eng and Wales, 190
—— Military Antiquities 243
—— Antiquities of Scotland 259
—— Antiquities of Ireland 269
—— Dict of the Vulgar Tongue, 353
—— Provincial Glossary, 354
Grosier, Description de la Chine, 303
Grotius de Veritate Rel Christ 42
—— de Baptismo et Eucharistia, 12
—— de Bello ac Pace, 68.
—— de Mare Libero, 68
—— Historia Gothorum, &c 274
—— Annales Belgici, 278
Grsepius de Salo et J dento Hebr 22
Gruchius de Comitiis Romanorum, 163
Gruner de Oblatione Primitiarum, 19
Gruteri (J) Inscriptiones Romanæ, 176
—— (W) Deliciæ Poetarum Gall Germ et Belg 361
Gundet sur les Girondins 287
Gualtern Siculiæ et Insularum adjacentium Tabula, 297
Guardian, 105
Guarnerii Hist Catanensis, 297

Gudius de Hebr. Obstetricum Origine, 23
Guiana (Travels in), 156
Guicciardini, Istoria d' Italia 298
Guignes (De), Histoire des Huns, &c 301
—— Dictionnaire Chinoise, 350
Guildford Trinity Hospital, 213
Guinguiné, Hist Litteraire d'Italie, 339
Guirani Numismata Nemausensium, 167
Guiscardi (Rob) Ducis Calabriæ, Vita, 296
Guizot, Synonymes Françaises 355
Guhelmus de Magistratibus Reip Rom 168
Gunpowder Treason, 232
Gunn on the Harp, 105
Gunton's Peterburgh, 203
Guidon on infidelity, 52
Gurnal's Christian Armour, 42
Gustavus Adolphus (Life of), 275.
Gustave Wasa (Histoire de), 275
Gutch's Collectanea Curiosa, 193
Gutherleth de Mysteriis Deorum Cabi 169
—— in Monumentum Herne, &c 169
—— in Ant Inscript Gr Smyrna, 169
—— de Solus Martis Sacerd 169
Gutherus de Vet Jure Pontincio Rom 164
—— de Jure Manium, 167
—— Choartius Major 167
—— de Officiis Domûs Augustæ, 168
Guttenberg (Monumens Topog de J), 341
Guy's (de) Greece, 144
Gwedir Family, 336
Gwilhin's Heraldry, 331
Gyllius de Bosphoro Thracio 160
—— de Topogr Constantinop 160
Gymnastic Arts, 127
Gyraldus (C. J B) de Ferrariâ, &c 294
—— (L G) de Comœdiâ, 161

Habington's (J) Edward IV 226
—— (W) Castara, 368
Haco's Expedition against Scotland, 262
Hadar Insula Melitæ, 297
Hahz (Life of), 321
Hiphtzi Ghazala, Reviczki, 378
Haguelon Calendarium Trilingue, 162
Hagustaldensis (Jo. Prior) Historia, 221
—— (Rogerus Prior) Historia, 221
Hahn de Usu Chronol in Jure, 70
Hailes (Lord) See D Dalrymple
Haji Khalifeh's Wars of the Turks, 300
Hakewell's Italy, 138
Hakluyt's Collection of Voyages, 131
Haldersonii Lexicon Islandico Danicum, 357
Hale's (Sir M) Works, 398
—— Life, 398
—— (W) Chronology 158
Halfpenny's York Cathedral, 216
Halhed's Gentoo Laws, 48
Halifax (S) on the Prophecies, 15
—— (Marq of) on Edward I and II &c 227
Hall's (B) Voyages and Travels, 131
—— Corea and Loo Choo, 151

Hall's (B.) North America, 153.
—— Etchings of N. America, 153.
—— Chili, Peru, and Mexico, 157.
—— (C. H.) on the Fulness of Time, 53.
—— (Sir J.) on Gothic Architecture, 122.
—— (Jos.) Works, 35
—— Life and Sufferings, 35
—— Horæ Vacivæ, 80
—— Satyrs, 368.
—— (R.) Works, 35
—— Life, 35
Hallam's Europe in the Middle Ages, 163
—— English Constitutional History, 245
Halle's Chronicle, 228
Hamilton (A.) Mem. de Grammont, 239
——'s (C.) Queen Anne, 241
—— Rohilla Afghans 304
—— (E.) Popular Essays, 77.
—— Novels, 382 383
—— (F.) Mysore, 150.
—— (H.) Works, 398.
—— Life, 398
—— (R.) on the Progress of Society, 83
—— (T.) Antar, 388
—— (W.) History of Medicine, &c. 101
—— Ægyptiaca, 116
—— F. India Gazetteer, 150.
—— Hindostan, 150
—— Lanark and Renfrew, 260
—— Antrim, 270
—— Hand-Book, 349
—— (Sir W.) Campi Phlegræi, 91
—— Etruscan Antiquities, 173.
—— Ancient Vases, 173
—— Outlines from Ancient Vases, 173
—— (Memoirs of J. and W. Dukes of), 266
Hampden and his Times 231
Hampshire Topography 201.
Han (the Sorrows of), 396
Hanbury's Ethiopia, 147
Hancarville (D') sur les Arts de la Grèce, 159
—— on Etruscan Antiquities, 173
Hancock on God, 51
Handel (Anecdotes of), 105
Hannekenius de Cura Domestica Rom 167
Hansenius de Jurejurando, 165
Hardouin de Nummis Herodiadum, 21.
—— de Nummis Samarit 23
Hardwicke's (L. of) Athenian Letters, 179
—— State Papers 218
Harding's Chronicle, 224
Hare Psalmorum Liber, 24
Haremberg Oculus Moysis et Christi, 17.
—— de Vocibus תושיה, &c. 19
—— de Domo inducta Minio, 23.
—— de רככב, רככב, &c. 23
Hargrove's Knaresborough, 217
Harkenroth de Monte Sublimi, 17.
—— de Λιβανου Hesychii, 17
—— de Ænone prope Salim, 18
—— de Rachele, 18
Harleian Catalogue, 345
—— Miscellany, 408
Harley Family History, 335.
Harmer on various Passages of Scripture, 26.

Harmonies of the Bible, 8
Harpsfeldii Hist Angl Ecclesiæ, 251.
Harraden's Cantabrigia depicta, 197
Harrington's (J.) Works, 398
—— Life, 398
—— (Sir J.) Nugæ Antiquæ, 248
—— Apologie for Poetrie, 362
—— Poems by various Authors, 364.
—— Epigrams, 368
Harris (J.) on the Attributes, 51.
—— Works, 398
—— Life, 398.
—— (M.) English Insects, 99
—— Aurelian, 99
—— (W.) Royal Institution Catalogue, 345
—— County of Down, 270
—— Hibernica, 270
Harrison's Chronicle, 225.
—— Description of Brittaine, 188.
Harry's (Blind) Wallace 263
—— (G. O.) Genealogy of James I 334
Hartford and Pomfret's Correspondence, 403
Harvey's Letters on Poetry, 362
Harwood's Litchfield, 212
Hasæus (J.) de הוברי, 17.
—— de היה בבל, &c. 23
—— de Inquinatis Sacrif Vestum 23
—— de Insc Psal xxii 21
—— (T.) de Monte Sublimi, 17
—— Dissertationes variæ de Ant Hebr. 18
—— de Voce Astartes, 21
Haslewood's British Bibliographer 343.
—— Ancient Essays on English Poetry, 362
—— England's Helicon 364
Hasselquist's Travels in the Levant, 148.
Hasted's Kent, 202
Hatim Tai, 389
Hatsell's Precedents of the House of Commons, 72
Hausset (Mémoires de Mad de), 284.
Hauy, Mineralogie, 91
Havercampi Sicilia Numismatica, 297
Hawes's Framlingham, 213
Hawke's Killing is Murder, 238.
Hawkeston (Description of), 211
Hawkhurst (History of), 203.
Hawking, 127
Hawkins (Sir J.) History of Music, 105
—— (J. S.) on Gothic Architecture, 122.
—— (T.) on the English Drama, 389.
—— (W.) Scripture Mysteries, 53
Hawkesworth's Voyages, 132
Haworth Lepidoptera Britannica, 99
Hay's Chichester, 213.
Haygarth's Greece, 368
Hayley's (T. A.) Memoirs, 321
—— (W.) Triumphs of Temper, 366.
—— Memoirs, 321
Haym, Biblioteca Italiana, 343
Haynes's Burleigh Papers, 249.
Hayward's Edward VI 230
Hazin (Life of), 321.
Head's (F. B.) Pampas, &c. 157
—— (G.) North America, 154
Headley's Beauties of Ancient English Poets, 363

Heard's Russian Grammar, 357
Hearne (T) Acta Apostolorum, 2
—— on the Oath of Allegiance, 71
—— Ductor Historicus, 176
—— Journeys to Reading, &c 189
—— Ectypa Varia, 190
—— Curious Discourses, 193.
—— Collected Works, 195
—— Antiq between Windsor and Oxford, 195
—— Antiq of Chilswell, 195
—— K Edward's Chapel, Islip, 209
—— Oxford Castle, &c. 209
—— Stunsfield Pavement, 209
—— Woodstocke Custom, 209
—— University of Oxford, 209
—— St Peter's, Oxford, 210
—— Glastonbury, 212
—— (Life of), 314
Heath's Chronicle, 235
Heber (R) Hymns, 31
—— Christian Comforter, 54
—— Sermons, 56
—— Journal in India, 150.
—— (Last Days of), 321
—— (Life of), 322
—— Palestine, 368
—— Poems, 368
Hebrew Bibles, 1
—— Language, 349
Heden Süssio Vestium Hebr usitata, 23
Hederici Lexicon Græcum, 351.
Hedgeland's St Neot's Church, 198
Heeren's Ancient History, 177
—— on the Carthaginians, &c 178
—— Antient Greece, 179.
Heineccius de Colloquiis Religiosorum, 27
Heinecken (le Bar), Coll d'Estampes, 120
—— Dictionnaire des Artistes, 120
—— [misprinted Heineker], 109
Heinsii Poemata, 361
Heliconia, 364
Heliodorus, 409
Helleus de Deo ignoto Athen 161
Helliried's English Attack on Denmark, 275.
Helyot, Hist des Ordres Ecclésiastiques, 65
Hemmingii Chart Eccles Wigornensis, 215
Hemmingford (W de) Hist Edwardi I II. III 221, 227
Henault, Cornelie, 395.
Henderson (A) on Wines, 126
—— (E) Iceland, 135.
Hendreich Missilia, 160.
Hemmius de Vitis Imp Rom 166
Henrices de Judæis Hebr 22
Henri IV 282
—— (Correspondance de), 282
Henry II —VIII 227–9
Henry VIII 's Primer, 30.
—— Formularies of Faith, 32
Henry (Life of Prince), 233
Henry's (M) Exposition of the Bible, 11
—— Sermons, 56
—— (R) Great Britain, 226
Henry the Minstrel's Wallace, 263
Henshall's Kent, 202
Hentzner's Itinerarium, 134

Hentzner's Journey into England, 189
Heraclidis Allegoriæ, 416
Heraldic History, 330
Heralds (Antiquity, &c of), 330
Heraldic Anomalies, 331
Herbelot (d'), Bibliotheque Orientale, 300.
Herbert (Lord) of Cherbury's Henry VIII 229
—— Life, 322
—— (G) Temple, Sacred Poems, &c. 368
—— (Life of), 313
—— (T) Travels, 133
—— (W) Inns of Court 207
—— Typographical Antiquities, 341
—— Helga, 368
Herculaneum see Drummond
Herefordshire Topography, 201
Heriot's Canadas, 153
Hermann de Ellipsibus Græcis, 350
Hermiæ Apostoli Opera, 31
Hernandez Historia Naturalis Mexicanorum, 89
Herodiani Historia, 416
—— translated, 416.
Herodoti Historia, 416
—— translated, 416.
—— (Rennel on the Geography of), 129
Herrara, Hist de lo Succedido en Escocia, &c 265
—— Hist de las Indias Occid 308
—— Descr de las Indias Occid 308.
Herrick's Select Poems, 368
Hertfordshire (Agriculture of), 124
Hertfordshire Topography, 201
Hertford s (E of) Expedition into Scotland, 263
Hervey s Meditations, 43
—— Letters, 43
Hesiodi Opera, 417.
—— Remains translated, 417
Hesychii Lexicon Græce, 350
Heubner de Academiis Hebr. 20
Heumann de חסד, 24
Hexapla Originis, 1
Heylin's Help to English History, 219
Heynii Opuscula, 398
Heywood's (S) Vindication of Fox's James II 240
—— (T) Exemplary Lives, 312
Hibbert's Catalogue 347.
Hicksii Thesaurus Lit Septent 356
Hieroclis Comment in Aurea Carmina, 417.
—— translated, 417
Hieroglyphics, 107.
Hieronymus de Marinis Genuæ, 293
Higden Historia, 221
—— Polychronicon, 223
Higgins's Spanish Dictionary, 356
Hill's Sermons, 57
—— Latin Synonymes, 252
—— (Memoir of Lord), 241.
Hiller de Vestibus Limbriatis Hebr 20
Hinderwell's Scarborough, 200
Hindostan (Travels in), 149
Hindostanese Costumes, 121
Hinton's (Sir J) Memoirs, 240
—— (J H) America, 310
Hippocratis Opera, 417
Histories of the Bible, 8

History 129
—— (*Universal*), 176
—— (*Ancient*) 177
—— *of the Middle Ages*, 183
—— (*Modern*), 183
—— *of Europe*, 183
Hitopodesa, 400
Hoare's (R) Shrievalty, 214.
—— (Sir R C) Italy, 138
—— Wiltshire, 214
—— English Historical Cat 219
—— Tour in Ireland, 269
—— Cat of Ital History, 292
—— (P) Epochs of the Arts, 108
Hobhouse's (J C) Albania, 143
—— Illustrations of Childe Harold, 366
Hockin's Pelew Isles, 151
Hodge's India, 150
—— Views in India 150
Hodgskin's Germany, 137.
Hodgson's (C) Q Anne's Bounty, 186
—— (Mem of Capt J), 236
Hofland's (J C) Views in Craven, 217
—— (Mrs) White Knights 195
Hogarth's (W) Analysis of Beauty, 110
—— Works, 115, 116
Hogg's Jacobite Relics, 373.
—— Poetical Works, 373
Hohersel de Mohs Manuscribus, 23
Holbein's Portraits, 316
Holden's Book of Proverbs, 6
—— Book of Ecclesiastes 6
Holderman, Grammaire Turque, 350
Holdsworth's Remarks on Virgil, &c 358
Hole (M) on the Liturgy, 31
—— (R) on the Arabian Nights, 398.
—— Ulysses, 418
Holinshed's Chronicle, 225
—— Scotland, 262
Holland See Low Countries and Netherlands
Holland's Agriculture of Cheshire, 214
—— Ionian Isles, &c 143
—— Monum Sepulch S Pauli, 206.
—— Basileologia, 315
—— Herologia 315
Hollar (Cat of the Works of), 120.
Holles, Family History, 335
Hollis (Memoirs of T), 322
Hollybushe's New Testament, 5
Holmes's (G) American Annals 308
—— (J) History of the United Brethren, 65
—— (R) Treatises, 43
—— on the Baptist's Prophecies, 53
Holstein de Iulieris Dianæ Ephes 161.
—— in Pictuiam Nymphæum, 164
Holy Scriptures, 1
Home's (Sir E) Comparative Anatomy, 102
—— (H) See Kaimes
—— (J) Rebellion in Scotland, 267.
Homeri Opera, 417
—— translated, 417
—— Ilias, 417
—— Batrachomyomachia, 417
—— Hymnus, 417
—— translated, 417
Homilies, 57.
Homodei Ætnæ Historia, 297

Hone's Every-Day Book, 194.
Hooke's (A) Bristolha, 196.
—— (N) Roman History, 180
—— (R) Micrographia, 100
—— (T) Sayings and Doings, 384
Hooker's (J) Exeter, 199
—— Chronicle, 225,
—— (R) Works, 28
—— (Life of), 28, 313
—— (W J) Exotic Flora, 92
—— Icones Filicum, 93.
—— Muscologia, 93
—— Musci Exotici, 93
—— Flora Boreali-Americana 95.
—— Botany of Beechey's Voyage, 95
—— Iceland, 145
Hooper's Medical Dictionary, 102.
Hope's Costume of the Ancients, 121.
—— on Household Furniture, 123.
—— Anastasius, 381.
Hôpital (Late of M de l'), 282.
Hopkins' (E) Works, 35
—— Life 35
—— (S) Doctrines of Revelation, 13.
Hopkinsoni Descriptio Paradisi, 17.
Hopkinson Manuscripts. 432
Horace's Art of Poetry, by Hurd, 359
Horatu Opera 418
—— translated, 418
Horace in London, 368
Horberry's Works, 35.
Horchins de Igne Sacro et de Musicâ, 24
Horne (G) on the Psalms, 12.
—— Sermons, 57
—— (T) Necessity of the Reformation, 54
—— (T H) Introduction to the Bible, 9
—— Doctrine of the Trinity, 43
—— Tour to the Lakes, 191.
—— Bibliography, 440
—— Classification of a Library, 345
Horsemanship, 127
Horsley's (J) Britannia Romana, 185
—— (S) Book of Psalms, 6
—— Biblical Criticism, 44.
—— Controversial Tracts, 43
—— Sermons and Charges, 57
—— Speeches, 246
Horticultural Transactions, 126
Hotman de Furoribus Gallicis, 282
Hotmanni Varia de Antiquitatibus Romani 165
Hottinger (H) de variis Orient Inscript 23
—— de Nummis Orient 23
—— (J C) de Decimis Hebræorum, 20
—— (J H) de Geogr Terra Chanaan, 17.
—— Jus Hebræorum, 17.
—— Cipp Hebraica, 25
Hottomanni Varia de Antiquitatibus Roman 163
Houbraken's Heads, 315
Hough (Life, &c of Bp), 322.
Houghton Hall Gallery, 117.
Hoveden (Roger de). Hist Anglicana 220
Howard's (C) Howard Family, 336
—— (G) Lady Jane Grey, 230
—— (Mem of H) Earl of Surrey, 399
—— (Mem of H) E of Northampton, 399

Howard's (J) State of Prisons 84
—— Lazarettos, 81.
—— (Memoirs of), 322
Howell (J) on Forreine Travel, 130
—— Character of England, &c 193
—— Londinopolis, 205
—— Character of the Low Countries, 279
Howes' Chronicle, 225
Howison's Upper Canada, 153
Hoyland's Poems, 368.
Hozier, l'Ordre de St Esprit, 332
Huber on Bees, 100.
—— on Ants, 100.
Hué, Louis XVI, 285
Huet de Situ Paradisi, 17.
—— de Navigationibus Salomonis, 17.
—— Hist of Romances, 379.
Hughes' (G) Barbadoes, 89
—— (J) South of France, 140.
Hulsean Lectures, 55.
Hulsius de Jehovâ, Deo, Rege, &c. 21.
—— de Sechinah, 21
—— de Corpore, Velo, et Sepul Moysis, 25.
Humbert, Manuel du Publiciste 69
Humboldt (A. de), Voyage dans l'Amérique, 155.
Hume's (D) Essays, 80
—— History of England, 226
—— (Sir D) Proceedings of the Parliament of Scotland, 267
Humfrey's Nobles, 332
Humphreys de Decanis Bangor 253.
Hungarian Bible, 7
Hungaricorum Poetarum Delitiæ, 361
Hunt's Tudor Architecture, 122
—— Architettura Campestre, 123
—— Designs for Parsonage-Houses, 123
Hunter's (H) Sacred Biography, 43.
—— (J.) New South Wales, 157
—— Doncaster, 217
—— Who wrote Cavendish's Wolsey? 229.
—— Library of Bretton, 345.
—— Hallamshire Glossary, 354.
—— (J D) N American Indians, 151
Hunting, 127
Huntingdomensis (Hen) Historia Ang. 220
Huntingdonshire Topography 202.
Hurd (R) on the Prophecies, 15
—— (Bp) Works, 398
Hurdis's Lectures on Poetry, 360.
—— Poems, 368
Hurtley's Malham, 217.
Hutchins' Dorset, 199.
Hutchinson (Memoirs of Col), 236
—— (Memoirs of Lucy), 237
—— (W) Excursion to the Lakes, 189
—— Cumberland, 198
—— Durham, 199
Hutten's Oxford, 209
Hutton's (C) Mathematical Dictionary, 102
—— Math Tracts, 102
—— Math Recreations, 102
—— Math Tables, 102
—— Conic Sections, 102
—— Mensuration, 102
—— (J) Theory of the Earth, 90

Hutton's (W) Derby 198.
—— Bosworth Field, 228.
—— on North Wales, 256
Hyde Veterum Persarum, &c. Religio, 67
—— Mandragorias, 128
Hyder Ali's Memoirs, 304
Hyett's Sepulchral Mem of Northamptonshire, 208
Hyginius de Castris Romanorum, 166

Iamblicus de Vitâ Pythagoricâ, 418
Ibbot on Freethinking, 52.
Iceland (Travels in), 135
Icelandic History, 274
—— Language, 357
Iconographie des Contemporains, 315
Ignatii Apostoli Opera, 34.
—— Epistolæ, 212
Ihre on the Icelandic Edda, 135
—— Glossarium Suio-Gothicum, 357
Ikenius de Funere, Sepulturâ, &c. 25
Illingworth's Scampton, 204
Inchbald's British Theatre, 391
—— Farces, 391
India (Travels in), 149
Indian History, 302
Inglis' Spain, 141
Ingram's (H) Flowers of the Wye, 368.
—— (J) Saxon Chronicle, 222
Ingulphi Abbatis Croylandensis Historia, 220 and 221
Inheritance (the), 383
Innes' Ancient Inhabitants of Scotland, 261
Innett's Origines Anglicanæ, 251.
Innisfalenses Annales, 271.
Inquisition, 65
Inquisitionum Post Mortem Calend. 247.
—— Ducatus Lancastriæ, 247
—— Scotiæ Abbreviatio, 247
Inscriptions, 176
Institut (Mémoires de l'), 340.
Intellectual Philosophy, 76
Inveges Carthago Secuh, 297
—— Panormus Antiqua, 297.
Iraihh, Querelles Litteraires, 337.
Ireland (Articles of the Church of), 33.
Ireland's (J) Paganism and Christianity, 44
—— (S) English Rivers, 192
—— Inns of Court, 207
—— (W H) Shakespeare Papers, 394
—— Confessions, 394
Irish Bible, 7
Irish Topography, &c. 269
—— Highlands (Letters from), 270
—— *History*, 270
—— *Ecclesiastical History*, 273.
—— Worthies, 314
—— *Language*, 354.
—— *Poetry*, 174
Ironside's Twickenham, 213
Irving's (D) Scottish Poets, 313.
—— (Wash) Novels, 381 and 383
—— Alhambra, 436
Isacke's Exeter, 199.
Iseus on the Athenian Law of Succession, 69
Islands Landnambok, 275
Isocratis Opera, 118

Isocrates' Orations translated, 421.
Italia (Giornale Letteraria d), 310
Italian Bible, 7
—— Costumes, 121.
Italian School of Painting, 111.
—— *History*, 292.
—— *Language* 355.
—— *Poetry*, 375
—— *Novels*, 387
—— *Drama*. 395.
Italorum Poemata Latina, 361
Italy (Travels in), 137

Jablonski Remphan Egypt Deus, 21
Jacob s (G) Law Dictionary by Tomlins [misp. Tomkins], 73
—— (J D) de Foro in Portis 22
—— (W) on the Coin-Trade, 85.
—— on Precious Metals, 85
—— South of Spain 141.
Jackson s (J. G) Morocco, 144.
—— (J) Works and Life, 35
Jacotius de Philosophorum Doctrinâ, 162
Jahr de Precibus Gentilium Expiat 20
Jahn's Hebrew Commonwealth, 60
James I of Scot. Poetical Remains 374
—— Life, 374
—— II 's Ant of Scottis Poetrie, 362
James VI. 264
—— (Historie of), 266.
—— I s Bible, 5
—— Basilikon Doron, 81
—— Reception at Oxford, 211.
—— Secret History, 232
—— Progresses, 243
—— I 232, II 240
James's (G P R) Charlemagne, 280
—— (W) Naval History, 243
Jameson's Mineralogy, 91
—— Roman Camps in Scotland, 258
Jamieson's (J) Ancient Culdees, 268.
—— Hermes Scythicus, 357
—— Scottish Dictionary, 354
—— (R) Ballads and Songs, 363.
Jannotti de Repub Venetorum, 293
Jansenius (Account of), 65
Janson Hortus Malabaricus, 94
Janus de Vite Aureâ Templi, 18
Japanese History, 306
—— Authors (List of), 306.
Jarrin's Confectioner, 126
Jeanne d'Arc, (Mémoires de) 281
Jeannin (Négotiations de), 283
Jebb's (J) Sacred Literature 10
—— Sermons, 57
—— (S) de Vita Scotorum Reginæ, 265
Jefferson's Memoirs, 310
Jeffrey of Monmouth's British Hist 222
—— See also Galfredus
—— (T) Dresses of different Nations, 193
—— Yorkshire, 216
Jehan's (Shah) Rules, 303.
—— (Hist de) de Sainctre, 390
Jehanguier (Mem of the Emperor) 303
Jchingus de Regione Tharsis, 17
Jenichen Thesaurus Juris Feudalis, 70
Jenkins' (A) Exeter 199
—— (Life and Letters of Sir L), 239.
Jenkinson's Wit's Theatre, 402.
Jennens's King Lear, 393

Jennings' Jewish Antiquities, 25
Jessen de Finnorum Rel. Pag &c 276
Jesuits (History of the) 65
Jewell's Works and Life, 36
—— Apologia 43.
Jewish History (Ancient), 16.
—— *(Modern)*, 60.
Joanna of Naples (Life of), 299
Jodrell's English Philology, 352.
Jofredi Nicæa Monumenta, 295
John III 's Letters Patent, 277
Johnson's (C) Highwaymen, 313.
—— (J) Manks Jurisprudence, 74
—— Typographia 107
—— Aristarchus Anti-Bentleianus, 418
—— (S) History of Magna Charta, 73
—— Tour to the Hebrides, 261
—— (Life of S), 322 and 398
—— Dictionary, 353
—— Works, 398
—— Letters by Piozzi, 403
Johnston Historia Rerum Brit 231
Johnstone's (Chev) Rebellion in 1745-6, 267.
—— (J) Chronicles of Man, 218
—— Antiquitates Sœlto-Scandiæ, 222
Joinville, Histoire de Loys IX, 281
Jona (A) Crymogæa, 275
—— (R) Grammatica Islandica 357
Jones's (D) Secret Hist of Whitehall, 239
—— (I) Stone-Heng, 215
—— (J) on the Canon of the New Test 9
—— Moral Tendency of Revelation, 54.
—— de Linguâ Shelhensi, 350
—— (R) Booke of Honour, 330.
—— (s) Sheridan's Dict improved, 353
—— (T) Brecknockshire, 257.
—— (T S.) Sermons, 57
—— (W.) Works, 36.
—— Life, 36
—— (Sir W) Works, 398
—— Life, 322
Jonson's Works, 391.
—— Life, 391
Jonston de Festis Græcorum, 161.
Jortin on the Christian Religion, 11.
—— Observations, 358
Joscelini Libri Saxonici, 219
Josephi Opera, 16
—— translated, 16
Josef (La Vie du Veritable Pére), 283
Joubertus de Gymnasiis 167.
—— de Balneis, 167.
Jouy (E), Œuvres, 398
Jovin (B) Hist Novocomensis, 293.
—— (P) Descriptiones, 129
—— de Rom Piscibus, 167
—— Historie de son Temps, 183
—— Descript Laclus Larii, 293.
—— Vitæ Vicecom Mediol 293
—— on the Turke's Chronicle, 300.
Jowett's Christian Researches, 65.
Juelli Apologia, 43
Julian's Works translated, 418
Jumiège, les Ducs de Normandie, 290.
Junius's Letters, 246.
—— de Picturâ Vet 108
—— (F) Biblia Latina, 4.
—— Etymologicon Anglicanum, 352
—— (H.) de Annis et Mensibus, 165

Junii Fastorum Liber, 165
Jurisprudence, 67
Jurisprudentia ante Justinianea, 69
Jus Provinciale Alemannicum, 70
Justelli Codex Canonum Ecc Afric 27
Justiciary Law, 74
Justin Martyr's Apology for Christianity, 44
Justinianus de Origine Urbis Venet 293.
—— Institutiones, 70
—— Corpus Juris, 70
—— Institutes translated, 419
Justini Historia, 418 and 419
Juvenalis Satyrs, 419
—— translated, 419.
Juvenis de Ant &c Tarentinorum, 293.
Juvigny, Bibliothèques Françoises, 343

Kæmpfer's History of Japan, 306
—— Life, 306
Kaimes' (Lord) History of Man, 77
—— on Education, 81.
—— (Memoirs of), 323.
Kalendarium Rom in and Maffieor 165
—— Frag in a d Capranicorum, 165
—— in Fasti Ovidii Libris, 165.
—— Rom sub Constantino, 165.
Kalm's North America, 153
Karamsin, Histoire de Russie, 276.
Karæorum Institutio, 20
Karæus in Librum Josuæ, 20.
Karinæ Faventia Rediviva, 294
Kay See Caius
Kay's Ecclesiastical History, 61.
Keach on Scripture Metaphors, 10
Keate's Pelew Islands, 151.
—— Geneva, 290.
Keating's Ireland, 271
Keating's Travels, 133
Keepsake, 107.
Keill on Burnet's Theory, 90
Keith's (A) Fulfilment of Prophecy, 15
—— (R) Scottish Bishops, 268
Kelly's Reminiscences, 390.
Kelsall's Arpino, 139
Kemble's (F A) Francis I 391
—— (J) Macbeth and Richard III 393
—— (Life of), 390
Kempis's (Thomas à) Imitation of Christ, 44.
Ken's (Bp) Life, 255
Kennedy's (J) Philosophy of the Creation, 12
—— (Vans) on the Languages of Asia and Europe, 348
—— Hindu Mythology, 438
—— (W) Aberdeen, 259
Kennet's Parochial Antiquities, 210
—— Complete History of Engl ind, 226.
Kenny's Chess Grammar, 126
Kent's (N) Agriculture of Norfolk, 125
—— (W) Dictionary of Heraldry, 331
Kentish Topography, 202
Kerr's (R) Agriculture of Berwickshire, 125
—— Collection of Voyages, 141
—— History of Scotl ind, 264
Kerner, le Raisin, 95
—— les Melons, 95
Keronis Interp Regula S Bened 65

Kersey's English Dictionary, 353
Kessler de Dimidio Siclo Argent. 22
Kett on the Prophecies, 15.
—— Opinions of Primitive Christians, 53
—— Flowers of Wit, 401
Kettell's American Poets, 364.
Kidder on the Messias, 51
Kidwilhe (State of), 297
Kilburne's Kent, 202
Kilham Etymologicon Teutonicon, 356
Killing no Murder, 238
King's (D) Vale Royal, 197
—— (E) Morsels of Criticism, 14
—— Monumenta Antiqua, 190
—— (M P) on Music, 105
—— (P P) Australia, 158
—— New Zealand, 158
—— (W) Own Times 241
Kingsborough (Lord) Mexican Antiquities, 172
Kinneir's Marches of Alexander, 129
—— Asia Minor, 148
—— Persia, 149
Kinschotti Poemata, 361
Kinsey's Portugal 143
Kip, Théâtre de la Grande Bretagne, 191
Kippis's Biographia Britannica, 312
Kirby's Suffolk Traveller, 212.
—— Entomology, 98
Kircher de Musica, &c 24.
—— de Musurgia, 24
—— Mundus Subterraneus, 90
—— Sphinx Mystagoga, 107
Kirk's Nature of Flyes, &c 259
Kirkmajer ad Tacit Hist de Relius Jud 16
Kirkpatrick's Nepaul, 151
Kuikton's Church of Scotland, 269
Khakani (Kulhat Hakim) 378
Klaproth, Supplément au Dict. Chinoise, 350
Klingsted sur les Samojedis, 135
Klopstock's Messiah, 44
Knevet's Rhodon and Iris, 392
Knights made by Abbots, 342
Knight's (E C) Latium, 189
—— (T) Divinity of Christ, 52
—— (R P) Greek Alphabet, 350
—— on Taste, 359
Knowles's Strafforde Papers, 250
Knox's (J) Forme of Prayers, &c 31
—— Reformation in Scotland, 268
—— Lettre to the Ladie Marie, 268
—— Appellation, 268
—— Against the Regiment of Women, 268
—— Life by Ruddiman, 268
—— by M Crie, 268
—— (R) Ceylon, 306
—— (V) Elegant Extracts, Verse, 361
—— Works, 398
Knyghton (Hen) Historia, 221.
Kobierzykius de Luxu Romanorum, 165
Koch de Numinorum Hebr Ins 23
—— Hist. des Traités de Paix, 68
Kohlius in Litteram Slavonum, 389
Kolan Nattinnawa, 378
Koran, translated by Sale, 60.
Koster's Brazil, 156.

Kotzebue's Voyage, 132
—— Italy, 138.
—— Paris, 110
—— Life, 323
Krantzii Wandalorum, &c Origo, 274
—— Rerum Germanic Hist 277
Krumbholtz Sacerdotium Hebraeorum, 18
Kunth Plantæ Æquinoctiales, 155
—— Révision des Graminées, 155
—— Mimoses, &c 155
Kuttner's German Dictionary, 356
Labat Voyage en Espagne 141
Labbæ (C) Glossarium, 351
Labbe (P) de Hist Byzant Scriptoribus, 181
—— Notitia Dignitatum, 182
Labeaume's Campaign in Russia, 276
Labitti Usus Pandectarum, 70
Laborde, Pavé d'Italica, 172
La Borde See Borde
Lacombe. Dict du Vieux Langage, 355
La Croix, de Calcul Différentiel, 102
La Croze de variis Linguis, 348
—— Histoire du Christianisme des Indes, 63
Lactantii Opera, 34
La Harpe, Cours de Littérature 317
—— Mélanges de Litterature, 347.
Laing's History of Scotland, 266
Lake's Works and Life, 36
Lakemacher de Gad et Meni, 21
Lalamantius de Tempore, 162
—— de Anno Romano, 165.
Lamarca, Henrique de Castro, 388
Lamb's English Dramatic Poets, 391
Lambard de Priscis Ang Legibus, 73.
—— Dict Angliæ Topographica, 185
Lambecii Notæ in Kalendarium Vetus, 165
Lambert's Canada and the United States, 153
Lamballe (Princesse de), Memoires, 285
Lambinet, Origine de l'Imprimerie, 340
Lamont's Diary, 266
Lamotte, le Nord de l'Europe, 136
Lampe de Cymbalis Veterum, 24
Lampridus Ælius, 409
Lamy de Levitis Cantoribus, 21
Lancashire Topography, 203.
Lancaster's Evidences of Christianity, 51
Lancastriæ Ducatûs Inquisitiones, 247
Lancelot's Tour to la Grand Chartreuse, 65
Lander's (R) Africa, 145
—— (R and J) Course of the Niger, 145
Landon, Œuvres des Peintres, 111
—— Annales de Musée, 117.
—— Galerie Historique, 311
Landseer (J) on Engraving, 119
—— (T) Sketches of Animals, 96
Landt's Feroe Islands, 275.
Laneham's Elizabeth's Entertainment at Kenilworth, 231
Langbaine's Eng Dramatic Poets, 390
Langbek Scriptores Danici, 274.
Langius de Vet Anno Romanorum, 165
Langres sur la Revolution Fr. no. 286
Language (on the Origin, &c of), 348.
Languasen de Mense Hebraeorum, 19
Languedocien (Dictionnaire), 355

Langhorne's Hist of England, 222
Lanigan's Eccles Hist of Ireland, 273
Lanjuinais (le Comte) sur le 31 Mai, 286
Lanquet's Chronicle, 224.
Landscape Annual, 407
Lansdowne MSS Catalogue, 345
Langtoft's Chronicle, 223
Lanté, Costumes de la France, 121
Lanzi, Storia Pittor della Italia, 109
—— translated, 109
Lanzonius (J) de Jatrophysicis Ferrariensibus, 296
—— (P) de Coronis Convivis, 168
—— de Luctû Mortuali, 168.
Lapland (Travels in), 135
—— (History of), 275.
—— (Language of), 357
Lardner's Works, 36.
—— Life, 36
Laræ (Historia VII Infantum), 120
Las Cases, Atlas Historique, 129
—— Journal, 288
Lastinaaa, Medallas Espanolas, 176
Latham's (J) Synopsis of Birds, 97
—— (S) Falconry, 128
Latimer's Sermons, 57
—— (Life of), 57
Latin Bibles 3 and 1
—— Language, 351
—— Poetry, 360
—— Romances, 379
Latour, le Langage des Fleurs, 402.
Latreille Hist des Crustacées et Insectes, 88
Latrobe's (J A) Music of the Church, 31
—— (C J) Alpenstock, 137.
—— Pedestrian, 438
Laud (Life of Abp), 234
—— Scotch Service-Book, 30
Laurembergii (J) Græcia Antiqua, 160
Laurentius (J) de Citharœdis, &c 24
—— Varia de Antiquitatibus Græcorum, 161-3
—— de Desponsatione Maris Adriaticæ, 294
—— de Monacis Eremius tertius, 294
Laval's Reformation in France, 63
Lavallée, la Grèce, 143
Lavater's Physiognomy, 79
Lavender's Travels 132
Lavington's Sermons, 57
—— (Life of), 57
Law, 67
Law (J) of Lauriston's Life 281
—— (W.) Christian Perfection, 44
—— Serious Call. 41
Lawrence (R) on the Calvinistical Articles, 53
—— Interests of Ireland 270
—— (Sir T) Portraits, 119
—— (Life of), 323
Lazri Græcia Antiqua, 160
Leake's (S M) English Money, 175
—— (W M) Morea, 143
—— Greek Revolution, 300
—— Researches in Greece, 351
Lebon (les Crimes de Joseph), 287
Le Brun's Battles of Alexander, 112
—— l'Escalier de Versailles, 114
—— Galerie de Peintres, 114

Leckie on the Balance of Power, 82
Le Clerc's Practical Geometry, 104
Ledwich's Antiquities of Ireland, 209
Lee's Collection of Butterflies, 99
—— (S.) Hebrew Grammar, 349
Lee Priory Poetical Works, 361
Leger, Histoire des Vaudoises, 62
Legh's (T.) Egypt, 146.
—— Syria, 148
Le Grand, Fabliaux, 374
Leemius de Lappombus, 276
Leibnitz de variis Linguis, 348
Leicester Gallery, 116
—— (E. of) Commonwealth 231 and 435
—— Life 231
Leicestershire Topography, 204
Leigh's Lancashire, 203.
—— (E.) on the Roman Emperors, 180
—— England described 188
—— French Proverbs, 401.
—— (G.) Armorie, 331
Leigh Court Gallery, 116
Leighton's Works, 36
—— Life, 36
Leith's Prince of Wales's Island 306
Leland's (J.) View of Deistical Writers, 44
—— on Christian Revelation, 44
—— (J.) Journey, 185
—— Itinerary. 188
—— Collectanea, 193
—— de Script Britannicis, 219
—— (Life of John), 314.
—— Genethliacon, 361
—— Cygnea Cantio, 361
—— (T.) Philip of Macedon, 179
—— on McPherson's British History, 219
—— Laus Galfredi Monumetensis, 222
—— Ireland, 271
Lelong Bibliotheca Sacra, 10
—— Bibliothèque Historique de la France, 279
Le Maitre, Sermons, 57
Le Mesurier on Schism, 54
Le Moine   See Moine
Lemon's State Papers 248
Lempriere's Classical Dictionary, 159
Le Neve's Monumenta Anglicana, 192
—— Fasti Ecclesiæ Anglicana, 253
Lenfant, Concile de Pise, 27
—— Concile de Constance, 27
—— Concile de Basle, 27
Leng on Revelation, 52
Lenoir (A.), Explication des Hiéroglyphes, 107
—— Hist. de l'Art en France, 108
—— Peintre sur Verre, 111
—— Monumens Français, 289
Lent de Judæorum pseudo-Messiis, 21
Leo Judæ's Germano-Swiss Bible, 7
Leo X. (Life of), 299
Leonis Africanus Africæ Descriptio, 144
—— translated by Pory, 306
—— Deaconi Hist. Byzant 182
—— (A.) Urbis Nolæ Descriptio, 295
Leontii Mechanici 410
Le Roux, Dictionnaire Comique, &c. 355
Le Roy   See Roy
Le Sage   See Las Casas

Le Sage, Gil Blas, 386
Lesleus (J.) de Origine, &c Scotorum, 262
—— de Titulo, &c Mariæ Scotorum, 264.
—— de Illustr Fœminarum Authoritate, 265
—— de Rebus Gestis regnante Maria 265
Lesley's History of Scotland, 263
—— Life, 265
—— Proceedings on his Embassie in England, 265
Leslie's (C.) Method with Deists, 44
—— (Sir J.) Natural Philosophy, 86
—— Philosophy of Arithmetic, 103.
—— (W.) Agriculture of Nairn and Moray, 125
Lesson, Histoire des Oiseaux-Mouches, 97
—— Histoire des Colibris, 438
—— Histoire des Trochilidées, 438
L'Estrange's Alliance of Divine Offices, 30
Lethieulliers, Baveux Tapestries, 194
Lettres Edifiantes, 64
Le Vaillant   See Vaillant
Le Vasor, Histoire de Louis XIII, 283
Levesque, Histoire de Russie, 276
Levizac, Bibliotheque des Vers Françoises, 375
Lewin's (J. W.) Lepidopterous Insects of N. S. Wales, 100
—— (W.) British Birds, 97
Lewis's (G.) Costume, &c of France and Germany, 121
—— (J.) on English Translations of the Bible, 10
—— Church Books, Vestments, &c 186.
—— on the Use of Seals 194
—— Faversham Church, 203
—— Isle of Thanet, 203
—— Suffragan Bishops, 253
Lewis and Clarke's Source of the Missouri, 151
Lewkenor on Forraine Cities, 184
Leicester's Chester 197
Leyden's Africa, 144
—— Complaint of Scotland, 263
—— Poetical Remains, 369
—— Life, 369
Leyser de Poesi Hebræorum, 24
Libanius translated, 418
Liber Quotidianus Garderobæ, 191
—— Niger Scaccarii, 246
Liberal Arts, 107
Libraries (on), 345
Liceti pro Cesenæ Ant Apologia, 291
Lichtenstein's South Africa, 146
Lichtenberger Initia Typographica, 340
Lichentantius de Terra Morijah, 18
Light (the) of Britayne, 219
Light's Sicilian Scenery, 140
Lightfoot Chorographia in Evangelios, 17
—— Descriptio Templi Hierus 18
—— Ministerium Templi, 18
—— Works, 36
—— Memoirs, 36
—— Flora Scotica, 94
Lights and Shadows of Scottish Life, 383
Ligorius de Vehiculis Antiquorum, 169

3 P

Lagoın Descriptio Villæ Tıburtinæ, 295.
Lilly's Life and Times, 78
—— Chronicon, 224
—— Monarchy and No Monarchy, 236
Lamborchi Theologia Christiana, 45
Lincoln (Earls of) Genealogy, 336
Lincolnshire (Agriculture of), 125
—— Topography, 204
Lindaldi Lexicon Lapponicum, 357
Lindenbrugii Codex Legum Antiquorum, 70
Lindley's Brazil, 156.
Lindsay See Lyndsay
Lingard's History of England, 226
Linnæus's Tour in Lapland, 155
—— System of Nature, 87
Linguet, Memoires sur la Bastile, 286
Lipenius de Navigationibus Salomonis et de Ophir, 17
—— Strenarum Historia, 166
Lipscomb's Buckinghamshire, 196
Lipsius de Vesta et Vestalibus, 164
—— Saturnalia, 166
—— de Amphitheatro, 166
Lister's Synopsis Conchyliorum, 100.
Literature, 336
Literary History 336
—— History of the Fourteenth and Fifteenth Centuries, 337
—— Souvenir, 407
Lithgow's Siege of Newcastle, 139
Littara de Rebus Neticus, 297
Little's Abingdon, 196
Liturgies, 29
Livii Historiæ, 419
—— translated, 419.
—— Forojuliensis Vita Henrici V 228
Lizars' Anatomical Plates, 102
Llorente, Histoire de l'Inquisition, 65
Lloyd's (D) State Worthies, 313
—— (L.) Northern Field Sports, 127
Lhuyd's (E) Archæologia Britannica, 354
—— (H) Breviary of Britayne, 187
Lobineau, Histoire de Bretagne, 290
Lobo Hist d'Abyssinie, 307
Locatus de Placentini Urbis Origine, 293
Locke's Works, 308
—— (Life of), 323
Lockhart's (G) Lockhart Papers, 268
—— (J G) Spanish Ballads, 377
—— Novels, 384 and 385
Lodge's (L) Illustrations of British Hist 248
—— Illustrious Portraits, 315.
—— English Peerage, 343
—— Existing Peerage 343
—— Genealogy of the Peerage, 335
—— (J) Desiderata Hibernica, 273
—— Irish Peerage, 334
—— (T) Glaucus and Silla, 369
Loeve-Veimars de la Litterature Allemande, 349
Loffredi Antiquitatis Puteolorum Desc 295.
Logan's (J) Privileges,&c of London, 206
—— Analogia Honorum 332
Logarithmici Scriptores, 103
Loggan's (D) Oxonia Illustrata, 210
Logic, 79

Lombardus de Balneis Puteolanis, 295
Lomejerus de Osculis, 23
Londinensis Synodi Articuli 2
London Architectura Ecclesiastica, 206
London (Topography of), 205
—— (Chronicle of), 205
—— (Diary of Events in), 431
—— (Description of), 431
—— (XII Companies of), 432.
—— Institution Catalogue, 345
Londonderry's War in Germany, &c 244
Long's (E) Jamaica, 311
—— (R.) Astronomy, 104.
Longinus de Sublimitate, 419 and 420.
—— translated, 420
Longland's (R) [misprinted Thomas] Piers Ploughman, 369
Longus, 169
Lonsdale (Life of Lord). 314
Looker-on, 405
Loon de Manumissione Servorum Romanorum, 169
Lope de la Vega (Life of C), 323
—— Obras, 398
Lopez de Ayala, Historia de Gibralter, 292
Lords of Session (Cat of the), 267
Lorenzo de Medicis (Life of), 299
Lorris, Rommant de la Rose, 374
Loskeil's Moravian Mission in N America, 66
Lossius de Epispasmo Judaico, 21
Lothian's History of the Netherlands, 279
Loudon (J) on Country Residences, 124.
—— (J C) Magazine of Nat Hist 89
—— Encyclopædia of Plants, 92
—— Encyc of Agriculture, 124
—— Encyc of Gardening 125.
Louis IX 281, XIII. and XIV 283; XV 284, XVI 285
—— le Grand (Médailles de), 176.
—— XIV. (Œuvres de), 283
Lounger (the), 405
Lovat's (Lord) Memoirs, 267
Lovell's Poems, 364
Lovelace's Lucasta, Epodes, &c 369
Low Countries (History of) 278
Lowe's Agriculture of Notts, 125
Lowman on the Revelations, 11
—— Jewish Civil Government, 25
—— Hebrew Ritual, 25
Lowndes's (T.) Romaic Lexicon, 351
—— (W T) Bibliographer's Manual, 343
Lowth's Isaiah, 6
—— de Sacra Poesi Hebræorum, 10, 24.
—— translated, 10
—— on the Prophets, 11
—— Oratio Creviana, 24
Lowther's (Von) Analysis of Nobility, 332
Lubeo de Decisionibus Pericularnenti Hebr 20
Lucani Pharsalia, 120
—— translated, 420
Luchet sur les Illuminés, 278
Luciani Opera, 420
—— translated, 420.
—— Opuscula, 420
Lucilii Satyræ, 413, 422

Lucius de Regno Illyrici, 297
—— Inscriptiones Dalmatica, 297
Lucius Ampellus, 116
Lucretius de Rerum Naturâ, 420.
—— translated, 420
Luders' Character of Henry V 228.
Ludlow's Memoirs, 236
—— Letters, 234
Ludolphi Historia Æthiopica, 307
—— Grammatica Amharica, 349
—— Lexicon Amharicum, 349
—— Lexicon Æthiopicum, 349.
Ludorum (de) Antiquorum Consuetudine, 161
Lupsete's Way of Dying Well, 45
Lutheri Biblia Germanica [Printer's name Hars, misprinted *A Luifft*], 7
—— Opera, 36.
—— Life, 63
Luzac Lectiones Atticæ, 358.
Lycophronis Alexandra, 420.
—— translated, 420
Lydus de Juramento, 22
—— de Re Militari Synt Sacrum, 22
Lve S Evangelia Gothica, 3
Lyell's Geology, 90.
Lyle's Euphues, 382
—— Euphues and his England, 382
Lyndsay's Complaint of Scotland, 263
—— Poetical Works, 374
—— Life, 374
Lynne's Scripture Texts for the Sycke, 45
Lyon's (G F) Northern Africa, 144.
—— Journal of the Hecla, 153
—— (J) Dover, 203
Lycerus de ⲟⲩⲟⲩ, &c 23
Lysiæ Orationes, 421
—— translated, 421
Lysons (D) Environs of London, 207
—— (D. and S) Magna Britannia, 208
—— (S) Roman Antiquities of Woodchester, 201
Lyttleton's (Lord) Henry II. 227.
—— Miscellaneous Works, 398.

Mably, le Droit Publique de l'Europe, 68
Macanei Verham Lacus Descriptio, 296
Maccaronicarum Carmina, 361
Macarius's Travels in Greece, 143
MacCarthy (Cat du Bibliotheque de), 346
Macartney's China, 151
—— (Life of), 323
M'Crie's Reformation in Italy, 64.
—— Reformation in Spain, 64
—— See also Bivsson, Knox, Melville, and Veitch
M'Curtin's Irish Dictionary, 354
Macculloch's (J) Highlands of Scotland, 260
—— Western Isles, 261
—— (J R) Commercial Dictionary, 85
Macdiarmid's British Statesmen, 313
Macdonald's Denmark and Sweden, 157
Macdonnel's Dictionary of Quotations, 348
Macfarlane's Constantinople, 142.
Macgregor's British America, 310
Mackenzie Genealogy, 336
—— (A) Voyages to the Frozen Sea, 153
—— (C) Haiti, 154.

Mackenzie (Sir G) on Precedency, 332.
—— (Sir G S) Agriculture of Ross and Cromarty, 121
—— Iceland, 135
—— (H) Works, 398
Mackintosh's Hist of the Revolution, 240
Macknight's Apostolical Epistles, 6.
—— Life of St Paul, 6
—— Harmony of the Gospels, 8
Maclaine's Sermons, 57
Macleod's Voyage of the Alceste, 152
Macklin's Bible, 5
Macmichael's Constantinople, 142.
Macneil's Poetical Works, 374
Macpherson's (D) Origin of Commerce, 85
—— (J) British History, 219
—— Original Papers, 250
Mackrell's King's Lynn, 208
Macrobu Opera, 421
Madeins de Coronis Nuptiarum, 165
Maddox (I) on Neal's Puritans, 256
—— (T) History of the Exchequer, 75
Maffei Teatro, 395
—— (M S) Verona, 139
—— de Amphitheatro Veronensi, 169.
—— de Amphitheatro et Theatro Gallico, 169
Magdeburg Centuriators, 62
Magee on the Atonement, 45.
Magius de Tintinnabulis, 168
—— de Equuleo, 168
Maghabechi (Parallel between) and R Hill, 328
Magna Charta, 73
Magnetism, 87
Magni (St) Vita, 261
—— (O) Historia Settentrionala, 274
Mahommedanism, 66
Mahon's Life of Belisarius, 182
—— War of the Succession, 438
Mailla, Histoire de la Chine, 305
Maillare, Histoire de la Convention Nat 286.
Mailros (Chronica de), 221
Maimbourg's History of the League, 239.
Maimonides de Templo, Vasis, &c Sanctuarii, 18
—— Vita, 18
—— de Novilunio, 19
—— de Luctu, 24
Maintenon (Memoires de Madame de) 284
—— Lettres inédites, 284.
—— Lettres, 403
Maitland (Memoirs of Secretary), 264
—— (Sir R) House of Setun, 336
—— Scottish Poems, 373
—— Poems, 374
—— (Sir J and T) Poems, 374
—— (W) London, 205.
—— Edinburgh, 260
Maittaire Annales Typographici, 311
—— English Grammar, 353
—— Miscellanea Græcorum Carmina, 408
—— Poetæ Latini, 409
Maus de Kijun et Remphan, 21
—— de Lustrationibus, &c Hebræorum, 21
—— de Purificatione Mirabili, 21

Manus de Philothesis, &c Hebræorum, 23
—— Specimina Linguæ Punicæ, 297
Majoragii de Senatu Romanorum, 168
Malabaric Dictionary, 150
Malaspinæ Rei Sicularum, 297
Malaterra de Gestis Rob Guiscardi, &c 296
—— Liberatio Messinæ à Saracenorum, 297
—— Genealogia Regum Siculæ, 297
Malayan Four Gospels and Acts, 8
—— Family's Memoirs, 323
Malcolm's (Sir J) Sketches of Persia, 149
—— (Sir J) History of Persia, 302
—— India, 303.
—— Central India, 304
—— Sikhs, 304,
—— (J. P) London, 205
—— Manners and Customs of London, 206
—— Manners and Customs of Europe, 184
Malden's King's College, Cambridge, 197
Malherbe, Poesies, 375
—— (Vie de), 375
Mallet's Northern Antiquities, 273
Malling, Traits Memorables de Danois, 274
Malhot, les Costumes Anciennes 121
Malmsburiensis (Gul) de Ecclesia Glastoniensi, 211
—— Historia Anglæ, 220 and 221
—— History, 223
—— (Anonymi) Historia 221
Malone's English Stage, 390.
—— on the Shakespeare Papers, 394
Meltebrun's Geography, 129
Malthus on Population, 84
Malton (Privileges of New), 217
Malynes's Canker of the Commonwealth, 85
Man's Reconciler of the Bible, 8
Manchester Phil Society's Memoirs, 340
—— Library Catalogue, 345
Mancy, Atlas des Littératures, 336.
Mandelslo, Voyages dans la Perse, &c 149.
Mandeville's Travels, 431
Manetti (Jannoctii) Vita, 296
Manfredi Monumenta Hist Lucæ, 296
—— de Archiep. Syracusæ, 296
—— de Panormitanâ Majestate, 297
Manilii Villæ Burghesiæ Descriptio, 295
Manks Bible, 7
Manni, Historia del Decamerone, 387
Manning's Surrey, 213.
Manoir's Armoric Gram and Vocab 354.
Mansonii Cesenæ Chronologia, 296
Mant's Common Prayer, 30
—— Gospel preached by the National Clergy, 34.
—— Sermons, 57.
Manufactures, 126.
Manuscripts, 131
Manutius (A) de Cælatura, 162
—— de Toga Rom 163
—— de Tunicâ Rom 163
—— de Tibiis Vet 163
—— de Reatina Urbe, 167
—— Villa de Ant Rom 167
—— (P) de Civitate et Comitiis Rom. 163
—— de Senatu et Legibus Rom 163

Marcel, Alphabet Irlandais, 354
Marcet's Political Economy, 83
—— Conversations on Chemistry, 87.
Marchand sur le Dict de Bayle, 311.
Marchangy, la Gaule Poétique, 289
Marchesii Foro-Livii Historia, 296
Marchmont Papers, 251.
Marco Polo's Travels, 117
Marganensis [misprinted Margmensis] Annales 221
Margaret Lindsay, 383
Marguerite de Valois, 386
Mariana Historia de Espana, 291.
Marie de Medicis (Vie de), 285
Marie Antoinette (Vie de), 285
Mariner's Tonga Islands, 157
Mariscottus de Personis et Lurvis, 166
Marivaux, Œuvres, 398
Markham's Cavaluer, 127
—— Carmina, 361
Marlborough's (Duchess of) Opinions, 241
—— (Duke of) Memoirs, 244
Marliani Romæ Topogr 164
Marlow's Hero and Leander, 369
Marmontel, Mémoires, 324
—— les Incas, 386
—— Contes Moraux, 386
Marmyon's Cupid and Psyche, 369
Marot, Œuvres, 375
Marottes a Vendre, 407
Marassis Breviarium Historicum, 182
Marriage, 363
Marriott's Sermons, 57
Mars (Field of), 244
Marsden Numismata Orientalia, 174
—— Sumatra, 306
—— Catalogue of Dictionaries, &c 344
Marshall (Office of Earl), 330
Marshall's Mortality of the Metropolis, 206
Marsillus de Ponte Trajani supra Danubium, 168
Marston's Ancient English Poesie, 363.
—— Works, 392
Martial de Paris, Poesies, 375
—— d'Auvergne, 386
Martialis Epigrammata, 421.
—— Græce, 421
Martin's (J) Illustrations of the Bible, 116
—— Illustr of Paradise Lost, 369
—— (M) Western Isles, 261.
—— (P), l Expédition Française en Egypte, 307
—— (T) Thetford, 268
—— (W) Petrificata Derbiensia, 91
Martine's St Andrews, 260
—— St Rule's Chapel, 260
Martinière, Dictionnaire Géographique, 130
Martinius de Theatro Saguntino, 169
Martini in Pugiorem Fidei Prooemium, 16.
Martius's Brazil, 156
Martii Historia Tiburtina, 293.
Martyn's (H) Sermons, 57
—— (T) Flora Rustica 121
Maruccini de Urbe Bassano, 256
Mary (Q), 229

Mary Queen of Scots' Execution, 208
—— Queen of Scots, 264 and 265
Maseres Scriptores Logarithmici, 103
Maskelyne's Astronomical Observations, 104
Mason's (G. H.) Costume of China, 121
—— (J.) Sermons, 57
—— (J. M.) on Shakespeare, 393
—— on Beaumont and Fletcher 391.
—— (W.) Works, 398
—— (W. M.) St. Patrick's, Dublin, 270
Massa de Origine, &c. Talismorum, 295
Massillon, Sermons, 57
—— Petit Careme, 57
Massinger's Plays, 392
Masters' Corpus Christi College, 197
Mathæus Ægyptus de Bacchinaliibus, 168
—— (B.) Memoriæ Historiæ Tusculi, 295
Mathematical Philosophy, 102
Mather's Eccles History of New Eng 64
Matter sur l'École d'Alexandrie, 337
Matthew Wald, 383
Matthews's Mahomedan Traditions, 66
—— Bible, 4
Matthias's Pursuits of Literature, 101
Matthiæ's Greek Grammar, 350
Matthieu, l Entrée de Marie de Medicis, 283
Matthioli Comment in Dioscoridem, 101
Maugist Davgremont (Hystoire de), 379
Maundrell s Journey to Jerusalem, 148
Maupertius on the Celestial Bodies, 104
Maurelli's Voyage, 154
Maurice's Indian Antiquities 302
—— Hindostan, 303
Maurisii Dominorum de Romano Marchiæ Hist 294
Maurolyci Sicaniæ Historia, 296
Maver's Phillipine Islands, 306
Mavor's Agriculture of Berks, 124
Mawe's Gardener s Calendar, 126.
—— (J.) Mineralogy of Derbyshire, 91
—— on Diamonds, 92
—— Conchology, 100
—— Brazil, 156
Maximilian's (Prince) Travels in Brazil, 156
Maximi Tyrii Dissertationes, 421
—— translated, 421
May's Hist. of the Long Parliament, 233
—— English History, 248
Mayart on Ireland, 273
Mayer, Aventures du Sire d'Armignac, 380
—— (F.) de Idolo בעל, 21
—— (L.) Views in Turkey, 142
—— Views in Egypt, 146
—— Views in Palestine, 148.
Mazarin (Hist du Cardinal), 283 and 284
Mazzellæ Puteolorum et Cumarum Desc. 295
Mazza Urbis Salernitanæ Historia, 295
Mazzochius in Mutilum Campani Amphi. 169
—— (J.) Veri Defensi, 295
—— Vejorum Defens Apologia, 295
Mechanics, 103
Meda, Le Souvre du 9 Thermidor, 267
Medals 174

Medals of George III's Reign, 175
Mede's Works, 36
—— Life, 36
Medici (History of the House of), 298
—— (L. de) Poesie, 376.
Medicine, 101
Meerman de l'Invention de l'Imprimerie, 341
Meer Hassan Ali's Mussulmauns in India, 151.
Meibomius (J. H.) de Cervisiis Veterum, 162
—— (M.) de Fabricà Triremium, 166
Meigh Constitutiones Servi Hebraci, 22
Meillan (Mémoires de), 286
Mejer de Suffitu, 18
Melancthonis Opera, 36
—— Life, 63
Melling, Voyage Pittoresque de Constantinople, 142
Melvil's Memoirs, 231
Melville (Life of Andrew), 268
Memory (Artificial), 107
Mendicity, 84
Mendoza, la Guerra de Grenada, 291
—— Lazarillo de Tormes, 388
Menestrier de Colo Mayerano 163
Menetrei Symbolicæ Dianæ Ephesianæ, 161
Mengin, Histoire de l Egypte, 307.
Mercurialis de Potionibus, 162
—— de Arte Gymnasticà, 169
Mercurius Aulicus, 234
—— Rusticus, 234
Meres' Comparison of English and Greek Poets, 262.
Merian Insecta Surinamensium, 100.
Merigot's Views in Rome, 139
Mernhard de Selenolatria, 17
Mersennus de Musicà Hebræorum, 24
Merula (G.) de Gallorum Cisalpin Antiquitate, 292
—— Alexandrinæ Vrbe cum Antiquitate, 293
—— (P.) de Maribus, 69
—— de Legibus Romanorum, 168
—— de Comitiis Romanorum, 168.
Messala Corvinus, 169 and 416
Metaphysics, 76
Metastasio (Memoirs of P.), 324
—— Opere, 398
—— translated, 395
Metellanum Registrum, 261
Meteorology, 86
Meung, Rommant de la Rose, 374
Meursius de Tubis Collectanea, 24
—— Varia de Antiq. Græcorum, 160, 61, and 62
—— Bibliothec Græc, 163
—— Attici, 163
—— de Funere, 164
—— de Luxu Rom 165
—— Glossarium Græco-Barbarum, 351
Mensehi Bibliotheca Historica, 176
Mexican Antiquities, 172
Meyer (C. G.) de Hominibus Prædiluvianis, 21
—— (J.) de Temporibus Sacris, 16
Meyrick on Ancient Armour 106
—— Cardigan, 257.

478   INDEX.

Mezeray, Histoire de France, 280
Michael Angelo See Buonarotti
Michaelis (C B) de Ant Economia Patriarchalis 21
—— (J B) de Judiciis Pœnisque in S S 22
—— (J D) Introduction to the New Testament, 9
—— on the Laws of Moses, 25.
—— sur la Arabie, 148
—— (J. L) Num Deus dicatur אלהים, 21
—— (J G) de Thuribulo Adyti, 18
—— (M A) Urbis Bergomatis Descriptio 296
Michaud, Histoire des Croisades, 183
Microcosm 405
Middle Ages (Hist of the), 183.
Middlesex (Topography of), 207
Middleton (C) on Swimming, 127
—— (E) Evangelical Biography, 312
—— (J) Agriculture of Middlesex, 125
—— (T F) on the Greek Article, 11
—— Sermons, 58
—— (Life of) 58
Midgley's Halifax, 217
Miers's Chile and La Plata, 157
Milburn's Oriental Commerce 85
Military Science 106
—— *History of Britain,* 243
Mill (D) de Altari Mediatore 18
—— de Corinbus Altaris ext 18.
—— Ahi Tractatus de Antiquitatibus Biblis, 21
—— de Mahomedismo ante Mohamedem, 21
—— (J) de Nilo et Euphrate, 17
—— (J.) British India, 303
Millar's Origin of Ranks, 82
—— (Life of), 82
Miller's (E) Doncaster, 217
—— (G) Philosophy of History, 184
—— Ely Cathedral, 197
—— (J) Divine Authority of the Scriptures, 54
—— Sermons, 58
—— (P) Gardener's Dictionary, 92
Milles's Catalogue of Honor, 333.
Millin, Galerie Mythologique, 170.
Millot's General History, 176
—— Hist des Troubadours, 337
Mills's (C) Hist of the Crusades, 183
—— Hist of Chivalry, 183
Milman on the Character of the Apostles, 54
—— Martyr of Antioch, 369.
—— Anne Boleyn, 369
—— Belshazzar, 369
—— Fall of Jerusalem, 369.
Milne's Botanical Dictionary, 92.
Milner's (I) Sermons, 58
—— (J) Winchester 201.
—— Defence of the Bible Society, 45
—— (Joseph) [misp John], Sermons, 58
—— (Life of), 58
—— Ecclesiastical History, 62
—— (T) History of the VII. Churches of Asia, 64
Milton de Doctrinâ Christianâ, 45
—— translated, 45
—— Poetical Works 369

Milton's Paradise Lost, 369
—— Regained, 369
—— Poems, 369
—— Prose Works, 398
—— Life, 324
Mineralogy, 91
Minot's Poems, 370.
Minutii Felicis Opera, 34.
—— Apology for Christianity, 34
Minutulus de Urbe Romæ, 167
—— de Rom. Ædificiis 167
Mirabeau, Hist de la Cour de Berlin, 278
Mirineus de Reb Hisp 290
Mirabellæ Ichnographia Syracusæ, 297
Mirkhond, Histoire des Sassanides, 302
Mirror (the), 405
—— for Magistrates, 364
Missale S Patrum Latinorum, 29
—— Romanum MS 29
—— Romanum s Conc Tridentini, 29
—— Dictum Mozarabes, 30
Missæ Defunctorum, 29
Miscellanea Antiqua Anglicana, 193.
—— Scotica, 267
Miscellanies, 406.
Miseries of Human Life, 407
Misincus Tractatus de Sacrificio Jugi, 20
Missionary Voyage to the South Sea, 157.
Missions (History of), 65
Mitford's (M R) Christina, 370
—— Our Village, 383
—— (W) History of Greece, 179
Moallakat, 378
Moat (Desc. of the) near Canterbury 203.
Moerum Belli Cameracensis Historia, 294.
Modern History, 183.
—— *Biography,* 312.
Modestus, 408
Modius de Triumphis, Ludis, &c Veterum, 163
Mohammed-Aly (Histoire de), 307
Moine (le), de Melanophoris, 169.
Molembecius de Juramento per Gentium Principis, 22
Molesworth's Denmark, 275.
Molière, Œuvres, 395
—— (Vie de), 395
Molin de Clavibus Veterum, 168
Molina's Chili 309
Molleville's French Revolution, 285
Mollien's Colombia, 158
Molloy's Irish Grammar, 354
Monarchy asserted, 248
Monboddo's Ancient Metaphysics, 78
—— on Language, 348
Money, 85
Mongitoris Siciliæ Delineatio, 296
—— Domus Ordinis Theuticorum Panormi, 297
Monmouth's (Carey, E. of) Memoirs, 230
Monmouthshire Topography, 208
Mons (Nouveau Testament de), 7.
Monstrelet, Chroniques, 281.
Montagu (B) on the Punishment of Death, 71
—— (E) on Ancient Republics, 68
—— (Eliz) Letters, 405
—— on Shakspeare, 393
—— (G) Ornithological Dictionary 97
—— Testacea Britannica 100

Montagu's (Lady M. W.) Works, 398.
—— Late, 398
Montaigne, l'Italie, 138
Monte (Rob de) Chronica Normannæ, 289
Montefeltrica's Persian and Turkish Dictionary, 350
Montelhon (History of), 380.
Montesquieu, l'Esprit des Loix, 68.
—— sur les Romains, 180
—— le Temple de Gnide, 386
Montfaucon's Antiquity explained, 159.
—— Palæographia Græca, 339
Montgomery's (J) Poetical Works, 370
—— (R) Oxford, 370
Monti, Tragedie, 395
Monticon, la Ville de Lyon, 288
Montpensier (le Duc de), Mémoires, 287
Montrose's (Marq of) Memoirs, 266
Montucla, Histoire des Mathematiques, 102
Monuments (Antique), 170
Moor's Hindu Pantheon 67
Moore's (J.) View of France, &c. 135
—— Society in Italy, 138
—— Residence in France, 286.
—— Zeluco, 385
—— (Sir J.) Campaign, 244
—— (T.) Lalla Rookh, 370
—— Loves of the Angels, 370
—— Anacreon, 410
Moral Philosophy, 79
Morant's Essex, 200
—— Jersey, 218
More's (H.) Practical Piety, 46
—— Christian Morals, 46
—— on St Paul, 46
—— Essays, 81.
—— on Female Education, 81
—— on the Character of a Young Princess, 81.
—— Cœlebs, 382
—— (Life of Dr H), 324.
—— (Thos de la) Historia Anglia, 220
—— (Sir T.) Coventry Religious Frenzy, 214
—— Edward V and Richard III 228.
—— Utopia, 82
—— Vita, 253 and 324.
—— Life, 324
—— Poemata, [Cayley's Life, misprinted Cowley's], 361
Moreland's Piedmontese Churches, 62
—— Cryptography, 107
Morelet (Memoires de l'Abbé), 285
Morelli (D J.), Notizia d' Opere di Disegno, 108
—— (T.) Lexicon Græcum, 351
Morclius de Veterum Philosophorum Origine, &c. 162
Morenæ Historia Laudensium, 293
Moreri, Dictionnaire Historique, 311
Morestelli Philomusus, 165.
—— Alypius, 165
—— Pompa Feralis, 167
Morgan's (H D.) Religious Principles of the Age, 54
—— (J.) Algiers, 307.
—— (W.) on Assurances, 103
Morghen, le Antichita di Puzzuoli, 172

Morier's Persia, 149
—— Hajji Baba, 383
Morin de Paradiso, 17
—— (Life of), 314
Morley (the Fortunes of Bp), 255.
Mornay (Du Plessis), Mémoires, 282
Mornington (Account of the Earl of), 105
Morres on Faith, 53
—— Tunstall in Kent, 203
Morrison's Chinese Grammar, 350.
Morton's Northamptonshire, 208
Moryasine's Itinerary, 134
Moschi Opera, 412 and 427.
—— translated, 427
Mosheim (J L.) on Christianity before Constantine, 61
—— Ecclesiastical History, 62
—— de Platonicis, 65
Mosis Chorenensis Historia Armeniaca, 302
Mothe le Vayer on Liberty and Servitude, 80
Motteville, Histoire d'Anne d'Autriche, 283
Moucke, Rittrati degli Pittori, 109
Moule's Bibliotheca Heraldica, 330
Mover Lectures, 52
Movsant, Bibliotheque de Vers Françoise, 375.
Moysie's (C A.) Doctrines of Unitarians, 54
—— (D.) Affairs in Scotland, 266
Mozart (Account of), 105
Mugnotii Eremi Camaldulensis Desc 295
Muleri Annus Judæorum et Turc-Arabum, 19
Muller's (C O.) Doric Race, 179
—— (D C.) St Petersbourg, 136
—— (J.) on Fortification, 106.
—— Histoire des Suisses, 290
—— (J G.) de Proselytis, 21.
—— (M J E.) de Davide ante Arcam saltante, 24
Munro's (Sir T.) Life, 304
Muntz's Encaustic Painting, 110
Muratori Nov Thes Veterum Inscriptionum, 176
—— de Coronâ Ferrei, 293
—— Annali d'Italia 297
—— della Poesia Italiana, 375.
Murdin's Burleigh Papers, 249.
Murdoch's Dictionary of Distinctions, 353.
Mure's Egyptian Calendar and Zodiac, 158.
Murillo (Life of B c), 321
Murphy's (A) Works 398.
—— (J) on Gothic Architecture, 122
—— Portugal, 142
—— Church of Batalha, 142
—— (J C) Arabian Antiquities, 172
—— Mahometan Empire in Spain, 291
Murray's (A) European Languages, 348
—— (H) Africa, 141.
—— Asia, 147.
—— North America, 152
—— (Memoirs of the Regent), 264
—— (L.) English Grammar, 353
—— (Mrs) Beauties of Scotland, 258
Musæi Poema, 421
—— translated, 421.
Muscovitarum Rerum Scriptores, 276.

Museum Florentinum, 170
—— Worsleyanum, 170
—— Thoresbyana, 171
Musgrave (G) Belgæ 186
—— (Su R) Irish Rebellions, 272.
Music, 105
Musicâ Hebræorum (Tractatus de), 24.
Musical Miscellany, 365
Musonius de Luxu Græcorum, 161
Mussati de Gestis Henrici VII 294
—— Tragœdia, 294
—— Poemata, 294
Mut's Balearick Isles, 292
Myer's Geography, 129.
Mythology 66
Myvyrian Archæology, 258

Nadir Chah (Histoire de), 302
Nagelius de Ludis Secularibus, 24
Naismith's Agriculture of Clydesdale, 125.
Naldii Vita Jannoctoi Manetti, 296.
Nalson's Collections, 233.
Napier's Peninsular War, 244.
Napoleon 288 See also Bonaparte
—— (Correspondance de), 288
Nardin, Predicateur Evangelique, 58
Nardini Roma Antica, 139
—— Roma Vetus, 164.
—— Veji Antiqui, 295
Nares (E) on the Creeds, 33.
—— Evidences of Christianity, 53
—— (R) Glossary, 353
Nash's Worcestershire, 215
Nattes Geometry, 104
Natural Philosophy, 86
—— *History* 87
Naturalist (Journal of a), 89.
Naturelles (Dictionnaire des Sciences), 87
Naudæus de Nomine Senæ, 294
—— Templi Reatini Instauratio, 296
Naudet l'Italie sous les Goths, 298
Nanmachius, 409
Naunton's Fragmenta Regalia, 230
Naval History of Britain, 243
Navigation and Naval Architecture, 105
Naylor's Helvetia, 290
Neal's Puritans, 255 and 6.
—— New England, 310
Neale's Views of Seats in Great Britain, 191
Neamet Ullah's Afghans, 304
Nearchus' Voyage, 131
Nebrissensis de Rebus Hispanicis, 290
Neff (Life of Felix), 436
Neil's Orkney and Shetland, 261
Nели Dialogus de Acad Cantabrigiensi, 197
—— Acad Oxoniensis Delineatio, 210.
Nelson (Life of Viscount), 243
—— (J) Islington, 207
—— (R) on the Fasts and Festivals, 31
Nennii Historia Britannorum 220, 221
Neocorus de Museo Alexandrino, 162
Neot (Life of Saint) 253
Nepotis (C) Imperatorum Vitæ, 421
Nesbet's Heraldry, 331
Neubrigensis (Gul) Historia, 220, 223
Neuf Preux (le Triomphe des), 379
Neve (P) on Milton and English Poets, 362

Neve's (T) Christ the Saviour 53
—— See Le Neve.
Nevill (Testa de), 247
Newcastle (Tracts on), 438 and 439
—— (Marq of) Discipline of War, 433
Newcomes (P) St Alban's, 202
—— (W) Ezekiel, 6
—— Minor Prophets, 6
—— on our Lord's Conduct, 46
Newcourt's Repertorium Ecclesiasticum, 206
Newenham on the Population of Ireland, 270
—— View of Ireland, 270
Newman's Spanish Dictionary, 356
Newton (I) Opera, 398
—— Life, 204
—— (J) Life 325
—— (T) Works, 36
—— Life, 36
—— (W) Maidstone, 202.
Nibby, Viaggio ne' contorni di Roma, 139
Nicami Concilii Epistolæ, &c 34
Nieander, 408
Nicephori Constantinopolitani Historia, 181
Nicholai IV Taxatio Ecclesiastica, 247.
Nicholas's New Zealand, 158
Nichols's (J) Topographia Britannica, 188
—— Miscellaneous Antiquities, 188
—— Leicestershire, 204
—— Canonbury House, 208
—— Lambeth, 213
—— Progresses of Queen Elizabeth, 230
—— of James I 233
—— Literary Anecdotes, 337.
—— Illustrations, 338
—— Six Old Plays, 393
Nicholson's German Dictionary, 356.
—— (G) Cambrian Guide, 256
—— (J) Cumberland, 198
—— Westmoreland, 214
—— (P) Architectural Dictionary, 122
—— Mechanical Exercises, 123
—— on Masonry, 123
Nicolai de Synedrio Ægyptiorum, 22
—— de Juramento Hebr Gr et Rom 22
—— de Phyllobolia, 23
—— de Sepulchris Hebræorum, 24
—— de Ritu Bacchanaliorum 161
Nicolas's Notitia Historica 159
—— Chronicle of London, 205
—— Siege of Carlaverock 227
—— Proceedings of Henry VI.'s Privy Council, 228
—— Herald's Visitations, 330
—— Rolls of Arms, 333
Nicolay's Turkie, 142
Nicolson de Jure Feudali, 73
—— Leges Marchiarum, 74
—— Historical Libraries, 219
—— (Abp W) Letters, 404
Niderstedt Melita, 160.
Niebuhr's (B G) History of Rome, 180
—— (C) l'Arabie, 148
Niersis (St) Preces, 40
Nigri Su thæ Descriptio 296
Nimmo's Stirlingshire, 260
Niphus de Auguriis, 164

Nizolii Lexicon Ciceronianum, 352
Nobility (the Rise of), 332
Noble's House of Medici, 298
—— Continuation to Granger, 315
—— College of Arms, 330
—— House of Stuart, 334
—— House of Cromwell, 335
Nolan's Poor-laws, 71
Non   See Saint Non
Nonarum Inquisitiones, 247
Norden's (F L) Egypt and Nubia, 146
—— (J) Guide for English Travellers, 189
—— Middlesex, 207
Norfolk's (D of) Match with Mary of Scotland, 265
Norfolk (Agriculture of), 125
—— (Topography of), 208.
Noris (F H) Cenotaphia Pisana, 295
—— (H) Fasti Consulares, 166
—— de Nummis Diocl et Licinii, 167
—— de Votis decennalibus, 167
Normannorum Nomina, &c. 220
—— Historia, 289
Normannos (Francos rythmico Teutonico contra), 289
Norris's (C) Tenby, 207
—— (R) Abomey, 115
—— King of Dahomy, 307.
North on Fish-ponds, 98
North (Life of Lord Keeper), 325
North of Europe (Travels in), 135
Northampton (Mem of H E of), 399
Northamptonshire Topography, 208
Northcote's Varieties of Art, 110
Northern History, 273
—— Antiquities (Illustrations of), 273
—— Languages, 356
—— *Poetry*, 377
—— Tales and Romances, 388
North Georgia Gazette, 407
Northumberland Household Book, 194
—— (*Topography of*), 209.
North-west Passage, 152
Northwick's (Lord) Ancient Coins, 174
Norton's Practices of Papists, 231
Norway (Travels in), 136
Norwegian History, 274
Norwich (Description of), 208
Nott on Religious Enthusiasm, 53
—— State of Eng Poetry, 362
Nottinghamshire Topography, 209
Nottingham's (E of) Entertainment in Spain, 233
Novellæ Leges, 70
Novels, 379
Novelle (Libro di), 387
—— Scelte, 387
Nowell's Catechismus, 32
Nowel (Life of Dean), 325
Nubia (Travels in), 146
Nugent's Hampden and his Times, 235.
Nugæ Curialium, 396
Numismatics, 173
Nunez Refianes, 401
Nut-brown Maid, 370
Nye on Religion, 46

Oberlin (Memoirs of J T), 325
Obsequens (Julius), 415, 424, and 429

Observer, 405
Ockley's History of the Saracens, 301
O'Clery Annales IV Magistrorum, 271
O'Connor's (A.) Chronicles of Eri, 271
—— (C) Scriptores Hibernicarum, 271
Occult Philosophy, 78
Occulti (Rime degli Academici), 375
Oethere's Voyage, 131.
Offer's Wiltshire, 214
O'Flaherty's Ogygia, 271
Ogden's (S) Sermons, 58
—— (Life of), 58
Oggeri, Annali d' Italia, 297
Ogilvie's Regalia of Scotland, 266
Oginski sur la Pologne 277
Ogle Family History, 335
O'Hara Family Tales, 383
Ohring Lexicon Lapponicum, 357
Oldcastell's Examination, &c 253
Oldfield's Representative History, 245
Oldmixon's England, 235
Oldys's British Librarian, 343
Olearius, Voyage en Muscovie, Perse, &c 119
Olivier, Entomologie, 98
—— Travels, 133
Olla Podrida, 405.
Oltmanns, Observations Astronomiques, &c 155
Olympius (M Aurelius), 409
Opelius de Fabrica Triremium, 166
Opitius (F) de Templi Custodia Nocturna, 18
—— (H) de Pharisæis, 20
—— de Clethi et Phlethi, 22
Oppianus de Piscatu, 421.
—— translated, 422
Optics, 104
Orange (Justification of the P of), 279
Oratio Dominica in diversis Linguis, 33
Oratory, 359
Orations of Arsanes the Venetian Ambassador, &c 359
Ordinaire's History of Volcanoes, 90
O'Reilly's Catalogue of Irish Writers, 271
Orem's Chanonry of Aberdeen, 260
Orford's Works, 399
Oriental Languages, 349
—— *Poetry*, 378
—— *Romances*, 388
—— *Drama*, 396
Origenis Philosophumenon Fragmenta, 162
—— Hexapla, 3.
Origin of Nations, 177
Orkneyinga Saga, 261
Orlandinus de Urbis Senæ Antiquitate, 295
Orleans's Poems, 370
Orme's (R) Mogul Empire, 303.
—— Indostan, 303
—— Memoirs, 303
—— (W) Bibliotheca Biblica, 10
Ormerod's Cheshire, 197
Ormonde (Life of James Duke of), 239
—— Papers, 250
Ornithology, 97
Orozco, Tesoro della Lingua Castellana, 356
Orphei Opera, 422
—— translated, 422

Ortelii Deorum Dearumque Capita, 161
Ortlob de Scutis et Clypeis Hebraeorum, 22
Osbaldiston's British Sportsman, 127
Osborne's Traditional Memorials, 231.
Osorius's Epistle, 230
Osorio's History of the Portuguese, 292
Osiander de Assylis Hebræorum, 22
—— de Assyliis Gentilium, 160.
Ossian's Poems, 374
Ostervald's Arguments of the Books of the Bible, 9
Otterbourne (Thomæ) Chronica, 224
Otthonis Historia Mismicorum, 20
Ottinelli de Firmo Elogium, 294
Ottius de Nummis Samaritanorum, 23
Ottley's Italian School, 112
—— Stafford Gallery, 116
—— History of Engraving, 119
Otto de Flumine Sabbathico, 18.
Otway's Works, 392
—— Life, 392
Oudin, Refranes, 401.
Oulton's Traveller's Guide, 189
Oupnek'hat, seu Doctrina Indorum, 67
Ouseley's Travels in the East, 149.
—— Persian Miscellanies, 349
Outovius de Montibus Sionis et Morijah, 18
—— de Sabbatho, 19
Overbury's Wife, 363
Overton's True Churchman, 46
Ovidii Opera, 422
—— Metamorphoses translated, 422.
Owen (H.) on Miracles, 52
—— (J.) on the Hebrews, 14
—— Latin Epigrams translated, 361
—— on the Bible Society, 236
—— (S.) River Thames, 192
—— (W.) Shrewsbury, 211
—— Welsh Dictionary, 354
Oxfordshire (Agriculture of), 125
Oxfordshire Topography, 209
Oxlee's Doctrine of the Trinity, 46
Oxley's New South Wales, 150
Oxoniensis Acad. Assertio Antiquitatis, 210
Oxoniana, 211

Pace Antiquitates Caltageronis, 297
Pachymeris Historia, 181
Paduani Monachi Chronica, 294
Pætus de Mensuris et Ponderibus, 166
Paganism, 66
Painter's Palace of Pleasure, 333
Painting, 109
Palaye, Histoire des Troubadours, 337.
Palermus de verâ C. Plinii Patriâ, 296
Palestine (Travels in) 147
Paley's Evidences of Christianity, 46
—— Horæ Paulinæ, 46
—— Natural Theology, 46
—— Clergyman's Companion, 46
—— Sermons and Tracts, 38.
—— Moral Philosophy, 80
—— (Life of), 325
Palgrave's Parliamentary Writs, 72.
—— English Commonwealth, 245.
Palissot de Beauvois, Insectes d'Afrique, &c. 99.

Palladio's Architecture, 122
Palladius de Olivis Rerum Foro-Juliensis, 294
—— de Oppugnatione Gradiscanâ, 294
Pallas, Voyages, 136
Palmer's Origines Liturgicæ, 30
Palmerin of England, 380
Palmerino d'Ingleterra, 380
Palmerus de Captivitate Pisarum, 295
Palmyra (Antiquities of), 171
Pamelii Liturgia Latina, 29.
Pananti's Algiers, 144
Panciroli Varia de Antiquitat. Rom. 164
—— Notitia Dignitatum, 165
Pancoucke, Proverbes François, 401.
—— Encyclopædiana, 401
Pandectæ Justinianæ, 70
Parvinius de Civitate Romanâ, 163.
—— de Imperio Romano, 163
—— Antiquæ Urbis Imago, 164
—— de Romanorum Nominibus, 164
—— de Ludis Circensibus, 165
—— de Ludis Sæcul. et de Triumpho, 166
—— de Antiquitatibus Veronensium, 298
Panzer Annales Typographici, 341
Paoli-Chigny, les Puissances de l'Europe, 184
Parænesis Germanicæ, 361
Paris (J. A.) on Diet, 102
—— (M.) Historia, 223
—— Vita Abbatum S. Albani, 253.
Parismus (Historie of), 380
Parival, Histoire de ce Siecle, 184.
Park's (J. J.) Hampstead, 207
—— (M.) Travels in Africa, 145
—— Life, 145
—— (T.) Heliconia, 361
Parker (M.) Historiæ Anglicanæ Scriptores, 220
—— de Antiquitate Britan. Ecclesiæ, 252
—— Cat. Cancellariæ Cantabrig. 252
—— de Scholarum, &c. Cantab. Patronis, 252
—— Life, 255
—— (R.) Skeletos Cantabrigiensis, 197.
—— (T. L.) Browsholme Hall, 218.
Parkes' Chemical Catechism, 87
Parkhurst's Hebrew Lexicon, 349
—— Greek Lexicon, 351
Parkin's Norfolk, 208
—— Norwich, 208.
Parkinson's (J.) Organic Remains, 91
—— (R.) Agriculture of Huntingdonshire, 124
—— Agriculture of Rutlandshire, 124
Parkyns' Inn Play, 127
Parliament (the Antiquity, Power, &c. of), 72
Parliamentary History of Britain, 244.
—— History, 245
Parnasso Espanol, 377
—— Lusitano, 377
Parochial Law, 74.
Parr's Character of Fox, 320
Parriana Bibliotheca, 346
Parry's (D.) British Etymologicon, 354
—— (Sir W. E.) Voyages for a North-west Passage, 153
—— Voyage to the North Pole, 153
Partenopex de Blois, 381

INDEX 483

Parutæ Sicilia Numismatica, 297
Pascal Pensees, 46
—— Letters 46
—— Life, 46
Paschius de חרם, 24
Pasley's Military Policy, 244
Paston Letters, 248
Patavini Marmoris Inscript Interp 167
Paterculus See Velleius
Paterson's Roads of England, &c. 189
Patlelin (la Farce de P), 395
Patinus de Numismate Augusti et Platonis, 162
—— in Inscriptiones Græcas, 169
—— in Monum Marcellinæ, 169.
—— in Cenotaph M Antonii, 169
Patres Ecclesiastici, 34
Patricii Res Militaris Roman 166
Patrick's Commentary on the Bible, 11
—— Sermons, 58
Patten's (R) Rebellion in Scotland, 267
—— (W)Somerset's Expedition, 230 and 264
Paul (Father). See Sarpi
Paul's Letters to his Kinsfolk, 244
Pausaniæ Græciæ Descriptio, 422
—— translated 422
Pavia (la Certosi di), 439
Peacham's Devises, 402
Pearce's Abyssinia, 147
Pearch's Collection of Poems, 364
Pearson (E) on the Prophecies, 15
—— (J) Annales Paulini, 13
—— on the Creed, 33.
Peck's Desiderata Curiosa, 193
—— Stamford, 204
—— Oliver Cromwell, 237
—— Memoirs of Milton's Poetical Works, 369.
Pecock's (Bp) Life, 253.
Pedrusi Museo Farnese, 174
Peele's Works, 392
—— Life, 392
—— Jests, 401
Pegge's Forme of Curv, 126
—— Coins of Archbishops of Canterbury, 175
—— Inscriptions of English Churches, 186
—— Bolsover and Peak Castles, 198
—— Roman Roads in Derbyshire, 198
—— Registrum Roffense, 202
—— Guy, Earl of Warwick, 214
—— Eccleshal Manor, 214
—— Lichfield House, 214
—— Suffragan Bishops, 253
—— Anonymiana, 338.
—— Anecdotes of the English Language, 353
Peignot, Dict de Bibliologie, 343
—— Dict des Livres Condamnes 343
—— Repertoire Bibliographique, 343
Pelham (Memoirs of H), 242
Pembrochiæ Numismata, 174
Peninsula (Recollections of the), 141
Pennant's British Zoology, 96
—— Indian Zoology, 96
—— Quadrupeds, 96
—— Genera of Birds, 97
—— Index to Buffon's Ornithology 97

Pennant's Arctic World, 135
—— Hindoostan, 150
—— Journey from Chester 189
—— Journey from London to Dover, 189
—— Tour from Downing, 189
—— London, 205
—— Tour in Wales. 256
—— Whiteford and Holywell, 257
—— Snowdon, 257
—— Tours in Scotland, 259
—— Literary Life, 338
Penrose on the Original of Christianity, 54
Pepys' Memoirs, 239
Peru Deliciæ Poet Hungaricorum, 361.
Perceval's (G) Italy, 298
—— (R) Ceylon, 306
—— Cape of Good Hope, 308
Percy's (T) Reliques of English Poetry, 363
—— (W) Celia, 370
Peregrini Hist Principum Longobard 295.
—— de Vet Signif. Vocis Portæ, 295
—— de Campaniâ Felice, 295
Perelli Antiquitates Sicili, 297
Perez, las Guerras de Grenada, 291
Perger, Galerie de Vienne, 117.
Perifixe, Histoire de Henri IV, 282
Perionius de Magistratibus Gr. et Rom 160
Periplus of the Erythræan Sea, 131
Peritsol Itinera Mundi, 17
Perlin, Description d Angleterre, &c 188
Perrault les Hommes Illustres, 314
Perrelli Ratio Lunæ, 162
Perrin's Luther's Forerunners, 62
Perrot's (Sir J) Memoirs, 272
—— (L C S on the Government of), 272
Perry's Conchology, 100
Persia (Travels in), 148.
Persian History, 302
—— Language, 349
—— Poems, MS 378
Persii Satyræ, 419 and 422
—— translated, 422
Perspective, 104
Perth (Chronicle of), 262
Pervigilium Veneris anon 413
Petachiæ Itinerarium, 17
Petavius de Ponderibus, &c 22
—— Kalendarium Vetus Romanum, 165
—— Supellectilis Portuuncula, 168
—— Vet Nummorum Γνωρισμα, 168
Petav, Chronologie de l'Histoire, 159
Peter the Great, 276
Peter's Letters to his Kinsfolk, 315.
Petit-Radel, l'Italie, 138
—— sur les Bibliothèques, 345
Petit (J. F), Chronique d'Hollande, 278
—— (S) Leges Atticæ, 69
—— de Anno Attico, 162
—— Ecloga Chronologicæ, 165
Petrarca le Rime, 376
—— (Translations from), 376
Petraique (Memoires de), 325.
Petroburgensis (Ben Ab) de Vitâ Hen. II 227
Petronii Satyricon, 422
—— translated, 422
Pettigrew's Bibliotheca Sussexiana, 316

Peyran's Defence of the Albigenses, 62
Peyton's House of Stuart, 235
Pezold de Promiscua Vestium utriusque Sexûs, 23.
Pfeifferi Antiquitates Hebræorum, 17
— de Theraphim, 21
— aha de Rebus Biblicis, 24
Pfeffinger de Nathinæis, 19
Phalaridis Epistolæ, 423
— translated, 423
Phæbonii Historia Marsorum, 295
Phædri Fabulæ, 423
Philadelphus de Valle Josaphat, 18
Philidor on Chess, 128
Philip II III and V 291
Philipses (Lives of the) Milton's Nephews, 237
Philippi (J) pro Rege, &c Anglicano Defensio, 72
Philippes s (M) Defence of Mary Queen of Scots, 265
Philpe's (Sir T) Plantations of the Londoners, 270
Phillipott's (T) Kent, 202.
Phillips's (A) Botany Bay, 157
—— Old Ballads, 363
—— (E) Charles I 225
—— Theatrum Poetarum 362.
—— (H) Silva Florifera, 95
—— Pomarium Britannicum, 95
—— on Cultivated Vegetables, 126
—— Floral Emblems, 402
—— (T) Shrewsbury. 211.
—— (W) Geology; 90
Philo Judaus on the Logos, 34
Philosophy, 76
—— (*History of*), 76
Philosophical Transactions, 340
Philostorgii Historia Ecclesiastica, 61.
Philostratus de Pictura, 162
Philoxeni Glossarium, 351
Philpott's Letters to C. Butler, 252.
Phocylides, 408
Phrantzæ (G) Chronicon, 181
Phrysius (T Popma) de Operis Servorum, 169
Physiognomy, 78
Physiognomical Portraits, 315
Picage, Galerie de Duseldorf, 117
Picart [misprinted Picard], Cérémonies et Coutumes Religieuses, 60
Piccolus (A) de Ant Jure Eccles Siciliæ, 296
Pietari ensis (Gul) Gesta Normannica, 220.
Picturesque Annual, 407
Picus of Mirandula's Memoirs, 314
Pidgeon's Cuvier's Fossil Mammalia, 96.
Piers Ploughman's Vision and Crede, 369
Pighii Themis Dea et Mythologia, 162
—— Fasti Magistr et Consularum Rom. 166
Pignorii M Deum matris Ideææ Initia, 161
—— de Servis, 169
—— Origines Patavinæ, 294
—— de Ritu Nuptiarum, 294.
—— Vita, Bibliotheca, et Museum, 294
Pignotti, Storia della Toscana, 298
Pike's Travels in North America, 154
Pilgrim Good Intent, 46.

Pilkington's (J) Derbyshire, 198
—— (M) Dict of Painters 109.
Pilpay's Fables, 400
Pincii de Timavo Dissert. 294.
Pindari Carmina, 423
—— translated 423
Pindemonte, Poësie, 376
Pine's Tapestry of the House of Lords, 243
Pingonii (P) Augustæ Taurinorum Chronicon, 295
Pinkerton's (J) Petralogy, 91.
—— Atlas, 130
—— on Medals, 173
—— Origin of Scythians and Goths, 178.
—— History of Scotland, 263
—— Iconographia Scotica, 316
—— Scottish Gallery, 315
—— Ballads, 373
—— Correspondence 404
Pinto, Peregrinaciones, 147
Piossens, Mémoires de la Regence, 284
Piranesi's Antiquities of Rome, 171
—— Vasi, Candelabri, &c 173
Piroli, Antiquités d'Herculaneum, 171.
Piri Siciliæ Sacræ, 296
—— Capelle S Petri in Panormo, 296
—— Chronologia Regum Siciliæ, 296.
Pisidæ Hist Byzantina Appendix, 182
Pitcairne's (R) Scottish Criminal Trials, 262
Pithæi Corpus Juris Canonici, 71.
—— Canones Ecclesia Rom 27
Pitisci Lexicon Antiquitatum Rom 169
Pitt (Anecdotes of), E of Chatham, 325
—— (Memoirs of W), 242
—— (W) Speeches, 242
—— Leicestershire Agriculture, 124
—— Northamptonshire Agriculture, 125
—— Staffordshire Agriculture, 125
—— Worcestershire Agriculture, 125.
Pius V's Bull, 255
Place (de la), Théorie de Probabilités, 103
—— Système du Monde, 104
—— Mechanique Céleste, 101
Placentini Itinerarium, 18
Placita temp Ric I usque ad Ed II 246
—— de quo Warranto, 247
Plague in London, 206
Planché, Dict de Langue Oratoire et Poétique, 355.
Planta's Helvetic Confederacy, 290
Plathnerus de Sandaligerulis Hebr 23
Platina's Lives of the Popes, 61
—— Historia Urbis Mantuæ, 293
Platonis Opera, 423
—— translated, 423
—— Republic translated, 423.
Plauti Comœdiæ, 423.
—— translated, 423
Playfair's Illustrations of the Huttonian Theory, 90
—— Geometry, 103
—— Trigonometry, 103
Pleskin de Columnis Æneis, 18.
Plinii Historia Naturalis, 423 and 424
—— translated, 424.
—— tradotta in Italiana, 424
—— Epistolæ &c 424.

INDEX.   485

Pliny's Letters, translated, 424
Plot's (Dr R) [misprinted Plat] Journey through England, 188
—— Oxfordshire, and Life, 209.
—— Staffordshire, 212
Plowden's Ireland, 272
Plumptre's Collection of Songs, 365
—— Letter to Aikin, 365
Plutarchi Proverbia Graeca, 162
—— Quaestiones Romanae, 165
—— Opera, 424
—— Lives translated, 424
Plymley's Church of Eng Doctrines, 46.
—— Agriculture of Shropshire, 125
Pocharis de Simulacris Solaribus Israel. 21.
Pococke's Travels, 133
Poetry, 359
—— (Art of), 359
Poetarum, Dictionnaire Suisse, 356
Poggius Florent de Fortuna Urbis Rom. 167.
—— Bracciolini Historia Florentina, 295
—— (Life of), 325
Poiteau et Risso, Histoire des Orangers, 95
Poitiers, Vie de Guillaume Conquerant, 290
Poland (Travels in), 136.
—— (History of), 277
Polemann de Urim et Thummim, 19
—— de Ritu precandi vet Hebr 20.
Poleni Thesauri Art Supplementa, 168.
Poleti Hist Fori Romani, 168
Poh Synopsis Criticorum, 11.
Police, 84
Polish Bible, 7
—— Language 357.
Polite Literature, 347
Politianus (Memoirs of Ang), 314
Politics, 81
Political Economy, 83
—— History of Britain, 244.
Pollio Trebellius, 409
Pollok's Course of Time, 370.
Polo   See Marco Polo
Polonorum Poetarum Pastoralia, 361.
Polwhele's Cornwall, 198
—— Devonshire, 198
—— Traditions and Recollections, 138
Polybius de Castris Romanorum, 166.
—— Historia, 424
—— translated, 424
—— trad en Françoise, 424
Polycarpi Apostoli Opera, 34
Polychronicon, 223.
Polyglot Bible, 2
Polygraphy, 396
Polynesian Voyages, 157
Pombal (Life of the Marquis de), 291
Pomponii Melae Orbis Descriptio, 415.
—— de Situ Orbis, 424
Pontani Historia Neapolitana, 295
Pontey's Planter, 125
—— Forest-Pruner, 125
Ponticus de Politiis Graecorum, 160
Pontificale Romanum, 30
Ponticract's (Lord) Letters, 433
Pope (Life of A), 326 and 399
—— Works, 399

Pope (Life of Sir T), 326
Popes (History of the), 64.
Population, 84
Porcius de Re Pecuniaria Vet 162.
Porphyrius de Vita Pythagora, 418.
Porphyrogenneta de Caeremoniis Byzant. 182
Porsoni Adversaria, 358
Porter's (H) Flowers of the Saints, 252
—— (M A) Novels, 381 and 395
—— (Sir R K) Russia and Sweden, 136.
—— Spain and Portugal, 141
—— Travels in Persia &c 149
—— Campaigns in Russia, 276
Porteus's Sermons, 58
—— Lectures, 58
Porti Lexicon Doricum, 427
Portraits, 117.
—— with Biographical Memoirs, 315
Portugal (Travels in), 141
Portuguese History 292
Portuguese Language, 356.
Portuguese Poetry, 377
Pory's Africa, 306
Postellus de Republica Atheniensium, 160
—— de Etruria, 295.
Pote's Windsor Castle, 195.
Potemkin (Memoirs of Prince), 276
Potts British Farmer, 124
Potter (J) on Church Government, 28
—— Archaeologia Graeca, 163
—— Grecian Antiquities, 170
—— (R) Aeschylus, 409
Pottinger's Beloochistan, 151.
Poulson's Beverley, 216.
Pouqueville, la Grèce, 143.
—— Greece, 143
Powell's (D) History of Cambria, 257.
—— (R) Life of Alfred, 222
—— Charles I 234
Pownall's Study of Antiquities, 159
Poyer's Barbadoes, 310
Pradt, la Révolution d'Espagne, 291.
Praetorii Orbis Gothicus, 274
—— Mars Gothicus, 274
Prasotius de Magistratibus Romanorum, 168
Pray Historia Regum Hungariae, 278.
Prayer (Book of Common), 30.
Predestination (Cambridge Tracts on), 46.
Praefectus Urbis Romanorum (Anon de), 166
Preston (Hist of), in Lancashire, 204
Price's (D) History of Arabia, 301
—— Mahommedan History, 302.
—— (J) Hereford, 201.
—— Leominster, 201
—— (U) on the Picturesque, 110
Pritchard's Physical Hist. of Mankind, 96
—— on Celtic Origin, 177
Prickett's Bridlington Priory, 216
Prideaux de Jure Pauperis, 18
—— Old and New Test connected, 26.
—— Life, 26
Priest's (St J) Agriculture of Bucks, 124
Priestley on Air, 86
Primaleone (l' Historia di), 380
Primer of Sarum, 30

Primer of Henry VIII 30
Prince's Worthies of Devon, 314
Prints, 111.
Printing, 107
—— (History of), 340
—— (Decree of the Star Chamber on), 341
Prior's Negotiations, 250.
Priscianus Cæs de Nummis, &c 166.
—— Periegesis, 124
Prise's Cambria 256
Prisons (Memoires sur les) Françaises, 287
Pritii Introductio in Nov Test 9
Procopii Historia, 181.
Prodici Hercules, 415.
Projector, 405
Promenades aux Cimetieres de Paris, 140
Propertius, 412
Property Laws, 74.
Prophecies (on the), 15
Prosperi Chronicon Integrum, 166
Protectorate, 237.
Proverbs, 401
Provinciæ Angliæ Partitio, 221.
Prudentii Opera, 424 and 425
Prynne's Soveraigne Power of Parliament, 72
—— Records 244 and 245
—— Histrio-Mastix, 390
Publii Syri Sententiæ, 423 and 427.
Puffendorf de Officio Hominis, 60.
Puget de St Pierre, Histoire des Druses, 301
Pulci Morgante Maggiore, 376.
Pulteney's Catalogue of Birds, Shells, and Plants of Dorsetshire, 89.
—— Life, 89
Purcell's Orpheus Britannicus, 105
Purchas his Pilgrimes, 131.
—— Relations of the World, 177
Puricelli Ambrosianæ Basilicæ, &c Desc 293
Purpurinus à Fav de Kalend Rom Amiterni, 168.
Puteani Olympiades, 162.
—— de Jurejurando, 165
—— varia de Antiquitatibus Rom 165 and 166
—— Pecuniæ Romanæ, 168
—— Historia Cisalpina, 293
Puttenham's Arte of Eng. Poesie, 362
Pym's Speech against Laud, 234.
Pyne's Costume of Britain, 121
—— Royal Residences, 191.
Pynnar's Survey of Ulster, 269
Pythagoræ Aurea Carmina, 425
—— les Vers Dorés, 425
Pythagoras's School Cambridge, 197

Quandt de Pont Max Suffragium, 19
—— de Cultris Circumcisionis, 21.
Quarles' Manual of Devotion, 46
—— Life, 46
Quarterly Review, 340.
Quatremère, Mém sur l'Egypte, 307
Quenstedt de Sepultura Vet. 25 and 163
Quérard, la France Littéraire, 343
Quesnel, Reflexions sur le N Test. 12

Quilman's Dunluce Castle, 370
—— Stanzas, 370.
Quiñones, Munedas Romanos, 174.
Quintiliani Opera, 424
—— de Inst Oratoria, 425
—— Declamationes, 425.
—— Institutes translated 425
Quintus Smyrnæus, 425
Quistorpii Nebo, 17

Rabelais, Œuvres, 386
Rabirius de Hastarum Origine, 164
Racan, Œuvres, 375
Racine, Hist de Port-Royal, 65
—— Œuvres et Vie 399
Racoviensis Catechesis, 33
Radcliffe (Life, &c of Sir G.), 326
—— (Mrs) Novels, 381, 383, and 384
Raffles's (Sir T S) Java, 306.
—— Life, 306
Ragman Roll, 263
Ragusæ Elogia Siculorum, 297
Ragecourt sur l'Affaire de Varennes, 236.
Raik's Somersetshire, 211
Raine's North Durham, 199.
Ralegh's (Sir W.) Poems, 370.
—— Works, 399
—— Life, 233 and 399
Ralfe's Naval Chronology, 243.
Rambach's Meditations, 47
Ramesensis Anonvmi Historia, 221.
Rammohun Roy's Translation of the Veds, 439
Ramsay's (A.) Tea-table Miscellany, 373
—— Poems, 374.
—— Gentle Shepherd, 392
—— Life, 392.
—— (Chev) Voyage de Cyrus, 386.
Ramus de Militia J Cæsaris, 166.
—— Vita 326
Ramusio, Navigationi e Viagi, 131.
Rancé (Account of the Abbé de), 65.
Randolph's Enchiridion Theologicum, 47
Randulphi Tuba Danica, 275.
Rantzovii Epigrammata, 439.
Ranzoviana Genealogia, 336
Raoul Rochette, Hist. des Colonies Grecques, 180
Raphaeli Imagines V et N Test, 112
—— Pinacotheca Hamptoniana, 112.
Rapin's History of England, 226
Rapiti Balnei ad Timavi ostium, 294
Rasche Lexicon Rei Nummariæ, 174
Raske's Danish Grammar, 357.
Rastell's Chronicles, 224
Rauthmell's Overborough, 204
Rawlinson's Vindication of the King's Ecc Rights, 28.
—— English Topographer, 185.
—— Bath Abbey, 211.
—— Salisbury Cathedral, 215.
Raii Historia Plantarum, 92.
—— Fowling, Falconry, and Singing-Birds, 97
—— N and S Country Words, 353.
—— Proverbs, 402.
Raynaudus de Pileo, 165.
Re (del) Antiquitates Tiburtinæ, 295.
Reading on the Lessons, 31

Rebati Delin Dianæ Arelatensis, 167
Rochenberg de Pharisæis, 20
Reconciler of the Bible, 8
Records (Public), 246
Recorde's Castle of Knowledge, 104.
Recreative Arts, 127.
Recueil des Historiens de France, 280
Reden, Tableaux Généalogiques Britan 334
Redouté, les Roses, 93
——— les Liliacees, 93
Reeves's Apologies of the Fathers, 34
Regan's Ireland, 271
Regnault-Warin, Mem sur La Fayette, &c 286
Rehfues, l Espagne 141
Res Accipitraria, 409
Reid on the Mind, 78
——— (Life of), 326.
Reine de חכם, 24
Reinhard de Sacco et Cinere, 25
Reinold de Inscriptionibus Legum, 70
Reiske de Baptismo Jud 21
Rejected Addresses, 370.
Relandi (H) Varia de Antiquitatibus Sacris, 17
——— de Spoliis Templi, 18
——— de Samaritanis, 20.
——— de Diis Cabiris, 21 and 169
——— de Galli Cantu Hieros audito, 22
——— de Nummis Samar 23
——— de Linguâ Ægyptia, 349.
Religion, 1.
——— (*History of*), 60
——— (*History of the Christian*), 61.
Religious Orders, 65
Relhan's Flora Cantabrigiensis, 94
Relics of Antiquity, 191
Rembrandt (Cat of the Works of), 120
Remonstrantis Confessio Fidei, 33
Renaudot Coll Liturgiarum Orient 29
Rennel s Geography of Herodotus, 129.
——— Expedition of Cyrus, 129
——— Western Asia, 147
——— Map of Hindostan, 149
Rénouard, Anna'es des Aldes, 342.
——— Cat. de sa Bibliotheque, 346
Repton (H) on Landscape Gardening, 126
Reresby's Travels, 134
——— Memoirs, 239
Resendii Antiquitates Lusitaniæ, 292.
Retz (Mem. du Card de), 284
Retzow, la Guerre de Sept Ans, 278
Reus's Register of Living Authors, 343.
Revett's Antiquities of Athens, 171.
Revickshy, Cat de ses Livres, 346
Revolution of 1688 (State Tracts on), 211
Reyna (Cass de) Biblia Hispanica, 8
——— (P) Messana Historia, 297
Reynard the Fox, 384
Reynolds's (L) Works, 36
——— Life, 36
——— [misprinted Reynold], 47.
——— (Sir J) Works, 399
——— Life, 326 and 399.
Rhemish (the) New Testament, 6
Rhemnius Fannius de Numinis, &c 166
Rhenferdius de Situ et Nominibus Loc Hebr 17.

Rhenferdii varia de Antiq Sacris, 20.
——— de Arabarcha Jud 21
——— Periculum Phœnicium, 23
Rhetoric, 359.
Rhetores Selecti, 408.
Rhorenscensius de Ritu scindendi Vestes, 23
Rhunkenii Vers Lat. Basilikon Libri, 70.
——— Opuscula, 458
Ribouldeald de Urim et Thummim, 19
Ricardo's Political Economy, 83
Ricciardi Vita S Bonifacii Comment 294
Riccio (Life of David), 264 and 326
Ricrobinus de Gymnasio Patavino, 294
Rich's Ireland, 269.
Richard I, Chansons, 371
——— la Tour Tenébreuse, 380
——— II Vita a Monacho anon 227
——— (Story of) in Ireland, 272.
——— III 228.
——— of Cirencester's Descrip of Britain, 187 and 188
——— (Account of), 188
——— de Situ Britanniæ, 220
——— (l'Abbé) Théorie des Songes, 79
Richarderie, Bibliothèque des Voyages, 131
Richards (G) on Prophecy, 53
——— (T) Welsh Dictionary, 354
Richardson's (C) English Philology, 353
——— (H) Hortus Bieiliensis, 91
——— (J) North American Zoology, 96
——— Account of the Statues, &c. in Italy, 108
——— on Painting, 110
——— Notes on Paradise Lost, 369
——— on Eastern Nations 301
——— Persian and Arabic Dictionary, 349
——— (R) Travels, 134
——— Correspondence, 437
——— (S) Novels, 382 and 384
——— (W) Sermons, 58.
——— (Life of), 58
——— on Shakespeare, 393
Richelieu (Histoire du Card), 283
Richmond's Fathers of the Eng Church, 37
Rickmann's Population Returns, 84.
Riddoch's Sermons, 58
Ridley (Bp) on Transubstantiation, 47
——— (Life of), 254.
——— (G) on the Holy Ghost, 53
Ridpath's Border History, 262
Rievallensis Ailredi Historia 221
Rigaltius de Populis Fundis, 164
Riley s Timbuctoo, 145
Riouffe, Mémoires d'un Détenu, 287
Ripamonti Historia Mediolanensis, 293
Ripperda (Life of the Duke de), 291
Risso et Poiteau, Histoire des Orangers, 95
Ritchie's Italy, &c 138
Ritus de Rebus Hispanicis, 290
——— de Regibus Siciliæ, 296
Ritson (J) on Courts Leet, 74
——— Bibliographia Poetica, 344
——— English Anthology, 363
——— Ancient Poetry, 363
——— Eng. Metrical Romances, 364.

488 INDEX.

Ritson's Ancient Songs, 365
—— Robin Hood, 365
—— English Songs, 365
—— Scottish Songs, 373
—— on Shakespeare, 393
Rituale Romanum, 30
Rivarol (Memoires de), 286
Robert (Life of St) of Knaresboro, 252
Robert the Devyll, 380
Roberts' Voyages, 132
—— (P.) Welsh Chronicles, 257
—— (W H) on the English Version of the Old Testament, 14
Robertson s (G) Agriculture of Kincardineshire, 125
—— (H) Romaic Grammar, 351
—— (J) Agriculture of Inverness-shire, 125
—— (W) Charles V 277
—— Scotland, 264
—— India, 302
—— America, 308
—— (Life of), 326
Robinson's (J) Theolog Dictionary, 16
—— (T) Prophecies of the Messiah, 15
—— Scripture Characters, 47
—— Christian System, 47.
—— on the Mosaic Creation, 47
—— Westmoreland, 214
—— (Life of), 326
—— Last Days of Bp Heber, 321
Robison's Mechanical Philosophy, 103
Robortelli varia de Antiquitatibus Romanorum, 164
—— de Mensium Appellatione, 165
—— de Legionibus Rom 166
—— Laconici, 166
Roby's Traditions of Lancashire, 384
Rocca de Campanis, 168
Rochefort, Histoire des Antilles, 310
Rochefoucault's Travels in N. America, 153
—— Maximes, 402
Rochester's (Lord) Diary in Poland, 239.
—— (Life of the Earl of), 326
Rocoles, les Impostures Insignes, 184.
Rodd's Spanish Ballads, 377
Roffensis Textus a Hearne, 203
Rogal Thuribulum, 18
Rogeri Comitis Siciliæ Vita, 296
Rogers's (S) Poems, 370
—— Italy, 370
—— Human Life, 370
—— (T) Lectures, 58
Roland (Memoires de Madame de), 287
Rolandini Grammatici Chronicon, 294
Rolin on the Roman Revenue, 170
—— Ancient History, and Life, 177
—— Belles Lettres, 347
Roman Antiquities, 163 and 168
Roman History, 180
—— *Topography of England*, 185
Romanies, 379
Rome (Description of), 139
—— in the 19th Century, 139
—— (Plates of the Antiquities of), 171
Romney (Life of G), 327.
Romoaldi Summarium Rationum, 265
Ronald's Pyrus Malus Brentfordiensis, 95
Rook's Sherwood Forest, 209

Roos's (Lord) Entertainment in Spain, 233.
Roquefort, Glossaire de la Langue Romaine, 355
Rosamond (on the Fair), 210
Roscoe's (T) Switzerland and Italy, 137.
—— Italy, 138
—— Italian Novelists, 387
—— German Novelists, 388
—— Spanish Novelists, 439.
—— (W.) Lorenzo di Medici, 299
—— Leo X 290
Rose (Rommant de la), 371
—— (Sir G) on Fox's James II 240
—— Marchmont Papers, 251.
—— (W S) Letters from Italy, 138.
Roser de Dagone, 21
Ross's Voyage for a North-west Passage, 152
Rossi (B de) Variæ Lectiones S Script 1.
—— (D) Raccolta di Statue, 172
—— (G G di) Scherzi Poetici, 376
—— (J) Hist Comitibus Warwicensibus, 214
—— Historia Angliæ, 224
Rossini, Vedute di Roma, 139
—— Antichità di Roma, 172
—— del Lazio, 172
Rostensch de Sepulchris Calce not. 25
Rostgaard Delitiæ Poet Danorum, 361
Rot de Velamine Capitis Virilis, 23
Rotuli Hundredorum, 247
—— Chartarum et Inquisitionum, 247
—— Patentium, 247
—— Originalium 247.
—— Scotiæ, 267
Roujoux Hist. des Sciences et des Arts, 106
Rouse on Chances, 103
Rousseau's Botany, 92
—— le Pachalik de Bagdad, 301.
—— and Hume's Quarrel, 337
Routh, Reliquiæ Sacræ, 34
Rovigo's (Duke de) Memoirs, 288
Rowland's (H) Mona Antiqua, 257
—— (S) Letting of Humours Blood, 370
Rowley's (T.) Poems, 370
Roxburghe Catalogue, 347
Roy (le) Achates Tiberianus, 168
Roy's (W) Military Antiquities, 185
Royal Household Ordinances, 194.
—— (the) Pilgrimage, 238
—— Institution Catalogue, 345.
Rubei (H) Italicarum Ravennatum Hist 294
—— (O) Monumenta Brixiana, 293
Rubenius de Re Vestiaria, 165
—— de Gemma Tib et Aug 166
—— de Urbibus Neocoris, 166
Rubens's Landscapes, 115
—— Galerie de Luxembourg, 115.
Ruchat Reformation en Suisse, 63.
Rudbeck's Lapland, 136
Rudder's Gloucestershire, 200.
Ruddiman (Life of T), 327.
Rudge's Agriculture of Gloucestershire, 124.
Ruding's British Coinage, 175
Rufus Sextus, 409
Rufus (S) de Regionibus Urbis, 164

Ruggle's Ignoramus, and Life, 389
Rulhiere, la Révolution de Russie, 276
—— l'Anarchie de Pologne, 277
Ruminator, 405
Rump Songs, 365
Rumphii Herbarium Amboiense, 94.
Ruphy, Dictionnaire Arabe 349
Rushworth's Historical Collections, 249.
Russell's (A.) Aleppo, 148
—— (J.) Germany, 137
—— Death of Archbishop Sharpe, 269
—— (Lord J.) History of Europe, 184.
—— (M.) Sacred and Profane History, 26
—— (R.) Patres Apostolici, 34.
—— (Lady R.) Letters, 259
—— (Trial of Lord W.), 239
Russia (Travels in), 136
—— *(Travels in Asiatic)*, 152
Russian Gallery of Pictures, 117.
—— Costumes, 121
—— *History*, 276,
—— Language, 357
Rutherford's Ancient History, 177
Rutilii Numatiani Itinerarium, 424
Rutland (Topography of), 211.
Rutter's Fonthill Abbey, 215
Ryan's Irish Worthies, 314.
Rymbegla, 275
Rymer's Fœdera, 248
Ryves's Mercurius Rusticus, 234.

Sabellicus de Situ Urbis Venetæ, 293.
—— de Vet Aquilejæ et Foro-Julii, 294
—— Vincentinus Crater, 294
Sacci Historia Ticinensis, 293.
Sacchetti, Novelle, 387
Sacheverell's Isle of Man, 218
Sackville's Induction, 363.
Sacontala 396
Sacred Philology, 9
Sacy (de), les Antiquités de la Perse, 302
—— Grammaire Arabe, 349
Sadé, la Litterature Françoise, 338
Sadeler Bavaria Sancta, 120
Sadler (M. T.) on Population, 84
—— (Sir R.) State Papers, 248
—— Life, 248
Sadv's Ethics, 80
Sagittarius de Nudipedalibus, 23
—— de Janus Veterum, 165
Sahidic New Testament, 3
Saint-Meard sur les Journees de Septembre, 286
Saint Non, Voyage Pittoresque de Naples, &c. 139
Saints (Lives of the), 64
Salame's Expedition to Algiers, 243
Sale's Translation of the Koran, 66
Salisburiensis (Jo.) Nugis Curialium, 396.
Saliæ Leges, 70
Salignac [misprinted Saligne], Hist de Pologne, 277
Sallengri Novus Thesaurus Antiquitatum Rom 167.
Sallustii Opera, 425
—— translated, 425
—— en Françoise, 425
—— en Espanola, 425
Salmasius de Secretariis, 167

Salmasius de Re Militari Rom. 166
—— Inscriptionum Vet. Explicatio, 169.
—— ad Dostadæ Aras, &c Notæ, 169
Salmon sur l'Etude des Conciles, 26
—— (N.) Essex, 200
—— (T.) Order of the Garter, 332
Salomon de Judiciis et Pœnis Rom 168
—— de Officiis Vitæ Civilis Rom 168.
Salt's Views in the East, 133
—— Travels in Abyssinia, 147
Salvator Rosa's Etchings, 112
Salviati sopra Lingua del Decamerone, 387
Sammes' Britannia Antiqua, 219
Sampson's Londonderry, 270
Samuel's Death of Captain Cook, 132
Sanazarius (Mem of A S), 314
Sanchoniathon's Phœnician History, 178
Sancroft's Fur Prædestinatus, 17
—— Sermons, 58
—— Life, 327
Sancti Itinerarium, 17.
Sandby's Landscapes of Great Britain, 191.
—— Virtuoso's Companion, 191
Sanders' Slienstone, 212
Sanderson's (R.) Sermons, 58.
—— (Life of), 313
—— (W.) History of Scotland, 264
Sandeus de Regibus Siciliæ et Apuliæ, 296
Sandford's Coronation of James II 333
—— Kings of England, 334
Sandoval, Vida del Carlos V. 291
Sandwich's (Earl) Voyage, and Life, 133
—— (E.) Sermons, 58
—— (Life of), 58
Sandys' (G.) Travels, 133
Sanfelicius de Situ, &c Campaniæ, 295
Sansoni Varia de Antiquitatibus Sacris, 17
Sansovino, Cento Novelle, 388
Santandrei, Catalogue de sa Bibliothèque, 346.
Santius (Rod) de Rebus Hispanicis, 290
Saracenic History, 301
Saraina de Civit Veronæ 296
—— Hist Veronensium, 296
Sarbiewii Carmina, 361
Sardus de Nummis, 166
Sarpi, Histoire du Concile de Trente, 27
—— (Life of), 314
Saturday Night, 41
Satyre Menippée, 283
Saubertus de Sacerdotibus Hebr. 18.
—— de Precibus Hebr 20
Saunderson's Aulicus Coquinariæ, 231
—— Charles I 233
Saurin, Discours sur la Bible, 11
—— Sermons, 58
Sauvagerie (De la), Antiquités des Gaules, 170
Savage's (J.) New Zealand, 158
—— (W.) Decorative Printing, 107.
—— Librarian, 343
Savary's Memoirs, 288
Savigny's Roman Law, 69
Saville (H.) Scriptores Ang post Bedam, 220
—— (Lord) Historical Collections, 433.
Savot de Nummis Ant 166
Savoy Confession of Faith, 33

3 R

Saxe Weimar — See Wimeren.
Saxonis Gram Danorum Regum Hist. 274
—— Historia Danica, 274.
Saxon Chronicle, 222
Say, Cours d Economie Politique, 83
—— Political Economy, 83
Scachius de Inauguratione Regum Israel 24
Scalæ Historia Florentinum, 295
—— Vita Vital Borihomæi 295
Scaliger de Comœdia et Tragœdiâ, 161.
—— de Versibus Comicis, 161
—— de Re Nummariâ, 162
—— de Vet Anno Rom 165
—— de Splendore Gentis Scaligeræ, 296
Scandinavian Metrical Tales, 378
Scardeonii Hist de Urbis Patav 294
—— de Sepulc Insignibus Patav 294
Scarron, le Roman Comique, 386
Scatcherd s Morley, 217.
Scattergood's Sermons. 58
Schaffors' Papierversuche, 126
Scharban de Luxu Hebræorum, 23
Scheffer s Lapland, 136
—— de Varietate Navium 163
—— Agrippa Liberator, 165
—— de Militiâ Navali Vet 169
—— de Re Vehiculari Vet 169
Scheidii Oleum Unctionis, 19.
Schelhorn de דרכי שלום, 23
Schelii Varia de Re Militari Rom 166.
Scheller's Latin Grammar, 352.
Scherzi Poetici, 376
Scheuchzer, Physique Sacree, 26.
Schickardi Jus Regium Hebr 21
Schiller, la Guerre de Trent Ans, 277
—— Song of the Bell, 396.
Schilteri Thes Antiquitatum Teutonicarum, et Vita, 274
Schimmelpenninck s Theory of Beauty, &c 79.
Schlegel sur la Littérature Orientale, 336
—— Lectures on Dramatic Literature, 389
Schleusneri Lexicon in LXX 351.
—— Lex in Novum Test 351
Schlichter de Mensâ et Pane Facierum, 18
—— de Laminâ Aureâ, 19
Schmid de Sectâ Pharisæorum, 20
—— de Usu Vestarum Albarum, 23
Schmidel Hist Navig in Americam 154
Schmidt de Drachmis à Christo solutis, 23
Schmidtmeyer's Chile, 157
Schoell, les Peuples de l'Europe, 184
—— la Littérature Grecque et Romaine, 336
Schoepflini Vindiciæ Typogr 341
Schoettgenii Antiq Triturae et Culoniæ in S Script 23
—— Hist Librariorum et Bibliopolorum, 169
—— Scriptores Hist Germanicæ, 277
Schoockii Achais Vetus, 160
Schotti Homericæ Apotheosis, 168.
Schoum in s Drawings of Flowers, 92
Schramm de Poesi Hebr 24
Schrieber, Pays du Rhine, 135

Schroederi Urbium Ferrariæ et Ravennæ Desc 294
—— Desc Regn Lepidi 296
—— de Rebus Armenicis 350
Schubart de Diluvio Deucalionis 163.
Schudt de Canticis Templi, 24
Schwabius de Moloch et Remphan, 23.
Scoresby's Arctic Regions, 135
Scot's Discovery of Witchcraft, 79.
Scotch Language, 352
—— Preacher, 58
Scotiæ Inquisitionum Abbrev. 247.
Scotland (Canons and Councils of the Ch of), 27
—— (Letters from the North of), 259
Scottish Law, 75
—— Topography and Antiquities, 258
—— History 261
—— Kings (Chronicle of), 262.
—— Parliament (Riding of the), 266
—— Documentary History, 267
—— Ecclesiastical History, 268
—— Ministers' Stipends (Register of), 269
—— Poetry, 372
Scotorum Poetarum Deliciæ, 361.
Scott's (J) Works, 36
—— Continuation of Milner's Church History, 62
—— Paris, 140
—— History of Bengal, 304
—— (F) Bible, 11
—— Works, 36
—— on Calvinism, 47
—— Life, 327
—— (Sir W) Border Antiquities, 192.
—— Provincial Antiquities, 259
—— Napoleon, 286
—— Poetical Works, 371
—— (Illustrations of), 371
—— Bridal of Triermain, 371.
—— Harold the Dauntless, 371
—— Border Minstrelsy, 373.
—— Waverley Novels 385.
—— Miscellaneous Prose Works, 399.
Scougal's Works, 47
Scriptores de Re Militari, 408
—— de Re Rustica, 408
—— Historiæ Romana , 409.
—— Hist Romani Minores, 409
—— Historiæ Augustæ, 409
—— Erotici, 409
Scripture Atlas, 130
Scriven on Copyholds 74
Scudamore (Memoirs of the Family of), 201
Sculpture, 122.
Sculleti Medulla Theologiæ Patrum, 34
Sebæ Rerum Naturalium Thesaurus, 89
Secker's Works, 36.
—— Life, 36
Seckendorf de Lutheranismo, 63
Sects (History of), 65
Sedano, Parnasso Espanola, 377
Seed's Moyer Lectures, 52
Seeley's (J) Description of Stowe, 196.
—— (J B) Flora, 151
Segar s Earl Marshal s Power, 330.
—— Booke of Honour, 330.
—— Baronagium, 333

INDEX

Segur's Frederick II. 276
—— Peter the Great, 276.
—— Expedition to Russia, 276
Seine (La) Homeri Nepenthes, 163
Selby's Ornithology, 439
Selden (J.) de Anno Civili Jud 19
—— de Successione Pontif Heb 19
—— de Diis Syris, 21 and 67
—— de Juramentis, 22
—— de Jure Nat et Gent Hebr 22.
—— de Synedriis et Successionibus Ebi 25
—— Opera, 399
—— Vita, 314 and 399
Senart (Mémoires de), 387.
Senecæ Opera, 425 and 426
—— Opera Rhetorica, 426
—— Tragœdiæ, 426
—— translated, 426.
—— Epistles translated, 426.
—— Morals translated, 426
Senstlebius de Alea Veterum, 161
Septuaginta Biblia, 2
—— (Translations of the), 5.
Seran de la Tour's Laves, 312
Serarii S J Herodes, 21.
Serenius Samonicus, 409
Serle's Horæ Solitariæ, 17
Sermons, 51
Seroux d'Agincourt, Hist de l'Art, 107.
—— Fragmens de Sculpture, 172
Serre, l'Entrée de Mary de Medici en G Brit 234
Serupius de Titulo Rabbi, 20.
Servetus (History of), 65.
Servilius de Mirandis Ant Operibus, 167
Servius de Odoribus, 162
Sestini Geographia Numismatica, 174
Seton Genealogy, 336
Seven Wise Masters of Rome, 387
Severus Alexandrinus, 408
—— Historia Sacra, &c 61.
Sevigné, Lettres, et Vie, 404
Seward's (A) Poetical Works, 371.
—— Life, 371.
—— Letters, 404
—— (W) Anecdotes, 314
—— Biographiana, 314
Sewell's History of the Quakers, 65
—— Dutch Dictionary, 356
Sextus Aurelius 409
Seyppel de Flagellandi Ritu Rom 22
Shaftesbury's Characteristics, 80
—— Memoirs 327
Shah Nameh, 302.
Shakespeare's Plays, 392
—— Works, 392
—— (Supplement to), 392
—— Life, 392
—— (the Novels and Tales of), 393
Sharp's Voyages, 132
Sharpe's (Sir C) Hartlepool, 209
—— (Death of Archbishop James), 269
—— (Archbishop John) on British Coins, 437
—— Life, 327
Shaw's (D) Philosophy of Judaism, 61
—— (G) Zoological Lectures, 96
—— General Zoology, 96
—— (L) Moray and Nairn, 260
—— (S) Topographer, 188

Shaw's (T.) Travels in Barbary and the Levant, 144
Shee's Elements of Art, 110
—— Rhymes on Art, 110.
Sheffield Castle (Letters found in), 434 and 435
Shefferus de Ant Torquibus, 167
Shepherd (J) on the Common Prayer, 31
—— Origin of Christianity, 47
—— (R) on the Christian Religion, 53
Sherborne Castle (Description of), 199
Sheridan's (R B) Works, 394
—— (Life of) 327
—— (Mrs) Sidney Biddulph, 385.
Sherlock's Works, 36
Sherwood's French Dictionary, 355
Shipwrecks and Disasters at Sea, 131.
Shires (on the Antiquity of), 193
Shirley's (J) Poems, 371
—— [misprinted W] Works, 394
Shrewsbury's (Duke of) Correspondence, 250
—— Family's Letters, 434 and 435.
Shropshire Topography, 211
Shukford's Sacred and Profane History connected, 26
Shurreef's Qanoon-e-Islam, 439
Siamese History, 305
Sibbald's (J.) Chronicle of Scottish Poetry, 373
—— (R) Prodromus Nat Hist Scotiæ, 89
—— Scotia Illustrata, 259
—— Fife and Kinross, 260.
—— de Gestis Gul Vallæ, 263
Sicard, les Journées de Septembre, 286
Siccama de Judicio C Virili, 163
—— in Festos Kalend Rom 165.
Sichemitarum Epistolæ, 20
Siciliæ Chronicon Anonym, 297
Siddons (Life of Mrs), 390
Sidney See Sydney
Sigonius de Republ Hebr 17.
—— de Republ Athen 160
—— de Lacedæmon Temporibus, 160
—— Varia de Antiquitatibus Romanorum, 163
—— de Nominibus Rom 164
Silius Italicus, 426
Simeon's Horæ Homileticæ, 58
Simeonis Mon. Dunhelm Historia, 221.
Simes's Musical Miscellany, 365
Simon's (J) Irish Coins, 175
—— (T) Medals, &c 175
Simon (St), Œuvres, 284
Simond's Switzerland, 137
—— Tour in England, 189
Simpson's (D) Sacred Literature, 10
—— Plea for Religion, 48
—— (T.) Hatfield Chase, 217
Simson's Euclid's Elements, 103
—— Trigonometry, 103
Sinclair on the Revenue, 85
Singer on Playing Cards, 128 and 311
Sini, Memorie Recondite, 183
—— Histoire de France, 280
Sismondi Républiques Italiennes, 298
—— de la Lit du Midi de l'Europe, 338
—— translated, 338
Skarbek, Théorie des Richesses, 84
Skeeler's Sermons, 59

Skelton's Oxonia Restaurata, 210
—— Works, 371
Skene's Regia Majestas, 75
Skinner's Eccles Hist of Scotland, 268
—— Scottish Episcopacy, 268
Skioldebrand's Journey to the North Cape, 145
Slacke's St. Mary's Hospital, Scroby, 218
Slade on the Epistles, 13
Slatyer's Pala-Albion, 225
—— Genethliacon, 334
Sleep-walker, 395
Sleidan's Chronicle, 63
Slevogt de Metempsychosi Hebr 20
—— de Proselytis Judæorum, 21
Slezer's Theatrum Scotia, 258
Slingsby (Life of Sir H), 236
—— (H) Grandmother's Guests, 382.
Sloane's Jamaica, &c 154
Sluiter Lectiones Andocideæ, 358
Smalcaldenses Articuli, 32
Smeaton's Reports, 123
—— Misc Papers, 123
Smellie (Life of W), 327
Smeregi Chronicon, 294
Smith's (A) Moral Sentiments, 80.
—— Wealth of Nations, 84
—— (Life of) 84 and 427.
—— (C) Cork, 270.
—— Waterford, 270.
—— Kerry, 270
—— (E) Book of Job, 6
—— (G) School of Arts, 106
—— (J) Agriculture of Argyle, 125.
—— Hist of Virginia, New England, &c 310
—— (Anecdotes of J C), 105.
—— (Sir J E) Corresp of Linnæus, 89.
—— Exotic Botany, 92
—— English Flora, 94
—— Lepidopterous Insects of Georgia, 100.
—— Hafod, 257
—— (J G) Forensic Medicine, 71
—— (J P) Scripture Testimony to the Messiah, 48
—— (J T) Westminster, 207.
—— (S) Agriculture of Gallowayshire, 125
—— (Sir T) de Republica Anglorum, 71.
—— (Life of), 231
—— (W) Nat Hist of Nevis, &c 89
—— Voyage to Guinea, 145
—— University College, Oxford, 211.
—— (Prof) Nat Hist of Congo, 145
—— Chart of Mountains, 99
Smithiana Dactylotheca, 173.
Smollett's History of England, 226
—— Miscellaneous Works, 399
—— Life, 399
Smyth's (J) Engravings from the Blenheim Collection, 116.
—— (Life of Bp. W), 314
—— (W) Description of London, 431
—— (W H) Sicily, 140.
—— Sardinia 439
Snelling's (T) English Coins, 175.
—— Eng Coins struck abroad, 175
—— Scottish Coins, 175
—— Coins of Europe, 176

Snellius de Re Nummaria, 162
Snorronis Sturl. Hist Septentrionalium, 274.
—— Historia Norvegiæ, 275.
—— Olave, the King of Man, 275
Soames's Doctrines of the Anglo-Saxon Church. 54
—— English Reformation, 254
Solueski (Histoire de), 277
Social Life in England and France, 240.
Societies Literary and Philosophical (History of), 339
Society of Arts' Transactions, 106.
Socinarum Catechismus, 33
Socratis Historia Ecclesiastica, 61.
Solinus Polyhistor, 246
Solis (De) Conquista de Mexico, 309
Solvet Etudes de la Fontaine, 400.
Solvyns' Hindoos, 121
Somers's Tracts, 108
Somerset's (D of) Expedition into Scotland, 264
Somersetshire Topography, 211
Somerville's (M) Mechanism of the Heavens, 104
—— (R) Agriculture of E Lothian, 125.
—— Booshuana Nation, 145
Somner's Gavelkind, and Life, 74.
—— Roman Ports and Forts in Kent, 202.
—— Canterbury, 202
—— Etymologicon Anglicanum, 352
Sonnini, Hist des Poissons et Cétacées, 88.
—— l'Egypte 146
Sotheby's Tour through Wales, and other Poems 256 and 371
South's Sermons, 59
Southern's Plays, 394
—— Life, 394
Southey on the Prospects of Society, 82
—— Spain and Portugal, 141.
—— Espriella's Letters, 189.
—— Peninsular War, 244
—— Book of the Church, 251.
—— Vindiciæ, 251
—— Chronicle of the Cid, 291.
—— Expedition of Orsua, 309.
—— History of Brazil, 309
—— Later English Poets, 364.
—— Poems, 361
—— Poetical Works, 371.
—— Omniana, 402
—— Essays, 407
Sophiani Gracia Descriptio, 160
Sephocles Tragœdiæ, 426
—— translated, 426
Sopwith's Fountain's Abbey, 438
Soutern Palamedes, 161
South Sea Voyages, 131 and 157
Sowerby's English Fungi, 93
—— English Botany, 94
—— Mineral Conchology, 101
Sozomeni Historia Ecclesiastica, 61
Sparke Anglicani Scriptores, 221
Spain (Travels in), 141
Spalding (Account of the Gent's Society at), 204
—— (J) Troubles in Scotland, 266
Spanheim's Ecclesiastical Annals, 61
—— de Nummo Smyrnensi, 164
—— Orbis Romanus, 166

Spanish Bible, 8
—— History, 290
—— Language, 356
—— Poetry, 377
—— Novels, 388
—— Drama, 396
Sparrman's Cape of Good Hope, 146
Spartianus Œlus, 409
Specialis Rei Sicularum, 297
Spectacle de la Nature, 89
Speed's Great Britain, 225
Spelman (H.) Leges Anglo-Saxonicæ, 73.
—— Aspilogia, 331
—— Glossarium Archaiologicum, 352.
—— (J.) Psalterium Saxonicum, 3.
Spence's (J.) Polymetis, 108
—— Meghabechi and Hill, 323.
—— Anecdotes, and Life, 338.
—— (W.) Entomology, 98
Spencer de Urim et Thummim, 19
—— de Professione Decimarum, 20.
—— de Solutione Primat. et Decim. 20
—— Alia de Antiquitatibus Sacris, 21 and 24
—— de Juramento per Anchialum, 22.
Spenceriana Bibliotheca, 346
Spenser's State of Ireland, 269
—— Letters on Poetry, 362.
—— Works, 371
—— Life, 371
Sperlingius de Nummis non cusis, 22.
—— de Crepidis, 162
—— de Ant. Græcis et Romanis, 169
Spiker's Travels in England, 189
Spix's (Von) Travels in Brazil, 156.
Spira (Judgment of God on F.), 42.
Spon. la Dalmatie, la Grèce, &c. 143.
—— Ignotorum, &c. Deorum Aræ, 161.
—— de Strenis, 162
—— Rei Ant. Quæstiones, 169
—— Miscellaneæ Antiquitates. 169
Spottiswood's Scottish Religious Houses, 258
—— Church of Scotland, 268
Spretus de Ravennæ Urbis Amplitud. 294.
Sprotti Chronica. 252.
Spry's Christian Unity, 54
Spurzheim's Physiognomical System, 79.
Squadroni Laudum Regi Lepidi, 296.
Squyer (Tragical Fiction of), 231
Stabback on the Gospels and Acts, 13.
Stace's Cromwelliana, 237
Stackhouse's History of the Bible, 8
Stael (Mad. de), l'Allemagne, 277
—— on the French Revolution, 285.
—— Corinne, 386
Stafford Gallery of Pictures, 116.
—— (Sir T.) Pacata Hibernica, 272
Staffordshire (Topography of), 212
Stanhope (G.) on Christianity, 51.
—— (J. S.) Battle of Platea, 143
—— Olympia, 143.
Stanihurst's Ireland, 269
Stanleiana Bibliotheca, 347
Stapfer, l'Oberland, 147
Stapleton Tres Thomæ, 253
Starke's Travels on the Continent, 134
State Papers, 248
Statii Opera, 426
—— Thebaid translated, 426

Statues (Ancient), 172
Statuæ Antiquæ in Thes. Florentino, 172
Statute Law, 73.
Statutes (the), 73
Staunton's Penal Code of China, 75.
—— China, 152
Staveley's English Churches, 186.
Stebbing's (H.) Christianity justified, 48
—— on Christianity, 52
—— (S.) Staffordshire, 212
Stedman's (C.) American War, 310.
—— (J. G.) Surinam, 156
Steele's Correspondence, 404
Steevens's Catalogue, 347
—— on Shakespeare, 392.
Stehlin's Traditions of the Jews, 60
Stellæ Elog. Venet. Navalis Pugnæ, 293.
Stenography, 107
Stephanidis Descriptio Londini, 205.
—— Vita St. Thomæ Cant. 221
Stephani Byzantini de Dodone Fragmentum, 161
Stephanus (H.) de Græcorum Moribus, 163
—— Katherine de Medicis, 282
—— Glossaria, 351.
—— Thesaurus Ling. Græcæ, 351
—— Poetæ Græci Principes, 408
—— (J.) de Jurisd. Vet. Græc. 160
—— (Sancti) Cadomensis Chronica, 220.
—— Regis Anglorum Gesta, 289
Stephens' Essayes and Characters, 80.
Sterne's Works, 399
—— Life, 399
Steuart's Planter's Guide, 125.
Stevenson's (M.) Florus Britannicus, 225.
—— (R.) Bell Rock Light, 123
—— (W.) Agriculture of Surrey, 125.
—— Progress of Discovery, 131.
—— Ely Cathedral, 197
—— Naval Commanders, 243
—— (W. B.) South America, 156.
Stewart's (C. J.) History of Bengal, 303
—— Catalogue of Tipoo's Library, 346
—— (Sir D.) Highlanders of Scotland, 259
—— (Dug.) on the Mind, 78
—— Philosophical Essays, 78
—— (J. H.) Redeemer's Advent, 48
—— (Lady Mary) Household Book, 259.
—— (W.) Scottish Church Government, 29
Stillingfleet's (B.) Select Works, 399
—— Life, 399
—— (E.) Works, 36.
—— Life, 36
Stoddart's Local Scenery of Scotland, 259
Stoll, les Punaises, Cigales, Spectres, &c. 99
Stonehenge (Account of), 215
Storrer's (J.) Fonthill Abbey, 215
—— (T.) Card. Wolsey, 229
Story's Wars of Ireland, 272
Stosch, Pierres Antiques, 173.
Stothard's Normandy, 140
Stourhead (Description of), 215
Stow's London and Westminster, 205
—— (Life of), 205
—— Chronicles, 225
Strabonis Geographia, 426

Strachey's Index to the Records 246
Strada, de Mariæ Reg Scot Vitâ 265
——— de Bello Belgico, 279
Strafforde Papers, 250
——— (Life of the Earl of), 250
Stranguage's Mary Queen of Scots, 264
Strauchius de Flagellandi Ritu Hebr 22.
Streinnius de Gentibus et Familis Rom 165
Stricker de Car Mag I'xpedit Hispanicâ, 183
Strutt's (J) Dictionary of Engravers, 120
——— English Manners and Customs, 193.
——— Dress and Habits, 193
——— Sports and Pastimes, 194
——— Chronicle, 222
——— Regal Antiquities [author's name omitted] 315
——— Queen-Hoo Hall, 384
——— (J G) Sylva Britannica, 95.
Struvii Bibliotheca Historica, 176
——— Corpus Hist Germanicæ, 277.
Strype's (J) Eccles Memorials, 254
——— Annals of the Reformation, 254
——— See also Aylmer, Cheke, Cranmer, Grindal, Parker, Smyth, and Whitgift.
Stuart s (J) Antiquities of Athens, 171.
——— (M) on the Hebrews, 14
Stubbes Historia Anglicana, 221
Stukeley's Med Hist of Carausius, 175
——— Itinerarium, 188.
——— Stone-Henge, 215
——— Abury, 215
Sturbridge Fair (Hist of), 197.
Sturlson See Snorro
Sturm's (C C) Reflections, 48
——— (L C) Sciographia Templi, 18
——— Mare Æneum, 20
Sturt's Common Prayer, 50
Suard, Mélange de Littérature 407
Suaresius de Foraminibus Lapidum, 167.
——— Prænestes Antiquæ, 295
Suckling's (Sir J.) Works, 399
Sudbury (Life of Dean), 311
Suetonius de claris Grammaticis, 424
——— Opera, 426
——— Lives, translated, 427
Suffolk (Agriculture of), 125.
——— (Topography of), 212
——— Papers, 251
Sugden's Law of Vendors, 74
Suger (Histoire de l'Abbé), 281
Suhm Scriptores Danici, 274
Suicen Thesaurus Patrum Græcorum, 34
Suidæ Lexicon Græcé, 350
Sully, Mémoires, 282 and 283
Sulpitii Severi Opera, 61
——— Satira, 409 and 410
Sumner's Records of the Creation, 48
——— Apostolical Preaching, 48
——— Evidences of Christianity, 48
——— Character of Christ, 48
——— Sermons, 59
Sanskrit New Testament, 8.
Superville, Sermons, 59
——— (le fils) Sermons, 59
Surgentis Neapolis illustrata, 295
Surgery, 101.
Surrey (Topography of), 213
Surrey (Memoirs of the Earls of), 345.

Surrey and Wyat's Works, 399
——— (Life of Henry, Earl of), 399.
Suttees' Durham, 199
Sussex (Topography of), 213
Sussexiana Bibliotheca, 346
Sutherland Genealogy, 336
Sutton (Life of sir R), 314
——— (T) Will and Testament, 207 and 328
Swammerdam Biblia Natura, 98
Swan's (C) Gesta Romanorum, 379.
——— (J) Speculum Mundi, 407
Sweden (Travels in) 136
Swedish History, 275
——— Language, 357
Sweet's Cistineæ, or Rock-Roses, 93.
——— Geraniaceæ, 93
Swift's Works, 399
——— Life, 328
Swimming, 127.
Swinburne's Travels in the Sicilies, 140
——— Travels in Spain, 141.
Swinden's Great Yarmouth, 208.
Swiss History, 290
Swiss-German Bible, 7
Switzerland (Travels in), 137
Sydenham (Life of Dr), 314
Sydney (A) on Government, 83.
——— (Sir P.) Psalms of David, 6.
——— (Life of), 328
——— Defence of English Poetry, 362
——— Misc Works, 399.
——— (the) Papers, 249.
——— (Memoirs of the), 249.
Sykes's Catalogue, 347
Sylva (De), el Unione de Portugal, 292
Sylvester's Posthumi, 371
Symeonis Monach Hist. Eccles Dunhelm. 199 and 233
Syncelli Chronographia, 181.
Synbus de Sabbatho Gentil, 19.
Syriaca Evangelia, à White, 3

Tachard, Voyage de Siam, 151
Taciti Opera 427.
——— translated, 427
Taffinus de Rom Anno Seculari, 165
Talbot Correspondence, 434 and 5
——— (E) Works, 399
——— Life, 399
Tales of the Wars, 385
Talleur, Chroniques de Normandie, 290.
Talmudical Writings, 60
Tanner's Notitia Monastica, 186
Tansillo's Nurse, 376
Tarsia (de) Historia Cupersanensium, 295
Tartary (History of), 305
Tasso, la Gierusalemme Liberata, 376.
——— translated, 376 and 377.
——— Life, 328
——— Aminta, 377
Tassoni (Life of Alexandro), 328
Tatham's Chart and Scale of Truth, 53
Tatius de Sacerdote Castrensi, 19
Tattam's Egyptian Grammar, 349.
Taverner's Bible, 4
Taxatio Ecclesiastica, 247.
Taylor's (F) Historical Collections, 434
——— (G L) Arch Antiq of Rome, 171.
——— (G W) Catalogue, 347

INDEX

Taylor's (G W) Profligate, 394
—— (Jer) Works, 36
—— Life 36
—— (J) Civil Law, 69
—— Gothic Ornaments in Lavenham Church, 122
—— (J. the Water Poet) Works, 399
—— (S) Harwich and Dover Court, 200
—— (T) Musiologia, 93.
Tempest's Religio Laici, 49.
Temple's (Sir J) Irish Rebellion, 272
—— (Sir W) Works, 399
—— Life, 399
Tenhove's (N) House of Medici, 299
Tennant's (C) Tour, 135
—— (W) Anster Fair, 374
Terentii Comœdia, 427.
—— translated, 427
Tertullian's Apology for Christianity, 34
Terry's East Indies, 151
Testa de Nevill, 247
Teutonici Poetæ Anonymi, 378
—— Metrical Tales, 378
Thebault's Frederick II 278
Themminck, Histoire des Pigéons, 97.
Theocriti Opera, 427
—— translated 427
Theodora and Didymus, 63
Theodoreti Historia Ecclesiastica, 61.
Theodosianus Codex, 69 and 70
Theodosii Tripolensis Sphæræ, 104
—— Diaconis Hist Byzantinæ, 182
Theognis, 408
Theophanis Hist Byzantina, 181
Theophrasti Characteres, 428
—— translated, 428
—— History of Stones translated, 428
Theophylacti Simoccatæ Historia, 181
—— Bulg Institutio Regia, 182
Theotisium Psalterium, 4
Thevenot, Voyages Curieux, 131
—— Travels, 133
Thibadeau sur la Convention Nationale, 287
Thistle (Statutes of the Order of the), 332.
Tholosanus de Nundinis et Mercatibus, 165
Thomas's (J) Printing in America, 342
—— (W) Worcester Cathedral, 215
Thomasinus de Donariis, &c 166
Thomassin, Figures dans Versailles, 172
Thomson's Scottish County Atlas, 130.
—— (Mrs) Henry VIII 229
—— (C) Transl of the Septuagint, 5
—— (J) Poetical Works, 371
—— Life, 371
—— (R) Chronicles of London Bridge, 206
—— (T) on Heat and Electricity, 86
—— System of Chemistry, 87
—— Travels in Sweden, 136
—— History of the Royal Society, 140
Thorne Historia Anglicana, 221.
Thoresby's (J) Leicestershire, 204
—— (R) Cat of his Antiquities, &c 171
—— on Yorkshire Antiquities, 216
—— Leedes, 217
—— Church of Leedes, 217.
—— Diary, 240
—— Correspondence,

Thorkelin's Fragments of Eng and Irish Hist 221
Thornbury Castle (Description of), 200
Thornton's Turkey, 500
Thoroton's Nottinghamshire, 209.
Thorpe's Antiquities of Kent, 202
—— Registrum Roffense, 203
—— Custumale Roffense, 203
Throckmorton (Legend of Sir N), 371
Thuani Historia sui Temporis, 183
—— (Life of), 328
Thuilleries (Bustes, &c au Palais des), 172
Thurlowe's State Papers, 250
Thucydides de Bello Pelop 428
—— translated, 428
Thwaites (E) Heptateuch, &c Anglo-Saxonice, 3
—— Gram Saxonica, 352
Thynne's Office of a Herald, 330
Thysius de Republica Atheniensium, 160.
Tiberius Rhetor, 408
Tibullus, 412
Tickell's Kingston upon Hull, 217
Tigernachi Annales Hibernicarum, 271
Tighe's (W) Kilkenny, 270
—— (Mrs) Psyche, 371.
Tillotson's Works, 36
—— Life, 36
Timur (Memoirs of the Emperor), 303.
Tindal's (N) Medallic Hist of England, 175.
—— Cont of Rapin's England, 226
—— (W) Evesham, 215
Tim Bobbin's Works, 354.
Tipoo's Library Catalogue, and Life, 346
Tiraboschi della Literatura Italiana, 339.
Tischbien's Ancient Vases, 173
Tissot de la Sante des Gens de Lettres, 102
Tituani Opera, 113
—— (Life of), 328
—— (C) Costume of Turkie, 142
Titsingh, Mem des Souverains du Japon, 306
Titus's Killing no Murder, 238
Tixall Poetry, 371
To-day in Ireland, 385
Toderini Literatura Turchescha, 349
Todd's (H J) Illustrations of Gower and Chaucer, 321.
—— Johnson's Dictionary, 353
—— (J) Rajast'han, 304
Toepfler de Tiara Sacerd Hebr 19.
Toldervy's Epitaphs, 192
Toleration (Religious), 27
Toletanus (Rod) de Rebus Hispanicis, 290
Tomasini Manūs Æneæ Cecropii, 162
—— de Tesseris, 162
Tombe, les Indes Orientales, 151
Tombs (on the Variety, &c), 193
Tomlins's Criminal Law, 74
Tomline's Refutation of Calvinism, 49
—— Christian Theology, 49
Tone's (T W) Life and Diary, 273, 328
Tongataboo (Residence at), 157
Tong-Kien-Kang-Mou, Hist de la China, 305
Tooke's (J H) Diversions of Purley, 348

496 INDEX.

Tooke's (W) Russia, 276
—— Catherine II 276.
Toone's Glossary, 353
Topography (Foreign), 130
—— *of England,* 195.
—— *of Wales,* 256
—— *of Scotland,* 258
—— *of Ireland,* 269
Topsell s Historie of Quadrupeds, 96.
—— Historie of Serpents, 93
Torfæi Orcades, 261
—— Groenlandia, 275.
Torr's York, 216
Torriano's Relation of Rome, 299
Tott (De) sur les Turcs, 300
Toulmin's Taunton, 211.
Toupn Emendationes in Suidam, 351.
Tournefort's Levant, and Life, 144.
Townley's Biblical Literature, 9
Townsend's (F) Calend. of Knights, 334.
—— (G) Harmony of the Bible. 8
—— Sermons, 59
—— on the Church of Rome 251.
—— (J) Character of Moses, 12
Townson's Works [2 vols. 8vo. omitted], 36
—— Life, 36 and 59
—— Discourses, 59
Tracts, 407
Tragicum Theatrum, 236
Trallianus de Rebus Mirab 161
—— de Longævis, 162
—— de Olympns, 162
Trapp on the Gospels, 13
—— Trinitarian Controversy, 52
Travels, 130
Travers on Eccles Discipline, 29.
Treherius de Jurejurando, 165
Tremellii Biblia Latina, 4
Tresham's British Gallery 116
Trevelyan's Heartburn, 209
—— (Pedigrees of the), 209
——'s Meldon Rivergreen, 209
Trevissa's Polychronicon, 223
Triglandius de Ritibus Mosaicis, 16
—— de Secta Karæorum, 20
—— de Dodone loco, 161.
Trissino, l' Italia liberata, 377
Trittenhem de Scriptoribus Eccles 61.
Trivett Chronicon, 223
Troil s (Von) Iceland, 135
Trojan Controversy, 143
Trokelowe (J. de) Annales Edwardi II. 227
Trollope's Americans, 154.
Troy (Destruction of), 380
Trumpet of Fame, 371
Trussell's Cont. of Daniel s England, 225
Truter's Booshuana Nation, 115
Truth brought to Light, 232
Tryphiordi Ilii Excidium, 428.
—— translated, 428
Tucker's Light of Nature, 49
—— Life, 49
Tuckey's Maritime Geography, 130
—— Congo, 145
Tuke's Agriculture of Yorkshire, 125.
Tully's Tripoli, 145
Turenne (Histoire du Visc. de), 284
Turkey (Travels in), 142 and 147.

Turkish Costumes, 121.
—— *History,* 299.
—— Language, 350
Turnbull on Ancient Painting, 108.
Turnebus de Vino, 162.
Turner's (D) Botanist's Guide, 93
—— Fuci, 93
—— Normandy, 140.
—— (E) Grantham, 204
—— (J) on Redemption, 52
—— (J M W) England and Wales, 191
—— (S) Theory of the World, 90
—— Anglo-Saxons, 222
—— History of England, 226
—— on Ancient British Poems, 374
—— Tibet, 152
—— (W) Levant, 144.
Turpin's Charles the Great and Orlando, 377.
Turre (a) Exp Inscr. Taurboln Lugd 168
—— de Beleno, &c 291
—— Monumenta Vet Antiq, 295
Turrigius ad Ursi Togati Notæ, 166
Tusser s Points of Husbandry, 124
Tweddell's (J.) Remains, 400
—— Life, 400.
Twells' (E) Moyer Lectures, 52
—— (L) Boyle Lectures, 52
—— (R) Sermons, 59
Twinus (J) de Rebus Anglicis, 222
Twiss (R) on Chess, 128.
—— Spain and Portugal, 141
Twyne's Garlande of Godly Flowers 49
Twysden Anglicani Scriptores, 221.
—— Anne Bullen, 229
Tyndall's Works, 36.
—— Life, 36
—— Parable of the Wicked Mammon, 49.
—— Practyse of Prelates, 229
Tyrtæus's Elegies translated 427
Tysilio's Welsh Chronicles, 257
Tytler's (A F) General History, 177.
—— on Petrarch, 325
—— Principles of Translation, 359
—— (W.) on Scottish Music, 105.
—— Life, 328

Ubaldini, Descrittione di Scotia, 258
Udall's Mary Queen of Scotland, 264
Ude s French Cook, 126
Ugolini Thesaurus Antiq Sacrarum, 16
—— Varia de Antiquitatibus Sacris, 18 and 19
—— de Phylacteriis et Sectis Hebr. 20
—— de Re Rustica Hebr 23
—— Uxor Hebræa, 23
—— de Veterum Funere, &c 25.
Ulloa's South America, 155
Ulster (British Undertakers of), 267
Ultonienses Annales, 271.
Unitarian Confession of Faith, 33.
Universal History, 177
Upcot's English Topography, 185
Upton (J) on Shakespeare, 395
—— (N) de Studio Militari, 331
Urquhart's (Sir T) Jewell, 266
—— Tracts, 407.
Ursatus de Notis Romanorum, 166
Ursins (Lettres de la Princesse des), 284.

Ursini (F) Effigies Virorum, &c 169
—— Familiæ Rom Nobiliores, 165.
—— ad Kalend Farnesianum Nota, 165
—— Fragmenta Historiarum, 180
—— Notæ ad Sc. de Re Rustica 409
—— (G) Antiquitates Hebr 20.
Usher See Usserius
—— (Life of Archbishop) 314
Usserius de Anno Solari, 162
—— Brit Eccl Antiquitates, 251
Utterson's (L V) Early Poetry, 363.
—— (Mrs) Tales of the Dead, 386
Vanbrugh's Plays, 394
Vanni Historia Infantum Laræ, 120
Vahram's Chronicle of Cilicia, 302
Vaillant (F. le), les Oiseaux de Paradis, &c 97
—— les Perroquets, 97
—— les Oiseaux de l'Amérique, &c 98
—— Voyages dans l'Afrique, 146
—— (J F) Numismata Seleucidæ, 174
Valaeri Spectacula Veneta, 294
Valenciennes, Histoire des Poissons, 98
Valentia's (Lord) Travels, 133
Valentinus de Theatro Saguntino, 169
—— de Circi Antiquitate, 169
Valerianus de Fulminum Significatione, 164
Valerii Flacci Argonautica, 128 and 129
—— Maximi Dicta Memorabilia, 129
Valesius de Populis Fundis, 163
Vallæ de Rebus Hispanicis, 290
Vallans' Tale of the Two Swannes, 202
Valle (della) Viaggi, 133
Vallency's Collectanea Hibernica, 271
Valor Ecclesiasticus temp. Hen VIII. 247.
Valguarnera de Panormo, 297
Van Alphen de Chadrach et Damasco, 17
Vancouver's (C) Agriculture of Devonshire, 124
—— of Hants, 124
—— (G) Voyage, 132
Van der Pyl's Dutch Grammar, 356
Van Dyk's Batavian Anthology, 378
Van Mildert on Infidelity, 52
—— on Scripture Interpretation, 54
Van Rheede Hortus Malabaricus, 94
Van-Til de Tabernaculo Movsis, 18
—— Cantus Poeseos, &c Hebr 24
Varamund de Furoribus Gallicis, 282
Varchi, le Guerre Fiorentina, 295
—— Istoria di Fiorentina, 295
Varro de Agricultura, 408
—— Lingua Latina, 429.
Vasari, Vite di Pittori, &c 108
Vasconcello de Antiquitatibus Thoracensis, 292
Vases, 173
Vassæus de Rebus Hispanicis, 290
Vattel, Droit de la Nature, 68
Vauchopius de Magistratibus Rom 168
Vaudoncourt's Ionian Isles, 144
Vaux on Baptism and the Lord's Supper, 54
Veceru Hist Seditionum Siciliæ, 297.
Vegetius de Arte Veterinaria, 408
Veitch (Life of W), 269
Vellei Paterculi Hist Romana, 129.
—— translated, 129

Velserus de Zeta et Zetaris, 169
Vence (Bible de), 12
Vendée (Mémoires sur la), 288
Vendéens (les Guerres de), 287
Venegas's California, 310
Veneroni, Maitre Italien, 355
Venerius de Oraculis, 161
Venetiarum Splendor, figuris illust 293
Venezia (le Fabriche di), 139
Venn's (H) Duty of Man, 49
—— on Zecharias, 49
—— (J) Sermons, 50
Vere Family History, 335
——'s (Sir F) Commentaries, 244, 279
Vergerius de Carneriensium Familia, 294.
Vergil (Pol) Anglicana Historia, 224
Verstigan's Decayed Intelligence, 193.
Vertot, les Révolutions de Suede, 276
Vertue's Anecdotes of Painting in Eng 108
—— (Life of), 120
—— Cat of Hollar's Works, 120
—— Medals, &c of T. Simon, 175.
—— Heads, 315
—— Views of Oxford Colleges, 210.
Verunnius Ponticus, 220
Verwey de Unctionibus, 24.
Vetusta Monumenta, 190
Veysie on the Atonement, 53
Vibius Sequester, 421
Vicars's Mischeefe's Mysterie, 232.
Victor de Regiombus Rom 164
Victor Sextus Aurelius, 409
Vida's Scacchia Ludus 128
Vieillot, les Oiseaux Dorés, 97.
—— les Chanteurs de Zone-Torride, 97
Vienna Gallery of Pictures, 117
Vieusseux's Italy in the 19th Century, 298
Views in Germany, 137.
—— in Italy, 139
—— in Naples, 140
—— in Malta, 140
—— in Lyons, 141
—— in the Pyrenees, 141
—— in the Netherlands, 141
—— in Great Britain, 191
—— in Yorkshire, 216
Vievra's Portuguese Grammar, 356.
—— Dictionary, 356
Villanus de Rubicone Antiquo, 294
—— Ariminensis Rubicon, 294
Villanova Laudes Urbis Hist 293
Ville (de) Pyrotechnia Veneta, 293.
—— Antiquitates Polæ, 294
Villehardouin, Hist de Constantinople, 181 and 182
Villon, Œuvres, 375
Vilate, Journées du 9 et 10 Thermidor, 287
Vince's (S misp James) Astronomy, 104.
Vincent's Periplus of the Erythrean Sea, &c 131
Vincentius Lirensis's Apology for Christianity, 44
Vincentius de Rubicone, 294
Vindingii Hellen 163
Vineyards (Topography of known), 126
Vinesalvi (Galf) Historia, 221
Violi de Rom Temporum Ratione, 165
Virgilii Opera, 429

Virgil's Works translated, 430.
—— 's Eneid translated, 430
—— Eneis en Françoise, 430
—— Georgics and Bucolics translated, 430
Virunium Pontici Hist Britann 222
Vitalis (O) Ecclesiastica Historia, 289
—— (S.) Annales Sardiniæ, 297
Viton de St Alais, Hist des Ordres Chiv 331
Vitringa de Decemviris Otiosis, 20
Vitruvius de Architectura, 122.
Vivian Grev, 385
Vltu Venatio, 127
Vocabolatio della Trusca, 355
Voet, les Coléoptères, 99
—— Comment in Pandectas, 70
Volpi-Communiana (Annali della Tipog) 342
Volaterranus de Magistratibus Rom 168
Voltaire's History of Europe, 183
—— Histoire de Charles XII, 275
—— Age of Louis XIV 283
Volusius Metianus de Nummis, &c. 166
Voraginis Legenda Sanctorum 64
Vorstius (A) de Obitu J Meursii, 162.
—— (J.) de Paradiso, 17.
—— de Synedriis Hebr 22
Vospiscus Flavius, 409
Vossius de Instr Hydraul, 24.
—— de Ant Romæ Magnitudine, 164
—— de Triremium Construct 166.
Vowell's Exeter, 199.
Voyages and Travels, 130
Vulgata Biblia, 3
Vulson, le Théâtre d'Honneui, 332

Waddington's Ethiopia, 147.
Wafer's Voyages, 132
Wagenseil de Sceptro Judæ 22.
Wakefield's (E) Ireland, 269
—— (G) Correspondence, 404
Walchius de Ponderibus &c 22
Walckenaer sur les Fabulistes, 397
Waldegrave's (Earl) Memoirs, 242.
Waldensian Confession of Faith, 32
—— History, 162
Walingfordensis (Joan) Historia, 221
Walker's (C) Hist of Independency, 236
—— (J) Sufferings of the Clergy, 255
—— Dress of the Irish, 270
—— Classical Pronunciation, 351.
—— Pronouncing Dictionary, 353
—— (J C) Irish Bards, 374
—— [misp Walter] on Irish Music, 103
—— on Italian Tragedy, 395
—— —— Drama, 395
—— (R) Sermons, 59
—— Life, 59
—— (S) Sermons, 59
Wall's Hist of Infant Baptism, 49
Wallace's (J) Orkney Isles, 261
—— History of Scotland, 262
—— (R) on the Numbers of Mankind, 81
—— (History of Sir W), 263
Wallich Plantæ Asiaticæ, 94
Wallis's (Capt) Voyage, 132.
—— (J) North Bishopric of Durham, 199
—— Northumberland, 209.

Walmsley's Physiognomical Portraits, 315
Walpole's (H) Anecdotes of the Arts in England, 168
—— Miscellaneous Antiquities, 193
—— Reminiscences, 241 and 242
—— George II 242
—— Own Conduct, 242
—— Memoirs, 242.
—— Royal and Noble Authors, 337
—— Works See Oxford
—— (Sir R) Memoirs, 241
—— (R) Memoirs on Turkey, 142.
—— Herculaneum, 171
Walsh's Constantinople, 142
—— Brazil, 156
Walsingham Y podigma Neustriæ, 220
—— Historia brevis Anglicana, 220.
Walter's Poems, 372
Waltheri Lexicon Juridicum, 69
—— Lexicon Diplomaticum, 339
Waltoni (B) in Bib Pol Prolegomena, 9.
—— (Life of Bp), 329
—— Vindication of the Polyglot, 329.
—— Introd ad Ling. Orient 349
—— (I) Angler, 128
—— Lives, 313
—— (W) South America, 156
Warburton's (J.) Vallum Romanum, 198.
—— Dublin, 269
—— (W) Works, 36
—— Life, 36
Warburtonian Lectures, 15
Ward's Novels 382, 384, and 385
—— (H G) Mexico, 154.
—— (J) Professors of Gresham College, 313
—— (T) England's Reformation 254.
—— (W) Hindoo Literature, 303.
Wardlaw on Unitarianism, 50
—— on Ecclesiastes, 59
—— Sermons, 59
Wareus de Scriptoribus Hiberniæ, 271
—— Rerum Hibern Annales, 272
Waring's Tour to Sheeraz, 149
Warner (L) de Karaits, 20
—— (R) Walks through the W Counties, 189
—— Tour through the N Counties, 189
—— Cornwall, 189
—— Antiquitates Culinariæ, 194.
—— Hampshire, 201
—— Isle of Wight, 201
—— Excursions from Bath, 211
—— Tour in Wales, 256
—— on Shakespeare 393
—— (W) Albion s England 225.
Warren (Memoirs of the Earls of), 335.
Warrington's Wales, 257
Warton's (J) Kiddington, 210.
—— (Jos) Life, 329
—— (T) Comp to Oxford Guide, 209
—— Hist of English Poetry, 362.
—— on Rowley s Poems, 370.
—— on the Fairie Queen, 371.
—— Poetical Works, and Life, 372.
Warwick's Charles I 233
Warwick (Black Book of), 214.
Warwickshire Topography, 214.
Washington (Life of), 310.

Water-colour Painters' Gallery, 116
Waterhouse's Fire of London, 205.
—— Apologie for Learning, 347
Waterland's (D) Works 37
—— Life, 37
Waterloo (Battle of), 244
Waterton's South America, 156
Wathen's Madras and China, 151
Watkins' Biddeford, 199
Watson's (J) Halifax, 217
—— Earls of Warren and Surrey, 335
—— (Rich) Two Apologies, 50
—— Theological Tracts, 50.
—— (Robt) Philip II and III 291
—— Taylor See Taylor
Watts's (I) Scripture History, 9
—— Logic, 79.
—— (R) Bibliotheca Britannica, 343
—— (W) Seats of Nobility, &c in Eng 191
Waverley Novels, 385
—— (Letters on the) 385
—— (Landscape Illustrations of), 259
—— (Portraits illustrative of), 315.
Waverleyensis Annales, 221
Way's (G) Fabliaux, 374
—— (L) Palingenesia, 372.
Waynflete (Life of Abp), 228
Weaver on Dancing 127
—— Funeral Monuments, 192
Webb's (T) Epitaphs, 192
—— (W) Irish History, 271
Webbe on English Poetrie, 362
Weber. Mém sur Marie Antoinette 285
—— (H) Northern Antiquities, 273
—— Metrical Romances, 364
—— Ancient Poems on Flodden Field, 367
Webster's Works, 394.
—— Life, 394
Weddel's Voyage to the South Pole, 157.
Weiske de Vocibus Græcis, 350.
Weld's North America, 153
—— Killarney, 270
Weldon's James I 232
—— Charles I 234
—— People of Scotland, 259
Wells' Sacred Geography, 25
Wellbeloved's St Mary's Abbey, 216
Welsh Bible, 7
—— Topography, 256
—— History, 257
—— Language, 354.
—— Poetry, 374
Wentworth on the Succession, 71
Werner (A G) on Mineralogical Veins, 91.
—— (D G) de Poculo Benedict 23
Wesley (Account of C and S), 105
—— (Life of J) 256
—— (S) History of the Bible, 8
Wesseling de Judæorum Archontibus, 22
West (G) on the Resurrection of Christ, 50
—— on the Olympic Games, 127
—— (J) Catalogue, 347.
—— (T) Furness, 204
—— (W) Guide to the Lakes, 169
West Indies (Voyages in the), 154
—— India Islands (History of the), 310.

Westminster Confession of Faith, 33
—— (Topography of), 205
Westmonasteriensis (Mat) Flores Historiæ, 223
Westmoreland (Topography of), 214
Wethamstede (Jo) Chronica, 224
—— de Processu contra Peacockum, 253
Weyland on the Poor-Laws, 84.
—— on Population, 84
Weymar de Suffitu, 18
—— de Unctione Sacrâ Hebr 19
Whalley's Northamptonshire, 208
Wharton (G) Calendarium Carolinum, 104
—— (P Lord) Household Book, 194.
Whately on Party Feeling in Religion, 54
Wheatley on the Common Prayer, 31.
—— on the Creeds, 52
Wheaton's Northmen, 274
Wheeler's (G) Greece, 143.
—— (Life of Sir G), 314
—— (R B) Stratford on Avon, 214
Whichcote's Sermons, 59
Whiston's Authentic Scriptural Records, 9
—— on the Prophecies, 52
Whitaker's (J) Ancient Cathedrals of Cornwall, 198
—— Manchester, 204
—— on M'Pherson's Introd 219
—— Mary Q of Scots vindicated, 266
—— (T D) Craven, 217
—— Leodis and Elmete, 217
—— Richmondshire, 218
—— Whalley, 218
Whitby on the New Testament, 11
White's (G) Selborne, 201
—— (J) Mahommedism and Christianity, 53
—— (J B) Evidence against Catholicism, 252
—— Doblado's Letters, 439
—— (K) Remains, 400
—— Life, 400
Whitelaw's Dublin, 269.
Whiter's Etymologicum Universale, 348.
Whitgift's (Abp) Life, 255
Whitlocke's (Sir B) Memorials, 226, 233
—— (Life of), 226
—— Swedish Embassy, 236
Whitney's Emblemes, 402
Whittington's Ecclesiastical Antiquities of France, 140
Whitworth's Russia, 276
Wicelii Historia St Bonifacii, 61
Wichmanshausen de Navig. Ophiriticâ, 17
—— de Thermis Tiberi 18
—— de Theraphim 21
—— de Divinationibus Babyl 21
—— de Calceo Hebr 23
—— de Laceratione Vestium 25
Wicliffe's New Testament, 4
—— Life, 4 and 253
Wieland's Oberon, 377
Wieling Index Chron Juris Justiniani, 70
Wigorniensis Florentii Chronicon, 222 and 223
Wikes (Th) Chronicon, 221.

Wilberforce on Christianity, 50.
Wilbraham's Cheshire Vocabulary, 353.
Wildman on Bees, 100
Wilford's (T.) Egypt, 307
—— (J.) Memorials, 312
Wilhelmi Worcestri Annales, 223.
Wilks's Mysore 304
Wilkins (D.) Concilia Magnæ Brit. 27
—— de Linguâ Copticâ, 349
—— (G.) on the Destruction of Jerusalem, 60
—— (W.) Magna Græcia, 172
Wilkinson (C H) on Galvanism 87
—— (R.) Sermon on Lord Hay's Marriage, 59
William the Conqueror, 226.
—— and Mary, 240
Williams' (D.) Monmouthshire, 208
—— (G.) Oxonia Depicta, 210
—— (H. W.) Travels in Italy, &c. 139
—— (J.) Concordance to the Greek Testament, 16
—— on Revelation, 51
—— (Late of Archbishop), 234
—— (W.) Primitive History, 158
—— Petrifactions in Derbyshire, 198.
Williamson (J.) on Revelation, 52
—— on the Truth of the Scriptures, 53
—— (T.) Oriental Field-Sports, 127
Willis's Cathedrals, 186
—— Parochiale, 186
—— St Asaph, 186
—— Bangor, 186
—— St Davids, 186.
—— Mitred Abbeys, 187
—— Buckingham, 196
—— Notitia Parliamentaria, 245.
Wills (Collection of Royal), 243.
Willughby's Ornithology, 97
—— Historia Piscium, 98.
Wilson's (Al.) American Ornithology, 98
—— (Life of), 98
—— (Arth.) James I 232
—— Life, 329.
—— Inconstant Lady, 394.
—— (D.) Sermons 59
—— Sermons and Tracts, 60.
—— (J.) History of Mountains, 90
—— Isle of Palms, 372
—— (R.) Trigonometry, 103.
—— (R T) B Expedition to Egypt, 244
—— Russian Campaign in Poland, 276
—— (Sir T) Arte of Logique, 79
—— Actio contra Mariam Scot 264
—— (T.) Archæological Dictionary, 159
—— Adversaria, 437
—— (Bishop T.) Bible, 5
—— Works 36
—— Life, 36
—— Sermons, 60
—— (W.) Jewish Opinions of Christ, 10.
Wilton House Antiquities, &c 170.
Wiltshire Topography, 214
Wimpfen's (B. von) Bloody Battle, 278
Winkelmann, Histoire de l'Art, 107.
—— (Vie de), 107
—— on the Painting, &c. of the Greeks, 108
—— Monumens Inédits, 170.

Winstanley's (H.) Grosvenor Gallery, 116
—— Audley End, 191.
—— Eddystone Lighthouse, 191
—— (W.) Loyal Martyrology, 236.
—— England's Worthies, 313.
Wintle's Daniel, 6
—— on Christian Redemption, 53.
Winwood's Memorials, 249
Wise, Nummi Scrinii Bodleianis, 174
Wisheart's Theologia, 60.
Wit's Recreations, 372
—— Commonwealth, 402
—— Theatre, 402
Withering's British Plants, 93
Withers's Fides Anglicana, 238
—— Abuses Stript, 372
—— Shepherd's Hunting, 372.
—— Fidelia, 372
—— Hymns and Songs of the Church, 372
Witherspoon's (J.) Works, 400.
—— Life, 400
Witsii Ægyptiaca, 16.
—— de Synedriis Hebr. 22.
Wittman's Travels, 133
Wodrow's Church of Scotland, 269.
Woodroephe's French Grammar, 355
Woide Fragmenta N Test Sahidica, 3
Wolfii Epitapha Judaica, 23
—— Jus Naturæ et Gentium, 68.
—— Lectiones Memorabiles, 407
Wolsey's (Cardinal) Life, 229.
Wood's (Capt) Voyages, 132.
—— (A.) Notes on Oxford, 209
—— Oxford University, 210
—— Athenæ Oxonienses, 313
—— (Life of A.), 314
—— (G.) Isle of Man, 218
—— (J.) Mechanics, 103.
—— Optics 104
—— Perspective, 104.
—— Bath, 211
—— (J. P.) Cramond, 260
—— (R.) Palymra, 171
—— Balbec, 171
—— (W.) Zoography, 89
—— Bowman's Glory, 127
Woodhouse on the Apocalypse, 7
Woodhouselee See Tytler
Woodville's Medical Botany, 93
Woodward on Religion, 52
—— Roman Antiquities near Bishopgate, 206
Worcester's (Marq.) Inventions 103 and 104
—— (Memoirs of), 104
Worcestershire (Topography of), 215.
—— Biography, 314
Wordsworth's (C.) Ecclesiastical Biography, 255
—— (W.) Ballads, 372
—— Excursion, 372
—— White Doe of Rylstone, 372
World, 405
Worlidge's Antique Gems, 173
Wormius (C.) de Corruptis Antiq Hebr apud Tacitum, 16
—— (O.) Danica Monumenta, 274
—— Regum Daniæ Series, 274
Worsleyanum Museum, 170
Worsley's Isle of Wight, 201

Worthington on Christianity, 52
Wortley's Characters and Elegies, 407.
Wotton (E) [misprinted Walton] de Animalibus, 96.
—— (H) Elementa Architecturæ, 122
—— (Life of Sir H), 313
—— Reliquiæ Wottonianæ, 400
—— (W) Traditions, &c of the Scribes, 61.
—— Leges Wallicæ, 73
—— de Confusione Linguarum, 348
—— View of Hickes' Treasure, 356.
Woyer de Polymathiá, 163
Wrangham's Works, 400
Wraxall's View of Europe, 184.
—— Own Times, 242
—— Courts of Berlin, &c 278
—— Race of Valois, 281
—— France, 282
Wrestling, 127
Wright's (G N) Dublin, 269
—— (J) Rutland, 211
—— Historia Histrionica, 390
—— (T) Halifax, 217
Writing, 107.
—— (History of), 339.
Wulterns de Siclo, 22
Wyat's (G) Anne Boleyn, 229
—— (Sir T) Works, 399.
—— Life, 399
Wycherley's Plays, 394
Wyerley's (W) Use of Armourie, 331
—— Poems, 372
Wyndham's Speeches, 246
—— Life, 246
Wynne's (E) Eunomus, 73
—— (Sir J) Gwedir Family, 336
—— (R) Itin Caroli I. in Hispaniam, 233
Wyntoun's Chronykill, 262

Xavier (Life of St Francis), 329
Ximenes (de Res Gest Card) 290
—— (Life of Card), 291
Xenophontis Opera, 430
—— de Socrate Comment 430

Xenophon's Cyropædia, translated, 430.
—— Anabasis, translated, 430
—— Hellenics, translated, 430.
—— Minor Works, translated, 430

Y's (D) Guernsey, 218
Yakstun Nattannawa, 378
Yates St Edmund's Bury, 212.
Year in Spain, 141
Yesterday in Ireland, 385
York's (on the Duchess of) Conversion, 51.
York (MSS relative to), 432 and 434-6.
Yorkshire Topography, 216
—— Biography, 314
Young's (Miss) Sketches of Italy, 138
—— (A) Agriculture of Sussex, 125
—— France, 140.
—— (E) Works, 400.
—— (G) Whitby, 218
—— (J) Angerstein Gallery, 116
—— Grosvenor Gallery, 116
—— Leigh Court Pictures, 116
—— (T) Egyptian Dictionary, 349
—— (Sir W.) History of Athens, 179
Yvery Genealogy, 336.

Zancaroli Antiquitates Foro-Julii, 294
Zanchii de Orobiorum Origine, 293
Zarlino (G), Institutione Harmoniche, 105
Zeal without Innovation, 51
Ziegra de Immolatione Molocho, 21.
Zimmerman on Solitude, 78
Zonaræ Annales, 181.
Zoology, 96
Zoroastre, le Zend Avesta, 67
Zorin Varia de Antiquitatibus Sacris, 18, 22, and 23
Zouche's (Lord) Dove, 372
—— (T) Works, 400
—— Life, 400
Zuniga's Philippine Isles, 306
Zurlauben, Tableaux de la Suisse, 137
Zuinglii Opera, 37.
—— Life, 63

THE END

LONDON
J NOYES, CASTLE STREET, LEICESTER SQUARE

Milton Keynes UK
Ingram Content Group UK Ltd.
UKHW010326010224
437068UK00004B/118